FOR
STUDENTS

Over the past four years we have spent time in classrooms across Canada, speaking to students just like you.

We've asked what you want to see in a textbook, how you learn, how many hours a week you spend online, and what you find most valuable when preparing for a test. Based on your feedback, we've developed a new hybrid learning solution—**MKTG**. Your textbook, the Chapter Review cards, and the online resources found at **www.icanmktg2.com** present a new, exciting, and fresh approach to learning. Check out the website for great tools like:

- Interactive quizzing
- Interactive e-book
- Flashcards
- Games
- Audio chapter summaries
- PowerPoint slides
- Videos
- **And more!**

Purestock/Getty Images

NELSON / EDUCATION

MKTG, Second Canadian Edition

by Charles W. Lamb; Joseph F. Hair, Jr.;
Carl McDaniel; Harish Kapoor;
Richard Appleby; and Janice Shearer

Vice President, Editorial Higher Education:
Anne Williams

Executive Editor:
Amie Plourde

Marketing Manager:
David Stratton

Developmental Editor:
Leslie Mutic

Photo Researcher/Permissions Coordinator:
Julie Pratt

Senior Content Production Manager:
Imoinda Romain

Copy Editor:
Mariko Obokata

Proofreader:
Erin Moore

Indexer:
Edwin Durbin

Manufacturing Manager:
Joanne McNeil

Design Director:
Ken Phipps

Managing Designer:
Franca Amore

Interior Design:
KeDesign, Mason, OH

Cover Design:
Martyn Schmoll

Cover Image:
Sam Janvanrough

Compositor:
Kyle Gell Design

Printer:
Webcom

Library and Archives Canada Cataloguing in Publication

MKTG / Charles W. Lamb... [et al.]. — 2nd Canadian ed.

Includes bibliographical references and index.

ISBN 978-0-17-650369-7

1. Marketing—Textbooks. 2. Marketing—Management—Textbooks. I. Lamb, Charles W II. Title: Marketing.

HF5415.M52 2012
658.8   C2011-905735-2

ISBN-13: 978-0-17-650369-7
ISBN-10: 0-17-650369-2

Brief Contents

© ISTOCKPHOTO.COM/KELLY CLINE

PHOTODISC/GETTY IMAGES

ALAN MARSH/FIRST LIGHT

Contents

BLOOMBERG VIA GETTY IMAGES

PART 1
MARKETING— LET'S GET STARTED

STEPHEN MCSWEENY/SHUTTERSTOCK.COM

REPRINTED WITH PERMISSION FROM OAKLEY, INC.

PART 2
ANALYZING MARKETING OPPORTUNITIES

PRNEWSFOTO/BOISE PAPER SOLUTIONS/ASSOCIATED PRESS

6 Business Marketing 90

7 Segmenting, Targeting, and Positioning 106

ISTOCKPHOTO.COM/JOHN VERNER

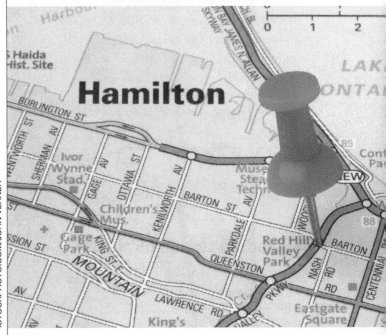

8 Customer Relationship Management (CRM) 124

© ISTOCKPHOTO.COM/FILONMAR

PART 3 PRODUCT DECISIONS

9 Product Concepts 140

10 Developing and Managing Products 154

LENSCAP/GETSTOCK.COM

11 Services and Nonprofit Organization Marketing 170

© JULIE PRATT

PART 4
DISTRIBUTION DECISIONS

12 Marketing Channels and Supply Chain Management 184

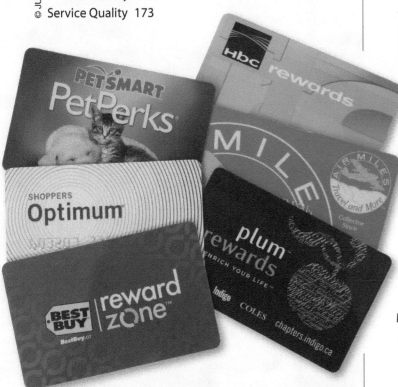

13 Retailing 204

14 Integrated Marketing Communications 224

ROSS ANANIA/TAXI/GETTY IMAGES

15 Advertising, Public Relations, and Direct Response 242

16 Social Media and Marketing 262

© AP PHOTO/CHRIS PIZZELLO

PART 6
PRICING DECISIONS

PART 7
GLOBAL MARKETING

20 Developing a Global Vision 332

PHOTODISC/GETTY IMAGES

An Overview of Marketing

> The aim of marketing is to know and understand the customer so well, the product or service fits him and sells itself.[1]
>
> —Peter Drucker

LO 1 What Is Marketing?

What does the term *marketing* mean to you? Many people think marketing is the same as personal selling. Others think marketing is the same as advertising. Still others believe marketing has something to do with making products available in stores, arranging displays, and maintaining inventories of products for future sales. Actually, marketing includes all of these activities and more.

Marketing has two facets. First, it is a philosophy, an attitude, a perspective, and a management orientation that stresses customer satisfaction. Second, marketing comprises the activities and set of processes used to implement this philosophy. The accepted definition of marketing encompasses both perspectives: **Marketing** refers to "the activity, set of institutions, and processes for creating, communicating, delivering, and exchanging offerings that have value for customers, clients, partners, and society at large."[2] Marketing is a broad organizational activity that crosses department boundaries.

Marketing is a process that focuses not just on selling goods, services, or ideas but also on delivering value and benefits to customers. Marketing uses communication, distribution, and pricing strategies to provide customers and other stakeholders with the goods, services, ideas, values, and benefits they desire when and where they want them. It involves building long-term, mutually rewarding relationships. In the often quoted words of Peter Drucker "the aim of marketing is to know and understand the customer so well, the product or service fits [the customer] and sells itself."[3] Marketing also entails an understanding that organizations have many connected

> **marketing** the activity, set of institutions, and processes for creating, communicating, delivering, and exchanging offerings that have value for customers, clients, partners, and society at large

What do you think?

Marketing is selling.

1 2 3 4 5 6 7
STRONGLY DISAGREE   STRONGLY AGREE

Find out what others think at the CourseMate for MKTG. Log in at NelsonBrain.com.

exchange people giving up one thing to receive another thing they would rather have

production orientation a philosophy that focuses on the internal capabilities of the firm rather than on the desires and needs of the marketplace

stakeholder "partners," including employees, suppliers, stockholders, distributors, and others.

Those companies that consistently reward their employees with recognition and incentives tend to perform better than other companies, which reinforces the direct link that has been found between customer satisfaction and employee satisfaction. Satisfied employees are loyal employees who positively influence customers, thereby creating loyalty. Loyalty will ultimately lead to higher profits and growth. Take, for example, Lululemon, a Canadian success story, whose core value of greatness reads: "we create the possibility of greatness in people because it makes us great. Mediocrity undermines greatness."[4]

One desired outcome of marketing is an exchange—people giving up one thing to receive another thing they would rather have. Normally, we think of money as the medium of exchange. We "give up" money to "receive" the goods and services we want. Exchange does not, however, require money. Two people may barter or trade such items as baseball cards or oil paintings. An exchange can take place only if the following five conditions exist:

CONDITIONS OF EXCHANGE

1. At least two parties are involved.
2. Each party has something that may be of value to the other party.
3. Each party is capable of communication and delivery.
4. Each party is free to accept or reject the exchange offer.
5. Each party believes it is appropriate or desirable to deal with the other party.[5]

Even when all these conditions exist, exchange will not necessarily take place. These conditions are necessary, however, for exchange to be possible. For example, you may place an advertisement on Kijiji to sell your cellphone. Several people may call you about the phone, some may even meet you to look at the phone, and a few may even make you an offer. However, unless you reach an agreement with one of the buyers and actually sell the cellphone, an exchange will not take place. All five conditions must exist for an exchange to occur. If you don't sell your old cellphone, an exchange did not occur because one party in the potential exchange did not perceive a benefit. Another important point to note is that an exchange results in a mutually beneficial situation—both parties are satisfied. If you sold your cellphone, you would have money to spend on something else, and the purchaser would have a new phone. Notice that marketing can occur even if an exchange does not occur. In the cellphone example, you would have engaged in marketing even if no one bought your used cellphone.

LO 2 Marketing Management Philosophies

Four competing philosophies strongly influence an organization's marketing processes. These philosophies are commonly referred to as production, sales, market, and societal marketing orientations.

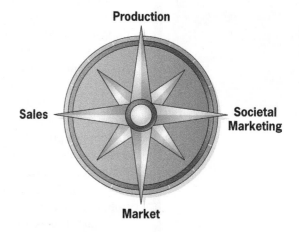

Production Orientation

A **production orientation** is a philosophy that focuses on the internal capabilities of the firm rather than on the desires and needs of the marketplace. A production orientation leads management to assess its resources and asks these questions: "What can we do best?" "What can our engineers design?" "What is easy to produce, given our equipment?" In a service organization, this orientation leads managers to ask, "What services are most convenient for the firm to offer?" and "Where do our talents lie?" Some have referred to this orientation as a *Field of Dreams* orientation, from the well-known movie line "If you build it, he will come." The furniture industry, infamous for both its disregard of customers and its slow cycle times, has historically been a production-oriented industry.

There is nothing wrong with assessing a firm's capabilities; in fact, such assessments are major considerations in strategic marketing planning (see Chapter 3). A production orientation falls short because it does not consider whether the goods and services that the firm produces most efficiently also meet the needs of the marketplace. Apple has a history of production orientation, creating computers, operating systems, and other gadgetry because they can, and hoping to sell the result. Some items have found a waiting market (early computers, iPod, iPhone). Other products, like the Newton, one of the first versions of a PDA, were simply flops. In other situations, such as when competition is weak or when demand exceeds supply, a production-oriented firm can survive and even prosper. More often, however, firms that succeed in competitive markets are led by managers who have a clear understanding that they must first determine what customers want and then produce it, rather than focusing on what management thinks should be produced.

Sales Orientation

A **sales orientation** reflects two ideas: that people will buy more goods and services if aggressive sales techniques are used and that high sales result in high profits. Not only are sales to the final buyer emphasized but intermediaries are also encouraged to push manufacturers' products more aggressively. For sales-oriented firms, marketing means selling goods or services and collecting money.

The fundamental problem with a sales orientation, as with a production orientation, is a lack of understanding of the needs and wants of the marketplace. Sales-oriented companies often find that, despite the quality of their sales force, they cannot convince people to buy goods or services that are neither wanted nor needed.

Some sales-oriented firms fail to understand the product or service qualities that are important to their customers. For example, many so-called dot-com businesses that came into existence in the late 1990s are no longer around because they focused on the technology rather than on the customer.

Market Orientation

The **marketing concept** is a simple and intuitively appealing philosophy that articulates a market orientation. It states that the social and economic justification for an organization's existence is the satisfaction of customers' wants and needs while also meeting organizational objectives. This concept is based on an understanding that a sale does not depend on an aggressive sales force, but rather on a customer's decision to purchase a product to meet an unsatisfied need. What a business thinks it produces is not of primary importance to its success. Instead, a business is defined by what customers' needs they are satisfying. The marketing concept includes the following:

▸▸ Focusing on customer wants and needs so that the organization can distinguish its offerings from those of its competitors

▸▸ Integrating all the organization's activities, including production, to satisfy customers' wants

▸▸ Achieving long-term goals for the organization by satisfying customers' wants and needs legally and responsibly

The key to success in today's highly competitive marketplaces is to continually delight the customer. This ability to delight is a result of the organization's commitment to ongoing customer research that seeks to unearth customers' changing wants and needs and is committed to holistically working to deliver the desired product or service experience. Firms that adopt and

sales orientation the idea that people will buy more goods and services if aggressive sales techniques are used and that high sales result in high profits

marketing concept the idea that the social and economic justification for an organization's existence is the satisfaction of customers' wants and needs while meeting organizational objectives

Zipcar is a car-sharing product and service. Zipcar's mission statement says it all: "To enable simple and responsible urban living."[6] Zipcar satisfies the *simple* in its mission statement by taking away the headaches of car ownership in an urban market. Zipcar members never need to worry about car maintenance, gas, insurance, or even parking. The company provides responsible urban living because each Zipcar replaces, or takes off the road, at least 15 personally owned vehicles. Through their memberships, users have access to a variety of automobile types for personal or business use whenever the need arises. The Zipcar membership card uses radio-frequency identification (RFID) technology to unlock a Zipcar located in a parking spot near where users need it; the gas card inside ensures that the user can fuel up for free. Membership can be completed online in a matter of minutes. For even more convenient use, an iPhone app is now available that allows members to reserve and unlock a Zipcar. Zipcar envisions a future in which car-sharing members outnumber car owners in major cities across the globe. The growth of Zipcar may ensure the company realizes this vision sooner rather than later.

zipcar

---

market orientation a philosophy that involves obtaining information about customers, competitors, and markets; examining the information from a total business perspective; determining how to deliver superior customer value; and implementing actions to provide value to customers

societal marketing orientation the idea that an organization exists not only to satisfy customers' wants and needs and to meet organizational objectives but also to preserve or enhance individuals' and society's long-term best interests

implement the marketing concept are said to be market oriented. Achieving a **market orientation** involves obtaining information about customers, competitors, and markets; examining the information from a total business perspective; determining how to deliver superior customer value; and implementing actions to provide value to customers.

For example, Speedy Auto Service, after speaking with female consumers and female suppliers, realized that women, for the most part, are uncomfortable dealing with the auto service sector. A survey commissioned by Speedy in 2009 found that 43 percent of women surveyed felt they received worse service than men when they took their car in to be fixed, and 42 percent believed that they were quoted higher prices than men. In response, Speedy launched clinics to educate women about automotive repair. These "Woman Driver Workshops," hosted by franchise owners, are designed to educate women about auto service repair, thereby improving their attitude about the service they receive.[7]

A critical component of a market orientation is understanding your competitive arena and the strengths and weaknesses of both your consumers and competitors. This understanding includes assessing both what your existing and potential competitors are doing today and what they might intend to do tomorrow.

Societal Marketing Orientation

A market-oriented organization may choose to *not* deliver the benefits sought by customers because these benefits may not be good for individuals or society. This philosophy, called a **societal marketing orientation**, states that an organization exists not only to satisfy customers' wants and needs and to meet organizational objectives but also to preserve or enhance individuals' and society's long-term best interests. According to a societal marketing orientation, organizations and businesses should market products and containers that are less toxic and more durable than the norm, contain reusable materials, or are made from recycled and/or recyclable materials. Even the 2010 Olympics recognized the societal marketing concept—all gold, silver, and bronze medals awarded at the 2010 Vancouver Olympic Games contained metal from recycled TVs, computers, and keyboards that might have otherwise ended up as e-waste.

LO3 Differences between Sales and Market Orientations

The differences between sales and market orientations are substantial. The two orientations can be compared in terms of five characteristics: the organization's focus, the firm's business, those to whom the product is directed, the firm's primary goal, and the tools used to achieve those goals.

The Organization's Focus

Personnel in sales-oriented firms tend to be "inward looking," focusing on selling what the organization makes rather than making what the market wants. Many of the past sources of competitive advantage—technology, innovation, and economies of scale—allowed companies to focus their efforts internally and prosper. Today, many successful firms derive their competitive advantage from an external, market-oriented focus. A market orientation has helped companies such as Dell, Tim Hortons, and WestJet to outperform their competitors. These companies put customers at the centre of their business in ways most companies do poorly or not at all.[8]

A sales orientation has led to the demise of many firms. For example, the demise of the video rental and sales retail giant Blockbuster can be traced to its continued reliance on retail sales and rentals despite a growing acceptance by consumers of online video rental sources and online video streaming.

Customer Value **Customer value** is the relationship between benefits and the sacrifice necessary to obtain those benefits. Customer value is not simply a matter of high quality. A high-quality product that is available only at a high price will not be perceived as a good value, nor will bare-bones service, nor low-quality goods selling for a low price. Instead, customers value goods and services that are of the quality they expect and are sold at prices they are willing to pay. Value can be

used to sell both a Mercedes-Benz and a $3 frozen chicken dinner.

The highly competitive and still-evolving market for smartphones and portable devices demonstrates the importance of offering enhanced customer value as a means of gaining a competitive advantage. The launch of the Apple tablet, the iPad, took the market by storm, and it quickly gained market share. In early 2011, Research In Motion (RIM) rolled out the BlackBerry PlayBook, which offered the functionality of the iPad and delivered better value to those in the corporate segment. The PlayBook has the ability to become a larger screen for a BlackBerry phone and offers the full web experience through its ability to display Flash Video and interactive formats, functions that the iPad can do, but only after third-party applications, or "apps," have been downloaded. RIM is counting on this added value to the corporate consumer to help maintain its stronghold in the business sector.[9] Marketers interested in customer value:

> **customer value** the relationship between benefits and the sacrifice necessary to obtain those benefits

- *Offer products that perform:* This is the bare minimum requirement. After grappling with the problems associated with its Vista operating system, Microsoft listened to its customers and made drastic changes for Windows 7, which received greatly improved reviews.

- *Earn trust:* According to Matthew Ryan, a Disney senior vice president, Disney guests "rely on Disney as a sure choice for their entertainment needs,"[10] which means that each time the consumer engages in the brand, it delivers. Delivering a reliable product or service earns consumers' trust in the brand and brings the consumer back to the brand time after time.

- *Avoid unrealistic pricing:* E-marketers leverage Internet technology to redefine how prices are set and negotiated. Because e-marketers have lower costs, they can often offer lower prices than their brick-and-mortar counterparts. The price of a product or service must

MARKETERS INTERESTED IN CUSTOMER VALUE:

- offer products that perform
- earn trust
- avoid unrealistic pricing
- give consumers the facts
- offer an organization-wide commitment to service and after-sales support
- partner with consumers to co-create experiences that consumers want

reflect the value that consumers place on the brand in the purchase and use situation. Determining this value requires that companies invest in research to continually understand consumer preferences.

▶▶ *Give consumers the facts:* Today's sophisticated consumers want informative advertising and knowledgeable salespeople. They want to access the information easily and at their convenience, which may or may not be at the point of purchase. Today's marketers must rely on a myriad of media to effectively reach the consumer to communicate how the brand will meet their unique needs.

▶▶ *Offer an organization-wide commitment to service and after-sales support:* People choose to fly WestJet because the airline offers superior value. WestJet's service is reliable and friendly and costs less than most major airlines. All WestJet employees participate in the effort to satisfy customers, which truly differentiates the brand in consumers' eyes.

▶▶ *Partner with consumers to co-create experiences that consumers want:* Companies can enhance both customer value and the relationship between the brand and the consumer by allowing consumers to create their own experience. For example, TiVo and built-in personal video recorders (PVRs) allow television viewers to take control over their program viewership.

Customer Satisfaction **Customer satisfaction** is the customer's evaluation of a good or service in terms of whether that good or service has met the customer's needs and expectations. Failure to meet a customer's needs and expectations results in the customer's dissatisfaction with the good or service.[11] Keeping current customers satisfied is just as important as attracting new customers—and a lot less expensive. One study showed that reducing customer attrition by just 5 to 10 percent could increase annual profits by as much as 75 percent.[12] A 2 percent increase in customer retention has the same effect on profits as cutting costs by 10 percent.[13] Firms that have a reputation for delivering high levels of customer satisfaction tend to do things differently from their competitors. When top management is obsessed with customer satisfaction, employees throughout the organization are more likely to understand the link between how they perform their

job and the satisfaction of customers. The culture of such an organization focuses on delighting customers rather than on selling products.

Richard Branson, founder of the Virgin Group, believes that good customer service stems from an environment that is founded on "a chain reaction of teamwork, one that is consistent from beginning to end."[14] One day, a Virgin agent, after recognizing a customer's high level of distress, acted in a very proactive manner to reduce the likelihood of potential negative effects. The agent used her own money to reimburse the customer for cab fare he shouldn't have incurred, and she then rushed him to his gate with 10 minutes to spare. The agent's great customer service turned a potentially negative incident into a positive experience. This agent, however, was subsequently chastised by her supervisor for not getting a receipt for the cab fare, and she was not reimbursed. You can imagine the negative effect this decision had on all employees who witnessed the supervisor's reaction. Fortunately, the supervisor's manager became aware of the situation and took steps to remind the supervisor that at Virgin it is important to "catch people doing something right" by the customer.[15]

Building Relationships Attracting new customers to a business is only the beginning. The best companies view new-customer attraction as the launching point for developing and enhancing a long-term relationship. Companies can expand their market share in three ways: attracting new customers, increasing business with existing customers, and retaining current customers. Building relationships with existing customers directly addresses two of the three possibilities and indirectly addresses the other.

Relationship marketing is a strategy that focuses on keeping and improving relationships with current customers. This strategy assumes that many consumers and business customers prefer to keep an ongoing relationship with one organization than to switch continually among providers in their search for value.[16] Disney is a good example of an organization focused on building long-term relationships with its customers. Disney managers understand that their company creates products and experiences that become an important part of peoples' lives and their memories. This understanding has led to Disney being a leader in doing "right by the

"KEEPING CURRENT CUSTOMERS **SATISFIED** IS JUST AS IMPORTANT AS ATTRACTING NEW CUSTOMERS—AND A LOT **LESS EXPENSIVE**."

TRAINING

McDonald's works hard to foster a collaborative environment where employees mentor each other. Off-site training programs are available to enhance employees' skills in leadership, communications, customer service, and time management.

DAVID LEVENSON/GETSTOCK.COM

customer," starting with the front-line cast member who interacts directly with the public and across employees in all departments who assess each decision made against the impact on the customer and the relationship the customer has with the Disney brand.[17]

Most successful relationship marketing strategies depend on customer-oriented personnel, effective training programs, teamwork, and employees who are given the authority to make decisions and solve problems.

Customer-Oriented Personnel For an organization to be focused on building relationships with customers, employees' attitudes and actions must be customer oriented. Any employee may be the only contact a customer has with the firm. In that customer's eyes, that one employee is the firm. Any person, department, or division that is not customer oriented weakens the positive image of the entire organization. For example, a potential customer who is greeted discourteously may well assume that the employee's attitude represents the whole firm.

For a fifth consecutive year, TD Canada Trust ranked highest in overall customer satisfaction among Canada's Big 5 banks, as measured by the J.D. Power and Associates 2010 Canadian Retail Banking Customer Satisfaction Study.[18] How did TD Canada Trust achieve such consistent ranking? By dedication to being the best-run, integrated, customer-focused financial institution and by adhering to its number-one guiding principle—"Be Customer Driven."[19] TD Canada Trust's leading customer satisfaction scores places it in a strong position among the Big 5 for "not only are highly satisfied customers more likely to stay with their banks longer than are less-satisfied

customers, they are also more likely to entrust a greater percentage of their deposits and investment dollars."[20]

The Role of Training Leading marketers recognize the role of employee training in customer service and relationship building. When employees make their customers happy, the employees are more likely to derive satisfaction from their jobs. Having contented workers who are committed to their jobs leads to better customer service and greater employee retention.

Empowerment In addition to training their employees, many market-oriented firms are giving employees more authority to solve customer problems on the spot. The term used to describe this delegation of authority is **empowerment**. Employees develop ownership attitudes when they are treated like part owners of the

empowerment
delegation of authority to solve customers' problems quickly—usually by the first person that the customer notifies regarding a problem

JEFF GREENBERG/GETSTOCK.COM

When a firm provides great value, word gets around.

A **MARKET-ORIENTED** FIRM DEFINES ITS BUSINESS IN TERMS OF THE **BENEFITS** ITS **CUSTOMERS** SEEK.

teamwork collaborative efforts of people to accomplish common objectives

business and are expected to act the part. These employees manage themselves, are more likely to work hard, account for their own performance and the company's, and take prudent risks to build a stronger business and sustain the company's success.

As mentioned earlier in the Virgin example, empowered employees continue to make a difference to the customer experience. Empowerment gives customers the feeling that their concerns are being addressed and gives employees the feeling that their expertise matters. The result is greater satisfaction for both customers and employees.

Teamwork Many organizations that are frequently noted for delivering superior customer value and providing high levels of customer satisfaction assign employees to teams and teach them team-building skills. **Teamwork** entails collaborative efforts of people to accomplish common objectives. When people in

the same department or work group support and assist each other and when they emphasize cooperation instead of competition, improvements are seen in job performance, company performance, product value, and customer satisfaction. Performance is also enhanced when people from a variety of departments in the organization join together to form cross-functional teams with the shared objective of enhancing customer needs.

The Firm's Business

A sales-oriented firm defines its business (or mission) in terms of goods and services. A market-oriented firm defines its business in terms of the benefits its customers seek. People who spend their money, time, and energy expect to receive benefits not just goods and services. This distinction has enormous implications.

When asked "What is your firm's business?" an employee can choose to respond in terms of the benefits customers seek, instead of in terms of the goods

WHEN SALES CONTINUE TO FALL —ACKNOWLEDGE THE CONSUMER AND RESPOND ACCORDINGLY

Sales of Polaroid cameras experienced continuous decline as consumers turned to digital cameras and cellphones for quality pictures that they could easily and instantly download and store on their computers. The instant picture that the Polaroid offered "back in the day" was no longer a significant competitive advantage, and the Polaroid film did not have as good picture quality as digital photos have today. But what was a competitive advantage was the tangible picture that was instantly available when using a Polaroid camera and film. Despite once being close to bankruptcy,

Polaroid is back, launching at the 2010 Consumer Electronics Show a product lineup that capitalizes on the brand's heritage and acknowledges consumers' demands for increased quality. The PIC 1000 is a redesigned and modernized version of the Polaroid OneStep camera in funky colours that uses the classic Polaroid Color 600 Instant Film to create Polaroid pictures for the true Polaroid-nostalgic consumer. For the consumer who is more picture-quality conscious, Polaroid launched an instant 12-megapixel digital camera with a built-in printer that produces 3" × 4" (7 cm × 10 cm) photos instantly. "People can snap, print and share images immediately without having to connect to a computer. People can view and crop images on the camera before they print and select from a range of borders from borderless to the classic Polaroid frame."[21]

and services sold. Responding in this way offers at least three important advantages:

- ▶▶ It ensures that the firm and it employees continue to focus on customers and avoid becoming preoccupied with goods, services, or the organization's internal needs.
- ▶▶ It encourages innovation and creativity by reminding employees that customer wants can be satisfied in many ways.
- ▶▶ It stimulates an awareness of changes in customer desires and preferences so that product offerings are more likely to remain relevant.

Having a market orientation and focusing on customer wants does not mean that customers will always receive everything they want. It is not possible, for example, to profitably manufacture and market $25 automobile tires that will last for 160,000 km. Furthermore, customers' preferences must be mediated by sound professional judgment in terms of how to deliver the benefits they seek. As one adage suggests, "People don't know what they want—they only want what they know." Consumers have a limited set of experiences and are unlikely to request anything beyond those experiences because they are not aware of benefits they may gain from other potential offerings. For example, before HDTV, people were very content to watch programs on their colour televisions and were convinced the picture quality was perfect.

Those to Whom the Product Is Directed

A sales-oriented organization targets its products at "everybody" or "the average customer." A market-oriented organization aims at specific groups of people. The fallacy of developing products aimed directed at the average user is that relatively few average users actually exist. Typically, populations are characterized by diversity. An average is simply a midpoint in some set of characteristics. Because most potential customers are not "average," they are not likely to be attracted to an average product marketed to the average customer. Consider the automobile market. Does the consumer really need another automobile, and, if so, what category should it fit into? Is it a compact, subcompact, sedan, van, or sport utility vehicle (SUV)? Nissan launched the Juke Sport Cross, a crossover SUV. The Juke is a car for the "urban adventurers, young people

who are very connected, savy and plugged in." The marketing plan for the Juke then will be "digitally focused" because that is where the consumer is.[22]

A market-oriented organization recognizes that different customer groups want different features or benefits. Such an organization may therefore need to develop different goods, services, and promotional appeals. A market-oriented organization carefully analyzes the market and divides it into groups of people who are fairly similar in terms of selected characteristics. The organization then develops marketing programs that will bring about mutually satisfying exchanges with one or more of those groups. Chapter 7 thoroughly explores the topic of analyzing markets and selecting those that appear to be most promising to the firm.

The Firm's Primary Goal

A sales-oriented organization seeks to achieve profitability through sales volume. Sales-oriented organizations place a higher premium on making a sale than on developing a long-term relationship with a customer. In contrast, the ultimate goal of most market-oriented organizations is to make a profit by creating customer value, providing customer satisfaction, and building long-term relationships with customers. The exception is nonprofit organizations that exist to achieve goals other than profits. Nonprofit organizations can and should adopt a market orientation. Nonprofit organization marketing is explored further in Chapter 11.

Tools the Organization Uses to Achieve Its Goals

Sales-oriented organizations seek to generate sales volume through intensive promotional activities, mainly personal selling and advertising. In contrast,

"PEOPLE DON'T KNOW WHAT THEY WANT—THEY ONLY **WANT WHAT THEY KNOW**."

market-oriented organizations recognize that promotion decisions are only one of four basic marketing mix decisions that need to be made: product decisions, place (or distribution) decisions, promotion decisions, and pricing decisions. A market-oriented organization recognizes that each of these four components is important. Furthermore, market-oriented organizations recognize that marketing is not just a responsibility of the marketing department. Interfunctional co-ordination means that skills and resources throughout the organization are needed to create, communicate, and deliver superior customer service and value.

A Word of Caution

This comparison of sales and market orientations is not meant to belittle, within the marketing mix, the role of promotion, especially the role of personal selling. Promotion is the means by which organizations communicate with present and prospective customers about the merits and characteristics of their organization and products. Effective promotion is an essential part of effective marketing. Salespeople who work for market-oriented organizations are generally perceived by their customers to be problem solvers and important relationship conduits. Chapter 17 examines the nature of personal selling in more detail.

LO 4 Why Study Marketing

Now that you understand the meaning of the term *marketing*, the importance of adopting a marketing orientation, how organizations implement this philosophy, and how one-to-one marketing is evolving, you may be asking, "What's in it for me?" or "Why should I study marketing?" These are important questions, whether you are majoring in a business field other than marketing (such as accounting, finance, or management information systems) or a nonbusiness field (such as journalism, education, or agriculture). Studying marketing is important for several reasons: marketing plays an important role in society, marketing is important to businesses, marketing offers outstanding career opportunities, and marketing affects your life every day.

Marketing Plays an Important Role in Society

The total population of Canada, as of 2010, is 34 million people. Think about how many transactions are needed each day to feed, clothe, and shelter a population of this size. The number is huge. And yet our country all works quite well, partly because the well-developed Canadian economic system efficiently distributes the output of farms and factories. Marketing functions within this economic system to make food available when we want it, in desired quantities, at accessible locations, and in sanitary and convenient packages and forms.

Marketing Is Important to Businesses

The fundamental objectives of most businesses are survival, profits, and growth. Marketing contributes directly to achieving these objectives. Marketing includes the following activities, which are vital to business organizations: assessing the wants and satisfactions of present and potential customers, designing and managing product offerings, determining prices and pricing policies, developing distribution strategies, and communicating with present and potential customers.

All business people, regardless of specialization or area of responsibility, need to be familiar with the terminology and fundamentals of accounting, finance, management, and marketing. People in all business areas need to be able to communicate with specialists in other areas. Furthermore, marketing is not just a job done by people in a marketing department. Marketing is a part of the job of everyone in the organization. Therefore, a basic understanding of marketing is important to all business people.

Marketing Offers Outstanding Career Opportunities

Marketers spend their time trying to understand consumers, their changing needs and wants, and their changing purchase behaviours. This task, in and of itself, results in a challenging and stimulating career area. Marketers create products or services to satisfy the consumer and ensure the consumer is able to efficiently access the product or service at an affordable price and is aware of the benefits they will receive upon purchase. Marketers require strong communication skills. They are natural leaders and resourceful team players, as the ability to develop and deliver need-satisfying goods and services is a result of the efforts of many under the guidance of the marketer. Marketing is the hub of the wheel within the organization, bringing together various departments that all have input to the final product created.

Within the field of marketing are numerous career opportunities. Strategic planning, product management, and project-planning skills are key on the business career side. Advertising or communication specialists work in the especially exciting communication career area within marketing, and they rely on their strong creative skills. In the marketing specialty areas of research, database development and mining, and supply chain management, a marketer's strong analytical skills are demanded.

Entry-level positions in marketing are plentiful and pay well. Advancement in the field can be rapid. Because marketing focuses on satisfying the customer, and the customer is always changing, the field of marketing is a dynamic area that is constantly changing. Marketers are lifelong learners who strive to stay on top of the technology that allows them to better understand and satisfy the customer. Marketers who have made their mark in history tend to be risk takers and problem solvers.

Marketing career opportunities exist in a variety of business and nonbusiness organizations. Some of the most exciting and rewarding career areas exist in the non-profit sector, in hospitals, museums, art galleries, and social service agencies. Career opportunities can be found online at a variety of resources. *Marketing Magazine* and *Strategy Magazine* are two very comprehensive online resources for marketing-specific employment opportunities. In addition, the Canadian Marketing Association is a good resource (http://www.the-cma.org/). The Institute of Communication Agencies, another great resource, has created a website specifically for those interested in the creative side of marketing entitled www.mybigfuture.ca.

Marketing Affects Your Life Every Day

Marketing plays a major role in your everyday life. You participate in the marketing process as a consumer of goods and services. You engage in a marketing activity that is part of the marketing process every time you purchase a product, research a product online, buy a magazine to read, or talk to your friends about a new product you have tried. By developing a better understanding of marketing, you will become a better-informed consumer. You will be better prepared to demand satisfaction when the goods and services you buy do not meet the standards promised by the manufacturer or the marketer.

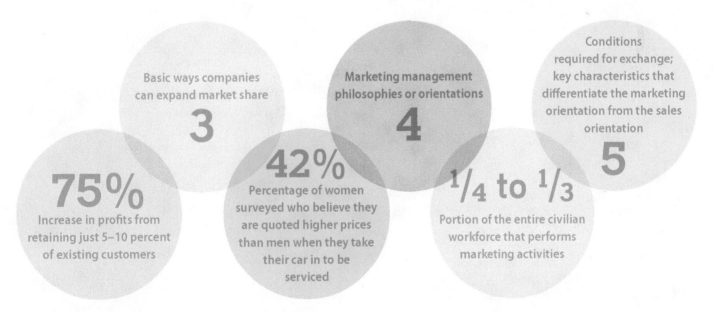

Basic ways companies can expand market share
3

Marketing management philosophies or orientations
4

Conditions required for exchange; key characteristics that differentiate the marketing orientation from the sales orientation
5

75%
Increase in profits from retaining just 5–10 percent of existing customers

42%
Percentage of women surveyed who believe they are quoted higher prices than men when they take their car in to be serviced

1/4 to 1/3
Portion of the entire civilian workforce that performs marketing activities

© JULIE PRATT

CHAPTER **2** The Marketing
Environment,
Social
Responsibility,
and Ethics

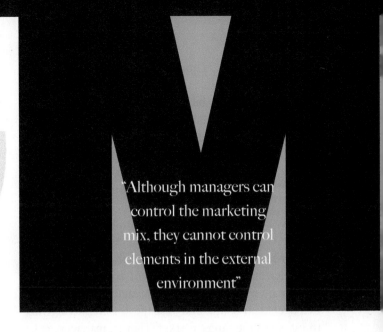

"Although managers can control the marketing mix, they cannot control elements in the external environment"

LO1 The External Marketing Environment

AFTER YOU FINISH THIS CHAPTER, GO TO WWW.ICANMKTG2.COM FOR STUDY TOOLS.

An extremely important decision made by marketing managers is the decision that relates to the creation of the marketing mix. Recall from Chapters 1 that a marketing mix is the unique combination of product, place (distribution), promotion, and price strategies. (The marketing mix is also addressed in Chapter 3.) The marketing mix is, of course, under the firm's control and is designed to appeal to a specific group of potential buyers. A **target market** is a defined group that managers feel is most likely to buy a firm's product.

target market a defined group most likely to buy a firm's product

Over time, managers alter the marketing mix to keep pace with changes in the environment in which consumers live, work, and make purchasing decisions. Also, as markets mature, some new consumers become part of the target market; others drop

What do you think?

The more similar consumers are to the target market that a company's marketing mix is designed to appeal to, the greater the likelihood the company will be successful.

1   2   3   4   5   6   7
STRONGLY DISAGREE   STRONGLY AGREE

ULTRA.F/PHOTODISC/JUPITERIMAGES

environmental management when a company implements strategies that attempt to shape the external environment within which it operates

component lifestyles choosing goods and services that meet one's diverse needs and interests rather than conforming to a single, traditional lifestyle

out. Those who remain may have different tastes, needs, incomes, lifestyles, and buying habits than the original target consumers.

Although managers can control the marketing mix, they cannot control elements in the external environment that continually mould and reshape the target market. Controllable and uncontrollable variables affect the target market, whether it consists of consumers or business purchasers. The uncontrollable elements of the environment continually evolve and create changes in the target market. In contrast, managers can shape and reshape the marketing mix to influence the target market. That is, managers react to changes in the external environment and attempt to create a more effective marketing program.

Understanding the External Environment

Unless marketing managers understand the external environment, the firm cannot intelligently plan for the future. Thus, many organizations assemble a team of specialists to continually collect and evaluate environmental information, a process called *environmental scanning*. The goal in gathering the environmental data is to identify future market opportunities and threats.

Environmental Management

No one business is large enough or powerful enough to create major change in the external environment. Marketing managers, therefore, are basically adapters rather than agents of change. A firm is not always completely at the mercy of the external environment, however. Sometimes a firm can influence external events, for example, through extensive lobbying. When a company implements strategies that attempt to shape the external environment within which it operates, it is engaging in **environmental management**.

The factors within the external environment that are important to marketing managers can be classified as social, demographic, economic, technological, political and legal, and competitive.

LO 2 Social Factors

Social change is perhaps the most difficult external variable for marketing managers to forecast, influence, or integrate into marketing plans. Social factors include our attitudes, values, and lifestyles. Social factors influence the products people buy, the prices paid for products, the effectiveness of specific promotions, and how, where, and when people expect to purchase products.

Marketing-Oriented Values

A *value* is a strongly held and enduring belief. Four basic values strongly influence attitudes and lifestyles of Canadian consumers:

▸▸ *Self-sufficiency:* Every person should stand on his or her own two feet.

▸▸ *Upward mobility:* Success should come to anyone who gets an education, works hard, and plays by the rules.

▸▸ *Work ethic:* Hard work, dedication to family, and frugality are moral and right.

▸▸ *Conformity:* No one should expect to be treated differently from everybody else.

These core values hold for a majority of Canadians today and have led to the perception that Canadians are trustworthy, family-oriented, conservative, and increasingly eco-conscious. Canadian society is known to be tolerant and respectful of other cultures. Our values are key determinants of what is important and not important, what actions we take or do not take, and how we behave in social situations.

Our values are typically formed through our interactions with family, friends, and other influencers, such as teachers, religious leaders, and politicians. The changing environment can also play a key role in shaping our values.

Values also influence our buying habits. Today's consumers are demanding, inquisitive, and discriminating. No longer willing to tolerate products that break down, we insist on high-quality goods that save time, energy, and often calories. Shoppers rank the characteristics of product quality as (1) reliability, (2) durability, (3) easy maintenance, (4) ease of use, (5) a trusted brand name, and (6) a low price. As shoppers, we are also concerned about nutrition and want to know what's in our food, and many of us have environmental concerns.

The Growth of Component Lifestyles

Canadian consumers today are piecing together **component lifestyles**. A lifestyle is a mode of living; it is the way we decide to live our lives. In other words, we choose products and services that meet our diverse needs and interests rather than conforming to traditional stereotypes.

In the past, a person's profession—for instance, banker—defined his or her lifestyle. Today, a person can be a banker and also a gourmet cook, a fitness enthusiast, a dedicated single parent, and an Internet guru. Each of these lifestyles is associated with different goods and services and represents a target audience. Component lifestyles increase the complexity of consumers' buying habits. The unique lifestyles of every consumer can require a different marketing mix.

Families Today

The Vanier Institute of the Family defines the family today as: Any combination of two or more persons who are bound together over time by ties of mutual consent, birth and/or adoption or placement and who, together, assume responsibilities for variant combinations of some of the following:

- ▸▸ Physical maintenance and care of group members
- ▸▸ Addition of new members through procreation or adoption
- ▸▸ Socialization of children
- ▸▸ Social control of members
- ▸▸ Production, consumption, distribution of goods and services
- ▸▸ Affective nurturance—love[1]

Despite a great deal of media coverage on the changing role of the family, it isn't so much the *role* of the family that has changed but the *makeup* of

FANCY/JUPITERIMAGES

the family. Canadian families have an unprecedented level of diversity. Some men and women are raising children on their own without a partner; others are living together unmarried, with or without children; and gay and lesbian couples are caring for each other and raising children together. In addition, some adult children are following a trend of returning to the nest and living with their parents, and an increasing number of people are living on their own.[2] Families today still demonstrate how, as individuals, we accept responsibility for each other.[3]

We face significant challenges in how we carry out our family responsibilities. For families today, two key resources are required—time and money—and they are both in short supply. The cost to raise children is ever increasing. Rising unemployment and the uncertainty of the economic system, coupled with some of the new family structures, continue to fuel a key Canadian social issue—child poverty. The currency for a successful career today is an investment of time and money in higher education, which too can be a challenge for some families. Families are also being challenged with caring for elderly parents in a system that appears to not be able to support them either fairly or equitably.[4]

The time poverty of Canadian families has led to an increase in use of social media not only as a communication tool but also as an information-gathering tool. Primary grocery shoppers in the home are increasingly using the Internet to do chores, plan trips, research products, find health information, read the news, seek out specials, and get coupons or participate in group savings. Consumers freely share the information they find with everyone in their personal networks.

LO 3 Demographic Factors

Another variable in the external environment and one extremely important to marketing managers is **demography**—the study of people's vital statistics, such as their age, race and ethnicity, and location. Demographics are significant because the basis for any market is people. Demographic characteristics are strongly related to consumer behaviour in the marketplace.

We turn our attention now to a closer look at age groups, their impact, and the opportunities they present for marketers. Why does tailoring the merchandise to particular age groups matter? One reason is that each generation enters a life stage with its own tastes and biases, and tailoring products to what customers value is key to sales. The cohorts have been given the names of tweens, Generation Y, Generation X, and baby boomers. You will find that each cohort group has its own needs, values, and consumption patterns.

Tweens and Teens

Canada's tweens, now often referred to as Gen-Zers, are pre-adolescents and early adolescents (aged 9 to 14). With attitudes, access to information, brand consciousness, technical sophistication well beyond their years, and purchasing power to match, these young consumers increasingly represent an attractive segment for marketers of all kinds of products.

The number of tweens owning cellphones has doubled over the past five years, with cellphone ownership among the 11- to 14-year-old age group reaching 69 percent. This age group represents the fastest-growing segment in the cellphone market.[5] Add to this, the dollar amounts that parents will spend on their tweens and one grasps the importance and potential of this market. Tweens overwhelmingly (92 percent) recognize television commercials for what they are—just advertising—and indicate that they tune out ads simply because they are boring. Despite such indifference, a recent proposal by the Toronto District School Board to expand in-school video advertising was turned down by the trustees after pressure by both parents and students. The consensus among 50 student councils across the school board was that the students didn't feel that school was an appropriate place to promote products.[6]

Teens, those aged 15 to 19, represent just over 2.1 million people in Canada. As a group, they are extremely important to marketers, because they wield significant purchasing power and are key influencers in family purchases. Teenagers are avid shoppers, spending on fashion, makeup, food, and entertainment. They are computer-savvy, heavy users of social media, and active digital music and movie downloaders.

Generation Y

Those designated by demographics as **Generation Y** were born between 1979 and 1994. They are about 6.4 million strong in Canada. And though Gen-Yers represent a much smaller group than the baby boomers, whose

birthdates span nearly 20 years, they are plentiful enough to put their own footprints on society. Most Gen-Yers are the children of baby boomers and so are sometimes referred to as echo boomers.

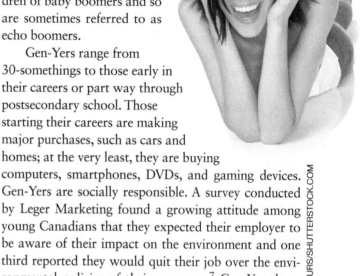

Gen-Yers range from 30-somethings to those early in their careers or part way through postsecondary school. Those starting their careers are making major purchases, such as cars and homes; at the very least, they are buying computers, smartphones, DVDs, and gaming devices. Gen-Yers are socially responsible. A survey conducted by Leger Marketing found a growing attitude among young Canadians that they expected their employer to be aware of their impact on the environment and one third reported they would quit their job over the environmental policies of their company.[7] Gen-Yers have been referred to as trophy kids as a result of their high expectations in the workforce and their increased sense of entitlement that leads to a desire for a better work–life balance. This is the generation that was rewarded for participation in a sport not just when their team won! Gen-Yers are more likely to be entrepreneurial. They have grown up in the face of a global financial crisis and significant meltdown in the financial markets. They are thus able to work with an uncertainty that other generations can't. They have the ability to network and can use social media to their advantage. They have seen people all around them forced out of work and are able to reinvent themselves as freelancers or consultants. They thus view self-employment positively.

Researchers have found Gen-Yers to be

▸▸ *Impatient.* Because they have grown up in a world that has always been automated, it's no surprise that they expect things to be done now.

YURI ARCURS/SHUTTERSTOCK.COM

BLOOMBERG VIA GETTY IMAGES

Gen-Yers are emerging as important to the survival of luxury brands. By 2017, Gen-Yers will outspend boomers. However, to appeal to the opinionated Gen-Yers, luxury brands will need to tell the Gen-Yer why their products should be considered luxury![8]

- *Family oriented.* Gen-Yers had relatively stable child-hoods and grew up in a very family-focused era, so they tend to have a stronger family orientation than the generation that preceded them.

- *Inquisitive.* Gen-Yers tend to want to know why things happen, how things work, and what they can do next.

- *Opinionated.* Today's youth have been encouraged to share their opinions by their parents, teachers, and other authority figures. As a result, Gen-Yers feel that their opinions are always needed and welcomed.

- *Diverse.* Gen Y is the most ethnically diverse generation the nation has ever seen, so they're much more accepting overall of people who are different from themselves.

- *Good managers of time.* Their entire lives have been scheduled—from playgroups to soccer camp to Little League, so they've picked up a knack for planning along the way.

- *Savvy.* Having been exposed to the Internet and 24-hour cable TV news at a young age, Gen-Yers are not easily shocked. They're much more aware of the world around them than earlier generations were.[9]

- *Connected.* More than 16 million Canadians are on Facebook, using their social networks for both communication and commerce.

Generation X

Generation X—people born between 1966 and 1978—consists of more than 7 million consumers across Canada. It is the first generation of latchkey children—products of dual-career households or, in roughly half of the cases, of divorced or separated parents. Gen-Xers have been bombarded by multiple media since their cradle days; thus, they are savvy and cynical consumers.

Their careers launched and their families started, Gen-Xers are at the stage in life when a host of demands are competing for their time—and their budgets. As a result, Gen X spending is quite diffuse: food, housing, transportation. Time is at a premium for harried Gen-Xers, so they're outsourcing the tasks of daily life, which include everything from housecleaning to dog walking to lawn care. Because of demands on their time, Gen-Xers spend much more on personal services than any other age group.[10] Many Gen-Xers work from home.

Over the next 10 years, most Gen-Xers will cross over into their 40s, historically the money-making years. Over the past 30 years, people aged 45 to 54 earned 60 percent more on average than any other age group. Gen-Xers face the reality, however, that the generation ahead of them, having experienced a financial recession, which started in late 2007, may opt not to retire, thereby affecting the Gen-Xers' ability to maximize their income. In addition, as an impending pension crisis looms, the Gen-Xers may find themselves funding the retirement years of the boomers. Although Gen-Xers are making and spending money, companies still tend to ignore them, focusing instead on the larger demographic groups—the baby boomers and Gen-Yers.

Baby Boomers—A Mass Market

Baby boomers make up the largest demographic segment of today's Canadian population. There are 9 million **baby boomers** (persons born between 1947 and 1965). The oldest have already turned 60 years old. With average life expectancy increasing, more and more Canadians over the age of 50 consider middle age to be a new start on life. People now in their 50s may well work longer than any previous generation; more men and women, given better health and uncertain economic cycles, are staying in the workforce longer than they ever have.

The boomers' incomes will continue to grow as they keep working. As a group, people aged 50 to 60 have more spending power per year, about double the spending power of today's 60- to 70-year-olds. In general, baby boomers are active and affluent, but a subsegment of boomers worry about the future and their own financial security.[11] Still, baby boomers are likely to be vigorous consumers in the future, and even though historically, consumers locked in their brand preferences by age 40, today's over-50 crowd is just as likely—and in some cases more likely—than younger generations to try different brands within a product category.[12] Nielsen research indicates that over the next decade Canadian households

KURHAN/SHUTTERSTOCK.COM

CANADIANS ON THE MOVE

Primary urban destinations in Canada are Toronto, Montreal, Calgary, and Vancouver.

multiculturalism
when all major ethnic groups in an area—such as a city, county, or census tract—are roughly equally represented

will be smaller. With a tougher economy, those smaller households will spend less, and the shrinking economy will affect the salaries of the Gen-Yers and Gen-Xers. Marketers must change their focus from youth to the boomers. They are a powerful demographic (as they have always been) with a spending power of more than $1 trillion. "According to Nielsen, baby boomers in 2010 account for approximately 38.5% of all dollars spent on consumer package-goods such as diapers, toothpaste and laundry detergent. They account for 40% of customers paying for wireless services and 41% of customers paying for Apple personal computers. And while brand alliances are often thought to be established by the time the consumer has turned 40, changing technology has unleased a steady spate of new devices and gadgets that are now available to all consumers"[13]

Population Shifts in Canada

Canada is a large country with a relatively small population that was, historically, spread out between rural and urban areas. Since the mid-1970s, however, the population has shifted out of rural areas so that now almost 80 percent of Canadians are considered to be urban dwellers. The majority of this 80 percent live in census metropolitan areas (CMAs), regions defined by Statistics Canada as comprising one or more municipalities situated around a major urban core, with a total population of at least 100,000.[14]

According to Statistics Canada, over 50 percent of the Canadian population lives in four major urban regions in Canada: the Golden Horseshoe in Ontario, Montreal and surrounding area, British Columbia's Lower Mainland, and the Calgary–Edmonton corridor. A recent Statistics Canada study observed that new parents and those between the ages of 25 and 44 were more likely than any others to move from an urban central municipality to a surrounding municipality or suburb.[15] The Toronto, Montreal, and Vancouver CMAs were home to 68.9 percent of recent immigrants in 2006, in contrast to 27.1 percent of the total Canadian population. Between 2001 and 2006, smaller CMAs were attracting immigrants, with 16.6 percent of immigrants settling in the CMAs of Calgary, Edmonton, Ottawa, Winnipeg, Hamilton, and London.[16] As a result, these urban core areas are the focus of many marketing programs by firms that are interested in reaching a large national yet very multicultural market.

LO 4 Growing Ethnic Markets

As anyone who lives and works in Canada will know, the population of our country is becoming more diverse. As a result, we are all being exposed to the languages, music, foods, and customs of a host of other cultures. The diversity will increase as more immigrants come to Canada. Given our relatively small population, immigration is an important source of the population growth needed to sustain and improve our economic growth. Each year, nearly 250,000 immigrants arrive in Canada. Close to three-quarters of these arrivals are classified as visible minorities.

Statistics Canada projects that by 2017, the visible minority population of Canada will be close to 7 million people and will account for 20 percent of the country's population.[17] And, if current trends continue, by that same year, fully 75 percent of this visible minority population will live in either Toronto, Vancouver, or Montreal (see Exhibit 2.1).[18] This multicultural environment will present both challenges and opportunities for firms developing marketing programs in these regions. Both domestic and international firms will need to adapt to this marketing reality.

Ethnic and Cultural Diversity

Multiculturalism occurs when all major ethnic groups in an area—such as a city, county, or census tract—are roughly equally represented. Because of its current demographic transition, the trend in Canada is toward greater multiculturalism.

The largest urban centres or census metropolitan areas in Canada experience the greatest impact of multiculturalism. The 2006 census revealed that between 17 and 44 percent of the populations of

Toronto, Vancouver, Montreal, Calgary, Ottawa, and Edmonton reported neither English nor French as their first language. This finding has major implications for any marketing program. Companies such as CIBC and Sears Canada have altered their advertising campaigns to reflect their changing customer profile and to provide information in other languages. The service sector, in particular, has had to adapt quickly to this change in Canada's demographic makeup. A visit to a local library or hospital in any urban centre will demonstrate the different needs that must be met in a culturally diverse population and the variety of languages that the services should be offered in. The City of Toronto reports that over 100 different languages are spoken in the city.[19]

As our immigrant population increases, many firms are either adapting or developing marketing plans to attract these segments. The World Cup of Soccer in 2010 saw Coke launch a World Cup anthem that became a number one iTunes hit in 17 countries. The song by Canadian K'naan and his label, A&M Octone Records, was the musical centrepiece of Coca-Cola's 160-country global marketing theme and it worked. The song "Wavin' Flag" crossed cultures. Marketers in Canada today are challenged to do the same. The cultural diversity of our country and the trend to multiculturalism will require multicultural marketing right at home.[20]

Another significant finding from the 2006 census is that 25 percent of the visible minority population is

EXHIBIT 2.1
Visible Minority Population in Selected Major Canadian Cities

	2001	**2006**	**2017**
Vancouver	36.9%	42.2%	51.0%
Toronto	36.8	41.9	50.5
Calgary	17.5	19.5	23.6
Ottawa	17.0	20.8	27.4
Edmonton	14.6	15.3	17.5
Montreal	13.6	15.4	19.4
Windsor	12.9	15.8	21.4
Winnipeg	12.5	13.3	15.7
Kitchener	10.7	12.0	15.1
Hamilton	9.8	11.1	14.5

SOURCE: Adapted from the Statistics Canada publication "Population Projections of Visible Minority Groups, Canada, Provinces and Regions," 2001 to 2017, Catalogue 91-541, released March 22, 2005, URL: http://www.statcan.ca/english/freepub/91-541-XIE/91-541-XIE2005001.pdf.

under 14 years of age.[21] This group will have a great impact in the decade ahead. Many of these young people will have the ability to understand and converse in multiple languages and will have adapted elements of numerous cultures into their lifestyle. These cultures will influence their response to marketing messages and ultimately determine their buying behaviour. What does being a Canadian really mean to a marketer?

Dramatic growth has been seen in Internet use across all ethnic groups.[22] Young people from various cultures use the Internet for accessing information and making purchases, which has spawned new strategies for using the Internet to reach the diverse youth markets. Every cultural group has access to websites that cater to their specific culture—everything from social networks, products, and events, to links to their native country. These culture-specific websites present opportunities for firms to target specific ethnic groups.

LO 5 Economic Factors

In addition to social and demographic factors, marketing managers must understand and react to the economic environment. The three economic areas of greatest concern to most marketers are consumers' incomes, inflation, and recession.

© KEN SEET/CORBIS

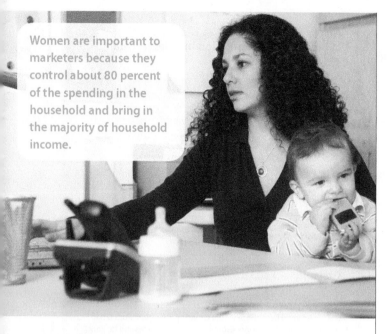

Women are important to marketers because they control about 80 percent of the spending in the household and bring in the majority of household income.

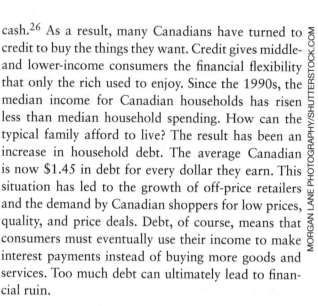

Consumers' Incomes

purchasing power
a comparison of income versus the relative cost of a set standard of goods and services in different geographic areas

As disposable (or after-tax) incomes rise, more families and individuals can afford the "good life." The median total family income in Canada was $68,410 in 2009.[23] Half of all Canadian households earned less, and the other half earned more than that amount.[24]

Education is the primary determinant of a person's earning potential. According to Human Resources and Skills Development Canada, the benefits of higher education include higher earnings, greater savings and assets, higher growth in earnings and higher income during retirement. In addition, higher education reduces the risk of experiencing low income and unemployment. The benefits of higher education are consistent across all provinces.[25] Along with "willingness to buy," or "ability to buy," income is a key determinant of target markets. The marketer who knows where the money is knows where the markets are. If you are seeking a store location for a new Louis Vuitton retail store, a brand that caters to high-income-earning consumers, you would probably concentrate on areas where residents have incomes that are significantly higher than the median. In Canada, 19 percent of consumers say that once they have paid for their essential living expenses they have no spare cash.[26] As a result, many Canadians have turned to credit to buy the things they want. Credit gives middle- and lower-income consumers the financial flexibility that only the rich used to enjoy. Since the 1990s, the median income for Canadian households has risen less than median household spending. How can the typical family afford to live? The result has been an increase in household debt. The average Canadian is now $1.45 in debt for every dollar they earn. This situation has led to the growth of off-price retailers and the demand by Canadian shoppers for low prices, quality, and price deals. Debt, of course, means that consumers must eventually use their income to make interest payments instead of buying more goods and services. Too much debt can ultimately lead to financial ruin.

Purchasing Power

Rising incomes don't necessarily mean a higher standard of living. Increased standards of living are a function of purchasing power. **Purchasing power** is measured by comparing income to the relative cost of a set standard of goods and services in different geographic areas, usually referred to as the cost of living. Another way to think of purchasing power is income minus the cost of living (i.e., expenses). In general, a cost-of-living index takes into account the costs of housing, food and groceries, transportation, utilities, health care, and miscellaneous expenses such as clothing, services, and entertainment. The cost of living is generally higher in major urban markets. For example, a worker living in Toronto must earn nearly three times as much to have the same standard of living as someone in Sydney, Nova Scotia.

When income is high relative to the cost of living, people have more discretionary income. That means they have more money to spend on nonessential items (in other words, on wants rather than needs). This information is important to marketers for obvious reasons. Consumers with high purchasing power can afford to spend more money without jeopardizing their budget for such necessities as food, housing, and utilities. They also have the ability to purchase higher-priced necessities, such as a more expensive car, a home in a more expensive neighbourhood, or a designer handbag versus a purse from a discount store.

"WOMEN CONTROL ABOUT 80 PERCENT OF THE SPENDING IN THE HOUSEHOLD."

Inflation

Inflation is a measure of the decrease in the value of money, generally expressed as the percentage reduction in value since the previous year, which is the rate of inflation. Thus, in simple terms, an inflation rate of 5 percent means 5 percent more money is needed today to buy the same basket of products that was purchased last year. If inflation is 5 percent, you can expect that, on average, prices have risen about 5 percent over prices in the previous year. Of course, if pay raises are matching the rate of inflation, then employees will be no worse off in terms of the immediate purchasing power of their salaries.

Inflation pressures consumers to make more economical purchases and still maintain their standard of living. When managers create marketing strategies to cope with inflation, they must realize that, despite what happens to the seller's cost, buyers will not pay more for a product than the subjective value they place on it. No matter how compelling the justification might be for a 10 percent price increase, marketers must always examine the impact of the price increase on demand. Many marketers try to hold prices level as long as is practical. (See Chapter 19 for more information on the strategies marketers use during periods of high inflation.)

Recession

A **recession** is a period of economic activity characterized by negative growth. More precisely, a recession occurs when the gross domestic product falls for two consecutive quarters. The recession that began in December 2007 affected Canada less than the rest of the world. Statistics Canada's official report on the 2008–09 slump shows it was a recession that was milder than two previously experienced economic dips. Canada experienced a recession that was less severe and shorter than in the other G7 nations, and our financial institutions ended up in a much better position than those in the United States, where many required government aid to stay afloat. Nonetheless, in the "technical" recession, Canada experienced a 3.3 percent drop in gross domestic product over the three quarters between the fall of 2008 and the summer of 2009, affecting consumer confidence, which ultimately affected consumer spending.[27] In the early fall of 2011 Canada's big banks issued warnings that the slowing economic growth could continue for a second quarter thereby suggesting another recession could occur before the close of 2011. To cope, many consumers switched to store brands, which on average cost less than manufacturers' brands. More consumers are using coupons than ever before. Group coupon sites are springing up all over. In a recession, consumers consider the price–value relationship deliberately before making purchases.

LO 6 Technological Factors

Technology is a critical factor in every company's external environment. Our ability, as a nation, to maintain and build wealth depends in large part on the speed and effectiveness with which we invent and adopt machines and technologies that lift productivity. External technology is important to managers for two reasons. First, by acquiring the technology, the firm may be able to operate more efficiently or create a better product. Second, a new technology may render existing products obsolete, as in the case of the traditional film-based camera being replaced by digital camera technology. Staying technologically relevant requires a great deal of research and a willingness to adopt new technologies.

> **inflation** a measure of the decrease in the value of money, expressed as the percentage reduction in value since the previous year
>
> **recession** a period of economic activity characterized by negative growth, which reduces demand for goods and services

THE **SUBJECTIVE VALUE** A BUYER PLACES ON THE PRODUCT IS **KEY** IN DETERMINING PURCHASE.

Research

Canada excels at both basic and applied research. **Basic research** (or *pure research*) attempts to expand the frontiers of knowledge but is not aimed at a specific, pragmatic problem. Basic research aims to confirm an existing theory or to learn more about a concept or phenomenon. For example, basic research might focus on high-energy physics. **Applied research**, in contrast, attempts to develop new or improved products. Canada is dramatically improving its track record in applied research. For example in Ontario, the recently rejuvenated auto industry is well positioned to release electric cars in the very near future.

RSS and Blogging

The recent explosion in the popularity of blogs has presented several intriguing opportunities for marketers. RSS (Really Simple Syndication) enables automated, seamless delivery of updated news content or marketing messages to blog sites or cellphones. For example, if you are interested in extreme sports, opera, and exotic fish (or other topics), you can set up an RSS feed that will pull down articles on those topics every day. Advancing technology also allows today's marketers to scan blogs and learn about consumer opinions as they are generated. By expanding their searches to include publicly posted blog content such as photos, user profiles, and hyperlinks, marketers are able to segment markets and profile individuals with newfound speed and accuracy.

LO 7 Political and Legal Factors

Every aspect of the marketing mix is subject to laws and restrictions. It is the duty of marketing managers or their legal assistants to understand these laws and conform to them because failure to comply with regulations can have major consequences for a firm. Sometimes just sensing trends and taking corrective action before a government agency acts can help avoid regulation.

Marketers must balance caution with risk. It is all too easy for a marketing manager, or sometimes a

TRAVEL NOW

78% of Canadians plan to **travel within Canada** in the coming year.

Youth travellers are a growing influence.

81% of Canadians plan to spend the same or more than they did on travel last year. Of all youth (those in the 18- to 24-year-old age group), 88% plan to travel more.

Those in the 18- to 24-year-old age group plan to travel most often in Canada, two trips on average.

According to 51% of those in the 18- to 24-year-old age group, "Travel is one of the most important things in my life."

Given the growing influence of youth travellers and their prolific use of social media, social media and mobile applications are key game changers for tourism![28]

lawyer, to say no to a marketing innovation that actually entails little risk. For example, an overly cautious lawyer could hold up sales of a desirable new product by warning that the package design could prompt a copyright infringement suit. Thus, marketers need a thorough understanding of the laws established by the various levels of government and regulatory agencies to govern marketing-related issues.

Federal Legislation

The federal legislation affecting how business is conducted in Canada is administered by the **Competition Bureau**, an independent agency of Industry Canada. This bureau, as can be seen in Exhibit 2.2, encompasses several branches and is responsible for enforcing laws covering such areas as bankruptcy, trade practices, competition, credit, labelling and packaging, copyrights, hazardous products, patents, and trademarks.[29] Some of

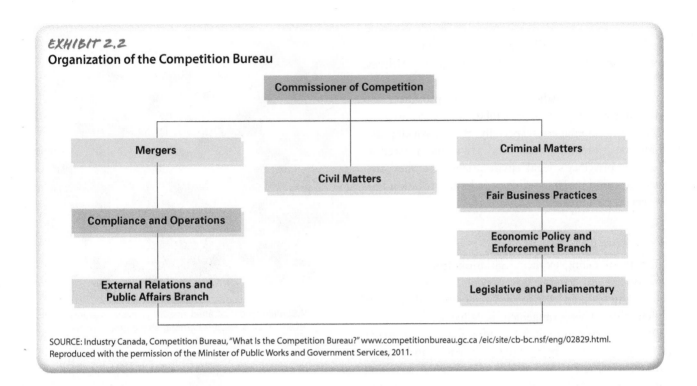

EXHIBIT 2.2
Organization of the Competition Bureau

SOURCE: Industry Canada, Competition Bureau, "What Is the Competition Bureau?" www.competitionbureau.gc.ca /eic/site/cb-bc.nsf/eng/02829.html. Reproduced with the permission of the Minister of Public Works and Government Services, 2011.

EXHIBIT 2.3
Specialized Federal Legislation Affecting Business

LEGISLATION	MAJOR PROVISIONS
Competition Act	Encourages free competition and efficiency in the marketplace. It prohibits mergers and governs specific marketing activities such as misleading advertising, price fixing, predatory pricing, and multilevel marketing fraud.
Consumer Packaging and Labelling Act	Ensures that full information regarding packaging (such as quantity and standard units of weight, volume, or measure) is provided to the consumer in both English and French.
Trade-marks Act	Regulates and protects brand names and trade marks.
Textile Labelling Act	Regulates the labelling of consumer textile goods, including clothing, bedding, and carpets.
Food and Drug Act	Monitors the sale of food, drugs, and cosmetics.
Motor Vehicle Safety Act	Regulates the safety standards for the manufacture of motor vehicles.
Personal Information Protection and Electronic Documents Act	Regulates the collection and use of personal information for commercial purposes. It protects the right of privacy of individuals while allowing for personal information to be used for appropriate purposes.
Privacy Act	Includes the ten privacy principles from the National Standard of Canada and outlines other laws and requirements to guide marketers regarding privacy issues.

SOURCE: From ZIKMUND/D'AMICO/BROWNE/DONVILLE. *Effective Marketing* ,1E. © 2008 Nelson Education Ltd. Reproduced by permission. www.cengage.com/permissions.

the specialized federal legislation that affects businesses and business dealings are listed in Exhibit 2.3.

Provincial and Territorial Laws

In Canada, our constitution divides legal jurisdictions between the provincial or territorial legislatures and the federal government, thus allowing each level of government to legislate in the areas for which it has been given responsibility. For example, Quebec's Bill 101 restricts the use of the English language in certain advertising and promotion material. A national company, such as Tim Hortons, may have to alter its advertising and store signage in Quebec to be in compliance. Alberta allows the sale of alcoholic beverages by retailers, whereas Ontario has provincially run Liquor Control Board of Ontario (LCBO) outlets. Airlines, on the other hand, are under federal jurisdiction, and the provinces do not have direct powers to regulate airline companies. Marketing managers, especially those working for national companies, must be aware of the differences in each province's legal environment, and they also need a sound understanding of federal legislation that affects their industry.

Self-Regulation

Instead of facing explicit legislation from either the provincial or federal governments, many business groups in Canada have formed associations that police themselves. This arrangement is called **self-regulation**. One such association is Advertising Standards Canada (ASC), established by Canada's advertising industry to monitor honesty and fairness in advertising. Advertising is a very visible form of communication strategy, and some firms come under fire from consumer groups regarding deception and honesty in their advertising. In an effort to achieve its mandate of "maintaining Canadian consumer confidence in advertising," ASC launched the campaign "Truth in Advertising" in November 2010. The strategy was to get the public's attention by purposefully exaggerating situations to make the point that dressing them up does not make them true. The intent was to inform consumers that truth in advertising is as important to the industry as it is to the public.[30] Another group, the Canadian Association of Broadcasters (CAB), has established a code of ethics for its member television and radio stations. The Canadian Marketing Association (CMA) has made great strides in developing guidelines and ethical practices for its thousands of member marketing firms.

Consumer Privacy A marketing manager must also be aware of the increasingly important area of consumer privacy, especially because of the vast amounts of data that almost any firm can collect and store by using the latest database technology. Everything from customer information to survey data is valuable to companies, but privacy issues need to be addressed. Firms should be able to justify the type of information they have and how it is to be used. Other issues of note are the security of information storage and the sale or transfer of information to others. Increasingly, and largely as a result of pressure from consumers'

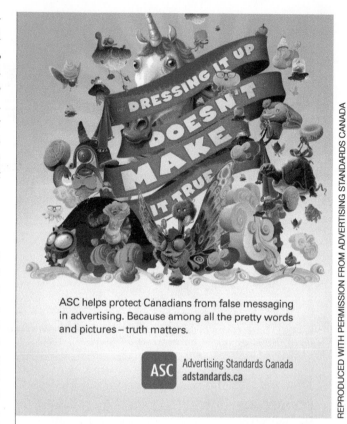

ASC helps protect Canadians from false messaging in advertising. Because among all the pretty words and pictures – truth matters.

ASC Advertising Standards Canada
adstandards.ca

groups, governments are looking at developing, or have already developed, privacy legislation.

Canada's federal government, similar to the governments of many other countries, already has legislation relating to privacy. The Privacy Act (PA) and the Personal Information Protection and Electronic Documents Act (PIPEDA) were put in place to protect the privacy of our personal information and to ensure that its collection, use, and disclosure are both legal and ethical. Canadian consumers are concerned about their privacy, but how many are aware of the details of this legislation? Marketers must, therefore, be proactive in ensuring consumer privacy.

LO8 Competitive Factors

The competitive environment encompasses the number of competitors a firm must face, the relative size of the competitors, and the degree of interdependence within the industry. Management has little control over the competitive environment confronting a firm.

Competition for Market Share and Profits

As Canadian population growth slows, costs rise, and available resources tighten, firms must work harder to maintain both their profits and market share regardless of the form of the competitive market. Firms often turn to innovative forms of advertising and communication to capture the minds of the target consumer. One such newer form is social media, a powerful form of communication. Firms also tap into socio-cultural trends by using these trends in their communications. For example, Pepsico, recognizing the growing consumer interest in product ingredients and the 100-mile challenge, launched a chip tracker for its "Lays Local" campaign. The tracker lets consumers discover the plant that produced their bag of chips and the farms that supplied the ingredients by entering the product's code on the tracker at lays.ca. Consumers can even drill down further to learn about the farms and the farmers.[31]

LO 9 Corporate Social Responsibility

Corporate social responsibility is a business's concern for society's welfare. This concern is demonstrated by managers who consider both the long-range best interests of the company and the company's relationship to the society within which it operates. The newest theory in social responsibility is called **sustainability**. This theory refers to the idea that socially responsible companies will outperform their peers by focusing on the world's social problems and viewing them as opportunities to build profits and help the world at the same time. It is also the notion that companies cannot thrive for long (i.e., lack sustainability) in a world where billions of people are suffering and are desperately poor. Thus, it is in business's interest to find ways to attack society's ills.

Another view is that business should focus on making a profit and leave social and environmental problems to nonprofit organizations and government. Economist Milton Friedman believed that the free market, and not companies, should decide what is best for the world.[32] Friedman argued that to the degree that business executives spend more money than they need to—purchasing delivery vehicles with hybrid engines, paying higher wages in developing countries, or even donating company funds to charity—they are spending shareholders' money to further their own agendas. Better to pay dividends and let the shareholders give the money away, if they choose.

Total corporate social responsibility has four components: economic, legal, ethical, and philanthropic.[33] The **pyramid of corporate social responsibility** portrays economic performance as the foundation for the other three responsibilities. At the same time that a business pursues profits (economic responsibility), however, it is also expected to obey the law (legal responsibility); to do what is right, just, and fair (ethical responsibilities); and to be a good corporate citizen (philanthropic responsibility). These four components are distinct but together constitute the whole. Still, if the company doesn't make a profit, then the other three responsibilities are moot.

Growth of Social Responsibility

The social responsibility of businesses is growing around the world. A recent study of social responsibility in seven countries, asked "Does your company consider social responsibility factors when making business decisions?" The percentage of each country's firms that said yes were as follows: Brazil, 62 percent; Canada, 54 percent; Australia, 52 percent; the United States, 47 percent; India, 38 percent; China, 35 percent; and Mexico, 26 percent.[34]

Furthermore, in Canada social responsibility has become increasingly professionalized and integrated across all levels within the organization. According to Imagine Canada, a national program supporting public and corporate charitable giving, businesses

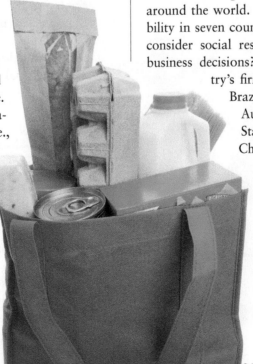

corporate social responsibility a business's concern for society's welfare

sustainability the idea that socially responsible companies will outperform their peers by focusing on the world's social problems and viewing them as opportunities to build profits and help the world at the same time

pyramid of corporate social responsibility a model that suggests corporate social responsibility is composed of economic, legal, ethical, and philanthropic responsibilities and that the firm's economic performance supports the entire structure

STEPHEN MCSWEENY/SHUTTERSTOCK.COM

green marketing
the development and marketing of products designed to minimize negative effects on the physical environment

ethics the moral principles or values that generally govern the conduct of an individual or a group

morals the rules people develop as a result of cultural values and norms

have moved beyond simply writing a cheque to a more engaged and integrated approach to social responsibility that includes in-kind gifts, employee volunteerism, and sponsorships.

Firms are realizing that corporate social responsibility isn't easy or quick. It works only when a firm engages a long-term strategy and effort, and the strategy is coordinated throughout the organization. It doesn't always come cheap, and the payoff, both to society and the firm itself, isn't always immediate. But consumers will patronize firms that are socially responsible.

Green Marketing

An outgrowth of the social responsibility movement is **green marketing**, the development and marketing of products designed to minimize negative effects on the physical environment. Not only can a company aid the environment through green marketing, but green marketing can often help the bottom line. Environmentally aware consumers tend to earn more and are more willing to pay a premium for green products.

To protect consumers from companies capitalizing on the "green movement" without substance, the Canadian Competition Bureau launched a guide that provides the business community with green marketing guidelines. While the guide is not law, the Competition Bureau will pursue deceptive environmental claims, fine violators, or remove products from store shelves. The guide suggests that environmental claims should be clear, specific, accurate, and not misleading; and all environmental claims should be verified and substantiated.

A company known for its green marketing practices is S. C. Johnson & Son. This company developed the Greenlist process, which requires that its scientists evaluate all the company's product ingredients to determine their impact and to reformulate products to reduce the ingredients' impact on the environment.[35] The use of this patented process led to the reformulation of Windex, resulting in a greener and more effective product.

LO 10 Ethical Behaviour in Business

Social responsibility and ethics go hand in hand. Ethics refers to the moral principles or values that generally govern the conduct of an individual or a group. Ethics can also be viewed as the standard of behaviour by which conduct is judged. Standards that are legal may not always be ethical, and vice versa. Laws are the values and standards enforceable by the courts. Ethics consists of personal moral principles and values rather than societal prescriptions.

Defining the boundaries of ethicality and legality can be difficult. Often, judgment is needed to determine whether an action that may be legal is an ethical or unethical act. Also, judgment is required to determine whether an unethical act is legal or illegal.

Morals are the rules people develop as a result of cultural values and norms. Culture is a socializing force that dictates what is right and wrong. Moral standards may also reflect the laws and regulations that affect social and economic behaviour. Thus, morals can be considered a foundation of ethical behaviour.

Morals are usually characterized as good or bad. "Good" and "bad" have different connotations, including effective and ineffective. A good salesperson makes or exceeds the assigned quota. If the salesperson sells a new stereo or television set to a disadvantaged consumer—knowing full well that the person can't keep up the monthly payments—is the salesperson still considered to be good? What if the sale enables the salesperson to exceed his or her quota?

Good and bad can also refer to conforming and deviant behaviours. Any doctor in Canada

THE CANADIAN PRESS/DON DENTON

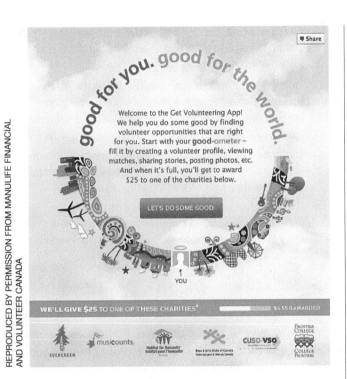

Manulife Financial and not-for-profit organization Volunteer Canada launched a marketing and social media initiative at www.getvolunteering.ca that was designed to increase the number of Canadian volunteers.

who charges extra fees for fast-tracking patients on waiting lists for provincially funded procedures would be considered unprofessional. Such a doctor would not be conforming to the norms and laws of the medical profession or to the laws regarding universal health-care set by our provincial legislatures and federal government. Bad and good are also used to express the distinction between criminal and law-abiding behaviour. And finally, different religions define good and bad in markedly different ways. A Muslim who eats pork would be considered bad, as would a fundamentalist Christian who drinks whisky.

Morality and Business Ethics

Today's business ethics actually consists of a subset of major life values learned since birth. The values business people use to make decisions have been acquired through family, educational, and religious institutions.

Ethical values are situation specific and time oriented. Nevertheless, everyone must have an ethical base that applies to conduct in the business world and in personal life. One approach to developing a personal set of ethics is to examine the consequences of a particular act. Who is helped or hurt? How long

GREEN IS GREEN

Mountain Equipment Co-op (MEC) is a Canadian company dedicated to providing quality outdoor gear and excellent value. For 40 years, MEC has operated under the philosophy of minimizing its environmental impact, by building products that last.

Here is how MEC puts it:

▸▸ Our goal is to make quality products for the outdoors. Central to this goal is a belief that our gear be made in a way that respects the people who manufacture it. Through our Ethical Sourcing Program we work to improve the human condition in factories. This means safer working conditions, legal working hours, and reasonable pay for work done.*

▸▸ The goal of our Ethical Sourcing Program is to improve the human condition in factories. This is no small feat. The causes of worker infractions are complex, varied, and driven by flaws in our

economy and society. Completely ending abuse of overtime, unlawful pay, and unsafe working conditions would require fundamental changes to factories, retailers, governments, economies, and to consumers' spending habits. Mindful of all this, we are working toward measured and incremental improvements.

Our Ethical Sourcing Program is run by a Director who reports directly to the CEO. At the Board level, a Sustainability Committee establishes and oversees the program's mandate and objectives. These are included in MEC Board Policies

Beyond the program itself, ethical sourcing requirements are integrated into our product design philosophy and purchasing decisions.[36]

SOURCE: Reproduced with the permission of Mountain Equipment Co-op.

lasting are the consequences? What actions produce the greatest good for the greatest number of people? A second approach stresses the importance of rules. Rules come in the form of customs, laws, professional standards, and common sense. "Always treat others as you would like to be treated" is an example of a rule.

The last approach emphasizes the development of moral character within individuals. Ethical development can be thought of as having three levels:[37]

▸▸ *Preconventional morality*, the most basic level, is childlike. It is calculating, self-centred, even selfish, and is based on what will be immediately punished or rewarded.

▸▸ *Conventional morality* moves from an egocentric viewpoint toward the expectations of society. Loyalty and obedience to the organization (or society) become paramount. A marketing decision maker at this level would be concerned only with whether the proposed action is legal and how it will be viewed by others.

▸▸ *Postconventional morality* represents the morality of the mature adult. At this level, people are less concerned about how others might see them and more concerned about how they see and judge themselves over the long run. A marketing decision maker who has attained a postconventional level of morality might ask, "Even though it is legal and will increase company profits, is it right in the long run?"

Ethical Decision Making

Ethical questions rarely have cut-and-dried answers. Studies show that the following factors tend to influence ethical decision making and judgments:[38]

▸▸ *Extent of ethical problems within the organization:* Marketing professionals who perceive fewer ethical problems in their organizations tend to disapprove more strongly of "unethical" or questionable practices than those who perceive more ethical problems. Apparently, the healthier the ethical environment, the more likely marketers will take a strong stand against questionable practices.

▸▸ *Top-management actions on ethics:* Top managers can influence the behaviour of marketing professionals by encouraging ethical behaviour and discouraging unethical behaviour.

▸▸ *Potential magnitude of the consequences:* The greater the harm done to victims, the more likely marketing professionals will recognize the behaviour as unethical.

▸▸ *Social consensus:* The greater the degree of agreement among managerial peers that an action is harmful, the more likely marketers will recognize the action as unethical.

▸▸ *Probability of a harmful outcome:* The greater the likelihood that an action will result in a harmful outcome, the more likely marketers will recognize the action as unethical.

▸▸ *Length of time between the decision and the onset of consequences:* The shorter the length of time between the action and the onset of negative consequences, the more likely marketers will perceive the action as unethical.

▸▸ *Number of people to be affected:* The greater the number of persons affected by a negative outcome, the more likely marketers will recognize the behaviour as unethical.

Ethical Guidelines

Many organizations have become more interested in ethical issues. One sign of this interest is the increase in the number of large companies that appoint ethics officers—from virtually none seven years ago to almost 33 percent of large corporations now. In addition, many companies of various sizes have developed a **code of ethics** as a guideline to help marketing managers and other employees make better decisions.

Creating ethics guidelines has several advantages:

▸▸ The guidelines help employees identify the business practices their firm recognizes as being acceptable.

▸▸ A code of ethics can be an effective internal control on behaviour, which is more desirable than external controls such as government regulation.

▸▸ A written code helps employees avoid confusion when determining whether their decisions are ethical.

▸▸ The process of formulating the code of ethics facilitates discussion among employees about what is right and wrong, which ultimately leads to better decisions.

Businesses must be careful, however, not to make their code of ethics too vague or too detailed. Codes that are too vague give little or no guidance to employees in their day-to-day activities. Codes that are too detailed encourage employees to substitute rules for judgment. For instance, if employees are involved in questionable behaviour, they may use the absence of a written rule as a reason to continue their behaviour, even though their conscience may be telling them otherwise. Following a set of ethical guidelines will not guarantee the "rightness" of a decision, but it will improve the chances that the decision will be ethical.

IT IS **IN BUSINESS'S INTEREST** TO FIND WAYS TO **ATTACK SOCIETY'S ILLS** AND LEND A HELPING HAND.

WHAT'S EXPECTED OF CANADIAN MARKETERS

The [Canadian Marketing Association's] Code of Ethics and Standards of Practice... is designed to establish and maintain standards for the conduct of marketing in Canada.

Marketers acknowledge that the establishment and maintenance of high standards of practice are a fundamental responsibility to the public, essential to winning and holding consumer confidence, and the foundation of a successful and independent marketing industry in Canada.

Members of the Canadian Marketing Association recognize an obligation—to the consumers and the businesses they serve, to the integrity of the discipline in which they operate, and to each other—to practice to the highest standards of honesty, truth, accuracy, fairness, and professionalism.

SOURCE: From Code of Ethics and Standards of Practice, Canadian Marketing Association, www.the-cma.org

Although many companies have issued policies on ethical behaviour, marketing managers must still put the policies into effect. They must address the classic "matter of degree" issue. For example, marketing researchers often resort to deception to obtain unbiased answers to their research questions. Asking for a few minutes of a respondent's time is dishonest if the researcher knows the interview will last 45 minutes. Not only must management post a code of ethics, it must also give examples of what is ethical and unethical for each item in the code. Moreover, top management must stress to all employees the importance of adhering to the company's code of ethics. Without a detailed code of ethics and top management's support, creating ethical guidelines becomes an empty exercise. The Canadian Marketing Association's code of ethics outlines its purpose.

6
the number of consumer-created ads that ran on Superbowl 2011

36%
percentage of consumers who find Facebook most useful for their travel experience

10
the number of years needed to make up lost economic ground if you graduate when the economy is in a recession

$1 trillion
annual spending power of boomers

Visit **icanmktg2.com** to find the resources you need today!

Located at the back of the textbook are rip-out Chapter Review cards. Make sure you also go online to check out other tools that MKTG offers to help you successfully pass your course.

- Interactive Quizzing
- Games
- Flashcards
- Audio Summaries
- PowerPoint Slides
- Videos and Assessments
- Cases
- Marketing Plans and Worksheets
- Animated Visual Summaries

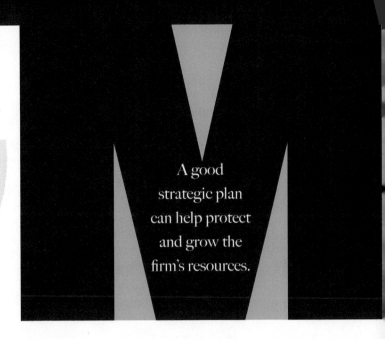

A good
strategic plan
can help protect
and grow the
firm's resources.

LO1   **The Nature of Strategic Planning**

AFTER YOU FINISH THIS CHAPTER, GO TO WWW.ICANMKTG2.COM FOR STUDY TOOLS.

Strategic planning is the managerial process of creating and maintaining a fit between the organization's objectives and resources and the evolving market opportunities. The goal of strategic planning is long-run profitability and growth. Thus, strategic decisions require long-term commitments of resources. A strategic error can threaten a firm's survival. On the other hand, a good strategic plan can help protect and grow the firm's resources.

Strategic marketing management addresses two questions: What is the organization's main activity at a particular time? How will the organization reach its goals? Strategic decisions affect an organization's long-run course, its allocation of resources, and ultimately its financial success. In contrast, an operating decision, such as changing the package design for Kellogg's Corn Flakes or altering the sweetness of a Kraft salad dressing, probably won't have a big impact on the long-run profitability of the company. However, the decisions that an organization makes at the operational and business levels directly link to and flow from the

strategic planning
the managerial process of creating and maintaining a fit between the organization's objectives and resources and evolving market opportunities

What do you think?

Things change so quickly that planning is a waste of time.

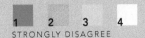

1   2   3   4   5   6   7
STRONGLY DISAGREE   STRONGLY AGREE

MICHAEL THOMAS/GETTY IMAGES

strategic decisions made at the highest level within the organization. For example, an organization might make a strategic decision to increase its presence in a particular market. This decision may result in one of its businesses units expanding its market share through new product introductions as a result of brand or line extensions.

How do companies go about planning strategic marketing? How do employees know how to implement the long-term goals of the firm? The answer is a marketing plan.

What Is a Marketing Plan?

Planning is the process of anticipating future events and determining strategies to achieve organizational objectives in the future. **Marketing planning** involves designing activities relating to marketing objectives and the changing marketing environment. Marketing planning is the basis for all marketing strategies and decisions. Issues such as product lines, distribution channels, marketing communications, and pricing are all delineated in the **marketing plan**. The marketing plan is a written document that acts as a guidebook of marketing activities for the marketing manager. In this chapter, you will learn the importance of writing a marketing plan and the types of information contained in a marketing plan.

Why Write a Marketing Plan?

By specifying objectives and defining the actions required to attain them, a marketing plan provides the basis by which actual and expected performance can be compared. Marketing can be one of the most expensive and complicated business activities, but it is also one of the most important. The written marketing plan provides clearly stated activities that help employees and managers understand and work toward common goals.

Writing a marketing plan allows you to examine the marketing environment in conjunction with the inner workings of the business. Once the marketing plan is written, it serves as a reference point for the success of future activities. Finally, the marketing plan allows the marketing manager to enter the marketplace with an awareness of possibilities and problems.

Marketing Plan Elements

Marketing plans can be presented in many different ways. Most businesses need a written marketing plan because a marketing plan is large and can be complex. Details about tasks and activity assignments may be lost if communicated orally. Regardless of the way a marketing plan is presented, some elements are common to all marketing plans. These include defining the business mission and objectives, performing a situation analysis, delineating a target market, and establishing components of the marketing mix. Exhibit 3.1 shows these elements, which are also described further below. Other elements that may be included in a plan are budgets, implementation timetables, required marketing research efforts, or elements of advanced strategic planning.

USED WITH PERMISSION FROM CHAPMAN'S ICE CREAM LTD.

Chapman's has adapted to a changing, health-conscious market by introducing Yogurt Plus, which is a source of active probiotic cultures and prebiotic fibre, and is low in fat.

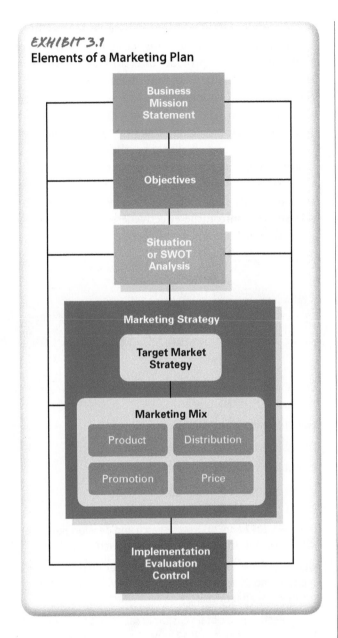

EXHIBIT 3.1
Elements of a Marketing Plan

Business Mission Statement

Objectives

Situation or SWOT Analysis

Marketing Strategy

Target Market Strategy

Marketing Mix

Product | Distribution

Promotion | Price

Implementation Evaluation Control

Writing the Marketing Plan

The creation and implementation of a complete marketing plan will allow the organization to achieve its marketing objectives and succeed. However, the marketing plan is only as good as the information it contains and the effort, creativity, and thought that went into its creation. Having a good marketing information system and a wealth of competitive intelligence is critical to a thorough and accurate situation analysis. The role of managerial intuition is also important in the creation and selection of marketing strategies. Managers must weigh any information against its accuracy and their own judgment when making a marketing decision.

Note that the overall structure of the marketing plan should not be viewed as a series of sequential planning

steps. Many of the marketing plan elements are decided on simultaneously and in conjunction with one another. Similarly, the skeletal sample marketing plan does not begin to cover the intricacies and detail of a full marketing plan. Further, every marketing plan has a different content, depending on the organization and its mission, objectives, targets, and marketing mix components.

There is no single correct format for a marketing plan. Many organizations have their own distinctive format or terminology for creating a marketing plan. As such, every marketing plan is unique to the firm for which it was created; although the format and order of presentation should be flexible, the same types of questions and topic areas should be covered in any marketing plan. Keep in mind that creating a complete marketing plan is not a simple or quick effort.

LO 2 Defining the Business Mission

The foundation of any marketing plan is the firm's **mission statement**, which answers the question: "What business are we in?" The way a firm defines its business mission profoundly affects the firm's long-run resource allocation, profitability, and survival. The mission statement is based on a careful analysis of benefits sought by present and potential customers and an analysis of existing and anticipated environmental conditions. The firm's mission statement establishes boundaries for all subsequent decisions, objectives, and strategies. As such, a mission statement should focus on the market or markets the organization is attempting to serve rather than on the goods or services offered. Otherwise, a new technology may quickly make the goods or services obsolete and the mission statement irrelevant to company functions.

Business mission statements that are stated too narrowly suffer from **marketing myopia**—defining a business in terms of goods and services rather than in terms of the benefits that customers seek. In this context, *myopia* means narrow, short-term thinking, which would be the case if the Wm. Wrigley Jr. Company defined its mission as being a gum manufacturer. (The company actually defines itself as a confectioner.) Alternatively, business missions may be stated too

mission statement
a statement of the firm's business based on a careful analysis of benefits sought by present and potential customers and an analysis of existing and anticipated environmental conditions

marketing myopia
defining a business in terms of goods and services rather than in terms of the benefits that customers seek

broadly. "To provide products of superior quality and value that improve the lives of the world's consumers" is probably too broad a mission statement for any firm except Procter & Gamble. Care must be taken when stating what business a firm is in. By correctly stating the business mission in terms of the benefits that customers seek, the foundation for the marketing plan is set.

The organization may also need to define a mission statement and objectives for a **strategic business unit (SBU)**, which is a subgroup of a single business or a collection of related businesses within the larger organization. A properly defined SBU should have a distinct mission and specific target market, control over its resources, its own competitors, and plans independent of the other SBUs in the organization. Thus, a large firm such as Kraft Foods may have marketing plans for each of its SBUs, which include breakfast foods, desserts, pet foods, and beverages.

LO 3 Setting Marketing Plan Objectives

Before the details of a marketing plan can be developed, objectives for the plan must be stated. Without objectives, a firm has no basis for measuring the success of its marketing plan activities.

A **marketing objective** is a statement of what is to be accomplished through marketing activities. To be useful, stated objectives should meet several criteria. First, objectives should be realistic, measurable, and time specific. It is tempting to state that the objective is "to be the best marketer of cat food." However, what is "best" for one firm might mean selling one million kilograms of cat food per year, whereas another firm might view "best" as having dominant market share. It may also be unrealistic for start-up firms or new products to command dominant market share, given other competitors in the marketplace. Finally, by what time should the objective be met? A more realistic objective would be "To achieve 10 percent dollar market share in the cat food market within 12 months of product introduction." Second, objectives must also be consistent with and indicate the priorities of the organization. Specifically, objectives flow from the business mission statement to the rest of the marketing plan.

Carefully specified objectives serve several functions. First, they communicate marketing management philosophies and provide direction for lower-level marketing managers so that marketing efforts are integrated and pointed in a consistent direction. Objectives also serve as motivators by creating goals for employees to strive toward. When objectives are attainable and challenging, they motivate those charged with achieving the objectives. Additionally, the process of writing specific objectives forces executives to clarify their thinking. Finally, objectives form a basis for control; the effectiveness of a plan can be gauged in light of the stated objectives.

JUDGE FOR YOURSELF

Poorly Stated Objectives

Our objective is to be a leader in the industry in terms of new-product development.

Our objective is to maximize profits.

Our objective is to better serve customers.

Our objective is to be the best that we can be.

Well-Stated Objectives

Our objective is to spend 12 percent of sales revenue between 2012 and 2013 on research and development in an effort to introduce at least five new products in 2013.

Our objective is to achieve a 10 percent return on investment during 2012, with a payback on new investments of no longer than four years.

Our objective is to obtain customer satisfaction ratings of at least 90 percent on the 2012 annual customer satisfaction survey, and to retain at least 85 percent of our 2012 customers as repeat purchasers in 2013.

Our objective is to increase market share from 30 percent to 40 percent in 2012 by increasing promotional expenditures by 14 percent.

LO 4 Conducting a Situation Analysis

Before specific marketing activities can be defined, marketers must understand the current and potential environment that the product or service will be marketed in. A situation analysis is sometimes referred to

	Strengths			**Opportunities**
I N T E R N A L	• production costs • marketing skills • financial resources • image • technology	**E X T E R N A L**		• social • demographic • economic • technological • political/legal • competitive
	Weaknesses			**Threats**

as a **SWOT analysis**; that is, the firm should identify its internal strengths (S) and weaknesses (W) and also examine external opportunities (O) and threats (T).

When examining internal strengths and weaknesses, the marketing manager should focus on organizational resources such as production costs, marketing skills, financial resources, company or brand image, employee capabilities, and available technology. For example, a potential weakness for AirTran Airways is the age of its airplane fleet, which could project an image of danger or low quality. A potential strength is the airline's low operating costs, which translate into lower prices for consumers. Another issue to consider in this section of the marketing plan is the historical background of the firm—its sales and profit history.

When examining external opportunities and threats, marketing managers must analyze aspects of the marketing environment. This process is called **environmental scanning**—the collection and interpretation of information about forces, events, and relationships in the external environment that may affect the future of the organization or the implementation of the marketing plan. Environmental scanning helps identify market opportunities and threats and provides guidelines for the design of marketing strategy. For example, H&R Block, a tax preparation service, benefits from complex changes in the tax codes that motivate citizens to have their tax returns prepared by a professional. Alternatively, tax-simplification or flat-tax plans would allow people to easily prepare their own returns and would have a dramatic impact on the company's revenues. The six most often studied macro-environmental forces are social, demographic, economic, technological, political and legal, and competitive. These forces were examined in detail in Chapter 2.

LO 5 Competitive Advantage

Performing a SWOT analysis allows firms to identify their **competitive advantage**. A competitive advantage is a set of unique features of a company and its products that are perceived by the target market as significant and superior to the competition. It is the factor or factors that cause customers to patronize a firm and not the competition. Firms may have three types of competitive advantages: cost, product/service differentiation, and niche strategies.

Cost Competitive Advantage

Cost leadership can result from obtaining inexpensive raw materials, creating an efficient scale of plant operations, designing products for ease of manufacture, controlling overhead costs, and avoiding marginal customers. Having a **cost competitive advantage** means being the low-cost competitor in an industry while maintaining satisfactory profit margins. A cost competitive advantage enables a firm to deliver superior customer value. Wal-Mart is the world's leading low-cost general merchandise store. It offers good value to customers because it focuses on providing a large selection of merchandise at low prices and good customer service. Wal-Mart is able to keep its prices down because it has strong buying power in its relationships with suppliers.

- Experience Curves
- Efficient Labour
- No-Frills Goods and Services
- Government Subsidies

- Product Design
- Re-engineering
- Production Innovations
- New Methods of Service Delivery

Cost Competitive Advantage

SWOT analysis
identifying internal strengths (S) and weaknesses (W) and also examining external opportunities (O) and threats (T)

environmental scanning collection and interpretation of information about forces, events, and relationships in the external environment that may affect the future of the organization or the implementation of the marketing plan

competitive advantage the set of unique features of a company and its products that are perceived by the target market as significant and superior to the competition

cost competitive advantage being the low-cost competitor in an industry while maintaining satisfactory profit margins

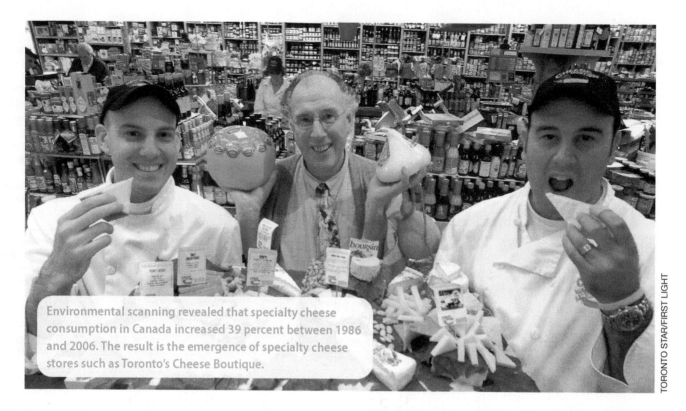

Environmental scanning revealed that specialty cheese consumption in Canada increased 39 percent between 1986 and 2006. The result is the emergence of specialty cheese stores such as Toronto's Cheese Boutique.

experience curves
curves that show costs declining at a predictable rate as experience with a product increases

Costs can be reduced in a variety of ways.

▸▸ *Experience curves:* **Experience curves** tell us that costs decline at a predictable rate as experience with a product increases. The experience curve effect encompasses a broad range of manufacturing, marketing, and administrative costs. Experience curves reflect learning by doing, technological advances, and economies of scale. Firms use historical experience curves as a basis for predicting and setting prices. Experience curves allow management to forecast costs and set prices based on anticipated costs as opposed to current costs. The experience curve was conceived by the Boston Consulting Group in 1966.

▸▸ *Efficient labour:* Labour costs can be an important component of total costs in low-skill, labour-intensive industries such as product assembly and apparel manufacturing. Many Canadian manufacturers have gone offshore to achieve cheaper manufacturing costs. Many Canadian companies are also outsourcing activities such as data entry and other labour-intensive jobs.

▸▸ *No-frills goods and services:* Marketers can lower costs by removing frills and options from a product or service. WestJet, for example, offers low fares but no seat assignments or meals. Low prices give WestJet a higher load factor and greater economies of scale, which, in turn, mean even lower prices.

▸▸ *Government subsidies:* Governments may provide grants and interest-free loans to target industries. Such government assistance enabled Japanese semiconductor manufacturers to become global leaders.

▸▸ *Product design:* Cutting-edge design technology can help offset high labour costs. BMW is a world leader in designing cars for ease of manufacture and assembly. Reverse engineering—the process of disassembling a product piece by piece to learn its components and obtain clues as to the manufacturing process—can also mean savings. Reverse-engineering a low-cost competitor's product can save research and design costs.

▸▸ *Re-engineering:* Re-engineering entails fundamental rethinking and redesign of business processes to achieve dramatic improvements in critical measures of performance. It often involves reorganizing from functional departments such as sales, engineering, and production to cross-disciplinary teams.

▸▸ *Production innovations:* Production innovations such as new technology and simplified production techniques help lower the average cost of production. Technologies such as computer-aided design and computer-aided

"THE **EXPERIENCE CURVE** WAS CONCEIVED BY THE BOSTON CONSULTING GROUP IN 1966."

manufacturing (CAD/CAM) and increasingly sophisticated robots help companies such as Boeing, Ford, and General Electric reduce their manufacturing costs.

▶▶ *New methods of service delivery:* Online bill delivery is not only an environmentally friendly alternative but also results in enormous cost savings. Airlines are lowering reservation and ticketing costs by encouraging passengers to use the Internet to book flights and by providing self-service check-in kiosks at the airport.

Product/Service Differentiation Competitive Advantage

Because cost competitive advantages are subject to continual erosion, product/service differentiation tends to provide a longer-lasting competitive advantage. The durability of this strategy tends to make it more attractive to many top managers. A **product/service differentiation competitive advantage** exists when a firm provides a unique benefit that is valuable to buyers beyond simply offering a low price. Examples include brand names (Lexus), a strong dealer network (Caterpillar for construction work), product reliability (Maytag appliances), image (Holt Renfrew in clothing), or service (FedEx). A great example of a company with a strong product/service differentiation competitive advantage is Oakley. Oakley's advantage is built around one simple idea—product innovation. This company lets its customers design their own sunglasses at its website, www.Oakley.ca/custom.

REPRINTED WITH PERMISSION FROM OAKLEY, INC.

Customize your look with Oakley

Niche Competitive Advantage

A **niche competitive advantage** seeks to target and effectively serve a single segment of the market (see Chapter 7). For small companies with limited resources that potentially face giant competitors, carving out a niche strategy may be the only viable option. A market segment that has good growth potential but is not crucial to the success of major competitors is a good candidate for developing a niche strategy. Many companies using a niche strategy serve only a limited geographic market. Other companies focus their product lines on specific types of products, as is the case with the Canadian company Booster Juice, which specializes in fruit juices, smoothie drinks, and other healthy, nutritious foods.

Building Sustainable Competitive Advantage

The key to having a competitive advantage is the ability to sustain that advantage. A **sustainable competitive advantage** is an advantage that cannot be copied by the competition. Examples of companies with a sustainable competitive advantage include Rolex (high-quality watches), Harry Rosen stores (customized service), and Cirque du Soleil (top-notch entertainment). Without a competitive advantage, target customers don't perceive any reason to patronize one organization over its competitors.

The notion of competitive advantage means that a successful firm will stake out a position unique in some manner from its rivals. Imitation by competitors indicates a lack of competitive advantage and almost ensures mediocre performance. Moreover, competitors rarely stand still, so it is not surprising that imitation causes managers to feel trapped in a seemingly endless game of catch-up. They are regularly surprised by the new accomplishments of their rivals.

Companies need to build their own competitive advantages rather than copy a competitor. The sources of tomorrow's competitive advantages are the skills and assets of the organization. Skills are functions such as customer service and promotion that the firm performs better than its competitors. Assets include patents, copyrights, locations, and equipment and technology that are superior to those of the competition. Marketing managers should continually focus the firm's skills and assets on sustaining and creating competitive advantages.

Remember, a sustainable competitive advantage is a function of the speed with which competitors can imitate a leading company's strategy and plans. Imitation requires a competitor to identify the leader's competitive advantage, determine how it is achieved, and then learn how to duplicate it.

product/service differentiation competitive advantage the provision of a unique benefit that is valuable to buyers beyond simply offering a low price

niche competitive advantage the advantage achieved when a firm seeks to target and effectively serve a single segment of the market

sustainable competitive advantage an advantage that cannot be copied by the competition

LO 6 Strategic Directions

The end result of the SWOT analysis and identification of a competitive advantage is to evaluate the strategic direction of the firm. A mission statement provides an organization with guidance for planning its business portfolio—the collection of its SBUs and products. One of the popular approaches for business portfolio analysis is the Boston Consulting Group (BCG) portfolio matrix.

BCG Portfolio Matrix

Recall that large organizations engaged in strategic planning may create strategic business units. Each SBU has its own rate of return on investment, growth potential, and associated risk. Management must find a balance among the SBUs that yields the overall organization's desired growth and profits with an acceptable level of risk. Some SBUs generate large amounts of cash, and others need cash to foster growth. The challenge is to balance the organization's "portfolio" of SBUs for the best long-term performance.

To determine the future cash contributions and cash requirements expected for each SBU, managers can use the Boston Consulting Group's portfolio matrix. The **portfolio matrix** is a tool for allocating resources among products and strategic business units on the basis of relative market share and market growth rate. Using the portfolio matrix requires classifying each SBU by its present or forecast growth and market share. The underlying assumption is that market share and profitability are strongly linked. The measure of market share used in the portfolio approach is relative market share, the ratio between the company's share and the share of the largest competitor. For example, if a firm has a 50 percent share and its competitor has 5 percent, the ratio is 10 to 1.

Exhibit 3.2 shows a portfolio matrix for a computer manufacturer. The size of the circle in each cell of the matrix represents dollar sales of

portfolio matrix a tool for allocating resources among products or strategic business units on the basis of relative market share and market growth rate

star in the portfolio matrix, a business unit that is a fast-growing market leader

cash cow in the portfolio matrix, a business unit that usually generates more cash than it needs to maintain its market share

problem child (question mark) in the portfolio matrix, a business unit that shows rapid growth but poor profit margins

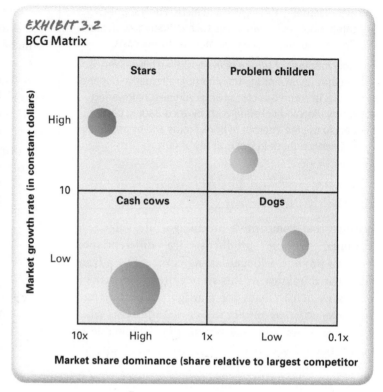

EXHIBIT 3.2
BCG Matrix

Market growth rate (in constant dollars)

Stars | Problem children

Cash cows | Dogs

High / 10 / Low

Market share dominance (share relative to largest competitor)

10x / High / 1x / Low / 0.1x

the SBU relative to dollar sales of the company's other SBUs. The following categories are used in the matrix:

▶▶ *Stars:* A **star** is a fast-growing market leader. For example, computer manufacturers have identified subnotebooks, hand-held models, and tablets as stars. Star SBUs have large profits but need lots of cash to finance growth. The best tactic is to protect existing market share by reinvesting earnings in product improvement, better distribution, more promotion, and production efficiency. Management must capture new users as they enter the market.

▶▶ *Cash cows:* A **cash cow** is an SBU that usually generates more cash than it needs to maintain its market share. The product has a dominant share in a low-growth market. Personal computers and laptops are categorized as cash cows in Exhibit 3.2. The strategy for a cash cow is to maintain market dominance by being the price leader and making technological improvements. Managers should not extend the basic line unless they can dramatically increase demand. Instead, they should allocate excess cash to the product categories where growth prospects are the greatest.

▶▶ *Problem children:* A **problem child**, also called a **question mark**, shows rapid growth but poor profit margins. It has a low market share in a high-growth industry. Problem children need lots of cash support to keep from becoming dogs. The strategies are to invest heavily to improve market share, acquire competitors to get the necessary market share, or drop the SBU. Sometimes a firm can reposition a problem child as a star.

BCG—A HISTORY

1963, Boston Consulting Group (BCG) is born.
1968, BCG introduced the growth share matrix, or portfolio matrix.

2007, BCG counted nearly **4,000** consultants in **66** offices in **38** countries and generated annual revenue of **$2.3** billion (the company's first month of billings totalled $500).[1]

▸▸ *Dogs:* A **dog** has low growth potential and a small market share. Most dogs eventually leave the marketplace. For computer manufacturers, the mainframe computer has become a dog. The options for dogs are to harvest or divest.

After classifying the company's SBUs in the matrix, managers must next allocate future resources for each SBU. Four basic strategies can be used:

▸▸ *Build:* An organization with an SBU that it believes has star potential (probably a problem child at present) may decide to give up short-term profits and use its financial resources to build. Procter & Gamble built Pringles from a money loser to a profit maker.

▸▸ *Hold:* If an SBU is a successful cash cow, a key goal is to preserve market share so that the organization can take advantage of the positive cash flow.

▸▸ *Harvest:* This strategy is appropriate for all SBUs except stars. The goal is to increase the short-term cash return without much concern for the long-run impact. This strategy is especially worthwhile when more cash is needed from a cash cow with unfavourable long-run prospects. For instance, Lever Brothers has harvested Lifebuoy soap for years with little promotional backing.

▸▸ *Divest:* Getting rid of SBUs with low shares of low-growth markets, such as problem children and dogs, is often a strategically appropriate decision. In a five-year period, General Electric exited four flagging businesses and entered seven new ones that were more promising.[2]

Strategic Alternatives

Once an organization decides on the portfolio of businesses, next it must identify opportunities to grow these businesses. To discover a marketing opportunity, management must know how to identify the alternatives. One method for developing alternatives is Ansoff's strategic opportunity matrix (see Exhibit 3.3), which matches products with markets. Firms can explore these four options:

▸▸ *Market penetration:* A firm using the **market penetration** alternative tries to increase market share among existing customers. If Kraft Foods started a major campaign for Maxwell House coffee by initiating aggressive advertising and offering cents-off coupons to existing customers, it would be following a penetration strategy. Customer databases, discussed in Chapters 4 and 8, would help managers implement this strategy.

▸▸ *Market development:* **Market development** involves attracting new customers to existing products. Ideally, new uses for old products stimulate additional sales among existing customers while also bringing in new buyers. For example, the growing emphasis on continuing education and executive development by colleges and universities is a market development strategy.

▸▸ *Product development:* A **product development** strategy entails the creation of new products for present markets. Several makers of men's suits have introduced new suits designed to be worn in hot weather, some of which contain the same fibres NASA developed for spacesuits to prevent astronauts from overheating.[3]

dog in the portfolio matrix, a business unit that has low growth potential and a small market share

market penetration a marketing strategy that tries to increase market share among existing customers

market development a marketing strategy that involves attracting new customers to existing products

product development a marketing strategy that entails the creation of new products for current customers

EXHIBIT 3.3
Ansoff's Strategic Opportunity Matrix

	Present Product	New Product
Present Market	**Market Penetration** Tim Hortons sells additional coffee to customers through Wal-Mart and leading grocery stores.	**Product Development** Tim Hortons develops Ice Coffee and Hot Chocolate Supreme.
New Market	**Market Development** Tim Hortons opens new stores in the United States.	**Diversification** Tim Hortons sells hats, coffee makers, Thermos bottles, and other merchandise.

NO COMPETITION

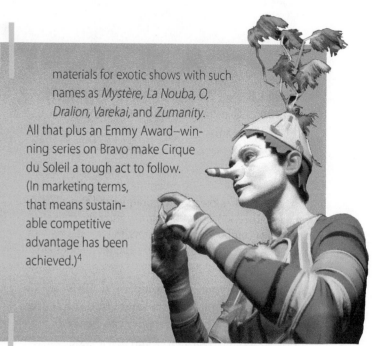

It's hard to find a direct competitor for Montreal's Cirque du Soleil. That's because

- They tell a story that goes beyond the acrobatic acts using animals that other circuses focus on.
- *More than 30 talent scouts* maintain a database containing 20,000 names of potential additions to the company's *2,700-member cast.*
- Each stage show has a life of 10–12 years.
- The company runs *five* world tours and maintains *five permanent* shows, each with a return approaching *$500 million.*
- More than *300 seamstresses*, engineers, and makeup artists sew, design, and build custom

materials for exotic shows with such names as *Mystère, La Nouba, O, Dralion, Varekai,* and *Zumanity.* All that plus an Emmy Award–winning series on Bravo make Cirque du Soleil a tough act to follow. (In marketing terms, that means sustainable competitive advantage has been achieved.)[4]

---

diversification a strategy of increasing sales by introducing new products into new markets

marketing strategy the activities of selecting and describing one or more target markets and developing and maintaining a marketing mix that will produce mutually satisfying exchanges with target markets

market opportunity analysis (MOA) the description and estimation of the size and sales potential of market segments that are of interest to the firm and the assessment of key competitors in these market segments

Managers following the product development strategy can rely on their extensive knowledge of the target audience. They usually have a good feel for what customers like and dislike about current products and what existing needs are not being met. In addition, managers can rely on established distribution channels.

▸▸ *Diversification:* **Diversification** is a strategy of increasing sales by introducing new products into new markets. Cirque du Soleil has begun to diversify its creative entertainment empire into apparel, accessories, fragrance, gifts, and cosmetics. The company is even considering opening its own stores.[5] A diversification strategy can be risky when a firm is entering unfamiliar markets, but diversification can be very profitable when a firm is entering markets that have little or no competition.

Selecting a Strategic Alternative Selecting which alternative to pursue depends on the overall company philosophy and culture. The choice also depends on the tool used to make the decision. Companies generally have one of two philosophies about when they expect profits. Even though market share and profitability are compatible long-term goals, companies either pursue profits right away or first seek to increase market share and then pursue profits.

Companies sometimes make the mistake of focusing on building market share, assuming that

profits will follow. The relationship between market share and profits is not always linear and depends on the industry, the company's product mix and the product life cycle stages the products are at. For example, in 2011, Hewlett-Packard's profitability was up by 5 percent over the previous year, even though its sales of personal computers declined.[6]

LO7 Describing the Target Market

Marketing strategy involves the activities of selecting and describing one or more target markets and developing and maintaining a marketing mix that will produce mutually satisfying exchanges with target markets.

Target Market Strategy

A market segment is a group of individuals or organizations that share one or more characteristics. They therefore may have relatively similar product needs. For example, parents of newborn babies need formula, diapers, and special foods.

The target market strategy identifies the market segment or segments on which to focus. This process begins with a **market opportunity analysis (MOA)—** the description and estimation of the size and sales potential of market segments that are of interest to the firm and the assessment of key competitors in these market segments. After the firm describes the market segments, it may choose to target one or more of these segments. Marketers use three general strategies for selecting target markets.

Target markets can be selected by appealing to the entire market with one marketing mix, concentrating on one segment, or appealing to multiple market segments using multiple marketing mixes. The characteristics, advantages, and disadvantages of each strategic option are examined in Chapter 7. Target markets could be individuals who are concerned about sensitive teeth (the target of Sensodyne toothpaste) or college students needing inexpensive about-town transportation (Yamaha Razz scooter).

Any market segment that is targeted must be fully described. Demographics, psychographics, and buyer behaviour should be assessed. Buyer behaviour is covered in Chapters 5 and 6. If segments are differentiated by ethnicity, multicultural aspects of the marketing mix should be examined. If the target market is international, it is especially important to describe differences in culture, economic and technological development, and political structure that may affect the marketing plan. Global marketing is covered in more detail in Chapter 20.

LO8 The Marketing Mix

The term **marketing mix** refers to a unique blend of product, place (distribution), promotion, and pricing strategies (often referred to as the **four Ps**) designed to produce mutually satisfying exchanges with a target market. The marketing manager can control each component of the marketing mix, but the strategies for all four components must be blended to achieve optimal results. Any marketing mix is only as good as its weakest component. The best promotion and the lowest price cannot save a poor product. Similarly, excellent products with poor placing, pricing, or promotion will likely fail.

Variations in marketing mixes do not occur by chance. Astute marketing managers devise marketing strategies to gain advantages over competitors and best serve the needs and wants of a particular target market segment. By manipulating elements of the marketing mix, marketing managers can fine-tune the customer offering and achieve competitive success.

Product Strategies

Typically, the marketing mix starts with the product "P." The heart of the marketing mix, the starting point, is the product offering and product strategy. Without knowing the product to be marketed, it is difficult to design a place strategy, decide on a promotion campaign, or set a price.

The product includes not only the physical unit but also its package, warranty, after-sale service, brand name, company image, value, and many other factors. A Godiva chocolate has many product elements: the chocolate itself, a fancy gold wrapper, a customer satisfaction guarantee, and the prestige of the Godiva brand name. We buy products not only for what they do (their benefits) but also for what they mean to us (their status, quality, or reputation).

Products can be tangible goods such as computers, ideas such as those offered by a consultant, or services such as medical care. Products should also offer customer value. Product decisions are covered in

marketing mix a unique blend of product, place, promotion, and pricing strategies designed to produce mutually satisfying exchanges with a target market

four Ps product, place, promotion, and price, which together make up the marketing mix

THE CANADIAN PRESS (RICHARD LAM)

Target Market for Lululemon:
Educated women (and men) who practise yoga and other activities to reduce stress and lead a healthier life and who also want to look stylish and feel comfortable.

"THE **BEST PROMOTION** AND THE **LOWEST PRICE** CANNOT SAVE A **POOR PRODUCT**."

Chapters 9 and 10, and services marketing is detailed in Chapter 11.

Place (Distribution) Strategies

Place, or distribution, strategies are concerned with making products available when and where customers want them. Would you rather buy a kiwi fruit at the 24-hour grocery store within walking distance or fly to New Zealand to pick your own? A part of the place "P" is physical distribution, which involves all the business activities concerned with storing and transporting raw materials or finished products. The goal is to ensure products arrive in usable condition at designated places when needed. Place strategies are covered in Chapters 12 and 13.

Promotion Strategies

Elements of the promotional mix include advertising, direct marketing, public relations, sales promotion, personal selling, and online marketing. Promotion's role in the marketing mix is to bring about mutually satisfying exchanges with target markets by informing, educating, persuading, and reminding consumers of the benefits of an organization or a product. A good promotion strategy can dramatically increase sales. Good promotion strategies do not guarantee success, however. Despite massive promotional campaigns, much-anticipated movies often have disappointing box-office returns. Each element of the promotion "P" is coordinated and managed with the others to create a promotional blend or mix. These integrated marketing communications activities are described in Chapters 14, 15, 16, and 17. Technology-driven aspects of promotional marketing are covered in Chapter 4.

Pricing Strategies

Price is what a buyer must give up to obtain a product. It is often the most flexible of the four marketing mix elements because it is the quickest element to change. Marketers can raise or lower prices more frequently and easily than they can change other marketing mix variables. Price is an important competitive weapon and is very important to the organization because price multiplied by the number of units sold equals total revenue for the firm. Pricing decisions are covered in Chapters 18 and 19.

LO 9 Following Up on the Marketing Plan

Implementation

Implementation is the process that turns a marketing plan into action assignments and ensures that these assignments are executed in a way that accomplishes the plan's objectives. Implementation activities may involve detailed job assignments, activity descriptions, timelines, budgets, and lots of communication. Although implementation is essentially "doing what you said you were going to do," many organizations repeatedly experience failures in strategy implementation. Brilliant marketing plans are doomed to fail if they are not properly implemented. These detailed communications may or may not be part of the written marketing plan. If they are not part of the plan, they should be specified elsewhere as soon as the plan has been communicated.

Evaluation and Control

After a marketing plan is implemented, it should be evaluated. **Evaluation** involves gauging the extent to which marketing objectives have been achieved during the specified time period. Four common reasons for failing to achieve a marketing objective are unrealistic marketing objectives, inappropriate marketing strategies in the plan, poor implementation, and changes in the environment after the objective was specified and the strategy was implemented.

Once a plan is chosen and implemented, its effectiveness must be monitored. **Control** provides the mechanisms both for evaluating marketing results in light of the plan's objectives and for correcting actions that do not help the organization reach those objectives within budget guidelines. Firms need to establish formal and informal control programs to make the entire operation more efficient.

"PRICE IS AN IMPORTANT **COMPETITIVE WEAPON**."

Perhaps the broadest control device available to marketing managers is the **marketing audit**—a thorough, systematic, periodic evaluation of the objectives, strategies, structure, and performance of the marketing organization. A marketing audit helps management allocate marketing resources efficiently.

Although the main purpose of the marketing audit is to develop a full profile of the organization's marketing effort and to provide a basis for developing and revising the marketing plan, it is also an excellent way to improve communication and raise the level of marketing consciousness within the organization. A marketing audit is a useful vehicle for selling the philosophy and techniques of strategic marketing to other members of the organization.

LO 10 Effective Strategic Planning

Effective strategic planning requires continual attention, creativity, and management commitment. Strategic planning should not be an annual exercise, in which managers go through the motions and forget about strategic planning until the next year. It should be an ongoing process because the environment is

4 CHARACTERISTICS OF A MARKETING AUDIT:

▶▶ *Comprehensive:* covers all major marketing issues facing an organization and not just trouble spots.

▶▶ *Systematic:* takes place in an orderly sequence and covers the organization's marketing environment, internal marketing system, and specific marketing activities. The diagnosis is followed by an action plan with both short-run and long-run proposals for improving overall marketing effectiveness.

▶▶ *Independent:* normally conducted by an inside or outside party who is independent enough to have top management's confidence and to be objective.

▶▶ *Periodic:* for maximum benefit, should be carried out on a regular schedule instead of only in a crisis.

continually changing and the firm's resources and capabilities are continually evolving.

Sound strategic planning is based on creativity. Managers should challenge assumptions about the firm and the environment and establish new strategies. And above all, the most critical element in successful strategic planning is top management's support and participation.

marketing audit a thorough, systematic, periodic evaluation of the objectives, strategies, structure, and performance of the marketing organization

Elements of the marketing mix; quadrants in the BCG matrix

4

Average cash rebate offered by a Big Three automaker

$2,500

Debut of the BCG portfolio matrix

1968

6

Macroenvironmental forces affecting marketing

$500 million
Approximate return on investment for a permanent Cirque du Soleil show

27
Number of languages spoken by Cirque du Soleil's 2,700-member cast

CHAPTER 4

Decision Support Systems and Marketing Research

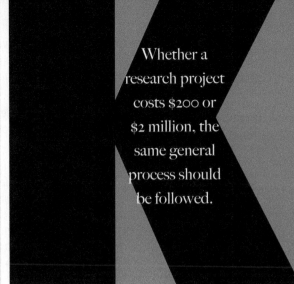

Learning Outcomes

Whether a research project costs $200 or $2 million, the same general process should be followed.

LO 1 Marketing Decision Support Systems

Accurate and timely information is the lifeblood of marketing decision making. Good information can help an organization maximize sales and efficiently use scarce company resources. To prepare and adjust marketing plans, managers need a system for gathering everyday information about developments in the marketing environment—that is, for gathering marketing information. The system most commonly used these days for gathering **marketing information** is called a *marketing decision support system*.

A marketing **decision support system (DSS)** is an interactive, flexible computerized information system that enables managers to obtain and manipulate information as they are making decisions. A DSS bypasses the information-processing specialist and gives managers access to useful data from their own desks.

A true DSS has the following characteristics:

▸▸ *Interactive:* Managers give simple instructions and see immediate results. The process is under their direct control; no computer programmer is needed. Managers don't have to wait for scheduled reports.

▸▸ *Flexible:* A DSS can sort, regroup, total, average, and manipulate the data in various ways. It will shift gears as the user changes topics, matching information to the issue at hand. For

marketing information
everyday information about developments in the marketing environment that managers use to prepare and adjust marketing plans

decision support system (DSS)
an interactive, flexible computerized information system that enables managers to obtain and manipulate information as they are making decisions

What do you think?

Participating in marketing research studies is fun.

1	2	3	4	5	6	7
STRONGLY DISAGREE						STRONGLY AGREE

GREG CEO/PHOTODISC/JUPITERIMAGES

example, the chief executive officer (CEO) can see highly aggregated figures, and the marketing analyst can view very detailed breakouts.

▶▶ *Discovery oriented:* Managers can probe for trends, isolate problems, and ask "what if" questions.

▶▶ *Accessible:* Managers who aren't skilled with computers can easily learn how to use a DSS. Novice users should be able to choose a standard, or default, method of using the system. They can bypass optional features so they can work with the basic system right away while gradually learning to apply its advanced features.

Perhaps the fastest-growing use of DSSs is for **database marketing**, which is the creation of a large computerized file of customers' and potential customers' profiles and purchase patterns. It is usually the key tool for successful one-to-one marketing, which relies on very specific information about a market. Today, many companies and organizations desiring to engage with their most valued clients and customers use customer relationship management, or CRM (CRM is discussed in Chapter 8). Consequently, there has been an increased emphasis on developing these databases so they can be easily accessed and can readily display key customer information. Companies are now equipping computer screens with **dashboards** (similar to the one in your car) to display computer-generated visual output easily accessed by employees for the purpose of maximizing customer relationship marketing interactions. For example, dashboards enable employees to see the customer's current exchanges of communications, sales, etc., and to tailor their responses and planned communications to their customers in a way to best meet the customer's needs and preferences.

LO 2 The Role of Marketing Research

Marketing research is the process of planning, collecting, and analyzing data relevant to a marketing decision. The results of this analysis are then communicated to management. Marketing research plays a key role in the marketing system. It provides decision makers with data on the effectiveness of the current marketing mix and with insights for necessary changes. Furthermore, marketing research is a main data source for both management information systems and DSS. In other words, the findings of a marketing research project become data in a DSS.

Marketing research has three types of roles: descriptive, diagnostic, and predictive. The *descriptive* role includes gathering and presenting factual statements. For example, what are the demographic characteristics of a firm's target market in terms of age, sex, income, etc.? What is the historic sales trend in the industry? What are consumers' attitudes toward a product and its advertising? The *diagnostic* role includes explaining data, such as determining the impact on sales of a change in the design of the package. The *predictive* function addresses "what if" questions. For example, how can the researcher use the descriptive and diagnostic research to predict the results of a planned marketing decision?

LO 3 Steps in a Marketing Research Project

Virtually all firms that have adopted the marketing concept engage in some marketing research because it offers decision makers many benefits. Some companies spend millions on marketing research; others, particularly smaller firms, conduct informal, limited-scale research studies.

Whether a research project costs $200 or $2 million, the same general process should be followed. The marketing research process is a scientific approach to decision making that maximizes the chance of receiving accurate and meaningful results. Exhibit 4.1 traces the seven steps in the research process, which begins with the recognition of a marketing issue or opportunity. As changes occur in the firm's external environment, marketing managers are faced with the questions "Should we change the existing marketing mix?" and, if so, "How?" Marketing research may be used to evaluate product promotion, place (distribution), or pricing alternatives.

During a recent summer, Starbucks wanted to learn whether its outdoor media—billboards, kiosk ads, and vehicle wraps (vinyl signage applied to cars and trucks)—reached and affected people as efficiently as its investments in television, radio, and print advertising.

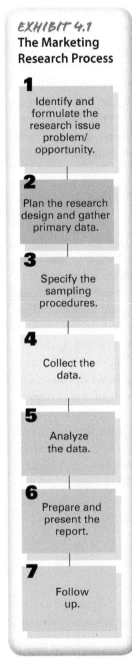

EXHIBIT 4.1
The Marketing Research Process

1
Identify and formulate the research issue problem/ opportunity.

2
Plan the research design and gather primary data.

3
Specify the sampling procedures.

4
Collect the data.

5
Analyze the data.

6
Prepare and present the report.

7
Follow up.

Starbucks was interested in customers' response to outdoor media because it was seeking the best avenue to get consumers to associate the Starbucks name with summertime drinks. So the company hired a market research firm to measure the effects of Starbucks' advertising.

Because the study was conducted online, the research company was able to show each respondent almost every piece of advertising that Starbucks had used over the summer. The research found that virtually all of Starbucks' advertising worked. When people noticed any of it, they ended up buying more of the summer drinks being advertised than people who didn't notice the advertising. The research also showed which of the advertising formats was most successful and that, in a number of cases, increased advertising spending did not produce buyers.[1]

The Starbucks story illustrates an important point about the issue/opportunity definition. The **marketing research issue** is information oriented. It is a statement that defines the focus for the information that is to be collected to aid any marketing decision making. As such, it involves determining what information is needed and how that information can be obtained efficiently and effectively. The **marketing research objective**, then, is to provide insightful decision-making information. It is the specific information needed to solve a marketing research issue. Managers must combine this information with their own experience and other information to make a proper decision. Starbucks' marketing research issue was to gather information online to determine the recall and impact of out-of-home media. The two marketing research objectives were to measure consumers' recall and their purchase of specific products featured in the promotions via billboards, kiosk ads, and vehicle wraps.

In contrast, the **management decision problem**, the broad-based problem that uses market research in order for managers to take proper actions, is action oriented. Management issues tend to be much broader in scope and far more general than marketing research issues, which must be narrowly defined and specific if the research effort is to be successful. Sometimes, several research studies must be conducted to solve a broad management issue. The management decision issue for Starbucks was: Does Starbucks' outdoor media reach and affect people as efficiently as Starbucks' investments in television, radio, and print advertising? Or, the Starbucks vice-president of promotion might simply ask, "How do I get the most bang for the bucks (sales) in my advertising budget?"

Secondary Data

A valuable tool throughout the research process but particularly in the issue/opportunity identification stage is **secondary data**—data previously collected for any purpose other than the one at hand. Secondary information originating within the company includes documents such as annual reports, reports to stockholders, product testing results (perhaps made available to the news media), the company's own marketing data, and house periodicals prepared by the company for communication to employees, customers, or others. Often this information is incorporated into a company's internal database.

Innumerable outside sources of secondary information also exist. These are principally business data summaries prepared by government departments and agencies (federal, provincial or territorial, and local), such as Statistics Canada. Still more data

marketing research issue a statement that defines the focus for the information that is to be collected to aid any marketing decision making

marketing research objective the specific information needed to solve a marketing research issue

management decision problem a broad-based problem that uses marketing research in order for managers to take proper actions

secondary data data previously collected for any purpose other than the one at hand

are available from online journals and research studies available from research and marketing associations such as the Marketing Research and Intelligence Association (MRIA) or the Canadian Institute of Marketing (CIM).

Trade and industry associations also publish secondary data that can be found in business periodicals and other news media that regularly publish studies and articles on the economy, specific industries, and even individual companies. The unpublished summarized secondary information from these sources corresponds to internal reports, memos, or special-purpose analyses with limited circulation. Economic considerations or priorities in the organization may preclude publication of these summaries. In addition, information on many topics, from a Nielsen PRIZM segmentation, to industry trends, to brands, etc., can be derived from polls, focus groups, surveys, panels, and interviews and are available from such companies as Environics Research Group and other sources on the Internet.

Secondary data save time and money if they help solve the researcher's problem. Even if the problem is not solved, secondary data have other advantages. They can aid in formulating the problem statement and can lead researchers to potential research methods and other types of data needed for solving the problem. In addition, secondary data can pinpoint the kinds of people to approach and their locations and can serve as a basis of comparison for other data. The disadvantages of secondary data stem mainly from a mismatch between the researcher's unique problem and the purpose for which the secondary data were originally gathered. For example, a company wanted to determine the market potential for a fireplace log made of coal rather than compressed wood by-products. The researcher found plenty of secondary data on total wood consumed as fuel, quantities consumed in each province and territory, and types of wood burned. Secondary data were also available on consumer attitudes and purchase patterns of wood by-product fireplace logs. The wealth of secondary data provided the researcher with many insights into the artificial-log market. Yet the researchers could not locate information on whether consumers would buy artificial logs made of coal.

The quality of secondary data may also pose a problem. Secondary data sources do not often give detailed information that would enable a researcher to assess the data's quality or relevance. Whenever possible, a researcher needs to address these important questions: Who gathered the data? Why were the data obtained? What methodology was used? How were classifications (such as heavy users versus light users) developed and defined? When was the information gathered?

The New Age of Secondary Information: The Internet

Although gathering secondary data is necessary in almost any research project, this task has traditionally been tedious and boring. The researcher often had to write to government agencies, trade associations, or other secondary data providers and then wait days or weeks for a reply that might never come. Often, one or more trips to the library were required, and the researcher might find that needed reports were signed out or missing. Now, however, the rapid development of the Internet has eliminated much of the drudgery associated with the collection of secondary data. Moreover, with libraries keeping with the times and needs of researchers, they now often have a designated librarian to aid the researcher (student) in advising as to what sites are available (some have limited or otherwise costs to access) and which sites may best help them find the information they desire.

Marketing Research Aggregators

The **marketing research aggregator** industry is a $100 million business that is growing about 6 percent a year. Companies in this field acquire, catalogue, reformat, segment, and resell reports already published by large and small marketing research firms. Even Amazon.com has added a marketing research aggregation area to its high-profile e-commerce site.

The role of aggregator firms is growing because their databases of research reports are getting bigger and more comprehensive—and more useful—as marketing research firms get more comfortable using resellers as a sales channel. Meanwhile, advances in Web technology are making the databases easier to search and deliveries speedier. By slicing and repackaging research reports

---

"SECONDARY DATA **SAVE TIME AND MONEY** IF THEY HELP SOLVE THE RESEARCHER'S PROBLEM."

into narrower, more specialized sections for resale to small- and medium-sized businesses that often cannot afford to commission their own studies or buy full reports, the aggregators are essentially nurturing a new target market for the information.

Youth Worries (% of Group)

	Age Group 18–24
Not having enough money	68
Grades	46
Someone close will get sick or die	46
Weight	41
Appearance	40
College too expensive	36
In car accident	35
Overweight	35
Environment	33
Parents lose jobs	17

SOURCE: Harris Interactive Youth Pulse 2010, *Trends & Tudes*, November 2010, http://www.harrisinteractive.com/vault/HI_TrendsTudes_2010_v09_i02.pdf. Reproduced with permission from Harris Interactive.

Prior to the emergence of research aggregators, a lot of marketing research was available only through premium-priced subscription services. For example, a 17-chapter, $2,800 report from Wintergreen Research Inc. was recently broken up and sold (on AllNetResearchers.com) for $350 per chapter, significantly boosting the overall revenue generated by the report.

In addition to AllNetResearch.com, other major aggregators are Profound.com, Bitpipe.com, eMarketer.com, and MarketResearch.com.

Planning the Research Design and Gathering Primary Data

Good secondary data can help researchers conduct a thorough Situation Analysis (SA) from internal and external data sources. Using that information, researchers can list their unanswered questions and rank them. Researchers must then decide the exact information still required to answer the questions. The **research design** specifies which research questions must be answered, how and when the data will be gathered, and how the data will be analyzed. Typically, the project budget is finalized after the research design has been approved.

Sometimes research questions can be answered by gathering more secondary data; otherwise, primary data may be needed. **Primary data**, or information collected for the first time, is used for solving the particular issue under investigation. The main advantage of primary data is that they will answer a specific research question that secondary data cannot answer. For example, suppose Pillsbury has two new recipes for refrigerated dough for sugar cookies. Which one will consumers like better? Secondary data will not help answer this question. Instead, targeted consumers must try each recipe and evaluate the taste, texture, and appearance of each cookie. Moreover, primary data are current and researchers know the source. Sometimes researchers gather the data themselves rather than assigning projects to outside companies. Researchers also specify the methodology of the research. Secrecy can be maintained because the information is proprietary. In contrast, much secondary data is available to all interested parties either for free or for relatively small fees.

Gathering primary data is expensive; costs can range from a few hundred dollars for a limited exploratory study comprising a few focus groups to several million for a nationwide study. For instance, a nationwide, 15-minute telephone interview with 1,000 adult males can cost $50,000, including a data analysis and report. Because primary data gathering is so expensive, firms may reduce the number of in-person interviews it conducts and use an Internet study instead. Larger companies that conduct many research projects use another cost-saving technique. They *piggyback* studies, or gather data on two different projects using one questionnaire. Nevertheless, the disadvantages of primary data gathering are usually offset by the advantages. Gathering primary data is often the only way of solving a research problem.

research **design** specifies which research questions must be answered, how and when the data will be gathered, and how the data will be analyzed

primary **data** information that is collected for the first time and is used for solving the particular problem under investigation

"THE **MOST POPULAR** TECHNIQUE FOR GATHERING PRIMARY DATA IS **SURVEY RESEARCH**."

survey research the most popular technique for gathering primary data, in which a researcher interacts with people to obtain facts, opinions, and attitudes

mall intercept interview interviewing people in the common areas of shopping malls

Because of the variety of techniques now available for research, including surveys, observations, and experiments, primary research can address almost any marketing question.

Survey Research The most popular technique for gathering primary data is **survey research**, in which a researcher interacts with people to obtain facts, opinions, and attitudes. Exhibit 4.2 summarizes the characteristics of traditional forms of survey research.

In-Home Personal Interviews Although in-home personal interviews often provide high-quality information, they tend to be very expensive because of the interviewers' travel time and mileage costs. Therefore, in-home personal interviews are rapidly disappearing from the North American and European researcher's survey toolbox. This method is, however, still popular in many countries around the globe.

Mall Intercept Interviews The **mall intercept interview** is conducted in the common area of a shopping mall or in a market research office within the mall. To conduct this type of interview, the research firm rents office space in the mall or pays a significant daily fee. One drawback is that it is difficult to get a representative sample of the population as not every consumer type comes to the mall at the same time, and many shoppers are often in a hurry, making them reluctant to participate in a survey. One advantage is the ability of the interviewer to probe when necessary—a technique used to clarify a person's response and ask for more detailed information.

Mall intercept interviews must be brief. Only the shortest interviews are conducted while respondents are standing. Usually, researchers invite respondents to their office for interviews, which are generally less than 15 minutes long. The overall quality of mall intercept interviews is about the same as telephone interviews.

Marketing researchers are applying computer technology in mall interviewing. The first technique

EXHIBIT 4.2
Characteristics of Traditional Forms of Survey Research

Characteristic	In-Home Personal Interviews	Mall Intercept Interviews	Central-Location Telephone Interviews	Self-Administered and One-Time Mail Surveys	Mail Panel Surveys	Executive Interviews	Focus Groups
Cost	High	Moderate	Moderate	Low	Moderate	High	Low
Time span	Moderate	Moderate	Fast	Slow	Relatively slow	Moderate	Fast
Use of interviewer probes	Yes	Yes	Yes	No	Yes	Yes	Yes
Ability to show concepts to respondent	Yes (also taste tests)	Yes (also taste tests)	No	Yes	Yes	Yes	Yes
Management control over interviewer	Low	Moderate	High	n/a	n/a	Moderate	High
General data quality	High	Moderate	High to moderate	Moderate to low	Moderate	High	Moderate
Ability to collect large amounts of data	High	Moderate	Moderate to low	Low to moderate	Moderate	Moderate	Moderate
Ability to handle complex questionnaires	High	Moderate	High, if computer-aided	Low	Low	High	n/a

is **computer-assisted personal interviewing**. The researcher conducts in-person interviews, reads questions to the respondent from a computer screen, and directly keys the respondent's answers into the computer. A second approach is **computer-assisted self-interviewing**. A mall interviewer intercepts and directs willing respondents to nearby computers. Each respondent reads questions from a computer screen or iPad and directly keys his or her answers into a computer. The third use of technology is fully automated self-interviewing. Respondents are guided by interviewers or independently approach a centrally located computer station or kiosk, read the questions from a screen, and directly key their answers into the station's computer.

Telephone Interviews Telephone interviews cost less than personal interviews, but the cost is rapidly increasing due to respondents' refusals to participate. Most telephone interviewing is conducted from a specially designed phone room called a **central-location telephone (CLT) facility**. A phone room has many phone lines, individual interviewing stations, and may include monitoring equipment and headsets. The research firm typically will interview people nationwide from a single location. The Canadian National Do Not Call List (Bill C-37) does not apply to survey research.

Most CLT facilities offer computer-assisted interviewing. The interviewer reads the questions from a computer screen and enters the respondent's data directly into the computer, saving time. Hallmark Cards found that an interviewer administered a printed questionnaire for its Shoebox Greeting cards in 28 minutes. The same questionnaire administered with computer assistance took only 18 minutes. The researcher can stop the survey at any point and immediately print out the survey results, allowing the research design to be refined as necessary.

Mail Surveys Mail surveys have several benefits: relatively low cost, elimination of interviewers and field supervisors, centralized control, and actual or promised anonymity for respondents (which may draw more candid responses). A disadvantage is that mail questionnaires usually produce low response rates because certain elements of the population tend to respond more than others. For example, the Citizen Survey 2006 of Kelowna, British Columbia, noted that respondent levels for those 18 to 24 years old were at only 0.4 percent, while this age group actually

makes up 11.2 percent of the city's population.[2] The resulting sample may therefore not represent the general population. Another serious problem with mail surveys is that no one probes respondents to clarify or elaborate on their answers.

Mail panels offer an alternative to the one-shot mail survey. A mail panel consists of a sample of households recruited to participate by mail for a given period. Panel members often receive gifts in return for their participation. Essentially, the panel is a sample used several times. In contrast to one-time mail surveys, the response rates from mail panels are high. Rates of 70 percent (of those who agree to participate) are not uncommon.

Executive Interviews An **executive interview** involves interviewing business people, at their offices, concerning industrial products or services, a process that is very expensive. First, individuals involved in the purchase decision for the product in question must be identified and located, which can itself be expensive and time-consuming. Once a qualified person is located, the next step is to get that person to agree to be interviewed and to set a time for the interview.

Finally, an interviewer must go to the particular place at the appointed time. Long waits are frequently encountered; cancellations are not uncommon. This type of survey requires the very best interviewers because they are frequently interviewing on topics that they know very little about.

Surveys where respondents select an answer from a list or rate the intensity of their response on a scale are relatively easy to evaluate.

computer-assisted personal interviewing the interviewer reads the questions from a computer screen and enters the respondent's data directly into the computer

computer-assisted self-interviewing the respondent reads questions off a computer screen and directly keys his or her answers into a computer

central-location telephone (CLT) facility a specially designed phone room used to conduct telephone interviewing

executive interview a type of survey that involves interviewing business people at their offices concerning industrial products or services

Focus Groups A **focus group** is a type of personal interviewing. Often recruited by random telephone screening, seven to ten people with certain desired characteristics form a focus group. These qualified consumers are usually offered an incentive (typically $30 to $50) to participate in a group discussion. The meeting place (sometimes resembling a living room, sometimes featuring a conference table) may be equipped with audiotaping and videotaping equipment. It also likely has a viewing room with a one-way mirror so that clients (manufacturers or retailers) may watch the session. A moderator, hired by the research company, leads the group discussion. Focus groups can be used to gauge consumer response to a product or promotion and are occasionally used to brainstorm new product ideas or to screen concepts for new products.

focus group seven to ten people who participate in a group discussion led by a moderator

open-ended question an interview question that encourages an answer phrased in the respondent's own words

closed-ended question an interview question that asks the respondent to make a selection from a limited list of responses

scaled-response question a closed-ended question designed to measure the intensity of a respondent's answer

Questionnaire Design All forms of survey research require a questionnaire. Questionnaires ensure that all respondents will be asked the same series of questions. Questionnaires include three basic types of questions: open-ended, closed-ended, and scaled-response. An **open-ended question** encourages an answer phrased in the respondent's own words. Researchers receive a rich array of information that is based on the respondent's frame of reference (What do you think about the new flavour?). In contrast, a **closed-ended question** asks the respondent to make a selection

from a limited list of responses. Closed-ended questions can either be what marketing researchers call *dichotomous* (Do you like the new flavour? Yes or No.) or *multiple choice*. A **scaled-response question** is a closed-ended question designed to measure the intensity of a respondent's answer. The "What do you think?" question that opened the chapter is a scaled-response question.

Closed-ended and scaled-response questions are easier to tabulate than open-ended questions because the response choices are fixed. On the other hand, unless the researcher designs the closed-ended question very carefully, an important choice may be omitted.

For example, suppose a food study asked this question: "Besides meat, which of the following items do you normally add to a taco that you prepare at home?"

Avocado	1	Olives (black/green)	6
Cheese (Monterey Jack/cheddar)	2	Onions (red/white)	7
Guacamole	3	Peppers (red/green)	8
Lettuce	4	Pimento	9
Mexican hot sauce	5	Sour cream	10

But a respondent may answer, "I usually add a green, avocado-tasting hot sauce" or "I cut up a mixture of lettuce and spinach." How would you code these replies? As you can see, the question needs both an "other" category and a place for respondents to elaborate on their answers.

Good questions address each of the previously set research objectives. Questions must also be clear and concise, and ambiguous language must be avoided. The answer to the question "Do you live within ten minutes of here?" depends on the mode of transportation (maybe the person walks), driving speed, perceived time, and other factors. Language should also be clear. As such, jargon should be avoided, and wording should be geared to the target audience. A question such as "What is the level of efficacy of your preponderant dishwasher soap?" would probably be greeted by blank stares. It would be much simpler to say "Are you (1) very satisfied, (2) somewhat satisfied, or (3) not satisfied with your current brand of dishwasher soap?"

Stating the survey's purpose at the beginning of the interview may improve clarity, but it may also increase the chances of receiving biased responses. Many times respondents will try to provide answers that they believe are "correct" or that the interviewer wants to hear. To avoid bias at the question level, researchers should avoid using leading questions and adjectives that cause respondents to think of the topic in a certain way.

Finally, to ensure clarity, the interviewer should avoid asking two questions in one; for example, "How did you like the taste and texture of the Betty Crocker coffee cake?" This should be divided into two questions, one concerning taste and the other texture.

Observation Research In contrast to survey research, **observation research** depends on watching what people do. Specifically, it is the systematic process of recording the behavioural patterns of people, objects, and occurrences with or without questioning them. A market researcher uses the observation technique and witnesses and records information as events occur or compiles evidence from records of past events. Carried a step further, observation may involve watching people or phenomena and may be conducted by human observers or machines.

For example, a machine may be used to track a person's eye movements to see how and what they read in a magazine or on a website. Examples of these various observational situations are shown in Exhibit 4.3.

Two common forms of people-watching-people research are mystery shoppers and one-way mirror observations. **Mystery shoppers** are researchers posing as customers who gather observational data about a store (i.e., are the shelves neatly stocked?) and collect data about customer–employee interactions. The interaction is not an interview, and communication occurs only so that the mystery shopper can observe the actions and comments of the employee. Mystery shopping is, therefore, classified as an observational marketing research method even though communication is often involved. One-way mirror observations allow researchers to see how consumers react to products or promotions.

Ethnographic Research Ethnographic research comes to marketing from the field of anthropology. The technique is becoming increasingly popular in commercial marketing research. **Ethnographic research**, or the study of human behaviour in its natural context, involves observation of behaviour and physical setting. Ethnographers such as Environics directly observe the population they are studying. As "participant observers," ethnographers can use their intimacy with the people they are studying to gain richer, deeper insights into culture and behaviour—in short, learning what makes people do what they do. Procter & Gamble sends researchers to people's homes for extended periods of time to see how customers do household chores, such as laundry and vacuuming. Cambridge Sound Works, a manufacturer of stereo equipment, assigned researchers to follow a dozen prospective customers over a two-week period to determine what was keeping men who wanted a high-end stereo from buying it. (Researchers discovered that the men's wives hated the unsightly appearance of the big, black stereo boxes.)[3] Today, speakers by Sony, Bose, and Bang & Olufsen, etc. are smaller with more aesthetically pleasing designs along with other consumer desires for them to be wireless and even vibration free.

observation research a research method that relies on four types of observation: people watching people, people watching an activity, machines watching people, and machines watching an activity

mystery shoppers researchers posing as customers who gather observational data about a store

ethnographic research the study of human behaviour in its natural context; involves observation of behaviour and physical setting

EXHIBIT 4.3
Observational Situations

Situation	Example
People watching people	Observers stationed in supermarkets watch consumers select frozen pizza; the purpose is to see how much comparison shopping people do at the point of purchase.
People watching phenomena	Observer stationed at an intersection counts traffic moving in various directions.
Machines watching people	Movie or video cameras record behaviour as in the people-watching-people example above.
Machines watching phenomena	Traffic-counting machines monitor traffic flow.

HSBN/SHUTTERSTOCK.COM

Experiments An **experiment** is a method a researcher can use to gather primary data. The researcher alters one or more variables—price, package design, shelf space, advertising theme, advertising expenditures—while observing the effects of those alterations on another variable (usually sales). The best experiments are those in which all factors are held constant except the ones being manipulated. The researcher can then observe, for example, how sales change as a result of changes in the amount of money spent on advertising.

Specifying the Sampling Procedures

Once the researchers decide how they will collect primary data, their next step is to select the sampling procedures to use. A firm can seldom interview or take a census of all possible users of a new product.

Therefore, a firm must select a sample of the group to be interviewed. A **sample** is a subset from a larger population.

Several questions must be answered before a sampling plan is chosen. First, the population, or **universe**, of interest must be defined. The universe is the group from which the sample will be drawn. It should include all the people whose opinions, behaviours, preferences, attitudes, and so on are of interest to the marketer. For example, in a study whose purpose is to determine the market for a new canned dog food, the population might be defined to include all current buyers of canned dog food.

After the population has been defined, the next question is whether the sample must be representative of that population. If the answer is yes, a probability sample is needed. Otherwise, a nonprobability sample might be considered. (See Exhibit 4.4.)

Probability Samples A **probability sample** is a sample in which every element in the population has a known

EXHIBIT 4.4
Types of Samples

Probability Samples	
Simple Random Sample	Every member of the population has a known and equal chance of selection.
Stratified Sample	The population is divided into mutually exclusive groups (such as gender or age); then random samples are drawn from each group.
Cluster Sample	The population is divided into mutually exclusive groups (such as geographic areas); then a random sample of clusters is selected. The researcher then collects data from all the elements in the selected clusters or from a probability sample of elements within each selected cluster.
Systematic Sample	A list of the population is obtained—i.e., all persons with a chequing account at XYZ Bank—and a skip interval is obtained by dividing the sample size by the population size. If the sample size is 100 and the bank has 1,000 customers, then the skip interval is 10. The beginning number is randomly chosen within the skip interval. If the beginning number is 8, then the skip pattern would be 8, 18, 28, etc.
Nonprobability Samples	
Convenience Sample	The researcher selects the easiest population members from which to obtain information.
Judgment Sample	The researcher's selection criteria are based on personal judgment that the elements (persons) chosen will likely give accurate information.
Quota Sample	The researcher finds a prescribed number of people in several categories—i.e., researcher selects a specific number of business students, arts students, science students, etc., so that each group has a specific number represented in the study. Respondents are not selected on probability sampling criteria.
Snowball Sample	Additional respondents are selected on the basis of referrals from the initial respondents. This method is used when a desired type of respondent is difficult to find—i.e., persons who have taken round-the-world cruises in the last three years are asked to refer others who they know that have taken long cruises and could be involved in the research study. This technique employs the old adage "Birds of a feather flock together."

statistical likelihood of being selected. Its most desirable feature is that scientific rules can be used to ensure that the sample represents the population.

One type of probability sample is a **random sample**—a sample arranged in such a way that every element of the population has an equal chance of being selected as part of the sample. For example, suppose a university is interested in receiving a cross section of student opinions on a proposed sports complex to be built using student activity fees. If the university can acquire an up-to-date list of all the enrolled students, it can draw a random sample by using random numbers from a table (found in most statistics books) to select students from the list. Common forms of probability and nonprobability samples are shown in Exhibit 4.4.

Nonprobability Samples Any sample in which little or no attempt is made to have a representative cross section of the population can be considered a **nonprobability sample**. Therefore, the probability of each sampling unit being selected is not known. A common form of a nonprobability sample is the **convenience sample**, which uses respondents who are convenient, or readily accessible, to the researcher—for instance, employees, friends, or relatives.

Nonprobability samples are acceptable as long as the researcher understands their nonrepresentative nature. Because of their lower cost, nonprobability samples are the basis of much marketing research.

Types of Errors Whenever a sample is used in marketing research, two major types of error may occur: measurement error and sampling error. **Measurement error** occurs when the information desired by the researcher differs from the information provided by the measurement process. For example, people may tell an interviewer that they purchase Crest toothpaste when they do not. Measurement error generally tends to be larger than sampling error.

Sampling error occurs when a sample does not represent the target population. A sampling error can be one of several types. A nonresponse error occurs when the sample interviewed differs from the sample drawn. This error happens because the original people selected to be interviewed either refused to cooperate or were inaccessible.

Frame error, another type of sampling error, arises when the sample drawn from a population differs from the target population. For instance, suppose a telephone survey is conducted to find out Calgary beer drinkers' attitudes toward Molson Canadian. If a Calgary telephone directory is used as the frame (the device or list from which the respondents are selected), the survey will contain a frame error. Not all Calgary beer drinkers have a phone, others may have unlisted phone numbers, and often young adults only have a cellphone. An ideal sample (for example, a sample with no frame error) matches all important characteristics of the target population to be surveyed. Can you suggest a perfect frame for Calgary beer drinkers?

Random error occurs when the selected sample is an imperfect representation of the overall population. Random error represents how accurately the chosen sample's true average (mean) value reflects the population's true average (mean) value. For example, we might take a random sample of beer drinkers in Calgary and find that 16 percent regularly drink Molson Canadian beer. The next day we might repeat the same sampling procedure and discover that 14 percent regularly drink Molson Canadian beer. The difference is due to random error. Error is common to all surveys, yet it is often not reported or is underreported. Typically, the only error mentioned in a written report is a sampling error.

Collecting the Data

Marketing research field service firms collect most primary data. A **field service firm** specializes in interviewing respondents on a subcontracted basis. Many have offices, often in malls, throughout the country. A typical marketing research study involves data collection in several cities, requiring the marketer to work with a comparable number of field service firms. Besides conducting interviews, field service firms provide focus-group facilities, mall intercept locations, test product storage, and kitchen facilities to prepare test food products.

Analyzing the Data

After collecting the data, the marketing researcher proceeds to the next step in the research process: data

random sample a sample arranged in such a way that every element of the population has an equal chance of being selected as part of the sample

nonprobability sample any sample in which little or no attempt is made to have a representative cross section of the population

convenience sample a form of nonprobability sample using respondents who are convenient, or readily accessible, to the researcher—for example, employees, friends, or relatives

measurement error an error that occurs when the information desired by the researcher differs from the information provided by the measurement process

sampling error a sample that does not represent the target population

frame error a sample drawn from a population differs from the target population

random error the selected sample is an imperfect representation of the overall population

field service firm a firm that specializes in interviewing respondents on a subcontracted basis

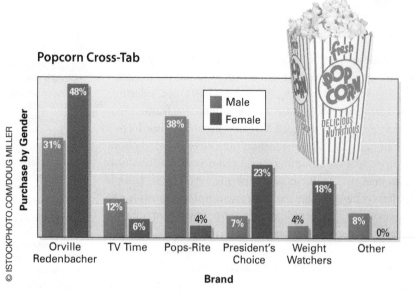

Popcorn Cross-Tab

Purchase by Gender

Legend: Male, Female

- Orville Redenbacher: Male 31%, Female 48%
- TV Time: Male 12%, Female 6%
- Pops-Rite: Male 38%, Female 4%
- President's Choice: Male 7%, Female 23%
- Weight Watchers: Male 4%, Female 18%
- Other: Male 8%, Female 0%

Brand

cross-tabulation a method of analyzing data that shows the analyst the responses to one question in relation to the responses to one or more other questions

analysis. The purpose of this analysis is to interpret and draw conclusions from the mass of collected data. The marketing researcher tries to organize and analyze those data by using one or more techniques common to marketing research: one-way frequency counts, cross-tabulations, and more sophisticated statistical analysis. Of these three techniques, one-way frequency counts are the simplest. One-way frequency tables simply record the responses to a question. For example, the answers to the question "What brand of microwave popcorn do you buy most often?" would provide a one-way frequency distribution. One-way frequency tables are always used in data analysis, at least as a first step, because they provide the researcher with a general picture of the study's results. A **cross-tabulation** shows the analyst the responses to one question in relation to the responses to one or more other questions. For example, what is the association between gender and the brand of microwave popcorn bought most frequently?

Researchers can use many other more powerful and sophisticated statistical techniques, such as hypothesis testing, measures of association, and regression analysis. A description of these techniques goes beyond the scope of this book but can be found in any good marketing research textbook. The use of sophisticated statistical techniques depends on the researchers' objectives and the nature of the data gathered.

Preparing and Presenting the Report

After data analysis has been completed, the researcher must prepare the report and communicate the conclusions and recommendations to management. This is a key step in the process. If the marketing researcher wants managers to carry out the recommendations, he or she must convince the managers that the results are credible and justified by the data collected.

Researchers are usually required to present both written and oral reports on the project. They should begin with a clear, concise statement of the research issue studied, the research objectives, followed by a complete but brief and simple explanation of the research design or methodology employed, including the nature of the sample and how it was selected. A summary of major findings should come next. The conclusion of the report should also present recommendations to management. Fuller reports will also contain any limitations that might have affected the research. These limitations will forewarn or advise the readers of any issues that could affect the reliability and validity of research. Awareness of these limitations may also help future researchers and may serve as cautions to managers when making their decision.

Most people who enter marketing will become research users rather than research suppliers. Thus, they must know what items to take note of in a report. As with many items we purchase, quality is not always readily apparent, and a high price does not guarantee superior quality. The basis for measuring the quality of a marketing research report is the research proposal. Did the report meet the objectives established in the proposal? Was the methodology outlined in the proposal followed? Are the conclusions based on logical deductions from the data analysis? Do the recommendations seem prudent, given the conclusions?

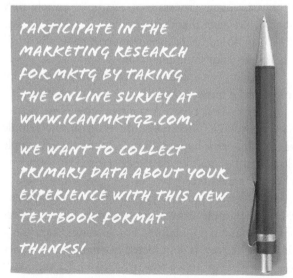

PARTICIPATE IN THE MARKETING RESEARCH FOR MKTG BY TAKING THE ONLINE SURVEY AT WWW.ICANMKTG2.COM.

WE WANT TO COLLECT PRIMARY DATA ABOUT YOUR EXPERIENCE WITH THIS NEW TEXTBOOK FORMAT.

THANKS!

- Better and faster decision making through much more rapid access to business intelligence
- Improved ability to respond quickly to customer needs and market shifts
- Follow-up studies and tracking research much easier to conduct and more fruitful
- Reduces labour- and time-intensive research activities (and associated costs) including mailing, telephone solicitation, data entry, data tabulation, and reporting

Following Up

The final step in the marketing research process is to follow up. The researcher should determine why management did or did not carry out the recommendations in the report. Was sufficient decision-making information included? What could have been done to make the report more useful to management? A good rapport is essential between the market researcher and the product manager or the person who authorized the project. Often, these individuals must work together on many studies throughout the year.

LO 4 The Profound Impact of the Internet on Marketing Research

The way survey research is conducted has changed forever because of the Internet. The vast majority (88 percent) of all North American research firms are now conducting marketing research online.[4]

In Canada, the online population is now closely tracking the population in most key demographic areas. In 2010, 79 percent of Canadians had Internet access, enabling them to log on each month to shop, email, find information, visit in chat rooms, and so forth. This usage exceeds 2009 predictions, which also showed Canada's Internet access to be the highest in North America. However, future increases may not continue at such a rapid

pace; more than one-half (56 percent) of those not having Internet access indicated they had no interest in having such access. The others without Internet access indicated their main reasons for not using the Internet as the cost of service and equipment, lack of a computer, and lack of confidence, skills, and knowledge.[5]

Advantages of Internet Surveys

The huge growth in the popularity of Internet surveys is the result of many advantages:

- *Rapid development, real-time reporting:* Internet surveys can be broadcast to thousands of potential respondents simultaneously. Respondents complete surveys simultaneously; then results are tabulated and posted for corporate clients to view as the returns arrive. Survey results can be in a client's hands in significantly less time than would be required for traditional surveys.

- *Dramatically reduced costs:* The Internet can cut costs by 25 to 40 percent and provide results in half the time required for traditional telephone surveys. Traditional survey methods are labour-intensive efforts incurring costs related to training, telecommunications, and management. Electronic methods eliminate these costs completely. While costs for traditional survey techniques rise proportionally with the number of interviews desired, electronic solicitations can grow in volume with little increase in project costs.

- *Personalized questions and data:* Internet surveys can be highly personalized for greater relevance to each respondent's own situation, thus speeding the response process.

- *Improved respondent participation:* Internet surveys take half as much time to complete as phone interviews, can

Internet Users and Penetration in North America by Country, 2008–2013 (millions and % of population)

	2008	2009	2010	2011	2012	2013
Canada	22.6	23.4	24.1	24.8	25.4	25.9
% of population	68.1%	69.2%	70.9%	71.9%	74.1%	74.9%
United States	192.8	199.2	205.3	210.9	216.0	221.1
% of population	63.4%	64.8%	66.2%	67.3%	68.3%	69.2%
North America	215.4	222.6	229.4	235.7	241.4	247.0

NOTE: An Internet user is a person of any age who uses the Internet from any location at least once per month.

SOURCE: eMarketer, February 2009, http://www.emarketer.com/images/chart_gifs/101001-102000/101419.gif. Reproduced by permission.

unrestricted Internet sample a survey in which anyone with a computer and Internet access can fill out the questionnaire

screened Internet sample an Internet sample with quotas that are based on desired sample characteristics

be accomplished at the respondent's convenience (after work hours), and can be much more stimulating and engaging. As a result, Internet surveys enjoy much higher response rates.

▸▸ *Contact with the difficult-to-reach:* Certain groups—doctors, high-income professionals, top management in Global 2000 firms—are among the most surveyed individuals on the planet and the most difficult to reach. Many of these groups are well represented online. Internet surveys provide convenient anytime/anywhere access that makes it easy for busy professionals to participate.

Problems with Internet Samples

1. ensuring only one response per person
2. ensuring the sample is representative of the population
3. lack of access for non-Internet computer users
4. avoiding professional and serial response users
5. self-selection only by current users and by interested parties

Uses of the Internet by Marketing Researchers

Marketing researchers are using the Internet to administer surveys, conduct focus groups, and perform a variety of other types of marketing research.

Internet Samples Internet samples may be classified as unrestricted, screened, or recruited. In an **unrestricted Internet sample**, anyone who desires can complete the questionnaire. It is fully self-selecting and probably representative of nothing except Web surfers. The problem is exacerbated if the same Internet user can access the questionnaire repeatedly. For example, *InfoWorld*, a computer-user magazine, decided to conduct its Readers Choice survey for the first time on the Internet. The results were so skewed

by repeat voting for one product that the entire survey was publicly abandoned and the editor asked for readers' help to avoid a recurrence of the problem. A simple solution to avoid repeat respondents is to lock respondents out of the site after they have completed the questionnaire.

Screened Internet samples adjust for the unrepresentativeness of the self-selected respondents by imposing quotas that are based on some desired sample characteristics. These characteristics are often demographic criteria, such as gender, income, and geographic region, or product-related criteria such as past purchase behaviour, job responsibilities, or current product use. The applications for screened samples are generally similar to those for unrestricted samples.

THE CHALLENGES OF GLOBAL MARKETING RESEARCH

In multicultural, multilingual research, questionnaires must be designed especially carefully. People in some cultures relate better to conversational interviewing than to fixed questionnaires. Some cultures require sensitive questions to be in a different order than others. In some places, people will only talk in particular settings. In Bosnia and Herzegovina, for example, questionnaires need to be administered in a neutral location not affiliated with any local ethnic group. In South Africa, many villages lack addresses and roads, and sampling has to be designed using satellite maps.[6]

Some Web survey systems can make immediate market segment calculations that first assign a respondent to a particular segment on the basis of screening questions and then select the appropriate questionnaire to match the respondent's segment. Alternatively, some Internet research providers maintain a "panel house" that recruits respondents who fill out a preliminary classification questionnaire. This information is used to classify respondents into demographic segments. Clients specify the desired segments, and the respondents who match the desired demographics are permitted to fill out the questionnaires of all clients who specify that segment.

Recruited Internet Samples

Recruited Internet samples are used in surveys that require more control over the makeup of the sample. Recruited samples are ideal for applications in which a database already exists from which to recruit the sample. For example, a good application would be a survey that uses a customer database to recruit respondents for a purchaser satisfaction study.

Respondents are recruited by telephone, mail, email, or in person. After respondents have qualified for the survey, they are either emailed the questionnaire or are directed to a website that contains a link to the questionnaire. At the website, passwords are normally used to restrict access to the questionnaire to recruited sample members. Since the makeup of the sample is known, completion of the questionnaires can be monitored; to improve the participation rate, follow-up messages can be sent to those who have not completed the questionnaire.

Recruited Panels

By far, the most popular form of Internet sampling is a recruited panel. In the early days of Internet recruiting, panels were created by means of Web-based advertising, or postings, that offered compensation for participation in online studies. This method allowed research firms to build large pools of individuals who were available to respond quickly to the demands of online marketing research. Internet panels have grown rapidly and now account for over 40 percent of all custom research sampling.[7]

Renting Internet Panels

Very few marketing research companies build their own Internet panels because of the huge expense involved. Instead, they rent a sample from an established panel provider, such as Survey Sampling International, which offers a huge Internet panel called Survey Spot. As with its other (non-Internet) panels,

Survey Sampling offers subsets of its main panel. Each subset is balanced to exactly reflect the demographics of the population, which is based on the 2006 Canadian census.

recruited Internet sample pre-recruited respondents must qualify to participate and are then emailed a questionnaire or directed to a secure website

Online Focus Groups

A recent development in qualitative research is the online, or cyber, focus group. A number of organizations are currently offering this new means of conducting focus groups. The process is fairly simple. The research firm builds

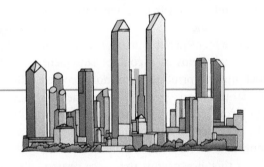

A system created by **Focus Vision Network** allows clients to view live focus groups in over 300 cities. The private satellite network lets a General Motors researcher observing a Vancouver focus group control two cameras in the viewing room. The researcher can get a full-group view or a close-up, zoom, or pan the participants. The researcher can also communicate directly with the moderator using an ear receiver.

www.focusvision.com

a database of respondents via a screening questionnaire on its website. When a client comes to a firm with a need for a particular focus group, the firm goes to its database and identifies individuals who appear to qualify. The firm sends an email to these individuals, asking them to log on to a particular site at a particular time scheduled for the group. The firm pays respondents an incentive for their participation.

The firm develops a discussion guide similar to the one used for a conventional focus group, and a moderator runs the group by typing in questions online for all to see. The group operates in an environment similar to that of a chat room so that all participants see all questions and all responses. The firm captures the complete text of the focus group and makes it available for review after the group has finished.

The Moderator's Role The basic way the moderator communicates with respondents in an online focus group is by typing all questions, instructions, and by probing into the text-entry area of the chat room in real time (live and on the spot). An advantage of the freestyle method is that it forces the moderator to adapt to the group rather than using a series of canned questions. A disadvantage is that typing everything freestyle (or even copying and pasting from a separate document) takes time.

Online focus groups enable respondents to view such items as a concept statement, a mock-up of a print ad, or a short product demonstration on video. The moderator simply provides a uniform resource locator (URL) reference for the respondents to enter in another browser window. One of the risks of doing this, however, is that once respondents open another browser, they have "left the room" and the moderator may lose their attention; researchers must hope that respondents will return within the specified amount of time.

More advanced virtual focus group software reserves a frame (section) of the screen for stimuli to be shown. Here, the moderator has control over what is shown in the stimulus area. The advantage of this approach is that the respondent does not need to do any work to see the stimuli.

Types of Online Focus Groups Online focus groups can be divided into two basic types:

The charge for online focus groups run by companies like Vancouver's Consumer Research Centre Ltd. compares very favourably to a cost in the range of $7,000, without travel costs, for conventional focus groups.

1. *Real-time online focus groups:* These are live, interactive sessions with four to six participants and a moderator in a chat room format. The typical session does not last longer than 45 to 50 minutes. The technique is best for simple, straightforward issues that can be covered in limited time. The results tend to be superficial compared with in-person focus groups—but this is acceptable for certain types of projects. Typically, three to four groups are recommended as a minimum. Clients can view the chat room as the session unfolds and communicate with the moderator. A variation of real-time online focus groups includes video capabilities, which allow participants to see and hear each other courtesy of webcams attached to their personal computers (PCs). Both verbal and nonverbal reactions can be recorded.

2. *Time-extended online focus groups:* These sessions follow a message board format and usually last five to ten days. The 15 to 20 participants must comment at least two or three times per day and spend 15 minutes a day logged on to the discussion. The moderator reviews respondents' comments several times per day (and night) and probes or redirects the discussion as needed. This technique provides three to four times as much content as the average in-person focus group. Time-extended online focus groups give participants time to reflect, talk to others, visit a store, or check the pantry. This extra time translates into richer content and deeper insights. Clients can view the online content as it is posted and may communicate with the moderator at any time.[8]

Advantages of Online Focus Groups Many advantages are claimed for cyber groups. Cyber Dialogue, a marketing research company specializing in cyber groups, lists the following benefits of online focus groups on its website:

▸▸ *Speed:* Typically, focus groups can be recruited and conducted, with delivery of results, within five days of client approval.

▸▸ *Cost-effectiveness:* Offline focus groups incur costs for facility rental, airfare, hotel, and food. None of these costs is incurred with online focus groups.

▸▸ *Broad geographic scope:* In a given focus group, you can speak to people in Edmonton, Alberta, and Halifax, Nova Scotia, at the same time.

▸▸ *Accessibility:* Online focus groups give you access to individuals who otherwise might be difficult to recruit (e.g., business travellers, doctors, mothers with infants).

▸▸ *Honesty:* From behind their screen names, respondents are anonymous to other respondents and tend to talk

Tech Meets Talk

Dad, pay my cellphone bill. Pleeeeaaaase.

3iYing, a market research firm, recruits panel members only from teenage females attending two New York art and design high schools because their students tend to have an advanced sense of design and be well-networked opinion leaders. The teens survey their networks of friends via email, instant messaging, or blog postings at Internet community sites, and then generate lists of what girls really want. The 3iYing design team then configures products and marketing campaigns for the client that resonate with the target audience. Virgin used what it learned from 3iYing to create a magazine ad designed to help girls shame parents into sharing money for either a real phone or more minutes. The ad contained a perforated cellphone and ran in *CosmoGIRL!*[9]

more freely about issues that might create inhibitions in a face-to-face group.

The Role of Blogs in Marketing Research Cutting-edge, technology-driven, marketing research companies, such as Nielsen BuzzMetrics (formerly Intelliseek), are now using more refined Internet search technologies to monitor, interpret, and report on comments, opinions, and feedback generated on blogs.[10] Arguably, the most revolutionary product is BuzzMetrics' BlogPulse, which monitors keywords and phrases, detects authors' sentiments, classifies data in terms of relevance, and unearths specific facts and data points about the brands, products, or companies that are the subject of bloggers' attention. Major clients such as Sony, AOL, Porsche, Yahoo!, and VH1 use BlogPulse to monitor consumers' opinions about their products or services on a daily, or even hourly, basis. BlogPulse can also identify the Internet's most influential bloggers, which marketers dearly love to know.

Other Uses of the Internet by Marketing Researchers The Internet revolution in marketing research has had an impact on more than just the way surveys and focus groups are conducted. The management of the research process and the dissemination of information have also been greatly enhanced by the Internet. Several key areas have been affected by the Internet:

▸▸ *The distribution of requests for proposals (RFPs) and proposals:* Companies can now quickly and efficiently send RFPs to a select email list of research suppliers. In turn, research suppliers can develop proposals and email them back to clients in a matter of hours.

▸▸ *Collaboration between the client and the research supplier in the management of a research project:* Now a researcher and client may both be looking at a proposal, RFP, report, or some type of statistical analysis at the same time on their respective computer screens while discussing it over the telephone. Changes to the research plan can be discussed and made immediately.

▸▸ *Data management and online analysis:* Clients can access their survey via the research supplier's secure website and monitor the data gathering in real time. The client can use sophisticated tools to analyze the data as the survey develops, allowing on-the-fly modifications to the elements of the project.

▸▸ *Publication and distribution of reports:* Reports can be published to the Web directly from numerous software programs, enabling the results to be made available to appropriate managers worldwide on an almost instantaneous basis.

▸▸ *Viewing of oral presentations of marketing research surveys by widely scattered audiences:* By placing oral presentations on password-protected websites, managers throughout the world can see and hear the actual client presentation.[11]

scanner-based research system for gathering information from a single group of respondents by continuously monitoring the advertising, promotion, and pricing they are exposed to and the products they buy

LO 5 Scanner-Based Research

Scanner-based research is a system for gathering information from a single group of respondents by continuously monitoring the advertising, promotion, and pricing they are exposed to and the products they buy. The variables measured are advertising campaigns, coupons, displays, and product prices. The result is a huge database of marketing efforts and consumer behaviour.

The two major scanner-based suppliers are Information Resources, Inc. (IRI), and The Nielsen Company. Although each has about half the market, IRI was the founder of scanner-based research. IRI's first product is called **BehaviorScan**. A household panel (a group of 3,000 long-term participants) has been recruited and maintained in each BehaviorScan town. Panel members shop with an ID card, which is presented at the checkout in scanner-equipped grocery stores and drugstores, allowing IRI to track electronically each household's purchases, item by item, over time. Microcomputers measure TV viewing in each panel member's household and send special commercials to panel members' television sets. With such a measure of household purchasing, it is possible to manipulate marketing variables (such as TV advertising or consumer promotions) and to introduce a new product and analyze real changes in consumer buying behaviour.

IRI's most successful product is **InfoScan**—a scanner-based, sales-tracking service for the consumer packaged goods industry. Retail sales, detailed consumer purchasing information (including measurement of store loyalty and total grocery basket expenditures), and promotional activity by manufacturers and retailers are monitored and evaluated for all bar-coded products. Data are collected weekly from more than 34,000 supermarkets, drugstores, and mass merchandisers.

The latest system in tagging for scanning, 1-TAG, has recently been developed by Leo Burnett partnering with Heidelberger Druckmaschinen, printing experts of Germany. This new system has some of the properties of radio-frequency identification (RFID) but is more complex. The 1-TAG is attached to the garments at the time of manufacture, allowing the manufacturer to control and customize the information content and production numbers in such a way that it is nearly impossible to make counterfeits. Customers and channel members can read the tags using a cellphone with a basic computer application (ap). The advantage to producers is preventing losses due to counterfeiting by unauthorized producers (also known as grey marketing). It also allows for supply chain inspections to

check goods in a very efficient and effective means by using standard mobile phones. In addition, the producer can improve information flow to the end user by loading intended destination, guarantees, expiry dates, and service information. The advantage for consumers is that a simple scan using an app on their cellphone can reassure them that the goods they purchased are authentic. Consumers can also use their cellphones to download other information from the tag, including the contact information for the manufacturer.[12]

LO 6 When Should Marketing Research Be Conducted?

When managers have several possible solutions to a problem, they should not instinctively call for marketing research. The first decision to make is whether to conduct marketing research at all.

Some companies have been conducting research in certain markets for many years. Such firms understand the characteristics of target customers and their likes and dislikes about existing products. Under these circumstances, further research would be repetitive and waste money. Procter & Gamble (P&G), for example, has extensive knowledge of the coffee market. After it conducted initial taste tests with Folgers Instant Coffee, P&G went into national distribution without further research. Sara Lee followed the same strategy with its frozen croissants, as did Quaker Oats with Chewy Granola Bars. This tactic, however, can backfire. Marketers may think they understand a particular market thoroughly and so bypass market research for a product, only to have the product fail and be withdrawn from the market.

If information were available and free, managers would rarely refuse more, but because marketing information can require a great deal of time and expense to accumulate, they might decide to forego additional information. Ultimately, the willingness to acquire additional decision-making information depends on managers' perceptions of its quality, price, and timing. In summary, research should be undertaken only when the expected value of the information is greater than the cost of obtaining it.

LO 7 # Competitive Intelligence

Derived from military intelligence, **competitive intelligence is an important tool for helping a firm overcome a competitor's advantage.** Specifically, competitive intelligence can help identify the advantage and play a major role in determining how it was achieved. Marketers can use this information for their Situation Appraisal in which they do their SWOT, Porter's Five Forces, and Stakeholder analysis to determine those factors that will influence the success of the business in the future.

Competitive intelligence (CI) helps managers assess their competitors and their vendors to become a more efficient and effective competitor. Intelligence is analyzed information. It becomes decision-making intelligence when it has implications for the organization. For example, a primary competitor may have plans to introduce a product with performance standards equal to ours but with a 15 percent cost advantage. The new product will reach the market in eight months. This intelligence has important decision-making and policy consequences for management. Competitive intelligence and environmental scanning

(where management gathers data about the external environment—see Chapter 3) combine to create marketing intelligence. Marketing intelligence is then used as input into a marketing decision support system.

In a survey of sports business professionals in each of five major professional leagues (the National Basketball Association, the National Football League, Major League Baseball, the National Hockey League, and Major League Soccer), 62 percent of all teams reported that they maintain a CI function, and nearly two-thirds of those teams have employed a CI function for three years or more. The CI assists in player personnel decisions and the identification of market opportunities.[13]

> **competitive intelligence (CI)** an intelligence system that helps managers assess their competition and vendors in order to become more efficient and effective competitors

Nine *out of ten* large companies have employees *dedicated* to the CI function.

IMAGE SOURCE/JUPITERIMAGES

Clearly, the Internet is an important resource for gathering competitive intelligence, but noncomputer sources can be equally valuable. Some examples include company salespeople, industry experts, CI consultants, government agencies, suppliers, periodicals, the Yellow Pages, and industry trade shows.

$250–$6,000
Cost for details of research reports on Canadian industries

Number of supermarkets, drugstores, and mass merchandisers providing IRI data every week
34,000

Percentage costs savings of online surveys versus traditional surveys
25–40%

88%
Percentage of research firms now conducting marketing research online

250,000+
Marketing research reports held by one of the top marketing research aggregators

2
Number of possible answers to a dichotomous question

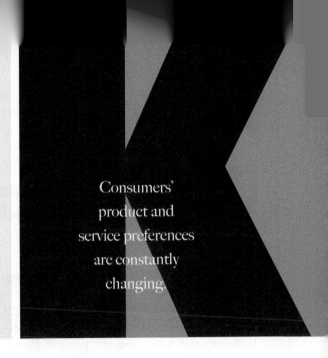

Consumers'
product and
service preferences
are constantly
changing.

LO 1 The Importance of Understanding Consumer Behaviour

AFTER YOU FINISH THIS CHAPTER, GO TO WWW. ICANMKTG2.COM FOR STUDY TOOLS.

Consumers' product and service preferences are constantly changing. To address this constant state of flux and to create a proper marketing mix for a well-defined market, marketing managers must have a thorough knowledge of consumer behaviour. **Consumer behaviour** describes how consumers make purchase decisions and how they use and dispose of the purchased goods or services. The study of consumer behaviour also includes an analysis of factors that influence purchase decisions and product use.

Understanding how consumers make purchase decisions can help marketing managers in several ways. For example, if a manager knows through research that gas mileage is the most important attribute for a certain target market, the manufacturer can redesign the product to meet that criterion. If the firm cannot change the design in the short run, it can use promotion in an effort to change consumers' decision-making criteria. When Virgin Mobile realized that Gen-Yers were looking for more flexibility and convenience and more value-added services than traditional cellphone plans offered, the company redesigned its marketing strategy to more closely match targeted consumers' needs, wants, and desires. Thus, depending on

consumer behaviour how consumers make purchase decisions and how they use and dispose of purchased goods or services; also includes the factors that influence purchase decisions and product use

What do you think?

Shopping just boils down to "buy" or "don't buy."

| 1 | 2 | 3 | 4 | 5 | 6 | 7 |
STRONGLY DISAGREE   STRONGLY AGREE

© ISTOCKPHOTO.COM/PAUL PIEBINGA

the amounts of time desired and when the consumer desires access, they can chose from different member plans at different prices.

The Consumer Decision-Making Process

When buying products, consumers generally follow the **consumer decision-making process** shown in Exhibit 5.1: (1) need recognition, (2) information search, (3) evaluation of alternatives, (4) purchase, and (5) postpurchase behaviour. These five steps represent a general process that can be used as a guide for studying how consumers make decisions. This guideline does not assume that consumers' decisions will proceed in order through all of the steps of the process. In fact, the consumer may end the process at any time or may not even make a purchase. The section on the types of consumer buying decisions later in the chapter discusses why a consumer's progression through these steps may vary. Before addressing this issue, however, we will describe each step in the process in greater detail.

Marketing managers can create wants on the part of the consumer.

Need Recognition

The first stage in the consumer decision-making process is need recognition. **Need recognition** occurs when consumers are faced with an imbalance between actual and desired states. Need recognition is triggered when a consumer is exposed to either an internal or an external **stimulus.** *Internal stimuli* are occurrences you experience, such as hunger or thirst. *External stimuli* are influences from an outside source such as someone's recommendation of a new restaurant, the design of a package, or an advertisement on television or radio.

Marketing managers can create wants on the part of the consumer. A **want** is a particular product or service that the consumer believes could

consumer decision-making process a five-step process used by consumers when buying goods or services

need recognition result of an imbalance between actual and desired states

stimulus any unit of input affecting one or more of the five senses: sight, smell, taste, touch, hearing

want a particular product or service that the consumer believes could satisfy an unfulfilled need

satisfy an unfulfilled need. A want can be for a specific product, or it can be for a certain attribute or feature of a product. For example, if your cellphone runs through the washing machine in your jeans pocket, you'll *need* to buy a replacement and may want one with greater speed, 12 MB camera, voice recognition, etc.

A marketing manager's objective is to get consumers to recognize an imbalance between their present status and their preferred state. Advertising and sales promotion often provide this stimulus. By surveying buyer preferences, marketers gain information about consumer needs and wants, which they can then use to tailor their products and services.

Another way marketers create new products and services is by observing trends in the marketplace. IKEA, the home furnishing giant, realized that Generation Y consumers prefer furniture that is stylish, easy to clean, multifunctional, and portable, so it created a line of products to meet those preferences. One item in the line is a space-saving, multifunction desk that can be converted into a dining table; it has wheels so that it can be easily moved.[1]

Consumers recognize unfulfilled wants in various ways. The two most common occur when a current product isn't performing properly and when the consumer is about to run out of something that is generally kept on hand. Consumers may also

BLOOMBERG/GETTY IMAGES

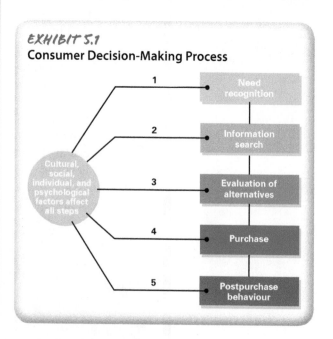

EXHIBIT 5.1
Consumer Decision-Making Process

1 — Need recognition
2 — Information search
3 — Evaluation of alternatives
4 — Purchase
5 — Postpurchase behaviour

Cultural, social, individual, and psychological factors affect all steps

recognize unfulfilled wants if they become aware of a product that seems superior to the one they currently used. Such is the case with cellphones. With increased options and usage, consumers desire longer battery life for their phones. Cellphone companies have thus replaced batteries with longer lasting Lithium-Ion batteries (300–500 rechargings) but this still means the batteries will die in 1–2 years. As the iPhone batteries are non-replaceable (unless returned to the company and costing $90) this means the consumer is faced with this inconvenience and expense as well as emerging new technological features. They are thus faced with a buying decision.

And as you will read in Chapter 20, marketers selling their products in global markets must carefully observe the needs and wants of consumers in various regions.

Information Search

After recognizing a need or want, consumers search for information about the various alternatives available to satisfy it. An information search can occur internally, externally, or both. An **internal information search** is the process of recalling information stored in one's memory. This stored information stems largely from previous experience with a product, for example, recalling whether a hotel where you stayed earlier in the year had clean rooms and friendly service.

In contrast, an **external information search** is the process of seeking information in the outside environment. There are two basic types of external information sources: nonmarketing-controlled and marketing-controlled. A **nonmarketing-controlled information source** is a product information source not associated with advertising or promotion. These information sources include personal experiences (trying or observing a new product); personal sources (family, friends, acquaintances, and co-workers who may recommend a product or service); and public sources, such as *Consumer*

Reports and other rating organizations that comment on products and services. For example, if you feel like seeing a movie, you may search your memory for past experiences at various cinemas when determining which one to go to (personal experience). To choose which movie to see, you may rely on the recommendation of a friend or family member (personal sources), or you may read the critical reviews in the newspaper or online (public sources). Marketers gather information on how these information sources work and use this information to attract customers.

On the other hand, a **marketing-controlled information source** is biased toward a specific product because it is a product information source that originates with marketers promoting the product. Marketing-controlled information sources include mass-media advertising (radio, newspaper, television, and magazine advertising), sales promotion (contests, displays, and premiums), salespeople, product labels and packaging, and the Internet. Many consumers, however, are wary of the information they receive from marketing-controlled sources, believing that most marketing campaigns stress the product's attributes and ignore its faults. These sentiments tend to be stronger among better-educated and higher-income consumers.

The extent to which an individual conducts an external search depends on his or her perceived risk, knowledge, prior experience, and level of interest in the good or service. Generally, as the perceived risk of the purchase increases, the consumer expands the search and considers more alternative brands. For example, you would probably spend more time researching the purchase of a laptop or

KEVIN WINTER/GETTY IMAGES

evoked set (consideration set) a group of the most preferred alternatives resulting from an information search, which a buyer can further evaluate to make a final choice

a car than the purchase of an energy drink. A consumer's knowledge about the product or service will also affect the extent of an external information search. A consumer who is knowledgeable and well informed about a potential purchase is less likely to search for additional information and will conduct the search more efficiently, thereby requiring less time to search.

The extent of a consumer's external search is also affected by confidence in one's decision-making ability. A confident consumer not only has sufficient stored information about the product but also feels self-assured about making the right decision. People lacking this confidence will continue an information search even when they know a great deal about the product. A third factor influencing the external information search is product experience. Consumers who have had a positive prior experience with a product are more likely to limit their search to items related to the positive experience. For example, when planning a trip, consumers are likely to choose airlines with which they have had positive experiences, such as consistent on-time arrivals, and will likely avoid airlines with which they had a negative experience, such as lost luggage.

Finally, the extent of the search is positively related to the amount of interest a consumer has in a product. A consumer who is more interested in a product will spend more time searching for information and alternatives. A dedicated runner searching for a new pair of running shoes may enjoy reading about the new brands available and, as a result, may spend more time

and effort than other buyers in deciding on the next shoe purchase.

The buyer's **evoked set** (or **consideration set**) is a group of the most preferred alternatives resulting from an information search, which a buyer can further evaluate to make a final choice. Consumers do not consider all brands available in a product category, but they do seriously consider a much smaller set. Having too many choices can, in fact, confuse consumers and cause them to delay the decision to buy or, in some instances, can cause them to not buy at all.

Evaluation of Alternatives and Purchase

After acquiring information and constructing an evoked set of alternative products, the consumer is ready to make a decision. A consumer will use the information stored in memory and obtained from outside sources to develop a set of criteria. These standards help the consumer to evaluate and compare alternatives. One way to begin narrowing the number of choices in the evoked set is to pick a product attribute and then exclude all products in the set without that attribute. For example, if you are buying a car and live in the mountains, you will probably exclude all cars without four-wheel drive.

Another way to narrow the number of choices is to use cutoffs. Cutoffs are either minimum or maximum levels of an attribute that an alternative must pass to be considered. If your budget for that new car is $25,000, you will not consider any four-wheel drive vehicle above that price point. A final way to narrow the choices is to rank the attributes under consideration in order of importance and evaluate the products on how well each performs on the most important attributes.

If new brands are added to an evoked set, the consumer's evaluation of the existing brands in that set changes. As a result, certain brands in the original set may become more desirable. If you discover that you can get the exact car you want, used, for $18,000 instead of spending $25,000 for a new model, you may revise your criteria and select the used car.

The goal of the marketing manager is to determine which attributes have the most influence on a consumer's choice. Several attributes may collectively affect a consumer's evaluation of products. A single attribute, such as price, may not adequately explain how consumers form their evoked set. Moreover, attributes the

THE CANADIAN PRESS/WAYNE GLOWACKI

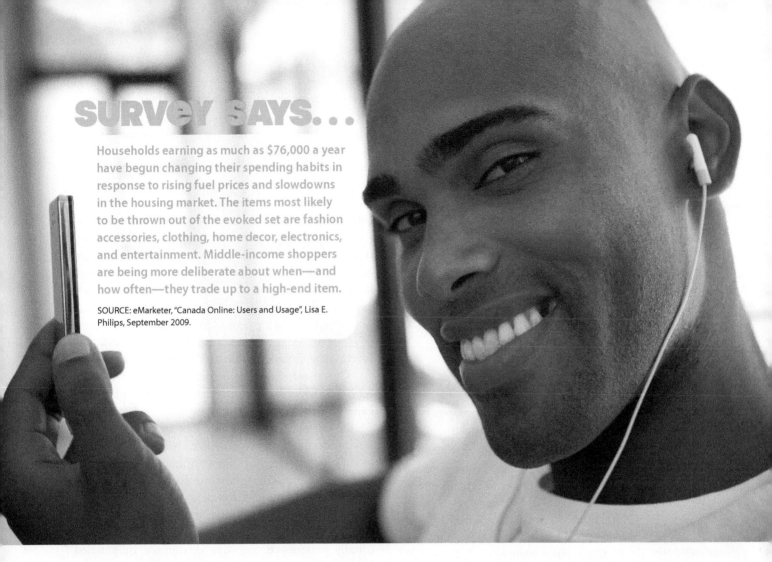

Households earning as much as $76,000 a year have begun changing their spending habits in response to rising fuel prices and slowdowns in the housing market. The items most likely to be thrown out of the evoked set are fashion accessories, clothing, home decor, electronics, and entertainment. Middle-income shoppers are being more deliberate about when—and how often—they trade up to a high-end item.

SOURCE: eMarketer, "Canada Online: Users and Usage", Lisa E. Philips, September 2009.

JUICE IMAGES/JUPITERIMAGES

marketer thinks are important may not be very important to the consumer. A brand name can also have a significant impact on a consumer's ultimate choice. By providing consumers with a certain set of promises, brands in essence simplify the consumer decision-making process so consumers do not have to rethink their options every time they need something.[2]

Following the evaluation of alternatives, the consumer decides which product to buy or decides not to buy a product at all. If he or she decides to make a purchase, the next step in the process is an evaluation of the product after the purchase.

Postpurchase Behaviour

When buying products, consumers expect certain outcomes from the purchase. How well these expectations are met determines whether the consumer is satisfied or dissatisfied with the purchase. For the marketer, an important element of any postpurchase evaluation is reducing any lingering doubts that the decision was sound. Eliminating such doubts is particularly important because 75 percent of all consumers say they had a bad experience in the last year with a product or service they purchased.[3]

When people recognize inconsistency between their values or opinions and their behaviour, they tend to feel an inner tension called **cognitive dissonance**. For example, suppose a regular tanning bed customer decides to try a more expensive airbrush tanning method called mystic tanning. Prior to purchase, the person may feel tension or anxiety, which is a feeling of dissonance. In her mind, the disadvantages (of higher costs) battle the advantages (of the lack of harmful ultraviolet rays).[4]

Consumers try to reduce dissonance by justifying their decision. They may seek new information that reinforces positive ideas about the purchase, avoid information that contradicts their decision, or revoke the original decision by returning the product. In some instances, people deliberately seek contrary information so they can refute it and reduce the dissonance. Dissatisfied customers sometimes rely on word of mouth to reduce cognitive dissonance, by letting friends and family know they are displeased.

Marketing managers can help reduce dissonance through effective communication with purchasers.

> **cognitive dissonance** inner tension that a consumer experiences after recognizing an inconsistency between behaviour and values or opinions

Postpurchase letters sent by manufacturers and dissonance-reducing statements in instruction booklets may help customers to feel more at ease with their purchase. Advertising that displays the product's superiority over competing brands or guarantees can also help relieve the possible dissonance of someone who has already bought the product. Ultimately, the marketer's goal is to ensure that the outcome meets or exceeds the customer's expectations rather than be a disappointment.[5]

LO 3 Types of Consumer Buying Decisions and Consumer Involvement

All consumer buying decisions generally fall along a continuum of three broad categories: routine response behaviour, limited decision making, and extensive decision making (see Exhibit 5.2). Goods and services in these three categories can best be described in terms of five factors: level of consumer involvement, length of time to make a decision, cost of the good or service, degree of information search, and the number of alternatives considered. The level of consumer involvement is perhaps the most significant determinant in classifying buying decisions. **Involvement** is the amount of time and effort a buyer invests in the search, evaluation, and decision processes of consumer behaviour.

Frequently purchased, low-cost goods and services are generally associated with **routine response behaviour**. These goods and services can also be called low-involvement products because consumers spend little time on the search and decision before making the purchase. Usually, buyers are familiar with several different brands in the product category but stick with one brand. Consumers engaged in routine response behaviour normally don't experience need recognition until they are exposed to

advertising or see the product displayed on a store shelf. These consumers buy first and evaluate later, whereas the reverse is true for consumers who engage in extensive decision making.

Limited decision making requires a moderate amount of time for gathering information and deliberating about an unfamiliar brand in a familiar product category. It typically occurs when a consumer has previous product experience but is unfamiliar with the current brands available. Limited decision making is also associated with lower levels of involvement (although higher than routine decisions) because consumers expend only moderate effort in searching for information or in considering various alternatives. If a consumer's usual brand is sold out, he or she will likely evaluate several other brands before making a final decision.

Consumers practise **extensive decision making** when considering the purchase of an unfamiliar, expensive product or an infrequently purchased item. This process is the most complex type of consumer buying decision and is associated with high involvement on the part of the consumer. This process resembles the model outlined in Exhibit 5.1. Because these consumers want to make the right decision, they want to know as much as they can about the product category and the available brands. People usually experience cognitive dissonance only when buying high-involvement products. Buyers use several criteria for evaluating their options and spend much time seeking information. Buying a home or a car, for example, requires extensive decision making.

PHIL WALTER/GETTY IMAGES

---

involvement the amount of time and effort a buyer invests in the search, evaluation, and decision processes of consumer behaviour

routine response behaviour the type of decision making exhibited by consumers buying frequently purchased, low-cost goods and services; requires little search and decision time

limited decision making the type of decision making that requires a moderate amount of time for gathering information and deliberating about an unfamiliar brand in a familiar product category

extensive decision making the most complex type of consumer decision making, used when considering the purchase of an unfamiliar, expensive product or an infrequently purchased item; requires the use of several criteria for evaluating options and much time for seeking information

EXHIBIT 5.2
Continuum of Consumer Buying Decisions

	Routine	Limited	Extensive
Involvement	low	low to moderate	high
Time	short	short to moderate	long
Cost	low	low to moderate	high
Information Search	internal only	mostly internal	internal and external
Number of Alternatives	one	few	many

The type of decision making that consumers use to purchase a product does not necessarily remain constant. If a routinely purchased product no longer satisfies, consumers may practise limited or extensive decision making to switch to another brand. Consumers who first use extensive decision making may then use limited or routine decision making for future purchases. For example, a family may spend a lot of time figuring out that their new puppy prefers hard food to soft, but once they know, the purchase will become routine.

Factors Determining the Level of Consumer Involvement

The level of involvement in the purchase depends on the following five factors:

▶▶ *Previous experience:* When consumers have had previous experience with a good or service, the level of involvement typically decreases. After repeated product trials, consumers learn to make quick choices. Because consumers are familiar with the product and know whether it will satisfy their needs, they become less involved in the purchase.

▶▶ *Interest:* Involvement is directly related to consumer interests, as in cars, music, movies, bicycling, or electronics. Naturally, these areas of interest vary from one individual to another. A person highly involved in bike racing will be more interested in the type of bike she owns than someone who rides a bike only for recreation.

▶▶ *Perceived risk of negative consequences:* As the perceived risk in purchasing a product increases, so does a consumer's level of involvement. The types of risks that

concern consumers include financial risk, social risk, and psychological risk. First, financial risk is exposure to loss of wealth or purchasing power. Because high risk is associated with high-priced purchases, consumers tend to become extremely involved. Therefore, price and involvement are usually directly related: as price increases, so does the level of involvement. Second, consumers take social risks when they buy products that can affect people's social opinions of them (for example, driving an old, beat-up car or wearing unstylish clothes). Third, buyers undergo psychological risk if they feel that making the wrong decision might cause some concern or anxiety. For example, some consumers feel guilty about eating foods that are not healthy, such as regular ice cream rather than fat-free frozen yogurt.

▶▶ *Situation:* The circumstances of a purchase may temporarily transform a low-involvement decision into a high-involvement one. High involvement comes into play when the consumer perceives risk in a specific situation. For example, an individual might routinely buy canned fruit and vegetables, but for dinner parties shop for high-quality fresh produce.

▶▶ *Social visibility:* Involvement also increases as the social visibility of a product increases. Products often on social display include clothing (especially designer labels), jewellery, cars, and furniture. All these items make a statement about the purchaser and, therefore, carry a social risk.

Marketing Implications of Involvement

Marketing strategy varies according to the level of involvement associated with the product. For high-involvement product purchases, marketing managers have several responsibilities. First, promotion to the target market should be extensive and informative. A good ad gives consumers the information they need for making the purchase decision and specifies the benefits and unique advantages of owning the product.

For low-involvement product purchases, consumers may not recognize their wants until they are in the store. Therefore, marketing managers focus on package design so the product will be eye-catching and easily recognized on the shelf. In-store promotions and displays also stimulate sales of low-involvement products. A good display can explain the product's purpose and prompt recognition of a want. Coupons, cents-off deals, and two-for-one offers also effectively promote low-involvement items.

Linking a product to a higher-involvement issue is another tactic that marketing managers can use to increase the sales of a low-involvement product. Although packaged food may normally

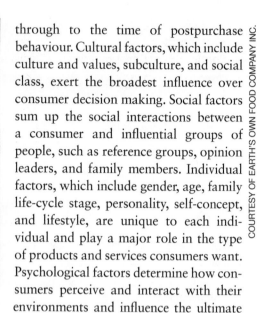

culture the set of values, norms, attitudes, and other meaningful symbols that shape human behaviour and the artifacts, or products, of that behaviour as they are transmitted from one generation to the next

be a low-involvement product, reference to health issues raises the involvement level. Makers of So Good soy milk and PC meatless burgers, both of which contain soy protein, tout soy's health benefits, such as reducing the risk of coronary heart disease, preventing certain cancers, and reducing the symptoms of menopause. Sales of soy-based products, long shunned in Canada for their taste, skyrocketed as a result of these health claims.[6]

Factors Influencing Consumer Buying Decisions

The consumer decision-making process does not occur in a vacuum. On the contrary, the decision process is strongly influenced by underlying cultural, social, individual, and psychological factors. These factors have an effect from the time a consumer perceives a stimulus

through to the time of postpurchase behaviour. Cultural factors, which include culture and values, subculture, and social class, exert the broadest influence over consumer decision making. Social factors sum up the social interactions between a consumer and influential groups of people, such as reference groups, opinion leaders, and family members. Individual factors, which include gender, age, family life-cycle stage, personality, self-concept, and lifestyle, are unique to each individual and play a major role in the type of products and services consumers want. Psychological factors determine how consumers perceive and interact with their environments and influence the ultimate decisions consumers make. They include perception, motivation, learning, beliefs, and attitudes. Exhibit 5.3 summarizes these influences.

LO 4 Cultural Influences on Consumer Buying Decisions

Of all the factors that affect consumer decision making, **cultural factors exert the broadest and deepest influence.** Marketers must understand the way people's culture and its accompanying values, as well as their subculture and social class, influence their buying behaviour.

Culture and Values

Culture comprises the set of values, norms, attitudes, and other meaningful symbols that shape human behaviour and the artifacts, or products, of that behavior as they are transmitted from one generation to the next. It is the essential character of a society that distinguishes it from other cultural groups.

Culture is pervasive. What people eat, how they dress, what they think and feel, and what language they speak are all dimensions of culture. Culture encompasses all the things consumers do without conscious choice because their culture's values, customs, and rituals are ingrained in their daily habits.

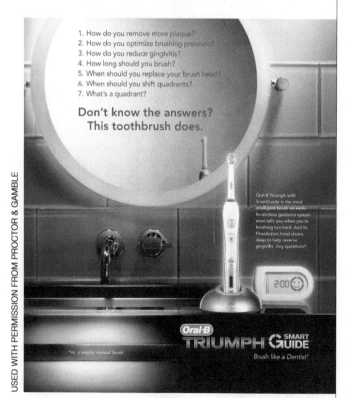

1. How do you remove more plaque?
2. How do you optimize brushing pressure?
3. How do you reduce gingivitis?
4. How long should you brush?
5. When should you replace your brush head?
6. When should you shift quadrants?
7. What's a quadrant?

Don't know the answers? This toothbrush does.

As the level of purchasing involvement increases, so does the marketing manager's responsibility to provide extensive and informative promotional materials to potential customers.

Culture is functional. Human interaction creates values and prescribes acceptable behaviour for each culture. By establishing common expectations, culture gives order to society. Sometimes these expectations are enacted into laws, such as the expectation that drivers will stop at red lights. Other times, these expectations are taken for granted: grocery stores and hospitals are open 24 hours, whereas banks are not.

Culture is learned. Consumers are not born knowing the values and norms of their society. Instead, they must learn what is acceptable from family and friends. Children learn the values that will govern their behaviour from parents, teachers, and peers.

Culture is dynamic. It adapts to changing needs and an evolving environment. The rapid growth of technology in today's world has accelerated the rate of cultural change. Although the amount of television viewing has remained relatively constant, the means of access (cable, NetFlix, etc.) and increased use of mobile devices and the Internet have changed entertainment patterns, family communications, and have heightened public awareness of political and other news events. Automation has increased the amount of leisure time we have and, in some ways, has changed the traditional work ethic. Another factor that contributes to cultural shifts in Canada is our rapidly increasing diversity, which influences our food, music, clothing, and entertainment. For example, students attending a postsecondary college or university often meet students from other countries and are introduced to their foods and celebrations, such as Chinese New Year. As a result, these students may change their preferences in foods and other areas.

The most defining element of a culture is its **values**— the enduring beliefs shared by a society that a specific mode of conduct is personally or socially preferable to another mode of conduct. People's value systems have a great effect on their consumer behaviour. Consumers with similar value systems tend to react alike to prices and other marketing-related inducements. Values also correspond to consumption patterns. For example, Canadians place a high value on convenience as we are thought to be in a time-starved society. This value has created lucrative markets for products such as breakfast bars, energy bars, and nutrition bars that allow consumers to eat on the go.[7] Those values considered central to the Canadian way of life include success, freedom, materialism, capitalism, progress, and youth.

> **value** the enduring belief shared by a society that a specific mode of conduct is personally or socially preferable to another mode of conduct

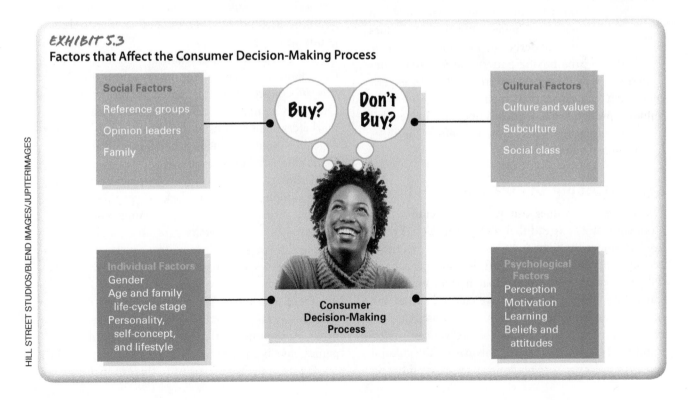

EXHIBIT 5.3
Factors that Affect the Consumer Decision-Making Process

HILL STREET STUDIOS/BLEND IMAGES/JUPITERIMAGES

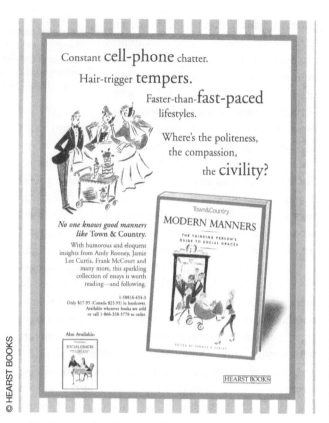

Constant **cell-phone** chatter.

Hair-trigger **tempers.**

Faster-than-**fast-paced**
lifestyles.

Where's the politeness,
the compassion,
the **civility?**

*No one knows good manners
like* Town & Country.

With humorous and eloquent
insights from Andy Rooney, Jamie
Lee Curtis, Frank McCourt and
many more, this sparkling
collection of essays is worth
reading—and following.

1-58816-454-3
Only $17.95 (Canada $25.95) in hardcover.
Available wherever books are sold
or call 1-866-338-3778 to order.

Also Available:

Town&Country
MODERN MANNERS
THE THINKING PERSON'S
GUIDE TO SOCIAL GRACES

HEARST BOOKS

Modern Manners explores the ways in which new technologies, like cellphones, have changed North American culture.

subculture a
homogeneous group of people
who share elements of the
overall culture and also have
their own unique cultural
elements

The personal values of target consumers have important implications for marketing managers. When marketers understand the core values that underlie the attitudes that shape the buying patterns of Canada's consumers and how these values were moulded by experiences, they can target their message more effectively. Values represent what is most important in people's lives. Therefore, marketers watch carefully for shifts in consumers' values over time.

Understanding Culture Differences

Underlying core values can vary across cultures. As more companies expand their operations globally, the need to understand the cultures of foreign countries becomes more important. A firm has little chance of selling products in a culture that it does not understand. Like people, products have cultural values and rules that influence their perception and use. Culture, therefore, must be understood before we can understand the behaviour of individuals within the cultural context. Colours, for example, may have different meanings in global markets than they do at home. In China, white is the colour of mourning, and brides wear red. Although, today the influence of western culture with Asian females is now seeing their desire to choose wedding dresses with both colours.

Language is another important aspect of culture that global marketers must consider. When translating product names, slogans, and promotional messages into foreign languages marketers must be careful not to convey the wrong message. Coors encouraged its English-speaking customers to "Turn it loose," but the phrase in Spanish means to suffer from diarrhea.

Though marketers expanding into global markets generally adapt their products and business formats to the local culture, some fear that increasing globalization and the proliferation of the Internet will result in a homogeneous world culture of the future.

Subculture

A culture can be divided into subcultures on the basis of demographic characteristics, geographic regions, national and ethnic background, political beliefs, and religious beliefs. A **subculture** is a homogeneous group of people who share elements of the overall culture and also have their own unique cultural elements. Within subcultures, people's attitudes, values, and purchase decisions are even more similar than they are within the broader culture. Subcultural differences may result in considerable variation within a culture in what, how, when, and where people buy goods and services.

In Canada's multicultural society, French Canadians represent a dominant subculture. While this subculture is mainly based in the province of Quebec, Canada is officially a bilingual nation, and marketers in all regions of the country must be knowledgeable about the language and lifestyle values of the French Canadian subculture.

Other subcultures are geographically dispersed. For example, computer hackers, people who are hearing impaired or visually impaired, Harley-Davidson bikers, university professors, and gays may be found throughout the country. Yet they have identifiable attitudes, values, and needs that distinguish them from the larger culture.

Once marketers identify subcultures, they can design special marketing programs to serve their needs. In response to the growing Asian market, companies have been spending a larger percentage of their marketing budgets advertising to this group. Canadian

Education seems to be the most reliable indicator of a person's social and economic status. Those with post-secondary degrees are more likely to fall into the upper classes, while those with some postsecondary experience tend to fall into the middle class.

banks such as TD Canada Trust and the CIBC have developed marketing campaigns targeting the Asian market, particularly in Vancouver and Toronto. Major league sports teams, such as the Vancouver Canucks and the Toronto Raptors, have used ethnic media outlets, such as Omni Television and CHIN Radio in the Toronto market, in campaigns that target this growing segment of potential fans.

Social Class

Like other societies, Canada has a class system. A **social class** is a group of people who are considered nearly equal in status or community esteem, who

EXHIBIT 5.4
Canadian Social Classes by Sex (%)

	Men	Women	Population Total
Capitalist/executive	8.8	2.7	6.2
New middle class	25.3	24.4	24.9
Old middle class	15.7	5.1	11.3
Working class	50.3	67.9	57.6
Total	100.1*	100.1*	100.0

*Totals may not equal 100 due to rounding.

SOURCE: Adapted from Simon Langlois, "Empirical Studies on Social Stratification in Quebec and Canada," in Yannick Lemel and Heinz-Herbert Noll, eds., *Changing structures of inequality: a comparative perspective*, Montreal: McGill-Queen's University Press, © 2002, p. 83. Reprinted with permission

regularly socialize among themselves both formally and informally, and who share behavioural norms.

One view of contemporary Canadian status structure is shown in Exhibit 5.4. The capitalist executive group comprises the small segment of affluent and wealthy Canadians who are more likely to own their own homes and purchase new cars and trucks and who are less likely to smoke. The most affluent consumers are more likely to attend art auctions and galleries, dance performances, operas, the theatre, museums, concerts, and sporting events.

The majority of Canadians today define themselves as middle class, regardless of their actual income or educational attainment. This phenomenon most likely occurs because working-class Canadians tend to aspire to the middle-class lifestyle while some of those who achieve affluence may downwardly aspire to respectable middle-class status as a matter of principle.

The working class is a distinct subset of the middle class. This group's interest in organized labour is one of its most common attributes. Members of the working class often rate job security as the most important reason for taking a job. The working-class person depends heavily on relatives and the community for economic and emotional support.

Lifestyle distinctions between the social classes are greater than the distinctions within a given class. The most significant difference between the classes occurs between the middle and working classes, which is differentiated by a major shift in lifestyles.

Social class is typically measured as a combination of occupation, income, education, wealth, and other variables. For instance, affluent upper-class consumers are more likely to be salaried executives or self-employed professionals with at least an undergraduate degree. Working-class or middle-class consumers are more likely to be hourly service workers or blue-collar employees with only a high-school education. Educational attainment, however, seems to be the most reliable indicator of a person's social and economic status. Those with university or college degrees or graduate degrees are more likely to fall into the upper classes, while those people with some postsecondary experience fall closer to traditional concepts of the middle class.

Marketers are interested in social class for two main reasons. First, social class often indicates which medium to use for advertising. An

social class a group of people who are considered nearly equal in status or community esteem, who regularly socialize among themselves both formally and informally, and who share behavioural norms

CHAPTER 5: CONSUMER DECISION MAKING 77

SOCIAL CLASS AND EDUCATION

Educational Profile	Median Earnings
Less than high school	$32,029
High school graduates	$37,403
Trades or apprenticeship	$39,996
College graduates	$42,937
University graduates, Bachelor	$56,048
Post Bachelor	$66,535

SOURCE: Statistics Canada. 2008. Median(1) 2005 earnings for full-year, full-time earners by education, both sexes, total—age group 25 to 64, for Canada, provinces and territories—20% sample data (table). Income and Earnings Highlight Tables. 2006 Census. Statistics Canada Catalogue no. 97-563-XWE2006002. Ottawa. Released May 1, 2008. http://www12.statcan.ca/english/census06/data/highlights/Earnings/Table803 .cfm?Lang=E&T=803&GH=4&SC=1&S=1&O=D (accessed July 17, 2008).

© PHOTODISC/GETTY IMAGES

reference group a group in society that influences an individual's purchasing behaviour

insurance company wanting to sell its policies to middle-class families might advertise during the local evening news because middle-class families tend to watch more television than other classes do, but if the company wanted to sell more policies to affluent individuals, it might place a print ad in a business publication such as the *Financial Post*. Second, knowing what products appeal to which social classes can help marketers determine where to best distribute their products.

LO 5 Social Influences on Consumer Buying Decisions

primary membership groups groups with which individuals interact regularly in an informal, face-to-face manner

secondary membership groups groups with which individuals interact less consistently and more formally than with primary membership groups

aspirational reference groups groups that an individual would like to join

norms the values and attitudes deemed acceptable by a group

Most consumers are likely to seek out the opinions of others to reduce their search and evaluation effort or uncertainty, especially as the perceived risk of the decision increases. Consumers may also seek out others' opinions for guidance on new products or services, products with image-related attributes, expensive products, or products where attribute information is lacking or uninformative. Specifically, consumers interact socially with reference groups, opinion leaders, and family members to obtain product information and decision approval.

Reference Groups

All the formal and informal groups that influence the purchasing behaviour of an individual are that person's **reference groups**. Consumers may use products or brands to identify with or become a member of a group. Consumers observe how members of their reference groups consume, and they use the same criteria to make their own consumer decisions.

Reference groups can be broadly categorized as being either direct or indirect (see Exhibit 5.5). Direct reference groups are face-to-face membership groups that touch people's lives directly. They can be either primary or secondary. **Primary membership groups** include all groups with which people interact regularly in an informal, face-to-face manner, such as family, friends, and co-workers. In contrast, people associate with **secondary membership groups** less consistently and more formally. These groups might include clubs, professional associations, and people who share a religious affiliation.

Consumers are also influenced by many indirect, nonmembership reference groups they do not belong to. **Aspirational reference groups** are those groups that a person would like to join. To join an aspirational group, a person must conform to that group's **norms**; that is, the values and attitudes deemed acceptable by the group. Thus, a person who wants to be elected to public office may begin to dress more conservatively, to match the attire of other politicians. He or she may patronize the same restaurants and attend the same social engagements that civic officials and business leaders attend, in an attempt to play a role that is acceptable to voters and people of influence. Similarly, teenagers today may dye their hair and experiment with body piercing and tattoos. Athletes are an aspirational group for several market segments. To appeal to the younger market, Coca-Cola signed basketball star LeBron James to be the spokesperson for its Sprite and Powerade brands, and Nike signed a sneaker deal with him reportedly worth $90 million. Coca-Cola and Nike assumed James would encourage consumers to drink Coke brands and buy Nike shoes because they would like to identify with James.[8]

Nonaspirational reference groups, or **dissociative groups**, influence our behaviour because we try to maintain distance from them. A consumer may avoid buying some types of clothing or cars, going to certain restaurants or stores, or even buying a home in a certain neighbourhood in order to avoid being associated with a particular group.

The activities, values, and goals of reference groups directly influence consumer behaviour. For marketers, reference groups have three important implications: (1) they serve as information sources and influence perceptions; (2) they affect an individual's aspiration levels; and (3) their norms either constrain or stimulate consumer behaviour. Understanding the effect of reference groups on a product is important for marketers as they track the life cycle of their products. Marketers continually face the challenge of identifying the trendsetters in a particular target market. For example, a snowboard manufacturer can determine what is considered cool in the snowboard market by seeking out the trendsetters on their favourite slopes. The unique ways in which these snowboarders personalize their equipment and clothing can be looked on as being desirable, and thus may be modified by the influencers who are seeking to express their own individual character. Once the fad look is embraced by the influencers, it has the potential to be adopted by the others in that socio-geographic group. However, as the adoption of the latest trend becomes more common, that trend loses its appeal to the trendsetters and they seek new ways to express their individualism. In the mean time, the product continues to be accepted by consumers who are influenced by seeing and hearing others who are receiving benefits they feel are desirable. Thus, marketers must understand and track the effects of reference groups on the sales of a product as it moves through its life cycle. The effects of reference groups are especially important both for products that satisfy such visible, unique, socially desirable, high-involvement needs as wine, fashion and the latest foods, and for personal services such as spa treatments and vacation destinations and activities.

Opinion Leaders

Reference groups frequently include individuals known as group leaders, or **opinion leaders**—those who influence others. Obviously, it is important for marketing managers to persuade such people to purchase their goods or services. Many products and services that are integral parts of Canadians' lives today received their initial boost from opinion leaders. For example, geothermal heating, iPads, hybrid vehicles, and electrical vehicles were purchased by opinion leaders well ahead of the general public.

Opinion leaders are often the first to try new products and services, usually as the result of pure curiosity. They are typically self-indulgent, making them more likely to explore unproven but intriguing products and services. Technology companies have found that teenagers, because of their willingness to experiment, are key opinion leaders for the success of new technologies. Texting became popular with teenagers before it gained widespread appeal. Today, tweeting has become a major means of communication. As a result, many technology companies include these in their marketing programs targeted to teens. By reaching opinion leaders, these companies hope to start a trend that will carry into the mass market.[9] Recent studies on opinion leaders in the pharmaceutical industry have uncovered the key influencer to be the **sociometric leader**, typically a well-respected collaborative professional who is socially and professionally well connected. These lower-profile individuals have certainly had marketers reflecting on whom they should be marketing to and with.[10]

After identifying potential opinion leaders, marketers will often endeavour to engage these people to support their products. For example, marketers may

nonaspirational reference groups (dissociative groups) groups that influence our behaviour because we try to maintain distance from them

opinion leader an individual who influences the opinions of others.

sociometric leader a low-profile, well-respected collaborative professional who is socially and professionally well connected

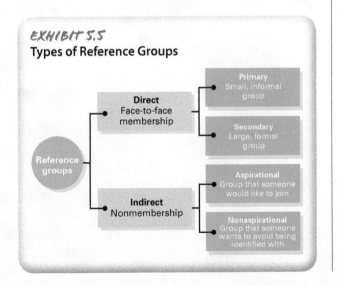

EXHIBIT 5.5
Types of Reference Groups

ask high-school cheerleaders to model new fall fashions or ask civic leaders to promote insurance, new cars, and other merchandise. Revatex, the maker of JNCO jeans, sponsors extreme-sports athletes, who appeal to the teen market. It also gives free clothes to trendsetters among teens in the hopes they will influence others to purchase the brand. JNCO also outfits big-name DJs in the rave scene and members of hip, alternative bands favoured by the teen crowd.

On a wider scale, large companies, groups, associations, and causes will seek out recognized organizations or individuals in sports, business, entertainment, religion, or politics to endorse or support the promotion of their product. The organization's or individual's familiarity, attractiveness, credibility, and relative association, can greatly influence a target group. Thus, while Justin Bieber can influence teens' fashion or desire to go to a summer music event, a promotion featuring Sidney Crosby might influence an athlete or hockey fan, and a local company's support of a new charity fundraiser or disaster relief (e.g., Big White Ski Resort's initiation of a fundraiser for flood disaster in Queensland, Australia, in 2011) can influence other companies, communities, and individuals to also support the cause.

How Blogs Are Defining Today's Opinion Leaders Increasingly, marketers are looking to blogs to find opinion leaders. In 2011, BlogsCanada.ca listed over 20 different categories in 12 regions, covering topics from athletics and dating to weddings and workouts. With new blogs coming online every day, it's getting harder to separate the true opinion leaders from Web users who are just looking to share random thoughts or vacation photos with family and friends. The fashion industry once dismissed bloggers as being snarky and small time, effectively limiting their access to hot events during semi-annual fashion week shows. Now, however, fashion bloggers have the attention of the fashion establishment because many are claiming bigger followings than the traditional media. Still, not all fashion blogs are equal. Bloggers from FashionTribes.com and Bagtrends.com received tickets to some fall 2006 shows, but those from Shopology.com and Coutorture.com were denied access because their audiences were too small.[11]

One way marketers are identifying true opinion leaders is by looking to teen blogs to identify the social trends that are shaping consumer behaviour. During the research phase of development for its teen-targeted RED Blogs service, AOL discovered that over 50 percent of teens did not mind sharing their feelings in public forums. Their openness is especially evident on social networking sites such as Facebook, YouTube, Tumblr, and Twitter, where teens and twentysomethings post extensive personal profiles, photo collections, links to user groups they belong to, and detailed descriptions of their social events.

Raised with MTV, 500-channel cable services, a rapidly maturing Internet, and ever-expanding cellphone capabilities, teens have unprecedented access to the world around them. They are no longer passive observers of the culture their parents have created. They can follow their favourite bands, actors, or athletes via their websites and blogs, and they expect to interact with

them instead of just admiring them from afar. With their unprecedented ability to network and communicate with each other, young people rely on each other's opinions more than marketing messages when making purchase decisions. Blogs, tweeting, etc. are becoming a key way that teens communicate their opinions. Consequently, today's marketers are reading teen blogs and tweets, developing products that meet the very specific needs that teens express there, and learning unique and creative ways to put key influencers in charge of marketing their brands for them.

Family

The family is the most important social institution for many consumers, strongly influencing their values, attitudes, self-concepts—and buying behaviour. For example, a family that strongly values good health will have a grocery list distinctly different from that of a family that views every dinner as a gourmet event. Moreover, the family is responsible for the **socialization process**, the passing down of cultural values and norms to children. Because children learn by observing their parents' consumption patterns, they will tend to shop in a similar pattern.

Decision-making roles among family members tend to vary significantly, depending on the types of items purchased. Family members assume a variety of roles in the purchase process. *Initiators* suggest, initiate, or plant the seed for the purchase process. The initiator can be any member of the family. For example, a sister might initiate the product search by asking for a new bicycle as a birthday present. *Influencers* are those members of the family whose opinions are valued. In our example, Mom might function as a price-range watchdog, an influencer whose main role is to veto or approve price ranges. A brother may give his opinion on certain makes of bicycles. The *decision maker* is the family member who actually makes the decision to buy or not to buy. For example, Dad or Mom is likely to choose the final brand and model of bicycle to buy after seeking further information from the sister regarding cosmetic features such as colour and after imposing additional parental criteria, such as durability and safety. The *purchaser* (probably Dad or Mom) is the one who actually exchanges money for the product. Finally, the *consumer* is the actual user—the sister, in the case of the bicycle.

Marketers should consider family purchase situations along with the distribution of consumer and decision-maker roles among family members. Ordinary marketing views the individual as both decision maker and consumer. Family marketing adds several other possibilities: sometimes more than one family member or all family members are involved in the decision; sometimes only children are involved in the decision; sometimes more than one consumer is involved; and sometimes the decision maker and the consumer are different people.

socialization process the passing down of cultural values and norms to children

LO 6 Individual Influences on Consumer Buying Decisions

A person's buying decisions are also influenced by personal characteristics that are unique to each individual, such as gender; age and life-cycle stage; and personality, self-concept, and lifestyle. Individual characteristics are generally stable over the course of one's life. For instance, most people do not change their gender, and the act of changing personality or lifestyle requires a complete reorientation of one's life. In the case of age and life-cycle stage, these changes occur gradually over time.

Gender

Physiological differences between men and women result in different needs. Just as important are the distinct cultural, social, and economic roles played by men and women and the effects that these roles have on their decision-making processes. Most car manufacturers have realized that men and women tend to look at different features when purchasing a vehicle. Generally speaking, men gravitate toward gadgets and performance-related items, while women prefer to focus on convenience features such as ease of access, carrying capacity, cup holders, and heated/cooled seats.

Indeed, men and women do shop differently. Studies show that men and women share similar motivations in terms of where to shop—that is, seeking reasonable prices, merchandise quality, and a friendly, low-pressure environment—but they don't necessarily feel the same about shopping in general. Most women enjoy shopping, while most men claim to dislike the experience and shop only out of necessity. Further,

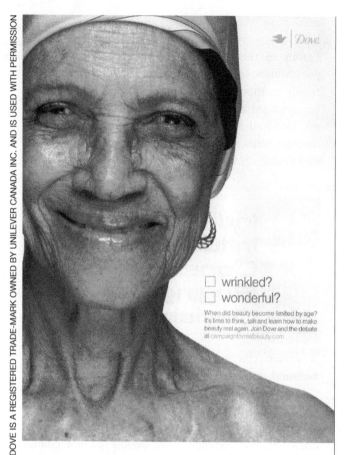

☐ wrinkled?
☐ wonderful?

When did beauty become limited by age? It's time to think, talk and learn how to make beauty real again. Join Dove and the debate at campaignforrealbeauty.com

men desire simple shopping experiences, stores with less variety and more convenience. Stores that appeal more to men than to women are easy to shop in, are near home or office, or have knowledgeable personnel.[12] The Internet appeals to men who find it an easy way to shop for clothing and gifts. Many Internet retailers are designing their sites to attract male gift buyers.

Trends in gender marketing are influenced by the changing roles of men and women in society. In October 2007, Satoru Iwata, Nintendo's president, noted that Japanese women had overtaken their male counterparts to become the biggest users of Nintendo's Wii and DS machines, which would have global implications.[13] Companies that have traditionally targeted women must develop new strategies that reflect the changing roles of women at home and work. Many industries—such as the video game industry and car racing—are attracting new customers by marketing to women.[14] But other changes also need to be considered by marketers. With recent changes in the views of millennial males to take more active roles in parenting and household duties, the

economic recession of 2008–10, and the higher education levels attained by females, males are now at home more, and, as of 2010, comprise the primary grocery shoppers (at 51 percent). This means that products, channels, and promotion need to change to meet the behaviours and needs of the male shopper.[15]

Age and Family Life-Cycle Stage

The age and family life-cycle stage of a consumer can have a significant impact on consumer behaviour. How old a consumer is generally indicates the products he or she may be interested in purchasing. Consumer tastes in food, clothing, technology, cars, furniture, and recreation are often age related. For example in a recent research study by Harris Interactive, the first Youth EquiTrend Study asked youths aged 8 to 24 years old to rate brands on familiarity, quality, and purchase consideration. The results showed marked differences in age groups. The 8- to 12-year-old tweens had listed as their top preferences: Nintendo, Doritos, Oreos, and M&Ms. The teens (aged 13 to 17 years old) had shifted to iPod, Google, M&Ms, and Oreos. The young adults' choices (aged 18 to 24 years old) were more tech-savvy products, listing Google, Facebook, iPod, and Gatorade.[16]

Related to a person's age is his or her place in the family life cycle. As Chapter 7 explains in more detail, the *family life cycle* is an orderly series of stages through which consumers' attitudes and behavioural tendencies evolve through maturity, experience, and changing income and status. Marketers often define their target markets in terms of family life cycle, such as "young singles," "young married with children,"

and "middle-aged married without children." As you can imagine, the spending habits of young singles, young parents, and empty nesters are very different. For instance, the presence of children in the home is the most significant determinant of the type of vehicle that's driven off the new-car lot. Parents are the ultimate need-driven car consumers, requiring larger cars and trucks to haul their children and all their belongings, which explains why sport utility vehicles (SUVs) and minivans were selling at a brisk pace before rising fuel costs became a major consideration when purchasing a vehicle.

Marketers should also be aware of the many non-traditional life-cycle paths that are common today and provide insights into the needs and wants of such consumers as divorced parents, lifelong singles, and childless couples.

Personality, Self-Concept, and Lifestyle

Each consumer has a unique personality. **Personality** is a broad concept that can be thought of as a way of organizing and grouping the consistency of an individual's reactions to situations. Thus, personality combines psychological makeup and environmental forces. It also includes people's underlying dispositions, especially their most dominant characteristics. Although personality is one of the least useful concepts in the study of consumer behaviour, some marketers believe that personality influences the types and brands of products purchased. For instance, the type of car, clothes, or jewellery a consumer buys may reflect one or more personality traits.

Self-concept, or self-perception, is how consumers perceive themselves in terms of attitudes, perceptions, beliefs, and self-evaluations. Although a self-concept may change, the change is often gradual. Through self-concept, people define their identity, which in turn provides for consistent and coherent behaviour.

Self-concept combines the **ideal self-image** (the way an individual would like to be) and the **real self-image** (the way an individual actually perceives himself or herself). Generally, we try to raise our real self-image toward our ideal (or at least narrow the gap). Consumers seldom buy products that jeopardize their self-image. For example, a woman who sees herself as a trendsetter wouldn't buy clothing that doesn't project a contemporary image.

Human behaviour depends largely on self-concept. Because consumers want to protect their identity as individuals, the products they buy, the stores they patronize, and the credit cards they carry support their self-image. By influencing the degree to which consumers perceive a good or service to be self-relevant, marketers can affect consumers' motivation to learn about, shop for, and buy a certain brand. Marketers also consider self-concept important because it helps explain the relationship between individuals' perceptions of themselves and their consumer behaviour.

An important component of self-concept is *body image*, the perception of the attractiveness of one's own physical features. For example, a person's perception of body image can be a stronger reason for weight loss than either good health or other social factors.[17] With the median age of Canadians rising, many companies are introducing products and services aimed at aging baby boomers who are concerned about their age and physical appearance. Marketers are also seeing boomers respond to products aimed at younger audiences. For instance, to the surprise of company managers, Starwood's "W" Hotels, designed and advertised to attract a young, hip crowd in cities from Montreal to San Francisco, are attracting large numbers of boomers as well.[18]

Personality and self-concept are reflected in lifestyle. A **lifestyle** is a mode of living, as identified by a person's activities, interests, and opinions. *Psychographics* is the analytical technique used to examine consumer lifestyles and to categorize consumers. Unlike personality characteristics, which can be difficult to describe and measure, lifestyle characteristics are useful in segmenting and targeting consumers. We, as consumers, are ever-changing in our affluence (income and spending focus), where we live (urban, suburban, or rural), and our relationships (family stage or life-stage groups). Lifestyle and psychographic analyses explicitly address the way consumers outwardly express their inner selves in their social and cultural environment. For example, to better understand their market segments, many companies now use psychographics such as PRIZM, which segments consumers into 66 different groups (e.g., Winner's Circle, a classification to which many of you aspire). Psychographics and lifestyle segmentation are discussed in more detail in Chapter 7.

personality a way of organizing and grouping the consistency of an individual's reactions to situations

self-concept how consumers perceive themselves in terms of attitudes, perceptions, beliefs, and self-evaluations

ideal self-image the way an individual would like to be

real self-image the way an individual actually perceives himself or herself

lifestyle a mode of living as identified by a person's activities, interests, and opinions

LO7 Psychological Influences on Consumer Buying Decisions

An individual's buying decisions are further influenced by psychological factors: perception, motivation, learning, and beliefs and attitudes. These factors are what consumers use to interact with their world, recognize their feelings, gather and analyze information, formulate thoughts and opinions, and take action. Unlike the other three influences on consumer behaviour, **psychological influences** can be affected by a person's environment because they are applied on specific occasions. For example, you will perceive different stimuli and process these stimuli in different ways depending on whether you are sitting in class concentrating on the instructor, sitting outside of class talking to friends, or sitting in your dorm room watching television.

psychological influences tools that consumers use to recognize, gather, analyze, and self-organize to aid in decision making

perception the process by which people select, organize, and interpret stimuli into a meaningful and coherent picture

selective exposure the process whereby a consumer decides which stimuli to notice and which to ignore

selective distortion a process whereby consumers change or distort information that conflicts with their feelings or beliefs

selective retention a process whereby consumers remember only information that supports their personal beliefs

Perception

The world is full of stimuli. A stimulus is any unit of input affecting one or more of the five senses: sight, smell, taste, touch, or hearing. The process by which we select, organize, and interpret these stimuli into a meaningful and coherent picture is called **perception**. In essence, perception is how we see the world around us and how we recognize that we need some help in making a purchasing decision.

People cannot perceive every stimulus in their environment. Therefore, they use **selective exposure**, a process whereby a consumer decides which stimuli to notice and which to ignore. The familiarity of an object, its contrast, movement, intensity (such as increased volume), and smell are cues that influence perception. Consumers use these cues to identify and define products and brands. The shape of a product's packaging, such as Coca-Cola's signature contour bottle, can influence perception. Colour is another cue, and it plays a key role in consumers' perceptions. Packaged foods manufacturers use colour to trigger unconscious associations for grocery shoppers who typically make their shopping decisions in the blink of an eye. Food marketers use green to signal environmental well-being and healthy, low-fat foods, whereas black, brown, and gold are used to convey premium ingredients.[19] The shape and look of a product's packaging can also influence perception.

What is perceived by consumers may also depend on the vividness or shock value of the stimulus. Graphic warnings of the hazards associated with a product's use are perceived more readily and remembered more accurately than less vivid warnings or warnings that are written in text. Sexier ads excel at attracting the attention of younger consumers. Companies such as Calvin Klein and Guess use sensuous ads to "cut through the clutter" of competing ads and other stimuli to capture the attention of the target audience.

Two other concepts closely related to selective exposure are selective distortion and selective retention. **Selective distortion** occurs when consumers change or distort information that conflicts with their feelings or beliefs. For example, suppose you buy a Sony Tablet. After the purchase, if you receive new information about an alternative brand, such as an Amazon Kindle, you may distort the information to make it more consistent with the prior view that the Tablet is just as good as the Kindle, if not better.

Selective retention is a process whereby consumers remember only information that supports their personal feelings or beliefs. The consumer forgets all information that may be inconsistent. Consumers may see a news report on suspected illegal practices by their favourite retail store but soon forget the reason the store was featured on the news.

Which stimuli will be perceived often depends on the individual. People can be exposed to the same stimuli under identical conditions but perceive them very differently. For example, two people viewing a TV

A TYPICAL CONSUMER IS EXPOSED TO MORE THAN **2,500 ADVERTISING MESSAGES** A DAY BUT NOTICES ONLY BETWEEN 11 AND 20.

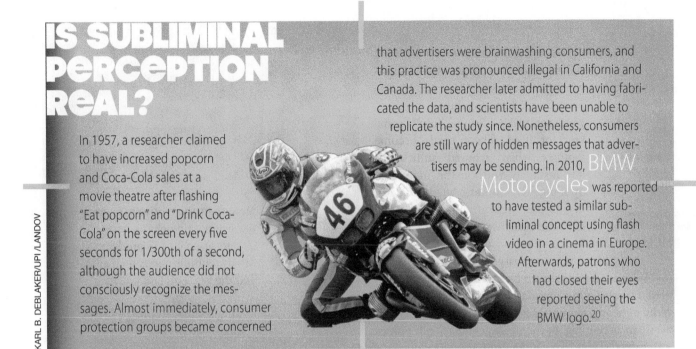

IS SUBLIMINAL PERCEPTION REAL?

In 1957, a researcher claimed to have increased popcorn and Coca-Cola sales at a movie theatre after flashing "Eat popcorn" and "Drink Coca-Cola" on the screen every five seconds for 1/300th of a second, although the audience did not consciously recognize the messages. Almost immediately, consumer protection groups became concerned that advertisers were brainwashing consumers, and this practice was pronounced illegal in California and Canada. The researcher later admitted to having fabricated the data, and scientists have been unable to replicate the study since. Nonetheless, consumers are still wary of hidden messages that advertisers may be sending. In 2010, BMW Motorcycles was reported to have tested a similar subliminal concept using flash video in a cinema in Europe. Afterwards, patrons who had closed their eyes reported seeing the BMW logo.[20]

commercial may have different interpretations of the advertising message. One person may be thoroughly engrossed by the message and become highly motivated to buy the product. Thirty seconds after the ad ends, the second person may not be able to recall the content of the message or even the product advertised.

Marketing Implications of Perception Marketers must recognize the importance of cues, or signals, in consumers' perception of products. Marketing managers first identify the important attributes that the targeted consumers want in a product, such as price, social acceptance, or quantity, and then design signals to communicate these attributes. Gibson Guitar Corporation briefly cut prices on many of its guitars to compete with Japanese rivals Yamaha and Ibanez but found instead that it sold more guitars when it charged more. Consumers perceived that the higher price indicated a better-quality instrument.[21]

Marketing managers are also interested in the *threshold level of perception:* the minimum difference in a stimulus that the consumer will notice. This concept is sometimes referred to as the "just-noticeable difference." For example, how much would Apple have to drop the price of its iPad before consumers recognized it as a bargain—$25? $50? or more? One study found that the just-noticeable difference in a stimulus is about a 20 percent change. That is, consumers will likely notice a 20 percent price decrease more quickly than a 15 percent decrease. This marketing principle can also be applied to other marketing variables, such as package size or loudness of a broadcast advertisement.[22]

Another study showed that the bargain-price threshold for a name brand is lower than that for a store brand. In other words, consumers perceive a bargain more readily when stores offer a small discount on a name-brand item than when they offer the same discount on a store brand; a larger discount is needed to achieve a similar effect for a store brand.[23] Researchers also found that for low-cost grocery items, consumers typically do not see past the second digit in the price. For instance, consumers do not perceive any real difference between two comparable cans of tuna, one priced at $1.52 and the other at $1.59, because they ignore the last digit.[24]

Marketing managers who intend to do business in global markets should be aware of how foreign consumers perceive their products. For instance, in Japan, product labels are often written in English or French, even though they may not translate into anything meaningful. Many Japanese associate the foreign words with products that are exotic, expensive, and of high quality.

CONSUMER MATH: **$1.52 = $1.59**

motive a driving force that causes a person to take action to satisfy specific needs

Maslow's hierarchy of needs a method of classifying human needs and motivations into five categories in ascending order of importance: physiological, safety, social, esteem, and self-actualization

learning a process that creates changes in behaviour, immediate or expected, through experience and practice

Motivation

By studying motivation, marketers can analyze the major forces influencing consumers to buy or not buy products. When you buy a product, you usually do so to fulfill some kind of need. These needs become motives when aroused sufficiently. For instance, you can be motivated by hunger to stop at McDonald's for, say, an Egg McMuffin before an early morning class. **Motives** are the driving forces that cause a person to take action to satisfy specific needs.

Why are people driven by particular needs at particular times? One popular theory is **Maslow's hierarchy of needs**, shown in Exhibit 5.6, which arranges needs in ascending order of importance: physiological, safety, social, esteem, and self-actualization. As a person fulfills each level to a somewhat satisfied level, a higher-level need becomes more important.

The most basic human needs are *physiological*—that is, the needs for food, water, and shelter. Because these needs are essential to survival, they must be satisfied first. *Safety* needs include security and freedom from pain and discomfort. Marketers sometimes appeal to consumers' fears and anxieties about safety to sell their products. After physiological and safety needs have been fulfilled, *social needs*—especially love and a sense of belonging—become the focus. Love includes acceptance by one's peers, as well as sexual and romantic love. Marketing managers probably appeal more to this need than to any other. The need to belong is also

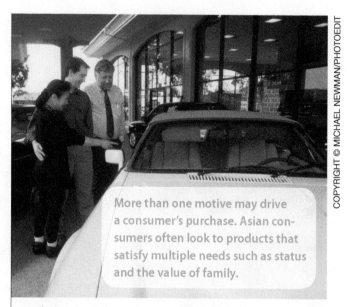

More than one motive may drive a consumer's purchase. Asian consumers often look to products that satisfy multiple needs such as status and the value of family.

a favourite of marketers, especially those marketing products to teens. Shoes and clothing brands, such as Nike, adidas, Hollister, and American Eagle Outfitters, score high with teenagers, who wear these labels to feel and look like they belong to the in crowd.

Whereas love is acceptance without regard to one's contribution, esteem is acceptance that is based on one's contribution to the group. *Self-esteem needs* include self-respect and a sense of accomplishment. Esteem needs also include prestige, fame, and recognition of one's accomplishments. Asian consumers, in particular, are strongly motivated by status and appearance and are always conscious of their place in a group, institution, or society as a whole. The importance of gaining social recognition motivates Asians to spend freely on premium brands. Indeed, marketers of luxury products such as Gucci, Louis Vuitton, Prada, BMW, and Mercedes Benz find that demand for their products is so strong among image-conscious consumers that their sales are generally unaffected by economic downturns.

The highest human need is *self-actualization*. It refers to finding self-fulfillment and self-expression, reaching the point in life at which "people are what they feel they should be." Maslow felt that very few people ever attain this level. Even so, advertisements may focus on this type of need. The platinum level for many credit-card companies appeals to this level.

Learning

Almost all consumer behaviour results from **learning**, which is the process that creates changes in behaviour, immediate or expected, through experience and practice. It is not possible to observe learning directly, but we can infer when it has occurred by a person's

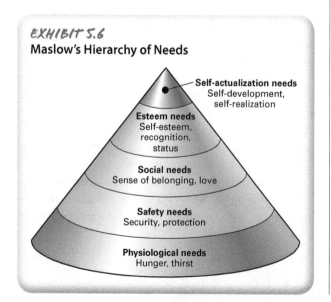

EXHIBIT 5.6
Maslow's Hierarchy of Needs

Self-actualization needs
Self-development, self-realization

Esteem needs
Self-esteem, recognition, status

Social needs
Sense of belonging, love

Safety needs
Security, protection

Physiological needs
Hunger, thirst

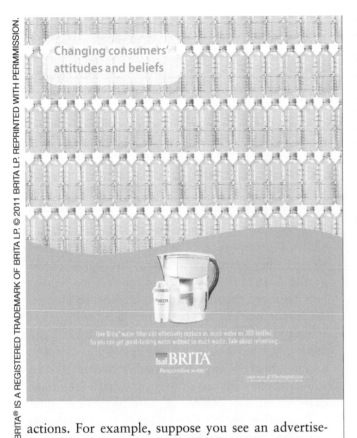

Changing consumers' attitudes and beliefs

One Brita® water filter can effectively replace as much water as 300 bottles. So you can get great-tasting water without so much waste. Talk about refreshing.

BRITA
Responsible water.

belief an organized pattern of knowledge that an individual holds as true about his or her world

attitude a learned tendency to respond consistently toward a given object

the behaviour pattern or to avoid it. Thus, if a new brand evokes neutral feelings, some marketing activity, such as a price change or an increase in promotion, may be required to induce further consumption. Learning theory is helpful for reminding marketers that concrete and timely actions are what reinforce desired consumer behaviour.

Repetition is a key strategy in promotional campaigns because it can lead to increased learning. Most marketers use repetitious advertising so that consumers will learn their unique advantage over the competition. Generally, to heighten learning, advertising messages should be spread over time rather than clustered together.

Beliefs and Attitudes

Beliefs and attitudes are closely linked to values. A **belief** is an organized pattern of knowledge that an individual holds as true about his or her world. A consumer may believe that Sony's camcorder makes the best home videos, tolerates hard use, and is reasonably priced. These beliefs may be based on knowledge, faith, or hearsay. Consumers tend to develop a set of beliefs about a product's attributes and then, through these beliefs, form a *brand image*—a set of beliefs about a particular brand. In turn, the brand image shapes consumers' attitudes toward the product.

An **attitude** is a learned tendency to respond consistently toward a given object, such as a brand. Attitudes rest on an individual's value system, which represents personal standards of good and bad, right and wrong, and so forth; therefore, attitudes tend to be more enduring and complex than beliefs. For an example of the nature of attitudes, consider the differing attitudes of North American and European consumers toward the practice of purchasing on credit. North Americans have long been enthusiastic about charging goods and services and are willing to pay high interest rates for the privilege of postponing payment. To many European consumers, however, doing what amounts to taking out a loan, even a small one, to pay for anything seems absurd.

Changing Beliefs If a good or service is meeting its profit goals, positive attitudes toward the product merely need to be reinforced. If the brand is not succeeding, however, the marketing manager must strive to change target consumers' attitudes toward it. This change can be accomplished in three ways: changing

actions. For example, suppose you see an advertisement for a new and improved cold medicine. If you go to the store that day and buy that remedy, we infer that you have learned something about the cold medicine.

There are two types of learning: experiential and conceptual. *Experiential learning* occurs when an experience changes your behaviour. For example, if the new cold medicine does not relieve your symptoms, you may not buy that brand again. *Conceptual learning*, which is not acquired through direct experience, is the second type of learning. Assume, for example, that you are standing at a pop machine and notice a new diet flavour with an artificial sweetener. Because someone has told you that diet beverages leave an aftertaste, you choose a different drink. You have learned that you would not like this new diet drink without ever trying it.

Reinforcement and repetition boost learning. Reinforcement can be positive or negative. For example, if you see a vendor selling frozen yogurt (a stimulus), and you buy it (your response), you may find the yogurt to be quite refreshing (your reward). In this example, your behaviour has been positively reinforced. On the other hand, if you buy a new flavour of yogurt and it does not taste good (negative reinforcement), you will not buy that flavour of yogurt again (your response). Without positive or negative reinforcement, a person will not be motivated to repeat

beliefs about the brand's attributes, changing the relative importance of these beliefs, or adding new beliefs. The first technique is to turn neutral or negative beliefs about product attributes into positive beliefs. For example, many consumers believed that it is easier and cheaper to take traditional film to be developed than it is to print their own digital photos. To change this belief, Kodak Corporation did two things. It set up kiosks in retail outlets that let consumers print their digital photos, and it launched kodakgallery.ca, a website where consumers can store digital photos and order prints of only the ones they want. Today, there are many on-line services available from Snapfish (a Hewitt Packard (HP) development company) to Costco offering these services in a convenient, high quality, cost effective way.

Changing consumers' beliefs about a service can be more difficult because service attributes are intangible. Convincing consumers to switch hairstylists or lawyers or to go to a mall dental clinic can be much more difficult than getting them to change their brand of razor blades. Image, which is also largely intangible, significantly determines service patronage. Service marketing is explored in detail in Chapter 11.

The second approach to modifying attitudes is to change the relative importance of beliefs about an attribute. For example, milk has always been considered a healthy beverage for children and adults. Now, however, dairies are aware of milk's added benefits, primarily the importance of calcium for bone strength, which they now actively promote on their packaging. Marketers can also emphasize the importance of some beliefs over others. The third approach to transforming attitudes is to add new beliefs, such as that breakfast cereal is also a great after-school snack.

Consumer Behaviour Elements— Working Together

As a result of their environment, individuals change, which, in turn, changes the nature of the goods and services they consume. By using the stages of the buying process to make the best choices, consumers become more experienced. This experience changes the parts of the buying process they use, the degree of effort and time they spend on each stage of buying, and the importance each of the psychological influences in their final buying decision. Effective marketers will carefully study their target markets, noting these changes and the degrees of difference. Then, after understanding the consumers' needs, these marketers can adjust their approach to the various elements in the marketing mix to meet the consumers' needs and help them move through the buying process.

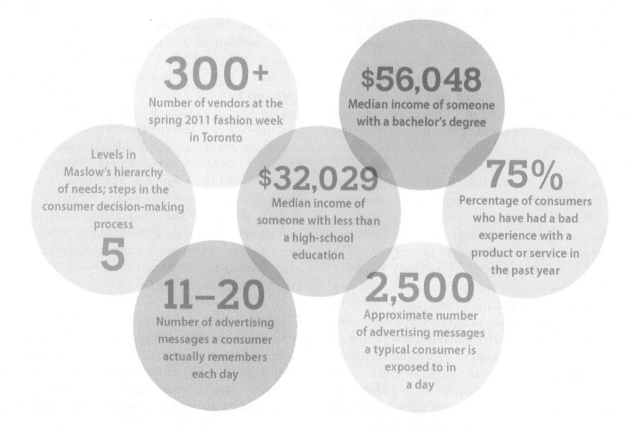

300+ Number of vendors at the spring 2011 fashion week in Toronto

$56,048 Median income of someone with a bachelor's degree

5 Levels in Maslow's hierarchy of needs; steps in the consumer decision-making process

$32,029 Median income of someone with less than a high-school education

75% Percentage of consumers who have had a bad experience with a product or service in the past year

11–20 Number of advertising messages a consumer actually remembers each day

2,500 Approximate number of advertising messages a typical consumer is exposed to in a day

71% The percentage of students who go online to study for a class.

© Andrew Rich/Getty Images

LOG IN!

MKTG was designed for students just like you—busy people who want choices, flexibility, and multiple learning options.

MKTG delivers concise, electronic resources such as flashcards, interactive quizzes, crossword puzzles and more!

At **www.icanmktg2.com**, you'll find electronic resources such as **printable interactive flashcards, downloadable study aids, games, quizzes,** and **videos** to test your knowledge of key concepts. These resources will help supplement your understanding of core **marketing** concepts in a format that fits your busy lifestyle.

"I really like how you use students' opinions on how to study and made a website that encompasses everything we find useful. Seeing this website makes me excited to study!"

—Abby Boston, Fanshawe College

Visit **www.icanmktg2.com** to find the resources you need today!

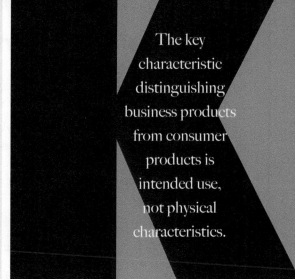

The key characteristic distinguishing business products from consumer products is intended use, not physical characteristics.

AFTER YOU FINISH THIS CHAPTER, GO TO WWW. ICANMKTG2.COM FOR STUDY TOOLS.

LO 1   What Is Business Marketing?

Business marketing is the marketing of goods and services to individuals and organizations for purposes other than personal consumption. The sale of a personal computer to your college or university is an example of business marketing. Business products include those that are used to manufacture other products, to become part of another product, or to aid the normal operations of an organization. The key characteristic distinguishing business products from consumer products is intended use, not physical characteristics. A consumer good is a product that is purchased for personal or family consumption or as a gift. If that same product, such as a personal computer or a cellphone, is bought for use in a business, it is a business product.

    The size of the business market in Canada and most other countries substantially exceeds that of the consumer market. In the business market, a single customer can account for a huge volume of purchases. For example, General Motors' purchasing department spends more than $85 billion per year on goods and services. General Electric, DuPont, and IBM spend more than $60 million per day on business purchases.[1]

business marketing the marketing of goods and services to individuals and organizations for purposes other than personal consumption

What do you think?

"Salespeople make shopping an uncomfortable experience."

1   2   3   4   5   6   7
STRONGLY DISAGREE   STRONGLY AGREE

YURI ARCURS/SHUTTERSTOCK.COM

LO 2 Business versus Consumer Markets

The basic philosophy and practice of marketing are the same whether the customer is a business organization or a consumer. Business markets do, however, have characteristics distinct from consumer markets.

Demand

Consumer demand for products is quite different from demand in the business market. Unlike consumer demand, business demand is derived, inelastic, joint, and fluctuating.

Derived Demand The demand for business products is called **derived demand** because organizations buy products to be used in producing their customers' products. For example, the market for central processing units (CPUs), hard drives, and CD-ROMs is derived from the demand for personal computers (PCs). These items are only valuable as components of computers. Demand for these items rises and falls with the demand for PCs.

Because demand is derived, business marketers must carefully monitor demand patterns and changing preferences in final consumer markets, even though their customers are not in those markets. Moreover, business marketers must carefully monitor their customers' forecasts because derived demand is based on expectations of future demand for those customers' products.

Some business marketers not only monitor final consumer demand and customer forecasts but also try to influence final consumer demand. Aluminum producers use television and magazine advertisements to point out the convenience and recycling opportunities that aluminum offers to consumers who can choose to purchase juice and pop in either aluminum or plastic containers.

Inelastic Demand The demand for many business products is inelastic with regard to price. *Inelastic demand* means that an increase or decrease in the price of the product will not significantly affect demand for the product. The elasticity of demand is discussed further in Chapter 18.

The price of a product used either in the production of another product or as part of another product is often a minor portion of the final product's total price. Therefore, demand for the final consumer product is not affected. If the price of automobile paint or spark plugs rises significantly—for example, 200 percent in one year—will the price increase affect the number of new automobiles sold that year? Probably not.

Joint Demand **Joint demand** refers to the demand for two or more items used together in a final product. For example, a decline in the availability of memory chips will slow the production of microcomputers, which will in turn reduce the demand for disk drives. Likewise, the demand for Apple operating systems exists as long as there is demand for Apple computers. Sales of the two products are directly linked.

Fluctuating Demand The demand for business products, particularly for new plants and equipment, tends to be less stable than the demand for consumer products. A small increase or decrease in consumer demand can produce a much larger change in demand for the facilities and equipment needed to make the consumer product. Economists refer to this phenomenon as the **multiplier effect** (or **accelerator principle**).

Purchase Volume

Business customers buy in much larger quantities than consumers. Just think how large an order Kellogg's typically places for the wheat bran and raisins used to manufacture Raisin Bran. Imagine the number of tires that DaimlerChrysler buys at one time.

derived demand
the demand for business products

joint demand the demand for two or more items used together in a final product

multiplier effect (accelerator principle) phenomenon in which a small increase or decrease in consumer demand can produce a much larger change in demand for the facilities and equipment needed to make the consumer product

© ISTOCKPHOTO.COM/EVGENY TERENTYEV

THE SIZE OF THE BUSINESS MARKET IN CANADA **SUBSTANTIALLY EXCEEDS** THAT OF THE CONSUMER MARKET.

Number of Customers

Business marketers usually have far fewer customers than consumer marketers. The advantage is that it is much easier to identify prospective buyers, monitor current customers' needs and levels of satisfaction, and personally attend to existing customers. The main disadvantage is that each customer becomes crucial—especially for those manufacturers that have only one customer. In many cases, this customer is the Canadian government. The success or failure of one bid can make the difference between prosperity and bankruptcy.

Location of Buyers

Business customers tend to be much more geographically concentrated than consumers. For instance, most of Canada's business-to-business (B2B) buyers are located in the large urban centres of Canada: Toronto, Montreal, Calgary, and Vancouver. The oil and gas industry is centred in Alberta, the automotive industry in southwestern Ontario, and the wine industry primarily in British Columbia and southern Ontario.

Distribution Structure

Many consumer products pass through a distribution system that includes the producer, one or more wholesalers, and a retailer. Because of many of the characteristics already mentioned, channels of distribution for business marketing are typically shorter. Direct channels, where manufacturers market directly to users, are much more common. The use of direct channels has increased dramatically in the past decade as a result of the introduction of various Internet buying and selling schemes. One such technique is called a **business-to-business online exchange**, which is an electronic trading floor that provides companies with integrated links to their customers and suppliers. The goal of B2B exchanges is to simplify business purchases and make them more efficient. These exchanges facilitate direct channel relationships between producers and their customers.

business-to-business online exchange an electronic trading floor that provides companies with integrated links to their customers and suppliers

Nature of Buying

Unlike consumers, business buyers usually approach purchasing rather formally. Businesses use professionally trained purchasing agents or buyers who spend their entire career purchasing a limited number of items. They get to know the items and the sellers well. Some professional purchasers earn the designation of Certified Purchasing Manager (CPM) after participating in a rigorous certification program.

Nature of Buying Influence

Typically, more people are involved in a single business purchase decision than in a consumer purchase. Experts from fields as varied as quality control, marketing, and finance, as well as professional buyers and users, may be grouped in a buying centre (discussed later in this chapter).

Type of Negotiations

Consumers are used to negotiating prices on automobiles and real estate. In most cases, however, Canadian consumers expect sellers

ALAN MARSH/FIRST LIGHT

"**RECIPROCITY** IS GENERALLY CONSIDERED A REASONABLE BUSINESS PRACTICE."

reciprocity a practice where business purchasers choose to buy from their own customers

original equipment manufacturers (OEMs) individuals and organizations that buy business goods and incorporate them into the products that they produce for eventual sale to other producers or to consumers

to set the price and other conditions of sale, such as time of delivery and credit terms. In contrast, negotiating is common in business marketing. Buyers and sellers negotiate product specifications, delivery dates, payment terms, and other pricing matters. Sometimes these negotiations occur during many meetings over several months. Final contracts are often very long and detailed.

Use of Reciprocity

Business purchasers often choose to buy from their own customers, a practice known as **reciprocity**. For example, General Motors (GM) buys engines for use in its automobiles and trucks from BorgWarner, which in turn buys many of the automobiles and trucks it needs from GM. This practice is neither unethical nor illegal unless one party coerces the other and the result is unfair competition. Reciprocity is generally considered a reasonable business practice.

Use of Leasing

Consumers normally buy products rather than lease them. But businesses commonly lease expensive equipment such as computers, construction equipment and vehicles, and automobiles. Leasing allows firms to reduce their capital outflow, acquire a seller's latest products, receive better services, and gain tax advantages.

The lessor, the firm providing the product, may be either the manufacturer or an independent firm. The benefits to the lessor include greater total revenue from leasing compared with selling and an opportunity to do business with customers who cannot afford to buy.

Primary Promotional Method

Business marketers tend to emphasize personal selling in their promotion efforts, especially for expensive items, custom-designed products, large-volume purchases, and situations requiring negotiations. The sale of many business products requires a great deal of personal contact. Personal selling is discussed in more detail in Chapter 17.

LO 3 Major Categories of Business Customers

The business market consists of four major categories of customers: producers, resellers, governments, and institutions.

Producers

The producer segment of the business market includes profit-oriented individuals and organizations that use purchased goods and services to produce other products, to incorporate into other products, or to facilitate the daily operations of the organization. Examples of producers include construction, manufacturing, transportation, finance, real estate, and food service firms. Canada is the world's third largest exporter of automotive products, with export revenues of $70.5 billion in 2007. Some of these firms are small, and others are among the world's largest businesses.

Producers are often called **original equipment manufacturers**, or **OEMs**. This term includes all individuals and organizations that buy business goods and incorporate them into the products that they produce for eventual sale to other producers or to consumers. Companies such as General Motors that buy steel, paint, tires, and batteries are said to be OEMs.

Resellers

The reseller market includes retail and wholesale businesses that buy finished goods and resell them for a profit. A retailer sells mainly to final consumers; wholesalers sell mostly to retailers and other organizational customers. Canada has approximately 220,000 retailers and 117,000 wholesalers. Consumer product firms such as Procter & Gamble, Kraft Foods, and Coca-Cola sell directly to large retailers and retail chains and through wholesalers to smaller retail units. Retailing is explored in detail in Chapter 13.

Business product distributors are wholesalers that buy business products and resell them to business customers. They often carry thousands of items in stock and employ sales forces to call on business customers. Businesses that wish to buy a gross of pencils or a hundred kilograms of fertilizer typically purchase these items from local distributors rather than directly from manufacturers.

Governments

A third major segment of the business market is government. Government organizations include thousands of federal, provincial or territorial, and municipal buying units. They make up what may be the largest single market for goods and services in Canada.

Contracts for government purchases are often put out for bid. Interested vendors submit bids (usually sealed) to provide specified products during a particular time. Sometimes the lowest bidder is awarded the contract. When the lowest bidder is not awarded the contract, strong evidence must be presented to justify the decision. Grounds for rejecting the lowest bid include lack of experience, inadequate financing, or poor past performance. Bidding allows all potential suppliers a fair chance at winning government contracts and helps ensure that public funds are spent wisely.

Federal Government Name just about any good or service and chances are that someone in the federal government uses it. The federal government buys goods and services valued at over $211 billion per year, making it the nation's largest customer.

Although much of the federal government's buying is centralized, no single federal agency contracts for all the government's requirements, and no single buyer in any agency purchases all that the agency needs. We can view the federal government as a combination of several large companies with overlapping responsibilities and thousands of small independent units.

Municipal, Academic, Social, and Hospitals (MASH) In 2006, municipal governments across Canada spent approximately $100 billion. In addition, the academic, social, and health care sectors, many of which are under the jurisdiction of provincial or territorial governments, spent the following amounts: colleges and universities, $32 billion; school boards, $42 billion; and health care providers, $67 billion.[2] In Canada, each province and territory sets its own regulations and buying procedures within this municipal, academic, social, and hospitals (MASH) sector. The potential for both large and small vendors is great,

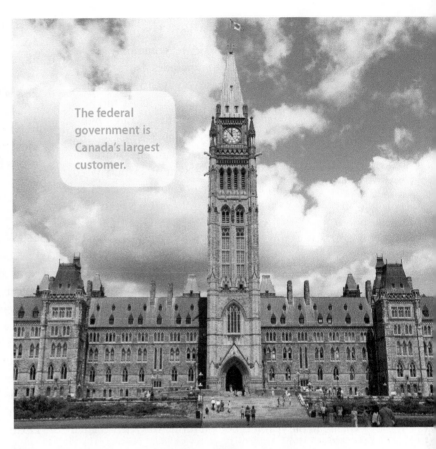

The federal government is Canada's largest customer.

ZHONG CHEN/SHUTTERSTOCK

however, as more than 6,000 municipal clients are spread across all the provinces and territories.

Institutions

The fourth major segment of the business market consists of institutions that seek to achieve goals other than the standard business goals of profit, market share, and return on investment. Excluding the MASH sector, this segment includes churches, labour unions, fraternal organizations, civic clubs, foundations, and other so-called nonbusiness organizations. Many firms have a separate sales force that calls on these customers.

LO 4 Types of Business Products

Business products generally fall into one of the following seven categories, depending on their use: major equipment, accessory equipment, raw materials, component parts, processed materials, supplies, and business services.

Major Equipment

major equipment (installations) such capital goods as large or expensive machines, mainframe computers, blast furnaces, generators, airplanes, and buildings

accessory equipment goods such as portable tools and office equipment that are less expensive and shorter-lived than major equipment

raw materials unprocessed extractive or agricultural products, such as mineral ore, lumber, wheat, corn, fruits, vegetables, and fish

Major equipment (commonly called **installations**) includes such capital goods as large or expensive machines, mainframe computers, blast furnaces, generators, airplanes, and buildings. Major equipment is depreciated over time rather than charged as an expense in the year it is purchased. In addition, major equipment is often custom designed for each customer. Personal selling is an important part of the marketing strategy for major equipment because distribution channels are almost always direct from the producer to the business user.

Accessory Equipment

Accessory equipment is generally less expensive and shorter-lived than major equipment. Examples include portable drills, power tools, microcomputers, and fax machines. Accessory equipment is often charged as an expense in the year it is bought rather than depreciated over its useful life. In contrast to major equipment, accessories are more often standardized and are usually bought by more customers. These customers tend to be widely dispersed. For example, all types of businesses buy microcomputers.

Local industrial distributors (wholesalers) play an important role in the marketing of accessory equipment because business buyers often purchase accessories from them. Regardless of where accessories are bought, advertising is a more vital promotional tool for accessory equipment than for major equipment.

Raw Materials

Raw materials are unprocessed extractive or agricultural products—for example, mineral ore, lumber, wheat, corn, fruits, vegetables, and fish. Raw materials become part of finished products. Extensive users, such as steel or lumber mills and food canners, generally buy huge quantities of raw materials. Because raw materials are typically sold by a relatively small numbers of sellers, none can greatly influence price or supply. Thus, the market tends to set the price of raw materials, and individual producers have little pricing flexibility. Promotion is almost always via personal

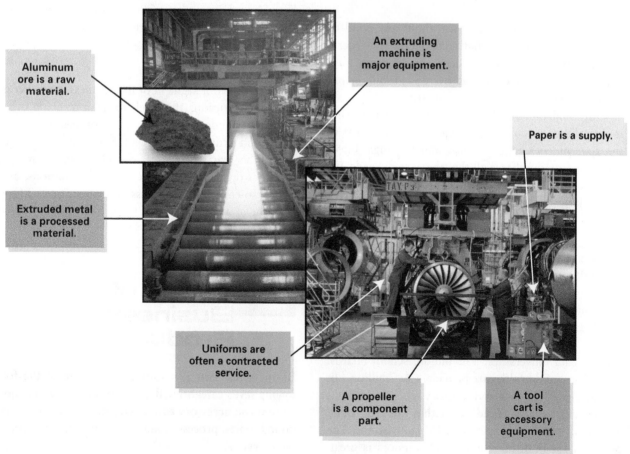

Aluminum ore is a raw material.

An extruding machine is major equipment.

Paper is a supply.

Extruded metal is a processed material.

Uniforms are often a contracted service.

A propeller is a component part.

A tool cart is accessory equipment.

DENIS SELIVANOV/SHUTTERSTOCK.COM, LUIS VEIGA/RISER/GETTY IMAGES, DREAMPICTURES/GETTY IMAGES

selling, and distribution channels are usually direct from producer to business user.

Component Parts

Component parts are either finished items ready for assembly or products that need very little processing before becoming part of some other product. Caterpillar diesel engines are component parts used in heavy-duty trucks. Other examples include spark plugs, tires, and electric motors for automobiles. A special feature of component parts is that they can retain their identity after becoming part of the final product. For example, automobile tires are clearly recognizable as part of a car. Moreover, because component parts often wear out, they may need to be replaced several times during the life of the final product. Thus, many component parts have two important markets: the original equipment manufacturer (OEM) market and the replacement market.

Many of the business features described in the previous section characterize the OEM market. The difference between unit costs and selling prices in the OEM market is often small, but profits can be substantial because of volume buying.

The replacement market is composed of organizations and individuals buying component parts to replace worn-out parts. Because components often retain their identity in final products, users may choose to replace a component part with the same brand used by the manufacturer—for example, the same brand of battery or automobile tires. The replacement market operates differently from the OEM market, however. Whether replacement buyers are organizations or individuals, they tend to demonstrate the characteristics of consumer markets. Consider, for example, an automobile replacement part. Its purchase volume is usually small, and there are many customers, geographically dispersed, who typically buy from car dealers or parts stores. Negotiations do not occur, and neither reciprocity nor leasing is usually an issue.

Manufacturers of component parts often direct their advertising toward replacement buyers. Cooper Tire & Rubber, for example, makes and markets component parts, automobile and truck tires, for the replacement market only. General Motors and other car makers compete with independent firms in the market for replacement automobile parts.

Processed Materials

Processed materials are products used directly in manufacturing other products. Unlike raw materials, they have had some processing. Examples include sheet metal, chemicals, specialty steel, lumber, corn syrup, and plastics. Unlike component parts, processed materials do not retain their identity in final products.

Most processed materials are marketed to OEMs or to distributors servicing the OEM market. Processed materials are generally bought according to customer specifications or to some industry standard, as is the case with steel and plywood. Price and service are important factors in choosing a vendor.

Supplies

Supplies are consumable items that do not become part of the final product, for example, lubricants, detergents, paper towels, pencils, and paper. Supplies are normally standardized items that purchasing agents routinely buy. Supplies typically have relatively short lives and are inexpensive compared with other business goods. Because supplies generally fall into one of three categories—maintenance, repair, or operating supplies—this category is often referred to as MRO items. Competition in the MRO market is intense. Staples and Grand & Toy, for example, battle for business purchases of office supplies.

Business Services

Business services are expense items that do not become part of a final product. Businesses often retain outside providers for such services as caretaking, advertising, legal counsel, management consulting, marketing research, and building maintenance. Hiring an outside provider makes sense when it costs less than hiring or assigning an employee to perform the task and when outside providers are needed for their specific expertise.

component parts either finished items ready for assembly or products that need very little processing before becoming part of some other product

processed materials products used directly in manufacturing other products

supplies consumable items that do not become part of the final product

business services expense items that do not become part of a final product

BUSINESS BUYING BEHAVIOUR HAS **FIVE IMPORTANT ASPECTS:** BUYING CENTRES, EVALUATIVE CRITERIA, BUYING SITUATIONS, BUSINESS ETHICS, AND CUSTOMER SERVICE.

LO 5 Business Buying Behaviour

As you probably have already concluded, business buyers behave differently from consumers. Understanding how purchase decisions are made in organizations is a first step in developing a business selling strategy.

Buying Centres

A **buying centre** includes all those people in an organization who become involved in the purchase decision. Membership and influence vary from company to company. For instance, in engineering-dominated firms, such as Bell Helicopter, the buying centre may consist almost entirely of engineers. In marketing-oriented firms, such as Toyota and IBM, marketing and engineering have almost equal authority. In consumer goods firms, such as Procter & Gamble, product managers and other marketing decision makers may dominate the buying centre. In a small manufacturing company, almost everyone may be a member.

The number of people involved in a buying centre varies with the complexity and importance of the purchase decision. The composition of the buying group will usually change from one purchase to another and sometimes even during various stages of the buying process. To make matters more complicated, buying centres do not appear on formal organization charts.

For example, although a formal committee may have been set up to choose a new plant site, such a committee is only part of the buying centre. Other people, such as the company president, often play informal yet powerful roles. In a lengthy decision-making process, such as finding a new plant location, some members may drop out of the buying centre when they can no longer play a useful role. Others whose talents are needed then become part of the centre. No formal announcement is ever made concerning "who is in" and "who is out."

buying centre all those people in an organization who become involved in the purchase decision

Roles in the Buying Centre As in family purchasing decisions, several people may play a role in the business purchase process.

BUSINESS PURCHASING ROLES

- ▸▸ *Initiator:* the person who first suggests making a purchase.
- ▸▸ *Influencers/evaluators:* people who influence the buying decision. They often help define specifications and provide information for evaluating options. Technical personnel are especially important as influencers.
- ▸▸ *Gatekeepers:* group members who regulate the flow of information. Frequently, the purchasing agent views the gatekeeping role as a source of his or her power. An administrative assistant may also act as a gatekeeper by determining which vendors schedule an appointment with a buyer.
- ▸▸ *Decider:* the person who has the formal or informal power to choose or approve the selection of the supplier or brand. In complex situations, it is often difficult to determine who makes the final decision.
- ▸▸ *Purchaser:* the person who actually negotiates the purchase. It could be anyone from the president of the company to the purchasing agent, depending on the importance of the decision.
- ▸▸ *Users:* members of the organization who will actually use the product. Users often initiate the buying process and help define product specifications.

Implications of Buying Centres for the Marketing Manager Successful vendors realize the importance of identifying who is in the decision-making unit, each member's relative influence in the buying decision, and each member's evaluative criteria. Successful selling strategies often focus on determining the most important buying influences and tailoring sales presentations to the evaluative criteria most important to these buying-centre members. For example, Loctite Corporation, the manufacturer of Super Glue and industrial adhesives and sealants, found that engineers were the most important influencers and deciders in adhesive and sealant purchase decisions. As a result, Loctite focused its marketing efforts on production and maintenance engineers.

Evaluative Criteria

Business buyers evaluate products and suppliers against three important criteria: quality, service, and price—in that order.

Quality In evaluative criteria, quality refers to technical suitability. A superior tool can do a better job in the production process, and superior packaging can increase dealer and consumer acceptance of a brand. Evaluation of quality also applies to the salesperson and the salesperson's firm. Business buyers want to deal with reputable salespeople and companies that are financially responsible. Quality improvement should be part of every organization's marketing strategy.

Service Almost as much as business buyers want satisfactory products, they also want satisfactory service. A purchase offers several opportunities for service. Suppose a vendor is selling heavy equipment. Prepurchase service could include a survey of the buyer's needs. After thorough analysis of the survey findings, the vendor could prepare a report and recommendations in the form of a purchasing proposal.

If a purchase results, postpurchase service might consist of installing the equipment and training those who will be using it. Postpurchase services may also include maintenance and repairs. Another service that business buyers seek is dependability of supply. They must be able to count on delivery of their order when it is scheduled to be delivered. Buyers also welcome services that help them to sell their finished products. Services of this sort are especially appropriate when the seller's product is an identifiable part of the buyer's end product.

Price Business buyers want to buy at low prices—at the lowest prices, in most circumstances. However, when a buyer pressures a supplier to cut prices to a point where the supplier loses money, the supplier is almost forced to take shortcuts on quality. The buyer also may, in effect, force the supplier to quit selling to him or her. The buyer will then need to find a new source of supply.

Buying Situations

Business firms, especially manufacturers, must often decide whether to make something or buy it from an outside supplier. The decision is essentially one of economics. Can an item of similar quality be bought at a lower price elsewhere? If not, is manufacturing it

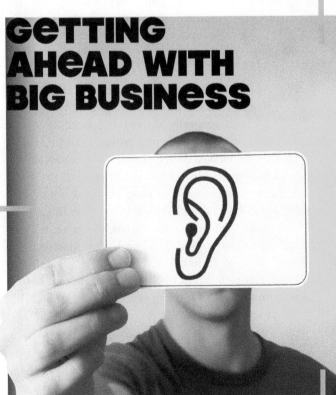

GETTING AHEAD WITH BIG BUSINESS

When a small manufacturer or supplier lands a contract with a large corporation, it's a big deal. But getting the attention of the decision maker at places such as Northrop Grumman, Coca-Cola, or Dell can be daunting and disheartening. The key to selling to large corporations requires spending time getting to know the company and how it operates. Most large corporations like working with small companies because of the easy access to the small firm's chief executive officer (CEO) and the small firm's ability to modify production or delivery dates quickly. Northrop Grumman wants its suppliers to highlight up front what their specialty is and how it will benefit Northrop—it doesn't want politicking. Dell is looking for companies that have long-term plans and a willingness to marry their culture to Dell's. Coca-Cola is looking for companies that offer a specific value Coke doesn't already have and that are willing to work within the system and not try to bypass it.[3]

in-house the best use of limited company resources? For example, Briggs & Stratton Corporation, a major manufacturer of four-cycle engines, might be able to save $150,000 annually on outside purchases by spending $500,000 on the equipment needed to produce gas throttles internally. Yet Briggs & Stratton could also use that $500,000 to upgrade its carburetor assembly line, which would save $225,000 annually. If a firm does decide to buy a product instead of making it, the purchase will be either a new buy, a modified rebuy, or a straight rebuy.

New Buy A **new buy** is a situation requiring the purchase of a product for the first time. For example, suppose a manufacturing company needs a better way to page managers while they are working on the shop floor. Currently, each of the several managers has a distinct ring, for example, two short and one long, which sounds over the plant intercom when a manager is being paged in the factory. The company decides to replace its buzzer system of paging with hand-held wireless radio technology that will allow managers to communicate immediately with the department initiating the page. This situation represents the greatest opportunity for new vendors. No long-term relationship has been established for this product, specifications may be somewhat fluid, and the buyers are generally more open to new vendors.

If the new item is a raw material or a critical component part, the buyer cannot afford to run out of supply. The seller must be able to convince the buyer that the seller's firm consistently deliver a high-quality product on time.

Modified Rebuy A **modified rebuy** is normally less critical and less time-consuming than a new buy. In a modified-rebuy situation, the purchaser wants some change in the original good or service. It may be a new colour, greater tensile strength in a component part, more respondents in a marketing research study, or additional services in a janitorial contract.

Because the two parties are familiar with each other and credibility has been established, buyer and seller can concentrate on the specifics of the modification. In some cases, though, modified rebuys are open

to outside bidders. The purchaser uses this strategy to ensure that the new terms are competitive. An example is the manufacturing company buying radios with a vibrating feature for managers who have trouble hearing the ring over the factory noise. The firm may open the bidding to examine the price/quality offerings of several suppliers.

Straight Rebuy A **straight rebuy** is the situation vendors prefer. The purchaser is not looking for new information or new suppliers. An order is placed and the product is provided as in previous orders. Usually, a straight rebuy is routine because the terms of the purchase have been agreed to in earlier negotiations. An example would be the previously cited manufacturing company purchasing, on a regular basis, additional radios from the same supplier.

One common instrument used in straight-rebuy situations is the purchasing contract. Purchasing contracts are used with high-volume products that are bought frequently. In essence, because of the purchasing contract, the buyer's decision making becomes routine and the salesperson is promised a sure sale. The advantage to the buyer is a quick, confident decision, and the advantage to the salesperson is reduced or eliminated competition.

Suppliers must remember not to take straight-rebuy relationships for granted. Retaining existing customers is much easier than attracting new ones.

Business Ethics

As we noted in Chapter 2, ethics refers to the moral principles or values that generally govern the conduct of an individual or a group. Ethics can also be viewed as the standard of behaviour by which conduct is judged.

Many companies also have codes of ethics that help guide buyers' and sellers' behaviour. In general, these codes deal both with "doing things right" and "the right thing to do." The Purchasing Management Association of Canada (PMAC) has developed the PMAC Code of Ethics to guide Canadian purchasing agents in their dealings with vendors; you can find this code at www.pmac.ca.

Customer Service

Business marketers are increasingly recognizing the benefits of developing a formal system to monitor customer

EIMANTAS BUZAS/SHUTTERSTOCK

opinions and perceptions of the quality of customer service. Companies should build their strategies around not only their products but also some highly developed service skills. Marketers need to understand that keeping current customers satisfied is just as important as attracting new customers, if not more so. Leading-edge firms are obsessed not only with delivering high-quality customer service but also with measuring satisfaction, loyalty, relationship quality, and other indicators of nonfinancial performance. Most firms find it necessary to develop measures unique to their own strategy, value propositions, and target market.

LO 6 The North American Industry Classification System

The North American Industry Classification System (NAICS) is an industry classification system for North American business establishments. The system, developed jointly by the United States, Canada, and Mexico, provides a common industry classification system for the North American Free Trade Agreement (NAFTA) partners. Goods- or service-producing firms that use identical or similar production processes are grouped together.

NAICS is an extremely valuable tool for business marketers engaged in analyzing, segmenting, and targeting markets. Each classification group is relatively homogeneous in terms of raw materials required, components used, manufacturing processes employed, and problems faced. The more digits in a code, the more homogeneous the group is. Therefore, if a supplier understands the needs and requirements of a few

HOW NAICS WORKS

NAICS Level	NAICS Code	Description
Sector	51	Information
Subsector	513	Broadcasting and telecommunications
Industry group	5133	Telecommunications
Industry	51332	Wireless telecommunications carriers, except satellite
Subdivision of industry	513321	Paging

firms within a classification, requirements can be projected for all firms in that category. The number, size, and geographic dispersion of firms can also be identified. This information can be converted to market potential estimates, market share estimates, and sales forecasts. It can also be used for identifying potential new customers. NAICS codes can help identify firms that may be prospective users of a supplier's goods and services. For a complete listing of all NAICS codes, visit **www.naics.com**.

North American Industry Classification System (NAICS) an industry classification system developed by the United States, Canada, and Mexico to classify North American business establishments by their main production processes

business-to-business electronic commerce the use of the Internet to facilitate the exchange of goods, services, and information between organizations

LO 7 Business Marketing on the Internet

The use of the Internet to facilitate the exchange of goods, services, and information between organizations is called **business-to-business electronic commerce** (B-to-B or B2B e-commerce). This method of conducting business has evolved and grown rapidly throughout its short history. In 2006, North America

STICKINESS = FREQUENCY × DURATION × SITE REACH

stickiness a measure of a website's effectiveness; calculated by multiplying the frequency of visits by both the duration of the visits and the number of pages viewed during each visit (site reach)

alone accounted for over $800 billion of B2B e-commerce.[4] Online B2B transactions in the European Union reached 2.2 trillion euros (about $1.8 trillion) in 2006, representing 22 percent of all B2B transactions.[5] This phenomenal growth is not restricted to large companies. (See Exhibit 6.1.)

It is difficult to imagine that commercial use of the Internet began as recently as the mid-1990s. In 1995, the commercial websites that did exist were static. Only a few had data-retrieval capabilities. Frames, tables, and styles were not available. Security of any sort was rare, and streaming video did not exist. In 2011, there were over two billion Internet users worldwide.

Measuring Online Success

To understand what works and what doesn't work online, marketers must understand the vast amount of data stored in the log files generated by their Web servers. Not all of these data are relevant for planning an online strategy, but by combining certain log file results with sales information, a marketer can fine-tune the marketing effort to maximize online success.

For marketers today, three of the most important things to measure are recency, frequency, and monetary value. *Recency* refers to customers who have made a purchase recently being more likely to purchase again in the near future than customers who haven't purchased for a while. *Frequency* data help marketers identify frequent purchasers who are definitely more likely to repeat their purchasing behaviour in the future. The *monetary value* of sales is important because big spenders can be the most profitable customers for your business.

> TWITTER IS HELPFUL IN MAINTAINING CONTACTS WITH NETWORKS!

NetGenesis, a company that has been purchased by SPSS, has devised a number of equations that can help online marketers better

understand their data. For example, multiplying the frequency of visits by both the duration of the visits and the number of site pages viewed during each visit (total site reach) can provide an analytical measure for your site's **stickiness** factor.

By measuring the stickiness factor of a website before and after a design or function change, the marketer can quickly determine whether visitors embraced the change. By adding purchase information to determine the level of stickiness needed to provide a desired purchase volume, the marketer gains an even more precise understanding of how a site change affected business. An almost endless number of factor combinations can be created to provide a quantitative method for determining buyer behaviour online. First, though, the marketer must determine the measurements required and which factors can be combined to arrive at those measurements.[6]

PHILIPPE WIDLING/DESIGN PICS/JUPITERIMAGES

Trends in B2B Internet Marketing

Over the last decade, marketers have become more and more sophisticated in the use of the Internet. Exhibit 6.2 compares three prominent Internet business marketing strategy initiatives from the late 1990s to five that are currently being pursued. In previous years, online marketing objectives focused on attracting new prospects and promoting brands. Today, savvy business marketers use the Internet to achieve a wide range of objectives.[7] The best online strategy integrates conventional and Internet marketing strategies. New applications that provide additional information about present and potential customers, increase efficiency, lower costs, increase supply chain efficiency, or enhance customer retention, loyalty, and trust are being developed each year. Chapter 8, Customer Relationship Management (CRM), describes several of these applications.

One term in Exhibit 6.2 that may be unfamiliar is **disintermediation**, which means eliminating intermediaries such as wholesalers or distributors from a marketing channel. A prime example of disintermediation is Dell, Inc., which sells directly to business buyers and consumers. Large retailers such as Wal-Mart use a disintermediation strategy to help reduce costs and prices.[8]

A few years ago, many people thought that the Internet would eliminate the need for distributors. Why would customers pay a distributor's markup when they could buy directly from the manufacturer with a few mouse clicks? Yet Internet disintermediation has

occurred less frequently than many expected. The reason is that distributors often perform important functions such as providing credit, aggregating supplies from multiple sources, delivering, and processing returns. Many business customers, especially small firms, depend on knowledgeable distributors for information and advice that are not available to them online. You will notice in Exhibit 6.2 that building channel partnerships and trust has replaced aggressive disintermediation initiatives as a priority for most firms. You will learn more about marketing channels in Chapter 12.

disintermediation the elimination of intermediaries such as wholesalers or distributors from a marketing channel

strategic alliance (strategic partnership) a cooperative agreement between business firms

LO 8 Relationship Marketing and Strategic Alliances

As Chapter 1 explained, relationship marketing is a strategy that involves seeking and establishing ongoing partnerships with customers. Relationship marketing has become an important business marketing strategy as customers have become more demanding and competition has become more intense. Loyal customers are also more profitable than those who are price-sensitive and who perceive little or no difference among brands or suppliers. For example, Dell provides a customized Web page for each of its premier customers that individual employees in the customer organization can access for information and technical support.

Although relationships are expected to produce win–win outcomes, these are not without constant challenges. Kodak, once a dominant firm in the film-processing business, has had to adjust its business model substantially to accommodate the sudden switch to digital images and photographs. Successful relationships with many retailers that had been based on film services had to be re-established by providing digital-based services instead. In the transition process, Kodak lost many customers to more nimble competitors. Kodak has had to work hard to form new relationships with former and future clients.[9]

Strategic Alliances

A **strategic alliance**, sometimes called a **strategic partnership**, is a cooperative agreement between business firms. Strategic alliances can take the form of licensing

EXHIBIT 6.2
Evolution of E-Business Initiatives

- Revenue generation
- Aggressive disintermediation initiatives
- Basic marketing communication strategies

- Reduce costs
- Build channel partnerships and trust
- Customer-focused technology and systems
- Brand building and development
- Integrate online and traditional media

Past initiatives → Present initiatives → Time

SOURCE: Andrew J. Rohm and Fareena Sultan, "The Evolution of E-Business," *Marketing Management*, January/February 2004, p. 35. Used by permission.

or distribution agreements, joint ventures, research and development consortia, and partnerships. They may be between manufacturers, manufacturers and customers, manufacturers and suppliers, and manufacturers and channel intermediaries.

Business marketers form strategic alliances to leverage what they have (technology, financial resources, access to markets) by combining these assets with those of other firms. Some alliances are formed with competitors to achieve increased productivity and lower costs for all participants. For example, Boeing Co. and Lockheed Martin have agreed to form a joint venture to launch military, spy, and civilian research rockets and satellites for the U.S. government. The joint venture will presumably end years of bitter rivalry and litigation between the two companies.[10]

For an alliance to succeed in the long term, it must be built on commitment and trust. **Relationship commitment** is a firm's belief that an ongoing relationship with some other firm is so important that it warrants maximum efforts at maintaining it indefinitely.[11] A perceived breakdown in commitment by one of the parties often leads to a reduction in the relationship.

Trust exists when one party has confidence in an exchange partner's reliability and integrity.[12] Some alliances fail when participants lack trust in their trading partners and benefits are not shared. An example of a failed alliance was a partnership between giant drug company Eli Lilly and a small biotechnology company, Amylin Pharmaceuticals, Inc.

The plan was to jointly develop and market a new diabetes drug. A low point in the relationship followed a shouting match between the marketing chiefs from Lilly and Amylin in a hallway following a joint presentation to senior management at Lilly. The main problem: mutual distrust.[13]

Relationships in Other Cultures

Although the terms *relationship marketing* and *strategic alliances* are fairly new, and popularized mostly by North American business executives and educators, the concepts have long been familiar in other cultures. Businesses in Mexico, China, Japan, Korea, and much of Europe rely heavily on personal relationships.

In Japan, for example, exchange between firms is based on personal relationships that are developed through what is called *amae*, or indulgent dependency. *Amae* is the feeling of nurturing concern for, and dependence upon, another. Reciprocity and personal relationships contribute to *amae*. Relationships between companies can develop into a **keiretsu**—a network of interlocking corporate affiliates. Within a keiretsu, executives may sit on the boards of their customers or their suppliers. Members of a keiretsu trade with each other whenever possible and often engage in joint product development, finance, and marketing activity. For example, the Toyota Group keiretsu includes 14 core companies and an additional 170 companies that receive preferential treatment. Toyota holds an equity position in many of these 170 member firms and is represented on many of their boards of directors. Many Canadian firms have found that the best way to compete in Asian countries is to form relationships with Asian firms.

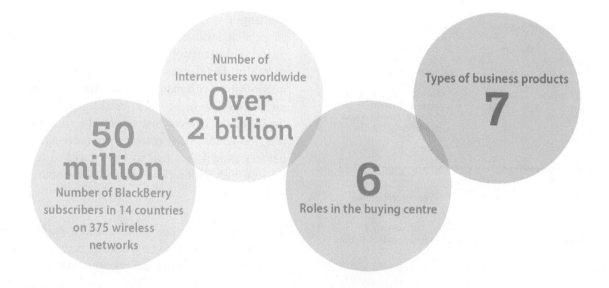

50 million — Number of BlackBerry subscribers in 14 countries on 375 wireless networks

Number of Internet users worldwide — Over 2 billion

6 — Roles in the buying centre

Types of business products — 7

CHAPTER **7** **Segmenting, Targeting, and Positioning**

Learning Outcomes

Market segmentation plays a key role in the marketing strategy of almost all successful organizations.

AFTER YOU FINISH THIS CHAPTER, GO TO WWW. ICANMKTG2.COM FOR STUDY TOOLS

GARY YEOWELL/STONE/GETTY IMAGES

LO 1   Market Segmentation

The term *market* means different things to different people. We are all familiar with the supermarket, stock market, labour market, fish market, and flea market. All these types of markets share several characteristics. First, they are composed of people (consumer markets) or organizations (business markets). Second, these people or organizations have wants and needs that can be satisfied by particular product categories. Third, they have the ability to buy the products they seek. Fourth, they are willing to exchange their resources, usually money or credit, for desired products. In sum, a **market** is (1) people or organizations with (2) needs or wants and with (3) the ability and (4) the willingness to buy. A group of people or an organization that lacks any one of these characteristics is not a market.

Within a market, a **market segment** is a subgroup of people or organizations sharing one or more characteristics that cause them to have similar product needs. At one extreme, we can define every person and every organization in the world as a market segment because each is unique. At the other extreme, we can define the entire consumer market as one large market segment and the business market as another large segment. All people have some similar characteristics and needs, as do all organizations.

market people or organizations with needs or wants and the ability and willingness to buy

market segment a subgroup of people or organizations sharing one or more characteristics that cause them to have similar product needs

What do you think?

It's pretty obvious when advertising is aimed at a certain group.

1   **2**   **3**   **4**   **5**   **6**   **7**
STRONGLY DISAGREE   STRONGLY AGREE

From a marketing perspective, market segments can be described as being somewhere between the two extremes. The process of dividing a market into meaningful, relatively similar, and identifiable segments or groups is called **market segmentation**. The purpose of market segmentation is to enable the marketer to tailor marketing mixes to meet the needs of one or more specific segments.

LO 2 The Importance of Market Segmentation

Until the 1960s, few firms practised market segmentation. When they did, it was more likely a haphazard effort than a formal marketing strategy. Before 1960, for example, the Coca-Cola Company produced only one beverage and aimed it at the entire pop market. Today, Coca-Cola offers more than a dozen different products to market segments on the basis of diverse consumer preferences for flavours and for calorie and caffeine content. Coca-Cola offers traditional pop flavours, energy drinks (such as POWERade), flavoured teas, fruit drinks (Fruitopia), and water (Dasani).

Market segmentation plays a key role in the marketing strategy of almost all successful organizations and is a powerful marketing tool for several reasons. Most importantly, nearly all markets include groups of people or organizations with different product needs and preferences. Market segmentation helps marketers define customer needs and wants more precisely. Because market segments differ in size and potential, segmentation helps decision makers more accurately define marketing objectives and better allocate resources. In turn, performance can be better evaluated when objectives are more precise.

LO 3 Criteria for Successful Segmentation

Marketers segment markets for three important reasons. First, segmentation enables marketers to identify groups of customers with similar needs and to analyze

the characteristics and buying behaviour of these groups. Second, segmentation provides marketers with information to help them design marketing mixes specifically matched with the characteristics and desires of one or more segments. Third, segmentation is consistent with the marketing concept of satisfying customer wants and needs while meeting the organization's objectives.

To be useful, a segmentation scheme must produce segments that meet four basic criteria:

1. *Substantiality:* A segment must be large enough to warrant developing and maintaining a special marketing mix. This criterion does not necessarily mean that a segment must have many potential customers. Marketers of custom-designed homes and business buildings, commercial airplanes, and large computer systems typically develop marketing programs tailored to each potential customer's needs. In most cases, however, a market segment needs many potential customers to make commercial sense.

2. *Identifiability and measurability:* Segments must be identifiable and their size measurable. Data on the population within geographic boundaries, the number of people in various age categories, and other social and demographic characteristics are often easy to get, and they provide fairly concrete measures of segment size.

3. *Accessibility:* The firm must be able to reach members of targeted segments with customized marketing mixes. Some market segments are more difficult to reach, for example, senior citizens (especially those with reading or hearing disabilities), individuals who don't speak English, and people who are illiterate.

4. *Responsiveness:* Markets can be segmented using any criteria that seem logical. Unless one market segment responds to a marketing mix differently from other segments, however, that segment need not be treated separately. For instance, if all customers are equally price-conscious about a product, marketers have no need to offer high-, medium-, and low-priced versions to different segments.

LO 4 Bases for Segmenting Consumer Markets

Marketers use **segmentation bases**, or **variables**, which are characteristics of individuals, groups, or organizations, to divide a total market into segments.

The choice of segmentation bases is crucial because an inappropriate segmentation strategy may lead to lost sales and missed profit opportunities. The key is to identify bases that will produce substantial, measurable, and accessible segments that exhibit different response patterns to marketing mixes.

Markets can be segmented by using a single variable, such as age group, or by using several variables, such as age group, gender, and education. Although a single-variable segmentation is less precise, it has the advantage of being simpler and easier to use than multiple-variable segmentation. The disadvantages of multiple-variable segmentation are that it is often more difficult to use than single-variable segmentation; usable secondary data are less likely to be available; and as the number of segmentation bases increases, the size of individual segments decreases. Nevertheless, the current trend is toward using more rather than fewer variables to segment most markets. Multiple-variable segmentation is clearly more precise than single-variable segmentation.

Consumer goods marketers commonly use one or more of the following characteristics to segment markets: geography, demographics, psychographics, benefits sought, and usage rate.

Geographic Segmentation

Geographic segmentation refers to segmenting markets by a region of a country or a region of the world, market size, market density, or climate. Market density means the number of people within a unit of land, such as a census tract. Climate is commonly used for geographic segmentation because of its dramatic impact on residents' needs and purchasing behaviour. Snow blowers, water and snow skis, clothing, and air-conditioning and heating systems are products with varying appeal, depending on climate. Not all Pizza Hut restaurants around the world serve the same pizza toppings that are commonly available in Canada. For example, Pizza Hut in Japan offers squid and other seafood toppings so it can meet the regional food preferences of its Japanese customers.

Demographic Segmentation

Marketers often segment markets on the basis of demographic information because such information is widely available and often relates to consumers' buying and consuming behaviour. Some common bases of **demographic segmentation** are age, gender, income, ethnic background, and family life cycle.

Age Segmentation Marketers use a variety of terms to refer to different age groups: newborns, infants, preschoolers, young children, tweens, teens, young adults, baby boomers, Generation X, Generation Y, and seniors. Age segmentation can be an important tool, as a brief exploration of the market potential of several age segments illustrates.

Through the spending of their allowances, earnings, and gifts, children account for, and influence, a great deal of consumption. Tweens (ages 9–14), which comprise approximately 2 million of Canada's total population, have direct spending power of $1.7 billion and an influence over how their families spend another $20 billion.[1] Tweens desire to be kids, but also want some of the fun of being a teenager. Many retailers such as Old Navy, American Eagle Outfitters, and Bluenotes serve this market with clothing that is similar in style to that worn by teenagers and young adults.

The teenage market (ages 15–19) includes more than 2 million individuals[2] and, like the tweens, this market accounts for substantial purchasing power, most of which is spent on clothing, entertainment, and food. Teens spend an average of 13 hours per week online compared with a weekly average of 19 hours for adults.[3] Magazines specifically designed to appeal to teenage girls include *Teen Vogue*, *Teen People*,

Hamilton

segmentation bases (variables) characteristics of individuals, groups, or organizations

geographic segmentation segmenting markets by region of a country or the world, market size, market density, or climate

demographic segmentation segmenting markets by age, gender, income, ethnic background, and family life cycle

3 REASONS TO GO REGIONAL

1. To find new ways to generate sales in sluggish and intensely competitive markets.
2. To appeal to local preferences.
3. To be able to react more quickly to competition.

Avon, a brand associated with older generations, is attempting to break into a more youthful market with its Mark brand of beauty products. From their dorms, college and university students sell the brightly coloured makeup in funky packaging.

CosmoGIRL!, Elle Girl, Seventeen, and *girlworks*.[4] Clothing marketers such as Ralph Lauren, Guess, DKNY, Dior, Giorgio Armani, and Juicy Couture advertise heavily in these magazines.[5]

The baby boom generation, born between 1947 and 1964, makes up the largest age segment with 9.2

million people in the group, approximately 30 percent of the entire Canadian population.[6] Together, baby boomers and the older generation, seniors, form a large and very lucrative market. Individuals 50 years old and older are continuing to lead active, fully involved lifestyles. Baby boomers represent tremendous current and future market potential for a wide range of products, including retirement properties, health and wellness products, automobiles with features designed for their age group, and other goods and services you might not expect. Not only are baby boomers often nostalgic and eager to continue their active lives, but they now can afford to buy top-of-the-line models of products from their youth. North Vancouver–based A&W is bringing back Chubby Chicken to appeal to the baby boom generation.[7]

Seniors (those aged 65 and older) are especially attracted to companies that build relationships by taking the time to get to know them and their preferences. Canadian seniors, who number 4.3 million, do not, however, think of themselves as old, or as seniors, despite their demands for traditional seniors' products. Mississauga-based Block Drug Company, having realized that today's seniors are healthier and perceive

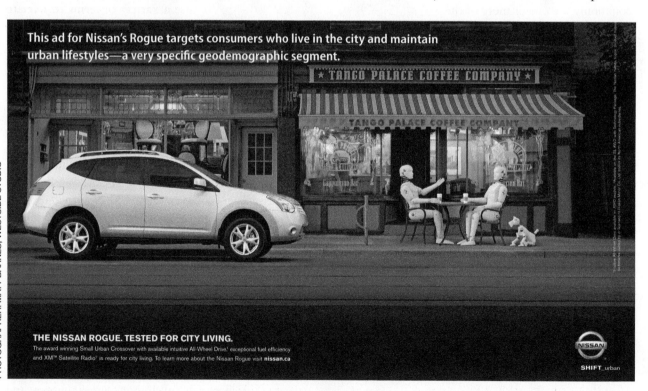

This ad for Nissan's Rogue targets consumers who live in the city and maintain urban lifestyles—a very specific geodemographic segment.

THE NISSAN ROGUE. TESTED FOR CITY LIVING.
The award winning Small Urban Crossover with available intuitive All-Wheel Drive,¹ exceptional fuel efficiency and XM™ Satellite Radio² is ready for city living. To learn more about the Nissan Rogue visit **nissan.ca**

SHIFT_urban

TWEENS, THOSE BETWEEN THE AGES OF 9 AND 14, HAVE A **SPENDING POWER** OF **$1.7 BILLION,** AND THEY INFLUENCE HOW THEIR FAMILIES SPEND ANOTHER $20 BILLION.[8]

themselves to be younger than any seniors before, launched a very different promotional campaign for its Polident brand of denture cleanser. Senior shoppers also prefer catalogue shopping over retail outlets because of their dissatisfaction with service at retail stores. Seniors are more likely than younger adults to have the combination of free time, money, and good health that allows them to pursue leisure-time activities, especially education and travel.[9]

Gender Segmentation Marketers of products such as clothing, cosmetics, personal-care items, magazines, jewellery, and footwear commonly continue to segment markets by gender. Many marketers that have traditionally focused almost exclusively on women have now recognized the importance and potential of the male segment. For example, males are increasingly involved in wedding planning, deciding on everything from the site, seating plans, and table decorations to the wedding cake and keepsakes for guests. As men become more involved with their weddings, businesses such as engagement consultants, resorts, and spas are beginning to create special packages designed to attract men.[10]

Other brands that have traditionally been targeted to men, such as Gillette razors and Rogaine hairloss treatment, are increasing their efforts to attract women and vice versa. Interactive Digital Software Association, a trade group, found that women are buying just as much game software as men. As a result, more game companies and websites are focusing their marketing efforts on girls and women.[11] Conversely, several Internet sites provide guidance for grooms: the WeddingChannel.com's groom-centric content includes holiday proposal do's and don'ts.[12]

Income Segmentation Income is a popular demographic variable for segmenting markets because income level influences consumers' wants and determines their buying power. Many markets are segmented by income, including the markets for housing, clothing, automobiles, and food. For example, in the auto industry, many car manufacturers have two different brands aimed at different income groups, such as Honda and Acura; Nissan and Infiniti; Toyota and Lexus. Honda, Nissan and Toyota are targeted at relatively lower-income consumers than Acura, Infiniti, and Lexus buyers.

Ethnic Segmentation Canada is a very culturally diverse country, and Canadian marketers are strongly aware of the multicultural makeup of the market. When considering Canada's ethnic communities, marketers might first focus on French Canadian and English Canadian markets, which are the largest, but they will then consider the other ethnic populations. Many companies are segmenting their markets according to ethnicity, and some marketers are developing unique approaches to sizable segments such as the Asian community. For example, the Toronto Symphony Orchestra (TSO) discovered that Chinese families had higher levels of musical literacy than the average for North Americans. The TSO decided to develop a Chinese-language promotional campaign that included, among other things, season brochures in Chinese.[14]

Regardless of the segment being targeted, marketers need to stay educated about the consumer they are pursuing, convey a message that is relevant to each particular market, use the Internet as a vehicle to educate ethnic markets about brands and products, and use

QUESTIONS TO ASK... ... WHEN SEGMENTING BY HERITAGE

What are the general characteristics of your total target population (size, growth rate, and spending power)?

Who are your target population (in terms of demographics, psychographics, attitudes, values, beliefs, and motivations)?

What are their behaviours (in terms of products, services, media, language, and so on)?

How does your target population differ from the general market and from each other, based on their country of origin?[15]

These recommendations apply to all ethnic groups that are generally segmented on the basis of ancestry.

THE AVERAGE CANADIAN FAMILY **INCOME** IS $74,600 PER YEAR WHILE AVERAGE FAMILY **SPENDING** IS $71,117; OF THIS, 19.8 PERCENT IS SPENT ON **SHELTER** WHILE 13.7 PERCENT GOES TO **TRANSPORTATION** COSTS.[13]

integrated marketing techniques to reinforce the message in various ways. Tracking ethnic communities is one of a multicultural marketer's most challenging and most important tasks. Some companies have found that segmenting according to the main ethnicities is not precise enough. The Asian Canadian segment, for example, comprises numerous other segments: those whose origin is Chinese, South Asian, Southeast Asian, Korean, and Japanese.

Alternatively, some companies have abandoned the notion that ethnic group youths require separate marketing mixes. Instead, they are focusing on "urban youth," regardless of race or ethnicity, because larger cities are the places where trends typically start.[16]

Family Life-Cycle Segmentation Consumer buying behaviour varies, and the variations are often not sufficiently explained by the demographic factors of gender,

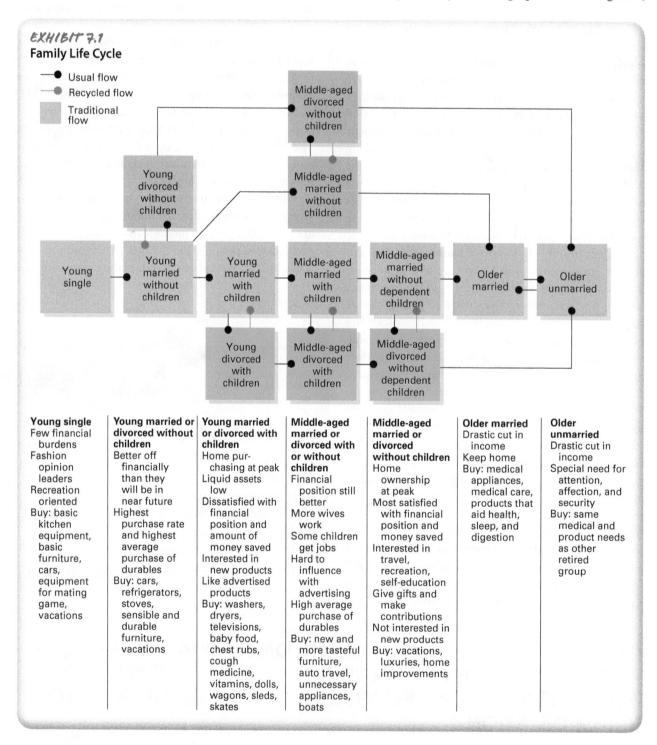

EXHIBIT 7.1
Family Life Cycle

— Usual flow
— Recycled flow
▨ Traditional flow

Young single	Young married or divorced without children	Young married or divorced with children	Middle-aged married or divorced with or without children	Middle-aged married or divorced without children	Older married	Older unmarried
Few financial burdens	Better off financially than they will be in near future	Home purchasing at peak	Financial position still better	Home ownership at peak	Drastic cut in income	Drastic cut in income
Fashion opinion leaders	Highest purchase rate and highest average purchase of durables	Liquid assets low	More wives work	Most satisfied with financial position and money saved	Keep home	Special need for attention, affection, and security
Recreation oriented	Buy: cars, refrigerators, stoves, sensible and durable furniture, vacations	Dissatisfied with financial position and amount of money saved	Some children get jobs	Interested in travel, recreation, self-education	Buy: medical appliances, medical care, products that aid health, sleep, and digestion	Buy: same medical and product needs as other retired group
Buy: basic kitchen equipment, basic furniture, cars, equipment for mating game, vacations		Interested in new products	Hard to influence with advertising	Give gifts and make contributions		
		Like advertised products	High average purchase of durables	Not interested in new products		
		Buy: washers, dryers, televisions, baby food, chest rubs, cough medicine, vitamins, dolls, wagons, sleds, skates	Buy: new and more tasteful furniture, auto travel, unnecessary appliances, boats	Buy: vacations, luxuries, home improvements		

ALAN GRAF/CULTURA/JUPITERIMAGES

age, and income. The consumption patterns among people of the same age and gender frequently differ because they are in different stages of the family life cycle. The **family life cycle (FLC)** is a series of stages determined by a combination of age, marital status, and the presence or absence of children.

Traditional families, that is, married couples with children under 24 years, constituted 34.6 percent of families according to 2006 census data.[17] The average number of persons in a family has been falling over the years. In 1961, the average family included 3.9 people, a number that has fallen to 3.0 persons per household.[18] Currently, household size seems to be stabilizing.

Exhibit 7.1 illustrates numerous FLC patterns and shows how families' needs, incomes, resources, and expenditures differ at each stage. The horizontal flow shows the traditional family life cycle. The lower part of the exhibit lists some of the characteristics and purchase patterns of families in each stage of the traditional life cycle. The exhibit also acknowledges that about half of all first marriages end in divorce. When young married couples move into the young-divorced stage, their consumption patterns often revert to those of the young-single stage of the cycle. About four out of five divorced persons remarry by middle age and re-enter the traditional life cycle, as indicated in the exhibit by the recycled flow.

At certain points in the life cycle, consumers are especially receptive to marketing efforts. Soon-to-be-married couples are typically considered to be most receptive because they are making brand decisions about products that could last longer than their marriages. Similarly, young parents are the target of companies promoting baby products, as these parents expect to have higher expenses. A thorough understanding of the FLC can help marketers to design, develop, and successfully sell their products in the most competitive manner.

Psychographic Segmentation

Age, gender, income, ethnicity, family life-cycle stage, and other demographic variables are usually helpful in developing segmentation strategies, but often they don't paint the entire picture. Demographics provides the skeleton, but psychographics adds meat to the bones. **Psychographic segmentation** is market segmentation on the basis of the variables in the box below.

Psychographic variables can be used individually to segment markets or can be combined with other variables to provide more detailed descriptions of market segments. One combination approach is the Environics PRIZM

PSYCHOGRAPHIC SEGMENTATION VARIABLES

▸▸ *Personality:* Personality reflects a person's traits, attitudes, and habits. Porsche Cars North America Inc. understood well the demographics of the Porsche owner: a fortysomething, male, university graduate earning over $100,000 per year. However, research discovered that this general demographic category actually included five personality types that more effectively segmented Porsche buyers. As a result, Porsche refined its marketing, and the company's sales rose by 48 percent.[19]

▸▸ *Motives:* Marketers of baby products and life insurance appeal to consumers' emotional motives—namely, to care for their loved ones. Using appeals to economy, reliability, and dependability, carmakers such as Subaru and Suzuki target customers by appealing to their rational motives.

▸▸ *Lifestyles:* Lifestyle segmentation divides people into groups according to the way they spend their time, the importance of the things around them, their beliefs, and socioeconomic characteristics such as income and education.

▸▸ *Geodemographics:* **Geodemographic segmentation** clusters potential customers into neighbourhood lifestyle categories. It combines geographic, demographic, and lifestyle segmentations. Geodemographic segmentation helps marketers develop marketing programs tailored to prospective buyers who live in small geographic regions, such as neighbourhoods, or who have very specific lifestyle and demographic characteristics.

C2 lifestyle segmentation system that divides the Canadian population into 66 different groups, clusters, or consumer types, all with catchy names. The clusters combine basic demographic data such as age, ethnicity, and income with lifestyle information, such as magazine and sports preferences, taken from consumer surveys. For example, the "Kids and Cul-de-Sacs" group comprises upscale, suburban families with a median household income of $68,900 who tend to shop online and visit Disney theme parks. The "Bohemian Mix" cluster refers to professionals aged 22 to 44 with a median income of $38,500, who are likely to shop at the Gap and read *Elle* magazine. The program also predicts to which neighbourhoods across the country the clusters are likely to gravitate.

Benefit Segmentation

Benefit segmentation is the process of grouping customers into market segments according to the benefits they seek from the product. Most types of market segmentation are based on the assumption that related subgroups of people or organizations share one or more characteristics that cause them to have similar product needs. Benefit segmentation is different because it groups potential customers on the basis of their needs or wants rather than using some other characteristic, such as age or gender.

Customer profiles can be developed by examining demographic information associated with people seeking certain benefits. This information can be used to match marketing strategies to selected target markets. The many different types of performance energy bars with various combinations of nutrients are aimed at consumers looking for different benefits. For example, PowerBar is designed for athletes looking for long-lasting fuel, while PowerBar Protein Plus is aimed at those who want extra protein for replenishing their muscles after strength training. Carb Solutions High Protein Bars are for those on low-carb diets; Luna Bars are targeted to women who want a bar with fewer calories, soy protein, and calcium; and Clif Bars are for people who want a natural bar made from such ingredients as rolled oats, soybeans, and organic soy flour.[20]

Usage-Rate Segmentation

Usage-rate segmentation divides a market by the amount of product bought or consumed. Categories vary depending on the product, but they are likely to include some combination of the following: former users, potential users, first-time users, light or irregular users, medium users, and heavy users. Segmenting by usage rate enables marketers to focus their efforts on heavy users or to develop multiple marketing mixes aimed at different segments. Because heavy users often account for a sizable portion of all product sales, some marketers focus on the heavy-user segment. Developing customers into heavy users is the goal behind many frequency and loyalty programs.

The **80/20 principle** holds that 20 percent of all customers generate 80 percent of the demand. Although the percentages usually are not exact, the general idea often holds true. For example, in the fast-food industry, heavy users account for only one of five fast-food patrons but represent 60 percent of all visits to fast-food restaurants. Thus, according to Statistics Canada, heavy users account for $9.36 billion of the $15.6 billion spent on fast food at Canada's 25,000 fast-food restaurants.[21]

LO 5 Bases for Segmenting Business Markets

The business market consists of four broad segments: producers, resellers, government, and institutions (for a detailed discussion of the characteristics of these segments, see Chapter 6). Whether marketers focus on only one or on all four of these segments, they are likely to find diversity among potential customers. Thus, further market segmentation offers just as many benefits to business marketers as it does to consumer-product marketers.

Company Characteristics

Company characteristics, such as geographic location, type of company, company size, and product use, can be

20 PERCENT OF ALL CUSTOMERS GENERATE **80 PERCENT** OF THE DEMAND.

important segmentation variables. Some markets tend to be regional because buyers prefer to purchase from local suppliers, and distant suppliers may have difficulty competing in terms of price and service. Therefore, firms that sell to geographically concentrated industries benefit by locating close to their markets.

Segmenting by customer type allows business marketers to tailor their marketing mixes to the unique needs of particular types of organizations or industries. Many companies are finding this form of segmentation to be quite effective. For example, Rona, one of the largest do-it-yourself retailers in Canada, has targeted professional repair and remodelling contractors in addition to consumers.

A commonly used basis for business segmentation is volume of purchase (heavy, moderate, light). Another is the buying organization's size, which may affect its purchasing procedures, the types and quantities of products it needs, and its responses to different marketing mixes. Many products, especially

SIX STEPS TO A SEGMENT

1. **SELECT A MARKET OR PRODUCT CATEGORY FOR STUDY:** Define the overall market or product category to be studied. It may be a market in which the firm already competes, a new but related market or product category, or a totally new market or category.

2. **CHOOSE A BASIS OR BASES FOR SEGMENTING THE MARKET:** This step requires managerial insight, creativity, and market knowledge. No scientific procedures guide the selection of segmentation variables. However, a successful segmentation scheme must produce segments that meet the four basic criteria discussed earlier in this chapter.

3. **SELECT SEGMENTATION DESCRIPTORS:** After choosing one or more bases, the marketer must select the segmentation descriptors. Descriptors identify the specific segmentation variables to use. For example, a company that selects usage segmentation needs to decide whether to pursue heavy users, nonusers, or light users.

4. **PROFILE AND ANALYZE SEGMENTS:** The profile should include the segments' sizes, expected growth, purchase frequency, current brand usage, brand loyalty, and long-term sales and profit potential. This information can then be used to rank potential market segments by profit opportunity, risk, consistency with organizational mission and objectives, and other factors important to the firm.

5. **SELECT TARGET MARKETS:** Selecting target markets is not a part of the segmentation process but is a natural outcome of the segmentation process. It is a major decision that influences and often directly determines the firm's marketing mix. This topic is examined in greater detail later in this chapter.

6. **DESIGN, IMPLEMENT, AND MAINTAIN APPROPRIATE MARKETING MIXES:** The marketing mix has been described as product, place (distribution), promotion, and pricing strategies intended to bring about mutually satisfying exchange relationships with target markets. Chapters 9 through 19 explore these topics in detail.

Tourism Vancouver uses all of these steps to keep the city a top destination for convention and meeting planners and tourists alike.

© MICHAEL K. MCCANN/FIRST LIGHT

raw materials such as steel, wood, and petroleum, have diverse applications. How customers use a product may influence the amount they buy, their buying criteria, and their selection of vendors.

Buying Processes

Many business marketers find it helpful to segment current and prospective customers on the basis of how they buy. For example, companies can segment some business markets by ranking key purchasing criteria, such as price, quality, technical support, and service. Atlas Corporation developed a commanding position in the industrial door market by providing customized products in just four weeks, which was much faster than the industry average of 12 to 15 weeks. Atlas's primary market is companies with an immediate need for customized doors.

The purchasing strategies of buyers may provide useful segments. Two purchasing profiles that have been identified are satisficers and optimizers. **Satisficers** are business customers who place their order with the first familiar supplier to satisfy their product and delivery requirements. **Optimizers**, on the other hand, are business customers who consider numerous suppliers (both familiar and unfamiliar), solicit bids, and study all proposals carefully before selecting one.

The personal characteristics of the buyers themselves (their demographic characteristics, decision styles, tolerance for risk, confidence levels, job responsibilities, etc.) influence their buying behaviour and thus offer a viable basis for segmenting some business markets. IBM computer buyers, for example, are sometimes characterized as being more risk-averse than buyers of less expensive computers that perform essentially the same functions. In advertising, therefore, IBM stressed its reputation for high quality and reliability.

LO 6 Steps in Segmenting a Market

The purpose of market segmentation, in both consumer and business markets, is to identify marketing opportunities. Markets are dynamic, so it is important that companies proactively monitor their segmentation strategies over time. Often, once customers or prospects have been assigned to a segment, marketers think their task is done. After customers are assigned to an age segment, for example, they stay there until they reach the next age bracket or category, which could be 10 years in the future. Thus, the segmentation classifications are static, but the customers and prospects are changing.

Dynamic segmentation reflects real-time changes made to market segments based on a customer's ongoing search and shopping behaviours. For example, the Chapters.Indigo.ca website suggests book titles based on a site visitor's browsing and purchase pattern. Similar segmentation techniques are also used by Netflix.ca. Dynamic segmentation uses advanced mathematical and computer programming techniques to offer highly customized solutions to customers.

LO 7 Strategies for Selecting Target Markets

So far, this chapter has focused on the market segmentation process, which is only the first step in deciding whom to approach about buying a product. The next task is to choose one or more target markets. A **target market** is a group of people or organizations for which an organization designs, implements, and maintains a marketing mix intended to meet the needs of that group, resulting in mutually satisfying exchanges. Because most markets will include customers with different characteristics, lifestyles, backgrounds, and income levels, a single marketing mix is unlikely to attract all segments of the market. Thus, if a marketer wishes to appeal to more than one segment of the market, it must develop different marketing mixes. For example, Sunlight Saunas makes saunas that retail at various prices between $1,695 and $5,595. The company segments its customer base into luxury and health markets based on data it gathers from visits to its website and conversations with potential customers. The same saunas appeal to both market segments, but the different groups require different marketing messages. Three general strategies are used for selecting target markets—undifferentiated, concentrated, and multisegment targeting. Exhibit 7.2 illustrates the advantages and disadvantages of each targeting strategy.

Advantages and Disadvantages of Target Marketing Strategies

Targeting Strategy	Advantages	Disadvantages
Undifferentiated Targeting	• Potential savings on production/ marketing costs	• Unimaginative product offerings • Company more susceptible to competition
Concentrated Targeting	• Concentration of resources • Can better meet the needs of a narrowly defined segment • Allows some small firms to better compete with larger firms • Strong positioning	• Segments too small, or changing • Large competitors may more effectively market to niche segment
Multisegment Targeting	• Greater financial success • Economies of scale in producing/ marketing	• High costs • Cannibalization

Undifferentiated Targeting

A firm using an **undifferentiated targeting strategy** essentially adopts a mass-market philosophy, viewing the market as one big market with no individual segments. The firm uses one marketing mix for the entire market. A firm that adopts an undifferentiated targeting strategy assumes that individual customers have similar needs that can be met through a common marketing mix. As such, marketers of commodity products, such as flour and sugar, are likely to use an undifferentiated targeting strategy.

The first firm in an industry sometimes uses an undifferentiated targeting strategy. With no competition, the firm may not need to tailor marketing mixes to the preferences of market segments. At one time, Coca-Cola used this strategy with its single product offered in a single size in a familiar green bottle. Undifferentiated marketing allows companies to save on production and marketing and achieve economies of mass production. Also, marketing costs may be lower when a company has only one product to promote and a single channel of distribution.

Too often, however, an undifferentiated strategy emerges by default rather than by design, reflecting a failure to consider the advantages of a segmented approach. The result is often sterile,

unimaginative product offerings that have little appeal to anyone. Another problem associated with undifferentiated targeting is the company's greater susceptibility to competitive inroads. Coca-Cola forfeited its position as the leading cola seller in supermarkets to Pepsi-Cola in the late 1950s, when Pepsi began offering its cola in several sizes.

Undifferentiated marketing can succeed. A grocery store in a small, isolated town may define all of the people that live in the town as its target market. It may offer one marketing mix that generally satisfies everyone in town. This strategy is not likely to be as effective, however, when a community has three or four grocery stores.

Concentrated Targeting

Firms using a **concentrated targeting strategy** select a market **niche** (one segment of a market) for targeting its marketing efforts. Because the firm is appealing to a single segment, it can concentrate on understanding the needs, motives, and satisfactions of that segment's members and on developing and maintaining a highly

undifferentiated targeting strategy a marketing approach that views the market as one big market with no individual segments and thus uses a single marketing mix

concentrated targeting strategy a strategy used to select one segment of a market for targeting marketing efforts

niche one segment of a market

RICHARD B. LEVINE/NEWSCOM

STARBUCKS BECAME **SUCCESSFUL** BY FOCUSING ON THE **NICHE** OF GOURMET COFFEE DRINKERS.

multisegment targeting strategy a strategy that chooses two or more well-defined market segments and develops a distinct marketing mix for each

cannibalization a situation that occurs when sales of a new product cut into sales of a firm's existing products

one-to-one marketing an individualized marketing method that utilizes customer information to build long-term, personalized, and profitable relationships with each customer

specialized marketing mix. Some firms find that concentrating resources and meeting the needs of a narrowly defined market segment is more profitable than spreading resources over several different segments.

Small firms often adopt a concentrated targeting strategy to compete effectively with much larger firms. Fatburger, which recently opened a store in Prince Albert, Saskatchewan, describes itself as "the last great hamburger stand."[22] Similarly, Starbucks became successful by focusing on customers who wanted gourmet coffee products.

Concentrated targeting violates the old adage "Don't put all your eggs in one basket." If the chosen segment is too small or if it shrinks because of environmental changes, the firm may suffer negative consequences. A concentrated strategy can also be disastrous for a firm that is not successful in its narrowly defined target market. For example, before Procter & Gamble introduced Head & Shoulders shampoo, several small firms were already selling antidandruff shampoos. Head & Shoulders was introduced with a large promotional campaign, and the new brand immediately captured over half the market. Within a year, several of the firms that had been concentrating on this market segment went out of business.

Multisegment Targeting

A firm that chooses to serve two or more well-defined market segments and develops a distinct marketing mix for each has a **multisegment targeting strategy**. Maple Leaf Foods offers many different kinds of bacon, such as regular and salt-reduced bacon. For convenience-seeking consumers, the company has developed Ready Crisp microwaveable bacon. For health-conscious segments, it offers turkey and chicken bacons. Cosmetics companies, on the other hand, seek to increase sales and market share by targeting multiple age and ethnic groups. Maybelline and CoverGirl, for example, market different lines catering to tween girls, teenage women, young adult women, older women, and visible minority women.

Multisegment targeting is used for stores and shopping formats, not just for brands. Marketers at Best Buy have identified five customer segments, which they have personalized by naming them: "Jill," a busy suburban mom; "Buzz," a focused, active younger male; "Ray," a family man who likes his technology practical; "BB4B" (Best Buy for Business), a small-business employer; and "Barry," an affluent professional male who's likely to drop tens of thousands of dollars on a home theatre system.

Multisegment targeting offers many potential benefits to firms, including greater sales volume, higher profits, larger market share, and economies of scale in manufacturing and marketing. Yet it may also involve greater product design, production, promotion, inventory, marketing research, and management costs. Before deciding to use this strategy, firms should compare the benefits and costs of multisegment targeting to those of undifferentiated and concentrated targeting.

Another potential cost of multisegment targeting is **cannibalization**, which occurs when sales of a new product cut into sales of a firm's existing products. In many cases, however, companies prefer to steal sales from their own brands rather than lose sales to a competitor. Marketers may also be willing to cannibalize existing business to build new business.

LO 8 One-to-One Marketing

Most businesses today use a mass-marketing approach designed to increase *market share* by selling their products to the greatest number of people. For many businesses, however, a more efficient and profitable strategy is to use one-to-one marketing to increase their *share of customers*—in other words, to sell more products to each customer. **One-to-one marketing** is an individualized marketing method that utilizes customer information to build long-term, personalized, and profitable relationships with each customer. The goal is to reduce costs through customer retention while increasing revenue through customer loyalty. One of the best-known examples of one-to-one marketing is Dell, which lets buyers customize the computer they order.

"**ONE-TO-ONE** MARKETERS LOOK FOR OPPORTUNITIES TO COMMUNICATE WITH EACH **INDIVIDUAL** CUSTOMER."

STANDARD TISSUE

You might think a firm producing a standard product such as toilet tissue would adopt an undifferentiated strategy. However, this market has industrial segments and consumer segments. Industrial buyers want an economical, single-ply product sold in boxes of a hundred rolls. The consumer market demands a more versatile product in smaller quantities. Within the consumer market, the product is differentiated with designer print or no print, cushioned or noncushioned, scented or unscented, economy priced or luxury priced, and single, double, or triple rolls. Fort Howard Corporation, the market share leader in industrial toilet paper, does not even sell to the consumer market.

The difference between one-to-one marketing and the traditional mass-marketing approach can be compared with shooting a rifle and a shotgun. If you have good aim, a rifle is the more efficient weapon to use. A shotgun, on the other hand, increases your odds of hitting the target when it is more difficult to focus. Instead of scattering messages far and wide across the spectrum of mass media (the shotgun approach), one-to-one marketers look for opportunities to communicate with each individual customer (the rifle approach). Anya Hindmarch, one of Britain's leading designers of handbags and accessories, invites her customers to participate in the creation of their handbags by providing a personal photograph that she then expertly transposes onto one of her beautifully designed bags. Customers may also participate in the design process in other ways to create a unique, customer-designed handbag.[23]

Several factors suggest that personalized communications and product customization will continue to expand as more and more companies understand why and how their customers make and execute purchase decisions. At least four trends will lead to the continuing growth of one-to-one marketing: personalization, time savings, loyalty, and technology.

Personalization: The one-size-fits-all marketing of yesteryear no longer fits. Consumers do not want to be treated like the masses. Instead, they want to be treated as the individuals they are, with their own unique sets of needs and wants. By its personalized nature, one-to-one marketing can fulfill this desire.

Time savings: Consumers will have little or no time to spend shopping and making purchase decisions. Because of the personal and targeted nature of one-to-one marketing, consumers can spend less time making purchase decisions and more time doing the things that are important.

Loyalty: Consumers will be loyal only to those companies and brands that have earned their loyalty and reinforced it at every purchase occasion. One-to-one marketing techniques focus on finding a firm's best customers, rewarding them for their loyalty, and thanking them for their business.

Technology: Advances in marketing research and database technology will allow marketers to collect detailed information on their customers, not just the approximation offered by demographics but specific names and addresses. Mass-media approaches will decline in importance as new technology offers one-to-one marketers a more cost-effective way to reach customers and enables businesses to personalize their messages to customers. With the help of database technology, one-to-one marketers can track their customers as individuals, even if they number in the millions.

One-to-one marketing is a huge commitment and often requires a 180-degree turnaround for marketers who spent the last half of the twentieth century developing and implementing mass-marketing efforts. Although mass marketing will probably continue to be used, especially to create brand awareness or to remind consumers of a product, the advantages of one-to-one marketing cannot be ignored.

> **positioning** a process that influences potential customers' overall perception of a brand, product line, or organization in general

LO 9 Positioning

The development of any marketing mix depends on **positioning**, a process that influences potential

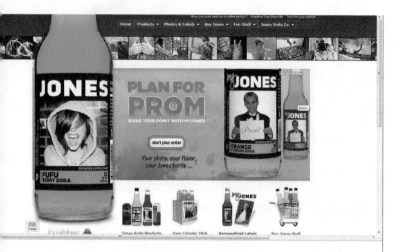

However, many everyday products, such as bleach, Aspirin, unleaded regular gasoline, and some soaps, are differentiated by such trivial means as brand names, packaging, colour, smell, or secret additives. The marketer attempts to convince consumers that a particular brand is distinctive and that they should demand it over competing brands.

Some firms, instead of using product differentiation, position their products as being similar to competing products or brands. For example, artificial sweeteners are advertised as tasting like sugar, and margarine is touted as tasting like butter.

Perceptual Mapping

Perceptual mapping is a means of displaying or graphing, in two or more dimensions, the location of products, brands, or groups of products in customers' minds. For example, Levi Strauss has developed for the youth market a range of products that range from different styles of jeans to nylon pants that can be unzipped into shorts. At the same time Levi's has strengthened its position in the adult apparel market by extending the Dockers and Slate brand casual clothing. Exhibit 7.3 presents a perceptual map that shows Levi's different brands and sub-brands for different market segments based on age, income, and lifestyle.

Positioning Bases

Firms use a variety of bases for positioning, including the following:

▶▶ *Attribute:* A product is associated with an attribute, product feature, or customer benefit. Rockport shoes are positioned as an always-comfortable brand that is available in a range of styles from working shoes to dress shoes.

▶▶ *Price and quality:* This positioning base may stress high price as a signal of quality or emphasize low price as an indication of value. Denmark-based Lego uses a high-price strategy for its toy building blocks, whereas Montreal-based Mega Bloks uses a low-price strategy.[24] Similarly, Wal-Mart has successfully followed the low-price and value strategy. The mass merchandiser Target has developed an interesting position that is based on price and quality. It is known as an upscale discounter, sticking to low prices but offering higher quality and design than most discount chains.

▶▶ *Use or application:* A company can stress a product's uses or applications as an effective means of positioning it with buyers. Snapple introduced a new drink called Snapple-a-Day that is intended for use as a meal replacement.

customers' overall perception of a brand, **product line, or organization** in general. **Position** is the place a product, brand, or group of products occupies in consumers' minds relative to competing offerings. Consumer goods marketers are particularly concerned with positioning. Procter & Gamble, for example, markets 11 different laundry detergents, each with a unique position.

Positioning assumes that consumers compare products on the basis of important features. Marketing efforts that emphasize irrelevant features are therefore likely to misfire. For example, Crystal Pepsi and a clear version of Coca-Cola's Tab failed because consumers perceived the "clear" positioning as more of a marketing gimmick than a benefit.

Effective positioning requires assessing the positions occupied by competing products, determining the important dimensions underlying these positions, and choosing a position in the market where the organization's marketing efforts will have the greatest impact. For example, Toyota Canada presents its philosophy of continuous improvement in three words—"make things better"—and positions itself as being environmentally friendly. With this positioning, Toyota is using product differentiation to create the perception that its products have very real advantages for the target market.

As the previous example illustrates, **product differentiation** is a positioning strategy that some firms use to distinguish their products from those of competitors. The distinctions can be either real or perceived. Companies can develop products that offer very real advantages for the target market.

position the place a product, brand, or group of products occupies in consumers' minds relative to competing offerings

product differentiation a positioning strategy that some firms use to distinguish their products from those of competitors

perceptual mapping a means of displaying or graphing, in two or more dimensions, the location of products, brands, or groups of products in customers' minds

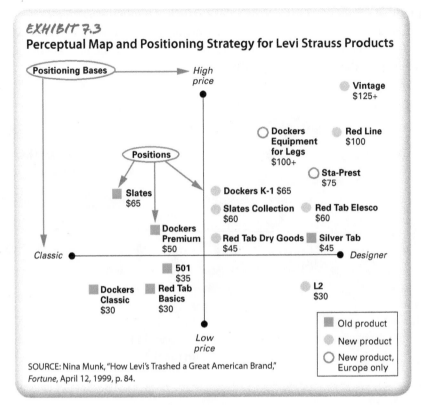

EXHIBIT 7.3
Perceptual Map and Positioning Strategy for Levi Strauss Products

SOURCE: Nina Munk, "How Levi's Trashed a Great American Brand," *Fortune*, April 12, 1999, p. 84.

who choose milk instead of sugary drinks tend to be leaner and the protein helps build muscle. So, shut up and drink.[25]

This ad reflects the following positioning bases:

▶▶ *Product attribute/benefit:* The emphasis that protein in milk "helps build muscle" describes a product attribute. Choosing milk instead of sugary drinks results in a leaner body, a benefit.

▶▶ *Use or application:* Rihanna values milk—"milk is more my move."

▶▶ *Product user:* The use of Rihanna, a successful Hollywood star, shows that milk is not just for kids.

▶▶ *Product class (disassociation):* The ad differentiates milk from other beverages showing that milk is healthier than sugary drinks.

▶▶ *Competitor (indirect):* She prefers milk over other drinks.

▶▶ *Product user:* This positioning base focuses on a personality or type of user. Zale Corporation has several jewellery store concepts, each positioned to a different user. The Zale stores cater to middle-of-the-road consumers who favour traditional styles. Its Gordon's stores project a contemporary look to appeal to a slightly older clientele, whereas People's Jewellers targets a wider market segment.

▶▶ *Product class:* The objective here is to position the product as being associated with a particular category of products, for example, positioning a margarine brand with butter. Alternatively, products can be disassociated with a category.

▶▶ *Competitor:* Positioning against competitors is part of any positioning strategy. The Avis rental car positioning as number two exemplifies a company positioning against specific competitors.

▶▶ *Emotion:* Positioning using emotion focuses on how the product makes customers feel. A number of companies use this approach. For example, Nike's "Just Do It" campaign didn't tell consumers what "it" is, but most got the emotional message of achievement and courage.

It is not unusual for a marketer to use more than one of these bases. A print ad in the "Got Milk?" campaign featuring pop singer Rihanna sporting a milk moustache reads as follows:

Drink it in. Pop star? Not exactly. Milk is more my move. Some studies suggest that teens

▶▶ *Emotion:* The ad conveys an upbeat, contemporary attitude.[26]

Repositioning

Sometimes products or companies are repositioned to sustain growth in slow markets or to correct positioning mistakes. **Repositioning** refers to changing consumers' perceptions of a brand in relation to competing brands.

Recently, Scott Paper had to change the name of its Cottonelle brand of toilet tissues to Cashmere brand because the company was losing its licence on the Cottonelle brand name. The new name, Cashmere, was developed from a marketing study of women who were asked, "What is softer than cotton?" The most common response was *cashmere.* Changing a brand name is the most demanding repositioning that a company can undertake. Scott Paper developed a multimedia campaign involving TV ads, radio ads, magazines, and point-of-purchase materials. TV advertising was the leading communication device. One ad begins by showing a bathroom with a 1970s motif. A woman wearing bell-bottoms enters the bathroom and puts a clearly marked package of Cottonelle in a cabinet. Fast-forward, and a woman wearing 1980s-style pants enters and

repositioning
changing consumers' perceptions of a brand in relation to competing brands

does the same thing. Fast-forward again to a modern-day bathroom with a woman dressed in contemporary fashion entering the bathroom, but this time with a package clearly marked "Cashmere." As she puts the Cashmere in the cabinet, the announcer's voice says, "We've changed Cottonelle over the years. Now we are giving it a softer name. Cottonelle is changing its name to Cashmere."[27]

Percentage of customers responsible for 80 percent of a company's demand

20%

Number of steps in segmenting a market

6

Number of supermarkets that go out of business for each Wal-Mart supercentre built

2

$1 trillion
Value of consumer spending related to trading down

13
Average number of hours a teen spends online each week

5 & 11
P&G has identified 5 different segments of detergent users in Canada and 11 in the U.S.

Visit **icanmktg2.com** to find the resources you need today!

Located at the back of the textbook are rip-out Chapter Review cards. Make sure you also go online to check out other tools that MKTG offers to help you successfully pass your course.

- Interactive Quizzing
- Games
- Flashcards
- Audio Summaries
- PowerPoint Slides

- Videos and Assessments
- Cases
- Marketing Plans and Worksheets
- Animated Visual Summaries

71% The percentage of students who go online to study for a class.

© Anderson Ross/Getty Images

GET ONLINE

The easy-to-navigate website for **MKTG** offers guidance on key topics in **marketing** in a variety of engaging formats. You have the opportunity to refine and check your understanding via interactive quizzes and flashcards. Videos and audio summaries provide inspiration for your own further exploration. And, in order to make **MKTG** an even better learning tool, we invite you to speak up about your experience with **MKTG** by completing a survey form and sending us your comments.

Get online and discover the following resources:

- Printable PowerPoint Slides
- Flashcards
- Interactive Quizzing
- Crossword Puzzles
- Audio Summaries

"I think this book is awesome for students of all ages. It is a much simpler way to study."

—Yasmine Al-Hashimi, Fanshawe College

Visit **www.icanmktg2.com** to find the resources you need today!

Customer Relationship Management (CRM)

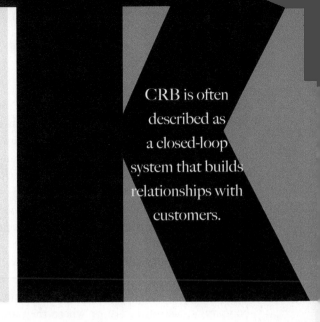

CRB is often described as a closed-loop system that builds relationships with customers.

AFTER YOU FINISH THIS CHAPTER, GO TO WWW. ICANMKTG2.COM FOR STUDY TOOLS

LO 1 What Is Customer Relationship Management?

Customer relationship management (CRM) is the ultimate goal of a new trend in marketing that focuses on understanding customers as individuals instead of as part of a large segment group. To achieve this goal, marketers are making their communications more customer specific. This movement was initially popularized as one-to-one marketing. However, CRM is a much broader approach to understanding and serving customer needs than one-to-one marketing.

Customer relationship management is a company-wide business strategy designed to optimize profitability, revenue, and customer satisfaction by focusing on highly defined and precise customer groups. This strategy is accomplished by organizing the company around customer segments, establishing and tracking customer interactions with the company, fostering customer-satisfying behaviours, and linking all processes of the company from its customers through its suppliers. CRM is a so-called rifle approach, whereas traditional mass marketing can be considered a shotgun approach. Instead of scattering messages far and wide across the spectrum of mass media (the shotgun approach), CRM marketers now are homing in on ways to effectively communicate with each individual customer (the rifle approach).

customer relationship management (CRM) a company-wide business strategy designed to optimize profitability, revenue, and customer satisfaction by focusing on highly defined and precise customer groups

What do you think?

When an email from a company pops into my inbox, I delete it right away.

1	2	3	4	5	6	7
STRONGLY DISAGREE   STRONGLY AGREE

© ISTOCKPHOTO.COM/ROBERT CHURCHILL

The Customer Relationship Management Cycle

On the surface, CRM may appear to be a rather simplistic customer service strategy. Although customer service is part of the CRM process, it is only a small part of a totally integrated approach to building customer relationships. CRM is often described as a closed-loop system that builds relationships with customers. Exhibit 8.1 illustrates this closed-loop system, which is continuous and circular with no predefined start or end point.[1]

To initiate the CRM cycle, a company must first *identify customer relationships with the organization*. This step may simply involve learning who the company's customers are or where they are located, or it may require more detailed information about the products and services these customers are using. Bridgestone Canada Inc., which produces Firestone tires and is a tire service company, uses a CRM system called OnDemand5, which initially gathers information from a point-of-sale interaction.[2] The information gathered includes basic demographic information, the frequency of consumers' purchases, how much they purchase, and how far they drive.

Next, the company must *understand its interactions with current customers*. Companies accomplish this task by collecting data on all types of communications a customer has with the company. Using its OnDemand5 system, Bridgestone Canada Inc. can add information that is based on additional interactions with the consumer, such as multiple visits to a physical store location and purchasing history. In this phase, companies build on the initial information collected and develop a more useful database.

Using this knowledge of its customers and their interactions, the company then *captures relevant customer data on interactions*. As an example, Bridgestone/Firestone can collect such relevant information as the date of the last communication with a customer, how often the customer makes purchases, and whether the customer redeemed coupons sent through direct mail.

How can marketers realistically analyze and communicate with individual customers? The answer lies in how information technology is used to implement the CRM system. Fundamentally, a CRM approach

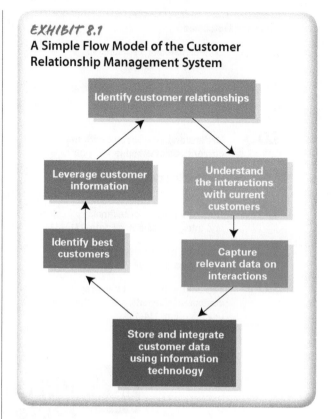

EXHIBIT 8.1
A Simple Flow Model of the Customer Relationship Management System

- Identify customer relationships
- Understand the interactions with current customers
- Capture relevant data on interactions
- Store and integrate customer data using information technology
- Identify best customers
- Leverage customer information

is no more than the relationship cultivated by a salesperson with the customer. A successful salesperson builds a relationship over time, constantly thinks about what the customer needs and wants, and is mindful of the trends and patterns in the customer's purchase history. The salesperson may also inform, educate, and instruct the customer about new products, technology, or applications in anticipation of the customer's future needs or requirements.

This kind of thoughtful attention is the basis of successful CRM systems. Information technology is used not only to enhance the collection of customer data but also to *store and integrate customer data* throughout the company and, ultimately, to get to know customers on a personal basis. Customer data are the first-hand responses that are obtained from customers through investigation or by asking direct questions. These initial data, which might include individual answers to questionnaires, responses on warranty cards, or lists of purchases recorded by electronic cash registers, have not yet been analyzed or interpreted.

The value of customer data depends on the system that stores the data and the consistency and accuracy

"HOW CAN MARKETERS REALISTICALLY **ANALYZE** AND **COMMUNICATE** WITH INDIVIDUAL CUSTOMERS?"

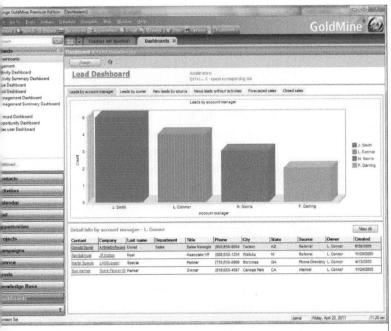

CRM is a strategy designed to optimize business performance by focusing on highly defined customer groups.

of the data captured. Obtaining high-quality, actionable data from various sources is a key element in any CRM system. Bridgestone Canada Inc. accomplishes this task by managing all information in a central database accessible by marketers. Different kinds of database management software are available, from extremely high-tech, expensive, custom-designed databases to standardized programs.

Every customer wants to be a company's main priority, but not all customers are equally important in the eyes of a business. Consequently, the company must identify *its profitable and unprofitable customers*. The Pareto Principle (the 80/20 rule mentioned in Chapter 7) would indicate that 80 percent of a business's profit will come from 20 percent of its customers.

Data mining is an analytical process that compiles actionable data on the purchase habits of a firm's current and potential customers. Essentially, data mining transforms customer data into customer information a company can use to make managerial decisions. Bridgestone Canada Inc. uses OnDemand5 to analyze its data to determine which customers qualify for the MasterCare Select program.

Once customer data are analyzed and transformed into usable information, the information must be *leveraged*. The CRM system sends the customer information to all areas of a business because the customer interacts with all aspects of the business. Essentially,

the company is trying to enhance customer relationships by getting the right information to the right person in the right place at the right time.

Bridgestone Canada Inc. utilizes the information in its database to develop different marketing campaigns for each type of customer. Customers are also targeted by promotions aimed at increasing their store visits, upgrading their vehicles to higher-end tires, and encouraging their purchases of additional services. Since the company customized its mailings to each type of customer, visits to stores have increased by more than 50 percent.[3]

Implementing a Customer Relationship Management System

Our discussion of a CRM system has assumed two key points. First, customers take centre stage in any organization. Second, the business must manage the customer relationship across all points of customer contact throughout the entire organization. In the next sections, we examine how a CRM system is implemented and follow the progression depicted in Exhibit 8.1 to explain each step in greater detail.

LO 2 Identify Customer Relationships

Companies that have a CRM system follow a customer-centric focus or model. Being **customer-centric** refers to an internal management philosophy similar to the marketing concept discussed in Chapter 1. Under this philosophy, the company customizes its product and service offering based on data generated through interactions between the customer and the company. This philosophy transcends all functional areas of the business, producing an internal system where all of the company's decisions and actions are a direct result of customer information.

A customer-centric company builds long-lasting relationships by focusing on what satisfies and retains valuable customers. For example, Sony's website (**http://www.playstation.ca/**) focuses on learning, customer knowledge management, and empowerment to market its PlayStation gaming computer entertainment system. The website offers online shopping,

data mining an analytical process that compiles actionable data on the purchase habits of a firm's current and potential customers.

customer-centric a philosophy under which the company customizes its product and service offering based on data generated through interactions between the customer and the company

learning in a CRM environment, the informal process of collecting customer data through customer comments and feedback on product or service performance

knowledge management the process by which learned information from customers is centralized and shared for the purpose of enhancing the relationship between customers and the organization

empowerment delegation of authority to solve customers' problems quickly—usually by the first person who learns of the customer's problem

interaction the point at which a customer and a company representative exchange information and develop learning relationships

opportunities to try new games, customer support, and information on news, events, and promotions. The interactive features include online gaming and message boards.

The PlayStation site is designed to support Sony's CRM system. When PlayStation users want to access amenities on the site, they are required to log in and supply information such as their name, email address, and birthdate. Users can opt to fill out a survey that asks questions about the types of computer entertainment systems they own, how many games are owned for each console, expected future game purchases, time spent playing games, types of games played, and level of Internet connectivity. Armed with this information, Sony marketers are then able to tailor the site, new games, and PlayStation hardware on the basis of players' replies to the survey and their use of the website.[4]

Customer-centric companies continually learn ways to enhance their product and service offerings. **Learning** in a CRM environment involves the informal process of collecting customer information through comments and feedback on product and service performance.

Each unit of a business typically has its own way of recording what it learns and may even have its own customer information system. The departments' different interests make it difficult to pull all of the customer information together in one place using a common format. To overcome this problem, companies using CRM rely on **knowledge management**, a process by which learned information from customers is centralized and shared for the purpose of enhancing the relationship between customers

and the organization. Information collected includes experiential observations, comments, customer actions, and qualitative facts about the customer.

As explained in Chapter 1, empowerment involves delegating authority to solve customers' problems quickly, usually by the first person who learns of the customer's problem. In other words, **empowerment** is the latitude organizations give their representatives to negotiate mutually satisfying commitments with customers. Usually, organizational representatives are able to make changes during interactions with customers through phone, fax, email, Web communication, or face-to-face.

An **interaction** occurs when a customer and a company representative exchange information and develop learning relationships. With CRM, the customer, and not the organization, defines the terms of the interaction, often by stating his or her preferences. The organization responds by designing products and services around customers' desired experiences. For example, students in Canada can purchase the Student Price Card for a nominal fee and use it to obtain discounts from affiliated retailers, such as The Source by Circuit City, Foot Locker, The Bay, and Aldo. Student Advantage tracks the cardholders' spending patterns and behaviours to gain a better understanding of what the student customer wants. Student Advantage then communicates this information to the affiliated retailers, who can tailor their discounts to meet the students' needs.[5]

The success of CRM—building lasting and profitable relationships—can be directly measured by the effectiveness of the interaction between the customer and the organization. In fact, CRM is further differentiated from other strategic initiatives by the organization's ability to establish and manage interactions with its current customer base. The more latitude (empowerment) a company gives its representatives, the more likely the interaction will conclude in a way that satisfies the customer.

TISH1/SHUTTERSTOCK.COM

ALEX STAROSELTSEV/SHUTTERSTOCK.COM

PAUL CONNORS/ASSOCIATED PRESS

"**EMPOWERMENT** INVOLVES **DELEGATING AUTHORITY** TO SOLVE CUSTOMERS' PROBLEMS QUICKLY."

LO 3 Understand Interactions of the Current Customer Base

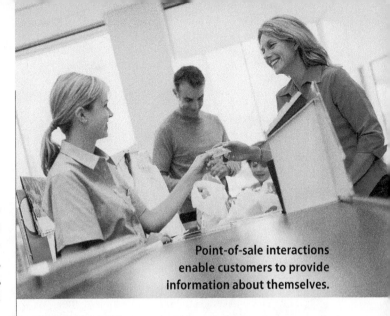

Point-of-sale interactions enable customers to provide information about themselves.

The *interaction* between the customer and the organization is the foundation on which a CRM system is built. Only through effective interactions can organizations learn about the expectations of their customers, generate and manage knowledge about customers, negotiate mutually satisfying commitments, and build long-term relationships.

Exhibit 8.2 illustrates the customer-centric approach for managing customer interactions. Following a customer-centric approach, an interaction can occur through a formal or direct communication channel, such as a phone, the Internet, or a salesperson. Any activity or touch point a customer has with an organization, either directly or indirectly, constitutes an interaction.

Companies that effectively manage customer interactions recognize that customers provide data to the organization that affect a wide variety of touch points. In a CRM system, **touch points** are all possible areas of a business where customers have contact with that business and data might be gathered. Touch points might include a customer registering for a particular service, a customer communicating with customer service for product information, a customer making direct contact electronically via QR code, email, or website visit, a customer completing and returning the warranty information card for a product, or a customer talking with salespeople, delivery personnel, and product installers. Data gathered at these touch points, once interpreted, provide information that affects touch points inside the company. Interpreted information may be redirected to marketing research, to develop profiles of extended warranty purchasers; to production, to analyze recurring problems and repair components; and to accounting, to establish cost-control models for repair service calls.

touch points all possible areas of a business where customers have contact with that business

point-of-sale interactions communications between customers and organizations that occur at the point of sale, usually in a store

Web-based interactions are an increasingly popular touch point for customers to communicate with companies on their own terms. Web users can evaluate and purchase products, make reservations, input preferential data, and provide customer feedback on services and products. Data from these Web-based interactions are then captured, compiled, and used to segment customers, refine marketing efforts, develop new products, and deliver a degree of individual customization to improve customer relationships.

Another touch point is through **point-of-sale interactions**, communications between customers and organizations that occur at the point of sale, usually in a store but also at information kiosks. Many point-of-sale software packages enable customers to easily provide information about themselves without feeling violated. The information

EXHIBIT 8.2
Customer-Centric Approach for Managing Customer Interactions

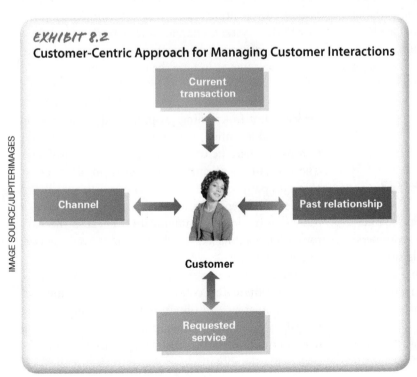

Current transaction

Channel

Past relationship

Customer

Requested service

MEMBER SERVICES

The British Columbia Automobile Association (BCAA) offers its members a wide variety of services, such as insurance, roadside assistance, travel planning, and savings and rewards. To offer its services effectively, BCAA asks for and collects basic information from its members, including name, address, and age. But BCAA goes beyond this basic contact information to acquire client information related to life-stage and behavioural patterns, which can include information related to past trips, services used, and level of satisfaction. This information led BCAA to develop a Voice of the Customer (VoC) program that includes customer service as one of its metrics. BCCA also integrates these measures into its employee compensation program. The result has been both a greater focus on customer centricity among employees and greater employee satisfaction with their workplace. In both 2008 and 2009, BCAA Home Insurance was ranked by J.D. Power and Associates as "Highest in Customer Satisfaction among Home Insurance Providers," which was followed, in 2010, by the Canadian Automobile Association (CAA) Best Practices Award for BCAA's "Inside Track" member panel research initiative and being named as one of the "50 Best Employers in Canada" for the fourth year in a row (2007, 2008, 2009, and 2010) by international human resources consultants Hewitt Associates and the Globe and Mail's *Report on Business* magazine.[6]

is then used in two ways: for marketing and merchandising activities and for accurately identifying the store's best customers and the types of products they buy. Data collected at point-of-sale interactions is also used to increase customer satisfaction through the development of in-store services and customer recognition promotions.

LO4 Capture Customer Data

Vast amounts of data can be obtained from the interactions between an organization and its customers. Therefore, in a CRM system, the issue is not how much data can be obtained, but rather what types of data should be acquired and how the data can effectively be used for relationship enhancement.

The traditional approach for acquiring data from customers is through channel interactions. Channel interactions include store visits, conversations with salespeople, interactions via the Web, traditional phone conversations, and wireless communications In a CRM system, channel interactions are viewed as prime information sources that are based on the channel selected to initiate the interaction rather than on the data acquired. For example, if a consumer logs on to the Sony website to find out why a Sony device is not functioning properly and the answer is not available online, the consumer is then referred to a page where he or she can describe the problem. The website then emails the problem description to a company representative, who will research the problem and reply via email. Sony continues to use the email mode of communication because the customer has established email as the preferred method of contact.[7]

Interactions between the company and the customer facilitate the collection of large amounts of data. Companies can obtain not only simple contact information (name, address, phone number) but also data pertaining to the customer's current relationship with the organization—past purchase history, quantity and frequency of purchases, average amount spent on purchases, sensitivity to promotional activities, and so forth.

In this manner, much information can be captured from one individual customer across several touch points. Multiply this information by the thousands of customers across all of the touch points within an organization, and the volume of data that company personnel deal with can rapidly become unmanageable. The large volumes of data resulting from a CRM initiative can be managed effectively only through technology. Once customer data are collected, the question of who owns those data becomes extremely salient. In its privacy statement, Toysmart.com declared it would never sell information registered at its website, including children's names and birthdates, to a third party. However, when the company filed for bankruptcy protection in the United States, it said the information collected constituted a company asset that needed to be sold off to pay creditors. Despite the outrage at this announcement, many dot-com companies closing their doors found they had little in the way of assets and followed Toysmart's lead. In Canada, the Personal Information Protection and Electronic Documents Act (PIPEDA), which deals with the protection of personal information, specifies only that disclosure must be made when third parties have access to personal information. PIPEDA does not address the selling of the information as a business asset.

LO 5 Store and Integrate Customer Data

Customer data are only as valuable as the system in which the data are stored and the consistency and accuracy of the data captured. Gathering data is further complicated because that data needed by one unit of the organization, such as sales and marketing, are often generated by another area of the business or even a third-party supplier, such as an independent marketing research firm. Thus, companies must use information technology to capture, store, and integrate strategically important customer information. This process of centralizing data in a CRM system is referred to as data warehousing.

A **data warehouse** is a central repository (*database*) of data collected by an organization. Essentially,

it is a large computerized file of all information collected in the previous phase of the CRM process, for example, information collected in channel, transaction, and product or service touch points. The core of the data warehouse is the **database**, "a collection of data, especially one that can be accessed and manipulated by computer software."[8] The CRM database focuses on collecting vital statistics on consumers, their purchasing habits, transactions methods, and product usage in a centralized repository that is accessible by all functional areas of a company. By utilizing a data warehouse, marketing managers can quickly access vast amounts of information required to make decisions.

When a company builds its database, usually the first step is to develop a list. A **response list** is a customer list that includes the names and addresses of individuals who have responded to an offer of some kind, such as by mail, telephone, direct-response television, product rebates, contests or sweepstakes, or billing inserts. It can also be a compiled list, created by an outside company that has collected names and contact information for potential consumers. Response lists tend to be especially valuable because past behaviour is a strong predictor of future behaviour and because consumers who have indicated interest in the product or service are more likely to purchase in the future. **Compiled lists** usually are prepared by an outside company and are available for purchase. A compiled list is a customer list that was developed by gathering names and addresses gleaned from telephone directories or membership rosters, sometimes enhanced with information from public records, such as census data, auto registrations, birth announcements, business start-ups, or bankruptcies. Lists range from those owned by large list companies, such as Dun & Bradstreet, for business-to-business data, and Cornerstone Group of Companies for consumer lists, to small groups or associations that are willing to sell their membership lists. Data compiled by large data-gathering companies are usually very accurate.

In this phase, companies are usually collecting channel, transaction, product, and service information,

data warehouse a central repository of data from various functional areas of the organization that are stored and inventoried on a centralized computer system so that the information can be shared across all functional departments of the business

database a collection of data, especially one that can be accessed and manipulated by computer software

response list a customer list that includes the names and addresses of individuals who have responded to an offer of some kind, such as by mail, telephone, direct-response television, product rebates, contests or sweepstakes, or billing inserts

compiled list a customer list that was developed by gathering names and addresses gleaned from telephone directories and membership rosters, sometimes enhanced with information from public records, such as census data, auto registrations, birth announcements, business start-ups, or bankruptcies

DATA MINING

Wal-Mart currently has over 4,000 terabytes (millions of characters) of customer transaction data—that's roughly twice the amount of data contained in the entire Internet. Wal-Mart uses its huge data warehouse to help each of its stores adapt its merchandising mix to local neighbourhood preferences.[9]

such as stores, salespersons, communication channels, contacts in formation, relationships, and brands.

A customer database becomes even more useful to marketing managers when it is enhanced to include more than simply a customer's or prospect's name, address, telephone number, and transaction history. Database enhancement involves purchasing information on customers or prospects to better describe their needs or to determine how responsive they might be to marketing programs. Enhancement data typically include demographic, lifestyle, or behavioural information.

Database enhancement can increase the effectiveness of marketing programs. By learning more about their best and most profitable customers, marketers can maximize the effectiveness of their marketing communications and cross-selling. Database enhancement also helps a company find new prospects.

Multinational companies building worldwide databases often face difficult problems when pulling together internal data about their customers. Differences in language, computer systems, and data-collection methods can be huge obstacles to overcome. In spite of the challenges, many global companies are committed to building databases.

LO 6 Identifying the Best Customers

CRM manages interactions between a company and its customers. To be successful, companies need to identify those customers who yield high profits or high potential profits. To identify these customers, significant amounts of data must be gathered from customers, stored and integrated in the data warehouse, and then analyzed and interpreted for common patterns that can identify homogeneous customers who differ from other customer segments. Because not all customers are the same, organizations need to develop interactions that target the top 20 percent high-value customers' want and needs. Therefore, the question becomes how to identify these customers. In a CRM system, the answer is data mining.

Data Mining

Data mining is used to find hidden patterns and relationships in the customer data stored in the data warehouse. It is a data analysis approach that identifies patterns of characteristics that relate to particular customers or customer groups. Although businesses have been conducting such analyses for many years, the procedures typically were performed on small data sets containing as few as 300 to 400 customers. Today, with the development of sophisticated data warehouses, millions of customers' shopping patterns can be analyzed.

Using data mining, marketers can search the data warehouse, capture relevant data, categorize significant characteristics, and develop customer profiles. When using data mining, it is important to remember that the real value is in the company's ability to transform its data from operational bits and bytes into information marketers' need for successful marketing strategies. Companies must analyze the data

"COMPANIES MUST ANALYZE THE DATA TO **IDENTIFY** AND **PROFILE** THE BEST CUSTOMERS."

A WIDE RANGE OF COMPANIES USE DATA MINING[10]

- The Bay
- BMO
- RBC
- Philips
- Save-On-Foods
- Future Shop
- Your academic institution
- Your favourite company?

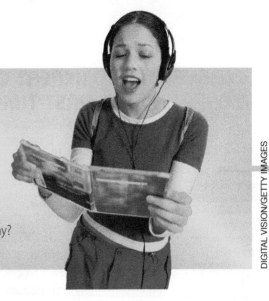

to identify and profile the best customers, calculate their lifetime value, and ultimately predict purchasing behaviour through statistical modelling. London Drugs uses data mining to identify commonly purchased items that should be displayed together on shelves and to learn what pop sells best in different parts of the country.

Before the information is leveraged, several types of analysis are often run on the data. These analyses include customer segmentation, recency-frequency-monetary (RFM) analysis, lifetime value (LTV) analysis, and predictive modelling.

Customer Segmentation Recall that *customer segmentation* is the process of breaking large groups of customers into smaller, more homogeneous groups. This type of analysis generates a profile, or picture, of the customers' similar demographic, geographic, and psychographic traits in addition to their previous purchase behaviour; it focuses particularly on the best customers. Profiles of the best customers can be compared and contrasted with other customer segments. For example, a bank can segment consumers on their frequency of usage, credit, age, and turnover.

Once a profile of the best customer is developed using these criteria, this profile can be used to screen other potential consumers. Similarly, customer profiles can be used to introduce customers selectively to specific marketing actions. For example, young customers with an open mind can be introduced to home banking. See Chapter 7 for a detailed discussion of segmentation.

Recency-Frequency-Monetary (RFM) Analysis Recency-frequency-monetary (RFM) analysis allows firms to identify customers who have purchased recently and often and who have spent considerable money, and are therefore the most likely to purchase again (see Exhibit 8.3). Firms develop equations to identify their best customers (often the top 20 percent of the customer base) by assigning a score to their customer records in the database on how often, how recently, and how much customers have spent. Customers are then ranked to determine which will move to the top of the list and which will fall to the bottom. The ranking provides the basis for maximizing profits by

> **recency-frequency-monetary (RFM) analysis** the analysis of customer activity as to recency, frequency, and monetary value

---

EXHIBIT 8.3
RFM Analysis: All Customers Are Not the Same

Best Customers	Average Customers	Poor Customers
High profit	Average profit	Low profit
Spent >$1,500	Spent approximately $400	Spent <$100
Multiple purchases	Two purchases	One purchase
Purchase in past 6 months	Purchase in past 18 months	Purchase in past two years
Lifetime value = high	Lifetime value = average	Lifetime value = low
$N = 2,500$ (18.5%)*	$N = 4,000$ (29.6%)*	$N = 7,000$ (51.9%)*
Total annual sales = $2.4 million	Total annual sales = $1.1 million	Total annual sales = $800,000

*N = number of customers in a category. The total number of customers is 13,500, and total annual sales are $4.3 million.

SOURCE: From LAMB/HAIR/MCDANIEL/FARIA/WELLINGTON. *MARKETING* 5E. © 2012 Nelson Education Ltd. Reproduced by permission. www.cengage.com/permissions.

"MARKETING TO **REPEAT CUSTOMERS** IS MORE PROFITABLE THAN MARKETING TO **FIRST-TIME BUYERS**."

lifetime value (LTV) analysis a data manipulation technique that projects the future value of the customer over a period of years using the assumption that marketing to repeat customers is more profitable than marketing to first-time buyers

predictive modelling a data manipulation technique in which marketers try to determine, based on some past set of occurrences, the odds that some other occurrence, such as an inquiry or purchase, will take place in the future

enabling the firm to use the information in its customer database to select those persons who have proved to be good sources of revenue.

Lifetime Value (LTV) Analysis Recency, frequency, and monetary data can also be used to create a lifetime value model on customers in the database. Whereas RFM looks at how valuable a customer currently is to a company, **lifetime value (LTV) analysis** projects the future value of the customer over a period of years. An example of LTV for a female aged 20 to 30 years old who has her hair done four times a year at an average cost of $120 per visit, given data-mined information of an average typical patronage life of five years, is $2,400 ($120/visit × 4 visits/year × 5 years). One of the basic assumptions in any LTV calculation is that marketing to repeat customers is more profitable than marketing to first-time buyers. That is, it costs more to find a new customer, in terms of promotion and gaining trust, than to sell more to a customer who is already loyal.

Customer lifetime value has numerous benefits. It shows marketers how much they can spend to *acquire* new customers, it tells them the level of spending to *retain* customers, and it facilitates targeting new customers who are identified as likely to be profitable customers.

Predictive Modelling The ability to reasonably predict future customer behaviour gives marketers a significant competitive advantage. Through **predictive modelling**, a data manipulation technique, marketers try to determine, using a past set of occurrences, the odds that some other occurrence, such as an inquiry or purchase, will take place in the future. SPSS Predictive Marketing is one tool marketers can use to answer questions about their consumers. The software requires minimal knowledge of statistical analysis. Users operate from a prebuilt model, which generates profiles in three to four days. SPSS also has an online product that predicts website users' behaviour.

LO7 Leverage Customer Information

Data mining identifies the most profitable customers and prospects. Managers can then design tailored marketing strategies to best appeal to the identified segments. In CRM, this activity is commonly referred to as leveraging customer information to facilitate enhanced relationships with customers.

Common CRM Marketing Database Applications

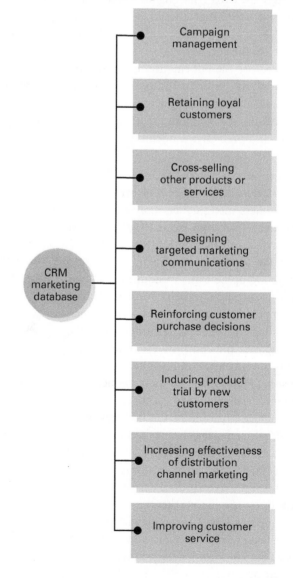

CRM marketing database

- Campaign management
- Retaining loyal customers
- Cross-selling other products or services
- Designing targeted marketing communications
- Reinforcing customer purchase decisions
- Inducing product trial by new customers
- Increasing effectiveness of distribution channel marketing
- Improving customer service

Campaign Management

Through campaign management, all areas of the company participate in the development of programs targeted to customers. **Campaign management** refers to developing product or service offerings customized for the appropriate customer segment and then pricing and communicating these offerings for the purpose of enhancing customer relationships. It involves monitoring and leveraging customer interactions to sell a company's products and to increase customer service. Campaigns are based directly on data obtained from customers through various interactions. Campaign management includes monitoring the success of the communications on the basis of customer reactions, such as customer inquiries, sales, orders, callbacks to the company, and the like. If a campaign appears unsuccessful, it is evaluated and changed to better achieve the company's desired objective.

Campaign management involves customizing product and service offerings, which requires managing multiple interactions with customers and giving priority to those products and services that are viewed as most desirable for a specifically designated customer. Even within a highly defined market segment, individual customer differences will emerge. Therefore, interactions among customers must focus on individual experiences, expectations, and desires.

Retaining Loyal Customers

After a company has identified its best customers, it should make every effort to maintain and increase their loyalty. When a company retains an additional 5 percent of its customers each year, profits will increase by as much as 25 percent. What's more, improving customer retention by a mere 2 percent can decrease costs by as much as 10 percent.[11]

Loyalty programs reward loyal customers for making multiple purchases. The objective is to build long-term mutually beneficial relationships between a company and its key customers. Marriott, Hilton, and Starwood Hotels, for instance, reward their best customers with special perks not available to customers who stay less frequently. Travellers who spend a specified number of nights per year receive reservation guarantees, welcome gifts such as fruit baskets and wine in their rooms, and access to concierge lounges. Loyal members who sign up to collect points can use their accumulated points to receive discounts at hotels in exotic locations, free nights, free flights, and reduced rates on car rentals. In addition to rewarding good customers, loyalty programs provide businesses with a wealth of information about their customers and shopping trends that can be used to make future business decisions.

campaign management developing product or service offerings customized for the appropriate customer segment and then pricing and communicating these offerings for the purpose of enhancing customer relationships

STAVING OFF THE COMPETITION

Stave Puzzles, the Rolls-Royce of puzzles, produces handcrafted wood puzzles. Each puzzle is unique and can be customized as the customer desires. Steve Richardson, the company's cofounder, has narrowed his customer base to his Hot Hundred most valuable customers. To manage his customer base and ensure they are receiving optimal service, he tracks not only standard information, such as contact data and orders, but also birthdays, anniversaries, relationships between customers, phone conversations, inquiries, and workshop visits.[12]

COURTESY OF STAVE PUZZLES

Loyal customers can receive special rewards!

Cross-Selling Other Products and Services

CRM provides many opportunities to cross-sell related products. Marketers can use the database to match product profiles with consumer profiles, enabling the cross-selling of products that match consumers' demographic, lifestyle, or behavioural characteristics. When the merger of Zellers and the Bay occurred, the resulting HBC Rewards Program had a database of some 500,000 names. Zellers used this database to identify customers who had bought fashion goods at the Bay but not at Zellers. These customers were sent direct-mail pieces about Zellers' new Mossimo line of fashions, resulting in a substantial increase in Zellers' sales to this target group.[13]

Internet companies use product and customer profiling to reveal cross-selling opportunities while a customer is surfing their site. Past purchases on a particular website and the website a surfer comes from provide online marketers with clues about the surfer's interests and what items to cross-sell. Similarly, profiles on customers enable sale representatives or customer service people to professionally personalize their communications while the customer is shopping. Knowing a customer's past purchases and preferences can enable the employee to provide more advice or suggestions that fit with the customer's tastes.

Designing Targeted Marketing Communications

By using transaction and purchase data, a database allows marketers to track customers' relationships to the company's products and services and to then modify their marketing message accordingly. Kraft Foods teamed with a supermarket chain to determine which advertising campaigns were most effective for frequent buyers of Kraft Macaroni & Cheese.[14]

Customers can also be segmented into infrequent users, moderate users, and heavy users. A segmented communications strategy can then be developed depending on the customer segment. Communications to infrequent users might encourage repeat purchases through a direct incentive, such as a limited-time coupon or price discount. Communications to moderate users may use fewer incentives and more reinforcement of their past purchase decisions. Communications to heavy users would be designed around loyalty and reinforcement of the purchase rather than price promotions.

Reinforcing Customer Purchase Decisions

As you learned in Chapter 5, cognitive dissonance is the feeling consumers get when they recognize an inconsistency between their values and opinions and their purchase behaviour. In other words, they doubt the soundness of their purchase decision and often feel anxious. CRM offers marketers an excellent opportunity to reach out to customers to reinforce the purchase decision. By thanking customers for their purchases and telling them they are important, marketers can help cement a long-term, profitable relationship.

Updating customers periodically regarding the status of their order reinforces purchase decisions. Postsale emails also afford the chance to provide more customer service or cross-sell other products.

Campion Boats of Kelowna, British Columbia, builds custom pleasure and recreational sport fishing boats that can cost upward of $200,000 each. The company uses its website to monitor customer profiles, broadcast company information, and communicate with its dealers and customers worldwide. For example, it can post pictures of a purchaser's boat in progress, thus both reinforcing the buyer's decision and perception of the quality of the craftsmanship and reducing the customer's likelihood of having feelings of cognitive dissonance.[15]

Inducing Product Trial by New Customers

Although significant time and money are expended on encouraging repeat purchases by the best customers, a marketing database is also used to identify new customers. Because a firm using a marketing database already has a profile of its best customers, it can easily use the results of modelling to profile potential customers. Bell Canada uses modelling to identify prospective residential and commercial telephone customers and successfully attract their business.

Marketing managers generally use demographic and behavioural data overlaid on existing customer data to develop a detailed customer profile that is a powerful tool for evaluating lists of prospects. For instance, if a firm's best customers are 35 to 50 years of age, live in suburban areas, and enjoy mountain climbing, the company can match this profile to prospects already in its database or to customers currently identified as using a competitor's product.

Increasing Effectiveness of Distribution Channel Marketing

In Chapter 12, you will learn that a marketing channel is a business structure of interdependent organizations, such as wholesalers and retailers, which move a

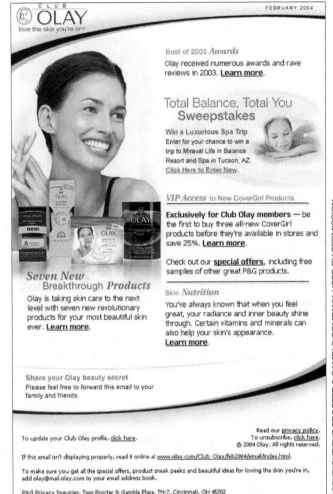

Olay, a brand of Procter & Gamble, invites customers to join Club Olay, which offers special discounts, free samples, and the opportunity to purchase products before they're available in stores. But members are also able to communicate with the company by sharing their beauty secrets and entering various sweepstakes.

product from the producer to the ultimate consumer. Most marketers rely on indirect channels to move their products to the end user. Thus, marketers often lose touch with the customer as an individual because the relationship is really between the retailer and the consumer. Marketers in this predicament often view their customers as aggregate statistics because specific customer information is difficult to gather.

Using CRM databases, manufacturers now have a tool to gain insight into who is buying their products. Instead of simply unloading products into the distribution channel and leaving marketing and relationship building to dealers, auto manufacturers today are using websites to keep in touch with customers and prospects, to learn about their lifestyles and hobbies, to understand their vehicle needs, and to develop relationships in hopes these consumers will reward them with brand loyalty in the future. BMW and other vehicle manufacturers have databases filled with contact information on the millions of consumers who have expressed an interest in their products.

With many brick-and-mortar stores setting up shop online, companies are now challenged to monitor purchases of customers who shop both in-store and online. This concept is referred to as multichannel marketing. After Lands' End determined that multichannel customers are the most valuable, the company targeted marketing campaigns toward retaining these customers and increased sales significantly.

Companies are also using radio-frequency identification (RFID) technology to improve distribution. This technology uses a microchip with an antenna that tracks anything from a pop can to a car. A computer can locate the product usually within two metres of a scanner but new technology and applications can, in some situations, enable detection up to 20 metres. The main implication of this technology is that companies will enjoy a reduction both in theft and in loss of merchandise shipments and will always know where merchandise is in the distribution channel. Moreover, as this technology is further developed, marketers will be able to gather essential information related to product usage and consumption.[16]

Improving Customer Service

CRM marketing techniques are increasingly being used to improve customer service. Many companies are using information and training webinars for their product or service in order to make personal contact with interested customers. Those interested in a topic are asked to register and provide a bit of information about themselves and their company's needs. Before or immediately after the webinar, a representative will contact them to answer questions and provide further information. Other companies, such as Canadian Tire, follow up customers' visits to the store with a call and a short survey to determine each customer's level of service satisfaction and whether any additional service is needed.

Privacy Concerns and CRM

Before rushing out to invest in a CRM system and build a database, marketers should consider consumers' reactions to the growing use of databases. Many customers are concerned about databases because of the potential for invasion of privacy. The sheer volume of information that is aggregated in databases makes this information vulnerable to unauthorized access and use. A fundamental aspect of marketing using CRM databases is providing valuable services to customers based on knowledge of what customers really value. It is critical, however, that marketers remember that these relationships should be built on trust. Although database technology enables marketers to compile ever-richer information about their customers that can be used to build and manage relationships, if these customers feel their privacy is being violated, then the relationship becomes a liability.

The popularity of the Internet for e-commerce and customer data collection and as a repository for sensitive customer data has alarmed privacy-minded customers. Online users complain loudly about being spammed, and Web surfers, including children, are routinely asked to divulge personal information to access certain screens or to purchase goods or services. Internet users are disturbed by the amount of information businesses collect on them as they visit various sites in cyberspace. Indeed, many users are unaware of how personal information is collected, used, and distributed. The government actively sells huge amounts of personal information to list companies. Consumer credit databases are often used by credit-card marketers to prescreen targets for solicitations. Online and off-line privacy concerns are growing and ultimately will have to be dealt with by businesses and regulators.

Privacy policies for Canadian companies are regulated by *Personal Information Protection and Electronic Documents Act* (PIPEDA) and the *Privacy Act*. But collecting data on consumers outside Canada is a different matter. For database marketers venturing beyond our borders, success requires careful navigation of foreign privacy laws. For example, under the European Union's European Data Protection

Directive, any business that trades with a European organization must comply with the EU's rules for handling information about individuals or risk prosecution. More than 50 nations have, or are developing, privacy legislation. Europe has the strictest legislation regarding the collection and use of customer data, and other countries look to that legislation when formulating their policies.

10%
Percentage decrease in costs resulting from a 2 percent increase in customer retention

Retaining 5% of customers can increase profits up to **25%**

Life expectancy of cellphones **2–3 years**

$8,000
Lifetime profit value of a loyal Pizza Hut customer

Lifetime value of a loyal Cadillac customer **$332,000**

4,000
Terabytes of customer data capacity in Wal-Mart's database

Visit **icanmktg2.com** to find the resources you need today!

Located at the back of the textbook are rip-out Chapter Review cards. Make sure you also go online to check out other tools that MKTG offers to help you successfully pass your course.

- Interactive Quizzing
- Games
- Flashcards
- Audio Summaries
- PowerPoint Slides

- Videos and Assessments
- Cases
- Marketing Plans and Worksheets
- Animated Visual Summaries

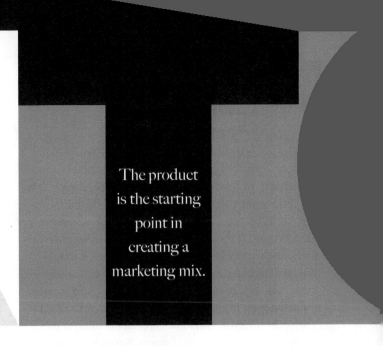

> The product is the starting point in creating a marketing mix.

AFTER YOU FINISH THIS CHAPTER, GO TO WWW. ICANMKTG2.COM FOR STUDY TOOLS.

DANA HOFF/BRAND X PICTURES/JUPITERIMAGES

LO1 What Is a Product?

The product offering, the heart of an organization's marketing program, is usually the starting point in creating a marketing mix. A marketing manager cannot determine a price, design a promotion strategy, or create a distribution channel until the firm has a product to sell. Moreover, an excellent distribution channel, a persuasive promotion campaign, and a fair price have no value when the product offering is poor or inadequate.

A **product** may be defined as everything, both favourable and unfavourable, received by a person in an exchange. A product may be a tangible good (a pair of shoes), a service (a haircut), an idea ("don't litter"), or any combination of these three. Packaging, style, colour, options, and size are some typical product features. Just as important are such intangibles as service, the seller's image, the manufacturer's reputation, and the way consumers believe others will view the product.

To most people, the term *product* means a tangible good, but services and ideas are also products. (Chapter 11 focuses specifically on the unique aspects of marketing services.) The marketing process identified in Chapter 1 is the same whether the product marketed is a good, a service, an idea, or some combination of these.

product everything, both favourable and unfavourable, received in an exchange

What do you think?

I pay attention to which brands I choose.

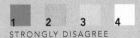

1   2   3   4   5   6   7
STRONGLY DISAGREE   STRONGLY AGREE

LO 2 Types of Consumer Products

Products can be classified as either business (industrial) or consumer products, depending on the buyer's intentions. The key distinction between the two types of products is their intended use. If the intended use is a business purpose, the product is classified as a business or industrial product. As explained in Chapter 6, a **business product** is used to manufacture other goods or services, to facilitate an organization's operations, or to resell to other customers. A **consumer product** is bought to satisfy an individual's personal wants. Sometimes the same item can be classified as either a business or a consumer product, depending on its intended use. Examples include light bulbs, pencils and paper, and computers.

We need to know about product classifications because business and consumer products are marketed differently. They are marketed to different target markets and tend to use different distribution, promotion, and pricing strategies.

Chapter 6 examined seven categories of business products: major equipment, accessory equipment, component parts, processed materials, raw materials, supplies, and services. This chapter examines an effective way of categorizing consumer products. Although they can be classified in several ways, the most popular approach includes these four types: convenience products, shopping products, specialty products, and unsought products. This approach classifies products according to how much effort is normally used to shop for them.

Convenience Products

A **convenience product** is a relatively inexpensive item that merits little shopping effort—that is, a consumer is unwilling to shop extensively for such an item. Candy, pop, small hardware items, dry cleaning, and car washes fall into the convenience product category.

Consumers buy convenience products regularly, usually without much planning. Nevertheless, consumers do know the brand names of popular convenience products, such as Coca-Cola, Colgate toothpaste, and Right Guard deodorant. Convenience products normally require wide distribution in order to sell sufficient quantities to make a profit. For example, the gum Dentyne Ice is available everywhere, including at Wal-Mart, Shoppers Drug Mart, Shell gas stations, newsstands, and vending machines.

Shopping Products

A **shopping product** is a product that requires comparison shopping because it is usually more expensive than a convenience product and is found in fewer stores. Consumers usually buy a shopping product only after comparing different brands' style, practicality, price, and lifestyle compatibility. Shoppers are typically willing to invest some effort into this process to get their desired benefits.

Shopping products can be divided into two types: homogeneous and heterogeneous. Consumers perceive *homogeneous* shopping products as being basically similar—for example, washers, dryers, refrigerators, and televisions. When shopping for homogeneous shopping products, consumers typically look for the lowest-priced brand that has the desired features. For example, consumers might compare Kenmore, Whirlpool, and General Electric refrigerators.

In contrast, consumers perceive *heterogeneous* shopping products as essentially different—for example, furniture, clothing, housing, and universities. Consumers often have trouble comparing heterogeneous shopping products because the prices, quality, and features vary so much. The benefit of comparing heterogeneous shopping products is that consumers can find the best product or brand for their needs, a decision that is often highly individual. For example, it can be difficult to compare a small, private university with a large, public university.

Specialty Products

When consumers search extensively for a particular item and are very reluctant to accept substitutes, that item is known as a **specialty product**. Patek Philippe watches,

---

business product (industrial product) a product used to manufacture other goods or services, to facilitate an organization's operations, or to resell to other customers

consumer product a product bought to satisfy an individual's personal wants

convenience product a relatively inexpensive item that merits little shopping effort

shopping product a product that requires comparison shopping because it is usually more expensive than a convenience product and is found in fewer stores

specialty product a particular item that consumers search extensively for and are very reluctant to accept substitutes for

---

Rolls-Royce automobiles, Bose speakers, Ruth's Chris Steak House, and highly specialized forms of medical care are generally considered specialty products.

Marketers of specialty products often use selective, status-conscious advertising to maintain their product's exclusive image. Distribution is often limited to one or a very few outlets in a geographic area. Brand names and quality of service are often very important.

Unsought Products

A product unknown to the potential buyer or a known product that the buyer does not actively seek is referred to as an **unsought product**. New products fall into this category until consumer awareness of them is increased through advertising and distribution.

Some goods are always marketed as unsought items, especially needed products that we do not like to think about or do not care to spend money on. Insurance, burial plots, and similar items require aggressive personal selling and highly persuasive advertising. Salespeople actively seek leads to potential buyers. Because consumers usually do not seek out this type of product, the company must approach customers directly through a salesperson, direct mail, or direct-response advertising.

LO 3 Product Items, Lines, and Mixes

Rarely does a company sell a single product. More often, it sells a variety of products. A **product item** is a specific version of a product that can be designated as a distinct offering among an organization's products. Campbell's Cream of Chicken soup is an example of a product item (see Exhibit 9.1).

A group of closely related product items is a **product line.** For example, the column in Exhibit 9.1 titled "Soups" represents one of Campbell's product lines. Different container sizes and shapes also distinguish items in a product line. Diet Coke, for example, is available in cans and various plastic containers. Each size and each container are separate product items.

An organization's **product mix** includes all the products it sells. All Campbell's products—soups, sauces, frozen entrées, beverages, and biscuits—constitute its product mix. Each product item in the product mix may require a separate marketing strategy. In some cases, however, product lines and even entire product mixes share some marketing strategy components. LG consumer electronics promotes all of its products with the same theme of "Life is Good." Organizations derive several benefits from organizing related items into product lines.

Product mix width (or breadth) refers to the number of product lines an organization offers. In Exhibit 9.1, for example, the width of Campbell's product mix is five product lines. **Product line depth** is the number of product items in a product line. As shown in Exhibit 9.1, the sauces

---

unsought product a product unknown to the potential buyer or a known product that the buyer does not actively seek

product item a specific version of a product that can be designated as a distinct offering among an organization's products

product line a group of closely related product items

product mix all products that an organization sells

product mix width the number of product lines an organization offers

product line depth the number of product items in a product line

---

EXHIBIT 9.1
Campbell's Product Lines and Product Mix

	Width of the Product Mix				
	Soups	**Sauces**	**Frozen Entrées**	**Beverages**	**Biscuits**
Depth of Product Line — DEPTH	Cream of Chicken	Mild Cheese	Chicken à la King	Tomato Juice	Arnott's:
	Cream of Mushroom	Alfredo	Beef Stew	V8 Juice	Water Cracker
	Vegetable Beef	Italian Tomato	Chicken Lasagna	V8 Splash	Butternut Snap
	Chicken Noodle	Marinara			Chocolate Chip
	Tomato				Fruit Oat
	Bean with Bacon				White Fudge
	Minestrone				
	Clam Chowder				
	French Onion				
	more…				

BENEFITS OF PRODUCT LINES

- **Advertising economies:** Product lines provide economies of scale in advertising. Several products can be advertised under the umbrella of the line. Campbell's can talk about its soup being "m-m-good" and promote the entire line.

- **Package uniformity:** A product line can benefit from package uniformity. All packages in the line may have a common look and still keep their individual identities. Again, Campbell's soup is a good example.

- **Standardized components:** Product lines allow firms to standardize components, thus reducing manufacturing and inventory costs. For example, General Motors uses the same parts on many automobile makes and models.

- **Efficient sales and distribution:** A product line enables sales personnel for companies such as Procter & Gamble to provide a full range of choices to customers. Distributors and retailers are often more inclined to stock the company's products if it offers a full line. Transportation and warehousing costs are likely to be lower for a product line than for a collection of individual items.

- **Equivalent quality:** Purchasers usually expect and believe that all products in a line are of equal quality. Consumers expect that all Campbell's soups and all Gillette razors will be of similar quality.

---

product modification
changing one or more of a product's characteristics

product line consists of four product items; the frozen entrée product line includes three product items.

Firms increase the *width* of their product mix to diversify risk. To generate sales and boost profits, firms spread risk across many product lines rather than depend on only one or two. Firms also widen their product mix to capitalize on established reputations. The Oreo Cookie brand has been extended to include items such as breakfast cereal, ice cream, Jell-O pudding, and cake mix.

Firms increase the *depth* of their product lines to attract buyers with different preferences, to increase sales and profits by further segmenting the market, to capitalize on economies of scale in production and marketing, and to even out seasonal sales patterns. P&G is adding some lower-priced versions of its namesake brands, including Bounty Basic and Charmin Basic. These brands are targeted to more price-sensitive customers, a segment that Procter & Gamble had not been serving with its more premium brands.[1]

Adjustments to Product Items, Lines, and Mixes

Over time, firms change product items, lines, and mixes to take advantage of new technical or product developments or to respond to changes in the environment. They may adjust by modifying products, repositioning products, or extending or contracting product lines.

Product Modification Marketing managers must decide if and when to modify existing products. **Product modification** changes one or more of a product's characteristics:

▸▸ *Quality modification:* a change in a product's dependability or durability. Reducing a product's quality may allow the manufacturer to lower the price, thereby appealing to target markets unable to afford the original product. Conversely, increasing quality can help the firm compete with rival firms. Increasing quality can also result in increased brand loyalty, greater ability to raise prices, or new opportunities for market segmentation. Inexpensive ink-jet printers have improved in quality to the point that they can now produce photo-quality images. These printers are now competing with camera film.

▸▸ *Functional modification:* a change in a product's versatility, effectiveness, convenience, or safety. Tide with Downy combines into one product the functions of both cleaning power and fabric softening.[2]

▸▸ *Style modification:* an aesthetic product change, rather than a quality or functional change. Clothing and auto manufacturers also commonly use style modifications to motivate customers to replace products before they are worn out.

Planned obsolescence describes the practice of modifying products so that those products that have already been sold become obsolete before they actually need replacement. Some argue that planned obsolescence is wasteful; some claim it is unethical. Marketers respond that consumers favour style modifications because they like changes in the appearance of goods like clothing and cars. Marketers also contend that consumers, not manufacturers and marketers, decide when styles are obsolete.

Repositioning Repositioning, as Chapter 7 explained, involves changing consumers' perceptions of a brand. Recently, Listerine, known for its antibacterial mouthwash qualities, has introduced among others, Listerine Whitening Plus Restoring, Listerine Total Care, and Listerine Zero to emphasize its new product positioning in the market. Similarly, Head & Shoulders has repositioned itself away from being a dandruff-only shampoo and introduced a total of ten different variations to suit different hair care needs. Changing demographics, declining sales, or changes in the social environment often motivate firms to reposition established brands.

GREAT TASTING & HEALTHY REFRESHMENT ON THE GO!

Adding new products to an existing line helps companies create variety and compete more broadly in their industries. Saputo extended its Milk2Go product line by introducing new flavours of milk as seen here at Milk2Go.com.

Product Line Extensions A **product line extension** occurs when a company's management decides to add products to an existing product line to compete more broadly in the industry. For example, the Diet Coke line includes multiple extensions: Diet Cherry Coke, Diet Coke with Lemon, and Diet Coke with Lime. Recently, Coca-Cola developed a brand extension for Diet Coke that was designed to appeal to men ages 18 to 34 who want a lower-calorie drink but see Diet Coke as a woman's drink. The product is called Coca-Cola Zero.[3]

planned obsolescence the practice of modifying products so those that have already been sold become obsolete before they actually need replacement

product line extension adding additional products to an existing product line to compete more broadly in the industry

Product Line Contraction Sometimes, marketers can get carried away with product extensions (Does the world really need 41 varieties of Crest toothpaste?) and some extensions are not embraced by the market, such as Vanilla Coke. Other times, contracting product lines is a strategic move. Heinz is deleting a number of product lines, such as vegetables, poultry, frozen foods, and seafood, to concentrate instead on the products it sells best: ketchup, sauces, frozen snacks, and baby food.[4]

Three major benefits are likely when a firm contracts its overextended product lines. First, resources become concentrated on the most important products. Second, managers no longer waste resources trying to improve the sales and profits of poorly performing products. Third, new product items have a greater

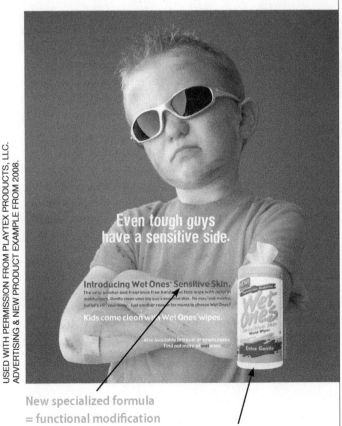

Even tough guys have a sensitive side.

Introducing Wet Ones® Sensitive Skin.

Kids come clean with Wet Ones® wipes.

New specialized formula = functional modification

New design or convenient transportation = style modification

YOUR BRAND'S OVEREXTENDED WHEN...

- some products in the line do not contribute to profits because of **low sales** or they cannibalize sales of other items in the line.
- manufacturing or marketing resources are disproportionately allocated to **slow-moving products**.
- some items in the line are **obsolete** because of new product entries in the line or new products offered by competitors.

chance of being successful because more financial and human resources are available to manage them.

LO 4 Branding

The success of any business or consumer product depends in part on the target market's ability to distinguish one product from another. Branding is the main tool marketers use to distinguish their products from the competition's.

A **brand** is a name, term, symbol, design, or combination thereof that identifies a seller's products and differentiates them from competitors' products. A **brand name** is that part of a brand that can be spoken, including letters (RIM, CML), words (Chevrolet), and numbers (WD-40, 7-Eleven). The elements of a brand that cannot be spoken are called the **brand mark**—for example, the well-known Mercedes-Benz and Air Canada symbols.

Benefits of Branding

Branding has three main purposes: product identification, repeat sales, and new-product sales. The most important purpose is *product identification*. Branding allows marketers to distinguish their products from all others. Many brand names are familiar to consumers and indicate quality.

The term **brand equity** refers to the value of company and brand names. A brand that has high awareness, high perceived quality, and high brand loyalty among customers is said to have high brand equity. Canadian Tire, Scotiabank, and Tim Hortons are companies with high brand equity. A brand with strong brand equity is a valuable asset.

The term **global brand** refers to a brand where at least 20 percent of the product is sold outside its home country or region. Yum! Brands, which owns Pizza Hut, KFC, and Taco Bell, is a good example of a company that has developed strong global brands. Yum! believes in adapting its restaurants to local tastes and different cultural and political climates. For example, in Japan, KFC sells tempura crispy strips; in northern England, it focuses on gravy and potatoes; and in Thailand, it offers rice with soy or sweet chili sauce.

The best generator of *repeat sales* is satisfied customers. Branding helps consumers identify those products they wish to buy again and avoid those they do not. **Brand loyalty**, a consistent preference for one brand over all others, is quite high in some product categories. More than half the users in product categories such as mayonnaise, toothpaste, coffee, headache remedies, photographic film, bath soap, and ketchup are loyal to one brand. Many students go to college or university and purchase the same brands they used at home rather than becoming price buyers. Brand identity is essential to developing brand loyalty.

The third main purpose of branding is to *facilitate new-product sales*. Having a well-known and respected company and brand name is extremely useful when introducing new products.

Branding Strategies

Firms face complex branding decisions, the first of which is whether to brand at all. Some firms actually

brand a name, term, symbol, design, or combination thereof that identifies a seller's products and differentiates them from competitors' products

brand name that part of a brand that can be spoken, including letters, words, and numbers

brand mark the elements of a brand that cannot be spoken

brand equity the value of company and brand names

global brand a brand where at least 20 percent of the product is sold outside its home country or region

brand loyalty a consistent preference for one brand over all others

EMILY BEREZIN

use the lack of a brand name as a selling point. These unbranded products are called generic products. Firms that decide to brand their products may choose to follow a policy of using manufacturers' brands, private (distributor) brands, or both. In either case, they must then decide among a policy of individual branding (different brands for different products), family branding (common names for different products), or a combination of individual branding and family branding.

Generic Products versus Branded Products A **generic product** is typically a no-frills, no-brand-name, low-cost product that is simply identified by its product category. (Note that a generic product is not the same as a brand name that becomes generic, such as cellophane.)

The main appeal of generics is their low price. Generic grocery products are usually 30 to 40 percent less expensive than manufacturers' brands in the same product category and 20 to 25 percent less expensive than retailer-owned brands. Pharmaceuticals are one example of a product category where generics have made large inroads. When patents on successful pharmaceutical products expire, low-cost generics rapidly appear on the market. For example, when the patent on Merck's popular anti-arthritis drug Clinoril expired, its sales declined by 50 percent almost immediately.

Manufacturers' Brands versus Private Brands The brand name of a manufacturer—such as Kodak, La-Z-Boy, and Fruit of the Loom—is called a **manufacturer's brand.** Sometimes *national brand* is used as

a synonym for *manufacturer's brand;* however, *national brand* is not always an accurate term because many manufacturers serve only regional markets. Using *manufacturer's brand* more precisely defines the brand's owner.

A **private brand**, also known as a private label or store brand, is a brand name owned by a wholesaler or a retailer. Private-label products made exclusively by retailers account for one of every five items sold in Canada, representing a large part of sales in some retail sectors.[5] The selection of private-branded products at Staples is growing by several hundred items a year, and these products account for approximately 20 percent of annual revenue. Staples is also unusual in that it is developing its own products rather than just putting its name on existing ones.[6] Part of the reason for the success of private brands is due to perceptions about quality. In 2005, a Nielsen online survey showed that more than two-thirds of global customers think private-label products are a good alternative to other

GLOBAL AND CANADIAN BRANDS

Top Five Global	Canadian
1. Coke	1. Thomson Reuters
2. IBM	2. TD Canada Trust
3. Microsoft	3. RBC
4. Google	4. BlackBerry
5. GE	5. Shoppers Drug Mart

SOURCES: http://www.interbrand.com/en/best-global-brands/best-global-brands-2008/best-globalbrands-2010.aspx, accessed February 9, 2011; http://www.interbrand.com/en/Interbrand-offices/Interbrand-Toronto/Best-Canadian-Brands-2010.aspx, accessed February 9, 2011.

Are you wasting your organization's most valuable advertising space?

You'd never run a blank advertisement for your organization. You'd never refuse to speak to a prospective buyer on the phone. So don't let your walking billboards, your people, travel silently around—empty canvasses for your image. Regardless of season or environment, we ensure you put forward a consistent, memorable image that's uniquely yours, with effective, integrated branded apparel and promotional programs.

Call one of our expert Corporate Sales Managers at 1.800.663.6275, email imagewear@erequest.ca or visit imagewear.ca

imagewear.ca
a division of Mark's Work Wearhouse

USED WITH PERMISSION FROM IMAGEWEAR, A DIVISION OF MARK'S WORK WEARHOUSE

The importance of integrated branding is reinforced by this Imagewear.ca advertisement.

individual branding using different brand names for different products

family brand marketing several different products under the same brand name

cobranding placing two or more brand names on a product or its package

brands, are an extremely good value, and offer quality that is at least as good as that of major manufacturer's brands.[7]

Retailers love consumers' greater acceptance of private brands. Because their overhead is low and these products have no marketing costs, private-label products bring 10 percent higher margins, on average, than manufacturers' brands. More than that, a trusted store brand can differentiate a chain from its competitors. Exhibit 9.2 illustrates key issues that wholesalers and retailers should consider in deciding whether to sell manufacturers' brands or private brands. Many firms offer a combination of both.

Individual Brands versus Family Brands Many companies use different brand names for different products, a practice referred to as **individual branding**. Companies use individual brands when their products vary greatly in use or performance. For instance, it would not make sense to use the same brand name for a pair of dress socks and a baseball bat. Procter & Gamble targets different segments of the laundry

detergent market with Bold, Cheer, Dash, Dreft, Era, Gain, Ivory Snow, Oxydol, Solo, and Tide.

In contrast, a company that markets several different products under the same brand name is using a **family brand**. Sony's family brand includes radios, television sets, stereos, and other electronic products. A brand name can only be stretched so far, however. Do you know the differences between Holiday Inn, Holiday Inn Express, Holiday Inn Select, Holiday Inn Sunspree Resort, Holiday Inn Garden Court, and Holiday Inn Hotel & Suites? Neither do most travellers.

Cobranding **Cobranding** involves placing two or more brand names on a product or its package. Three common types of cobranding are ingredient branding, cooperative branding, and complementary branding. *Ingredient branding* identifies the brand of a part that makes up the product, for example, an Intel microprocessor in a personal computer, such as Dell or Apple. *Cooperative branding* occurs when two brands receiving equal treatment (in the context of an advertisement) borrow on each other's brand equity. When Intel launched its Centrino wireless processor, it established cobranding relationships with Via Rail

---

EXHIBIT 9.2

Comparing Manufacturers' and Private Brands from the Reseller's Perspective

Key Advantages of Carrying Manufacturers' Brands	Key Advantages of Carrying Private Brands
• Heavy advertising to the consumer by well-known manufacturers such as Procter & Gamble helps develop strong consumer loyalties.	• A wholesaler or retailer can usually earn higher profits on its own brands. In addition, because the private brand is exclusive, the retailer is under less pressure to mark the price down to meet competition.
• Well-known manufacturers' brands, such as Kodak and Fisher-Price, can attract new customers and enhance the dealer's (wholesaler's or retailer's) prestige.	• A manufacturer can decide to drop a brand or a reseller at any time or even to become a direct competitor to its dealers.
• Many manufacturers offer rapid delivery, enabling the dealer to carry less inventory.	• A private brand ties the customer to the wholesaler or retailer. A person who wants Motomaster batteries must go to Canadian Tire.
• If a dealer happens to sell a manufacturer's brand of poor quality, the customer may simply switch brands and remain loyal to the dealer.	• Wholesalers and retailers have no control over the intensity of distribution of manufacturers' brands. Canadian Tire store managers don't have to worry about competing with other sellers of Motomaster automotive products. They know that these brands are sold only at Canadian Tire.

"**PRIVATE-LABEL** PRODUCTS MADE EXCLUSIVELY BY RETAILERS ACCOUNT FOR **ONE OF EVERY FIVE** ITEMS SOLD IN CANADA."

BETTER LETTERS?

For decades, cars had comprehensible names: Lincoln called its top-of-the-line model the Town Car, and Cadillac models included the DeVille and Eldorado. Recently, however, luxury automakers have favoured alphanumeric combinations, like the BMW M5, the Audi A8, the Lexus LS 450, and the renowned Mercedes S-class. The idea behind alphanumeric branding is to build the image of a whole brand, not just one model. But some letters are more popular than others, leading to brand confusion. For example, car models include the Mercedes S-class, the Audi S series, and the Jaguar S type; in addition, there is an Acura MDX and a Lincoln MKX.[8]

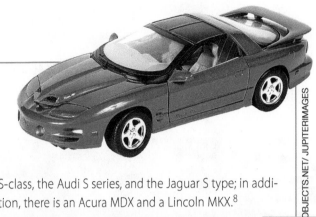

ZEDCOR WHOLLY OWNED/PHOTOOBJECTS.NET/ JUPITERIMAGES

Hot	Not	No Chance
X, S, and Z	O, P, U, Y	B (b-movie; second-class)
		F (failing; F-word)
		N (no; sounds like M)

---

and hotel chains Marriott International and Westin Hotels & Resorts because of the mutual value in establishing these relationships. Via Rail was able to set up WiFi access to reach Intel's target market of mobile professionals, while the hotel chains enabled Intel to target business professionals.[9] Finally, with *complementary branding*, products are advertised or marketed together to suggest usage, such as a spirits brand (Seagram's) and a compatible mixer (7-Up).

Cobranding is a useful strategy when a combination of brand names enhances the prestige or perceived value of a product or when it benefits brand owners and users. Cobranding may be used to increase a company's presence in markets where it has little or no market share. For example, Coach was able to build a presence in a whole new category when its leather upholstery with logo was used in Lexus automobiles.[10]

Trademarks

A **trademark** is the exclusive right to use a brand or part of a brand. Others are prohibited from using the brand without permission. A **service mark** performs the same function for services, such as H&R Block and Weight Watchers. Parts of a brand or other product identification may qualify for trademark protection. Some examples are

▶▶ shapes, such as the Jeep front grille and the Coca-Cola bottle

▶▶ ornamental colour or design, such as the decoration on Nike tennis shoes, the black-and-copper colour combination of a Duracell battery, Levi's small tag on the left side of the rear pocket of its jeans, or the cut-off black cone on the top of Cross pens

▶▶ catchy phrases, such as Sun Life Financial's "Life's brighter under the sun," Nike's "Just do it," and Budweiser's "This Bud's for you"

▶▶ abbreviations, such as Bud, Coke, or FedEx

▶▶ sounds, such as General Electric Broadcasting Company's ship's bell clock sound and the MGM lion's roar

It is important to understand that trademark rights come from use rather than registration. In Canada, trademarks are registered under the Trade-marks Act and Regulations. When a company registers a trademark, it must have a genuine intention to use it and must actually use it within three years of the application being granted. Trademark protection typically lasts

> **trademark** the exclusive right to use a brand or part of a brand
>
> **service mark** a trademark for a service

MGM PICTURES LOGO © TOPHAM/THE IMAGE WORKS

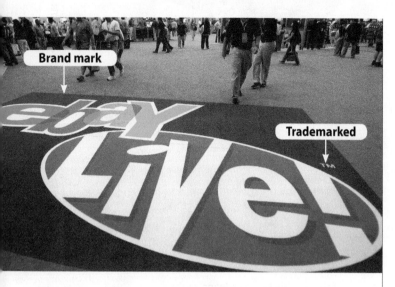

Brand mark

Trademarked

generic product name a term that identifies a product by class or type and cannot be trademarked

for 15 years. To renew the trademark, the company must prove it is using the mark. Rights to a trademark last as long as the mark is used. Normally, if the firm does not use a trademark for an extended period, it is considered abandoned, allowing a new user to claim exclusive ownership.

The Canadian Intellectual Property Office (CIPO) is responsible for registering trademarks and patents. Canada's Trade-marks Act and Regulations were updated in December 2008 to deal with the ever-increasing challenges posed by the complexities of modern business.

Companies that fail to protect their trademarks face the possibility that their product names will become generic. A **generic product name** identifies a product by class or type and cannot be trademarked. Former brand names that were not sufficiently protected by their owners and were subsequently declared to be generic product names by courts include cellophane, linoleum, thermos, kerosene, monopoly, cola, and shredded wheat.

Companies such as Rolls-Royce, Cross, Xerox, Levi Strauss, Frigidaire, and McDonald's aggressively enforce their trademarks. Rolls-Royce, Coca-Cola, and Xerox even run newspaper and magazine ads stating that their names are trademarks and should not be used as descriptive or generic terms. Some ads threaten lawsuits against competitors that violate trademarks.

Despite severe penalties for trademark violations, trademark infringement lawsuits are not uncommon. Some of the major battles involve brand names that

closely resemble an established brand name. Donna Karan filed a lawsuit against Donnkenny, Inc., whose NASDAQ trading symbol—DNKY—was too close to Karan's DKNY trademark.

Companies must also contend with fake or unauthorized brands. Knockoffs of Burberry's trademarked tan, black, white, and red plaid are easy to find in cheap shops all over the world, and loose imitations are also found in some reputable department stores. One website sells a line of plaid bags, hats, and shoes that it says are "inspired by Burberry." Burberry says it spends a couple million pounds a year running ads in trade publications and sending letters to trade groups, textile manufacturers, and retailers reminding them about its trademark rights. It also sues infringers, works with customs officials and local law enforcement to seize fakes, and scans the Internet to pick up online chatter about counterfeits.[11]

In Europe, you can sue counterfeiters only if your brand, logo, or trademark is formally registered. Until recently, formal registration was required in each country in which a company sought protection. Now, a company can use just one application to register its trademark in all European Union (EU) member countries.

LO5 Packaging

Packages have always served a practical function—that is, they hold contents together and protect goods as they move through the distribution channel. Today, however, packaging is also a container for promoting the product and making it easier and safer to use.

Packaging Functions

The three most important functions of packaging are to contain and protect products, to promote products, and to facilitate the storage, use, and convenience of products. A fourth function of packaging that is becoming increasingly important is to facilitate recycling and reduce environmental damage.

Containing and Protecting Products The most obvious function of packaging is to contain products that are liquid, granular, or otherwise divisible.

Packaging also enables manufacturers, wholesalers, and retailers to market products in specific quantities, such as kilograms.

Physical protection is another obvious function of packaging. Most products are handled several times between the time they are manufactured, harvested, or otherwise produced and the time they are consumed or used. Many products are shipped, stored, and inspected several times between production and consumption. Some products, such as milk, need to be refrigerated. Others, such as beer, are sensitive to light. Still others, such as medicines and bandages, need to be kept sterile. Packages protect products from breakage, evaporation, spillage, spoilage, light, heat, cold, infestation, and many other conditions.

Promoting Products Packaging does more than identify the brand, list the ingredients, specify features, and give directions. A package differentiates a product from competing products and may associate a new product with a family of other products from the same manufacturer. Welch's repackaged its line of grape juice–based jams, jellies, and juices to unify the line and get more impact on the shelf.

Packages use designs, colours, shapes, and materials to try to influence consumers' perceptions and buying behaviour. For example, marketing research shows that health-conscious consumers are likely to think that any food is probably good for them as long as it comes in green packaging. Packaging can also influence consumer perceptions of quality and prestige. And packaging has a measurable effect on sales. Quaker Oats revised the package for Rice-a-Roni without making any other changes in marketing strategy and experienced a 44 percent increase in sales in one year.

Facilitating Storage, Use, and Convenience Wholesalers and retailers prefer packages that are easy to ship, store, and stock on shelves. They also like packages that protect products, prevent spoilage or breakage, and extend the product's shelf life.

Consumers' requirements for storage, use, and convenience cover many dimensions. Consumers are constantly seeking items that are easy to handle, open, and reclose, and some consumers want packages that are tamper-proof or childproof. Research indicates that hard-to-open packages are among consumers' top complaints.[12] Surveys conducted by *Sales & Marketing Management* magazine revealed that consumers dislike—and avoid buying—leaky ice cream boxes, overly heavy or fat vinegar bottles, immovable pry-up lids on glass bottles, key-opener sardine cans, and hard-to-pour cereal boxes. Such packaging innovations as zipper tear strips, hinged lids, tab slots, screw-on tops, and pour spouts were introduced to solve these and other problems. Easy openings are especially important for kids and aging baby boomers.

Some firms use packaging to segment markets. For example, a C&H sugar carton with an easy-to-pour, reclosable top is targeted to consumers who don't do a lot of baking and are willing to pay at least 20 cents more for the package. Different-size packages appeal to heavy, moderate, and light users. Campbell's soup is packaged in single-serving cans aimed at the elderly and singles market segments. Packaging convenience can increase a product's utility and, therefore, its market share and profits.

Facilitating Recycling and Reducing Environmental Damage One of the most important packaging issues today is compatibility with the environment. Some firms use their packaging to target environmentally concerned market segments. Brocato International markets shampoo and hair conditioner in bottles that are biodegradable in landfills. Products as different as deodorant and furniture polish are packaged in eco-friendly, pump-spray packages that do not rely on aerosol propellants.

Labelling

An integral part of any package is its label. Labelling generally takes one of two forms: being persuasive or informational. **Persuasive labelling** focuses on a promotional theme or logo, and consumer information is

"PACKAGING CAN ALSO INFLUENCE CONSUMER **PERCEPTIONS OF QUALITY**."

persuasive labelling package labelling that focuses on a promotional theme or logo, and consumer information is secondary

informational labelling package labelling designed to help consumers make proper product selections and to lower their cognitive dissonance after the purchase

universal product codes (UPCs) a series of thick and thin vertical lines (bar codes), readable by computerized optical scanners that match the codes to brand names, package sizes, and prices

secondary. Note that the standard promotional claims—such as "new," "improved," and "super"—are no longer very persuasive. Consumers have been saturated with "newness" and thus discount these claims.

Informational labelling, in contrast, is designed to help consumers make proper product selections and to lower their cognitive dissonance after the purchase. Sears attaches a "label of confidence" to all its floor coverings. This label gives such product information as durability, colour, features, cleanability, care instructions, and construction standards. Most major furniture manufacturers affix labels to their wares that explain the products' construction features, such as type of frame, number of coils, and fabric characteristics. The Consumer Packaging and Labelling Act mandated detailed nutritional information on most food packages and standards for health claims on food packaging. An important outcome of this legislation has been guidelines from Health Canada for the use of such terms as *low fat, light, reduced cholesterol, low sodium, low calorie, low carb,* and *fresh*.

Universal Product Codes

The **universal product codes (UPCs)** that now appear on most items in supermarkets and other high-volume outlets were first introduced in 1974. Because the numerical codes appear as a series of thick and thin vertical lines, they are often called *bar codes*. The lines are read by computerized optical scanners that match the codes to brand names, package sizes, and prices. They also print information on cash register tapes and help retailers rapidly and accurately prepare records of customer purchases, control inventories, and track sales. The UPC system and scanners are also used in single-source research (see Chapter 4).

LO 6 Global Issues in Branding and Packaging

When planning to enter a foreign market with an existing product, a firm has three options for handling the brand name:

▸▸ *One brand name everywhere:* This strategy is useful when the company markets mainly one product and the brand name does not have negative connotations in any local market. The Coca-Cola Company uses a one-brand-name strategy in 195 countries around the world. The advantages of a one-brand-name strategy are greater identification of the product from market to market and ease of coordinating the promotion from market to market.

▸▸ *Adaptations and modifications:* A one-brand-name strategy is not possible when the name cannot be pronounced in the local language, when the brand name is owned by someone else, or when the brand name has a negative or vulgar connotation in the local language. The Iranian detergent "Barf," for example, might encounter some resistance in the Canadian market.

▸▸ *Different brand names in different markets:* Local brand names are often used when translation or pronunciation problems occur, when the marketer wants the brand to appear to be a local brand, or when regulations require localization. Henkel's Silkience hair conditioner is called Soyance in France and Sientel in Italy. The adaptations were deemed to be more appealing in the local markets. Coca-Cola's Sprite brand had to be renamed Kin in Korea to satisfy a government prohibition on the unnecessary use of foreign words.

In addition to global branding decisions, companies must consider global packaging needs. Three aspects of packaging especially important in international marketing are labelling, aesthetics, and climate considerations. The major concern is properly translating ingredient, promotional, and instructional information on labels. Care must also be employed in meeting all local labelling requirements. Several years ago, an Italian judge ordered that all bottles of Coca-Cola be removed from retail shelves because the ingredients were not properly labelled. In Canada, by law, labelling is required to be bilingual.

Package *aesthetics* may also require some attention. Even though simple visual elements of the brand, such as a symbol or logo, can be a standardizing element across products and countries, marketers must stay attuned to cultural traits in host countries. For example, colours may have different connotations. In some countries, red is associated with witchcraft, green may be a sign of danger, and white may be symbolic of death. Aesthetics also influence package sizes. Pop is not sold in six-packs in countries that lack refrigeration. In some countries, products such as detergent may be bought only in small quantities because of a lack of storage space. Other products, such as cigarettes, may be bought in small quantities, and even single units, because of the low purchasing power of buyers.

Extreme *climates* and long-distance shipping necessitate sturdier and more durable packages for goods sold overseas. Spillage, spoilage, and breakage are all more important concerns when products are shipped long distances or are frequently handled during shipping and storage. Packages may also have to ensure a longer product life if the time between production and consumption lengthens significantly.

LO 7 Product Warranties

Just as a package is designed to protect the product, a warranty protects the buyer and provides essential information about the product. A **warranty** confirms the quality or performance of a good or service. An **express warranty** is a written guarantee. Express warranties range from simple statements—such as "100 percent cotton" (a guarantee of quality) and "complete satisfaction guaranteed" (a statement of performance)—to extensive documents written in technical language. In contrast, an **implied warranty** is an unwritten guarantee that the good or service is fit for the purpose for which it was sold.

Although court rulings might suggest that all products sold in Canada carry an implied warranty, actual warranties do vary depending on the province or territory. At the federal level, protection against misleading warranties is provided under the Competition Act. In general, products sold must be free from encumbrances (the seller must have clear title to ownership), the descriptions of the product on the package must be accurate, the product must be fit for its intended purpose, and the product must be of reasonable durability.

warranty a confirmation of the quality or performance of a good or service

express warranty a written guarantee

implied warranty a n unwritten guarantee that the good or service is fit for the purpose for which it was sold

4
Types of consumer products; functions of packaging

195
Number of countries where the Coca-Cola brand name is used

1974
Year the bar code was introduced

20%
Percentage of a brand's revenue that has to come from international sources before it can be considered a global brand

Developing and Managing Products

The average fast-moving consumer goods company introduces 70 to 80 new products per year.

HIROSHI WATANABE/DIGITAL VISION/JUPITERIMAGES

LO 1 The Importance of New Products

New products are important to sustain growth, increase revenues and profits, and replace obsolete items. According to a Boston Consulting Group survey of senior executives, more than two-thirds cite innovation as a priority but 57 percent are dissatisfied with the returns on their innovation investments.[1] It is no wonder. Despite spending huge sums on research and development, most companies have many more failures than successes. According to Doblin Group, innovation consultants, the overall innovation initiative success rate is a dismal 4.5 percent.[2] Companies that do a particularly good job at product innovation include Apple, 3M, GE, and Sony.[3] The average fast-moving consumer goods company introduces 70 to 80 new products per year.[4] In one recent year, PepsiCo introduced more than 200 new products. In 2011, Kellogg's announced it would launch more than $800 million worth of new products during the year. For both PepsiCo and Kellogg's, their share of sales from new products far exceeds their respective industry averages.[5]

new product a product new to the world, new to the market, new to the producer or seller, or new to some combination of these

Categories of New Products

The term **new product** can be confusing because its meaning varies widely. Actually, the term has several correct definitions. A product can be new to the world, new

What do you think?

Getting the newest products is always extremely exciting.

1   2   3   4   5   6   7
STRONGLY DISAGREE   STRONGLY AGREE

TEN OF THE MOST IMPORTANT

new-to-the-world products introduced in the past 100 years are:

1. Penicillin
2. Transistor radio
3. Polio vaccine
4. Mosaic (the first graphic Web browser)
5. Microprocessor
6. Black-and-white television
7. Plain paper copier
8. Alto personal computer (prototype of today's PCs)
9. Microwave oven
10. Arpanet network (the groundwork for the Internet)[6]

to the market, new to the producer or seller, or new to some combination of these. New products have six categories:

▸▸ *New-to-the-world products (also called discontinuous innovations):* These products create an entirely new market. New-to-the-world products represent the smallest category of new products.

▸▸ *New product lines:* These products, which the firm has not previously offered, allow the firm to enter an established market. After Procter & Gamble purchased Iams pet food brand, its worldwide sales doubled and profits tripled. The brand moved from the fifth best-selling pet food brand in the United States to the top spot in less than five years.[7]

▸▸ *Additions to existing product lines:* This category includes new products that supplement a firm's established line. Examples of product line additions include Huggies Pull-Ups, Pampers Kandoo baby wipes, and other personal care products for kids.

▸▸ *Improvements or revisions of existing products:* The new and improved product may be significantly or slightly changed. Gillette's Fusion and Fusion Power razors are examples of product improvements. Another type of revision is package improvement. The Heinz EZ Squirt

Ketchup bottle is short and made from easy-to-squeeze plastic; its needle-shaped nozzle lets small hands use it to decorate food. Most new products fit into the revision or improvement category.

▸▸ *Repositioned products:* These are existing products targeted at new markets or new market segments. For example, General Motors successfully repositioned its tired, defeated Cadillac luxury brand as a direct competitor to European brands such as BMW and Lexus.[8] BMW and Mercedes have been competing for the top spot in the Canadian luxury car market for many years. In 2010, Mercedes took the first place from BMW in Canada.[9]

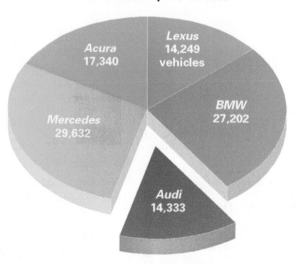

2010 Sales Volume in the Canadian Luxury Car Market

- Acura 17,340
- Lexus 14,249 vehicles
- BMW 27,202
- Mercedes 29,632
- Audi 14,333

▸▸ *Lower-priced products:* This category refers to products that provide performance similar to competing brands at a lower price. Hewlett-Packard Laser Jet 3100 is a scanner, copier, printer, and fax machine combined. This new product is priced lower than many conventional colour copiers and much lower than the combined price of the four items purchased separately.

LO 2 The New-Product Development Process

The management consulting firm Booz Allen Hamilton has studied the new-product development process for more than 30 years. After analyzing five major studies undertaken during this period, the firm concluded that the companies most likely to succeed in developing

EXHIBIT 10.1
New-Product Development Process

1 New-product strategy
2 Idea generation
3 Idea screening
4 Business analysis
5 Development
6 Test marketing
7 Commercialization

New product

and introducing new products are those that take the following actions:

▶▶ Make the long-term commitment needed to support innovation and new-product development.

▶▶ Use a company-specific approach, driven by corporate objectives and strategies, with a well-defined new-product strategy at its core.

▶▶ Capitalize on experience to achieve and maintain competitive advantage.

▶▶ Establish an environment—a management style, organizational structure, and degree of top-management support—conducive to achieving company-specific new-product and corporate objectives.

Most companies follow a formal new-product development process, usually starting with a new-product strategy. Exhibit 10.1 traces the seven-step process, which is discussed in detail in this section. The exhibit is funnel-shaped to highlight the fact that each stage acts as a screen. The purpose is to filter out unworkable ideas.

New-Product Strategy

A **new-product strategy** links the new-product development process with the objectives of the marketing department, the business unit, and the corporation. A new-product strategy must be compatible with these objectives, and, in turn, all three objectives must be consistent with one another.

A new-product strategy is part of the organization's overall marketing strategy. It sharpens the focus and provides general guidelines for generating, screening, and evaluating new-product ideas. The new-product strategy specifies the roles that new products must play in the organization's overall plan and describes the characteristics of products the organization wants to offer and the markets it wants to serve.

The importance of having a well-thought-out new-product strategy is illustrated by a Dun & Bradstreet finding that for each successful new product introduced, a company needs another 50 to 60 new-product ideas in the new-product development process.[10] Gillette aims for 40 percent of annual sales to be generated from products less than five years old.[11]

Idea Generation

New-product ideas come from many sources, including customers, employees, distributors, competitors, vendors, research and development (R&D), and consultants.

▶▶ *Customers:* The marketing concept suggests that customers' wants and needs should be the springboard for developing new products. Many of today's most innovative and successful marketers have taken the approach of introducing fewer new products, but taking the necessary steps to ensure these chosen few are truly unique, better, and, above all, really do address unmet consumer needs. How do they do that? They begin and end development with the customer.[12] The most common

KAYROS STUDIO "BE HAPPY"/SHUTTERSTOCK.COM

"FOR **EACH SUCCESSFUL NEW PRODUCT** INTRODUCED, A COMPANY NEEDS ANOTHER **50 TO 60 NEW-PRODUCT IDEAS** IN THE NEW-PRODUCT DEVELOPMENT PROCESS."

techniques for gathering new-product ideas from consumers are surveys, focus groups, observation, and mining blogs. Umbria Communications scours 13 million blogs to determine what consumers are saying about new products and trends. Electronic Arts uses Umbria to determine what bloggers are saying about upcoming games so it can predict demand.[13]

▶▶ *Employees:* Marketing personnel—advertising and marketing research employees, as well as salespeople—often create new-product ideas because they analyze and are involved in the marketplace. Encouraging employees from different divisions to exchange ideas is also a useful strategy. The developers of Mr. Clean AutoDry turned to scientists who worked on PUR water purification and Cascade dishwashing detergent to learn how to dry dishes without spotting.[14] Some firms reward employees for coming up with creative new ideas. Procter & Gamble, for example, offers stock options as a reward. At Google, employees can spend up to 20 percent of their time working on individual projects called Googlettes.[15]

▶▶ *Distributors:* A well-trained sales force routinely asks distributors about needs that are not being met. Because distributors are closer to end users, they are often more aware of customer needs than are manufacturers. The inspiration for Rubbermaid's Sidekick, a litter-free lunch box, came from a distributor's suggestion that the company place some of its plastic containers inside a lunch box and sell the set as an alternative to wrapping lunches in plastic wrap and paper bags.

▶▶ *Competitors:* No firms rely solely on internally generated ideas for new products. A big part of any organization's marketing intelligence system should be monitoring the performance of competitors' products. One purpose of competitive monitoring is to determine which, if any, of the competitors' products should be copied. Many companies form alliances with competitors to market new and existing products. Procter & Gamble and Clorox combined the patented adhesive-film technology that P&G uses in its packaging to develop Glad Press'n Seal food storage wrap.[16]

▶▶ *Vendors:* 7-Eleven regularly forges partnerships with vendors to create proprietary products such as Candy Gulp

PR NEWSWIRE/ASSOCIATED PRESS

(a plastic cup filled with Gummies) and Blue Vanilla Laffy Taffy Rope candy developed by Nestlé's Wonka division exclusively for 7-Eleven.

▶▶ *Research and development:* R&D is carried out in four distinct ways. You learned about basic research and applied research in Chapter 3. The other two ways are product development and product modification. **Product development** goes beyond applied research by converting applications into marketable products. Product modification makes cosmetic or functional changes in existing products. Many new-product breakthroughs come from R&D activities. Balancing the need to develop new products with pressure to lower costs creates a difficult dilemma for many managers. Although companies spend billions of dollars every year on research and development, as many as 40 percent of managers think their companies are not doing enough to develop new products.[17] Two companies have made major commitments to building competitive advantage through R&D: Procter & Gamble, with 7,500 researchers located in 20 technical facilities in nine countries, and Toyota Motor Corporation, which spends $8 billion per year on research and product development—twice as much as either General Motors or Ford spends.[18] Some companies are establishing innovation laboratories to complement or even replace traditional R&D programs. Idea labs focus on substantially increasing the speed of innovation. Despite the important role that idea labs play in the systematic development of new products, it is critical to realize that not all new products are developed in this manner. For example, the glass touchscreen used on iPhones had been initially developed by Corning, but it was never commercially produced. Steve Jobs, in a conversation with the then–Corning CEO, realized that Corning had the capability to produce the kind of glass he wanted for iPhone screens.

▶▶ *Consultants:* Outside consultants are always available to examine a business and recommend product ideas. Examples include the Weston Group, Booz Allen Hamilton, and Management Decisions. Traditionally, consultants determine whether a company has a balanced portfolio of products and, if not, which new-product ideas are needed to offset the imbalance.

Creativity is the wellspring of new-product ideas, regardless of who comes up with them. A variety of approaches and techniques have been developed to stimulate creative thinking. The two considered most useful for generating new-product ideas are brainstorming and focus-group exercises. The goal of **brainstorming** is to get a group to think of unlimited ways to vary a product or solve a problem. Group members avoid criticism of an idea, no matter how ridiculous it may seem. Objective evaluation is postponed. The sheer quantity of ideas is what matters. As noted in Chapter 4, an objective of focus-group interviews is to stimulate insightful comments through group interaction. Focus groups usually consist of seven to ten people. Sometimes consumer focus groups generate excellent new-product ideas. In the industrial market, focus groups have led to the evolution of machine tools, keyboard designs, aircraft interiors, and backhoe accessories.

Idea Screening

After new ideas have been generated, they pass through the first filter in the product development process. This stage, called **screening**, eliminates ideas that are inconsistent with the organization's new-product strategy or are obviously inappropriate for some other reason. The screening review is performed by the new-product committee, the new-product department, or some other formally appointed group. General Motors' Advanced Portfolio Exploration Group (APEx) knows that only one out of every twenty new car concepts developed by the group will ever become a reality. That's not a bad percentage. In the pharmaceutical business, one new product out of 5,000 ideas is not uncommon.[19] Most new-product ideas are rejected at the screening stage.

Concept tests are often used at the screening stage to rate concept (or product) alternatives. A **concept test** is an evaluation of a new-product idea, usually before any prototype has been created. Typically, researchers survey consumer reactions to descriptions and visual representations of a proposed product.

Concept tests are considered fairly good predictors of success for line extensions. They have also been relatively precise predictors of success for new products that are not copycat items, are not easily classified into existing product categories, and do not require major changes in consumer behaviour—such as Betty Crocker Tuna Helper and Libby's Fruit Float. Concept tests are usually inaccurate, however, in predicting the success of new products that create new consumption patterns and require major changes in consumer behaviour—such as microwave ovens, videocassette recorders, computers, and word processors.

Business Analysis

New-product ideas that survive the initial screening process move to the **business analysis** stage, the second stage of the screening process, where preliminary figures for demand, cost, sales, and profitability are calculated. For the first time, costs and revenues are estimated and compared. Depending on the nature of the product and the company, this process may be simple or complex.

The newness of the product, the size of the market, and the nature of the competition all affect the accuracy of revenue projections. In an established market such as the pop business, industry estimates of total market size are available. Forecasting market share for a new entry is a bigger challenge.

Analyzing overall economic trends and their impact on estimated sales is especially important in product categories that are sensitive to fluctuations in the business cycle. If consumers view the economy as uncertain and risky, they will put off buying durable goods such as major home appliances, automobiles, and homes. Likewise, business buyers postpone major equipment purchases if they expect a recession.

Answering questions during the business analysis stage may require studying the new product's markets, competition, costs, and technical capabilities. But at the end of this stage, management should have a good understanding of the product's market potential. This understanding is important because costs increase dramatically once a product idea enters the development stage.

Development

In the early stage of **development**, the R&D or engineering department may develop a prototype of the product. During this stage, the firm should start sketching a marketing strategy. The marketing department should decide on the product's packaging, branding, labelling, and so forth. In addition, it should map out strategies for the product's preliminary promotion, price, and distribution. The feasibility of manufacturing the product at an acceptable cost should be thoroughly examined. The development stage can last

brainstorming the process of getting a group to think of unlimited ways to vary a product or solve a problem

screening the first filter in the product development process, which eliminates ideas that are inconsistent with the organization's new-product strategy or are obviously inappropriate for some other reason

concept test evaluation of a new-product idea, usually before any prototype has been created

business analysis the second stage of the screening process, where preliminary figures for demand, cost, sales, and profitability are calculated

development the stage in the product development process in which a prototype is developed and a marketing strategy is outlined

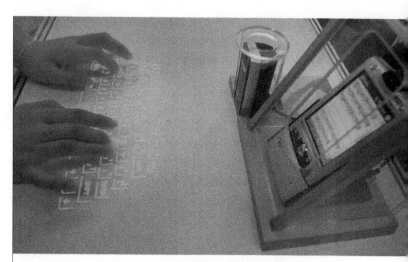

simultaneous product development a team-oriented approach to new-product development

a long time and thus be very expensive. It took 10 years to develop Crest toothpaste, 15 years to develop the Polaroid Colorpack camera, 15 years to develop the Xerox copy machine, 18 years to develop Minute Rice, and 51 years to develop television. Gillette developed three shaving systems over a 27-year period (TracII, Atra, and Sensor) before introducing the Mach3 in 1998 and Fusion in 2006.[20] Gillette Fusion is the P&G product that has reached the $1 billion sales mark in the shortest time.[21]

The development process works best when all the involved areas (R&D, marketing, engineering, production, and even suppliers) work together rather than sequentially, a process called **simultaneous product development**. This approach allows firms to shorten the development process and reduce costs. In simultaneous product development, all relevant functional areas and outside suppliers participate in all stages of the development process. Rather than proceeding through highly structured stages, the cross-functional team operates in unison. Involving key suppliers early in the process capitalizes on their knowledge and enables them to develop critical component parts. In 1996, General Motors took more than 48 months to develop a new

A hostess demonstrates a prototype of a touch-sensitive screen that can be rolled or folded and used as a computer or tablet at the Asus stand at the CeBIT Technology Fair on March 3, 2010, in Hanover, Germany.

CHINAFOTOPRESS/GETTY IMAGES

vehicle. Simultaneous product development helped GM to reduce that time to approximately 18 months.[22]

The Internet is a useful tool for implementing simultaneous product development. On the Net, multiple partners from a variety of locations can meet regularly to assess new-product ideas, analyze markets and demographics, and review cost information. Ideas judged to be feasible can quickly be converted into new products. Without the Internet, it would be impossible to conduct simultaneous product development from different parts of the world. Global R&D is important for two reasons. First, large companies have become global and no longer focus on only one market. Global R&D is necessary to connect with customers in different parts of the world. Second, companies want to tap into the world's best talent—which isn't always found in North America.[23]

Some firms use online brain trusts to solve technical problems. InnoCentive Inc. is a network of 80,000 self-selected science problem solvers in 173 countries. Its clients include Boeing, DuPont, and Procter & Gamble. More than one-third of the two dozen requests submitted to InnoCentive's network by P&G have been solved. Problem solvers are paid $10,000 or more for their solutions. As a result of working with InnoCentive and other initiatives, P&G has increased the proportion of its new products derived from outside sources from 20 to 35 percent in a three-year period.[24] Innovative firms are also gathering a variety of R&D input from customers online. Google polls millions of Web page creators to determine the most relevant search results.[25]

THE BUSINESS ANALYSIS STAGE— COMMON QUESTIONS

▸▸ What is the likely demand for the product?

▸▸ What impact is the new product likely to have on total sales, profits, market share, and return on investment?

▸▸ How will the introduction of the product affect existing products? Will the new product cannibalize existing products?

▸▸ Will current customers benefit from the product?

▸▸ Does the product enhance the image of the company's overall product mix?

▸▸ Will the new product affect current employees in any way? Will it lead to hiring more people or reducing the size of the workforce?

▸▸ What new facilities, if any, are needed?

▸▸ How might competitors respond?

▸▸ What is the risk of failure? Is the company willing to take the risk?

Laboratory tests are often conducted on prototype models during the development stage. User safety is an important aspect of laboratory testing, which actually subjects products to much more severe treatment than is expected by end users. The Canada Consumer Product Safety Act requires manufacturers to conduct a reasonable testing program to ensure that their products conform to established safety standards.

Many products that test well in the laboratory are also tried out in homes or businesses. Examples of product categories well suited for such tests include human and pet food products, household cleaning products, and industrial chemicals and supplies. These products are all relatively inexpensive, and their performance characteristics are apparent to users. For example, Procter & Gamble tests a variety of personal and home-care products in the community around its Cincinnati, Ohio, headquarters.

Test Marketing

After products and marketing programs have been developed, they are usually tested in the marketplace. **Test marketing** is the limited introduction of a product and a marketing program to determine the reactions of potential customers in a market situation. Test marketing allows management to evaluate alternative strategies and to assess how well the various aspects of the marketing mix fit together. Even established products are test marketed to assess new marketing strategies.

The cities chosen as test sites should reflect market conditions in the new product's projected market area. Yet no city exists that can universally represent market conditions, and a product's success in one city doesn't guarantee it will be a nationwide hit. When selecting test market cities, researchers should therefore find locations where the demographics and purchasing habits mirror the overall market. The company should also have good distribution in test cities. Moreover, test locations should be isolated from the media. If the TV stations in a particular market reach a very large area outside the test market, the advertising for the test product may pull in many consumers from outside the market. The product may then appear to be more successful than it really is.

The High Costs of Test Marketing Test marketing frequently takes one year or longer, and costs can exceed $1 million. Some products remain in test markets even longer. Despite the cost, many firms believe it is much better to fail in a test market than in a national introduction. Because test marketing is so expensive,

some companies do not test line extensions of well-known brands. For example, because its Sara Lee brand is well known, Consolidated Foods Kitchen faced little risk in distributing its frozen croissants nationally. Other products introduced without being test marketed include General Foods' International Coffees and Quaker Oats' Chewy Granola Bars.

The high cost of test marketing is not just financial. One unavoidable problem is that test marketing exposes the new product and its marketing mix to competitors before its introduction. Thus, the element of surprise is lost. Competitors can also sabotage, or jam, a testing program by introducing their own sales promotion, pricing, or advertising campaign. The purpose is to hide or distort the normal conditions that the testing firm might expect in the market.

Alternatives to Test Marketing Many firms are looking for cheaper, faster, safer alternatives to

> **test marketing** the limited introduction of a product and a marketing program to determine the reactions of potential customers in a market situation

CHECKLIST FOR SELECTING TEST MARKETS

In choosing a test market, many criteria need to be considered, especially the following:

▸▸ Similarity to planned distribution outlets

▸▸ Relative isolation from other cities

▸▸ Availability of cooperative advertising media

▸▸ Diversified cross-section of ages, religions, cultural-societal preferences, etc.

▸▸ No atypical purchasing habits

▸▸ Representative population size

▸▸ Typical per capita income

▸▸ Good record as a test city, but not overly used

▸▸ Not easily jammed by competitors

▸▸ Stability of year-round sales

▸▸ No dominant television station; multiple newspapers, magazines, and radio stations

▸▸ Availability of research and audit services

▸▸ Availability of cooperative retailers

▸▸ Freedom from unusual influences, such as one industry's dominance or heavy tourism

simulated (laboratory) market testing the presentation of advertising and other promotion materials for several products, including a test product, to members of the product's target market

commercialization the decision to market a product

traditional test marketing. In the early 1980s, Information Resources, Inc. pioneered one alternative: single-source research using supermarket scanner data (discussed in Chapter 4). A typical supermarket scanner test costs about $300,000. Another alternative to traditional test marketing is **simulated (laboratory) market testing**, which involves the presentation of advertising and other promotional materials for several products, including the test product, to members of the product's target market. These people are then taken to shop at a mock or real store, where their purchases are recorded. Shopper behaviour, including repeat purchasing, is monitored to assess the product's likely performance under true market conditions. Research firms offer simulated market tests for $25,000 to $100,000, compared with $1 million or more for full-scale test marketing.

Despite these alternatives, most firms still consider test marketing essential for most new products. The high price of failure simply prohibits the widespread introduction of most new products without testing. Many firms are finding that the Internet offers a fast, cost-effective way to conduct test marketing. Procter & Gamble is an avid proponent of using the Internet as a means of gauging customer demand for potential new products. The company reportedly conducts 40 percent of its product tests and other studies online and hopes to cut its $140 million annual research budget in half by shifting efforts to the Internet.[26] Many products that are not available in grocery stores or drugstores can be sampled or purchased from P&G's corporate website www.pg.com. Before launching Crest Whitestrips, management ran an eight-month campaign offering the strips exclusively on http://whitestrips.com at a test price of $44 per kit. In eight months, 144,000 whitening kits were sold online, and when P&G introduced the product in retail outlets, it sold $50 million worth of kits in the first three months at the initial test price.[27]

Commercialization

The final stage in the new-product development process is **commercialization**, the decision to market a product. The decision to commercialize the product sets several tasks in motion: ordering production materials and equipment, starting production, building inventories, shipping the product to field distribution points, training the sales force, announcing the new product to the trade, and advertising to potential customers.

The time from the initial commercialization decision to the product's actual introduction varies. It can range from a few weeks for simple products that use existing equipment to several years for technical products that require custom manufacturing equipment. And the total cost of development and initial introduction can be staggering. Gillette spent $750 million developing Mach3, and the first-year marketing budget for the new three-bladed razor was $300 million.

The most important factor in successful new-product introduction is a good match between the product and market needs—as the marketing concept would predict. Successful new products deliver a meaningful and perceivable benefit to a sizable number of people or organizations and are different in some meaningful way from their intended substitutes. Firms that routinely experience success in new-product introductions tend to share the following characteristics:

▶▶ a history of carefully listening to customers

▶▶ an obsession with producing the best product possible

▶▶ a vision of what the market will be like in the future

▶▶ strong leadership

▶▶ a commitment to new-product development

▶▶ a project-based team approach to new-product development

▶▶ getting every aspect of the product development process right

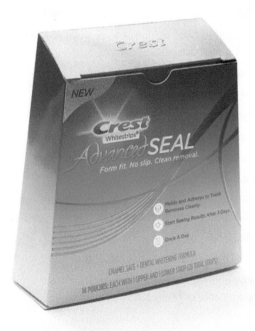

LO 3 Global Issues in New-Product Development

Increasing globalization of markets and of competition encourages multinational firms to consider new-product development from a worldwide perspective. A firm that starts with a global strategy is better able to develop products that are marketable worldwide. In many multinational corporations, every product is developed for potential worldwide distribution, and unique market requirements are built in whenever possible.

Some global marketers design their products to meet regulations in their major markets and then, if necessary, meet smaller markets' requirements country by country. Nissan develops lead-country car models that, with minor changes, can be sold in most markets. By using this approach, Nissan has been able to reduce the number of its basic models from 48 to 18. Some products, however, have little potential for global market penetration without modification. In other cases, companies cannot sell their product at affordable prices and still make a profit in many countries. To counter this problem, Procter & Gamble uses subcontractors to combine proprietary ingredients with standard chemicals and package the products.[28] The result is lower cost to P&G.

We often hear about the popularity of American products in foreign countries. Recently, Canadian companies have been finding that products popular in foreign markets can become hits in Canada. Haagen-Dazs introduced *Dulce de leche* in Canada after having it successfully introduced in Argentina.

Developed in the UK; would work or be accepted in Canada.

LO 4 The Spread of New Products

Managers have a better chance of successfully marketing products if they understand how consumers learn about and adopt products. A person who buys a new product never before tried may ultimately become an **adopter**, a consumer who was happy enough with his or her trial experience with a product to use it again.

Diffusion of Innovation

An **innovation** is a product perceived as new by a potential adopter. It really doesn't matter whether the product is new to the world or belongs to some other category of new product. If the product is new to a potential adopter, in this context, it is considered an innovation. **Diffusion** is the process by which the adoption of an innovation spreads.

Early adopters are opinion leaders who encourage others to buy a new product; they are often essential to successful product innovation. Eco-Handbags is a Canadian company that hopes to attract early adopters with its trendy and ecologically friendly products.

Five categories of adopters participate in the diffusion process:

▸▸ *Innovators:* the first 2.5 percent of all those who adopt the product. Innovators are eager to try new ideas and products, almost to the point of obsession. In addition to having higher incomes, innovators are typically more worldly and more active outside their community than noninnovators. Innovators also rely less on group norms and are more self-confident.

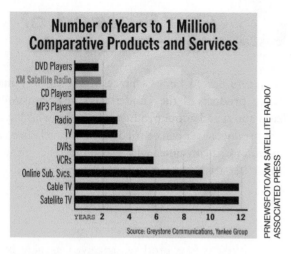

Number of Years to 1 Million Comparative Products and Services

	YEARS
DVD Players	
XM Satellite Radio	
CD Players	
MP3 Players	
Radio	
TV	
DVRs	
VCRs	
Online Sub. Svcs.	
Cable TV	
Satellite TV	

YEARS 2   4   6   8   10   12

Source: Greystone Communications, Yankee Group

PRNEWSFOTO/XM SATELLITE RADIO/ ASSOCIATED PRESS

Because they tend to be well educated, they are more likely to get their information from scientific sources and experts. Innovators are characterized as being venturesome.

▸▸ *Early adopters:* the next 13.5 percent to adopt the product. Although early adopters are not the very first, they do adopt early in the product's life cycle. Compared with innovators, early adopters rely much more on group norms and values. They are also more oriented to the local community, in contrast to the innovators' worldly outlook. Early adopters are more likely than innovators to be opinion leaders because of their closer affiliation with groups. The respect of others is a dominant characteristic of early adopters.

▸▸ *Early majority:* the next 34 percent to adopt. The early majority weighs the pros and cons before adopting a new product. They are likely to collect more information and evaluate more brands than early adopters, thereby extending the adoption process. They rely on the group for information but are unlikely to be opinion leaders themselves. Instead, they tend to be opinion leaders' friends and neighbours. The early majority is an important link in the process of diffusing new ideas because they are positioned between earlier and later adopters. A dominant characteristic of the early majority is deliberateness. Most of the first residential broadband users were classic early adopters—white males, well educated, and wealthy, with a great deal of Internet experience.

▸▸ *Late majority:* the next 34 percent to adopt. The late majority adopts a new product because most of their friends have already adopted it. Because they also rely on group norms, their adoption stems from pressure to conform. This group tends to be older and below average in income and education. They depend mainly on word-of-mouth communication rather than on the mass media. The dominant characteristic of the late majority is skepticism.

▸▸ *Laggards:* the final 16 percent to adopt. Like innovators, laggards do not rely on group norms. Their

independence is rooted in their ties to tradition. Thus, the past heavily influences their decisions. By the time laggards adopt an innovation, it has probably been outmoded and replaced by something else. For example, they may have bought their first black-and-white TV set after colour television was already widely diffused. Laggards have the longest adoption time and the lowest socioeconomic status. They tend to be suspicious of new products and alienated from a rapidly advancing society. The dominant value of laggards is tradition. Marketers typically ignore laggards, who do not seem to be motivated by advertising or personal selling.

Note that some product categories may never be adopted by 100 percent of the population. The percentages noted in the adopter categories above refer to the percentage of all of those who will eventually adopt a product, not to percentages of the entire population.

Product Characteristics and the Rate of Adoption

Five product characteristics can be used to predict and explain the rate of acceptance and diffusion of a new product:

▸▸ *Complexity:* the degree of difficulty involved in understanding and using a new product. The more complex the product, the slower is its diffusion.

▸▸ *Compatibility:* the degree to which the new product is consistent with existing values and product knowledge, past experiences, and current needs. Incompatible products diffuse more slowly than compatible products.

▸▸ *Relative advantage:* the degree to which a product is perceived as superior to existing substitutes. Because it can store and play back thousands of songs, the iPod has a clear relative advantage over the portable CD player.

▸▸ *Observability:* the degree to which the benefits or other results of using the product can be observed by others and communicated to target customers. For instance, fashion items and automobiles are highly visible and more observable than personal-care items.

▸▸ *Trialability:* the degree to which a product can be tried on a limited basis. It is much easier to try a new toothpaste or breakfast cereal than a new automobile or microcomputer.

Marketing Implications of the Adoption Process

Two types of communication aid the diffusion process: *word-of-mouth communication* among consumers and communication from marketers to consumers. Word-of-mouth communication within and across groups speeds diffusion. Opinion leaders discuss new products with their followers and with other opinion leaders. Marketers must therefore ensure that opinion leaders receive the types of information that are desired in the media they use. Suppliers of some products, such as professional and healthcare services, rely almost solely on word-of-mouth communication for new business.

The second type of communication aiding the diffusion process is *communication directly from the marketer to potential adopters*. Messages directed toward early adopters should normally use different appeals than messages directed toward the early majority, the late majority, or the laggards. Early adopters are more important than innovators because they make up a larger group, are more socially active, and are usually opinion leaders.

As the focus of a promotional campaign shifts from early adopters to the early majority and the late majority, marketers should study these target markets' dominant characteristics, buying behaviour, and media characteristics. They should then revise their messages and media strategy to fit these target markets. The diffusion model helps guide marketers in developing and implementing promotion strategy.

LO5 Product Life Cycles

The **product life cycle (PLC)**, one of the most familiar concepts in marketing, is a concept that traces the stages of a product's acceptance, from its introduction (birth) to its decline (death). Few other general concepts have been so widely discussed. Although some researchers and consultants have challenged the theoretical basis and managerial value of the PLC, many believe it is a useful marketing management diagnostic tool and a general guide for marketing planning in various life-cycle stages.[29]

As Exhibit 10.2 shows, a product progresses through four major stages: introduction, growth, maturity, and decline.

The PLC concept can be used to analyze a brand, a product form, or a product category. The PLC for a product form is usually longer than the PLC for any one brand. The exception would be a brand that was the first and last competitor in a product form market. In that situation, the brand and product form life cycles would be equal in length. Product categories have the longest life cycles. A **product category** includes all brands that satisfy a particular type of need, such as shaving products, passenger automobiles, or colas.

The time a product spends in any one stage of the life cycle may vary dramatically. Some products, such as trendy items, move through the entire cycle in weeks. Others, such as electric clothes washers and dryers, stay in the maturity stage for decades. Exhibit 10.2 illustrates the typical life cycle for a consumer durable good, such as a washer or dryer. In contrast, Exhibit 10.3 illustrates typical life cycles for styles (such as formal, business, or casual clothing), fashions (such as miniskirts or baggy jeans), and fads (such as leopard-print clothing). Changes in a product, its uses, its image, or its positioning can extend that product's life cycle.

The PLC concept does not tell managers the length of a product's life cycle or its duration in any stage. It does not dictate marketing strategy. It is simply a tool to help marketers forecast future events and suggest appropriate strategies.

> **product life cycle (PLC)** a concept that traces the stages of a product's acceptance, from its introduction (birth) to its decline (death)
>
> **product category** all brands that satisfy a particular type of need

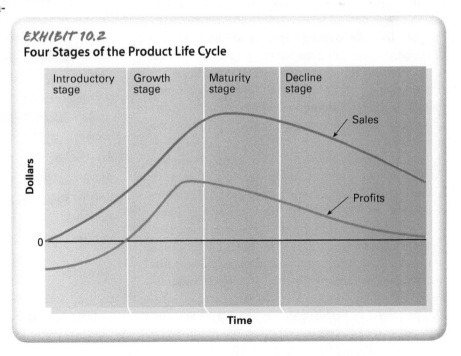

EXHIBIT 10.2
Four Stages of the Product Life Cycle

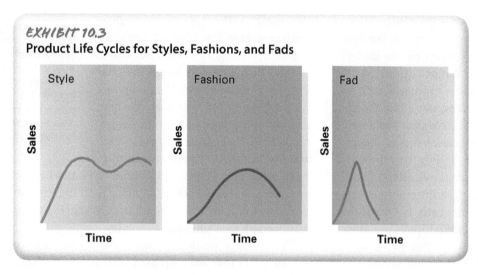

EXHIBIT 10.3
Product Life Cycles for Styles, Fashions, and Fads

Introductory Stage

introductory stage the full-scale launch of a new product into the marketplace

growth stage the second stage of the product life cycle when sales typically grow at an increasing rate, many competitors enter the market, large companies may start to acquire small pioneering firms, and profits are healthy

The **introductory stage** of the PLC represents the full-scale launch of a new product into the marketplace. Product categories that have recently entered the product life cycle include computer databases for personal use, room-deodorizing air-conditioning filters, and wind-powered home electric generators. A high failure rate, little competition, frequent product modification, and limited distribution typify the introductory stage of the PLC.

Marketing costs in the introductory stage are normally high for several reasons. High dealer margins are often needed to obtain adequate distribution, and incentives are needed to convince consumers to try the new product. Advertising expenses are high because of the need to educate consumers about the new product's benefits. Production costs are also often high in this stage, as a result of product and manufacturing flaws being identified and then corrected and because of efforts undertaken to develop mass-production economies.

Sales normally increase slowly during the introductory stage. Moreover, profits are usually negative because of R&D costs, factory tooling, and high introduction costs. The length of the introductory phase is largely determined by product characteristics, such as the product's advantages over substitute products, the educational effort required to make the product known, and management's commitment of resources to the new item. A short introductory period is usually preferred to help reduce the impact of negative earnings and cash flows. As soon as the product gets off the ground, the financial burden should begin to diminish. Also, a short introduction helps dispel some of the uncertainty as to whether the new product will be successful.

Promotion strategy in the introductory stage focuses on developing product awareness and informing consumers about the product category's potential benefits. At this stage, the communication challenge is to stimulate primary demand—demand for the product in general rather than for a specific brand. Intensive personal selling is often required to gain acceptance for the product among wholesalers and retailers. Promotion of convenience products often requires heavy consumer sampling and couponing. Shopping and specialty products demand educational advertising and personal selling to the final consumer.

The PLC seems to vary among European countries, from just under four years in Denmark to about nine years in Greece. Cultural factors seem to be largely responsible for these differences. Scandinavians are often more open to new ideas than people in other European countries.[30]

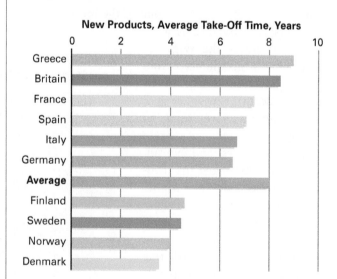

New Products, Average Take-Off Time, Years

Growth Stage

If a product category survives the introductory stage, it advances to the **growth stage** of the life cycle. The growth stage is the second stage of the product life cycle when sales typically grow at an increasing rate, many competitors enter the market, large companies may start to acquire small pioneering firms, and profits are healthy. Profits rise rapidly in the growth stage, reach their peak, and begin declining as competition intensifies. Emphasis switches from primary demand promotion (for example, promoting personal digital assistants, or PDAs) to aggressive brand advertising and communication of the differences between brands (for example, promoting Casio versus Palm and Visor).

Distribution becomes a major key to success during the growth stage and later stages. Manufacturers scramble to sign up dealers and distributors and to build long-term relationships. Without adequate distribution, it is impossible to establish a strong market position.

Maturity Stage

A period during which sales increase at a decreasing rate signals the beginning of the **maturity stage** of the life cycle. New users cannot be added indefinitely, and, sooner or later, the market approaches saturation. Normally, the maturity stage is the longest stage of the product life cycle. Many major household appliances are in the maturity stage of their life cycles.

For shopping products such as durable goods and electronics, and for many specialty products, annual models begin to appear during the maturity stage. Product lines are lengthened to appeal to additional market segments. Service and repair assume more important roles as manufacturers strive to distinguish their products from others. Product design changes tend to become stylistic (How can the product be made different?) rather than functional (How can the product be made better?).

As prices and profits continue to fall, marginal competitors start dropping out of the market. Dealer margins also shrink, resulting in less shelf space for mature items, lower dealer inventories, and a general reluctance to promote the product. Thus, promotion to dealers often intensifies during this stage in order to retain loyalty.

Heavy consumer promotion by the manufacturer is also required to maintain market share. Cutthroat competition during this stage can lead to price wars. Another characteristic of the maturity stage is the emergence of niche marketers that target narrow, well-defined, underserved segments of a market. Starbucks Coffee targets its gourmet line at the only segment of the coffee market that is growing: new, younger, more affluent coffee drinkers.

Decline Stage

A long-run drop in sales signals the beginning of the **decline stage**. The rate of decline is governed by how rapidly consumer tastes change or substitute products are adopted. Many convenience products and trendy items lose their market overnight, leaving large inventories of unsold items, such as designer jeans. Others die more slowly. Canadian sales of traditional 35mm cameras have been on a steady decline since 2000. In one recent year, film camera sales dropped 15 percent. The worldwide shift to digital photography has led Eastman Kodak to stop selling reloadable film-based consumer cameras in the United States, Canada, and Europe. Instead, Kodak now focuses on the development of digital cameras and imaging systems.[31]

Some firms have developed successful strategies for marketing products in the decline stage of the product life cycle. They eliminate all nonessential marketing expenses and let sales decline as more and more customers discontinue purchasing the products. Eventually, the product is withdrawn from the market.

Management sage Peter Drucker said that all companies should practise organized abandonment, which involves reviewing every

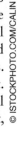

CHAPTER 10: DEVELOPING AND MANAGING PRODUCTS

product, service, and policy every two or three years and asking the critical question "If we didn't do this already, would we launch it now?" If the answer is no, it's time to begin the abandonment process.[32]

Implications for Marketing Management

The product life cycle concept encourages marketing managers to plan so that they can take the initiative instead of reacting to past events. The PLC is especially useful as a predicting, or forecasting, tool. Because products pass through distinctive stages, it is often possible to estimate a product's location on the curve using historical data. Profits, like sales, tend to follow a predictable path over a product's life cycle.

Exhibit 10.4 shows the relationship between the adopter categories and stages of the PLC. Note that the various categories of adopters first buy products in different stages of the life cycle. Almost all sales in the maturity and decline stages represent repeat purchasing.

Kodak's first consumer camera was introduced in 1888. Look how far that discontinuous innovation has come.

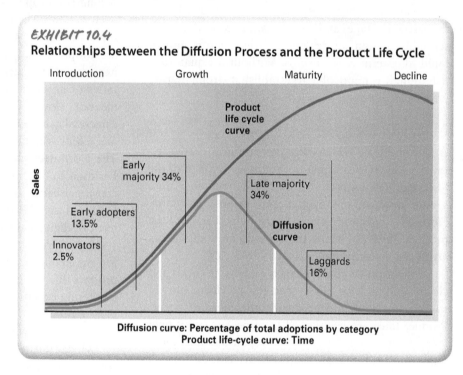

EXHIBIT 10.4
Relationships between the Diffusion Process and the Product Life Cycle

Introduction   Growth   Maturity   Decline

Product life cycle curve

Early majority 34%

Late majority 34%

Early adopters 13.5%

Diffusion curve

Innovators 2.5%

Laggards 16%

Sales

Diffusion curve: Percentage of total adoptions by category
Product life-cycle curve: Time

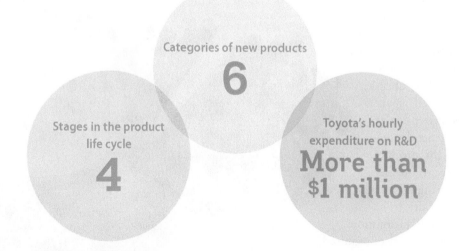

Categories of new products

6

Stages in the product life cycle

4

Toyota's hourly expenditure on R&D

More than $1 million

CHAPTER **11** Services and Nonprofit Organization Marketing

Canada has one of the strongest banking systems globally and has one of the most highly developed financial services sectors on the planet.

AFTER YOU FINISH THIS CHAPTER, GO TO WWW. ICANMKTG2.COM FOR STUDY TOOLS.

© ISTOCKPHOTO.COM/RAFAEL RAMIREZ LEE

LO1 The Importance of Services

A service is the result of applying human or mechanical efforts to people or objects. Services involve a deed, a performance, or an effort that cannot be physically possessed. Today, the service sector substantially influences the Canadian economy, According to Statistics Canada, in 2010 the service sector accounted for 78 percent of all employment. Canadian economic growth continues to be driven by growth in the service sector.[1] The growing service sector is a key area for employment opportunities. Canadian services are of world-class quality, and our financial services sector is regarded even more highly in the wake of the recent global financial crisis. The demand for services is expected to continue. Much of this demand results from demographics. An aging population will need nurses, home health care, physical therapists, and social workers. Demand for information managers, such as computer engineers and systems analysts, will also increase. There is also a growing market for Canadian service companies worldwide.

Whether you are marketing a good or a service, the marketing process discussed in Chapter 1 is the same. In addition, although a comparison of goods and services marketing can be beneficial, in reality it is difficult to distinguish clearly between manufacturing and service firms. Indeed, many manufacturing firms can point to service as a major factor in their success. One example is the mining

service the result of applying human or mechanical efforts to people or objects

What do you think?

Opportunities for employment in the service sector are plentiful.

| 1 | 2 | 3 | 4 | 5 | 6 | 7 |
STRONGLY DISAGREE   STRONGLY AGREE

industry. Canada's natural resources have resulted in many producers of mined commodities. To support these producers, mining service providers emerged. Now, despite the softening of this sector in terms of Canada's economic growth, Canada is still considered a major player because of the expertise of these service providers that can be easily exported.[2] Nevertheless, services have some unique characteristics that distinguish them from goods, and marketing strategies need to be adjusted for these characteristics.

LO 2 How Services Differ from Goods

Services have four unique characteristics that distinguish them from goods. Services are intangible, inseparable, heterogeneous, and perishable.

Intangibility

The basic difference between services and goods is that services are intangible performances. Because of their **intangibility**, they cannot be touched, seen, tasted, heard, or felt in the same manner that goods can be sensed.

Evaluating the quality of services before or even after making a purchase is harder than evaluating the quality of goods because, compared with goods, services tend to exhibit fewer search qualities. A **search quality** is a characteristic that can be easily assessed before purchase—for instance, the colour of a car or the keyboard on a cellphone. At the same time, services tend to exhibit more experience and credence qualities. An **experience quality** is a characteristic that can be assessed only after use, such as the quality of a meal in a restaurant. A **credence quality** is a characteristic that consumers may have difficulty assessing even after purchase because

intangibility the inability of services to be touched, seen, tasted, heard, or felt in the same manner that goods can be sensed

search quality a characteristic that can be easily assessed before purchase

experience quality a characteristic that can be assessed only after use

credence quality a characteristic that consumers may have difficulty assessing even after purchase because they do not have the necessary knowledge or experience

inseparability the inability of the production and consumption of a service to be separated; consumers must be present during the production

they do not have the necessary knowledge or experience. Medical and consulting services are examples of services that exhibit credence qualities.

These characteristics also make it more difficult for marketers to communicate the benefits of an intangible service than to communicate the benefits of tangible goods. Thus, marketers often rely on tangible cues to communicate a service's nature and quality. For example, Ronald McDonald House uses the symbol of a house drawn as a child would, with a heart coming out of the chimney, to symbolize the warmth and love provided to families of critically ill children who stay in a Ronald McDonald House.

The facilities that customers visit, or from which services are delivered, are a critical tangible part of the total service offering. Messages about the organization are communicated to customers through such elements as the décor, the clutter or neatness of service areas, and the staff's manners and dress. Think of how you assess the service of a new hairdresser prior to your first appointment. Undoubtedly, you consider the appearance of both the salon and the hairdresser to get a sense of whether the salon's style suits your needs. This assessment, which is based on the physical surroundings, is critical in your decision to proceed with the appointment.

Inseparability

Goods are produced, sold, and then consumed. In contrast, services are often sold, produced, and consumed at the same time. In other words, their production and consumption are inseparable activities. This **inseparability** means that, because consumers must be present during the production of services such as haircuts or surgery, they are actually involved in the production of the services they buy. Such consumer involvement is rare in goods manufacturing.

Simultaneous production and consumption also means that services normally cannot be produced in a centralized location and consumed in decentralized locations, as goods typically are. Services are also inseparable from the perspective of the service provider. Thus, the quality of service that firms are able to deliver depends on the quality of their employees.

Heterogeneity

One great strength of McDonald's is consistency. Whether customers order a Big Mac in Tokyo or Moscow, they know exactly what they will get. This is not the case with many service providers. Because services have greater **heterogeneity** or variability of inputs and outputs, they tend to be less standardized and uniform than goods. For example, physicians in a group practice or hairstylists in a salon differ in their technical and interpersonal skills. Because services tend to be labour-intensive and production and consumption are inseparable, consistency and quality control can be difficult to achieve.

Standardization and training help increase consistency and reliability. IKEA invests in its employees from the get-go. New hires do not hit the sales floor until they've had two weeks of upfront training, and the training continues. Egos are parked at the door, creating a team environment in which employees are rewarded for their efforts with higher salaries, benefit packages, paid holidays, and opportunities to travel. In December 2010, 12,400 IKEA workers in the United States received a bicycle as a holiday gift. It was IKEA's way of saying "thanks for being strongly committed to working together."[3] Such training and commitment to staff leads to exceptional customer service.

Perishability

The fourth characteristic of services is their **perishability**, which refers to their inability to be stored, warehoused, or inventoried. An empty hotel room or vacant airplane seat produces no revenue. The possible revenue has been lost. Yet service organizations are often forced to turn away full-price customers during peak periods.

One of the most important challenges in many service industries is finding ways to synchronize supply and demand. The philosophy that some revenue is better than none has prompted many hotels to offer deep discounts on weekends and during the off-season.

LO 3 Service Quality

Because of the four unique characteristics of services, service quality is more difficult to define and measure than the quality of tangible goods. Business executives rank the improvement of service quality as one of the most critical challenges facing them today.

Research has shown that customers evaluate service quality by the following five components:[4]

▸▸ **Reliability:** the ability to perform the service dependably, accurately, and consistently. Reliability refers to performing the service right the first time. This component has been found to be the one most important to consumers.

▸▸ **Responsiveness:** the ability to provide prompt service. Examples of responsiveness include returning customers' calls quickly, serving lunch fast to someone in a hurry, or mailing a transaction slip immediately. The ultimate in responsiveness is offering service 24 hours a day, seven days a week.

▸▸ **Assurance:** the knowledge and courtesy of employees and their ability to convey trust. Skilled employees exemplify assurance when they treat customers with respect and when they make customers feel that they can trust the firm.

▸▸ **Empathy:** caring, individualized attention to customers. Firms whose employees recognize customers and learn their specific requirements are providing empathy.

▸▸ **Tangibles:** the physical evidence of the service. The tangible parts of a service include the physical facilities, tools, and equipment used to provide the service, and the appearance of personnel.

Overall service quality is measured by combining customers' evaluations for all five components.

The Gap Model of Service Quality

A model of service quality called the **gap model** identifies five gaps that can cause problems in service delivery and influence customer evaluations of service quality.[5] These gaps are illustrated in Exhibit 11.1:

▸▸ *Gap 1:* Knowledge Gap—the gap between what customers want and what management thinks customers want. This gap results from a lack of understanding or a misinterpretation of the customers' needs, wants, or desires. A consumer's expectations may vary for a variety of reasons, including the consumer's past experiences and the type of situation. A firm that does little or no customer satisfaction research is likely to experience this

heterogeneity the variability of the inputs and outputs of services, which causes services to tend to be less standardized and uniform than goods

perishability the inability of services to be stored, warehoused, or inventoried

reliability the ability to perform a service dependably, accurately, and consistently

responsiveness the ability to provide prompt service

assurance the knowledge and courtesy of employees and their ability to convey trust

empathy caring, individualized attention to customers

tangibles the physical evidence of a service, including the physical facilities, tools, and equipment used to provide the service

gap model a model identifying five gaps that can cause problems in service delivery and influence customer evaluations of service quality

Ronald McDonald House looks like a home with all the amenities a home would provide.

gap. To close gap 1, firms must stay attuned to customer wishes by researching customer needs and satisfaction and by increasing the interaction and communication between management and employees.

▸▸ *Gap 2:* Standards Gap—the gap between what management thinks customers want and the quality

specifications that management develops to provide the service. Essentially, this gap is the result of management's inability to translate customers' needs into delivery systems within the firm. In other words, the gap is a result of management not having provided the appropriate service designs and standards. The reduction in this gap is achieved not only through training and development of employees but also by involving employees in establishing the service quality goals.

▸▸ *Gap 3:* Delivery Gap—the gap between the service quality specifications and the service that is actually provided. If both gaps 1 and 2 have been closed, then gap 3 results from the inability of management and employees to do what should be done. Management needs to ensure that employees have the skills and the proper tools to perform their jobs, including effective training programs and ongoing feedback. Management also needs to commit to service quality being paramount.

▸▸ *Gap 4:* Communication Gap—the gap between what the company provides and what the customer is told it provides. To close this gap, companies need to create realistic customer expectations through honest, accurate communication regarding what they can provide.

▸▸ *Gap 5:* Expectation Gap—the gap between the service that customers expect they should receive and the perceived service after the service has been provided. This gap can be positive or negative and clearly influences consumers' perception of service quality. Ongoing research is necessary to understand consumers' perceptions and to manage their expectations.

When one or more of these gaps is large, service quality is perceived as being low. As the gaps shrink, service quality perception improves.

LO 4 Marketing Mixes for Services

Services' unique characteristics—intangibility, inseparability of production and consumption heterogeneity, and perishability—make the marketing of services more challenging. Elements of the marketing mix (product, place, promotion, and pricing) need to be adjusted to meet the special needs created by these

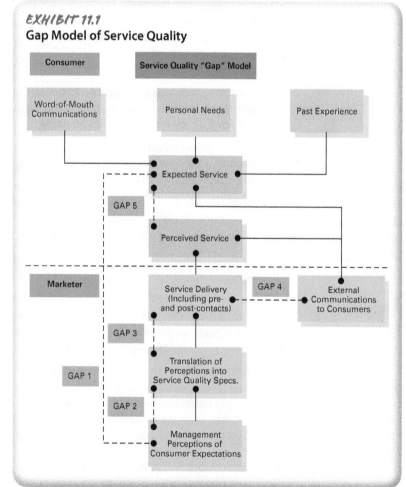

EXHIBIT 11.1
Gap Model of Service Quality

characteristics. In addition, effective marketing of services requires the management of 4 additional Ps: people, process, productivity, and physical environment.

Product (Service) Strategy

A product, as defined in Chapter 9, is everything a person receives in an exchange. In the case of a service organization, the product offering is intangible and consists in large part of a process or a series of processes. This definition suggests then that the service firm must attempt to make the intangible tangible by providing physical cues of the service quality and positioning. Logos, tag lines, and promotional materials attempt to create tangible evidence of the service offering.

Service as a Process Two broad categories of things are processed in service organizations: people and objects. In some cases, the process is physical, or tangible, whereas, in other cases, the process is intangible. Using these characteristics, service processes can be placed into one of four categories:[6]

» *People processing* takes place when the service is directed at a customer. Examples are transportation services and health care.

» *Possession processing* occurs when the service is directed at customers' physical possessions. Examples are lawn care and veterinary services.

JustJunk is an example of a possession-processing service. This service focuses less on the attractiveness of its physical environment than would a people-processing service, such as a massage therapist, but emphasis is still paid to the logo and the look of the physical cues that represent the company.

» *Mental stimulus processing* refers to services directed at people's minds. Examples are theatre performances and education.

» *Information processing* describes services that use technology or brainpower directed at a customer's assets. Examples are insurance and consulting.

Because customers' experiences and involvement differ for each of these types of services processes, marketing strategies may also differ. Take, for example, a season's pass to the games of a Canadian Football League (CFL) team. It is a mental stimulus–processing service where the quality of the product (the service) is very much dependent on the quality of the players and the coaching staff. The game outcome can never be controlled but the individual clubs can control other aspects of the game to ensure the game attendee has a positive experience. The half-time shows, the game day give-aways, the stadium itself, and the food and drink are elements of the product that can be controlled to enhance the service experience.

core service the most basic benefit the consumer is buying

supplementary services a group of services that support or enhance the core service

Core and Supplementary Service Products The service offering can be viewed as a bundle of activities that includes the **core service**, which is the most basic benefit the customer is buying, and a group of **supplementary services** that support or enhance the core service. For the Fowler Kennedy Sport Medicine Clinic at the University of Western Ontario and Fanshawe College, the core service is the treatment of sports-related injuries. The supplemental services offered include sports-related research, pedorthic care, custom bracing, and the sale of braces, back supports, orthotics, and first-aid supplies through the clinic's retail store.

Sports medicine and physiotherapy could be considered a commodity, but through the continued emphasis on research and the development of innovative ways to treat sports-related injuries, Fowler Kennedy continues to attract elite athletes from all over Canada, which helps to further differentiate the clinic.

The Service Mix Most service organizations market more than one service. For example, TD Canada Trust

provides a wide range of banking and investment services to both individuals and organizations. Each organization's service mix represents a set of opportunities, risks, and challenges. Each part of the service mix should make a different contribution to achieving the firm's goals. To succeed, each service may also need a different level of financial support. Designing a service strategy therefore means deciding what new services to introduce to which target market, what existing services to maintain, and what services to eliminate.

Process Strategy

Because services are delivered before or while being consumed, the marketing mix for services includes the strategic decisions surrounding the process. Here, *process* refers to the establishing of standards to ensure the service delivery is consistent and compatible with the service positioning. To establish these processes, the knowledge gap must be reduced through market research that seeks to understand consumer expectations; a process protocol must then be established to ensure the service delivery meets customers' expectations. Process is fluid, which means that customer satisfaction should be evaluated on an ongoing basis and processes should be updated to ensure service delivery continues to meet expectations. The more standardized the delivery, the less likely the need for ongoing evaluation of process.

People Strategy

The standards gap and the delivery gap must be managed to improve the service. The service is provided by a service provider, but distinguishing between the two is often very difficult. Thus, managing the employee who is the service provider is highly strategic. Strategies include providing incentives, training, and recognition programs that management consistently supports. Employees who are well trained, empowered, and rewarded will deliver on the service promise. Take Lululemon as an example. Founded in British Columbia in 1988, Lululemon has grown into an international company specializing in athletic clothing for yoga and running. The company started as a small store where the sale of clothing was secondary to the store being a community hub for the "discussion of healthy living and the mental aspects of a powerful life of possibilities." However, the sale of the clothing quickly took over, and the store became very much a retail store first and a community hub second. Training of employees then became critically important for they now had to inspire the healthy living philosophy and create the dialogue. Lululemon employees are team members who are provided with a "success" library and training tools. All team members work interactively to set goals in both their professional and personal lives. The organization strives through this commitment to its employees to maintain a culture of integrity and dedication to living a healthy fun life.[7]

Place (Distribution) Strategy

Distribution strategies for service organizations must focus on such issues as convenience, number of outlets, direct versus indirect distribution, location, and scheduling. One of the key factors influencing the selection of a service provider is *convenience*. Hence, the place strategy is important to service firms.

An important distribution objective for many service firms is the *number of outlets* to use or the number of outlets to open during a certain time. Generally, the intensity of distribution should meet, but not exceed, the target market's needs and preferences. Having too few outlets may inconvenience customers; having too many outlets may boost costs unnecessarily. Intensity of distribution may also depend on the image desired. Having only a few outlets may make the service seem more exclusive or selective.

The next service distribution decision is whether to distribute services to end-users *directly* or *indirectly* through other firms. Because of the nature of services, many service firms choose to use direct distribution or franchising. Examples include legal, medical, accounting, and personal-care services. The Internet has provided some service providers with the opportunity to intensify their distribution or even to automate part of the service to better satisfy the customer. Most of the major airlines are now using online services to sell tickets directly to consumers, which results in lower distribution costs for the airline companies. Other firms with standardized service packages have developed indirect channels. For example, the Government of Ontario has created ServiceOntario kiosks as a fast, easy, and more accessible way for Ontario residents to renew their driver's licence or health card. This strategy is likely to succeed because the level of customer service required in renewing a driver's licence or health card is minimal.

The *location* of a service most clearly reveals the relationship between its target market strategy and its distribution strategy. For time-dependent service providers, such as airlines, physicians, and dentists, *scheduling* is often a more important factor.

Physical Evidence Strategy

Closely associated with managing place strategies to maintain service quality is managing the physical evidence surrounding the service delivery. All four categories of service processes can benefit from attention paid to both the physical environment in which the service is being offered and the quality of the equipment used to deliver the service. For example, when you arrive at your dental appointment, an untidy office and old equipment may lead you to question the ability of the dentist to provide the best oral care with the least amount of pain.

McMaster Children's Hospital in Hamilton, Ontario, states its vision is "advancing health and integrating care for children and youth through excellence, innovation and partnerships." To this end, in April 2011, the Emergency Department at McMaster Children's Hospital became a children's-only service, treating teenagers and children ages 17 and under. When the renovations of the Emergency Department are complete, changes will include a Pediatric Clinical Decision Unit, where children who need to be treated in the Emergency Department for several hours can be cared for comfortably, larger treatment rooms to allow for family care at the bedside, and special consideration of the interior environment below the one-metre-high level so as to enhance the view and involvement of young children and those in wheelchairs. Such attention to physical surroundings further establishes in the minds of the family of the sick child that they are in the best place for the care of a child.[8]

Promotion Strategy

Consumers and business users have more trouble evaluating services than goods because services are less tangible. In turn, marketers have more trouble promoting intangible services than tangible goods. Here are four promotion strategies for services:

▸▸ *Stressing tangible cues:* A tangible cue is a concrete symbol of the service offering. Free newspapers and attentive concierge staff are ways that hotels attempt to make their service offering tangible.

▸▸ *Using personal information sources:* A personal information source is someone consumers are familiar with (such as a celebrity) or someone they know or can relate to personally. Service firms can set up blogs and stimulate customer interaction on the blogs to generate positive word of mouth. Facebook and Twitter are two social media tools that service firms include in their promotion strategy to capitalize on the potential for consumer discussion around their service offerings. Of course, there is always the possibility of negative word of mouth, which requires a comprehensive and often swift crisis communication plan.

▸▸ *Creating a strong organizational image:* One way to create an image is to manage the evidence, including the physical environment of the service facility, the appearance of the service employees, and the tangible items associated with a service, such as the firm's website, stationery, and brochures. The Toronto Zoo, for example, has created a strong, first-class image with its consistent look and messaging in all communication pieces and in all consumer touch points at the zoo itself. In other words the Toronto Zoo has created a strong image through branding that it carries out in all its communications.

Same planet. Different world.

▸▸ *Engaging in postpurchase communication:* Postpurchase communication refers to the follow-up activities that a service firm might engage in after a customer transaction. Postcard surveys, telephone calls, and other types of follow-up show customers that their feedback matters.

Price Strategy

Considerations in pricing a service are similar to the pricing considerations to be discussed in Chapters 18 and 19. However, the unique characteristics of services present special pricing challenges. See Exhibit 11.2.

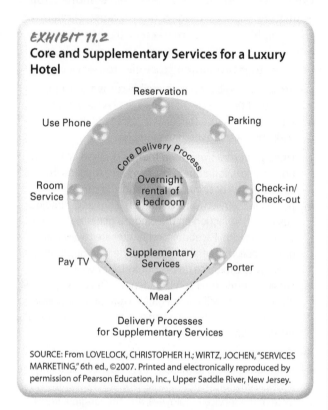

EXHIBIT 11.2
Core and Supplementary Services for a Luxury Hotel

Reservation
Use Phone
Parking
Core Delivery Process
Room Service
Overnight rental of a bedroom
Check-in/ Check-out
Pay TV
Supplementary Services
Porter
Meal
Delivery Processes for Supplementary Services

SOURCE: From LOVELOCK, CHRISTOPHER H.; WIRTZ, JOCHEN, "SERVICES MARKETING," 6th ed., ©2007. Printed and electronically reproduced by permission of Pearson Education, Inc., Upper Saddle River, New Jersey.

Marketers should first set performance objectives when pricing each service. Three categories of pricing objectives have been suggested:[9]

▸▸ *Revenue-oriented pricing* focuses on maximizing the surplus of income over costs. A limitation of this approach is that determining costs can be difficult for many services.

▸▸ *Operations-oriented pricing* seeks to match supply and demand by varying prices. For example, matching hotel demand to the number of available rooms can be achieved by raising prices at peak times and decreasing them during slow times.

▸▸ *Patronage-oriented pricing* tries to maximize the number of customers using the service. Thus, prices vary with different market segments' ability to pay, and methods of payment (such as credit) are offered to increase the likelihood of a purchase.

A firm may need to use more than one type of pricing objective. In fact, all three objectives may need to be included to some degree in a pricing strategy, although the importance of each type may vary depending on the type of service provided, the prices that competitors are charging, the differing ability of various customer segments to pay, or the opportunity to negotiate price.

Productivity Strategy

Because services are often tied to a service provider and because the delivery of a service cannot be inventoried if supply exceeds demand, it is critical that the service firm work to manage the supply or the availability of the service without affecting service quality. Such a strategy is often referred to as capacity management. A trip to Florida during your February break is likely much more expensive than the same trip in September. Student demand for holidays to Florida is high in February, and hotels and airlines try to capitalize on the demand. In September, on the other hand, school has just started, student and families are thus otherwise engaged, so hotels and airlines offer lower prices to stimulate demand. After all, the plane still has to fly despite empty seats, and the hotels are still open despite empty rooms. This method of capacity management is referred to as off-peak pricing, and every day we see plenty of examples of it.

LO 5 Relationship Marketing in Services

Many services involve ongoing interaction between the service organization and the customer. Thus, these services can benefit from relationship marketing, the strategy described in Chapter 1, as a means of attracting, developing, and retaining customer relationships. The idea is to develop strong loyalty by creating satisfied customers who will buy additional services from the firm and are unlikely to switch to a competitor. Satisfied customers are also likely to engage in positive word-of-mouth communication, thereby helping to bring in new customers.

Many businesses have found it more cost-effective to hang on to the customers they have than to focus only on attracting new customers.

EFFECTIVE MARKETING OF SERVICES REQUIRES THE MANAGEMENT OF AN ADDITIONAL **4 Ps:** PEOPLE, PROCESS, PRODUCTIVITY, AND PHYSICAL ENVIRONMENT.

RELATIONSHIP MARKETING IS USED TO **ATTRACT, DEVELOP,** AND **RETAIN CUSTOMERS.** HOW LIKELY IS IT THAT THE CUSTOMER WILL USE THIS SERVICE **AGAIN?**

Services that purchasers receive on a continuing basis (for example, prescriptions, banking, and insurance) can be considered membership services. This type of service naturally lends itself to relationship marketing. When services involve discrete transactions (for example, a movie screening, a restaurant meal, or public transportation), it may be more difficult to build membership-type relationships with customers. Nevertheless, services involving discrete transactions may be transformed into membership relationships by using marketing tools. For example, the service could be sold in bulk (for example, a subscription to a theatre season or a commuter pass on public transportation). Or a service firm could offer special benefits to customers who choose to register with the firm (for example, loyalty programs for hotels and airlines). The service firm that has a more formalized relationship with its customers has an advantage because it knows who its customers are and how and when they use the services offered.[10]

Relationship marketing can be practised at three levels:[11]

▶▶ *Level 1:* Pricing incentives are used to encourage customers to continue doing business with a firm. Frequent flyer programs are an example of level-1 relationship marketing. This level of relationship marketing is the least effective in the long term because its price-based advantage is easily imitated by other firms.

▶▶ *Level 2:* This level of relationship marketing also uses pricing incentives but seeks to build social bonds with customers. The firm stays in touch with its customers, learns about their needs, and designs services to meet those needs. Level-2 relationship marketing is often more effective than level-1 relationship marketing.

▶▶ *Level 3:* At this level, the firm again uses financial and social bonds but adds structural bonds to the formula. Structural bonds are developed by offering value-added services that are not readily available from other firms. Members of Hertz's #1 Club Gold program can call and reserve a car, board a courtesy bus at the airport, tell the driver their name, and get dropped off in front of their car. Marketing programs like this one have the strongest potential for sustaining long-term relationships with customers.

Companies use loyalty cards to build customer relationships.

LO 6 Internal Marketing in Service Firms

The service and the service provider are inseparable. Thus, the quality of a firm's employees is crucial to delivering a consistently superior product and to building long-term relationships with customers. Employees who like their jobs and are satisfied with the firm they work for are more likely to deliver superior service to customers. Their superior service, in turn, increases the likelihood of retaining customers. Thus, it is critical that service firms practise **internal marketing**, which means treating employees as customers and developing systems and benefits that satisfy their needs. To satisfy employees, companies have designed and instituted a wide variety of programs, such as flextime and on-site daycare. The *Financial Post* once again selected TD Bank Financial Group as one of Canada's Top 100 Employers because it demonstrates commitment to its employees. The company supports new moms, dads, and adoptive parents with leave top-up payments; provides employees with excellent financial benefits, including low-interest home loans and year-end bonuses; and the head office social committee hosts an impressive holiday party for children of employees, complete with carnival rides, a petting zoo, pony rides, and over 3,000 gifts delivered from Santa.[12]

LO 7 Global Issues in Services Marketing

According to Foreign Affairs and International Trade Canada, both Canada's merchandise trade and its services trade contracted in 2009 due to the global recession. However, Canada's services trade fell less than merchandise trade. Canada continues to trade strongly in services but a services trade deficit persists. In 2010, Canada's exports of services were $66 billion, a decline over the three previous years.[13] Despite the trade declines, the international marketing of services is a major part of global business. To be successful in the global marketplace, service firms must first determine the nature of their core product. Next, the marketing mix elements should be designed to take into account each country's cultural, technological, and political environments.

Because of their competitive advantages, many Canadian service industries have been able to enter the global marketplace. Banks, for example, have advantages in customer service and collections management.

LO 8 Nonprofit Organization Marketing

A **nonprofit organization** is an organization that exists to achieve some goal other than the usual business goals of profit, market share, and return on investment. Both nonprofit organizations and private-sector service firms market intangible products, and both often require the customer to be present during the production process. Both for-profit and nonprofit services vary greatly from producer to producer and from day to day, even from the same producer.

Canada's nonprofit and voluntary sector is the second largest in the world, behind the Netherlands. In Canada, more than two million people are employed in the nonprofit sector, representing 11.1 percent of the economically active population. The nonprofit sector represents $79.1 billion or 7.1 percent of Canada's gross domestic product (GDP), which is larger than the manufacturing or automotive industries.[14] The nonprofit sector includes hospitals, colleges, and universities. If these organizations are removed from the picture, the remaining organizations are what Statistics Canada calls the core nonprofit sector, which contributes more than $35 billion to the Canadian economy, accounting for about 2.5 percent of GDP.[15]

What Is Nonprofit Organization Marketing?

Nonprofit organization marketing is the effort by nonprofit organizations to bring about mutually satisfying exchanges with target markets. Although these organizations vary substantially in size and purpose and operate in different environments, most perform the following marketing activities:

▸ Identifying the customers they wish to serve or attract (although they usually use another term, such as clients, patients, members, or sponsors)

▸ Explicitly or implicitly specifying objectives

▸ Developing, managing, and maintaining programs and services

▸ Deciding on prices to charge (although they may use other terms, such as *fees, donations, tuition, fares, fines,* or *rates*)

▸ Scheduling events or programs, and determining where they will be held or where services will be offered

▸ Communicating their availability through brochures, signs, public service announcements, or advertisements

Unique Aspects of Nonprofit Organization Marketing Strategies

Like their counterparts in for-profit business organizations, nonprofit managers develop marketing strategies to bring about mutually satisfying exchanges with their target markets. However, marketing in nonprofit organizations is unique in many ways—including the setting of marketing objectives, the selection of target markets, and the development of appropriate marketing mixes.

Objectives In the private sector, the profit motive is both an objective for guiding decisions and a criterion for evaluating results. Nonprofit organizations do not seek to make a profit for redistribution to owners or shareholders. Rather, their focus is often on generating enough funds to deliver the service while covering expenses.

Most nonprofit organizations are expected to provide equitable, effective, and efficient services that respond to the wants and preferences of their multiple constituencies, which may include users, donors, politicians, appointed officials, the media, and the general public. Nonprofit organizations cannot measure their success or failure in strictly financial terms.

Nonprofit managers may find it difficult to prioritize objectives, make decisions, and evaluate performance because of the lack of a financial bottom line and the existence of multiple, diverse, intangible, and sometimes vague or conflicting objectives. These managers must often use approaches different from those commonly used in the private sector.

Target Markets Two issues relating to target markets are unique to nonprofit organizations:

▸▸ *Apathetic or strongly opposed targets:* Private-sector organizations usually give priority to developing those market segments that are most likely to respond to particular offerings. In contrast, some nonprofit organizations must, by nature of their service, target those who are apathetic about or strongly opposed to receiving their services, such as people requiring vaccinations or psychological counselling.

▸▸ *Pressure to adopt undifferentiated segmentation strategies:* Nonprofit organizations often adopt undifferentiated strategies (see Chapter 7) by default. Sometimes they fail to recognize the advantages of targeting, or an undifferentiated approach may appear to offer economies of scale and low per capita costs. In other instances, nonprofit organizations are pressured or required to serve the maximum number of people by targeting the average user.

Positioning Decisions Because of the unique issues relating to target markets, positioning decisions are critical to the nonprofit. The mission and vision of the nonprofit must be clearly articulated and communicated through the nonprofit's positioning statement, also referred to as the nonprofit's value proposition, which then drives all messaging. Because nonprofit organizations are pressured to adopt undifferentiated segmentation strategies and are often in complementary roles with those offering similar services in the public sector, a single-minded positioning is key to maintaining an accurate perception of the nonprofit among all constituent groups.

Product Decisions Three product-related characteristics distinguish business organizations from nonprofit organizations:

▸▸ *Benefit complexity:* Nonprofit organizations often market complex and emotional behaviours or ideas. Examples include the need to exercise or eat properly and the need to quit smoking. The benefits that a person receives are complex, long term, and intangible, and therefore are more difficult to communicate to consumers. Ronald McDonald House offers a home away from home for families of ill children receiving treatment at area hospitals. This nonprofit enables families to stay close to their child at a very critical time. The benefit is enormous but unless you have experienced having nowhere to sleep but in your car or in a chair at your child's bedside, how do you fully and accurately communicate the service benefits of Ronald McDonald House?

▸▸ *Benefit strength:* The benefit strength of many nonprofit offerings is not immediate or is indirect. What are the direct, personal benefits to you of driving 80 km per hour or volunteering at your local hospice? In contrast, most private-sector service organizations can offer customers immediate and direct, personal benefits.

RONALD McDONALD HOUSE CHARITIES

public service advertisement (PSA) an announcement that promotes a program of a nonprofit organization or of a federal, provincial or territorial, or local government

▶ *Involvement:* The involvement level of the products offered by nonprofit organizations varies greatly by nature of the intangibility of the product and the perceived importance of the product to the target market. ("I don't have children so why would I pay attention to the Ronald McDonald House organization?") Many nonprofit organizations market products that elicit very low involvement ("Prevent forest fires") or very high involvement ("Stop smoking"). The typical range for private-sector goods is much narrower. Traditional promotional tools may be inadequate to motivate adoption of either low- or high-involvement products.

Place (Distribution) Decisions A nonprofit organization's capacity for distributing its service offerings to potential customer groups when and where they want them is typically a key variable in determining the success of those service offerings. For example, many large universities have one or more satellite campus locations to provide easier access for students in other areas. Canadian Blood Services has placed a heavy emphasis on mobile donor sites that take the opportunity to donate to the donor's place of business, in essence intensifying distribution.

The extent to which a service depends on fixed facilities has important implications for distribution decisions. Services such as those offered by the Ronald McDonald House are limited only by the number of rooms in each house.

Promotion Decisions Many nonprofit organizations are explicitly or implicitly prohibited from advertising, thus limiting their promotion options. Other nonprofit organizations simply do not have the resources to retain advertising agencies, promotion consultants, or marketing staff. However, nonprofit organizations have a few special promotion resources to call on:

▶ *Professional volunteers:* Nonprofit organizations often seek out marketing, sales, and advertising professionals to help them develop and implement promotion strategies. In some instances, an advertising agency donates its services in exchange for potential long-term benefits.

Donated services create goodwill, personal contacts, and general awareness of the donor's organization, reputation, and competency. One such example is john st., a Toronto advertising firm that does creative work for the Canadian-based nonprofit War Child.

▶ *Sales promotion activities:* Sales promotion activities that make use of existing services or other resources are increasingly being used to draw attention to the offerings of nonprofit organizations. Sometimes nonprofit charities even team up with other companies for promotional activities. Special events are a great way to reach many targets while partnering with both profit and nonprofit companies. The Princess Margaret Weekend to End Breast Cancer is a great example.

▶ *Public relations:* Public relations is a valuable tool used by nonprofits. But organizations must ensure that their message is compelling and meaningful. One form of public relations used effectively by nonprofits is public service advertising. A **public service advertisement (PSA)** is an announcement that promotes a program of a nonprofit organization or of a federal, provincial or territorial, or local government. Unlike a commercial advertiser, the sponsor of the PSA does not pay for the time or space. Instead, the time or space is donated by the medium as a public service.

Pricing Decisions Five key characteristics distinguish the pricing decisions of nonprofit organizations from those of the profit sector:

▶ *Pricing objectives:* The main pricing objective in the profit sector is revenue or, more specifically, profit maximization, sales maximization, or target return on sales or investment. Many nonprofit organizations must also be concerned about revenue. Often, however, nonprofit organizations seek to either partially or fully defray costs rather than achieve a profit for distribution to stockholders. Nonprofit organizations also seek to redistribute income through the delivery of their service. Moreover, they strive to allocate resources fairly among individuals or households or across geographic or political boundaries.

▶ *Nonfinancial prices:* In many nonprofit situations, consumers are not charged a monetary price but instead must absorb nonmonetary costs. Nonmonetary costs include time and maybe even embarrassment, depending on the service being provided. Habitat for Humanity requires the recipients of a home to contribute sweat equity as part of the price of the building of their new home.

OBEDIENCE IS KEY

•HELPCHILDSOLDIERS.COM•

COURTESY OF WAR CHILD

- ➤➤ *Indirect payment:* Indirect payment through taxes is common to marketers of free services, such as libraries, fire protection, and police protection. Indirect payment is not a common practice in the profit sector.

- ➤➤ *Separation between payers and users:* By design, the services of many charitable organizations are provided to those who are relatively poor and are largely paid for by those who are better off financially. Although examples of separation between payers and users can be found in the profit sector (such as insurance claims), the practice is much less prevalent.

- ➤➤ *Below-cost pricing:* An example of below-cost pricing is university tuition. Virtually all private and public colleges and universities price their services below their full costs.

NONPROFIT MARKETING STRATEGY AT A GLANCE

Objectives
- May be multiple and intangible

Positioning
- Single-minded

Place
- Intensity of distribution

Price
- Objectives
- Nonfinancial pricing
- Indirect payment
- Separation between payers and users
- Below-cost pricing

Target Markets
- Apathetic or strongly opposed
- Pressure to adopt an undifferentiated strategy

Product
- Benefit complexity
- Benefit strength
- Involvement

Promotion
- Professional volunteers
- Sales promotion activities
- Public relations

Possible gaps in service quality

5

Categories of service processes

4

Number of charities registered with the Canada Revenue Agency

78,000

Percentage of Canadian GDP provided by service sector

70%

52

The number of countries that have a Ronald McDonald House

Visit **icanmktg2.com** to find the resources you need today!

Located at the back of the textbook are rip-out Chapter Review cards. Make sure you also go online to check out other tools that MKTG offers to help you successfully pass your course.

- Interactive Quizzing
- Games
- Flashcards
- Audio Summaries
- PowerPoint Slides
- Videos and Assessments
- Cases
- Marketing Plans and Worksheets
- Animated Visual Summaries

CHAPTER 12

Marketing Channels and Supply Chain Management

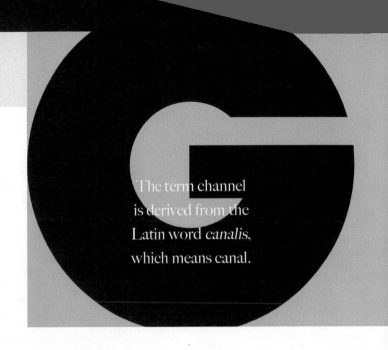

The term channel is derived from the Latin word *canalis*, which means canal.

LO 1 Marketing Channels

AFTER YOU FINISH THIS CHAPTER, GO TO WWW. ICANMKTG2.COM FOR STUDY TOOLS.

A marketing channel can be viewed as a large canal or pipeline through which products, their ownership, communication, financing and payment, and accompanying risk flow to the consumer. Formally, a **marketing channel** (also called a **channel of distribution**) is a business structure of interdependent organizations that reach from the point of product origin to the consumer, with the purpose of moving products to their final consumption destination. In other words, a marketing channel is a set of interdependent organizations that ease the transfer of ownership as products move from producer to business user or consumer. Marketing channels facilitate the physical movement of goods through the supply chain, representing *place* or *distribution* in the marketing mix (product, price, promotion, and place) and encompassing the processes involved in getting the right product to the right place at the right time.

marketing channel (channel of distribution) a set of interdependent organizations that ease the transfer of ownership as products move from producer to business user or consumer

What do you think?

I prefer to download my music online compared to buying it at a store.

1   2   3   4   5   6   7
STRONGLY DISAGREE   STRONGLY AGREE

© ISTOCKPHOTO.COM/ROBERT BYRON

channel members all parties in the marketing channel that negotiate with one another, buy and sell products, and facilitate the change of ownership between buyer and seller in the course of moving the product from the manufacturer into the hands of the final consumer

supply chain the connected chain of all of the business entities, both internal and external to the company, that perform or support the marketing channel functions

discrepancy of quantity the difference between the amount of product produced and the amount an end-user wants to buy

discrepancy of assortment the lack of all the items a customer needs to receive full satisfaction from a product or products

Many different types of organizations participate in marketing channels. **Channel members** (also called *intermediaries* and

resellers) comprise all parties in the marketing channel that negotiate with one another, buy and sell products, and facilitate the change of ownership between buyer and seller in the course of moving the product from the manufacturer into the hands of the final consumer. An important aspect of marketing channels is the joint effort of all channel members to create a continuous and seamless supply chain. The **supply chain** is the connected chain of all of the business entities, both internal and external to the company, that perform or support the marketing channel functions. As products move through the supply chain, channel members facilitate the distribution process by providing specialization and division of labour, overcoming discrepancies, and providing contact efficiency.

Providing Specialization and Division of Labour

According to the concept of *specialization and division of labour,* breaking down a complex task into smaller, simpler tasks and then allocating them to specialists will both create greater efficiency and lower average production costs. Manufacturers achieve economies of scale through the use of efficient equipment capable of producing large quantities of a single product.

Marketing channels can also attain economies of scale through specialization and division of labour by aiding producers who lack the motivation, financing,

or expertise to market directly to end-users or consumers. In some cases, as with most consumer convenience goods, such as pop, the cost of marketing directly to millions of consumers—taking and shipping individual orders—is prohibitive. For this reason, producers hire channel members, such as wholesalers and retailers, to do what the producers are not equipped to do or what channel members are better prepared to do. Channel members can do some things more efficiently than producers because they have built good relationships with their customers. Therefore, their specialized expertise enhances the overall performance of the channel.

Overcoming Discrepancies

Marketing channels also aid in overcoming discrepancies of quantity, assortment, time, and space created by economies of scale in production. For example, assume that Quaker Oats can efficiently produce its Aunt Jemima instant pancake mix at a rate of 5,000 units in a typical day. Not even the most ardent pancake fan could consume that amount in a year, much less in a day. The quantity produced to achieve low unit costs has created a **discrepancy of quantity**, which is the difference between the amount of product produced and the amount an end-user wants to buy. By storing the product and distributing it in the appropriate amounts, marketing channels overcome quantity discrepancies by making products available in the quantities that consumers desire.

Mass production creates not only discrepancies of quantity but also discrepancies of assortment. A **discrepancy of assortment** occurs when a consumer does not have all of the items needed to receive full satisfaction from a product. For pancakes to provide maximum satisfaction, several other products are required to complete the assortment. At the very least, most people want a knife, fork, plate, butter, and syrup. Even though Quaker is a large consumer-products company, it does not come close to providing the optimal assortment to go with its Aunt Jemima pancakes. To overcome discrepancies of assortment, marketing channels assemble in one place many of the products necessary to complete a consumer's needed assortment.

A **temporal discrepancy** is created when a product is produced but a consumer is not ready to buy it. Marketing channels overcome temporal discrepancies by maintaining inventories in anticipation of demand. For example, manufacturers of seasonal merchandise, such as Christmas or Halloween decorations, operate year-round, despite consumer demand being concentrated only during certain months of the year.

Furthermore, because mass production requires many potential buyers, markets are usually scattered over large geographic regions, creating a **spatial discrepancy**. Often global, or at least nationwide, markets are needed to absorb the outputs of mass producers. Marketing channels overcome spatial discrepancies by making products available in locations convenient to consumers. For example, if all the Aunt Jemima pancake mix is produced in Peterborough, Ontario, then the Quaker Oats Company must use an intermediary to distribute the product to other regions of Canada.

Providing Contact Efficiency

The third need fulfilled by marketing channels is the contact efficiency provided by reducing the number of stores customers must shop in to complete their purchases. Suppose you had to buy your milk at a dairy and your meat at a stockyard. You would spend a great deal of time, money, and energy shopping for just a few groceries. Supply chains simplify distribution by cutting the number of transactions required to move products from manufacturers to consumers and by making an assortment of goods available in one location.

Consider the example illustrated in Exhibit 12.1. Four consumers each want to buy an HD television. Without a retail intermediary such as Future Shop, television manufacturers JVC, Zenith, Sony, Toshiba, and RCA would each have to make four contacts to reach the four buyers who are in the target market, for a total of 20 transactions. However, when Future Shop acts as an intermediary between the producer and consumers, each producer makes only one contact, reducing the number of transactions to nine. Each producer sells to one retailer rather than to four consumers. In turn, consumers buy from one retailer instead of from five producers. Information technology has enhanced contact efficiency by making information on products and services easily available over the Internet. Shoppers can find the best bargains without physically searching for them.

LO 2 Channel Intermediaries and Their Functions

Intermediaries in a channel negotiate with one another, facilitate the change of ownership between buyers and sellers, and physically move products from the manufacturer to the final consumer. The most prominent difference separating intermediaries is whether they take title to the product or not. *Taking title* means they own the merchandise and control the terms of the sale—for example, price and delivery date. Retailers and merchant wholesalers are examples of intermediaries that

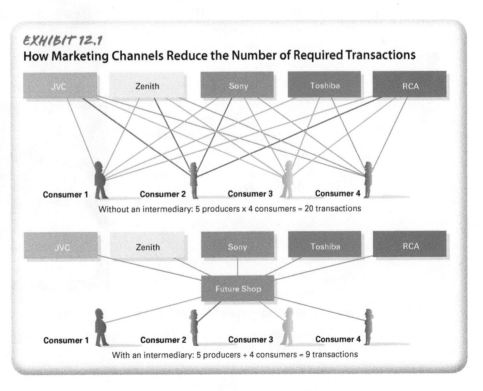

EXHIBIT 12.1
How Marketing Channels Reduce the Number of Required Transactions

Without an intermediary: 5 producers × 4 consumers = 20 transactions

With an intermediary: 5 producers + 4 consumers = 9 transactions

retailer a channel intermediary that sells mainly to consumers

take title to products in the marketing channel and resell them. **Retailers** are firms that sell mainly to consumers. Retailers will be discussed in more detail in Chapter 13.

Variations in channel structures are due in large part to variations in the numbers and types of wholesaling intermediaries. (See Exhibit 12.2.) Generally, product characteristics, buyer considerations, and market conditions determine the type of intermediary the manufacturer should use.

▸▸ *Product characteristics* that may require a certain type of wholesaling intermediary include whether the product is standardized or customized, the complexity of the product, and the gross margin of the product. For example, a customized product such as insurance is sold through an insurance agent or broker who may represent one or multiple companies. In contrast, a standardized product such as gum is sold through a merchant wholesaler that takes possession of the gum and reships it to the appropriate retailers.

▸▸ *Buyer considerations* affecting the wholesaler choice include how often the product is purchased and how long the buyer is willing to wait to receive the product. For example, at the beginning of the school term, a student may be willing to wait a few days for a textbook if it means paying a lower price by ordering online. Thus, this type of product can be distributed directly. But, if the student waits to buy the book until right before an exam and needs the book immediately, the student will need to purchase it for full price at the school bookstore.

▸▸ *Market characteristics* that determine the wholesaler type include the number of buyers in the market and whether they are concentrated in a general location or are widely dispersed. Gum and textbooks, for example, are produced in one location and consumed in many

EXHIBIT 12.2
Marketing Channel Functions Performed by Intermediaries

Type of Function	Description
Transactional Functions	**Contacting and promoting:** Contacting potential customers, promoting products, and soliciting orders
	Negotiating: Determining how many goods or services to buy and sell, type of transportation to use, when to deliver, and method and timing of payment
	Risk taking: Assuming the risk of owning inventory
Logistical Functions	**Physically distributing:** Transporting and sorting goods to overcome temporal and spatial discrepancies
	Storing: Maintaining inventories and protecting goods
	Sorting: Overcoming discrepancies of quantity and assortment by
	Sorting out: Breaking down a heterogeneous supply into separate homogeneous stocks
	Accumulating: Combining similar stocks into a larger homogeneous supply
	Allocating: Breaking a homogeneous supply into smaller and smaller lots ("breaking bulk")
	Assorting: Combining products into collections or assortments that buyers want available at one place
Facilitating Functions	**Researching:** Gathering information about other channel members and consumers
	Financing: Extending credit and other financial services to facilitate the flow of goods through the channel to the final consumer

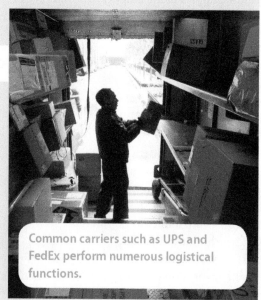

Common carriers such as UPS and FedEx perform numerous logistical functions.

© CHARLES REX ARBOGAST/ASSOCIATED PRESS

other locations. Therefore, a merchant wholesaler is needed to distribute the products. In contrast, in a home sale, the buyer and seller are localized in one area, which facilitates the use of an agent or broker relationship.

Channel Functions Performed by Intermediaries

Retailing and wholesaling intermediaries in marketing channels perform several essential functions that enable the flow of goods between producer and buyer. The three basic functions that intermediaries perform are summarized in Exhibit 12.2.

Although individual members can be added to or deleted from a channel, someone must still perform these essential functions. They can be performed by producers, end-users or consumers, channel intermediaries such as wholesalers and retailers, and sometimes by nonmember channel participants. For example, if a manufacturer decides to eliminate its private fleet of trucks, it must still move the goods to the wholesaler. This task may be accomplished by the wholesaler, which may have its own fleet of trucks, or by a nonmember channel participant, such as an independent trucking firm. Nonmembers also provide many other essential functions that may at one time have been provided by a channel member. For example, research firms may perform the research function; advertising agencies may provide the promotion function; transportation and storage firms, the physical distribution function; and banks, the financing function.

LO 3 Channel Structures

A product can take many routes to reach its final consumer. Marketers search for the most efficient channel from the many alternatives available. Marketing a consumer convenience good such as gum or candy differs from marketing a specialty good such as a Prada handbag. The next sections discuss the structures of typical and alternative marketing channels for consumer and business-to-business products.

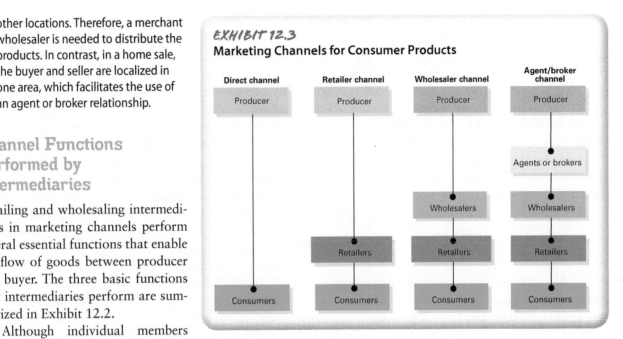

EXHIBIT 12.3
Marketing Channels for Consumer Products

Direct channel	Retailer channel	Wholesaler channel	Agent/broker channel
Producer	Producer	Producer	Producer
			Agents or brokers
		Wholesalers	Wholesalers
	Retailers	Retailers	Retailers
Consumers	Consumers	Consumers	Consumers

Channels for Consumer Products

Exhibit 12.3 illustrates the four ways manufacturers can route products to consumers. Producers use the **direct channel** to sell directly to consumers. Direct-marketing activities—including telemarketing, mail-order and catalogue shopping, and forms of electronic retailing such as online shopping and shop-at-home television networks—are a good example of this type of channel structure. Direct channels have no intermediaries. Producer-owned stores and factory outlet stores—such as Danier Leather, Roots 73, and Rocky Mountain Chocolate Factory—are examples of direct channels. Direct marketing and factory outlets are discussed in more detail in Chapter 13.

By contrast, an *agent/broker channel* is fairly complicated and is typically used in markets characterized by many small manufacturers and many retailers that lack the resources to find each other. Agents or brokers bring manufacturers and wholesalers together for negotiations, but they do not take title to merchandise. Ownership passes directly to one or more wholesalers and then to retailers. Finally, retailers sell to the ultimate consumer of the product. For example, a food broker represents buyers and sellers of grocery products. The broker acts on behalf of many different producers and negotiates the sale of their products to wholesalers that specialize in foodstuffs. These wholesalers in turn sell to grocers and convenience stores.

direct channel a distribution channel in which producers sell directly to consumers

dual distribution (multiple distribution) the use of two or more channels to distribute the same product to target markets

Most consumer products are sold through distribution channels similar to the other two alternatives: the retailer channel and the wholesaler channel. A *retailer channel* is most common when the retailer is large and can buy in large quantities directly from the manufacturer. Wal-Mart, Sears, and car dealers are examples of retailers that often bypass a wholesaler. A *wholesaler channel* is commonly used for low-cost items that are frequently purchased, such as candy, gum, and magazines.

Channels for Business and Industrial Products

As Exhibit 12.4 illustrates, five channel structures are common in business and industrial markets. First, direct channels are typical in business and industrial markets. For example, manufacturers buy large quantities of raw materials, major equipment, processed materials, and supplies directly from other manufacturers. Manufacturers that require suppliers to meet detailed technical specifications often prefer direct channels. The direct communication required between Chrysler Canada and its suppliers, for example, along with the tremendous size of the orders, makes anything but a direct channel impractical. The channel from producer to government buyers is also a direct channel. Since much government buying is done through bidding, a direct channel is attractive.

Companies selling standardized items of moderate or low value often rely on *industrial distributors*. In many ways, an industrial distributor is like a supermarket for organizations. Industrial distributors are wholesalers and channel members that buy and take title to products. Moreover, they usually keep inventories of their products and sell and service them. Often small manufacturers cannot afford to employ their own sales force. Instead, they rely on manufacturers' representatives or selling agents to sell to either industrial distributors or users such as Sysco.

The Internet has enabled virtual distributors to emerge and thereby has forced traditional industrial distributors to expand their business model. Many manufacturers and consumers are bypassing distributors and going direct, often via the Internet. Companies looking to drop the intermediary from the supply chain have created exchanges. Retailers use the Worldwide Retail Exchange to make purchases (that in the past would have required telephone, fax, or face-to-face sales calls), and, in so doing, save approximately 15 percent in their purchasing costs. Finally, a third type of Internet marketplace is a private exchange. Private exchanges allow companies to automate their supply chains while sharing information only with select suppliers. Dell, IBM, and Hewlett-Packard, for example, use private exchanges to manage their inventory supplies and save on distribution and freight costs.[1]

Alternative Channel Arrangements

Rarely does a producer use just one type of channel to move its product. It usually employs several different or alternative channels, which include multiple channels, nontraditional channels, and strategic channel alliances.

Multiple Channels When a producer selects two or more channels to distribute the same product to target markets, this arrangement is called **dual distribution** (or **multiple distribution**). As more people have access to the Internet and embrace online shopping, an increasing number of retailers are choosing to use multiple distribution channels. For example, companies such as Roots, which includes Roots Home Design, Roots Business to Business, and Roots Yoga, sells in-store, online, and through catalogues.

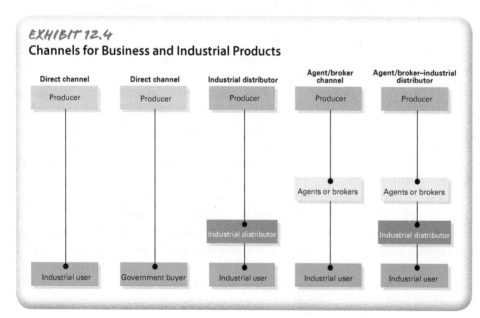

EXHIBIT 12.4
Channels for Business and Industrial Products

Direct channel: Producer → Industrial user
Direct channel: Producer → Government buyer
Industrial distributor: Producer → Industrial distributor → Industrial user
Agent/broker channel: Producer → Agents or brokers → Industrial user
Agent/broker–industrial distributor: Producer → Agents or brokers → Industrial distributor → Industrial user

Nontraditional Channels Often nontraditional channel arrangements help differentiate a firm's product from the competition. Nontraditional channels include the Internet, mail-order channels, and infomercials. Although nontraditional channels may limit a brand's coverage, for a producer serving a niche market, they provide a way to gain market access and customer attention without having to establish channel intermediaries. Nontraditional channels can also provide another avenue of sales for larger firms. For example, vending machines often associated with dispensing pop, snacks, or cash are taking on new roles. A London publisher sells short stories through vending machines in the London underground. Instead of the traditional book format, the stories are printed like folded maps, making them an easy-to-read alternative for commuters. An Ontario company, PharmaTrust, in 2011 initiated placement of pharmaceutical drug dispensing machines that receive the prescriptions by video-phone taken by head office, read patient's benefit cards, take payment, and dispense the patient's drugs in Ontario hospitals.

Strategic Channel Alliances Companies often form **strategic channel alliances**, which are cooperative agreements between business firms to use one of the manufacturer's already established channels. Alliances are used most often when the creation of marketing channel relationships may be too expensive and time-consuming. Nearly 15 years ago, Starbucks contracted with Pepsi to develop and bottle a Starbucks brand of ready-to-drink (RTD) coffee. The resulting Frappuccino and Doubleshot were an immediate success. Today, the Pepsi Bottling Group is still the sole distributor for Starbucks RTD beverages, and Starbucks has continued access to the thousands of outlets where Pepsi is sold.[2] Strategic channel alliances are proving to be more successful for growing businesses than mergers and acquisitions. This success is especially true in global markets where cultural differences, distance, and other barriers can prove challenging.

TORONTO STAR/FIRST LIGHT

The successful logistics systems for Oh Henry! chocolate bars starts with its manufacturing facility.

© JULIE PRATT

LO 4 Supply Chain Management

Many modern companies are turning to supply chain management to gain a competitive advantage. The goal of **supply chain management** is to coordinate and integrate all of the activities performed by supply chain members into a seamless process, from the source to the point of consumption, ultimately giving supply chain managers total visibility of the supply chain, both inside and outside the firm. The philosophy behind supply chain management is that by visualizing the entire supply chain, supply chain managers can maximize strengths and efficiencies at each level of the process to create a highly competitive, customer-driven supply system that is able to respond immediately to changes in supply and demand.

Supply chain management is completely customer driven. In the mass-production era, manufacturers produced standardized products that were pushed down through the supply channel to the consumer. In today's marketplace, however, products are being driven by customers, who expect to receive product configurations and services matched to their unique needs. The focus is on pulling products into the marketplace and partnering with members of the supply chain to enhance customer value. Customizing an automobile is now possible because of new supply chain relationships between the automobile manufacturers and the aftermarket auto-parts industry.[3]

This reversal of the flow of demand from a push to a pull has resulted in a radical reformulation of

strategic channel alliance a cooperative agreement between business firms to use one of the manufacturer's already established distribution channels

supply chain management a management system that coordinates and integrates all of the activities performed by supply chain members into a seamless process, from the source to the point of consumption, resulting in enhanced customer and economic value

market expectations and traditional marketing, production, and distribution functions. Integrated channel partnerships allow companies to respond with the unique product configuration and mix of services demanded by the customer. Today, supply chain management is both a *communicator* of customer demand that extends from the point of sale all the way back to the supplier, and a *physical flow* process that engineers the timely and cost-effective movement of goods through the entire supply pipeline.

WHY USE A SUPPLY CHAIN? WELL, YOU'LL BENEFIT FROM...
- AN ALMOST 20% INCREASE IN CASH FLOW
- A MORE THAN 50% INCREASE IN FLEXIBILITY OF CHAIN ACTIVITIES
- A 5–10% REDUCTION IN SUPPLY CHAIN COSTS[4]

Benefits of Supply Chain Management

Supply chain management is both a key means of differentiation for a firm and a critical component in marketing and corporate strategy. Companies that focus on supply chain management commonly report lower costs of inventory, transportation, warehousing, and packaging; greater supply chain flexibility; improved customer service; and higher revenues. Research has shown a clear relationship between supply chain performance and profitability.

LO5 Making Channel Strategy Decisions

Devising a marketing channel strategy requires several critical decisions. Supply chain managers must decide what role distribution will play in the overall marketing strategy. In addition, they must be sure that the channel strategy chosen is consistent with product, promotion, and pricing strategies. In making these decisions, marketing managers must determine which factors will influence the choice of channel and the appropriate level of distribution intensity.

Factors Affecting Channel Choice

Supply chain managers must answer many questions before choosing a marketing channel. The final choice depends on their desired distribution channel objectives in terms of coverage, costs, and control of their products. To determine the final choice means first analyzing several factors that often interact with each other. These factors can be grouped as market factors, product factors, and producer factors.

Market Factors Among the most important market factors affecting the choice of distribution channel are target customer considerations. Specifically, supply chain managers should answer the following questions: Who are the potential customers? What do they buy? Where do they buy? When do they buy? How do they buy? Additionally, the choice of channel depends on whether the producer is selling to consumers or to industrial customers. Industrial customers tend to buy in larger quantities and often require more customer service than consumers. For example, Toyota Industrial Equipment manufactures the leading lift truck used to move materials in and out of warehouses and other industrial facilities. Its business customers buy large numbers of trucks at one time and require additional services such as data tracking on how the lift truck is used.[5] In contrast, consumers usually buy in very small quantities and sometimes do not mind if they receive little or no service, such as when shopping in discount stores Wal-Mart and Zellers.

The geographic location and the size of the market are also important in channel selection. As a rule, if the target market is concentrated in one or more specific areas, then direct selling through a sales force is appropriate. When markets are more widely dispersed, intermediaries would be less expensive. The size of the market also influences channel choice. Generally, larger markets require more intermediaries. For instance, Procter & Gamble has to reach millions of consumers with its many brands of household goods. As a result, it needs many intermediaries, including wholesalers and retailers.

Product Factors Products that are more complex, customized, and expensive tend to benefit from shorter and more direct marketing channels. These types of products sell better through a direct sales force. Examples include pharmaceuticals, scientific instruments, airplanes, and mainframe computer

intensive distribution a form of distribution aimed at having a product available in every outlet where target customers might want to buy it

coverage ensuring product availability in every outlet where potential customers might want to buy it

systems. On the other hand, the more standardized a product is, the longer its distribution channel can be and the greater the number of intermediaries that can be involved. For example, with the exception of flavour and shape, the formula for chewing gum is about the same from producer to producer. Chewing gum is also very inexpensive, so the distribution channel for gum tends to involve many wholesalers and retailers.

The product's life cycle is also an important factor in choosing a marketing channel. In fact, the choice of channel may change over the life of the product. As products become more common and less intimidating to potential users, producers tend to look for alternative channels. For example, iPods are now available in special vending machines located in airports, as a result of initiatives by companies such as ZoomSystems.

Another factor is the delicacy of the product. Perishable products, such as vegetables and milk, have a relatively short lifespan. Therefore, they require fairly short marketing channels. Today, consumers' desire for fresh (often organic) produce and other farm products has led to a renewed growth across Canada in farmers'

markets and in businesses delivering these products from the farm directly to consumers' homes.

Producer Factors Several factors pertaining to the producer itself are important to the selection of a marketing channel. In general, producers with large financial, managerial, and marketing resources are better able to use more direct channels. These producers have the ability to hire and train their own sales force, warehouse their own goods, and extend credit to their customers. Smaller or weaker firms, on the other hand, must rely on intermediaries to provide these services. Compared with producers that have only one or two product lines, producers that sell several products in a related area are able to choose channels that are more direct. Their sales expenses then can be spread over more products.

A producer's desire to control pricing, positioning, brand image, and customer support also tends to influence channel selection. For instance, firms that sell products with exclusive brand images, such as designer perfumes and clothing, usually avoid channels in which discount retailers are present, preferring instead to sell their wares only in expensive stores to maintain an image of exclusivity. Many producers have opted to risk their image, however, and test sales in discount channels. Levi Strauss expanded its distribution to include Sears and Wal-Mart. Wal-Mart is now Levi Strauss's biggest customer.

Levels of Distribution Intensity

Organizations have three options for intensity of distribution: intensive distribution, selective distribution, or exclusive distribution.

Intensive Distribution **Intensive distribution** is a form of distribution aimed at maximum market coverage. **Coverage** refers to ensuring product availability in every outlet where potential customers might want to buy it. If buyers are unwilling to search for a product (as is true of convenience goods and operating supplies), the product must be very accessible to buyers.

Most manufacturers pursuing an intensive distribution strategy sell to a large percentage of the wholesalers willing to stock their products. Retailers' willingness (or unwillingness) to handle items tends to control the manufacturer's ability to achieve intensive distribution. For example, a retailer already carrying

selective distribution a form of distribution achieved by screening dealers to eliminate all but a few in any single area

exclusive distribution a form of distribution that involves only one or a few dealers within a given area

channel power a marketing channel member's capacity to control or influence the behaviour of other channel members

channel control a situation in which one marketing channel member intentionally affects another member's behaviour

channel leader (channel captain) a member of a marketing channel who exercises authority and power over the activities of other channel members

ten brands of gum may show little enthusiasm for carrying one more brand.

Selective Distribution **Selective distribution** is achieved by screening dealers and retailers to eliminate all but a few in any single area. Because only a few are chosen, the consumer must seek out the product. For example, when Heeling Sports Ltd. launched Heelys, thick-soled sneakers with a wheel embedded in each heel, the company needed to create demand. It hired a group of 40 teens to perform Heelys exhibitions in targeted malls, skate parks, and college and university campuses across the country. The company then made the decision to avoid large stores such as Sears, preferring instead to distribute the shoes only through selected mall retailers and skate and surf shops, where the Heelys could be positioned as "cool and kind of irreverent."[6]

Selective distribution strategies often hinge on a manufacturer's desire to maintain a superior product image so as to be able to charge a premium price.

Exclusive Distribution The most restrictive form of market coverage is **exclusive distribution**, which is a form of distribution that involves only one or a few dealers within a given area. Because buyers may have to search or travel extensively to buy the product, exclusive distribution is usually confined to consumer specialty goods, a few shopping goods, and major industrial equipment. Sometimes, exclusive territories are granted by new companies (such as franchisers) to obtain market coverage in a particular area. Limited distribution may also serve to project an exclusive image for the product.

Retailers and wholesalers may be unwilling to commit the time and money necessary to promote and

service a product unless the manufacturer guarantees them an exclusive territory. This arrangement shields the dealer from direct competition and enables it to be the main beneficiary of the manufacturer's promotion efforts in that geographic area. In an exclusive distribution, channels of communication are usually well established because the manufacturer works with a limited number of dealers rather than many accounts.

Exclusive distribution also takes place within a retailer's store rather than a geographic area—for example, when a retailer does not sell competing brands. Mark's Work Wearhouse partners with manufactures to produce its Dakota and WindRiver lines, brands sold only in its stores.

LO 6 Managing Channel Relationships

A marketing channel is more than a set of institutions linked by economic ties. Social relationships play an important role in building unity among channel members. A critical aspect of supply chain management, therefore, is managing the social relationships among channel members to achieve synergy. The basic social dimensions of channels are power, control, leadership, conflict, and partnering.

Channel Power, Control, and Leadership

Channel power is a channel member's capacity to control or influence the behaviour of other channel members. **Channel control** occurs when one channel member intentionally affects another member's behaviour. To achieve control, a channel member assumes channel leadership and exercises authority and power. This member is termed the **channel leader**, or **channel captain**. In one marketing channel, a manufacturer may be the leader because it controls new-product

iPhone 4S sales alone topped 4 million in the first weekend of release in October 2011.

IN THE FIRST QUARTER OF 2011, **APPLE STORE SALES** TOPPED $3.85 BILLION, A **95% JUMP** FROM THE SAME QUARTER OF THE PRIOR YEAR.

designs and product availability. In another marketing channel, a retailer may be the channel leader because it wields power and control over the retail price, inventory levels, and postsale service.

The exercise of channel power is a routine element of many business activities in which the outcome is often greater control over a company's brands. Apple started its line of retail stores because management was dissatisfied with how distributors were selling the company's computers (i.e., with its lack of control). Macintosh computer displays were often buried inside other major retail stores, surrounded by personal computers running Microsoft's more popular Windows operating systems. To regain channel power, Apple hired a retail executive to develop a retail strategy that relied heavily on company-owned stores reflecting Apple's design sensibilities. While still selectively adding to its number of stores in Canada, the United States, Spain, and elsewhere in 2011, Apple has also seen this expansion as an excellent way to control its channel development in China, where it plans to open 25 stores in 2012 alone.[7]

Channel Conflict

Inequitable channel relationships often lead to **channel conflict**, which is a clash of goals and methods among distribution channel members. In a broad context, conflict may not be bad. Often it arises because staid, traditional channel members refuse to keep pace with the times. Removing an outdated intermediary may result in reduced costs for the entire supply chain. The Internet has forced many intermediaries to offer online services such as merchandise tracking and inventory availability.

Conflicts among channel members can be due to many different situations and factors. Oftentimes, conflict arises because channel members have conflicting goals, as was the case with Apple and its distributors. Conflict can also arise when channel members fail to fulfill expectations of other channel members—for example, when a franchisee does not follow the rules set down by the franchiser or when communications channels break down between channel members. Further, ideological differences and different perceptions of reality can also cause conflict among channel members. For instance, some retailers,

believing the customer is always right, may offer a very liberal return policy. Conversely, some wholesalers and manufacturers may feel that people often try to get something for nothing or don't follow product instructions carefully. These differing views of allowable returns will undoubtedly conflict with those of retailers.

Conflict within a channel can be either horizontal or vertical. **Horizontal conflict** is a channel conflict that occurs among channel members on the same level, such as two or more different wholesalers or two or more different retailers that handle the same manufacturer's brands. This type of channel conflict is found most often when manufacturers practise dual or multiple distributions. Horizontal conflict can also occur when channel members feel that other members on the same level are being treated differently by the manufacturer, such as only some channel members receiving substantial discounts.

Many regard horizontal conflict as healthy competition. Much more serious is **vertical conflict**, which occurs between different levels in a marketing channel, most typically between the manufacturer and wholesaler or the manufacturer and retailer. Producer-versus-wholesaler conflict occurs when the producer chooses to bypass the wholesaler and deal directly with the consumer or retailer.

Dual distribution strategies can also cause vertical conflict in the channel, such as when high-end fashion designers sell their goods through their own boutiques and luxury department stores. Similarly, manufacturers experimenting with selling to customers directly over the Internet create conflict with their traditional retailing intermediaries. For instance, Kodak's U.S. launch of Ofoto[Kodak Gallery].com, a site where customers can upload digital pictures and purchase prints directly from Kodak, cost the company a $500 million contract with Walgreens, a U.S. chain that sells about 2 billion photo prints a year, all of which once were printed on Kodak paper using Kodak chemicals.[8] Producers and retailers may also disagree over the terms of the sale or other aspects of the business relationship.

ASSOCIATED PRESS/KODAK

channel conflict a clash of goals and methods among distribution channel members

horizontal conflict a channel conflict that occurs among channel members on the same level

vertical conflict a channel conflict that occurs between different levels in a marketing channel, most typically between the manufacturer and wholesaler or between the manufacturer and retailer

Channel Partnering

Regardless of the locus of power, channel members rely heavily on one another. Even the most powerful manufacturers depend on dealers to sell their products; and even the most powerful retailers require the products provided by suppliers. In sharp contrast to the adversarial relationships of the past between buyers and sellers, contemporary management emphasizes the development of close working partnerships among channel members. **Channel partnering**, or **channel cooperation**, is the joint effort of all channel members to create a supply chain that serves customers and creates a competitive advantage. Channel partnering is vital if each member is to gain something from other members. By cooperating, retailers, wholesalers, manufacturers, and suppliers can speed up inventory replenishment, improve customer service, and reduce the total costs of the marketing channel.

Channel alliances and partnerships help supply chain managers create the parallel flow of materials and information required to leverage the supply chain's intellectual, material, and marketing resources. The rapid growth in channel partnering is due to new technology and the need to lower costs. Collaborating channel partners meet the needs of consumers more effectively, thus boosting sales and profits. Forced to become more efficient, many companies are turning formerly adversarial relationships into partnerships.

L07 Managing the Logistical Components of the Supply Chain

Critical to any supply chain is orchestrating the physical means through which products move through it. **Logistics** is the process of strategically managing the efficient flow and storage of raw materials, in-process inventory, and finished goods from point of origin to point of consumption. As mentioned earlier, supply chain management coordinates and integrates all of

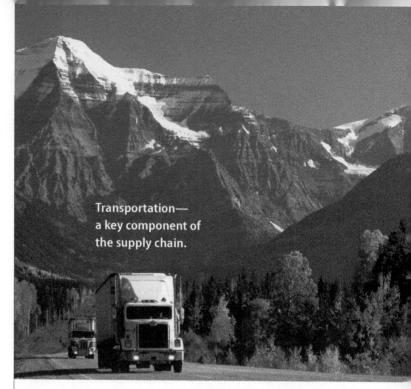

Transportation— a key component of the supply chain.

the activities performed by supply chain members into a seamless process. The supply chain consists of several interrelated and integrated logistical components: (1) sourcing and procurement of raw materials and supplies, (2) production scheduling, (3) order processing, (4) inventory control, (5) warehousing and materials handling, and (6) transportation.

The **logistics information system** is the link connecting all of the logistics components of the supply chain. The components of the system include, for example, software for materials acquisition and handling, warehouse management and enterprise-wide solutions, data storage and integration in data warehouses, mobile communications, electronic data interchange, radio-frequency identification (RFID) chips, and the Internet. Working together, the components of the logistics information system are the fundamental enablers of successful supply chain management.

The **supply chain team**, in concert with the logistics information system, orchestrates the movement of goods, services, and information from the source to the consumer. Supply chain teams typically cut across organizational boundaries, embracing all parties that participate in moving the product to market. The best supply chain teams also move beyond the organization to include the external participants in the chain, such as suppliers, transportation carriers, and third-party logistics suppliers. Members of the supply chain communicate, coordinate, and cooperate extensively.

Sourcing and Procurement

One of the most important links in the supply chain occurs between the manufacturer and the supplier.

Purchasing professionals are on the front lines of supply chain management. Purchasing departments plan purchasing strategies, develop specifications, select suppliers, and negotiate price and service levels.

The goal of most sourcing and procurement activities is to reduce the costs of raw materials and supplies. Purchasing professionals have traditionally relied on tough negotiations to get the lowest price possible from suppliers of raw materials, supplies, and components. Perhaps the biggest contribution purchasing can make to supply chain management, however, is in the area of vendor relations. Companies can use the purchasing function to strategically manage suppliers in order to reduce the total cost of materials and services. Through enhanced vendor relations, buyers and sellers can develop cooperative relationships that reduce costs and improve efficiency with the aim of lowering prices and enhancing profits. By integrating suppliers into their companies' businesses, purchasing managers have become better able to streamline purchasing processes, manage inventory levels, and reduce overall costs of the sourcing and procurement operations.

Production Scheduling

In traditional mass-market manufacturing, production begins when forecasts call for additional products to be made or when inventory control systems signal low inventory levels. The firm then makes a product and transports the finished goods to its own warehouses or those of intermediaries, where the goods wait to be ordered by retailers or customers. For example, many types of convenience goods, such as toothpaste, deodorant, and detergent, are manufactured on the basis of past sales and demand and then sent to retailers to resell. Production scheduling that is based on pushing a product down to the consumer obviously has its disadvantages, the most notable being that companies risk making products that may become obsolete or that consumers don't want in the first place.

In a customer "pull" manufacturing environment, which is growing in popularity, production of goods or services is not scheduled until an order is placed by the customer specifying the desired configuration. As you read in Chapter 11, this process, known as **mass customization**, or **build-to-order**, uniquely tailors mass-market goods and services to the needs of the individuals who buy them. Companies as diverse as BMW, Dell, Levi Strauss, Mattel, and a host of Web-based businesses are adopting mass customization to maintain or obtain a competitive edge.

As more companies move toward mass customization—and away from mass marketing—of goods, the need to stay on top of consumer demand is forcing manufacturers to make their supply chains more flexible. Flexibility is critical to a manufacturer's success when responding to dramatic swings in demand. To meet consumers' demand for customized products, companies must adapt their manufacturing approach or even create a completely new process. For years, Nike sold its shoes through specialty retailers to hardcore runners who cared little what the shoes looked like. Over time, however, runners began to demand more stylish designs and more technologically

> **mass customization (build-to-order)** a production method whereby products are not made until an order is placed by the customer; products are made according to customer specifications

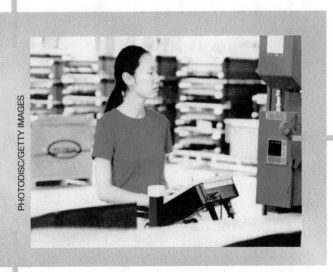

BUILD IT—FAST!

@ Dell, using specialized automation software, it takes:

< 6 workers

< 8 hours

To assemble ≈ several hundred computers

Which equals +160% increase in productivity per person per hour.[9]

PHOTODISC/GETTY IMAGES

"FOR THE SUPPLIER, **JIT** MEANS SUPPLYING CUSTOMERS WITH PRODUCTS IN JUST **A FEW DAYS,** OR EVEN **A FEW HOURS,** RATHER THAN WEEKS."

just-in-time production (JIT) a process that redefines and simplifies manufacturing by reducing inventory levels and delivering raw materials just when they are needed on the production line

order processing system a system whereby orders are entered into the supply chain and filled

electronic data interchange (EDI) information technology that replaces the paper documents that usually accompany business transactions, such as purchase orders and invoices, with electronic transmission of the needed information to reduce inventory levels, improve cash flow, streamline operations, and increase the speed and accuracy of information transmission

advanced footwear. To keep pace with rapidly changing fashions and trends, Nike launched NikeiD, a set of specialty stores and a website through which consumers can design and order athletic shoes.[10]

Just-in-Time Manufacturing An important manufacturing process common today among manufacturers is just-in-time manufacturing. Borrowed from the Japanese, **just-in-time production** (JIT), sometimes called *lean production*, requires manufacturers to work closely with suppliers and transportation providers to get necessary items to the assembly line or factory floor at the precise time they are needed for production. For the manufacturer, JIT means that raw materials arrive at the assembly line in guaranteed working order "just in time" to be installed, and finished products are generally shipped to the customer immediately after completion. For the supplier, JIT means supplying customers with products in just a few days, or even a few hours, rather than weeks. For the ultimate end-user, JIT means lower costs, shorter lead times, and products that more closely meet the consumer's needs. For example, Zara, a European clothing manufacturer and retailer with more than 600 stores in 48 countries, uses the JIT process to ensure that its stores are stocked with the latest fashion trends. Using its salespeople to track which fashions are selling fastest, the company can increase production of hot items and ship them to its stores in just a few days. Because Zara stores do not maintain

large inventories, they can respond quickly to fashion trends and offer their products for less, giving Zara a distinct advantage over more traditional retailers such as Gap that place orders months in advance.[11]

Order Processing

The order is often the catalyst that sets the supply chain in motion, especially in build-to-order environments. The **order processing system** processes the requirements of the customer and sends the information into the supply chain via the logistics information system. The order goes to the manufacturer's warehouse. If the product is in stock, the order is filled and arrangements are made to ship it. If the product is not in stock, it triggers a replenishment request that finds its way to the factory floor.

Proper order processing is critical to good service. As an order enters the system, management must monitor two flows: the flow of goods and the flow of information. Good communication among sales representatives, office personnel, and warehouse and shipping personnel is essential to accurate order processing. Shipping incorrect merchandise or partially filled orders can create just as much dissatisfaction as stockouts or slow deliveries. The flow of goods and information must be continually monitored so that mistakes can be corrected before an invoice is prepared and the merchandise shipped.

Order processing is becoming more automated through the use of computer technology known as **electronic data interchange (EDI)**. The basic idea of EDI is to replace the paper documents that usually accompany business transactions, such as purchase orders and invoices, with electronic transmission of the needed information. A typical EDI message includes all the information that would traditionally be included on a paper invoice, such

© IMAGE 100/CORBIS

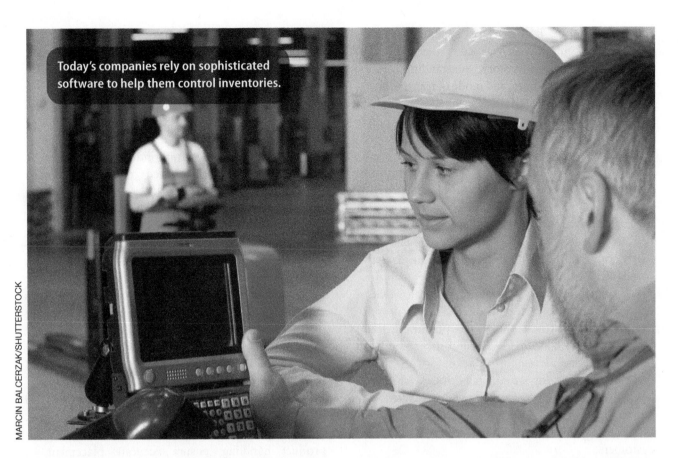

Today's companies rely on sophisticated software to help them control inventories.

MARCIN BALCERZAK/SHUTTERSTOCK

as product code, quantity, and transportation details. The information is usually sent via private networks, which are more secure and reliable than the networks used for standard email messages. Most importantly, the information can be read and processed by computers, significantly reducing costs and increasing efficiency. Companies that use EDI can reduce inventory levels, improve cash flow, streamline operations, and increase the speed and accuracy of information transmission. EDI also creates a closer relationship between buyers and sellers.

Retailers such as Wal-Mart and the Bay have become major users of EDI because logistics speed and accuracy are crucial competitive tools in the overcrowded retail environment. EDI works hand in hand with retailers' *efficient consumer response* programs to ensure the right products are on the shelf, in the right styles and colours, at the right time, through improved techniques for tracking inventory, ordering, and distribution.

Inventory Control

The **inventory control system** develops and maintains an adequate assortment of materials or products to meet a manufacturer's or a customer's demands.

Inventory decisions, for both raw materials and finished goods, have a big impact on supply chain costs and the level of service provided. If too many products are kept in inventory, costs increase—as do risks of obsolescence, theft, and damage shrinkage. If too few products are kept on hand, then the company risks product shortages, angry customers, and ultimately lost sales. The goal of inventory management, therefore, is to keep inventory levels as low as possible while maintaining an adequate supply of goods to meet customer demand.

Managing inventory from the supplier to the manufacturer is called **materials requirement planning (MRP)**, or **materials management**. This system also encompasses the sourcing and procurement operations, signalling when raw materials, supplies, or components will need to be replenished for the production of more goods. The system that manages the finished goods inventory from manufacturer to end-user is commonly referred to as **distribution resource planning (DRP)**.

inventory control system a method of developing and maintaining an adequate assortment of materials or products to meet a manufacturer's or a customer's demand

materials requirement planning (MRP) (materials management) an inventory control system that manages the replenishment of raw materials, supplies, and components from the supplier to the manufacturer

distribution resource planning (DRP) an inventory control system that manages the replenishment of goods from the manufacturer to the final consumer

Both inventory systems use various inputs, such as sales forecasts, available inventory, outstanding orders, lead times, and mode of transportation to be used, to determine what needs to be done to replenish goods at all points in the supply chain. Marketers identify demand at each level in the supply chain, from the retailer back up the chain to the manufacturer, and use EDI to transmit important information throughout the channel.

As you would expect, JIT has a significant impact on reducing inventory levels. Because supplies are delivered exactly when they are needed on the factory floor, little inventory of any kind is needed, and companies can order materials in smaller quantities. Those lower inventory levels can give firms a competitive edge through the flexibility to halt production of existing products in favour of those gaining popularity with consumers. Savings also come from having less capital tied up in inventory and from the reduced need for storage facilities. At the retail level, the reduced need for storage space allows for more extensive use of the retail store's area (its real estate space) for the display of more products to their customers.

Warehousing and Materials Handling

Although JIT manufacturing processes may eliminate the need to warehouse many raw materials, manufacturers may often keep some safety stock on hand in the event of an emergency, such as a strike at a supplier's plant or a catastrophic event that temporarily stops the flow of raw materials to the production line. The 2011 tsunami in Japan caused difficulties for automakers, such as Toyota and Honda, when lack of component parts resulted in car production being cut up to 25 percent in North American factories.[12]

The final user may not need or want the goods at the same time the manufacturer produces and wants to sell them. Products such as grain and corn are produced seasonally, but consumers demand them year-round. Other products, such as Christmas ornaments and turkeys, are produced year-round, but most consumers do not want them until autumn or winter. Therefore, management must have a storage system to hold these products until they are shipped.

Storage helps manufacturers manage supply and demand, or production and consumption. It provides time utility to buyers and sellers, which means that the seller stores the product until the buyer wants or needs it. But storing additional product does have disadvantages, including the costs of insurance on the stored product; taxes; the risks of obsolescence, spoilage, or theft; and warehouse operating costs. Another drawback is opportunity costs—that is, the opportunities lost because money is tied up in stored product instead of being used elsewhere.

Because businesses are focusing on cutting supply chain costs, the warehousing industry is investing in services that use sophisticated tracking technology such as **materials-handling systems**. An effective materials-handling system moves inventory into, within, and out of the warehouse quickly with minimal handling. With a manual, nonautomated materials-handling system, a product may be handled more than a dozen times. Each time it is handled, the cost and risk of damage increase; each lifting of a product stresses its package. Consequently, most manufacturers today have moved to automated systems. Scanners quickly identify goods entering and leaving a warehouse through bar-coded labels affixed to the packaging and pallets holding the goods.

Automatic storage and retrieval systems store and pick goods in the warehouse or distribution centre. Automated materials-handling systems decrease product handling, ensure accurate placement of product, and improve the accuracy of order picking and the rates of on-time shipment.

Transportation

Transportation typically accounts for 5 to 10 percent of the price of goods. Supply chain logisticians must

decide which mode of transportation to use to move products from supplier to producer and from producer to buyer. These decisions are, of course, related to all other logistics decisions. The five major modes of transportation are rail, truck, pipeline, water, and air. Supply chain managers generally choose a mode of transportation on the basis of several criteria:

▸▸ *Cost:* The total amount a specific carrier charges to move the product from the point of origin to the destination

▸▸ *Transit time:* The total time a carrier has possession of goods, including the time required for pickup and delivery, handling, and movement between the point of origin and the destination

▸▸ *Reliability:* The consistency with which the carrier delivers goods on time and in acceptable condition

▸▸ *Capability:* The ability of the carrier to provide the appropriate equipment and conditions for moving specific kinds of goods, such as those that must be transported in a controlled environment (for example, under refrigeration)

▸▸ *Accessibility:* A carrier's ability to move goods over a specific route or network

▸▸ *Traceability:* The relative ease with which a shipment can be located and transferred

The mode of transportation used depends on how the needs of the shipper relate to these six criteria. Exhibit 12.5 compares the basic modes of transportation on these criteria.

In many cases, especially in a JIT manufacturing environment, the transportation network replaces the warehouse or eliminates the expense of storing inventories as goods are timed to arrive the moment they're needed on the assembly line or for shipment to customers.

LO 8 Trends in Supply Chain Management

Several technological advances and business trends affect the job of today's supply chain manager. Three of the most important trends are advanced computer technology, outsourcing of logistics functions, and electronic distribution.

outsourcing (contract logistics) a manufacturer's or supplier's use of an independent third party to manage an entire function of the logistics system, such as transportation, warehousing, or order processing

Advanced Computer Technology

Advanced computer technology has boosted the efficiency of logistics dramatically with tools such as automatic identification systems (auto ID) using barcoding and radio-frequency technology, communications technology, and supply chain software systems that help synchronize the flow of goods and information with customer demand. At Amazon.com's state-of-the-art distribution centres, sophisticated order systems utilize computer terminals to guide workers through the picking and packing process. Radio-frequency technology, which uses radio signals that work with scanned bar codes to identify products, directs Amazon's workers to the exact locations in the warehouse where the product is stored. These supply chain technology tools have resulted in a 70 percent improvement in operational efficiency.[13]

Many companies use radio-frequency identification (RFID) tags in shipments to Wal-Mart stores. RFID tags are chips attached to a pallet of goods that allow the goods to be tracked from the time they are packed at the manufacturing plant until the consumer purchases them. Benefits include increased revenue for Wal-Mart because the shelves are always full and reduced inventory management costs because time spent counting items and overstocking are minimized.[14]

Outsourcing Logistics Functions

External partners are becoming increasingly important in the efficient deployment of supply chain management. **Outsourcing,** or **contract logistics,** is a rapidly growing segment of the distribution industry in which a manufacturer or supplier uses an

EXHIBIT 12.5
Criteria for Ranking Modes of Transportation

	Highest				Lowest
Relative Cost	Air	Truck	Rail	Pipeline	Water
Transit Time	Water	Rail	Pipeline	Truck	Air
Reliability	Pipeline	Truck	Rail	Air	Water
Capability	Water	Rail	Truck	Air	Pipeline
Accessibility	Truck	Rail	Air	Water	Pipeline
Traceability	Air	Truck	Rail	Water	Pipeline

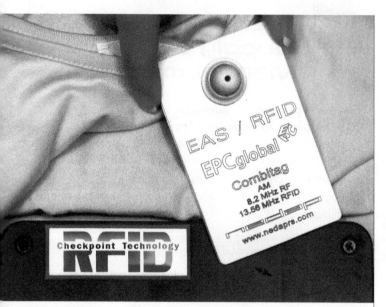

RFID tags can be attached to pallets of products or to individual items, such as clothing tags.

Electronic Distribution

Electronic distribution is the most recent development in the logistics arena. Broadly defined, **electronic distribution** includes any kind of product or service that can be distributed electronically, whether over traditional forms such as fibre-optic cable or through satellite transmission of electronic signals. Companies such as eTrade, iTunes, and Movies.com have built their business models around electronic distribution.

LO 9 Channels and Distribution Decisions for Global Markets

With the spread of free-trade agreements and treaties, global marketing channels and management of the supply chain have become increasingly important to corporations that export their products or manufacture abroad.

Developing Global Marketing Channels

Manufacturers introducing products in global markets must decide which type of channel structure to use. Using company salespeople generally provides more control and is less risky than using foreign intermediaries. However, setting up a sales force in a foreign country also involves a greater commitment, both financially and organizationally.

Channel structures and types abroad may differ from those in North America. For instance, the more highly developed a nation is economically, the more specialized its channel types. Therefore, a marketer wishing to sell in Germany or Japan will have several channel types to choose from. Conversely, developing countries such as India, Ethiopia, and Venezuela have limited channel types available: typically, these countries have few mail-order channels, vending machines, or specialized retailers and wholesalers. Some countries also regulate channel choices. Until 2004, Chinese regulations required foreign retailers to have a local partner. So, IKEA, the Swedish home furnishings retailer, used joint ventures to open its first two Chinese stores. When the regulations were lifted, IKEA opened its first wholly owned store in Guangzhou, followed by the opening of an enormous Beijing store,

electronic distribution a distribution technique that includes any kind of product or service that can be distributed electronically, whether over traditional forms such as fibre-optic cable or through satellite transmission of electronic signals

independent third party, such as SDV Logistics, to manage an entire function of the logistics system, including transportation, warehousing, and order processing. To focus on their core competencies, some companies choose to turn their logistics functions over to firms with expertise in that area. Partners create and manage entire solutions for getting products where they need to be, when they need to be there. Because a logistics provider is focused, clients receive service in a timely, efficient manner, thereby increasing customers' level of satisfaction and boosting their perception of added value to a company's offerings.

Third-party contract logistics allow companies to cut inventories, locate stock at fewer plants and distribution centres, and still provide the same service level or even better. The companies can then refocus investment on their core business. In the hospitality industry, Sysco negotiates with suppliers to obtain virtually everything that a hotel might need in terms of food and beverages. By relying on Sysco to manage many aspects of the supply chain, hotels such as Fairmont Hotels & Resorts and Intercontinental Hotels Group can concentrate on their core function—providing hospitality.[15] Many firms are taking outsourcing one step further by allowing business partners to take over the final assembly of their product or its packaging in an effort to reduce inventory costs, speed delivery, or better meet customer requirements.

second in size only to the company's flagship store in Stockholm.[16]

Global Logistics and Supply Chain Management

One of the most critical global logistical issues for importers of any size is coping with the legalities of trade in other countries. Shippers and distributors must be aware of the permits, licences, and registrations they may need to acquire and, depending on the type of product they are importing, the tariffs, quotas, and other regulations that apply in each country. This multitude of different rules is why multinational companies are committed to working through the World Trade Organization to develop a global set of rules and to encourage countries to participate.

Transportation can also be a major issue for companies dealing with global supply chains. Uncertainty regarding shipping usually tops the list of reasons why companies, especially smaller ones, resist international markets. In some instances, poor infrastructure makes transportation dangerous and unreliable. And the process of moving goods across the borders of even the most industrialized nations can still be complicated by government regulations. To make the process easier, Wide Range Transportation Services operates a 3,700 square metre (40,000 sq. foot) facility in Grimsby, Ontario, between Hamilton and Buffalo, New York. It offers brokerage, warehousing, fleet, and logistics services to help its clients reduce costs and save time shipping goods across the border.[17] The company uses technology similar to E-Z pass to automate the border crossings. The new system sends short-range radio signals containing information on the load to tollbooths, weigh stations, and border crossings. If the cargo meets requirements, the truck or train receives a green light to go ahead. Questionable cargo is set aside for further inspection. Transportation industry experts say the system can reduce delivery times by more than three hours.[18]

STEPHEN CHERNIN/GETTY IMAGES

Delivery of packages and documents in Canada:
>4.0 billion annually
≈ 15 million daily by ground
≈ 2.2 million daily by air

Service area:
More than 220 countries and territories; every address in North America and Europe

Daily delivery of packages & documents:
15.8 million

Delivery Fleet:
27,950 package cars, vans, tractors, motorcycles

UPS Jet Aircraft Fleet:
227;
ninth largest airline in the world

SOURCE: www.ups.com

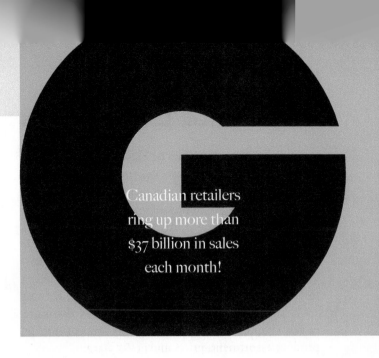

Canadian retailers ring up more than $37 billion in sales each month!

LO 1 The Role of Retailing

AFTER YOU FINISH THIS CHAPTER, GO TO WWW. ICANMKTG2.COM FOR STUDY TOOLS.

Retailing—all the activities directly related to the sale of goods and services to the ultimate consumer for personal, nonbusiness use—has enhanced the quality of our daily lives. When we shop for groceries, hairstyling, clothes, books, and many other products and services, we are involved in retailing. The millions of goods and services provided by retailers mirror the needs and styles of Canadian society.

Retailing affects all of us directly or indirectly. The retailing industry is one of the largest employers; more than 200,000 Canadian retailers employ over 1.8 million people. Retail trade accounts for 12.5 percent of all Canadian employment. At the store level, retailing is still largely a mom-and-pop business. Almost eight out of ten retail companies employ fewer than ten employees, and, according to Statistics Canada, over 97 percent of all retailers employ fewer than 50 employees.[1]

The Canadian economy is heavily dependent on retailing. Retailers ring up over $440 billion in sales annually, about 6 or 7 percent of the gross domestic product (GDP).[2] Although most retailers are quite small, a few giant organizations dominate the industry (see Canada's Top 10 Retailers).

retailing all the activities directly related to the sale of goods and services to the ultimate consumer for personal, nonbusiness use

What do you think?

When shopping, I use my cellphone to scan items for information and comparison.

1	2	3	4	5	6	7
STRONGLY DISAGREE				STRONGLY AGREE		

© ESCHCOLLECTION/PHOTONICA/GETTY IMAGES

LO 2 Classification of Retail Operations

A retail establishment can be classified according to its ownership, level of service, product assortment, and price. Specifically, retailers use the latter three variables to position themselves in the competitive marketplace. (As noted in Chapter 7, positioning is the strategy used to influence how consumers perceive one product in relation to all competing products.) These three variables can be combined in several ways to create distinctly different retail operations. Exhibit 13.1 lists the major types of retail stores discussed in this chapter and classifies them by level of service, product assortment, price, and gross margin.

Ownership

Retailers can be broadly classified by form of ownership: independent, part of a chain, or franchise outlet. Retailers owned by a single person or partnership and not operated as part of a larger retail institution are **independent retailers**. Around the world, most retailers are independent, operating one or a few stores in their community. Local florists and ethnic food markets typically fit this classification.

Chain stores are owned and operated as a group by a single organization. Under this form of ownership, many administrative tasks are handled by the home office for the entire chain. The home office also buys most of the merchandise sold in the stores. Gap and Starbucks are examples of chains.

Franchises, such as Subway and Quiznos, are owned and operated by individuals but are licensed by a larger supporting organization. The franchising approach combines the advantages of independent ownership with those of the chain store organization.

Level of Service

The level of service that retailers provide can be classified along a continuum, from full service to self-service. Some retailers, such as exclusive clothing stores, offer high levels of service. They provide alterations, credit, delivery, consulting, liberal return policies, layaway, gift wrapping, and personal shopping. Other retailers, such as factory outlets and warehouse clubs, offer virtually no services.

Product Assortment

The third basis for positioning or classifying stores is by the breadth and depth of their product line. Specialty stores—for example, Hallmark card stores—have the most concentrated product assortments, usually carrying single or narrow product lines but in considerable depth. On the other end of the spectrum, full-line discounters typically carry broad assortments of merchandise with limited depth. For example, Costco carries automotive supplies, household cleaning products,

independent retailers retailers owned by a single person or partnership and not operated as part of a larger retail institution

chain stores stores owned and operated as a group by a single organization

franchise the right to operate a business or to sell a product

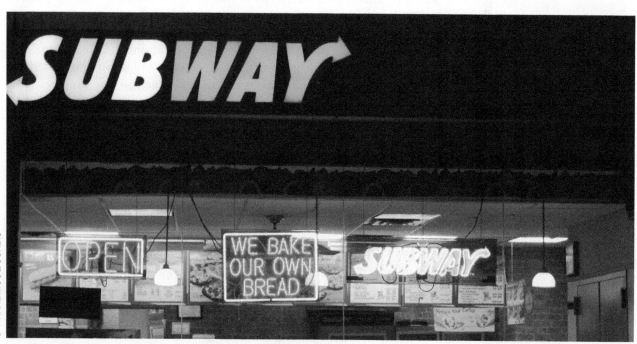

© VIVIANE MOOS/CORBIS

CANADA'S TOP 10 RETAILERS

Ranking in Canada	Top Canadian Retail Companies, 2011	Worldwide Ranking	Number of Stores	2010 Sales (in billions of dollars)
1	Loblaw Companies Ltd. Hypermarket: Supercentre/ Superstore/Joe Fresh	40	1,027	31
2	Alimentation Couche-Tard Inc. Convenience: Couche-Tard/ Mac's/Becker's/Mike's Mart	48	1,483	16.4
3	Empire Company Ltd. (Sobeys) Supermarket: Sobeys/IGA/ThriftyFoods/Price Chopper/ FreshCo/Lawtons Drug Stores	58	1,344	15.5
4	Metro Inc. Supermarket: Metro/SuperC/GP Foods/Brunet/ Pharmacy (drug stores)	87	831	11
5	Shoppers Drug Mart Corp. Shoppers Drug Mart/Shoppers Simply/Pharmacy/ Pharmaprix Simplement Santé/Murale	99	1,239	10.4
6	Canadian Tire Corp., Ltd. Canadian Tire Stores/Canadian Tire Petroleum/ Part Source/Mark's Work Wearhouse	127	485	10.3
7	Katz Group Inc. Drug Store/Pharmacy: Guardian/IDA/Rexall/ Pharma Plus/Herbie's	148	1,800	8.2
8	Jim Pattison Group Supermarket: Overwaitea/ Save-On-Foods/Urban Fare/ Buy-Low Foods/Ripley Entertainment Company	213	455	7.2
9	Liquor Control Board Ontario Specialty Retail	237	611	4.3
10	RONA Inc. Home Improvement	243	911	4.8

SOURCES: http://retailindustry.about.com/od/famousretailers/a/canada_2010_largest_retailers_world.htm; http://www.loblaw.ca/Theme/ Loblaw/files/doc_financials/2010_Annual_Report_complete_report.pdf; http://www.couche-tard.com/corporatif/modules/AxialRealisation/ img_repository/files/documents/relation-investisseur/Presentations%20corporatives/Annual%20General%20Meeting%202010.pdf; http:// www.sobeyscorporate.com/App_Themes/SobeysCorporate/media/en/Empire_AR_10_ENG.pdf; http://metro.altitudesolutions.com/client/ page1.asp?page=2&clef=1&clef2=1; http://www.shoppersdrugmart.ca/english/corporate_information/investor_relations/financial_information/ financial_statements/Q4_2010.pdf; http://corp.canadiantire.ca/EN/Investors/FinancialReports/Annual%20Reports%20Library/CTC_AR_2010.pdf; http://www.katzgroup.ca/contact.htm; http://www.jimpattison.com/; http://www.lcbo.com/aboutlcbo/annualreport2010.shtml; http://www.rona.ca/ content/2010-annual-report_2010_annual-reports-other-documents_investor-relations

and pet food. Typically, though, it carries only four or five brands of dog food. In contrast, a specialty pet store, such as PetSmart, may carry as many as 20 brands in a wide variety of flavours, shapes, and sizes.

Other retailers, such as factory outlet stores, may carry only part of a single line. Nike stores sell only certain items of its own brand. Discount specialty stores, such as Rona and Toys "R" Us, carry a broad assortment in concentrated product lines, such as building and home supplies and toys.

Price

Price is a fourth way to position retail stores. Traditional department stores and specialty stores typically charge the full suggested retail price. In contrast, discounters, factory outlets, and off-price retailers use low prices as a major lure for shoppers.

The last column in Exhibit 13.1 shows the typical **gross margin**—the amount of money the retailer

gross margin the amount of money the retailer makes as a percentage of sales after the cost of goods sold is subtracted

EXHIBIT 13.1
Types of Stores and Their Characteristics

Type of Retailer	Level of Service	Product Assortment	Price	Gross Margin
Department store	Moderately high to high	Broad	Moderate to high	Moderately high
Specialty store	High	Narrow	Moderate to high	High
Supermarket	Low	Broad	Moderate	Low
Convenience store	Low	Medium to narrow	Moderately high	Moderately high
Drugstore	Low to moderate	Medium	Moderate	Low
Full-line discount store	Moderate to low	Medium to broad	Moderately low	Moderately low
Discount specialty store	Moderate to low	Medium to broad	Moderately low to low	Moderately low
Warehouse clubs	Low	Broad	Low to very low	Low
Off-price retailer	Low	Medium to narrow	Low	Low
Restaurant	Low to high	Narrow	Low to high	Low to high

makes as a percentage of sales after the cost of goods sold is subtracted. The level of gross margin and the price level generally match. For example, a traditional jewellery store has high prices and high gross margins of approximately 50 percent. Because of the highly competitive market, new car dealers must work to keep their prices as low as possible and thus have low gross margins Gross margins can decline as a result of markdowns on merchandise (about 15 percent) during sale periods and price wars among competitors, when stores lower their prices on certain items in an effort to win customers.

LO 3 Major Types of Retail Operations

Traditionally, retail stores have been of several distinct types, with each offering a different product assortment, type of service, and price level, according to its customers' shopping preferences.

In a recent trend, however, retailers are experimenting with alternative formats that are more difficult to classify. For instance, supermarkets are expanding their nonfood items and services, discounters are adding groceries, drugstores are becoming more like convenience stores, and

department store a store housing several departments under one roof

buyer a department head who selects the merchandise for his or her department and may also be responsible for promotion and for personnel

department stores are experimenting with smaller stores. Nevertheless, many stores still fall into one of the basic types.

Department Stores

A **department store** is a store housing several departments under one roof. It usually carries a wide variety of shopping and specialty goods, including apparel, cosmetics, housewares, electronics, and sometimes furniture. Purchases are generally made within each department rather than at one central checkout area. Each department is treated as a separate buying centre to achieve economies in promotion, buying, service, and control. Each department is usually headed by a **buyer**, a department head who selects the merchandise for his or her department and may also be responsible for promotion and for personnel. For a consistent, uniform store image, central management sets broad policies about the types of merchandise carried and price ranges. Central management is also responsible for the overall advertising program, credit policies, store expansion, customer service, and so on. Large independent department stores are rare today. Most are owned by national chains. Canada's department store market is dominated by Sears and the Bay.

The $1.8 billion takeover of 220 Zellers stores by Target (USA) in January of 2011 will undoubtedly change the current environment of the large department stores. The acquisition by Target—whose stores are typically larger than Zellers and carry a more diverse product selection, including groceries—is forecast to be completed by 2014.

Specialty Stores

Specialty store formats allow retailers to refine their segmentation strategies and tailor their merchandise to specific target markets. A **specialty store** is not only a type of store but also a method of retail operations—namely, specializing in a given type of merchandise. Examples include children's clothing, baked goods, and pet supplies. A typical specialty store carries a deeper but narrower assortment of specialty merchandise than a department store. Generally, specialty stores' knowledgeable sales clerks offer more attentive customer service. The format has become very powerful in the apparel market and other areas. In fact, consumers buy more clothing from specialty stores than from any other type of retailer. Tim Hortons, M&M Meats, and Mountain Equipment Co-op are examples of successful chain specialty retailers.

In specialty outlets, consumers usually consider price to be secondary. Instead, a store's popularity is determined by distinctive merchandise, the store's physical appearance, and the calibre of the staff. Because of these stores' limited product line and their attention to customers, manufacturers often favour introducing new products in small specialty stores before moving on to larger retail and department stores.

Supermarkets

Canadian consumers spend about a tenth of their disposable income in **supermarkets**. Supermarkets are large, departmentalized, self-service retailers that specialize in food and some nonfood items. Supermarkets have experienced declining sales in recent years, some of which has resulted from increased competition from discounters Wal-Mart and Costco. But demographic and lifestyle changes have also affected the supermarket industry, as families eat out more or are just too busy to prepare meals at home.

Conventional supermarkets are being replaced by bigger *superstores*, which are usually twice the size of supermarkets. Superstores meet the needs of today's customers for convenience, variety, and service by offering one-stop shopping for many food and non-food needs, in addition to many services—including pharmacies, flower shops, salad bars, in-store bakeries, takeout food sections, sit-down restaurants, health food sections, DVD rentals, dry-cleaning services, shoe repair, photo processing, and banking. Some even offer family dentistry or optical shops, and many now have gas stations. This tendency to offer a wide variety of nontraditional goods and services under one roof is called **scrambled merchandising**.

To stand out in an increasingly competitive marketplace, many supermarket chains are tailoring their marketing strategies to appeal to specific consumer segments. Most notable is the shift toward *loyalty marketing programs* in which repeat customers use their frequent shopper cards to earn discounts or gifts. After frequent shopper cards are scanned at the checkout, they help supermarket retailers electronically track shoppers' buying habits to aid their CRM programs.

Drugstores

Drugstores stock pharmacy-related products and services as their main draw, but they also carry an extensive selection of over-the-counter (OTC) medications, cosmetics, health and beauty aids, seasonal merchandise, specialty items such as greeting cards and a limited selection of toys, and even refrigerated convenience foods. As competition has increased from mass merchandisers and supermarkets that have their own pharmacies and from direct-mail prescription services, drugstores have added such services as 24-hour, drive-through pharmacies and low-cost health clinics staffed by nurse practitioners.

Demographic trends in Canada look favourable for the drugstore industry. The average 60-year-old purchases 15 prescriptions per year, nearly twice as many as the average 30-year-old. Because baby boomers are attentive to their health and keenly sensitive about their looks, the increased traffic at the pharmacy counter in the future should also spur sales in other traditionally strong drugstore merchandise categories,

specialty store a retail store specializing in a given type of merchandise

supermarket a large, departmentalized, self-service retailer that specializes in food and some nonfood items

scrambled merchandising the tendency to offer a wide variety of nontraditional goods and services under one roof

drugstore a retail store that stocks pharmacy-related products and services as its main draw

ALICE/SHUTTERSTOCK.COM

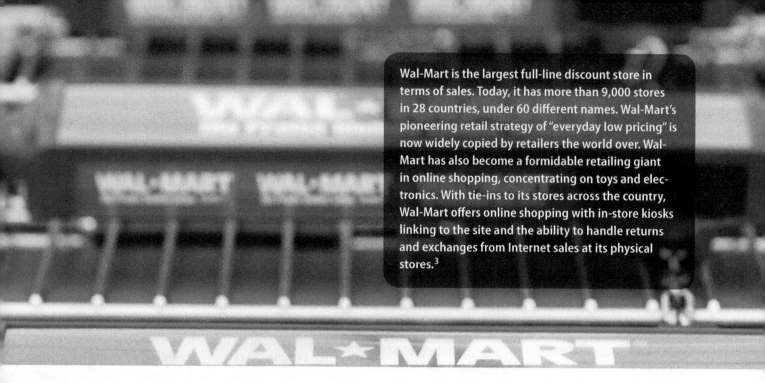

Wal-Mart is the largest full-line discount store in terms of sales. Today, it has more than 9,000 stores in 28 countries, under 60 different names. Wal-Mart's pioneering retail strategy of "everyday low pricing" is now widely copied by retailers the world over. Wal-Mart has also become a formidable retailing giant in online shopping, concentrating on toys and electronics. With tie-ins to its stores across the country, Wal-Mart offers online shopping with in-store kiosks linking to the site and the ability to handle returns and exchanges from Internet sales at its physical stores.[3]

convenience store a miniature supermarket, carrying only a limited line of high-turnover convenience goods

discount store a retailer that competes on the basis of low prices, high turnover, and high volume

full-line discount stores a retailer that offers consumers very limited service and carries a broad assortment of well-known, nationally branded "hard goods"

mass merchandising a retailing strategy using moderate to low prices on large quantities of merchandise and lower levels of service to stimulate high turnover of products

supercentre a retail store that combines groceries and general merchandise goods with a wide range of services

specialty discount store a retail store that offers a nearly complete selection of single-line merchandise and uses self-service, discount prices, high volume, and high turnover

category killers specialty discount stores that heavily dominate their narrow merchandise segment

most notably OTC drugs, vitamins, and health and beauty aids.

Convenience Stores

A **convenience store** can be defined as a miniature supermarket, carrying only a limited line of high-turnover convenience goods. These self-service stores, such as 7/Eleven and Mac's, are typically located near residential areas and many are open 24 hours, seven days a week. Convenience stores offer exactly what their name implies: a convenient location, long hours, fast service. However, prices are almost always higher at a convenience store than at a supermarket. Thus, the customer pays for the convenience.

In response to recent heavy competition from gas stations and supermarkets, convenience store operators have changed their strategy. They have expanded their offerings of nonfood items with DVD rentals and health and beauty aids, and some have added upscale sandwich and salad lines and more fresh produce. Some convenience stores are even selling pizzas, hot dogs, and tacos that are prepared in the store.

Discount Stores

A **discount store** is a retailer that competes on the basis of low prices, high turnover, and high volume.

Discounters can be classified into four major categories: full-line discount stores, specialty discount stores, warehouse clubs, and off-price discount retailers.

Full-Line Discount Stores Compared with traditional department stores, **full-line discount stores** offer consumers very limited service and carry a much broader assortment of well-known, nationally branded hard goods, including housewares, toys, automotive parts, hardware, sporting goods, and garden items, in addition to clothing, bedding, and linens. As with department stores, national chains dominate the discounters. Full-line discounters are often called mass merchandisers. **Mass merchandising** is the retailing strategy whereby retailers use moderate to low prices on large quantities of merchandise and lower levels of service to stimulate high turnover of products.

Supercentres combine a full line of groceries and general merchandise with a wide range of services, including pharmacy, dry cleaning, portrait studios, photo finishing, hair salons, optical shops, and restaurants—all in one location. For supercentre operators such as Wal-Mart, food is a customer magnet that sharply increases the store's overall volume, while taking customers away from traditional supermarkets.

Specialty Discount Stores Another discount niche includes the single-line **specialty discount stores**—for example, stores selling sporting goods, electronics, auto parts, office supplies, housewares, or toys. These stores offer a nearly complete selection of single-line merchandise and use self-service, discount prices, high volume, and high turnover to their advantage. Specialty discount stores are often termed **category killers** because

THE CANADIAN PRESS/STEVE WHITE

RICHARD APPLEBY

they heavily dominate their narrow merchandise segment. Examples include Future Shop and Best Buy in electronics, Staples and Office Depot in office supplies, and IKEA in home furnishings.

Category killers have also emerged in other specialty segments, creating retailing empires in highly fragmented mom-and-pop markets. For instance, the home improvement industry, which for years was served by professional builders and small hardware stores, is now dominated by The Home Depot and Rona. Category-dominant retailers like these serve their customers by offering a large selection of merchandise, stores that make shopping easy, and low prices every day, which eliminates the need for time-consuming comparison shopping. Sporting goods

stores in Canada face similar competitive challenges from Bass Pro Shops, which has launched stores in Vaughan (north of Toronto), Calgary, and is planning a store in Montreal.

Warehouse Membership Clubs **Warehouse membership clubs** sell a limited selection of brand-name appliances, household items, and groceries. These goods are usually sold in bulk from warehouse outlets on a cash-and-carry basis to members only. Individual members of warehouse clubs are charged low or no membership fees. Warehouse club members tend to be more educated and more affluent and have a larger household than regular supermarket shoppers. These core customers use warehouse clubs to stock up on staples; then they go to specialty outlets or food stores for perishables. Currently, the leading store in this category is Costco.

Off-Price Retailers An **off-price retailer** sells at prices 25 percent or more below traditional department store prices because it pays cash for its stock and usually doesn't ask for return privileges. Off-price retailers buy manufacturers' overruns at or below cost. They also absorb goods from bankrupt stores, irregular merchandise, and unsold end-of-season output. Nevertheless, much off-price retailer merchandise is first-quality, current goods. Because buyers for off-price retailers purchase only what is available or what they can get a good deal on, merchandise styles and brands often change monthly. Today, there are dozens of off-price retailers. One of the best known in Canada is Winners.

Factory outlets are an interesting variation on the off-price concept. A **factory outlet** is an off-price retailer that is owned and operated by a manufacturer. Thus, it carries one line of merchandise—its own. Each season, 5 to 10 percent of a manufacturer's output does not sell through regular distribution channels because it consists of closeouts (merchandise being discontinued), factory seconds, and cancelled orders. By operating factory outlets, manufacturers can regulate where their surplus is sold, and they can realize higher profit margins than if they disposed of the goods through independent wholesalers and retailers. Factory outlet malls typically locate in out-of-the-way rural areas or near vacation destinations.

warehouse membership clubs limited-service merchant wholesalers that sell a limited selection of brand-name appliances, household items, and groceries on a cash-and-carry basis to members, small businesses, and groups

off-price retailer a retailer that sells at prices 25 percent or more below traditional department store prices because it pays cash for its stock and usually doesn't ask for return privileges

factory outlet an off-price retailer that is owned and operated by a manufacturer

Most are situated 10 to 15 km from urban or suburban shopping areas so the manufacturers don't alienate their department store accounts by selling the same goods virtually next door at a discount.

Restaurants

Restaurants straddle the line between retailing establishments and service establishments. Restaurants do sell tangible products—food and drink—but they also provide a valuable service for consumers in the form of food preparation and food service. Most restaurants could even be defined as a specialty retailer, given that most concentrate their menu offerings on a distinctive type of cuisine—for example, Swiss Chalet and Starbucks coffee shops.

As a retailing institution, restaurants deal with many of the same issues as a more traditional retailer, such as personnel, distribution, inventory management, promotion, pricing, and location. Restaurants and food-service retailers run the spectrum from those offering limited service and inexpensive food, such as fast-food chains and the local snack bar, to those that offer sit-down service and moderate to high prices, such as the The Keg or a local trendy French bistro.

Eating out is an important part of Canadians' daily activities and is growing in strength. According to Statistics Canada, food away from home accounts for about 25 percent of the household food budget for the average family. The trend toward eating out has been fuelled by the increase in working mothers and dual-income families who have more money to eat out and less time to shop and prepare meals at home.[4] However, several external issues affect this potential market growth. The first are regulator and taxation issues. As a result of the introduction of the harmonized sales tax (HST) in five provinces (in New Brunswick, Nova Scotia, and Newfoundland and Labrador in 1997 and joined by British Columbia and Ontario in 2010), and a lowering of society's alcohol tolerance levels, restaurant sales have reportedly dropped by 15 to 20 percent.[5] Additional public awareness of obesity in Canadians and the call for

PRNEWSFOTO/STONYFIELD FARM/THE ASSOCIATED PRESS

local foods are also having an increased effect on the menu choices restaurants are offering.

LO 4 Nonstore Retailing

The retailing methods discussed so far are in-store methods, requiring customers to physically shop at stores. In contrast, **nonstore retailing** is shopping without visiting a store. Because consumers demand convenience, nonstore retailing is currently growing faster than in-store retailing. The major forms of nonstore retailing are automatic vending, direct retailing, direct marketing, and electronic retailing.

Automatic Vending

A low-profile yet important form of retailing is **automatic vending**, the use of machines to offer goods for sale—for example, the vending machines dispensing pop, candy, and snacks typically found in cafeterias and office buildings. Vending machines sell $63 million in goods annually in Canada.[6] Food and beverages account for about 85 percent of all sales from vending machines. Consumers are willing to pay higher prices for products from a convenient vending machine than for the same products in a traditional retail setting.

Retailers constantly seek new opportunities to sell via vending machines. Many moviegoers have the option of purchasing hot popcorn and chicken fingers from a vending machine instead of waiting in line at the concession stand. Many vending machines today also sell nontraditional kinds of merchandise, such as videos, toys, stickers, sports cards, office-type supplies, disposable cameras, and even ice cream.

Direct Retailing

In **direct retailing**, representatives sell products door-to-door, office-to-office, or at home sales parties. Companies such as Avon and The Pampered Chef have used this approach for years, and both have typically hired women as direct sellers and have targeted women as their primary customers. Recently, however, direct retailers' sales have suffered as a result of women having entered the traditional workforce. Although most direct sellers such as Avon and Tupperware still advocate the party plan method, the realities of the marketplace have forced them to be more creative in reaching their target customer. Direct sales representatives now hold parties in offices, parks, and even parking lots. Others hold informal gatherings where shoppers can drop in at their convenience or offer self-improvement classes. Many direct retailers are also turning to direct mail, telephone, or more traditional retailing venues to find new avenues to their customers and increase sales. Avon, for instance, has begun opening cosmetics kiosk counters in malls, called Avon Beauty Centers. Avon has also launched a new brand—Mark, promoted as a beauty experience for young women. Most Mark representatives are students who typically sell the product as an after-school part-time job. Prospective representatives and consumers can buy products or register to be a representative in person, online, or over the phone.[7]

Direct retailers are also using the Internet as a channel to reach more customers and increase sales. Amway launched Quixtar.com, an online channel for its products that generated over $1 billion in revenues in its first year. Customers access the site using a unique referral number for each Amway rep, a system that ensures that the reps earn their commissions.

Direct Marketing

Direct marketing, sometimes called **direct-response marketing**, refers to the techniques used to get consumers to make a purchase from their home, office, or other nonretail setting. Those techniques include direct mail, catalogues and mail order, telemarketing, and electronic retailing. Shoppers using these methods are less bound by traditional shopping situations. Time-strapped consumers and those who live in rural or suburban areas are most likely to be direct-response shoppers because they value the convenience and flexibility provided by direct marketing.

Direct Mail Direct mail can be the most efficient or the least efficient retailing method, depending on the quality of the mailing list and the effectiveness of the mailing piece. Canadian companies have generated $3.6 billion in revenue using direct marketing.[8] By using direct mail, marketers can precisely target their customers according to demographics, geographics, and even psychographics. Good mailing lists come from an internal database or are available from list brokers for about $35 to $150 per thousand names.

Direct mailers are becoming more sophisticated in targeting the right customers. Using statistical methods to analyze census data, lifestyle and financial information, and past purchase and credit history, direct mailers can pick out those most likely to buy their products. Because direct mail has average response rates of 1 to 3 percent, marketers have found it important to initialize their direct campaign materials by trying different formats, as in a controlled experiment. If one method generates a better return or response rate, such as 3 percent, then its best qualities are used for the overall campaign; when compared with a lower response rate of, say, 1.5 percent, a 3 percent return can easily mean twice the number of customers.

Catalogues and Mail Order Consumers can now buy just about anything through the mail, from the mundane to the outlandish. Although women comprise the majority of catalogue shoppers, the percentage of male catalogue shoppers has recently soared. As changing demographics have shifted more shopping responsibility to men, they are viewing shopping via catalogue, mail order, and the Internet as more sensible than a trip to the mall.

Successful catalogues are usually created and designed for highly segmented markets. Certain types of retailers use mail order successfully. For example, computer manufacturers have discovered that mail order is a lucrative way to sell personal computers to home and small-business users, evidenced by the huge successes of Dell, whose direct business model has made it a $55 billion company and the number one personal computer (PC) seller worldwide. With a global market share of almost 20 percent, Dell sells about $50 million in computers and equipment online every day.[9]

Telemarketing Telemarketing is the use of the telephone to sell directly to consumers. It consists of outbound sales calls, usually unsolicited, and inbound calls, which are usually customer orders made through toll-free 800 numbers or fee-based 900 numbers.

direct marketing (direct-response marketing) techniques used to get consumers to make a purchase from their home, office, or another nonretail setting

telemarketing the use of the telephone to sell directly to consumers

Rising postage rates and decreasing long-distance phone rates have made *outbound* telemarketing an attractive direct-marketing technique. The skyrocketing costs of field sales have also led marketing managers to use outbound telemarketing. Searching for ways to keep costs under control, marketing managers have learned how to pinpoint prospects quickly, zero in on serious buyers, and keep in close touch with regular customers. Meanwhile, marketing managers reserve expensive, time-consuming in-person calls for closing sales. So many consumers complained about outbound telemarketing, however, that the Canadian Radio-television Telecommunications Commission (CRTC) established the National Do Not Call List for consumers who do not want to receive unsolicited telephone calls. Additional regulations also stipulate that companies must allow consumers the option of opting out of email marketing (spam) and prohibits them from camouflaging their identity through false addresses and misleading subject lines. Some industry experts say the lists help them by eliminating non-buyers, but others believe these regulations could have a long-term negative effect on telemarketing sales.[10]

Inbound telemarketing programs, which use 800 and 900 numbers, are mainly used to take orders, generate leads, and provide customer service. Inbound 800 telemarketing has successfully supplemented direct-response TV, radio, and print advertising for more than 25 years. The more recently introduced 900 numbers, which customers pay to call, are gaining popularity as a cost-effective way for companies to target customers. One of the major benefits of 900 numbers is that they allow marketers to generate qualified responses. Although the charge may reduce the total volume of calls, the calls that do come are from customers who have a true interest in the product.

© ISTOCKPHOTO.COM/MARTIN CARLSSON

Electronic Retailing

Electronic retailing includes the 24-hour, shop-at-home television networks and online retailing.

Shop-at-Home Networks The shop-at-home television networks are specialized forms of direct-response marketing. The shows on these networks display merchandise, with the retail price, to home viewers. Viewers can phone in their orders directly on a toll-free line and shop with a credit card. The shop-at-home industry has quickly grown into a billion-dollar business with a loyal customer following. Shop-at-home networks can reach nearly every home with a television set. The best-known shop-at-home network is The Shopping Channel. Home shopping networks attract a broad audience through diverse programming and product offerings and are now adding new products to appeal to more affluent audiences. For instance, cooking programs attract both men and women, fashion programs attract mostly women, and electronics attract primarily men.

Online Retailing For years, shopping at home meant looking through catalogues and then placing an order over the telephone. For many people today, however, shopping at home now means turning on a computer, surfing retail websites, and using the click of a mouse to select and order products online. **Online retailing**, or *e-tailing*, is a type of shopping available to consumers who have personal computers and access to the Internet. Almost 80 percent of Canadians have Internet access either at home or at work.

Online retailing has exploded in the last several years as consumers have found this type of shopping convenient and, in many instances, less costly. Consumers can shop without leaving home, choose from a wide selection of merchants, use shopping comparison services to search the Web for the best price, and then have the items delivered to their doorsteps. As a result, online shopping continues to grow at a rapid pace, with online sales accounting for $15.1 billion in sales in Canada. Online retailing is also increasing in popularity outside North America.

Most traditional retailers have now jumped on the Internet bandwagon, allowing shoppers to purchase the same merchandise found in their stores from their website. Online retailing also fits well with traditional catalogue companies, such as Lands' End and Eddie Bauer, which already have established distribution networks.

e-COMMERCE FACTOID

In 2009, about 39 percent of Canadians aged 16 and over used the Internet to place more than **95 million orders**. These figures are up from the 32 percent of Canadians and the 70 million orders placed in 2007, when the survey was last conducted. Relatively more residents of British Columbia (47 percent) and Alberta (45 percent) made an online order in 2009.

Statistics Canada, e-Commerce, 2009 Canadian Internet Use Survey, www.statcan. gc.ca/imdb-bmdi/4432-eng.htm, accessed August 30, 2011.

As the popularity of online retailing grows, it is becoming critical that retailers offer their products online and that their stores, websites, and catalogues are integrated. Customers expect to find the same brands, products, and prices whether they purchase online, on the phone, or in a store. Therefore, retailers are increasingly using in-store kiosks to help tie the channels together for greater customer service.

Popular e-tailers don't necessarily need a physical presence in the market. For example, eBay and Amazon have created tremendously successful formulas without selling in a single retail store.

LO5 Franchising

A *franchise* is a continuing relationship in which a franchiser grants to a franchisee the business rights to operate or to sell a product. The **franchiser** originates the trade name, product, methods of operation, and so on. The **franchisee**, in return, pays the franchiser for the right to use its name, product, or business methods. A franchise agreement between the two parties usually lasts for 10 to 20 years, at which time the agreement can be renewed if both parties are agreeable.

To be granted the rights to a franchise, a franchisee usually pays an initial, one-time franchise fee. The amount of this fee depends solely on the individual franchiser, but it generally ranges from $50,000 to $250,000 or higher. In addition to this initial franchise fee, the franchisee is expected to pay royalty fees, usually in the range of 3 to 7 percent of gross revenues. The franchisee may also be expected to pay advertising fees, which usually cover the cost of promotional materials and, if the franchise organization is large enough, regional or national advertising. A McDonald's franchise, for example, costs an initial $45,000 per store plus a monthly fee that is based on the restaurant's sales performance and base rent. In addition, a new McDonald's franchisee can expect start-up costs for equipment and pre-opening expenses to range from $500,000 to more than $1 million. The size of the restaurant facility, area of the country, inventory, selection of kitchen equipment, signage, and style of décor and landscaping all affect new restaurant costs.[11] Fees such as these are typical for all major franchisers, including Burger King and Subway.

Two basic forms of franchises are used today: product and trade name franchising and business format franchising. In *product and trade name franchising*, a dealer agrees to sell certain products provided by a manufacturer or a wholesaler. This approach has been used most widely in the auto and truck, pop bottling, tire, and gasoline service industries. For example, a local tire retailer may hold a franchise to sell Michelin tires.

Business format franchising is an ongoing business relationship between a franchiser and a franchisee. Typically, a franchiser sells a franchisee the rights to use the franchiser's format or approach to doing business. This form of franchising has rapidly expanded since the 1950s through retailing, restaurant, food-service, hotel and motel, printing, and real estate franchises.

franchiser the originator of a trade name, product, methods of operation, and so on that grants operating rights to another party to sell its product

franchisee an individual or business that is granted the right to sell a franchiser's product

WELL-KNOWN CANADIAN FRANCHISERS

Franchiser	Total Units	Initial Investment (in thousands of dollars)
Apple Auto Glass	Franchised Units: 118 Company Owned: 4	$100–$300
Canadian Tire	Franchised Units: 475 Company Owned: 0	$125+
Harvey's Restaurants	Franchised Units: 197 Company Owned: 46	$150–$250
The Keg Steakhouse & Bar	Franchised Units: 54 Company Owned: 43	$3,000–$4,500
Mr. Sub	Franchised Units: 400 Company Owned: 2	$50
M&M Meat Shops	Franchised Units: 468 Company Owned: 4	$260–$400
Mister Transmission	Franchised Units: 85 Company Owned: 0	$120–$150
Pearle Vision	Franchised Units:2 Company Owned: 83	$250–$350
Sandler Training	Franchised Units:16 Company Owned: 0	$80
Survivor Bootcamp Inc.	Franchised Units: 47 Company Owned: 2	$8
Tim Hortons	Franchised Units: 3,000 Company Owned: 18	$194

Source: Canadian Franchise Association, http://www.cfa.ca (accessed May 2011).

IT'S A BEAUTIFUL THING.

LO 6 Retail Marketing Strategy

Retailers must develop marketing strategies that are based on overall goals and strategic plans. Retailing goals might include more traffic, higher sales of a specific item, a more upscale image, or heightened public awareness of the retail operation. The strategies that retailers use to obtain their goals might include a sale, an updated décor, or a new advertisement. The key tasks in strategic retailing are defining and selecting a target market and developing the retailing mix to successfully meet the needs of the chosen target market.

Defining a Target Market

The first and foremost task in developing a retail strategy is to define the target market. This process begins with market segmentation, the topic of Chapter 7. Successful retailing has always been based on knowing the customer. Sometimes retailing chains flounder when management loses sight of the customers the stores should be serving. For example, Gap built a retail empire by offering updated, casual classics, such as white shirts and khaki pants that appealed to everyone from high school through middle age; however, Gap began losing customers when it shifted toward trendier fashions with a limited appeal.

Target markets in retailing are often defined by demographics, geographics, and psychographics. For instance, Bluefly.com, a discount fashion e-tailer, targets both men and women in their thirties who have a higher-than-average income, read fashion magazines, and favour high-end designers. By understanding who its customers are, the company has been able to tailor its website to appeal specifically to its audience. The result is a higher sales rate than most e-tailers.[12]

Gap was highly successful selling casual, preppy classics. However, when it started offering trendier clothing, it no longer met the needs of its established customer base and began to lose business.

Determining a target market is a prerequisite to creating the retailing mix. For example, Costco's merchandising approach for sporting goods is to match its product assortment to the demographics of the local store and region.

Choosing the Retailing Mix

Retailers combine the elements of the retailing mix to come up with a single retailing method to attract the target market. The **retailing mix** consists of six Ps: the four Ps of the marketing mix (product, place, promotion, and price) plus presentation and personnel (see Exhibit 13.2).

The combination of the six Ps projects a store's image, which influences consumers' perceptions. Using these impressions of stores, shoppers position one store against another. A retail marketing manager must ensure that the store's positioning is compatible with the target customers' expectations. As discussed at the beginning of the chapter, retail stores can be positioned on three broad dimensions: service provided by store personnel, product assortment, and price. Management should use everything else—place, presentation, and promotion—to fine-tune the basic positioning of the store.

The Product Offering The first element in the retailing mix is the **product offering**, also called the *product assortment* or *merchandise mix*. Retailers decide what to sell on the basis of what their target market wants to buy. They can base their decision on market research, past sales, fashion trends, customer requests, and other sources. A recent approach, called data mining, uses complex mathematical models to help retailers make better product mix decisions. The Bay/Zellers and Wal-Mart use data mining to determine which products to stock at what price, how to manage markdowns, and how to advertise to draw target customers.

Developing a product offering is essentially a question of the width and depth of the product assortment. *Width* refers to the assortment of products offered; *depth* refers to the number of different brands offered within each assortment. Price, store design, displays, and service are important to consumers in determining where to shop, but the most critical factor is merchandise selection. This reasoning also holds true for online retailers. Amazon.com, for instance, is building the world's biggest online department store so that shoppers can get whatever they want with one click on their Web browsers. Like a traditional department store or mass merchandiser, Amazon offers considerable width in its product assortment with millions of different items, including books, music, toys, videos, tools and hardware, health and beauty aids, electronics, and software. Conversely, online specialty retailers, such as 1-800-Flowers.com and polo.com clothing, focus on a single category of merchandise, hoping to attract loyal customers with their larger depth of products at lower prices and better customer service. Many online retailers purposely focus on single-product-line niches that could never garner enough foot traffic to support a traditional brick-and-mortar store. For instance, Fridgedoor.com claims to be the single largest stop for all things magnetic: novelty magnets, custom magnets, and magnetic supplies. It is the Web's largest refrigerator magnet retailer, with over 1,500 different types of magnets for sale.[13]

After determining which products will satisfy target customers' desires,

retailing mix a combination of the six Ps—product, place, promotion, price, presentation, and personnel—to sell goods and services to the ultimate consumer

product offering the mix of products offered to the consumer by the retailer; also called the product assortment or merchandise mix

EXHIBIT 13.2

The Retailing Mix

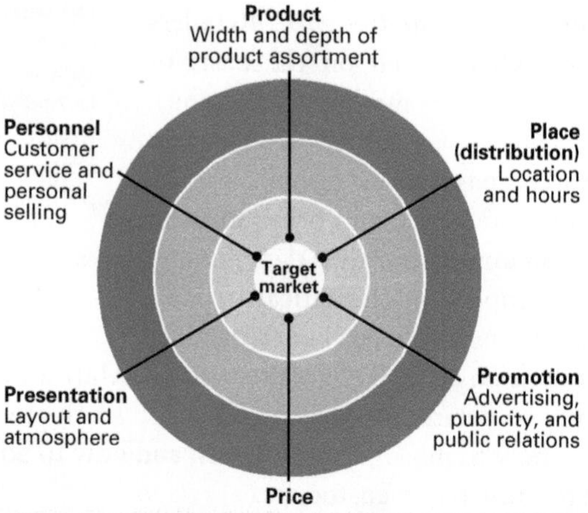
Product
Width and depth of product assortment
Personnel
Customer service and personal selling
Place (distribution)
Location and hours
Target market
Presentation
Layout and atmosphere
Promotion
Advertising, publicity, and public relations
Price

retailers must find sources of supply and evaluate the products. When the right products are found, the retail buyer negotiates a purchase contract. The buying function can either be performed in-house or be delegated to an outside firm. The goods must then be moved from the seller to the retailer, which means shipping, storing, and stocking the inventory. The trick is to manage the inventory, both by cutting prices to move slow goods and by keeping adequate supplies of hot-selling items in stock. As in all good systems, the final step is to evaluate the entire process to seek more efficient methods and eliminate problems and bottlenecks.

Promotion Strategy Retail promotion strategy includes advertising, public relations and publicity, and sales promotion. The goal is to help position the store in consumers' minds. Retailers design intriguing ads, stage special events, and develop promotions aimed at their target markets. Today's grand openings are a carefully orchestrated blend of advertising, merchandising, goodwill, and glitter. All the elements of an opening—press coverage, special events, media advertising, and store displays—are carefully planned.

Retailers' advertising is carried out mostly at the local level. Local advertising by retailers usually provides specific information about their stores, such as location, merchandise, hours, prices, and special sales. In contrast, national retail advertising generally focuses on image. Wal-Mart, since entering Canada, has emphasized its lower pricing strategy.

Advertising campaigns also take advantage of cooperative advertising, another popular retail advertising practice. Traditionally, marketers paid retailers to feature their products in store mailers, or a marketer developed a TV campaign for the product and simply tacked on several retailers' names at the end. Today advertising makes use of a more collaborative trend by integrating products such as Tide laundry detergent or Coca-Cola into the actual campaign. Another common form of cooperative advertising involves the promotion of exclusive products. For example, Shoppers Drug Mart recently acquired the rights to Nativa Organics products.

The Proper Location The retailing axiom "location, location, location" has long emphasized the importance of place to the retail mix. The location decision is important first because the retailer is making a large, semi-permanent commitment of resources that can reduce its future flexibility. Second, the location will affect the store's future growth and profitability.

Site location begins by choosing a community. Important factors to consider are the area's economic growth potential, the amount of competition, and geography. For instance, Wal-Mart often builds stores in new communities that are still under development. On the other hand, while population growth is an important consideration for fast-food restaurants, most also look for an area with other fast-food restaurants because being located in clusters helps to draw customers for each restaurant. Finally, for many retailers, geography remains the most important factor in choosing a community. For example, Starbucks seeks densely populated urban communities for its stores.

After settling on a geographic region or community, retailers must choose a specific site. In addition to growth potential, the important factors are neighbourhood socioeconomic characteristics, traffic flows, land costs, zoning regulations, and public transportation. A particular site's visibility, parking, entrance and exit locations, accessibility, and safety and security issues are also considered. Additionally, a retailer should consider how its store would fit into the surrounding environment. Retail decision makers probably would not locate a Dollarama next to a Holt Renfrew department store.

Retailers face one final decision about location: whether to have a freestanding unit or to become a tenant in a shopping centre or mall.

Freestanding Stores An isolated, freestanding location can be used by large retailers such as Wal-Mart or

Sears and sellers of such shopping goods as furniture and cars because they are known as destination stores. **Destination stores** are stores consumers seek out and purposely plan to visit. An isolated store location may have the advantages of low site cost or rent and no nearby competitors. On the other hand, it may be difficult to attract customers to a freestanding location, and no neighbouring retailers are around to share costs.

Freestanding units are increasing in popularity as retailers strive to make their stores more convenient to access, more enticing to shop in, and more profitable. More and more retailers are deciding not to locate in pedestrian malls. Perhaps the greatest reason for developing a freestanding site is greater visibility. Retailers often feel they get lost in huge shopping centres and malls, but freestanding units can help stores develop an identity with shoppers. Also, an aggressive expansion plan may not allow time to wait for the shopping centre to be built. Drugstore chains such as Shoppers Drug Mart have been aggressively relocating their existing shopping centre stores to freestanding sites, especially street corner sites for drive-through accessibility.

Shopping Centres Shopping centres began in the 1950s when Canadians started migrating to the suburbs. The first shopping centres were *strip malls*, typically located along busy streets. They usually included a supermarket, a variety store, and perhaps a few specialty stores. Next, *community shopping centres* emerged, with one or two small department stores, more specialty stores, a couple of restaurants, and several apparel stores. These community shopping centres provided off-street parking and a broader variety of merchandise.

Regional malls offering a much wider variety of merchandise started appearing in the mid-1970s. Regional malls are either entirely enclosed or roofed to allow shopping in any weather. Most are landscaped with trees, fountains, sculptures, and the like to enhance the shopping environment. They have acres of free parking. The *anchor stores* or *generator stores* (often major department stores) are usually located at opposite ends of the mall to create heavy foot traffic.

According to shopping centre developers, *lifestyle centres* are emerging as the newest generation of shopping centres. Lifestyle centres typically combine outdoor shopping areas that comprise upscale retailers and restaurants, plazas, fountains, and pedestrian streets. They appeal to retail developers looking for an alternative to the traditional shopping mall, a concept rapidly losing favour among shoppers.

Retail Prices Another important element in the retailing mix is price. Retailing's ultimate goal is to sell products to consumers, and the right price is critical in ensuring sales. Because retail prices are usually based on the cost of the merchandise, an essential part of pricing is efficient and timely buying.

Price is also a key element in a retail store's positioning strategy. Higher prices often indicate a level of quality and help reinforce the prestigious image of retailers, as they do for Harry Rosen and Birks. On the other hand, discounters and off-price retailers, such as Zellers and Winners, offer good value for the money. There are even stores, such as Dollarama, where most items cost one dollar. Dollarama's single-price-point strategy is aimed at getting customers to make impulse purchases through what analysts call the wow factor—the excitement of discovering that an item costs only a dollar.

Presentation of the Retail Store The presentation of a retail store helps determine the store's image and positions the retail store in consumers' minds. For instance, a retailer that wants to position itself as an upscale store would use a lavish or sophisticated presentation.

RICHARD APPLEBY

"THE **LAYOUT** OF RETAIL STORES IS A **KEY FACTOR** IN THEIR SUCCESS."

atmosphere the overall impression conveyed by a store's physical layout, décor, and surroundings

The main element of a store's presentation is its **atmosphere**, the overall impression conveyed by a store's physical layout, décor, and surroundings. The atmosphere might create a relaxed or busy feeling, a sense of luxury or of efficiency, a friendly or cold attitude, a sense of organization or of clutter, or a fun or serious mood. HMV Music stores, targeted to Generation Y consumers, use a recording studio feel.

The layout of retail stores is a key factor in their success. The goal is to use all of the store's space effectively, including aisles, fixtures, merchandise displays, and nonselling areas. In addition to making shopping easy and convenient for the customer, an effective layout has a powerful influence on traffic patterns and purchasing behaviour. IKEA uses a unique circular store layout, which encourages customers to pass all of a store's departments to reach the checkout lanes. The shopper thus is exposed to all of IKEA's merchandise assortment.

Layout also includes the placement of products in the store. Many technologically advanced retailers are using a technique called *market-basket analysis* to analyze the huge amounts of data collected through their point-of-purchase scanning equipment. The analysis looks for products that are commonly purchased together to help retailers find ideal locations for each product. Wal-Mart uses market-basket analysis to determine where in the store to stock products for customer convenience. Kleenex tissues, for example, are in the paper-goods aisle and beside the cold medicines.

The following factors are the most influential in creating a store's atmosphere:

▸▸ *Employee type and density:* Employee type refers to an employee's general characteristics—for instance, being neat, friendly, knowledgeable, or service oriented. Density is the number of employees per thousand square feet of

Over 800 stores! More than 100 eating establishments! Nine major attractions! Spanning the area of 48 city blocks, the West Edmonton Mall is North America's largest entertainment and shopping centre.

selling space. Whereas low employee density creates a do-it-yourself, casual atmosphere, high employee density denotes readiness to serve the customer's every whim.

▸▸ *Merchandise type and density:* A prestigious retailer such as Sony carries the best brand names and displays them in a neat, uncluttered arrangement. Discounters and off-price retailers often carry seconds or out-of-season goods crowded into small spaces and hung on long racks by category—tops, pants, skirts, etc.—creating the impression that "We've got so much stuff, we're practically giving it away."

▸▸ *Fixture type and density:* Fixtures can be elegant (rich woods), trendy (chrome and smoked glass), or consist of old, beat-up tables, as in an antiques store. The fixtures should be consistent with the general atmosphere the store is trying to create.

▸▸ *Sound:* Sound can be pleasant or unpleasant for a customer. Music can entice customers to stay in the store longer and buy more or eat quickly and leave a table for others. It can also control the pace of the store traffic, create an image, and attract or direct the shopper's attention.

▸▸ *Odours:* Smell can either stimulate or detract from sales. Research suggests that people evaluate merchandise more positively, spend more time shopping, and are generally in a better mood when an agreeable odour is present. Retailers use fragrances as an extension of their retail strategy.

▸▸ *Visual factors:* Colours can create a mood or focus attention and therefore are an important factor in atmosphere. Red, yellow, and orange are considered warm colours and are used when a feeling of warmth and closeness is desired. Cool colours, such as blue, green, and violet, are used to open up closed-in places and create an air of elegance and cleanliness. Many retailers have found that natural lighting, either from windows or skylights, can lead to increased sales. Outdoor lighting can also affect consumer patronage.

Personnel and Customer Service People are a unique aspect of retailing. Most retail sales involve a customer–salesperson relationship, if only briefly. When customers shop at a grocery store, the cashiers check and bag their groceries. When customers shop at a prestigious clothier, the sales clerks may assist in the fitting process, offer alteration services, wrap purchases, and even offer a glass of champagne. Sales personnel provide their customers with the amount of service prescribed in the retail strategy of the store.

Retail salespeople serve another important selling function: they persuade shoppers to buy. They must therefore be able to persuade customers that what they are selling is what the customer needs. Salespeople are trained in two common selling techniques: trading up and suggestion selling. Trading up means persuading customers to buy a higher-priced item than they originally intended to buy. To avoid selling customers something they do not need or want, however, salespeople should take care when practising trading-up techniques. Suggestion selling, a common practice among most retailers, seeks to broaden customers' original purchases with related items. For example, if you buy a new printer at Staples, the sales representative will ask whether you want to purchase paper, a USB cable, or extra ink cartridges. Suggestion selling and trading up should always help shoppers recognize true needs rather than sell them unwanted merchandise.

Providing great customer service is one of the most challenging elements in the retail mix because customer expectations for service are so varied. What customers expect in a department store is very different from their expectations for a discount store. Customer expectations also change. Ten years ago, shoppers wanted personal one-on-one attention. Today, most customers are happy to help themselves as long as they can easily find what they need.

Customer service is also critical for online retailers. Online shoppers expect a retailer's website to be easy to use, products to be available, and returns to be simple. Therefore, customer-friendly retailers, such as Bluefly.com, design their sites to give their customers the information they need such as what's new and what's on sale. Other companies such as Amazon.com and LandsEnd.com offer product recommendations and personal shoppers. Some retailers that have online catalogues and traditional brick-and-mortar stores, such as Chapters/Indigo and Sears, now allow customers to return goods bought through the catalogue or online to their traditional store to make returns easier.

LO7 New Developments in Retailing

In an effort to better serve their existing customers and to attract new customers, retailers are constantly

Apple stores use large open tables to display company products, making it easier for visitors to play with them.

adopting new strategies. Two recent developments are interactivity and m-commerce.

Interactivity

Adding interactivity to the retail environment is one of the most popular retailing strategies of the past few years. Small retailers and national chains are using interactivity in stores to differentiate themselves from the competition. The new interactive trend gets customers involved rather than just catching their eye. For example, Build-a-Bear enables customers to make their own stuffed animal by choosing which animal to stuff and then dressing and naming it.

M-Commerce

M-commerce (mobile e-commerce) enables consumers who have wireless mobile devices to connect to the Internet and shop. M-commerce enjoyed early success overseas and has been gaining acceptance and popularity in Canada. Essentially, m-commerce goes beyond text message advertisements to allow consumers to purchase goods and services using wireless mobile devices, such as cellphones, pagers, personal digital assistants (PDAs), and handheld computers. M-commerce users adopt the new technology because it saves time and offers more convenience in a greater number of locations. One study of m-commerce users who use Web-enabled devices to conduct transactions found that they consider relevant content, easy site navigation, and mobile device compatibility to be very important.[14] Quick Response (QR) codes are rapidly being affixed to many products and services. These codes enable customers to easily access more detailed information using their smartphones. QR codes are discussed further in Chapter 17. Vending machines are an important venue for m-commerce. Both PepsiCo and Coca-Cola have developed smart vending technologies. Coca-Cola's Intelligent Vending, a cashless payment system, accepts credit cards, radio-frequency identification (RFID) devices, and hotel room keys, and can be accessed via cellphone.[15]

INTERACTIVE RETAILING

Build-A-Bear is a 100 percent interactive retailing concept. Children choose an empty fabric shell and take it to a special station where they place a plush heart into their animal before a sales associate adds the stuffing. Children move to the next station to simulate washing and fluffing their animal. Finally they select an outfit to dress their animal before proceeding to the checkout.

© BUILD-A-BEAR WORKSHOP/ PRNEWSFOTO (AP TOPIC GALLERY)

80%
Percentage of retailers that have fewer than 10 employees

46%
Percentage of all store-based revenues that come from chain stores

$3 billion
Average amount Canadians spend per month on groceries

$37 billion
Average monthly retail sales in Canada

11.2%
Percentage of all Canadian employment that is in retail sector

$525 million
Average monthly sales for women's clothing and accessories

Visit **icanmktg2.com** to find the resources you need today!

Located at the back of the textbook are rip-out Chapter Review cards. Make sure you also go online to check out other tools that MKTG offers to help you successfully pass your course.

- Interactive Quizzing
- Games
- Flashcards
- Audio Summaries
- PowerPoint Slides

- Videos and Assessments
- Cases
- Marketing Plans and Worksheets
- Animated Visual Summaries

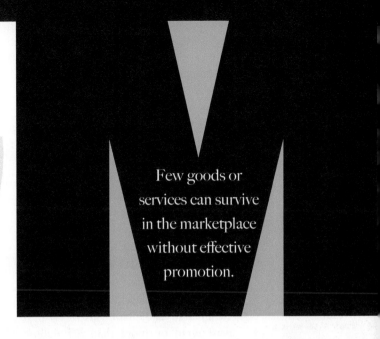

Few goods or services can survive in the marketplace without effective promotion.

AFTER YOU FINISH THIS CHAPTER, GO TO WWW. ICANMKTG2.COM FOR STUDY TOOLS.

© PHIL ASHLEY/LIFESIZE/JUPITERIMAGES

LO 1 The Role of Promotion in the Marketing Mix

Few goods or services, no matter how well developed, priced, or distributed, can survive in the marketplace without effective **promotion**—communication by marketers that informs, persuades, and reminds potential buyers of a product for the purpose of influencing their opinion or eliciting a response.

Promotional strategy is a plan for the optimal use of the elements of promotion (the promotion mix elements): advertising, direct marketing, public relations, personal selling, sales promotion, and online marketing. As Exhibit 14.1 shows, the marketing manager determines the goals of the company's promotional strategy in light of the firm's overall goals for the marketing mix—product, place (distribution), promotion, and price. Using these overall goals, marketers combine the elements of the promotional strategy (the promotional mix) to form a coordinated plan. The promotion plan then becomes another integral part of the marketing strategy for reaching the target market.

The main function of a marketer's promotional strategy is to convince target customers that the goods and services offered provide a competitive advantage over

promotion
communication by marketers that informs, persuades, and reminds potential buyers of a product for the purpose of influencing an opinion or eliciting a response

promotional strategy a plan for the optimal use of the elements of promotion: advertising, direct marketing, public relations, personal selling, sales promotion, and online marketing

What do you think?

Flashy promotions get my attention.

1 2 3 4 5 6 7
STRONGLY DISAGREE   STRONGLY AGREE

the competition. A **competitive advantage** is the set of unique features of a company and its products that are perceived by the target market as significant and superior to the competition. Such features can include high product quality, rapid delivery, low prices, excellent service, or a feature not offered by the competition. For example, General Motors launched the new 2011 Chevrolet Cruze in Canada and immediately won the 2011 Canadian Car of the year in the compact category. The Cruze is second to none for fuel efficiency and is globally engineered. It was tested on more than 9.5 million km of roads around the globe on every continent. Chevrolet effectively communicates its competitive advantage in all communication pieces by referring to consumers' preference for the car in major global markets, by communicating the awards the car has won, by comparing the car to two key competitors on its website, and by always referring to "designed in Asia, engineered in Europe and built in North America."[1] Promotion is a vital component of the marketing mix, informing consumers of a product's benefits and thereby positioning the product in the marketplace.

LO 2 The Promotional Mix

Most promotional strategies use several ingredients—which may include advertising, public relations, sales promotion, personal selling, direct-response communication, and online marketing—to reach a target market. That combination is called the **promotional mix**. The proper promotional mix is the one that management believes will meet the needs of the target market and fulfill the organization's overall goals. The more funds allocated to each promotional tool and the more managerial emphasis placed on each tool, the more important that element is thought to be in the overall mix.

Advertising

Almost all companies selling a good or service use advertising, whether in the form of a multimillion-dollar campaign or a poster placed on the side of a

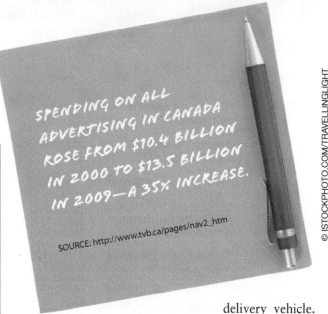

SPENDING ON ALL ADVERTISING IN CANADA ROSE FROM $10.4 BILLION IN 2000 TO $13.5 BILLION IN 2009—A 35% INCREASE.

SOURCE: http://www.tvb.ca/pages/nav2_htm

delivery vehicle.

Advertising is any form of impersonal, one-way mass communication about a product or organization that is paid for by a marketer. Traditional media—such as television, radio, newspapers, magazines, billboards, and transit cards (advertisements on buses and taxis and at bus stops)—are most commonly used to transmit advertisements to consumers. With the increasing fragmentation of traditional media choices, marketers are now sending their advertisements to consumers through new methods, such as websites, email, blogs, mobile messaging, social media tools, and interactive video technology located in department stores and supermarkets.

One of the primary benefits of advertising is its ability to communicate to a large number of people at

EXHIBIT 14.1
Role of Promotion in the Marketing Mix

Overall marketing objectives

Marketing mix
• Product
• Place (distribution)
• Promotion
• Price

Target market

Promotional mix
• Advertising
• Direct marketing
• Public relations
• Sales promotion
• Personal selling
• Online marketing

Promotion plan

one time. Cost per contact, therefore, is typically very low. Advertising has the advantage of being able to reach the masses (for instance, through national television networks), but it can also be used to microtarget smaller groups of potential customers by placing print ads in special interest magazines or commercials on specialty television programs. Although the *cost per contact* in advertising is very low, the *total cost* to advertise is typically very high. This hurdle tends to restrict advertising on a national basis. Chapter 15 examines advertising in greater detail.

Public Relations

Because organizations are concerned about how they are perceived by their target markets, they often spend large sums to build a positive public image. **Public relations** is the marketing function that evaluates public attitudes, identifies areas within the organization the public may be interested in, and executes a program of action to earn public understanding and acceptance, such as the Pepsi Refresh Project. Public relations helps an organization communicate with its customers, suppliers, stockholders, government officials, employees, and the community in which it operates. Marketers use public relations not only to maintain a positive image but also to educate the public about the company's goals and objectives, introduce new products, achieve a competitive advantage, and help support the sales effort.

In recent years, many organizations have been criticized for contributing to childhood obesity, including manufacturers of cereal targeted specifically to children. The Kellogg Company is on the front line of such criticism and, as such, is working both internally and externally to assist in the movement to reduce childhood obesity. The company has launched new cereals and modified others. The Healthy Weight Commitment Foundation (HWCF) is a U.S. nation-wide, multi-year effort to reduce obesity—especially childhood obesity—by 2015. It's a first-of-its-kind coalition that brings together numerous organizations, including the Kellogg Company. Kellogg's is passionate about working with HWCF members and made a $1 million commitment to the foundation. In addition, since 2005, Kellogg's has been the proud supporter of Active Healthy Kids Canada, sponsoring its annual *Report Card on Physical Activity for Children and Youth*, a report designed to offer insight into how well the country provides physical activity opportunities for young people. In 2010, Kellogg Canada was a sponsor of the 3rd International Congress on Physical Activity and Public Health held in Toronto.[2]

A public relations program can generate favourable **publicity**—public information about a company, product, service, or issue appearing in the mass media as a news item. Organizations generally do not pay for the publicity and are not identified as the source of the information, but they can benefit tremendously from it. For example, we all know that Tim Hortons is a Canadian passion, but a passion McDonald's is assaulting with its coffee strategy. McDonald's invested heavily in the delivery of a consistently good cup of coffee. Yet, not enough people knew it, nor were enough people willing to try it so McDonald's began a sampling program. The fast-food restaurant offered a free coffee over a two-week period starting in April 2009 and has since repeated the coffee offer during key times of the year. An important outcome of this sampling program has been the publicity McDonald's has received. Countless blogs, articles in newspapers, and news coverage have been generated on the program and how good the coffee is. The program worked—McDonald's share of the coffee market is growing against Tim Hortons'.[3]

Although organizations do not directly pay for publicity, it should not be viewed as being free. Preparing news releases, staging special events, and persuading media personnel to broadcast or print publicity messages costs money. Public relations and publicity are examined further in Chapter 15.

public relations the marketing function that evaluates public attitudes, identifies areas within the organization the public may be interested in, and executes a program of action to earn public understanding and acceptance

publicity public information about a company, product, service, or issue appearing in the mass media as a news item

HELEN SESSIONS/GETSTOCK.COM

VEGAS/GETSTOCK.COM

Sales Promotion

Sales promotion consists of all marketing activities—other than personal selling, advertising, direct marketing and public relations—that stimulate consumer purchasing, dealer effectiveness, and sales force enthusiasm. Sales promotion is generally a short-run tool used to stimulate immediate increases in demand. Sales promotion can be aimed at end consumers, trade customers, or a company's employees. Sales promotions include free samples, contests and sweepstakes, premiums, trade shows, and coupons. A major promotional campaign might use several of these sales promotion tools.

Marketers often use sales promotion to improve the effectiveness of other ingredients in the promotional mix, especially advertising and personal selling. Adding value to the brand is the main intent of sales promotion, which makes it a particularly valuable activity for promoting new brands or brands in highly competitive marketplaces. Research shows that sales promotion complements advertising by yielding faster short-term sales responses.

Personal Selling

Personal selling is a purchase situation involving a personal, paid-for communication between two people in an attempt to influence each other. In this dyad, both the buyer and the seller have specific objectives they wish to accomplish. The buyer may need to minimize cost or ensure a quality product, whereas the salesperson may need to maximize revenue and profits.

Traditional methods of personal selling include a planned presentation to one or more prospective buyers for the purpose of making a sale. Whether the personal selling takes place face-to-face or over the phone, it attempts to persuade the buyer to accept a point of view.

Today, personal selling is characterized by the relationship that develops between a salesperson and a buyer. Initially, this concept was more typical in business-to-business selling situations, involving the sale of such products as heavy machinery and computer systems, which tended to take a long time to close and often resulted in modifications to the product to meet the unique needs of the buyer. More recently, both business-to-business and business-to-consumer

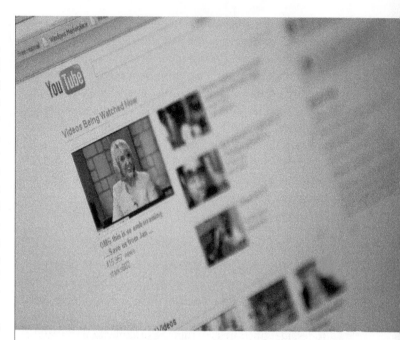

NICHOLAS KAMM/AFP/GETTY IMAGES

selling tend to focus on building long-term relationships rather than on making a one-time sale.

Relationship selling emphasizes a win–win outcome and the accomplishment of mutual objectives that benefit both buyer and salesperson in the long term. Rather than focusing on a quick sale, relationship selling attempts to create a long-term, committed relationship that is based on trust, increased customer loyalty, and a continuation of the relationship between the salesperson and the customer. Personal selling, like other promotional mix elements, is increasingly dependent on the Internet. Most companies use their websites to attract potential buyers seeking information on products and services and to drive customers to their physical locations where personal selling can close the sale. Personal selling is discussed further in Chapter 17.

Direct-Response Communication

Direct-response communication, often referred to as direct marketing, is the communication of a message directly from a marketing company and directly to an intended individual target audience. The objective is to generate profitable business results through targeted communications to a specific audience. Direct response communication utilizes a combination of relevant messaging and offers that can be tracked, measured, analyzed, stored, and leveraged to drive future marketing initiatives.

Direct-response communication has grown in importance in integrated marketing communication programs for many reasons but two factors have played key roles: (1) the results of the communication program can be measured and, hence, immediately altered (if necessary) to improve performance; and (2) the use of the Internet as a communication tool provides one-to-one communication to the intended target, which is the foundation of direct-marketing communication.

Direct-marketing communication uses a variety of media to deliver the personalized message, including television and radio, referred to as direct-response broadcast; newspaper and magazines, referred to as direct-response print; telephone, referred to as tele-marketing; the Internet, both email and websites; and postal mail, referred to as direct mail. The most common form of direct-response communication is direct mail.

Direct-response communication can be highly successful because the consumer often finds the targeted communication to be more appealing as it is more personal. Direct marketing is designed to meet consumers' unique needs. Potential buyers can learn about the product and make a purchase all at the same time.

Online Marketing

Online Marketing is communication delivered through the Internet. The rapid growth of consumers' use of the Internet and its pervasive impact on consumers' daily lives have led to new communication opportunities for marketers today. The Internet creates real-time, two-way communication with consumers. This allows the marketer to alter the message to better suit the consumer. Consumers can not only immediately respond to the marketer's message with further inquiries or even a purchase, but as a result of email and social media, they can also share it instantly with their friends and family.

A common interactive tool is a website. Companies develop their own websites (corporate websites) to provide the consumer with product or service information. Often, the website goes beyond product information and contains news on upcoming events, new product launches, contests, and special offers. The information contained on a website can help to engage the consumer more fully, thereby strengthening the company/consumer relationship. Non-corporate websites have been developed to entertain, provide information, and to provide online shopping opportunities, which all make the consumer's life more convenient. The website www.beyondtherack

.com is a member-based shopping site profiling designer-brand clothing and accessories at prices up to 80 percent off through limited-timed shopping events. Members are notified in advance of the brands on special according to their preferences for the limited-time period. This makes shopping much more convenient for the brand- and price-conscious consumer.

The increasing use of digital technology has contributed to users' growing participation in social media. Nowhere is this more evident than in Canada, where 60 percent of Internet users now have a social networking profile. All age groups are using social media, even those 55 and older, 43 percent of whom report having a social networking profile. Frequency of use of social networking sites has increased in the last two years, and the most commonly visited social networking site in Canada is Facebook.[4] In this increasingly connected world, social media provide organizations with the opportunity to hold intimate conversations with individual consumers that can be shared through "likes" on Facebook and retweets on Twitter. In the same way social media allow consumers to speak to one another. This conversation is often in a public forum, such as on Facebook, providing instantaneous and wide-reaching word-of-mouth. The consumer using social media is in control of the message, the medium, and the response. This relinquishing of control is hard for marketers, but for those that do, the reward can be increased brand loyalty. If the marketer can listen and learn, he or she can engage more successfully.

LO 3 Marketing Communication

Promotional strategy is closely related to the process of communication. As humans, we assign meaning to feelings, ideas, facts, attitudes, and emotions. **Communication** is the process by which we exchange or share meanings through a common set of symbols. When a company develops a new product, changes an old one, or simply tries to increase sales of an existing good or service, marketers use promotion programs to communicate information about the firm and its products to potential customers and various publics.

Communication can be divided into two major categories: interpersonal communication and mass

online marketing two-way communication of a message delivered through the Internet to the consumer

communication the process by which we exchange or share meanings through a common set of symbols

communication. **Interpersonal communication** is direct, face-to-face communication between two or more people. When communicating face-to-face, each person can see the other's reaction and can respond almost immediately. A salesperson speaking directly with a client is an example of an interpersonal marketing communication.

Mass communication involves communicating a concept or message to large audiences. A great deal of marketing communication is directed to consumers as a whole, usually through a mass medium such as television or magazines. When a company uses mass communication, it generally does not personally know the people with whom it is trying to communicate. Furthermore, the company is unable to respond immediately to consumers' reactions to its message. Instead, the marketing manager must wait to see whether people react positively or negatively to the mass-communicated promotion. Any clutter from competitors' messages or other distractions in the environment can reduce the effectiveness of the mass-communication effort.

The Communication Process

Marketers are both senders and receivers of messages. As *senders*, marketers attempt to inform, persuade, and remind the target market to adopt a particular course of action. As *receivers*, marketers attune themselves to the target market so they can develop the appropriate messages, adapt existing messages, and spot new communication opportunities. In this way, marketing communication is a two-way, rather than one-way, process. The two-way nature of the communication process is shown in Exhibit 14.2.

The Sender and Encoding The **sender** is the originator of the message in the communication process. In an interpersonal conversation, the sender may be a parent, a friend, or a salesperson. For an advertisement or press release, the sender is the company or organization. For example, Unilever Canada was challenged to breathe new life into its Knorr Sidekicks, a brand in a highly competitive category. The competitive advantage to communicate was that Sidekicks now have 25 percent less salt. The company introduced Salty, a lovable yet sad fellow who was nothing more than an underused salt shaker because he was needed 25 percent less. His cute face and dejected persona were extremely appealing to the target audience. Salty soon started showing up on social media sites, and Unilever Canada began selling Salty saltshakers. The creation of Salty led to outstanding business results.[5]

Encoding is the conversion of the sender's ideas and thoughts into a message, usually in the form of words or signs. The Knorr Sidekicks ad uses encoded words and encoded visuals, in the form of Salty, the dejected salt shaker, to deliver the advertising message.

According to a basic principle of encoding, what matters is not what the source says but what the receiver *hears*. One way to convey a message that the receiver will hear properly is to use concrete words and pictures.

EXHIBIT 14.2
Communication Process

Sender	Encoding the message	Message channel	Decoding the message	Receiver
• Marketing manager • Advertising manager • Advertising agency	• Advertisement • Sales presentation • Store display • Coupon • Press release	• Media • Salesperson • Retail store • Local news show	• Receiver interpretation of message	• Customers • Viewers/listeners • News media • Clients

Noise
• Other advertisements
• News articles
• Other store displays

Feedback channel
• Market research
• Sales results
• Change in market share

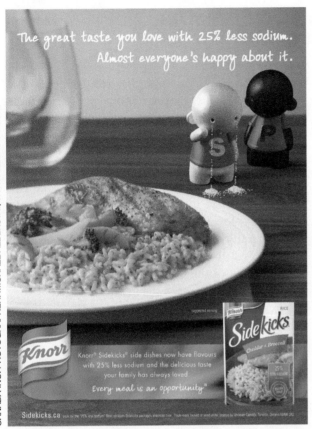

Message Transmission Transmission of a message requires a **channel**—a voice, radio, newspaper, or other communication medium. A facial expression or gesture can also serve as a channel.

Reception occurs when the message is detected by the receiver and enters his or her frame of reference. In a two-way conversation, such as a sales pitch given by a sales representative to a potential client, reception is normally high. In contrast, the desired receivers may or may not detect the message when it is mass communicated because most media are cluttered by **noise**—anything that interferes with, distorts, or slows down the transmission of information. In some media that are overcrowded with advertisers, such as newspapers and television, the noise level is high and the reception level is low. For example, in the case of the Knorr Sidekicks television commercial featuring Salty, its reception may be affected by television advertisements for other meal ideas, the nature of the program that features the advertisement, and other television programs aired during the time the commercial is playing. Transmission can also be hindered by situational factors in the physical surroundings, such as light, sound, location, and weather; the presence of other people; or the temporary moods consumers might bring to the situation.

Mass communication may not even reach all the right consumers. Although some members of the Knorr Sidekicks target audience may have been watching the television program that featured the commercial, others likely were not.

The Receiver and Decoding Marketers communicate their message through a channel to customers, or **receivers**, who will decode the message. **Decoding** is the interpretation of the language and symbols sent by the source through a channel. Effective communication requires a common understanding between two communicators or a common frame of reference. Therefore, marketing managers must ensure a proper match between the message to be conveyed and the target market's attitudes and ideas.

Even though a message has been received, it will not necessarily be properly decoded—or even seen, viewed, or heard—because of selective exposure, perception, and retention. Even when people receive a message, they tend to manipulate, alter, and modify it to reflect their own biases, needs, knowledge, and culture. Differences in age, social class, education, culture, and ethnicity can lead to miscommunication. Further, because people don't always listen or read carefully, they can easily misinterpret what is said or written. In fact, researchers have found that consumers misunderstand a large proportion of both printed and televised communications.

Feedback In interpersonal communication, the receiver's response to a message is direct **feedback** to the source. Feedback may be verbal, as in saying "Yes I will buy," or nonverbal, as in nodding, smiling, frowning, or gesturing.

Because mass communicators such as Unilever are often cut off from direct feedback, they must rely on market research or analysis of viewer responses for indirect feedback. Unilever, the marketer of Knorr Sidekicks, could use a variety of advertising research methods to determine the awareness, perception, and comprehension of the Salty ad. In addition, an analysis of sales both before and after airing of the ad could help to determine the ads effectiveness. As marketers like Unilever continue to shift advertising budgets to social media and the Internet, direct feedback will become increasingly available.

channel a medium of communication—such as a voice, radio, or newspaper—used for transmitting a message

noise anything that interferes with, distorts, or slows down the transmission of information

receiver the person who decodes a message

decoding interpretation of the language and symbols sent by the source through a channel

feedback the receiver's response to a message

OF ALL BUSINESS OWNERS USING **SOCIAL MEDIA,** 75 PERCENT SAY IT HAS **BENEFITED** THEIR BUSINESS.[6]

The Communication Process and the Promotional Mix

The six elements of the promotional mix differ in their ability to affect the target audience. Exhibit 14.3 outlines differences among the promotional mix elements with respect to mode of communication, marketer's control over the communication process, amount and speed of feedback, direction of message flow, marketer's control over the message, identification of the sender, speed in reaching large audiences, and message flexibility.

From Exhibit 14.3, you can see that most elements of the promotional mix are indirect and impersonal when used to communicate with a target market, providing only one direction of message flow. For example, advertising, public relations, and sales promotion are generally impersonal, one-way means of mass communication. Because these elements of the promotional mix provide no opportunity for direct feedback, it is more difficult to alter the promotional message of these elements to adapt to changing consumer preferences, individual differences, and personal goals.

Personal selling, on the other hand, is personal, two-way communication. The salesperson receives immediate feedback from the consumer and can adjust the message in response. Personal selling, however, is very slow in dispersing the marketer's message to large audiences. Direct-response communication intention is to be targeted, two-way communication but the extent of the personalization is dependent on the medium used to reach the intended target.

The Impact of the Internet on Marketing Communication

Marketing communication has been profoundly affected by the Internet and by related technologies,

EXHIBIT 14.3
Characteristics of the Elements in the Promotional Mix (including Direct-Response Communication)

	Advertising	Public Relations	Sales Promotion	Personal Selling	Direct-Response Communication	Online Marketing
Mode of Communication	Indirect and impersonal	Usually indirect and impersonal	Usually indirect and impersonal	Direct and face-to-face	Direct but often impersonal	Direct and sometimes personal
Communicator Control over the Situation	Low	Moderate to low	Moderate to low	High	Some, depending on mode of communication	Some, depending on mode of communication
Amount of Feedback	Little	Little	Little to moderate	Much	High	High
Speed of Feedback	Delayed	Delayed	Varies	Immediate	Varies	Quick
Direction of Message	Flow one-way	One-way	Mostly one-way	Two-way	Mostly two-way	Two-way
Control over Message Content	Yes	No	Yes	Yes	Some	Some
Identification of Sponsor	Yes	No	Yes	Yes	Yes	Yes
Speed in Reaching Large Audience	Fast	Usually fast	Fast	Slow	Slow	Depends
Message Flexibility	Same message to all audiences	Usually no direct control over message audiences	Same message to varied target	Tailored to prospective buyer	Tailored to prospective target	Tailored to prospective target

such as **social networking sites**, also called **social media sites**, websites where users create and share information about themselves, brands, and other mutual interests. The increased use of social networking sites, such as Facebook, Twitter, and YouTube, has created a completely new way for marketers to manage their image, connect with consumers, and generate interest in and desire for their companies' products. A report released by Bank of Montreal in September 2010 indicates that business owners in Canada are using social networking sites, and 75 percent of those users indicate their usage has had a positive impact on business.[7]

Users of social networking sites tend to be multiusers—that is, they often use more than one platform, on an ongoing basis. Although these users also tend to be younger than the general population, social networking usage is not limited to youth; the fastest growing age group on Facebook is the 55 and older demographic.[8] In addition to participating on social networking sites like Twitter, consumers today are also actively blogging. They are participating in conversations on a variety of sites that result in frequent and ongoing dialogues on subjects they are interested in. Tumblr is a combination of a social network site and a blog. Its focus is not on connecting as is Twitter's but rather on providing a forum for personal expression. It is easy to create posts that are quite robust on Tumblr and it offers the social networking element of Twitter by allowing users to follow other blogs and to re-blog. Blogs are discussed further in Chapter 16.

So what is the value for companies of using social media sites in their communications campaign? One of the key advantages is the opportunity for easy two-way communication with individuals and large groups of people. The data gathered in such interactions is immediate and allows marketers to alter their messages accordingly. In addition, social networking sites such as Facebook generate instant consumer engagement. When businesses utilize this engagement appropriately, they can generate much consumer loyalty.

Not only has the Internet created the opportunity for two-way communication through blogging and social networking sites but it has changed the nature of communication between marketer and consumer. A 2010 Statistics Canada study noted that 80 percent of Canadians are using the Internet. Although using email is the number one online activity (by 93 percent of Internet users), an increasing number of users are involved in interactive communication. Some 27 percent of users contribute content to blogs and discussion groups (the percentage increases to 45 percent for those users under the age of 30), 27 percent were communicating with governments, and 45 percent were using an instant messenger.[9] Interactive forms of communication change the traditional model of communication depicted in Exhibit 14.2. In the past, feedback was traditionally impersonal and numbers- driven: if the communication program did not achieve its goals, the marketer reviewed the program's aims relative to its results to determine what changes were needed. Today, however, the acceptance of the Internet by all age groups has led to instantaneous and continual feedback. Companies actively seek consumer feedback by creating their own blogs, Facebook pages, and by using Twitter. Social media puts a face on what were once largely impersonal corporations.

A perfect example of the power of the Internet—and, in particular, social media sites and blogs—to encourage quick and far reaching communication is Gap's 2010 introduction of its new logo. Launched on October 4, 2010, the new logo drew immediate public reaction—and it was not positive. On October 6, Gap acknowledged the outcry by asking consumers to submit their own new designs, in an example of **crowdsourcing**, the channelling of the power of online crowds to gather feedback on marketing programs for almost immediate improvements and changes. The consumer-created designs never materialized. On October 10, the company issued a press release,

PHOTOEDIT/GETSTOCK.COM

© ISTOCKPHOTO.COM/GALATAPARTNERS

which stated, "we've been listening and watching all of the comments this past week. We heard [people] say over and over again they are passionate about our blue box logo, and they want it back. So we've made the decision to do just that—we will bring it back across all channels."[10]

Feedback on Gap's new logo occurred, and it occurred quickly and was widespread, as blogs, Twitter feeds, and Facebook sites were created quickly to provide all consumers the opportunity to voice their opinions. The Gap story reminds us that the consumer, as a result of the power of the Internet, is often in control. It is yet another change in communication that marketers are learning to embrace and use to their advantage.

<table><tr><td>**LO 4**</td><td></td></tr></table>

The Goals and Tasks of Promotion

People communicate with one another for many reasons. They seek amusement, ask for help, give assistance or instructions, provide information, and express ideas and thoughts. Promotion, on the other hand, seeks to modify behaviour and thoughts in some way. For example, promoters may try to persuade consumers to drink coffee at McDonald's rather than at Tim Hortons. Promotion also strives to reinforce existing behaviour—for instance, encouraging consumers to continue to drink McDonald's coffee and to eat more from their menu. The source (the seller) hopes to project a favourable image or to motivate a purchase of the company's goods and services.

Promotion can perform one or more of three tasks: *inform* the target audience, *persuade* the target audience, or *remind* the target audience. Often a marketer will try to accomplish two or more of these tasks at the same time.

Informing

Informative promotion seeks to convert an existing need into a want or to stimulate interest in a new product. This type of promotion is generally more prevalent during the early stages of the product

life cycle. People typically will not buy a product or service or support a nonprofit organization until they understand its purpose and its benefits to them. Complex and technical products, such as automobiles, computers, and investment services, often continue to use informative promotion well after the product or service has moved beyond the introductory stage of the product life cycle. This continued promotion is due to the nature of the purchase decision and the risk involved in the purchase. For example, shortly after Apple launched the iPad, its advertisements changed to focus on unique features, such as the versatility of use, the superiority of the graphics, and the endless number of apps that could be downloaded to make the user's life so much better. Informative promotion is also important for when a new brand being introduced into an old product class. The new product cannot establish itself against more mature products unless potential buyers are aware of it, value its benefits, and understand its positioning in the marketplace.

Persuading

Persuasive promotion is designed to stimulate a purchase or an action. Persuasion normally becomes the main promotion goal when the product enters the growth stage of its life cycle. By this time, those in the target market should have general awareness of the product category and some knowledge of how the category can fulfill their wants. Therefore, the company's promotional task switches from informing consumers about the product category to persuading them to buy its brand rather than the competitor's. The promotional message thus emphasizes the product's real and perceived competitive advantages, often appealing to emotional needs such as love, belonging, self-esteem, and ego satisfaction.

Persuasion can also be an important goal for very competitive mature product categories, such as many household items and pops. In a marketplace characterized by many competitors, the promotional message often encourages brand switching and aims to convert some buyers into loyal users. Critics believe that some promotional messages and techniques can be too persuasive, causing consumers to buy products and services they really don't need.

Reminding

Reminder promotion is used to keep the product and brand name in the public's mind. This type of promotion prevails during the maturity stage of the life cycle. A reminder promotion assumes that the target market has already been persuaded of the merits of the good or service. Its purpose is simply to trigger a memory. Crest toothpaste and other consumer products often use reminder promotion.

LO5 Promotional Goals and the AIDA Concept

The ultimate goal of any promotion is to have someone buy a good or service or, in the case of nonprofit organizations, to take some action (such as donate blood). A classic model for achieving promotional goals is called the **AIDA concept**.[11] The acronym stands for *attention, interest, desire,* and *action*—the stages of consumer involvement with a promotional message.

This model proposes that consumers respond to marketing messages in a cognitive (thinking), affective (feeling), and conative (doing) sequence. First, a promotion manager may focus on attracting a consumer's *attention* by training a salesperson to use a friendly greeting and approach, by using music that is relevant to the target, or by using bold headlines, movement, bright colours, and the like in an advertisement. Next, a good sales presentation, demonstration, or advertisement creates *interest* in the product and then, by illustrating how the product's features will satisfy the consumer's needs, arouses desire. Finally, a special offer or a strong closing sales pitch may be used to obtain purchase action.

The AIDA concept assumes that promotion propels consumers along the following four steps in the purchase-decision process:

1. *Attention:* The advertiser must first gain the attention of the target market. A firm cannot sell its product if the market does not know that the good or service exists. When Apple introduced the iPad, the company needed to create awareness and gain attention for the new product, so Apple used publicity and sampling, limited the supply to only certain countries and retailers, and then advertised and promoted it extensively through ads on TV, in magazines, and on social media sites. Because the iPad was a brand extension of the Apple computer, it required less effort than the introduction of an entirely new brand. At the same time, because the iPad was an innovative new product, the promotion had to attract customers' attention and create awareness of a new idea from an established company.

2. *Interest:* Simple awareness of a brand seldom leads to a sale. The next step is to create interest in the product. A print ad cannot tell potential customers all the features of the iPad. Thus, to create interest, Apple had to arrange iPad demonstrations and target its messages to innovators and early adopters.

3. *Desire:* Potential customers for the Apple iPad may like the concept of a tablet-style computer, but may not feel it is necessarily better than their current laptop computer. Thus, Apple had to create brand preference by highlighting unique features not found on a laptop, such as the touch screen, the vertical and horizontal readability of the screen, and the tablet's light weight and convenience. Specifically, Apple had to convince potential consumers that the iPad was the newest and best solution for their portable computing, communicating, viewing, and listening needs.

4. *Action:* Some potential target market customers may have been convinced to buy an iPad but had not yet made the actual purchase. To motivate them to take action, Apple continued advertising to more effectively communicate the

OLEKSIY MAKSYMENKO PHOTOGRAPHY/GETSTOCK.COM

features and benefits. It also used promotions, widened the distribution, and limited online discounts. In the first six months of the iPad's launch, 7.4 million devices were sold.[12]

Most buyers involved in high-involvement purchase situations pass through the four stages of the AIDA model on their way to making a purchase. The promoter's task is to first determine where on the purchase ladder most of the target consumers are located and to then design a promotion plan to meet their needs. For instance, if Apple learned from its market research that many potential customers were in the desire stage but had not yet bought an iPad, then Apple could alter its promotional strategy to utilize messages and media that the target consumer would be attentive to.

The AIDA concept does not explain how all promotions influence purchase decisions. The model suggests that promotional effectiveness can be measured in terms of consumers progressing from one stage to the next. However, much debate surrounds the order of the stages and whether consumers go through all steps. A purchase can occur without interest or desire, such as when a low-involvement product is bought on impulse. Regardless of the order of the stages or consumers' progression through these stages, the AIDA concept helps marketers by suggesting which promotional strategy will be most effective.[13]

AIDA and the Promotional Mix

Exhibit 14.4 depicts the relationship between the promotional mix and the AIDA model. It shows that, although advertising does have an impact in the later stages, it is most useful in gaining attention for goods or services. In contrast, personal selling reaches fewer people at first. Salespeople are more effective at creating customer interest for merchandise or a service and at creating desire. For example, advertising may help a potential computer purchaser to gain knowledge about competing brands, but the salesperson may be the one

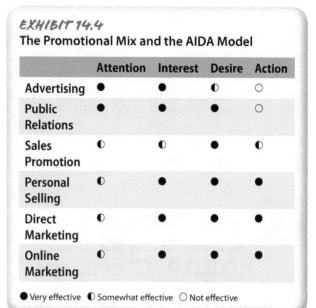

EXHIBIT 14.4
The Promotional Mix and the AIDA Model

	Attention	Interest	Desire	Action
Advertising	●	●	◐	○
Public Relations	●	●	●	○
Sales Promotion	◐	◐	●	◐
Personal Selling	◐	●	●	●
Direct Marketing	◐	●	●	●
Online Marketing	◐	●	●	●

● Very effective   ◐ Somewhat effective   ○ Not effective

who actually encourages the buyer to decide a particular brand is the best choice. The salesperson also has the advantage of having the product, such as a computer, physically there to demonstrate its capabilities to the buyer.

Public relations' greatest impact is gaining attention for a company, good, or service. Many companies can attract attention and build goodwill by sponsoring community events that benefit a worthy cause, such as antidrug and antigang programs. Such sponsorships project a positive image of the firm and its products into the minds of consumers and potential consumers. Book publishers push to get their titles on the bestseller lists of major publications, such as *The Globe and Mail*. Authors also make appearances on talk shows and at bookstores to personally sign books and speak to fans.

Sales promotion's greatest strength is in creating strong desire and purchase intent. Coupons and other price-off promotions are techniques used to persuade customers to buy new products. Frequent buyer sales promotion programs, popular among retailers, allow

"THE **COSTS** AND **RISKS** ASSOCIATED WITH A PRODUCT ALSO INFLUENCE THE **PROMOTIONAL MIX**."

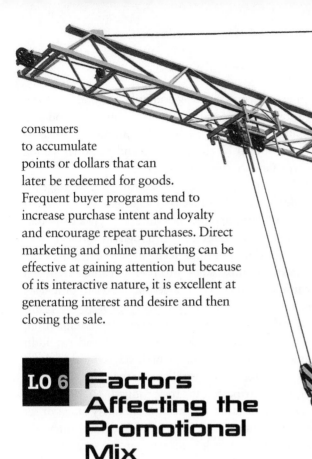

consumers to accumulate points or dollars that can later be redeemed for goods. Frequent buyer programs tend to increase purchase intent and loyalty and encourage repeat purchases. Direct marketing and online marketing can be effective at gaining attention but because of its interactive nature, it is excellent at generating interest and desire and then closing the sale.

LO 6 Factors Affecting the Promotional Mix

Promotional mixes vary a great deal from one product and one industry to the next. Normally, advertising and personal selling are used to promote goods and services, supported and supplemented by sales promotion. Public relations helps to develop a positive image for the organization and the product line. However, a firm may choose not to use all six promotional elements in its promotional mix, or it may choose to use them only in varying degrees. The particular promotional mix chosen by a firm for a product or service depends on several factors: the nature of the product, the stage in the product life cycle, target market characteristics, the type of buying decision, funds available for promotion, and whether a push or a pull strategy will be used.

Nature of the Product

Characteristics of the product itself can influence the promotional mix. For instance, a product can be classified as either a business product or a consumer product. (Refer to Chapters 6 and 9.) As business products are often custom-tailored to the buyer's exact specifications, they are often not well suited to mass promotion. Therefore, producers of most business goods, such as computer systems or industrial machinery, rely more heavily on personal selling than on advertising. Advertising, however, still serves a purpose in promoting business goods. Advertising in trade media can help locate potential customers for the sales force.

For example, print media advertising often includes coupons soliciting the potential customer to "fill this out for more detailed information."

In contrast, because consumer products generally are not custom-made, they do not require the selling efforts of a company representative to tailor them to the user's needs. Thus, consumer goods are promoted mainly through advertising to create brand familiarity. Television and radio advertising, consumer-oriented magazines, and increasingly the Internet and other highly targeted media are used to promote consumer goods, especially nondurables. Sales promotion, the brand name, and the product's packaging are about twice as important for consumer goods as for business products. Persuasive personal selling is important at the retail level for shopping goods such as automobiles and appliances.

The costs and risks associated with a product also influence the promotional mix. As a general rule, when the costs or risks of buying and using a product increase, personal selling becomes more important. In fact, inexpensive items cannot support the cost of a salesperson's time and effort unless the potential volume is high. On the other hand, expensive and complex machinery, cars, and new homes represent a considerable investment. A salesperson must assure buyers that they are spending their money wisely and not taking an undue financial risk.

Social risk is also an issue. Many consumer goods are not products of great social importance because they do not reflect social position. People do not experience much social risk when buying a loaf of bread. However, buying many specialty products such as jewellery and clothing involves a social risk. Many consumers depend on sales personnel for guidance in making the proper choice.

PURESTOCK/JUPITERIMAGES

Stage in the Product Life Cycle

The product's stage in its life cycle is a big factor in designing a promotional mix (see Exhibit 14.5). During the *introduction stage*, the basic goal of promotion is to inform the target audience that the product is available. Initially, the emphasis is on the general product class—for example, electric cars. This emphasis gradually changes to gaining attention for a particular brand, such as the Toyota Scion. Typically,

both extensive advertising and public relations inform the target audience of the product class or brand and heighten awareness levels. Sales promotion encourages early trial of the product, and personal selling gets retailers to carry the product.

When the product reaches the *growth stage* of the life cycle, the promotion blend may shift. Often a change is necessary because different types of potential buyers are targeted. Although advertising and public relations continue to be major elements of the promotional mix, sales promotion can be reduced because consumers need fewer incentives to purchase. The promotional strategy is to emphasize the product's differential advantage over the competition. Persuasive promotion is used to build and maintain brand loyalty during the growth stage. By this stage, personal selling has usually succeeded in achieving adequate distribution for the product.

As the product reaches the *maturity stage* of its life cycle, competition becomes fiercer, and thus persuasive; and reminder advertising is more strongly emphasized. Sales promotion comes back into focus as product sellers try to increase their market share.

All promotion, especially advertising, is reduced as the product enters the *decline stage*. Nevertheless, personal selling and sales promotion efforts may be maintained, particularly at the retail level.

Target Market Characteristics

A target market that is characterized by widely scattered potential customers, highly informed buyers, and brand-loyal repeat purchasers generally requires a promotional mix with more advertising and sales promotion and less personal selling. Sometimes, however, personal selling is required even when buyers are well informed and geographically dispersed. Although industrial installations may be sold to well-educated people with extensive work experience, salespeople must be present to explain the product and work out the details of the purchase agreement.

EXHIBIT 14.5
Product Life Cycle and the Promotional Mix

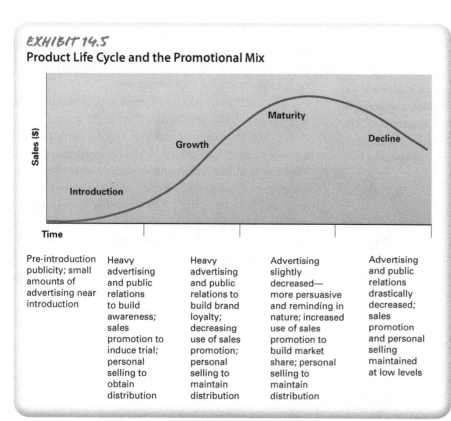

Introduction	Growth	Maturity	Decline
Pre-introduction publicity; small amounts of advertising near introduction	Heavy advertising and public relations to build awareness; sales promotion to induce trial; personal selling to obtain distribution	Heavy advertising and public relations to build brand loyalty; decreasing use of sales promotion; personal selling to maintain distribution	Advertising slightly decreased—more persuasive and reminding in nature; increased use of sales promotion to build market share; personal selling to maintain distribution	Advertising and public relations drastically decreased; sales promotion and personal selling maintained at low levels

Firms often sell goods and services in markets where potential customers are difficult to locate. Direct-response print advertising can be used to find these customers. The reader is invited to call for more information, mail in a reply card for a detailed brochure, visit a website, or scan a Quick Response (QR) code located within the ad to receive more information.

Type of Buying Decision

The promotional mix also depends on the type of buying. For routine consumer decisions, such as buying toothpaste, the most effective promotion calls attention to the brand or reminds the consumer about the brand. Advertising and, especially, sales promotion are the most productive promotion tools to use for routine decisions.

If the decision is neither routine nor complex, advertising and public relations help establish awareness for the good or service. Suppose a man is looking for a bottle of wine to serve to his dinner guests. As a beer drinker, he is not familiar with wines, yet he has read an article in a popular magazine about the Pyramid at Summerhill Winery in the Okanagan and seen an advertisement for the wine. He may be more likely to buy this brand because he is already aware of it.

In contrast, consumers who make complex buying decisions are more extensively involved. They rely on large amounts of information to help them reach a purchase decision. Personal selling is effective in helping these consumers decide. For example, consumers thinking about buying a car often depend on a salesperson to provide the information they need to reach a decision. Increasingly, social media is playing an important role as the nature of social media makes it very easy for the purchaser to seek advice from peers to acquire the information they need. Such information is perceived as unbiased and trustworthy. Print advertising may also be used for high-involvement purchase decisions because it can often provide a large amount of information to the consumer.

Available Funds

Money, or the lack of it, may easily be the most important factor in determining the promotional mix. A small, undercapitalized manufacturer may rely heavily on free publicity if its product is unique. If the situation warrants a sales force, a financially strained firm may turn to manufacturers' agents, who work on a commission basis with no advances or expense accounts. Even well-capitalized organizations may not be able to afford the advertising rates of such publications as *Canadian Living*, *Sports Illustrated*, and *The Globe and Mail*, or the cost of running television commercials on *CSI* or during the Stanley Cup playoffs. The price of a high-profile advertisement in these media could support several salespeople for an entire year.

When funds are available to permit a mix of promotional elements, a firm will generally try to optimize its return on promotion dollars while minimizing the *cost per contact*, or the cost of reaching one member of the target market. In general, the cost per contact is very high for personal selling, public relations, and sales promotions such as samplings and demonstrations. On the other hand, given the number of people national advertising reaches, it has a very low cost per contact. Usually, a trade-off is made among the funds available, the number of people in the target market, the quality of communication needed, and the relative costs of the promotional elements.

Push and Pull Strategies

The last factor that affects the promotional mix is whether a push or a pull promotional strategy will be used. Manufacturers may use aggressive personal selling and trade advertising to convince a wholesaler or a retailer to carry and sell their merchandise. This approach is known as a **push strategy** (see Exhibit 14.6). The wholesaler, in turn, must often push the merchandise forward by persuading the retailer to handle the goods. The retailer then uses advertising, displays, and other forms of promotion to convince the consumer to buy the pushed products. This concept also applies to services.

At the other extreme is a **pull strategy**, which stimulates consumer demand to obtain product distribution. Rather than trying to sell to the wholesaler,

push strategy a marketing strategy that uses aggressive personal selling and trade advertising to convince a wholesaler or a retailer to carry and sell particular merchandise

pull strategy a marketing strategy that stimulates consumer demand to obtain product distribution

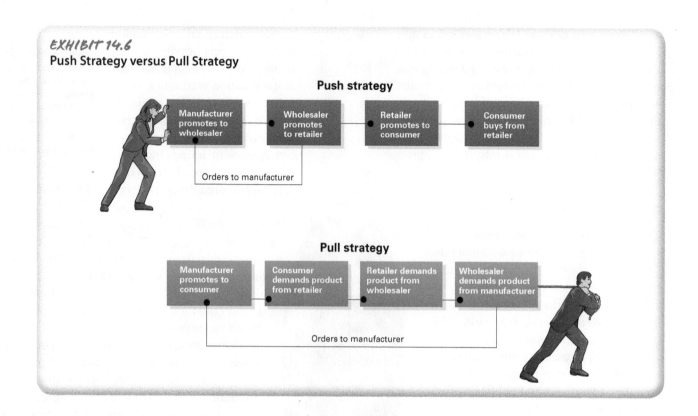

EXHIBIT 14.6
Push Strategy versus Pull Strategy

Push strategy

Manufacturer promotes to wholesaler → Wholesaler promotes to retailer → Retailer promotes to consumer → Consumer buys from retailer

Orders to manufacturer

Pull strategy

Manufacturer promotes to consumer → Consumer demands product from retailer → Retailer demands product from wholesaler → Wholesaler demands product from manufacturer

Orders to manufacturer

integrated marketing communications (IMC) the careful coordination of all promotional messages for a product or a service to ensure the consistency of messages at every contact point where a company meets the consumer

the manufacturer using a pull strategy focuses its promotional efforts on end consumers or opinion leaders. For example, Colgate often hires dental assistants or hygienists to visit area dentists to provide them with free product samples. These samples are used on the dentist's patients, thereby creating buzz about the new product. As consumers begin demanding the product, the retailer orders the merchandise from the wholesaler. The wholesaler, confronted with rising demand, then places an order for the pulled merchandise from the manufacturer. Consumer demand pulls the product through the channel of distribution (see Exhibit 14.6). Heavy sampling, introductory consumer advertising, cents-off campaigns, and couponing are all part of a pull strategy.

Rarely does a company use a pull or a push strategy exclusively. Instead, the mix will usually emphasize one of these strategies. For example, pharmaceutical companies generally use a push strategy, through personal selling and trade advertising, to promote their drugs and therapies to physicians. Sales presentations and advertisements in medical journals give physicians the detailed information they need to prescribe medication to their patients. Most pharmaceutical companies supplement their push promotional strategy with

a pull strategy targeted directly to potential patients through advertisements in consumer magazines and on television.

LO 7 Integrated Marketing Communications

Ideally, marketing communications from each promotional mix element (personal selling, advertising, sales promotion, direct marketing, and public relations) should be integrated—that is, the message reaching the consumer should be the same regardless of whether it is from an advertisement, a salesperson in the field, a magazine article, or a coupon in a newspaper insert.

Consumers do not think in terms of the six elements of promotion: advertising, sales promotion, direct marketing, public relations, personal selling, and online marketing. Instead, everything is an ad. The only people who recognize the distinctions among these communications elements are the marketers themselves.

Many companies today have adopted the concept of **integrated marketing communications (IMC)**. IMC is the careful coordination of all promotional messages—traditional advertising, direct marketing, online, public relations, sales promotion, personal selling, and other communications—for a product or service to ensure the consistency of messages at every contact point where a company meets the consumer. Following the concept of IMC, marketing managers carefully work out the roles that various promotional elements will play in the marketing mix. The timing of promotional activities is coordinated, and the results of each campaign are carefully monitored to improve future use of the promotional mix tools.

Movie marketing campaigns benefit greatly from an IMC approach. Those campaigns that are most integrated generally have more impact and make a deeper impression on potential moviegoers, leading to higher box-office sales. It is not uncommon for movie marketing to include premieres, fast-food tie-ins, toys, contests, games, books, music CDs, and even podcasts. Automobile marketing campaigns also utilize an IMC approach, particularly when targeting a younger audience, which tends to be more multimedia-oriented.

The IMC concept has been growing in popularity for several reasons. First, the proliferation of thousands of media choices beyond traditional television has made promotion a more complicated task. Instead of promoting a product through only mass-media options, such as television and magazines, promotional messages today can appear in many varied sources. Further, the mass market has also been fragmented—that is, more selectively segmented markets and an increase in niche marketing have replaced the traditional broad

market groups that marketers promoted to in years past. Finally, marketers have slashed their advertising spending in favour of promotional techniques that generate immediate sales responses and those that are more easily measured, such as direct marketing. Thus, the interest in IMC is largely a reaction to the scrutiny that marketing communications has been subjected to and, in particular, to suggestions that uncoordinated promotional activity leads to a strategy that is wasteful and inefficient.

General Motors utilized very energetic television ads to establish the look and feel of the launch campaign for the Chevy Cruze. These ads were supported by extensive print, out-of-home, online, and experiential elements. Online promotions included a fan page on Facebook and an opportunity to experience the car in 3D on the GM website.[14]

JAE C. HONG/ASSOCIATED PRESS

$50 billion
Dollar value of Facebook

450,000
Number of Facebook friends of Molson Canadian, making it one of the most popular brands on Facebook

Time it took Gap to revert to its original logo
1 week

$10 million+
Amount spent by the Hudson's Bay Company to promote its 2010 Olympic apparel line

26
Number of Apple iPads sold per minute

CHAPTER 15

Advertising, Public Relations, and Direct Response

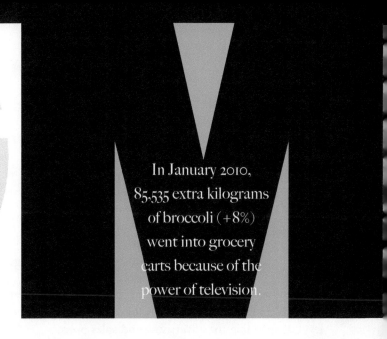

In January 2010, 85,535 extra kilograms of broccoli (+8%) went into grocery carts because of the power of television.

LO 1 The Effects of Advertising

Advertising is defined in Chapter 14 as any form of impersonal, paid communication in which the sponsor or company is identified. It is a popular form of promotion, especially for consumer packaged goods and services. Advertising revenues have historically increased annually. Between 2007 and 2008, they increased 3.8 percent; however, between 2008 and 2009, advertising revenue actually fell 7.9 percent with softening in all advertising media with the exception of the Internet, which experienced a gain in revenue of 13.7 percent.[1]

Although Canada has a fair number of strong domestic advertising agencies, international advertising agencies are beginning to have a significant presence here. This industry shift has occurred as a result of the globalization of the industry during the past 20 years, whereby many smaller domestic agencies were acquired or formed alliances with larger agencies. The mergers, acquisitions, and partnerships are a result of clients demanding a greater breadth and depth of service that can best be met by smaller domestic agencies partnering with larger international firms.

In September 2010, it was reported that the Canadian government's 2009–10 ad budget had hit a record $130 million, more than $50 million over the previous year's budget.[2] Canada's top advertisers, other than the federal government, include Procter & Gamble and General Motors Canada. Spending on advertising varies by industry.

What do you think?

Television advertising helps me to know which brands have the features I am looking for.

1	2	3	4	5	6	7
STRONGLY DISAGREE				STRONGLY AGREE		

Advertising and Market Share

Today's most successful brands of consumer goods, such as Ivory soap and Coca-Cola, were built long ago by heavy advertising and marketing investments. Today's advertising dollars are spent on maintaining brand awareness and market share.

New brands with a small market share tend to spend proportionately more for advertising and sales promotion than new brands with a large market share, typically for two reasons. First, beyond a certain level of spending for advertising and sales promotion, diminishing returns set in. That is, sales or market share begins to decrease no matter how much is spent on advertising and sales promotion. This phenomenon is called the **advertising response function**. Understanding the advertising response function helps marketers to use their budgets wisely. A market leader such as Johnson & Johnson's Neutrogena typically spends proportionately less on advertising than a newcomer such as L'Oréal's Men Expert Hydra Sensitive 24H Moisturizer. Neutrogena has already captured the attention of the majority of its target market. It only needs to remind customers of its product.

The second reason that new brands tend to require higher spending for advertising and sales promotion is that a certain minimum level of exposure is needed to measurably affect purchase habits. If L'Oréal advertised Men Expert Hydra Sensitive 24H in only one or two publications and bought only one or two television spots, it would not achieve the exposure needed to penetrate consumers' perceptual defences, and thereby affect purchase intentions.

The Effects of Advertising on Consumers

Advertising affects consumers' daily lives, informing them about products and services and influencing their attitudes, beliefs, and ultimately their purchases. Advertising affects the TV programs people watch, the content of the newspapers they read, the politicians they elect, the medicines they take, and the toys their children play with. Consequently, the influence of advertising on the North American socioeconomic system has been the subject of extensive debate in nearly all corners of society.

Though advertising cannot change consumers' deeply rooted values and attitudes, advertising may succeed in transforming a person's negative attitude toward a product into a positive one. For instance, serious or dramatic advertisements are more effective at changing consumers' negative attitudes. Humorous ads, on the other hand, have been shown to be more effective at shaping attitudes when consumers already have a positive image of the advertised brand.[3]

To reinforce its positioning as a brewer of lower-priced beer, the James Ready Brewing Company has executed a series of out-of-home ads that creatively assist consumers in saving money.

Advertising also reinforces positive attitudes toward brands. When consumers have a neutral or favourable frame of reference toward a product or brand, advertising often positively influences them. When consumers are already highly loyal to a brand, they may buy more of it when advertising and promotion for that brand increase.[4] This behaviour is why market leaders spend billions of dollars annually to reinforce and remind their loyal customers about the benefits of their products.

Advertising can also affect the way consumers rank a brand's attributes. For example, in years past, car ads emphasized such brand attributes as roominess, speed, and low maintenance. Today, however, car marketers have added fuel efficiency, safety, economy, and customization to the list.

LO 2 Major Types of Advertising

The firm's promotional objectives determine the type of advertising it uses. If the goal of the promotion plan is to build up the image of the company or the industry, **institutional advertising** may be used. In contrast, if the advertiser wants to enhance the sales of a specific good or service, **product advertising,** which promotes the benefits of a specific good or service, is used.

Institutional Advertising

Historically, advertising in Canada has been product oriented. Today, many companies market multiple products and need a different type of advertising. Institutional advertising, or corporate advertising, promotes the corporation as a whole and is designed to establish, change, or maintain the corporation's identity. It usually does not ask the audience to do anything but maintain a favourable attitude toward the advertiser and its goods and services. Ideally, this favourable attitude will transfer to the products being marketed by the company, thereby creating a competitive advantage over competitors.

Advocacy advertising is a form of institutional advertising in which an organization expresses its views on a particular cause, issue, or cause. This form of advertising has increased as companies seek to gain public favour by linking their marketing campaigns to social issues or causes, such as global warming or childhood obesity.

Product Advertising

Unlike institutional advertising, product advertising promotes the benefits of a specific good or service. The product's stage in its life cycle often determines whether the product advertising used is pioneering advertising, competitive advertising, or comparative advertising.

Pioneering Advertising Pioneering advertising is intended to stimulate primary demand for a new product or product category. Heavily used during the introductory stage of the product life cycle, pioneering advertising offers consumers in-depth information about the benefits of the product class.

Pioneering advertising also seeks to create interest. Pharmaceutical companies are the latest players in pioneering advertising. The launch of the Apple iPad is a good example of a pioneering campaign.

Competitive Advertising Firms use competitive or brand advertising when a product enters the growth phase of the product life cycle and other companies begin to enter the marketplace. Instead of building demand for the product category, the goal of **competitive advertising** is to influence demand for a specific brand. During this phase, promotion often becomes less informative and, instead, appeals more to emotions. Advertisements may begin to stress subtle differences between brands, with heavy emphasis on building recall of a brand name and creating a favourable attitude toward the brand. Automobile advertising has long used very competitive messages, drawing distinctions on the basis of such factors as quality, performance, and image.

Comparative Advertising Comparative advertising directly or indirectly compares two or more competing brands on one or more specific attributes. Some advertisers even use comparative advertising against their own brands. Products experiencing sluggish growth or those entering the marketplace against strong competitors are more likely to employ comparative claims in their advertising.

Before the 1970s, comparative advertising was allowed only if the competing brand was veiled and unidentified. In 1971, the FTC (Federal Trade Commission) in the United States fuelled the growth of comparative advertising, claiming it provided consumers with useful information. The Competition Act in Canada prohibits advertisers from falsely describing competitors' products and allows competitors to sue if ads show their products or mention their brand names in an incorrect or false manner. Advertising Standards Canada guidelines also prevent advertisers from making false claims about their own products. PepsiCo and Coca-Cola have often used comparative advertising as a tool to communicate product benefits.

product advertising a form of advertising that promotes the benefits of a specific good or service

advocacy advertising a form of advertising in which an organization expresses its views on a particular issue or cause

pioneering advertising a form of advertising designed to stimulate primary demand for a new product or product category

competitive advertising a form of advertising designed to influence demand for a specific brand

comparative advertising a form of advertising that compares two or more competing brands on one or more specific attributes

Researchers estimate that the average North American viewer watches at least six hours of commercial television messages a week.

LO 3 Creative Decisions in Advertising

Advertising strategies are typically organized around an advertising campaign. An **advertising campaign** is a series of related advertisements focusing on a common theme, slogan, and set of advertising appeals. It is a specific advertising effort for a particular product that extends for a defined period of time.

Before any creative work can begin on an advertising campaign, it is important to determine what goals or objectives the advertising should achieve. An **advertising objective** is the specific communication task that a campaign should accomplish for a specified target audience during a specified period. The objectives of a specific advertising campaign often depend on the overall corporate objectives, the product being advertised, and consumers' position with respect to the product and the AIDA model (as discussed in Chapter 14). Depending on where consumers are in the AIDA process helps to determine whether the advertising objective is to create awareness, arouse interest, stimulate desire, or create a purchase.

The DAGMAR approach (Defining Advertising Goals for Measured Advertising Results) establishes a protocol for writing advertising objectives. According to this method, all advertising objectives should precisely define the target audience, the desired percentage change in a specified measure of effectiveness, and the time frame during which that change is to occur.

Once the advertising objectives are defined, creative work can begin on the advertising campaign. Specifically, creative decisions include identifying product benefits, developing and evaluating advertising appeals, executing the message, and evaluating the effectiveness of the campaign.

Identifying Product Benefits

A well-known rule of thumb in the advertising industry is "Sell the sizzle, not the steak." In other words, the advertising goal is to sell the benefits of the product, not its attributes. An attribute is simply a feature of the product, such as its easy-open package or a particular scent. A benefit is what consumers will receive or achieve by using the product. A benefit should answer the consumer's question "What's in it for me?" Benefits might include such things as convenience or savings. A quick test to determine whether you are offering attributes or benefits in your advertising is to ask, "So?" Consider this example:

Attribute: Tim Hortons coffee is fresh brewed every 20 minutes. So...??

Benefit: So you will receive a fresh, good-tasting cup of coffee each and every time.

Marketing research and intuition are usually used to unearth the perceived benefits of a product and to rank consumers' preferences for these benefits.

Developing and Evaluating Advertising Appeals

An **advertising appeal** identifies a reason for a person to buy a product. Developing advertising appeals, a challenging task, is generally the responsibility of the creative people in the advertising agency. Advertising appeals typically play off consumers' emotions or address consumers' needs or wants.

Advertising campaigns can focus on one or more advertising appeals. Often the appeals are quite general, thereby allowing the firm to develop a number of subthemes or minicampaigns using both advertising and sales promotion. Several possible advertising appeals are listed in Exhibit 15.1.

Choosing the most appropriate appeal normally requires market research. Criteria for evaluation include desirability, exclusiveness, and believability. The appeal first must make a positive impression on and be desirable to the target market. It must also

---

advertising campaign a series of related advertisements focusing on a common theme, slogan, and set of advertising appeals

advertising objective a specific communication task that a campaign should accomplish for a specified target audience during a specified period

advertising appeal a reason for a person to buy a product

EXHIBIT 15.1

Common Advertising Appeals

Profit	Informs consumers whether the product will save them money, make them money, or keep them from losing money
Health	Appeals to those who are body conscious or who want to be healthy
Love or Romance	Often used to sell cosmetics and perfumes
Fear	Can centre around fears of social embarrassment, growing old, or losing one's health; because of the power of fear, advertisers need to exercise care when using this type of appeal
Admiration	Often leads to the use of celebrity spokespeople in advertising
Convenience	Often used to promote fast-food restaurants and microwave-ready foods
Fun and Pleasure	Are the key to advertising vacations, beer, amusement parks, and more
Vanity and Egotism	Are used most often for expensive or conspicuous items such as cars and clothing
Environmental Consciousness	Centres around protecting the environment and being considerate of others in the community

be exclusive or unique; consumers must be able to distinguish the advertiser's message from competitors' messages. Most important, the appeal should be believable. An appeal that makes extravagant claims not only wastes promotional dollars but also creates ill will for the advertiser.

The advertising appeal selected for the campaign becomes what advertisers call its **unique selling proposition**. The unique selling proposition usually becomes the campaign's slogan. Tim Hortons' advertising campaign aimed at coffee drinkers carries the slogan "Always Fresh. Always Tim Hortons." Effective slogans often become so ingrained that when consumers hear the slogan, they can immediately conjure up images of the product.

Executing the Message

Message execution is the way an advertisement portrays its information. Again, the AIDA plan (see Chapter 14) is a good blueprint for executing an advertising message. Any ad should immediately draw the attention of the reader, viewer, or listener. The advertiser must then use the message to hold interest, create desire for the good or service, and ultimately motivate a purchase.

The style in which the message is executed is one of the most creative elements of an advertisement. Exhibit 15.2 lists examples of executiconal styles used by advertisers. Executional styles often dictate what

unique selling proposition a desirable, exclusive, and believable advertising appeal selected as the theme for a campaign

NAME THAT BRAND

Memorable tag lines are often a hallmark of a **strong brand**. Can you identify the brands advertised with each tag line?

1. I'm lovin' it.
2. Zoom-Zoom.
3. The Ultimate Driving Machine
4. Just do it.
5. I am Canadian.
6. Melts in your mouth, not in your hands.
7. Diamonds are forever.

1) McDonald's, 2) Mazda, 3) BMW, 4) Nike, 5) Molson (Canadian), 6) M&Ms, 7) De Beers

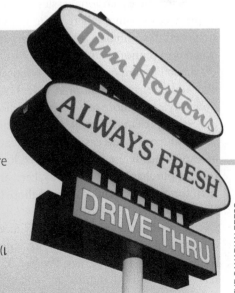

THE CANADIAN PRESS (STEVE WHITE)

EXHIBIT 15.2
Ten Common Executional Styles for Advertising

Slice-of-Life	Depicts people in normal settings, such as at the dinner table or in their car. McDonald's often uses slice-of-life styles showing youngsters munching French fries and Happy Meals on family outings.
Lifestyle	Shows how well the product will fit in with the consumer's lifestyle. As a new family moves in, the child of the new family meets the child living next door. Although neither speaks the other's language, they both have a glass of milk and an Oreo cookie, and you know they will become fast friends.
Spokesperson/ Testimonial	Can feature a celebrity, a company official, or a typical consumer making a testimonial or endorsing a product. Andie MacDowell endorses L'Oréal Excellence Crème hair colour, while Carrie Fisher endorses Jenny Craig. Galen Weston appears in television ads, touting the great taste of President's Choice Blue Menu products available at Loblaws.
Fantasy	Creates a fantasy for the viewer built around use of the product. Carmakers often use this style to let viewers fantasize about how they would feel speeding around tight corners or down long country roads in their cars.
Humorous	Advertisers often use humour in their ads, such as Bell Sympatico's Frank and Gordon.
Real/Animated Product Symbols	Creates a character that represents the product in advertisements, such as the Energizer Bunny, Starkist's Charlie the Tuna, or General Mills' long-time icon, Betty Crocker, redesigned for the new millennium.
Mood or Image	Builds a mood or image around the product, such as peace, love, or beauty. De Beers ads depicting shadowy silhouettes wearing diamond engagement rings and diamond necklaces portrays passion and intimacy while extolling that a "diamond is forever."
Demonstration	Shows consumers the expected benefit. Many consumer products use this technique. Laundry-detergent spots are famous for demonstrating how their product will clean clothes whiter and brighter. CLR demonstrates in television commercials how it removes calcium, lime, and rust around the house.
Musical	Conveys the message of the advertisement through song. For example, Honda's ad for the 2008 Accord coupe depicted the car driving alongside moving images of family events, environmental beauty, feats of athleticism, and wonders of technology to a soundtrack of ELO's "Hold on Tight to Your Dreams."
Scientific	Uses research or scientific evidence to depict a brand's superiority over competitors. Pain relievers such as Advil, Bayer, and Excedrin use scientific evidence in their ads.

type of media is to be employed to convey the message. Scientific executional styles lend themselves well to print advertising, where more information can be conveyed. Testimonials by athletes are one of the more popular executional styles.

Injecting humour into an advertisement is a popular and effective executional style. Humorous executional styles are more often used in radio and television advertising than in print or magazine advertising where humour is less easily communicated. Humorous ads are typically used for lower-risk, low-involvement, routine purchases such as candy, beer, and casual jeans than for higher-risk purchases or those that are expensive, durable, or flamboyant.[5]

Sometimes a company will modify its executional styles to make its advertising more relevant. For decades, Procter & Gamble has advertised shampoo in China using a

After the Super Bowl, consumers are asked to vote on their favourite ads, and the rankings are then posted on various sites. While not entirely scientific, this survey does provide marketers with a sense of the ability of different ads to generate awareness and arouse interest.

demonstrational executional style. Television ads first showed how the science of shampoo worked and then showed a woman with nice shiny hair. Because today's urban Chinese no longer make solely utilitarian purchases, P&G now uses emotional appeals in its advertisements. One shows a woman emerging from an animated cocoon as a sophisticated butterfly, while a voice purrs, "Head & Shoulders metamorphosis—new life for hair."[6]

Postcampaign Evaluation

Evaluating an advertising campaign can be the most demanding task facing advertisers. How can they assess whether the campaign led to an increase in sales or market share or elevated awareness of the product? Many advertising campaigns aim to create an image for the good or service instead of asking for action, so their real effect is unknown. So many variables shape the effectiveness of an ad that advertisers often must guess whether their money has been well spent. Nonetheless, marketers spend considerable time studying advertising effectiveness and its probable impact on sales, market share, or awareness.

Testing ad effectiveness can be done either before or after the campaign. Before a campaign is released, marketing managers use pretests to determine the best advertising appeal, layout, and media vehicle. After advertisers implement a campaign, they use several monitoring techniques to determine whether the campaign has met its original goals. Even if a campaign has been highly successful, advertisers still typically do a postcampaign analysis to identify how the campaign might have been more efficient and which factors contributed to its success.

LO4 Media Decisions in Advertising

A major decision for advertisers is the choice of **medium**—the channel used to convey a message to a target market. **Media planning**, therefore, is the series of decisions advertisers make regarding the selection and use of media, allowing the marketer to optimally and cost-effectively communicate the message to the target audience. Specifically, advertisers must determine which types of media will best communicate the benefits of their product or service to the target audience and when and for how long the advertisement will run.

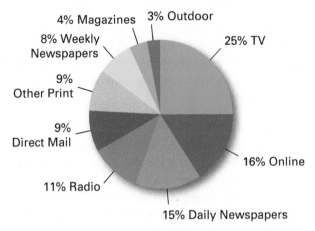

Canadian Net Advertising Revenue by Medium

- 4% Magazines
- 3% Outdoor
- 8% Weekly Newspapers
- 25% TV
- 9% Other Print
- 9% Direct Mail
- 16% Online
- 11% Radio
- 15% Daily Newspapers

NOTE: Percentage do not total to 100, due to rounding.

SOURCE: Television Bureau of Canada, http://www.tvb.ca/pages/nav2_htm/?from=search.

Promotional objectives and the appeal and executional style of the advertising strongly affect the selection of media. Both creative and media decisions are made at the same time. Creative work cannot be completed without knowing which medium will be used to convey the message to the target market. In many cases, the advertising objectives dictate the medium and the creative approach to be used. For example, if the objective is to demonstrate how fast a product operates, the best medium to show this action is likely a TV commercial.

Canadian advertisers spend roughly $14 billion annually on media monitored by national reporting services—newspapers, magazines, phone directories, Internet, radio, television, and outdoor media. The remainder is spent on unmonitored media, such as direct mail, trade exhibits, cooperative advertising, brochures, coupons, catalogues, and special events. About 24 percent of every media dollar goes toward TV ads, 9 percent toward direct mail, and about 23 percent to newspaper ads. But these traditional mass-market media are declining in usage as more advertisers turn to targeted media.

Media Types

Advertising media are channels that advertisers use in mass communication. The eight major advertising media are newspapers, magazines, radio, television, outdoor media, phone directories, catalogue/direct mail, and the Internet. Exhibit 15.3

medium the channel used to convey a message to a target market

media planning the series of decisions advertisers make regarding the selection and use of media, allowing the marketer to optimally and cost-effectively communicate the message to the target audience

summarizes the advantages and disadvantages of these major channels. In recent years, however, alternative media channels have emerged that give advertisers innovative ways to reach their target audience and avoid advertising clutter.

Newspapers The advantages of newspaper advertising include geographic flexibility and timeliness. Because copywriters can usually prepare newspaper ads quickly and at a reasonable cost, local merchants can reach their target market almost daily. Because newspapers are generally a mass-market medium, they may not be the best vehicle for marketers trying to reach a very narrow market; however, newspapers are attempting to counter that negative by creating lifestyle sections. Newspaper advertising also encounters many distractions from competing ads and news stories; thus, one company's ad may not be particularly visible. Newspapers are responding to the growing demand for online news through creation of and support of their own interactive Web-based news sites. These sites allow for consumer dialogue and are constantly updated to bring the news to the reader as it happens.

The main sources of newspaper ad revenue are local retailers, classified ads, and cooperative advertising. In **cooperative advertising**, the manufacturer and the retailer split the costs of advertising the manufacturer's brand. Cooperative advertising encourages retailers to devote more effort to the manufacturer's lines.

Magazines Compared with the costs of advertising in other media, the cost per contact in magazine advertising is usually high. The cost per potential customer may be much lower, however, because magazines are often targeted to specialized audiences and thus reach more potential customers.

One of the main advantages of magazine advertising is its target market selectivity. Magazines are published for virtually every market segment. For instance, *Elle Canada* is a leading Canadian fashion

---

EXHIBIT 15.3
Advantages and Disadvantages of Major Advertising Media

Medium	Advantages	Disadvantages
Newspapers	Geographic selectivity and flexibility; short-term advertiser commitments; news value and immediacy; year-round readership; high individual market coverage; co-op and local tie-in availability; short lead time; highly credible	Little demographic selectivity; limited colour capabilities; low pass-along rate; may be expensive
Magazines	Good reproduction, especially for colour; demographic selectivity; regional selectivity; local market selectivity; relatively long advertising life; high pass-along rate	Long-term advertiser commitments; slow audience buildup; limited demonstration capabilities; lack of urgency; long lead time
Radio	Low cost; immediacy of message; can be scheduled on short notice; relatively no seasonal change in audience; highly portable; short-term advertiser commitments; entertainment carryover	No visual treatment; short advertising life of message; high frequency required to generate comprehension and retention; distractions from background sound; commercial clutter
Television	Ability to reach a wide, diverse audience; low cost per thousand; creative opportunities for demonstration; immediacy of messages; entertainment carryover; demographic selectivity with cable specialty stations; emotional medium	Short life of message; some consumer skepticism about claims; high campaign cost; little demographic selectivity with network stations; long-term advertiser commitments; long lead times required for production; commercial clutter
Outdoor Media	Repetition; moderate cost; flexibility; geographic selectivity; high creativity	Short message; lack of demographic selectivity; high "noise" level distracting audience
Internet	Fastest-growing medium; ability to reach a narrow target audience; relatively short lead time required for creating Web-based advertising; moderate cost; interactive medium	Difficult to measure ad effectiveness and return on investment; ad exposure relies on "click-through" from banner ads; not all consumers have access to the Internet

are more likely to respond to certain kinds of ads and products. Radio listeners tend to listen habitually and at predictable times. The most popular listening time is drive-time, when commuters form a vast captive audience. Radio is thus a highly effective medium for targeting mobile consumers while they are in market for a specific product or service, such as meal options on the drive home, or Registered Retirement Savings Plan (RRSP) rates during February.[7] Like magazines and newspapers, radio stations are embracing the Internet through the creation of their own websites, which highly engage the listener and offer advertisers an alternative way to reach station-loyal consumers. Radio personalities are embracing social media by using Facebook and Twitter to engage with their listeners and create the personal connection that they get through the phone-in call, but in a way that reaches so many so quickly.

Television Television broadcasters include network television, independent stations, cable television, and satellite television. Network television reaches a wide and diverse market, whereas cable television and satellite television broadcast a multitude of specialty channels devoted to highly segmented markets. Because of its targeted channels, cable television is often characterized by media buyers as *narrowcasting*.

Advertising time on television can be very expensive, especially for network and popular cable channels. Specials events and first-run prime-time shows for top-ranked TV programs command the highest rates for a typical 30-second spot, with the least-expensive ads costing about $300,000 and the more expensive ones $500,000. A 30-second spot during the Super Bowl in 2011 was reported to cost approximately $3 million.[8]

A recent development in television commercial creative is what the industry refers to as *user-created content*. For the past few Super Bowls, Doritos has run a Crash the Super Bowl commercial, encouraging fans to create their own ads. The finalists are voted on by the public on the contest website, and the top three ads are then aired on the Super Bowl. In addition to the notoriety of having the commercial run on the Super Bowl, a million-dollar prize is offered if the commercial is voted number one on the *USA Today* ad meter.[9]

Infomercials continue to be a successful television format as they are relatively inexpensive to produce and air. Advertisers use infomercials when

> **infomercial** a 30-minute or longer advertisement that looks more like a TV talk show than a sales pitch

magazine, *Shape* is a personal fitness magazine targeting women, *Canadian Business* is a business resource magazine, and *Up* is a magazine for WestJet patrons. On May 12, 2011, Toronto's new free weekly city magazine, *The Grid*, was launched. This magazine targets a young urban crowd with articles that capture the vibe and the energy of Toronto. The magazine was launched simultaneously with www.thegridto.com, to keep the information current and to stimulate dialogue with the reader.

Radio Radio has several strengths as an advertising medium: selectivity and audience segmentation, a large out-of-home audience, low unit and production costs, timeliness, and geographic flexibility. Local advertisers are the most frequent users of radio advertising, contributing more than three-quarters of all radio ad revenues. Like newspapers, radio also lends itself well to cooperative advertising.

The ability to target specific demographic groups is a major selling point for radio stations, attracting advertisers pursuing narrowly defined audiences that

HARD-ROCKING COMMERCIALS

1. When was the first rock song used in a commercial?
What was the song?
What was the product being advertised?

2. What year marked the beginning of regular use of rock music in commercials?
What was the song?
What product did it pitch?

1) 1974, Carly Simon's "Anticipation," Heinz ketchup 2) 1995, Rolling Stones' "Start Me Up," Microsoft's launch of Windows [10]

the information to be presented to the consumer is relatively complicated. Some companies are now producing infomercials that have a more polished look, which is being embraced by mainstream marketers.

Probably the most significant recent trend to affect television is the acceptance of personal video recorders (PVRs) and digital cable, which allow consumers to watch their favourite programs whenever they want and to skip the commercial messages. A July 2010 Television Bureau of Canada survey found that just over 63 percent of Canadians subscribe to digital cable and 38 percent own a PVR. Although viewers are inclined to skip the ads to avoid the interruption, they are less likely to do so when the ad is for a product or service they are interested in or when the commercial appears to be entertaining. In addition, a significant number of PVR-owning consumers said that even when they skipped the ads, they were aware of the product or service being featured in the commercials.[11] PVRs have made television more user-friendly in so far as consumers are in control of when they watch their favourite show.

Another key trend in television viewing today is Internet TV, which allows consumers the luxury of watching what they want when they want it. Canadian consumers enjoy watching television programs, and their behaviour today suggests a preference for more control as to when they enjoy those programs. Like marketers and advertisers, networks are also highly concerned about ad skipping. If consumers are not watching advertisements, then marketers will spend a greater proportion of their advertising budgets on alternative media, leading to the disappearance of a critical revenue stream for networks.

Out-of-Home Media Outdoor, or out-of-home, advertising is a flexible, low-cost medium that may take a variety of forms. Examples include billboards, skywriting, giant inflatables, mini-billboards in malls and

FOR EVERY **HOUR** OF TELEVISION PROGRAMMING, AN AVERAGE OF **15 MINUTES** IS DEDICATED TO **NONPROGRAM** MATERIAL.

on bus stop shelters, signs in sports arenas, lighted moving signs in bus terminals and airports, and ads painted on cars, trucks, buses, water towers, manhole covers, drinking glass coasters, and even people, referred to as *living advertising*. The plywood scaffolding surrounding downtown construction sites often holds ads, which, in places like the Eaton Centre and other redevelopment projects in any Canadian city, can reach thousands daily.

One of the fastest growing areas of out-of-home media is place-based media. Place-based media communicates to consumers where they live, work, and play. Its content is created to be personalized and relevant. A variety of place-based media allow marketers to reach the right consumer at the right place at the right time, such as washroom ads in bars, restaurants, schools and fitness facilities. When you consider that approximately 70 percent of all decisions are made at the point of purchase, place-based media is critical to include in the media mix. Some other examples of place-based media include ads on pizza boxes, golf course hospitality carts, dry-cleaning bags and hangers, and food carriers used in stadiums, arenas, and movie theatres.

Outdoor advertising reaches a broad and diverse market, making it ideal both for promoting convenience products and services and for directing consumers to local businesses. One of the main advantages of outdoor media over other media is its very high exposure frequency and very low clutter from competing ads. Outdoor advertising can also be customized to local marketing needs, which is why local businesses are often the leading outdoor advertisers in any given region.

The Internet With ad revenues approaching $1.8 billion in 2009, the Internet has become a solid advertising medium. Online advertising reached 72 percent of the Canadian population in 2008.[12] Internet advertising provides an interactive, versatile platform that offers rich data on consumer usage, enabling advertisers to improve their ad targetability and achieve measurable results.[13]

Canadians spend an average of 45.5 hours online each month, which is almost double the worldwide average of 26.6 hours.[14] Popular Internet sites and search engines generally sell advertising space to marketers to promote their goods and services. The Internet offers companies both large and small a highly effective way to reach many consumers.

One of the most popular approaches for Internet advertising is the use of search engine ads. Marketers'

primary objective in using search engine ads is to enhance brand awareness. They do this through paid placement of ads tied to key words used in search engines searches—when someone clicks on the ad, the advertiser pays the search engine a fee. Search engine advertising accounts for just under half of all money spent on Internet advertising.

Ad space bought on websites in a variety of formats is another common approach for Internet advertising. The ad space can be purchased directly from a website or media buyers can buy on networks that represent a variety of websites. This form of advertising can be highly effective as Web analytics provide excellent information on website visitors ensuring the opportunity for precise targeting.

Blogs have evolved to very robust sites with a wealth of information for members, allowing for conversations to evolve through comment threads. A **blog** is a publicly accessible Web page that functions as an interactive journal, whereby readers can post comments on the author's entries. Bloggers often become key influencers who need to be harnessed by marketers. A great example is www.savvymoms.ca. Finally, the popularity of social media sites such as Facebook, LinkedIn, and YouTube has made them popular advertising sites. Chapter 16 discusses the use of social media sites in greater detail.

Alternative Media To cut through the clutter of traditional advertising media, advertisers are developing new media vehicles, including shopping carts in grocery stores, computer screen savers, DVDs, interactive kiosks in department stores, advertisements run before movies at the cinema, and *advertainments*— mini movies that promote a product and are shown via the Internet.

Marketers are looking for more innovative ways to reach captive and often bored commuters. For instance, subway systems now show ads via lighted boxes installed along tunnel walls.

Video games and **advergaming** are emerging as excellent mediums for reaching males aged 18 to 34. Massive Inc. started a video game advertising network and established a partnership with Nielsen Entertainment Inc. to provide ad ratings. Massive can insert ads with full motion and sound into games played on Internet-connected computers. This ability is a big improvement over previous ads, which had

blog a publicly accessible Web page that functions as an interactive journal, whereby readers can post comments on the author's entries

advergaming placing advertising messages in Web-based or video games to advertise or promote a product, service, organization, or issue to be inserted when the games were made and therefore quickly became obsolete.[15]

Marketing communication using a mobile device has exploded. Penetration of mobile phone subscribers in Canada was estimated to be about 73 percent in 2010, reaching 85 percent by 2014. Smartphone penetration in 2010 was estimated at 31 percent, growing to 50 percent by 2014. Smartphones are mobile devices that offer businesses a new media platform. According to Ipsos Reid, Canadian marketers expect to increase their online, email, and mobile ad spending in 2011.[16] See the table below.

Estimated Change in Ad Spending in 2010* According to Marketers in Canada, by Media, Percentage of Respondents

	Increase	Stay the Same	Decrease
Online	81%	18%	1%
Email	63%	31%	6%
Mobile	49%	49%	3%
Direct Mail	23%	55%	23%
Out-of-Home Digital	12%	73%	14%
TV	10%	67%	22%
Radio	11%	63%	26%
Print	9%	49%	41%

NOTE: Numbers may not add up to 100% due to rounding; *vs. 2009.
SOURCE: Ipsos Reid as cited by eMarketer.com

Media Selection Considerations

An important element in any advertising campaign is the **media mix**, the combination of media to be used. Media mix decisions are typically based on several factors: cost per contact, reach, frequency, target audience considerations, flexibility of the medium, noise level, and the life span of the medium.

Cost per contact is the cost of reaching one member of the target market. Naturally, as the size of the audience increases, so does the total cost. Cost per contact enables an advertiser to compare media vehicles, such as television versus radio, magazine versus newspaper, or, more specifically, *Chatelaine* versus *Flare*. An advertiser debating whether to spend local advertising dollars for TV spots or radio spots could consider the cost per contact of each. The advertiser might then pick the vehicle with the lowest cost per contact to maximize advertising punch for the money spent.

Reach is the number of different target consumers who are exposed to a commercial at least once during a specific period, usually four weeks. Media plans for product introductions and attempts at increasing brand awareness usually emphasize reach. For example, an advertiser might try to reach 70 percent of the target audience during the first three months of the campaign. Reach is related to a medium's ratings, generally referred to in the industry as *gross ratings points*, or GRP. A television program with a higher GRP means that more people are tuning in to the show and the reach is higher. Accordingly, as GRP increases for a particular medium, so does cost per contact.

Because the typical ad is short-lived and because often only a small portion of an ad may be perceived at one time, advertisers repeat their ads so that consumers will remember the message. **Frequency** is the number of times an individual is exposed to a message during a specific period. Advertisers use average frequency to measure the intensity of a specific medium's coverage. For example, Coca-Cola might want an average exposure frequency of five for its POWERade television ads. In other words, Coca-Cola wants each television viewer to see the ad an average of five times.

Media selection is also a matter of matching the advertising medium with the product's target market. If marketers are trying to reach teenage females, they might select advertising on the retailer Aritzia's website. A medium's ability to reach a precisely defined market is its **audience selectivity**. Some media vehicles, such as general newspapers and network television, appeal to a wide cross-section of the population. Others—such as *Zoomer, Runners World, TSN, HGTV, OLN,* and Christian radio stations—appeal to very specific groups.

The *flexibility* of a medium can be extremely important to an advertiser. For example, because of layouts and design, the lead time for magazine advertising is considerably longer than for other media types and so is less flexible. By contrast, radio and Internet advertising provide maximum flexibility. If necessary, an advertiser can change a radio ad on the day it is aired.

Noise level is the level of distraction to the target audience in a medium. Noise can be created by competing ads, as when a street is lined with billboards or when a television program is cluttered with competing ads. Whereas newspapers and magazines have a high noise level, direct mail is a private medium with a low noise level. Typically, no other advertising media or news stories compete for direct-mail readers' attention.

CONTENTS BROUGHT TO YOU BY ...

The media buys for the **James Ready Brewing Company** focused on beer drinkers in southern Ontario and celebrated the beer's value positioning by offering discounts at local retailers in its efforts to build a relationship with beer drinkers in the local community.

ultimately must select an approach that is most likely to result in the ad being understood and remembered when a purchase decision is being made.

Advertisers also evaluate the qualitative factors involved in media selection, including attention to the commercial and the program, involvement, program liking, lack of distractions, and other audience behaviours that affect the likelihood that a commercial message is being seen and, ideally, absorbed. While advertisers can advertise their product in as many media as possible and repeat the ad as many times as they like, the ad still may not be effective if the audience is not paying attention. Research on audience attentiveness for television, for example, shows that the longer viewers stay tuned to a particular program, the more memorable they find the commercials. Contrary to long-held assumptions, when selecting media vehicles, *holding power* can be more important than ratings (the number of people tuning in to any part of the program).

Media have either a short or a long *lifespan*, which means that messages can either quickly fade or persist as tangible copy to be carefully studied. A radio commercial may last less than a minute, but advertisers can overcome this short lifespan by repeating radio ads often. In contrast, a magazine has a relatively long lifespan, which is further increased by a high pass-along rate.

Media planners have traditionally relied on the above factors for selecting an effective media mix, with reach, frequency, and cost often being the overriding criteria. Well-established brands with familiar messages probably need fewer exposures to be effective, whereas newer or unfamiliar brands likely need more exposures to become familiar. In addition, today's media planners have more media options than ever before.

The proliferation of media channels is causing *media fragmentation* and forcing media planners to pay as much attention to where they place their advertising as to how often the advertisement is repeated. That is, marketers should evaluate reach *and* frequency when assessing the effectiveness of advertising. In certain situations, it may be important to reach potential consumers through as many media vehicles as possible. When this approach is considered, however, the budget must be large enough to achieve sufficient levels of frequency to have an impact. In evaluating reach versus frequency, therefore, the media planner

Media Scheduling

After choosing the media for the advertising campaign, advertisers must schedule the ads. A **media schedule** designates the media to be used (such as magazines, television, or radio), the specific vehicles (such as *Flare* magazine, the TV show *The Good Wife*, or the radio show *The Dean Blundell Show*), and the insertion dates of the advertising.

Media schedules are divided into three basic types:

▶▶ Products in the latter stages of the product life cycle, which are advertised on a reminder basis, use a **continuous media schedule**. A continuous schedule allows the advertising to run steadily throughout the advertising period. Examples include L'Oréal Excellence Crème and Molson Canadian , which may have an ad in the newspaper every Sunday and a TV commercial on Global every Wednesday at 7:30 p.m. over a three-month time period.

▶▶ With a **flighted media schedule**, the advertiser may schedule the ads heavily every other month or every two weeks to achieve a greater impact with

media schedule designation of the media, the specific publications or programs, and the insertion dates of advertising

continuous media schedule a media scheduling strategy in which advertising is run steadily throughout the advertising period; used for products in the latter stages of the product life cycle

flighted media schedule a media scheduling strategy in which ads are run heavily every other month or every two weeks, to achieve a greater impact with an increased frequency and reach at those times

an increased frequency and reach at those times. Movie studios might schedule television advertising on Wednesday and Thursday nights, when moviegoers are deciding which films to see that weekend.

▸▸ A **pulsing media schedule** combines continuous scheduling with a flighted media schedule. Continuous advertising is simply heavier during the best sale periods. A retail department store may advertise on a year-round basis but place more advertising during certain sale periods, such as Thanksgiving, Christmas, and back-to-school.

▸▸ Certain times of the year call for a **seasonal media schedule**. COLD-FX and Coppertone sunscreen, which are typically used more during certain times of the year, tend to follow a seasonal strategy.

New research comparing continuous media schedules versus flighted ones finds that continuous schedules for television advertisements are more effective in driving sales than flighted schedules. The research suggests that it may be more important to get exposure as close as possible to the time when a consumer makes a purchase. Therefore, the advertiser should maintain a continuous schedule over as long a period of time as possible. Often called *recency planning*, this theory of scheduling is now commonly used for scheduling television advertising for frequently purchased products, such as Coca-Cola or Tide detergent. Recency planning's main premise is that advertising works by influencing the brand choice of people who are ready to buy.

ROSE ALCORN

LO 5 Direct-Response Communication

Direct-response communication is often referred to as *direct marketing*. It involves generating profitable business results through targeted communications to a specific audience. Direct-response communication utilizes a combination of relevant messaging and offers that can be tracked, measured, analyzed, stored, and leveraged to drive future marketing initiatives.

Direct-response communication provides the opportunity for one-to-one communication resulting in more targeted messaging and relationship building. Not-for-profits, whose objective is to raise awareness and generate donations, rely heavily on this form of communication because it can be tailored, its effectiveness is measurable, and it builds relationships that are key to effective stewardship.

Direct-response communication can be highly successful because the targeted communication is often more appealing to the consumer than mass-market communication. It is designed to meet consumers' unique needs, and they can learn about the product and make a purchase all at one time.

When creating a direct-response marketing campaign, keep in mind the following five key elements:

▸▸ *The offer:* the offer is the catalyst that stimulates the consumer to respond to the sales proposition in the message. The more time-sensitive the offer, the more immediate the need for a response.

▸▸ *The creative:* special considerations are needed when developing a direct-response campaign; industry experts exist to assist marketers in this task.

▸▸ *The media:* to deliver a personalized message, direct response communication can utilize television, radio, newspapers, magazines, telephone, the Internet, mail, or any combination of these media. The most common form of direct response communication is direct mail.

▸▸ *Response and tracking mechanism:* the strength of direct-response communication is the ability to track results and report progress relative to the advertising objective. Such metrics must be in place.

▸▸ *Customer call service:* because direct response is built around an immediate consumer response, a call centre must exist to handle the calls.

The Tools of Direct-Response Communication

Direct-Response Broadcast Direct-response broadcast utilizes television and radio. **Direct-response television (DRTV)** refers to television commercials that end with a call to action. DRTV can vary in length:

short-form DRTV can be 15, 30, 60, 90, or 120 seconds in length. Long-form DRTV typically run for 30 to 60 minutes and are often referred to as *infomercials*. Because the return on investment with direct response is measured and is a critical key success factor, marketers don't want to pay regular rates for the spots. Thus, stations offer discounts on inventory not sold, which explains why much DRTV is seen at odd hours in the day. Direct-response radio isn't as widely used as direct-response television due to the nature of radio as a medium (portable and no visuals), but some advertisers will create messaging around the call-to-action tool (the phone number) to enhance the success of using radio as a direct-response medium.

Direct-Response Print **Direct-response print** includes newspapers, magazines, and inserts. Often marketers will want to capitalize on the subscriber base of the magazine or newspaper to reach a certain demographic or psychographic. The ad is a direct-response print ad if it includes a direct call to action.

Telemarketing **Telemarketing** refers to outbound (a company calling the customer) and inbound (a customer calling the company) sales calls, to secure an order. Inbound telemarketing is what we do each time we call a number to place an order. Outbound telemarketing is what we often are annoyed with. In September 2008, the federal government launched a federal **Do Not Call List (DNCL)**. Consumers can voluntarily choose to register on this list, and companies that use telemarketing must update their database every 30 days to ensure that those registered on the DCNL are not contacted. Companies will be fined if they are found in violation of the DNCL.

Almost 8.7 million numbers had been listed by May 2011, and 102 investigations of potential violations were underway. The Canadian Radio-television Telecommunications Commission, or CRTC, (the agency charged with monitoring the DNCL and complaints) has imposed 25 monetary penalties since the program was introduced. In December 2010, Xentel DM Inc. was fined $500,000 for unauthorized telemarketing practices relating to the DNCL.[17] Also in December, Bell Canada was fined $1.5 million—the largest fine yet.

Direct Mail **Direct mail** is printed communications distributed to the consumer via Canada Post or independent contractors. The key is that the piece is delivered directly to the consumer. Direct mail has two forms—addressed and unaddressed—and addressed direct mail generally receives higher response rates. A successful campaign must obviously reach the right person, be read by that person, and be persuasive enough to lead to a response. A critical element in a direct-mail campaign is the mailing list. Mailing lists can be internal (such as a company-created database) or can be rented or purchased from companies that specialize in lists. Another critical element is the creative—the envelope must be interesting and intriguing enough to be opened, and the enclosed letter must be persuasive enough to prompt a response.

Direct Response Using the Internet The nature of the Internet suggests it can be a valuable direct-response tool, as it easily provides targeted communication that can be measured and analyzed. A common form of direct response using the Internet is email. When used with the intent to acquire new customers or convince customers to purchase something immediately, email communication can be a cost-effective direct-response tool. Email communication is targeted communication that provides the recipient with the opportunity to seek additional information or to place an order with the click of a mouse.

LO6 Public Relations

Public relations is the element in the promotional mix that evaluates public attitudes, identifies issues that may elicit public concern, and executes programs to

direct-response print advertising in a print medium that includes a direct call to action

telemarketing the use of telecommunications to sell a product or service; involves both outbound and inbound calls

Do Not Call List (DNCL) a free service whereby Canadians register their telephone number to reduce or eliminate phone calls from telemarketers

direct mail a printed form of direct-response communication that is delivered directly to consumers' homes

product placement a public relations strategy that involves getting a product, service, or company name to appear in a movie, television show, radio program, magazine, newspaper, video game, video or audio clip, book, or commercial for another product; on the Internet; or at special events

gain public understanding and acceptance. Public relations is a vital link in a progressive company's marketing communication mix. Marketing managers plan solid public relations campaigns that fit into overall marketing plans and focus on targeted audiences. These campaigns strive to maintain a positive image of the corporation in the eyes of the public. As such, they should capitalize on the factors that enhance the firm's image and minimize the factors that could generate a negative image.

Publicity is the effort to capture media attention—for example, through articles or editorials in publications or through human-interest stories on radio or television programs. Corporations usually initiate publicity by issuing a media release that furthers their public relations plans. A company that is about to introduce a new product or open a new store may send out media releases in the hope that the story will be published or broadcast. Savvy publicity can often create overnight sensations or build up a reserve of goodwill with consumers. Corporate donations and sponsorships can also create favourable publicity.

Public relations departments may perform any or all of the following functions:

» *Media relations:* placing positive, newsworthy information in the news media to attract attention to a product, a service, or a person associated with the firm or institution

» *Product publicity:* publicizing specific products or services

» *Corporate communication:* creating internal and external messages to promote a positive image of the firm or institution

» *Public affairs:* building and maintaining national or local community relations

» *Lobbying:* influencing legislators and government officials to promote or defeat legislation and regulation

» *Employee and investor relations:* maintaining positive relationships with employees, shareholders, and others in the financial community

» *Crisis management:* responding to unfavourable publicity or a negative event

Major Public Relations Tools

Public relations professionals commonly use several tools, many of which require an active role on the part of the public relations professional, such as writing media releases and engaging in proactive media relations. Sometimes, however, these techniques create their own publicity.

Product Publicity Publicity is instrumental in introducing new products and services. Publicity can help advertisers explain the special features of their new product by prompting free news stories or positive word of mouth. During the introductory period, an especially innovative new product often needs more exposure than conventional paid advertising affords. Public relations professionals write media releases or develop videos in an effort to generate news about their new product. They also jockey for exposure of their product or service at major events, on popular television and news shows, or in the hands of influential people. For example, to promote the DVD and Blu-ray release of the movie *Inception*, Warner Home Entertainment set up a giant re-creation of a maze from the movie in Toronto's Yonge-Dundas Square. Participants who made it through the 1.6 km maze in less than two minutes received prizes. This stunt received tremendous publicity and was just one of numerous communication tactics used to reach the 18- to 34-year-old male target.[18]

Product Placement Marketers are increasingly using product placement to reinforce brand awareness and create favourable attitudes. **Product placement** is a strategy that involves getting a product, service, or company name to appear in a movie, television show, radio program, magazine, newspaper, video game, video or audio clip, book, or commercial for another product; on the Internet; or at special events. Including an actual product, such as a can of Pepsi, adds a sense of realism to a movie, television show, video game, book, or similar vehicle that cannot be created by a can simply marked *pop*. Product placements are arranged through barter (trade of product for placement), through paid placements, or at no

JOSE IGNACIO SOTO/SHUTTERSTOCK.COM

charge when the product is viewed as enhancing the vehicle in which it is placed.

Product placement expenditures are growing as a result of increasing audience fragmentation and the spread of ad-skipping technology. More than two-thirds of product placements are in movies and TV shows, but placements in other media are growing, particularly on the Internet and in video games. Digital technology now enables companies to *virtually* place their products in any audio or video production. Virtual placement not only reduces the cost of product placement for new productions but also enables companies to add product placement to previously produced programs, such as reruns of television shows. Overall, companies obtain valuable product exposure, brand reinforcement, and increased sales through product placement, often at a much lower cost than advertising in mass media, such as television ads.

Sponsorship Sponsorships are increasing both in number and as a proportion of companies' marketing budgets, with worldwide sponsorship spending topping $30 billion annually. Probably the biggest reason for the increasing use of sponsorships is the difficulty of reaching audiences and differentiating a product from competing brands through the mass media.

With **sponsorship**, a company spends money to support an issue, cause, or event that is consistent with corporate objectives, such as improving brand awareness or enhancing corporate image. Most commonly, companies sponsor events such as festivals and fairs, conventions, expositions, sporting events, arts and entertainment spectaculars, and charity benefits. BMO Financial Group's sponsorship of the Calgary Stampede is a typical example of an event sponsorship. The Toronto Waterfront Marathon now called the Scotiabank Toronto Waterfront Marathon is another example.

Although the most popular sponsorship events continue to be those involving sports, music, or the arts, companies have recently been turning to more specialized events, such as tie-ins with schools, charities, and other community service organizations. Marketers sometimes even create their own events tied around their product.

Corporations also sponsor issues. Sponsorship issues are quite diverse, but the three most popular are education, health care, and social programs. Firms often donate a percentage of sales or profits to a worthy cause that is favoured by their target market.

A special type of sponsorship, **cause-related marketing**, involves the association of a for-profit company with a nonprofit organization. Through the sponsorship, the company's product or service is promoted, and money is raised for the nonprofit. In a common type of cause-related sponsorship, a company agrees to donate a percentage of the purchase price for a particular item to a charity, but some arrangements are more complex. The Canadian Football League (CFL) in cooperation with Purolator Inc. started a unique program called Purolator Tackle Hunger. During the CFL regular season, every time a CFL quarterback gets sacked, Purolator will donate the equivalent of the quarterback's weight in food to the CFL team's hometown food bank. In addition, Purolator encourages all fans coming to a game to bring a non-perishable food item or cash. Several studies indicate that some consumers consider a company's reputation when making purchasing decisions and that a company's community involvement boosts employee morale and loyalty.[19]

The Internet Companies increasingly are using the Internet in their public relations strategies. Company websites are used to introduce new products, promote

> **sponsorship** a public relations strategy in which a company spends money to support an issue, cause, or event that is consistent with corporate objectives, such as improving brand awareness or enhancing corporate image
>
> **cause-related marketing** a type of sponsorship involving the association of a for-profit company with a nonprofit organization; through the sponsorship, the company's product or service is promoted, and money is raised for the nonprofit

Supporting your local food bank. Check.
With your help, we can tackle hunger one can at a time. 100% of your donations will be delivered to your local food bank.

Purolator TackleHunger

Please donate

existing products, obtain consumer feedback, post news releases, communicate legislative and regulatory information, showcase upcoming events, provide links to related sites, release financial information, and perform many more marketing activities. Online reviews from opinion leaders and other consumers help marketers to sway consumers' purchasing decisions in their favour. On PlayStation. com, Sony has online support, events and promotions, game trailers, and new and updated product releases. The site also includes message boards where the gaming community can exchange tips on games, vote on lifestyle issues such as music and videos, and learn about promotional events.[20]

Websites are also key elements of integrated marketing communications strategies. A visitor to the website of media giant Astral can follow advertising links to Astral Television, Radio, Out-of-Home, and Digital. Astral also offers the visitor Astral Mix, which represents the truest sense of integrated marketing. Astral Mix brings together experienced media professionals to assist advertisers in the development of highly targeted campaigns, using the right combination of Astral's various media platforms.

More and more often, companies are also using blogs—both corporate and noncorporate—as a tool to manage their public image. **Corporate blogs** are sponsored by a company or one of its brands and are maintained by one or more of the company's employees. They disseminate marketing-controlled information and are effective platforms for developing thought leadership, fostering better relationships with stakeholders, maximizing search engine optimization, and attracting new customers, endearing the organization to them with anecdotes and stories about brands. Because blogs are designed to be updated daily, corporate blogs are dynamic and highly flexible, giving marketers the opportunity to adapt their messages more frequently than any other communication channel.

Noncorporate blogs cannot be controlled, but marketers must monitor them both to encourage positive content and to be aware of and respond to negative information. In addition to getting the message out, companies are using blogs to create communities of consumers who feel positively about the brand.

Managing Unfavourable Publicity

Although marketers try to avoid unpleasant situations, crises do happen. In our free-press environment, publicity is not easily controlled, especially in a crisis. **Crisis management** is the coordinated effort to handle the effects of unfavourable publicity or an unexpected unfavourable event, ensuring fast and accurate communication in times of emergency.

One of the best recent examples of poor crisis management was BP's handling of the 2010 Gulf of Mexico oil spill. A public relations nightmare ensued from BP's lack of quick response, its lack of transparency, and the comment by Tony Hayward, BP's chief executive officer, "I would like my life back."[21]

Percentage of marketers that say social media is the new marketing initiative they'll spend more on in 2011
55%

Percentage of marketers in 2010 who said they have not made social media part of their core marketing strategy
4%

Worldwide downloads of Ben & Jerry's iPhone app
45,000

2 billion
Videos watched on Facebook each month

2.5 billion
Average number of Google searches per day

Social Media and Marketing

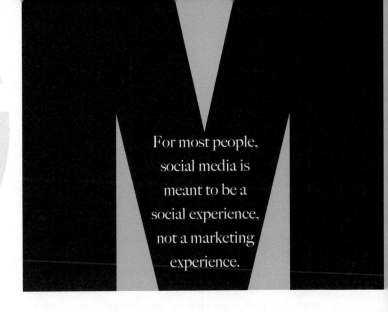

For most people, social media is meant to be a social experience, not a marketing experience.

AFTER YOU FINISH THIS CHAPTER, GO TO WWW. ICANMKTG2.COM FOR STUDY TOOLS.

LO 1 What Is Social Media?

The most exciting thing to happen to marketing and promotion is the increasing use of online technology, particularly social media, to promote brands. Social media has changed the way that marketers can communicate—from mass messages to intimate conversations. As marketing moves into social media, marketers must remember that, for most people, social media is meant to be a social experience, not a marketing experience. In fact, social media is many things to different people, though most people think of it as digital technology. Brian Solis, of FutureWorks, defines **social media** as "any tool or service that uses the Internet to facilitate conversations."[1] However, social media can also be defined relative to traditional advertising, such as television and magazines, in that traditional marketing media offers a mass media method of interacting with consumers, while social media offers more one-to-one ways to meet consumers. Also, compared with traditional advertising, social media also has more sophisticated methods of measuring how marketers meet and interact with consumers. Currently, social media includes tools and platforms, such as social networks, blogs, microblogs, and media sharing sites, which can be accessed through a growing number of devices, such as computers, laptops, smartphones, e-readers, tablets, and netbooks. This technology changes daily, offering consumers new ways to experience social media platforms, which must constantly innovate to keep up with consumer demands.

social media any tool or service that uses the Internet to facilitate conversations

What do you think?

Marketers are adept at using social media as a marketing tool.

1   2   3   4   5   6   7

STRONGLY DISAGREE   STRONGLY AGREE

At the basic level, social media consumers want to exchange information, collaborate with others, and have conversations. Social media has changed how and where conversations take place, making human interaction global through popular technology. Research shows that more than 73 percent of active online users have read a blog and more than half belong to at least one social network. Marketing consultant John Haydon said, "The real value of social media is that it exponentially leverages word-of-mouth."[2] Clearly, conversations are happening online; marketers today must determine how best to leverage these conversations to the benefit of their brand and the relationships they are trying to create with the targeted consumer.

Marketers are interested in online communications because more than 60 percent of Canadians are using social media at least once per day.[3] This widespread use has led brands, companies, individuals, and celebrities to promote their messages online. Today, even in death, Michael Jackson continues to be the most popular celebrity on Facebook, where he has more than 26 million friends. Today, Lady Gaga reigns as the queen of social media: on her fan page, she posts about her music career, upcoming tours, and her

current recordings. She even goes so far as to chat with her fans. Her music video for the song "Bad Romance" was recently usurped as the most viewed video by "Baby," the video by teen sensation Justin Bieber, which in March 2011 had more than 500.4 million views. Interestingly, the video scored 1.1 million "dislikes" compared with 578,000 "likes" from viewers.[4] Lady Gaga's celebrity is due in large part to being a highly effective brand—her messages resonate with audiences worldwide, and she makes her brand easily accessible through popular social media platforms. Her carefully crafted social media strategy has translated into real money; Lady Gaga recently debuted on the Forbes Celebrity 100 Power List for 2010 at number 4, earning more than $62 million (including her corporate sponsorships and endorsements) in the past 12 months.[5] As far as brands go, very few marketers have done a better job than Lady Gaga of leveraging social media to drive sales of core products.[6]

How Consumers Use Social Media

Hoping to replicate some of Lady Gaga's social media success, many marketers are looking to get their message on the fastest-growing social media platform—Facebook. Facebook originated as a community for college students that opened to the general public as its popularity grew. Facebook has hundreds of millions of users, and usage growth has been phenomenal: consumer use has grown from 77 percent in 2009 to 87 percent in 2011, and business professional use has grown from 58 percent in 2009 to 81 percent in 2011.[7] If Facebook were a country, it would be the third largest in the world. The largest area of growth in new profiles is the baby boomer segment, who use Facebook to connect with old friends and keep up with family. Other social networks, such as MySpace, Twitter, and YouTube, offer alternative networks to other demographics. MySpace, aimed at the Gen Y crowd, provides a highly personalized experience around all things entertainment. MySpace creates connections between people and artists. Videos are one of the most popular tools by which marketers reach consumers, and YouTube is by far the largest online video repository—it has more content than any major television network. Due to its connection with Google, YouTube also offers a powerful search tool.[8] Flickr is a popular photo sharing site, where millions of people upload new photos daily. Twitter boasts hundreds of millions of registered users who average billions of tweets daily. At the MTV Video Music Awards on August 29, 2011, Beyoncé's performance

sparked a Twitter record. During her performance, which started at 10:35 p.m., fans set a Twitter record, sending 8,868 tweets per second.[9] Technorati tracks hundreds of millions of blogs and indexes an estimated two million new blog posts per day.[10] More than half of Technorati's active users have uploaded photos, and almost a quarter have uploaded videos. According to the Leger Marketing study, Social Media Reality Check 2011 Research Findings, "social media is the new normal" and "it has not replaced any channels—it's simply another one."[11]

Increased usage of alternative platforms such as smartphones and tablet computers has further contributed to the proliferation of social media usage. Canadians spend more time online than the rest of the world's population, and Canadians' time online continues to grow. People aged 55 years and older have the fastest online penetration, exhibiting 12 percent growth between 2009 and 2010. Canadians are also among the highest consumers of blogs and social networks sites, such as Facebook. Those aged 55 and older have been the drivers of social networking growth in Canada.[12] Canadians access the Internet from both their computers and their mobile devices. Seventy-five percent of Canadian households have access to a mobile device, a penetration rate lower than in many other countries. Canadians are using their mobile phones to access social networking sites and are considered to be text friendly, sending over 122 million text messages a day.[13] In April 2010, Apple released the much anticipated iPad tablet computer. More than 8,500 native iPad apps (many of which connect to social networks) are available for download, and within the first two months of the tablet's release, 35 million downloads had already been recorded.[14] The overall impact of tablet computing on social media (and thus the discipline of marketing) is yet to be seen, but given the incredible impact that the smartphone has had in its short lifespan, tablets could prove to be game changing.

Social Commerce A new area of growth in social media is **social commerce**, which combines social media with the basics of e-commerce. Social commerce is a subset of e-commerce that involves the interaction and user contribution aspects of social online media to assist online buying and selling of products and services.15 Basically, social commerce relies on user-generated content on websites to assist consumers with

purchases. On Polyvore.com, members create collages of photographs of clothing items that create a fashionable look. Photographs come from various retailers and include accessories, clothes, shoes, and makeup. Once the look is complete, other members view the looks and can click on the individual items to see price and retailers. Social commerce sites often include ratings and recommendations (such as on Amazon) and social shopping tools (such as Groupon). In general, social commerce sites are designed to help consumers make more informed decisions on purchases or services.

Social Media and Integrated Marketing Communications

While marketers typically employ a social media strategy alongside traditional channels such as print and broadcast media, many budget pendulums are swinging toward social media. In 2010, Canadian advertising continued to increase in the online environment. The top two online advertisers in Canada in 2010 were Proctor & Gamble and GMAC/Ally, together accounting for nearly 17 billion ad impressions throughout the year. Social networking experienced the largest gain in ad impressions.[16] In the U.S. Interactive Marketing Forecast, 2009–2014, Forrester Research predicts that mobile marketing, social media, email marketing, display advertising, and search marketing will grow from 13 percent of advertising spending in 2010 to more than 21 percent of spending by 2014. The bulk of this budget will still go to search marketing (almost doubling in 2014), but substantial investments will also be made in mobile marketing and social media.[17]

IAB Canada reported that 2010 Canadian online advertising revenue exceeded budgeted expectations, growing to $2.23 billion. These figures place the Internet ahead of daily newspapers in terms of share of total Canadian media advertising revenue, second only to television. The top three online ad revenue categories were automotive, packaged goods, and financial services.[18] A unique consequence of social media is the widespread shift from one-to-many communication to many-to-many communication. Instead of simply putting a brand advertisement on television with no means for feedback,

social commerce a subset of e-commerce that involves the interaction and user contribution aspects of social online media to assist online buying and selling of products and services

social media allows marketers to have conversations with consumers, forge deeper relationships, and build brand loyalty. Social media also allow consumers to connect with each other, share opinions, and collaborate on new ideas according to their interests. In 2009, Grey Goose vodka created an online community exclusively for bartenders. This community enabled mixologists to chat with each other and share ideas and anecdotes about their common trade. The Grey Goose online community was intended not so much to advertise the brand but to create a shared space and provide genuine value to bartenders. The brand advocacy then came naturally.[19] With social media, the audience is often in control of the message, the medium, the response, or all three. This distribution of control is often difficult for companies to adjust to, but the focus of social marketing is unavoidably on the audience, and the brand must adapt to succeed. The interaction between producer and consumer becomes less about entertaining and more about listening, influencing, and engaging.

In 2009, Hewlett-Packard used social media to avert a public relations (PR) crisis after a video claiming that HP was racist garnered two million views on YouTube. Because it was aware of its customers' social dialogues, HP learned about the groundswell early on and was able to quell the story before it gained too much momentum.[20] Mountain Dew's marketing team tested the limits of consumer control and the power of social media by moving the brand's advertising almost entirely online. The team tapped into the brand's core consumer demographic—18- to 39-year-old males with strong Facebook, MySpace, and YouTube presences—to build line extensions and help choose a marketing partner.

Social media and the Internet provides the opportunity for crowdsourcing, which captures the input of many people that is then leveraged to make decisions that used to be based on the input of only a few people.[21] Companies get feedback on marketing campaigns, new product ideas, and other marketing decisions by asking customers to weigh in. Ben & Jerry's has always relied on fan feedback in product development but in 2010 it went one step further, capitalizing on social media and crowdsourcing by launching "Do the World a Flavour." This contest invited fans to invent their own flavour online, with the chance to win a trip to the Dominican Republic to see a sustainable fair trade cocoa farm. In addition, the winning flavour was produced as an official Ben & Jerry's product. The crowdsourced-based contest provided the opportunity to reach consumers globally while

communicating Ben & Jerry's belief in the fair trade model.[22] Crowdsourcing offers a way for companies to engage heavy users of a brand and receive input, which in turn increases those users' brand advocacy and lessens the likelihood that a change will be disliked enough to drive away loyal customers.

LO 2 Creating and Leveraging a Social Media Campaign

Social media is an exciting new field, and its potential for expanding a brand's impact is enormous. Because its costs are often minimal and its learning curve is relatively low, some organizations are tempted to dive headfirst into social media. However, as with any marketing campaign, it is always important to start with a strategy. For most organizations, this means starting with a marketing or communications plan, as covered in Chapter 3.

The new communication paradigm created by a shift to social media marketing raises questions about

A young woman holds a glass of red wine during an online wine tasting. People from all parts of Germany regularly meet online to taste wine and exchange opinions via Twitter, generating earned media buzz for the winery whose wine they are drinking.

categorization. In light of the convergence of traditional and digital media, researchers have explored different ways that interactive marketers can categorize media types. One such researcher, Sean Corcoran of Forrester Research, devised a distinction between owned, earned, and paid media. **Owned media** is online content that an organization creates and controls. Owned media includes blogs, websites, Facebook pages, and other social media presences. The purpose of owned media is to develop deeper relationships with customers. **Earned media** is a public relations term connoting free media such as mainstream media coverage. In an interactive space, media is earned through word of mouth or online buzz about something the brand is doing. Earned media includes viral videos, retweets, comments on blogs, and other forms of customer feedback resulting from a social media presence. **Paid media** is content paid for by the company to be placed online. Paid media is similar to marketing efforts that utilize traditional media, such as newspapers, magazines, and on television. In an interactive space, paid media includes display advertising, paid search words, and other types of direct online advertising.[23]

To leverage all three types of media, marketers must follow a few key guidelines. First, they must maximize owned media by reaching out beyond their existing websites to create portfolios of digital touch points. This approach is especially helpful for brands with tight budgets, as the organization may not be able to afford much paid media. Second, marketers must recognize that aptitude at public and media relations no longer translates into earned media. Instead, markets must learn how to listen and respond to stakeholders. This will stimulate word of mouth. Finally, marketers must understand that paid media is not dead but should serve as a catalyst to drive customer engagement.[24] If balanced correctly, all three types of media can be powerful tools for interactive marketers.

The Listening System

The first action a marketing team should take when initiating a social media campaign is simple—it should just listen. Developing an effective listening system is necessary to both understanding and engaging an online audience. Marketers must not only hear what is being said about the brand, the industry, the competition, and the customer—they must pay attention to who is saying what. The specific ways that customers and noncustomers rate, rank, critique, praise, deride, recommend, snub, and generally discuss brands are all important. Negative comments and complaints

are of particular importance, both because they can illuminate unknown brand flaws and because they are the comments that tend to go viral. Online tools such as Google Alerts, Google Blog Search, Twitter Search, SiteVolume, Social Mention, and Socialcast are extremely helpful in the development of efficient, effective listening. In Exhibit 16.1, social media strategist Jeremiah Owyang outlines eight stages of effective listening. Listening to customers communicate about one's own brand can be very revealing, but social media is also a great way to monitor competitors' online presences, fans, and followers. Paying attention to the ways that competing brands attract and engage with their customers can be particularly enlightening for both small businesses and global brands.

Social Media Objectives

After establishing a listening platform, the organization should develop a list of objectives for its social media team to accomplish. These objectives must be developed with a clear understanding of how social media changes the communication dynamic with and for customers. Remember—attempting to reach a mass audience with a static message will never be as successful as influencing people through conversation. Marketing managers must set objectives that reflect this reality. Here are some practical ideas that marketing managers should consider when setting social media objectives:

▸▸ *Listen and learn.* Monitor what is being said about the brand and competitors, and glean insights about audiences. Use online tools and do research to implement the best social media practices. If you have established a listening strategy, this objective should have already been accomplished.

▸▸ *Build relationships and awareness.* Open dialogues with stakeholders by giving them compelling content across a variety of media. Engage in conversations, and answer customers' questions candidly, which will both increase Web traffic and boost your search engine ranking.

▸▸ *Promote products and services.* The clearest path to increasing the bottom line using social media is to get customers talking about products and services, which ultimately translates into sales.

▸▸ *Manage your reputation.* Develop and improve the brand's reputation by responding to comments and criticism that appear on blogs and forums. Additionally, organizations

owned media online content that an organization creates and controls
earned media a public relations term connoting free media such as mainstream media coverage
paid media content paid for by a company to be placed online

EXHIBIT 16.1
Eight Stages of Effective Listening

Stage	Description	Resources Required	Purpose
Stage 1: Without Objective	The organization has established a listening system but has no goals.	Social media notification tools (Google Alerts)	To keep up with brand and competitor information.
Stage 2: Tracking brand mentions	The organization tracks mentions in social space but has no guidance on next steps.	A listening platform with key word report capabilities (Radian6)	To track discussions, understand sentiment, and identify influencers to improve overall marketing strategy.
Stage 3: Identifying market risks and opportunities	The organization seeks discussions online that may result in identification of problems and opportunities.	A listening platform with a large staff dedicated to the client (Converseon)	To seek out discussions and reports to other teams, such as product development and sales. These teams then engage the customers directly or conduct further research.
Stage 4: Improving campaign efficiency	The organization uses tools to acquire real-time data on marketing efficiency.	Web analytics software (Google Analytics)	To gather a wealth of information about consumers' behaviour on their websites (and social media).
Stage 5: Measuring customer satisfaction	The organization collects information about satisfaction, including measures of sentiment.	Insight platforms that offer online focus group solutions	To measure the impact of satisfaction or frustration during interaction.
Stage 6: Responding to customer inquiry	The organization identifies customers where they are (e.g., Twitter).	A customer service team is allowed to make real-time responses	To generate a high sense of satisfaction for customers.
Stage 7: Better understanding of customers	The organization adds social information to demographics and psychographics to gain better consumer profiles.	Social customer relationship management (CRM) systems to sync data	To create a powerful analytical tool by marrying the organization's database and social media. (See Chapter 8 for more on CRM.)
Stage 8: Being proactive and anticipating customer demands	The organization examines previous patterns of data and social behaviour to anticipate needs.	Advanced customer database with predictive application (yet to be created)	To modify the social media strategy to preempt consumer behaviour modifications on the basis of trends.

SOURCES: Jeremiah Owyang, "Web Strategy Matrix: The Eight Stages of Listening," *Web Strategy*, November 10, 2009; and Jim Sterne, *Social Media Metrics* (Hoboken, NJ: John Wiley & Sons, 2010).

BUILDING TRUST ONLINE

To succeed with any marketing campaign, customers' trust must be earned. Here are some guidelines for **earning customer trust:**

▸▸ Online content must be up to date, easy to understand, and valuable. Be the translator for your customers as they wade through message after message.

▸▸ Make sure that your website is easy to navigate and gives customers quick access to the information and media they seek.

▸▸ Make your social space fun and interactive. Interactivity is all about forging relationships. Treat customers like people, not data, and they will treat you as a person, not junk mail.

▸▸ Follow contemporary design trends. Your audience will inevitably judge your book by its cover.[25]

SOURCE: Jonathon Hensley, "How to Build Trust Online," *Marketing News*, March 15, 2010.

can position themselves as helpful and benevolent by participating in other forums and discussions.

▸▸ *Improve customer service.* Customer comments about products and services will not always be positive. Use social media to search out displeased customers and engage them directly in order to solve their service issues.

LO 3 Evaluation and Measurement of Social Media

Social media has the potential to revolutionize the way organizations communicate with stakeholders. Given the relative ease and efficiency with which organizations can use social media, a positive return on investment (ROI) is likely for many—if not most—organizations. A Forrester Research report found that 95 percent of marketers planned to increase or maintain their investments in social media. However, though they understand that it is a worthwhile investment, most marketers have not been able to figure out how to measure the benefits of social media. As social media evolves, so do the measurements and metrics

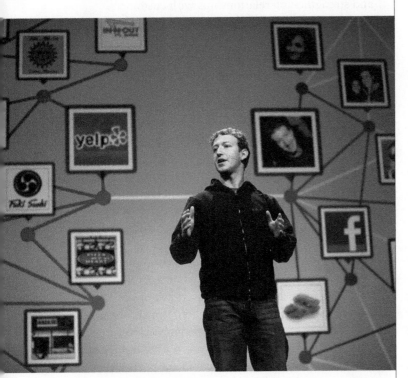

Facebook CEO Mark Zuckerberg introduces new features for Facebook during a one-day developer conference sponsored by Facebook. Behind him is an illustration of the myriad ways social networking sites can interact.

THREE AREAS OF MEASUREMENT:

▸▸ *Social media measurement:* Ever-changing metrics that are used to determine the ROI of each tool. Social media measurement determines, for example, the conversion rate of a Facebook friend. Tools include Google Analytics, Social Mention, Twinfluence, Twitalyzer, and Klout, among others.[26]

▸▸ *Public relations measurement:* Since many modern PR campaigns entail social media, PR measurement exists to calculate the impact of social media on press coverage and other elements of PR. Tools include DIY Dashboard, Tealium, and Vocus, which quantizes information such as share of voice relative to competitors, stories by location, and a sentiment analysis for each press hit.

▸▸ *Social media monitoring:* Tools that are used less for campaign metrics and more for customer service improvement, brand management, and prospecting. Tools include BlogPulse, Technorati, Trendrr, Google Trends, TweetDeck, Visible Technologies, and Trackur. Google News Alerts, a free online tool, leverages Google's search technology to report relevant news stories and blog posts about any topic or organization.

that track it.[27] Yet, as with traditional advertising, marketers lack hard evidence as to the relative effectiveness of these tools. Some marketers accept this unknown variable and focus on social media being less about ROI than about deepening relationships with customers; others work tirelessly to better understand the measurement of social media's effectiveness. The Leger Study, Social Media Reality Check 2011 Research Findings provides evidence to the value of social media from a relationship perspective. This research shows that 46 percent of consumers agreed that information found on social media sites was more credible than information found in advertising, and 43 percent agreed that reading about a product or service in the social media space made them feel more positive about the product or service.[28] While literally hundreds of metrics have been developed to measure social media's value, these metrics are meaningless unless they are tied to key performance indicators.[29] For example, a local coffee shop manager may measure the success of her social media presence by her accumulated number of friends on Facebook and followers on Twitter. But these numbers depend entirely on context. The rate of accumulation, investment per fan and follower, and comparison to similarly sized coffee shops are all important variables to consider. Without context, measurements are meaningless.

LO 4 Social Behaviour of Consumers

Once objectives have been determined and measurement tools have been implemented, it is important to identify the consumer. Who is using social media? What types of social media do they use? Does Facebook attract younger users? Do Twitter users retweet viral videos? These types of questions must be considered because they determine not only which tools will be most effective but also, more importantly, whether launching a social media campaign even makes sense for a particular organization.

Understanding an audience necessitates understanding how that audience uses social media. In *Groundswell*, Charlene Li and Josh Bernoff of Forrester Research identify six categories of social media users, which are listed below.

1. *Creators:* Those who produce and share online content such as blogs, websites, articles, and videos

2. *Critics:* Those who post comments, ratings, and reviews of products and services on blogs and forums

3. *Collectors:* Those who use RSS feeds to collect information and vote for websites online

4. *Joiners:* Those who maintain a social networking profile and visit other sites

5. *Spectators:* Those who read blogs, listen to podcasts, watch videos, and generally consume media

6. *Inactives:* Those who do none of these things[30]

A 2009 study determined that 24 percent of social media users functioned as creators, 37 percent functioned as critics, 21 percent functioned as collectors, 51 percent functioned as joiners, and 73 percent functioned as spectators. While participation in each of these categories trended upward, inactives decreased from 44 percent in 2007 to only 18 percent in 2009.[31] However, recent Forrester research shows that the number of people who contribute content is slowing down. Participation in most categories fell slightly, prompting analysts to recommend that marketers re-examine how they are engaging with their customers online. Despite the apparent slowdown, research also shows that more social networking "rookies" are classified as joiners. Another bright spot is a new category, *conversationalists*, or people who post status updates on social networking sites and microblogging services such as Twitter. Conversationalists represent 31 percent of users.[32]

LO 5 Social Media Tools: Consumer- and Corporate-Generated Content

Several tools and platforms can be employed as part of an organization's social media strategy. Blogs, microblogs, social networks, media creation and sharing sites, social news sites, location-based social networking sites, review sites, and virtual worlds and online gaming all have their place in a company's social marketing plan. These are all tools in a marketing manager's toolbox, available when applicable to the marketing plan but not necessarily to be used all at once. Because of the breakneck pace at which technology changes, this list of resources will surely look markedly different five years from now. More tools emerge every day, and branding strategies must keep up with the ever-changing world of technology. For now, the resources highlighted in this section remain a marketer's strongest set of platforms for conversing and strengthening relationships with customers.

Blogs

Blogs have become staples in many social media strategies and are often a brand's social media centerpiece. Some experts believe that every company should have a blog that speaks to current and potential customers, not as consumers, but as people.[33] Blogs allow marketers to create content in the form of posts, which ideally build trust and a sense of authenticity in customers. Once posts are made, audience members can provide feedback through comments. Because the comments section of a blog post opens a dialogue and gives customers a voice, it is one of the most important avenues of conversation between brands and consumers.

Several brands use blogs effectively. GM's FastLane Blog is considered a corporate best. It is packed with audio, video, and photos and is organized into categories that offer something for everyone. One of FastLane Blog's biggest draws is its high-quality writing. Each reader comment is answered in a fun and pithy tone, encouraging participation and continued readership (http://fastlane.gmblogs.com). Vans Girls Blog, the official blog for Vans Shoes, is another corporate success. By posting fashion photos,

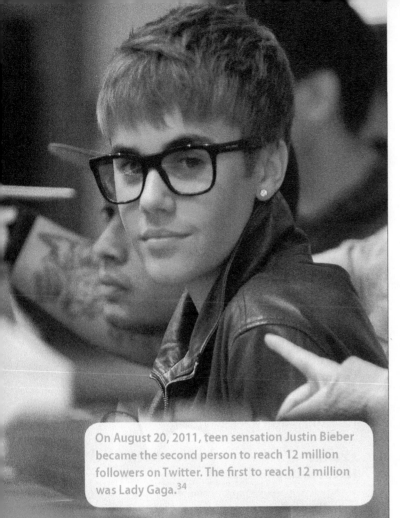

On August 20, 2011, teen sensation Justin Bieber became the second person to reach 12 million followers on Twitter. The first to reach 12 million was Lady Gaga.[34]

organizing events, and highlighting style and celebrity news, Vans Girls Blog captivates its dedicated audience with content that is both interesting and relevant to the Vans brand. This blog is a great example of a corporate blog aimed at a singular audience (http://offthewallvansgirls.wordpress.com). The Canadian Marketing Association produces a successful blog, http://www.canadianmarketingblog.com/, which has become a wealth of information and source of conversation for many Canadian marketers.

In contrast, noncorporate blogs are independent and not associated with the marketing efforts of any particular company or brand. Because these blogs contain information not controlled by marketers, they are perceived to be more authentic than corporate blogs. Mommy bloggers, women who review children's products and discuss family related topics on their personal blogs, use noncorporate blogs. The goal of mommy blogs is to share parenting tips and experiences and become part of a community. Because of the popularity of these and other types of blogs, many bloggers receive products and/or money from companies in exchange for a review. These reviews have high potential for social buzz; four out of five noncorporate bloggers post brand or product reviews. Even

if a company does not have a formal social media strategy, chances are the brand is still out in the blogosphere, whether or not a marketing manager approached a blogger.

microblogs blogs with strict limits on the length of posts

Microblogs

Microblogs are blogs with strict limits on the length of posts. Twitter, the most popular microblogging platform, requires that posts be no more than 140 characters in length. Other microblogging platforms, include Jaiku, Tumblr, Plurk, and, of course, Facebook's status updates. Originally designed as a short messaging system used for internal communication, Twitter has gained global popularity and is now used as a communication and research tool by individuals and brands around the world. A large part of Twitter's success stems from its extremely versatile platform: Posts and private messages can be sent and received via text messages, smartphone apps, desktop clients, external websites, tablet computers, and email. Twitter posts, commonly called tweets, can be amended with photos, videos, and external links. Recently, Twitter has changed its interface to include video and photos and has added new products to try to monetize the site. It has also developed promoted tweets, which are ads that appear in search results and user feeds, both on Twitter.com and third-party clients that access the service, such as TweetDeck, twhirl, TwitterBerry, and Tweetie.

Despite its strict character limit, Twitter has proven effective for disseminating breaking news, promoting longer blog posts and campaigns, sharing links, announcing events, and promoting sales. By following, retweeting, responding to potential customers' tweets, and by tweeting content that inspires customers to engage the brand, corporate Twitter users can quickly and efficiently lay a foundation for meaningful two-way conversation. Research has found that when operated correctly, corporate Twitter accounts are well respected and well received. Twitter can be used to build communities; aid in customer service; gain prospects; increase awareness; and, in the case of nonprofits, raise funds.

The ways a business can use Twitter to successfully engage with customers are almost limitless. Cupcake Diner provides sweet treats to residents of Hamilton, Ontario, and area all day long from the Cupcake Diner mobile van. Natalie, the owner, uses Twitter to inform customers of her van's location throughout the day. Because the tweets are informative, useful, and relevant, Cupcake Diner has built a following of more than 1,500 in a very short time.[35]

Social Networks

Social networking sites allow individuals to connect—or network—with friends, peers, and business associates. Connections may be made around shared interests, shared environments, or personal relationships. Depending on the site, connected individuals may be able to send each other messages, track each other's activity, see each other's personal information, share multimedia, or comment on each other's blog and microblog posts. Depending on its goals, a marketing team might engage several social networks as part of its social media strategy: Facebook is the largest and fastest-growing network; MySpace caters to younger audiences; LinkedIn is geared toward professionals and businesses who use it to recruit professionals; and niche networks like Bebo, Last.fm, WeAreTeachers, BlackPlanet, and Match.com cater to specialized markets. There is a niche social network for just about every demographic and interest. Beyond those already established, an organization may decide to develop a brand-specific social network or community. While all social networking sites are different, some marketing goals can be accomplished on any such site. Given the right strategy, increasing awareness, targeting audiences, promoting products, forging relationships, highlighting expertise and leadership, attracting event participants, performing research, and generating new business are attainable marketing goals on any social network.

Facebook is by far the largest social networking site. While individual Facebook users create profiles, brands, organizations, and nonprofit causes operate as pages (see Exhibit 16.2). As opposed to individual profiles, all pages are public and are thus subject to search engine indexing. By maintaining a popular Facebook page, a brand not only increases its social media presence, it also helps to optimize search engine results. Pages often include photo and video albums, brand information, and links to external sites. The most useful page feature, however, is the Wall. The Wall allows a brand to communicate directly with fans via status updates, which enables marketers to build databases of interested stakeholders. When an individual becomes a fan of your organization or posts on your Wall, that information is shared with the individual's friends, creating a mini viral marketing campaign. Other Facebook marketing tools include groups, applications, and ads. Facebook is an extremely important platform for social marketers.

Facebook has proved to be fertile ground for new marketing ideas and campaigns. By creating a Facebook application called Real or Fake, Adobe used the social network's built-in software platform to advertise student editions of the Photoshop photo editing software to college students. When users installed the Real or Fake application, they gained access to weekly images, which they were challenged to distinguish as authentic or digitally manipulated. After they took the challenge, users were directed to tutorials that demonstrated how the altered photos were manipulated using Photoshop. By the end of the campaign, Adobe had earned additional Facebook fans and had witnessed an increase in page views from 5,057 to 53,000 per week. More than 6 percent of Real or Fake users actually purchased the Photoshop software. Through this campaign, Adobe did not just establish a social media presence but also created a novel way to engage its fans.[36] Coca-Cola's Facebook

EXHIBIT 16.2
Facebook Lingo

Non-Individual (Usually Corporate)	Individual
Page	Profile
Fan of a page, tells fan's friends that the user is a fan, creates mini viral campaign	Friend a person, send private messages, write on the Wall, see friend-only content
Public, searchable	Privacy options, not searchable unless user enabled

© Cengage Learning 2011

© SAEED KHAN/AFP/GETTY IMAGES

page, boasting five million fans, was developed by two individuals in California. Rather than taking on the management of its own page, Coca-Cola decided to work with fans to maintain the page. Again, to succeed in social media, organizations must learn to share control with the customer.

LinkedIn features many of the same services as Facebook (profiles, status updates, private messages, company pages, and groups) but is oriented around business and professional connections. Unlike Facebook, LinkedIn features a question-and-answer forum, where users can ask for advice and share expertise in specific fields, and a file hosting service, where users can upload intellectual property like slides, presentations, and other shared documents.[37] LinkedIn is used primarily by professionals who wish to build their personal brands online and businesses who are recruiting employees and freelancers.

Media Sharing Sites

Media sharing sites allow users to upload and distribute multimedia content, such as videos and photos. Sites such as YouTube and Flickr are particularly useful to brands' social marketing strategies because they add a vibrant interactive channel on which to disseminate content. The distribution of user-generated content has changed markedly over the past few years. Today, organizations can tell compelling brand stories through videos, photos, and audio.

Photo sharing sites allow users to archive and share photos. Flickr, Picasa, TwitPic, Photobucket, Facebook, and Imgur all offer free photo hosting services that can be utilized by individuals and businesses alike.

These images were used as part of Adobe's Real or Fake game on Facebook. Can you tell which is real and which is fake? The chameleon is fake (those are goat horns imposed on its head), and the road is real (it's in Morocco).

Video creation and distribution have also gained popularity among marketers because of video's rich ability to tell stories. YouTube, the highest-trafficked video-based website and the sixth highest-trafficked site overall, allows users to upload and stream their videos to an enthusiastic and active community.[38] YouTube is not only large (in terms of visitors), it attracts a diverse base of users: Age and gender demographics are remarkably balanced.

Many entertainment companies and movie marketers have used YouTube as a showcase for new products, specials, and movie trailers. For example, Lions Gate Entertainment purchased ad space on the YouTube home page in 15 countries to promote the *Avatar* movie trailer. Some teen clothing brands, such as Forever 21 and West 49, build followings on YouTube by posting hauls—videos made by teens that focus on fashion. Clearly, user-generated content can be a powerful tool for brands that can use it effectively.

A podcast, another type of user-generated media, is a digital audio or video file that is distributed serially for other people to listen to or watch. Podcasts can be streamed online, played on a computer, uploaded to a portable media player (like an iPod), or downloaded onto a smartphone (like HTC's Droid Incredible). Podcasts are like radio shows that are distributed through various means and not linked to a scheduled time slot. While they have not experienced the exponential growth rates of other digital platforms, podcasts have amassed a steadily growing number of loyal devotees. A good example of effective use of the medium is BMO Capital Products Podcast Services, which offers clients and nonclients alike free information about stock market investment.[39]

Social News Sites

Social news sites allow users to decide which content is promoted on a given website by voting for or against the content. Users post news stories and multimedia for the community to vote on crowd-sourced communities such as Reddit, Digg, and Yahoo! Buzz. The more interest from readers, the higher the ranking of the story or video. Marketers have found that these

© KENNETH JOW/© ISTOCKPHOTO.COM/ERIC ISSELÉE

sites are useful for promoting campaigns, creating conversations around related issues, and building website traffic.[40] If it is voted up, discussed, and shared enough to be listed among the most popular topics of the day, content posted to a crowd sourced site can go viral across other sites and, eventually, the entire Web. Social bookmarking sites such as Del.ici.ous and StumbleUpon are similar to social news sites but the objective of their users is to collect, save, and share interesting and valuable links. On these sites, users categorize links with short, descriptive tags. Users can search the site's database of links by specific tags or can add their own tags to others' links. In this way, tags serve as the foundation for information gathering and sharing on social bookmarking sites.[41]

Location-Based Social Networking Sites

Considered by many to be the next big thing in social marketing, location sites such as Gowalla and Foursquare should be on every marketer's radar. Essentially, **location-based social networking sites** combine the fun of social networking with the utility of location-based GPS technology. Foursquare, one of the most popular location sites, treats location-based micronetworking as a game: Users earn badges and special statuses that are based on their number of visits to particular locations. Users can write and read short reviews and tips about businesses, organize meet-ups, and see which Foursquare-using friends are nearby. Foursquare updates can also be posted to linked Twitter and Facebook accounts for followers and friends to see. Location sites such as Foursquare are particularly useful social marketing tools for local businesses, especially when combined with sales promotions such as coupons, special offers, contests, and events. Location sites can be harnessed to forge lasting relationships with and deeply engrained loyalty in customers.[42] For example, a local restaurant can allow consumers to check in on Foursquare using their smartphone and receive a coupon for that day's purchases. Since the location site technology is relatively new, many brands are still figuring out how best to utilize Foursquare. Facebook added Places to capitalize on this location-based technology, which allows people to "check in" and share their location with their online friends. It will be interesting to see how use of this technology grows over time.

© HANDOUT/MCT/NEWSCOM

Review Sites

Individuals tend to trust other people's opinions when it comes to purchasing. According to Nielsen Media Research, more than 70 percent of consumers said that they trusted online consumer opinions. This percentage is much higher than that of consumers who trust traditional advertising. Based on the early work of Amazon and eBay to integrate user opinions into product and seller pages, countless websites have sprung up that allow users to voice their opinions across every segment of the Internet market. **Review sites** allow consumers to post, read, rate, and comment on opinions regarding all kinds of products and services. For example, Yelp, the most active local review directory on the Web, combines customer critiques of local businesses with business information and elements of social networking to create an engaging, informative experience. On Yelp, users scrutinize local restaurants, fitness centres, tattoo parlours, and other businesses, each of which has a detailed profile page. Business owners and representatives can edit their organizations' pages and respond to Yelp reviews both privately and publicly.[43] By giving marketers the opportunity to respond to their customers directly and to position their businesses in a positive light, review sites serve as useful tools for local and national businesses.

Virtual Worlds and Online Gaming

Virtual worlds and online gaming present additional opportunities for marketers to engage with consumers. These include massive multiplayer online games (MMOGs) such as *World of Warcraft* and *The Sims Online* as well as online communities (or virtual worlds) such as Second Life, Poptropica, and Habbo Hotel. Consultancy firm KZero Worldswide reported that almost 800 million people have participated in some sort of virtual world experience, and the sector's annual revenue is approaching $1 billion. Much of this revenue has come from in-game advertising—virtual world environments are often fertile grounds for branded content. Several businesses, such as IBM and consultancy firm Crayon, have developed profitable trade presences in Second Life. IBM has used its Second Life space to hold virtual conferences with more than 200 participants, while Crayon has held a number of virtual networking events and meet and greets in the virtual world.[44] While unfamiliar to and even intimidating for many traditional marketers, the field of virtual worlds is an important, viable, and growing consideration for social media marketing.

One area of growth is social gaming. Nearly 25 percent of people play games within social networking sites such as Facebook and MySpace. The typical player is a 43-year-old woman with a full-time job and some postsecondary education. Women are most likely to play with real-world friends or relatives as opposed to strangers. Most play multiple times per week and more than 30 percent play daily. Facebook is by far the largest social network for gaming. The top five games on Facebook are Farmville, Bejeweled Blitz, Texas Hold'em Poker, Café World, and Mafia Wars. Because of the popularity of gaming with friends and relatives through these sites, marketers need to integrate their message based on the social network platforms and the demographic participating in social gaming.[45]

Another popular type of online gaming targets a different group—MMOGs target 18- to 34-year-old males. In these environments, thousands of people play simultaneously, and the games have revenues of more than $400 billion annually. Regardless of the type of experience, brands must be creative in how they integrate into games. Social and real-world–like games are the most appropriate for marketing and advertising (as opposed to fantasy games), and promotions typically include special events, competitions, and sweepstakes. In some games (e.g., Sims), having ads increases the authenticity. For example, Nike offers shoes in *Sims Online* that allow the player to run faster.

LO6 Social Media and Mobile Technology

While much of the excitement in social media has been based on websites and new technology uses, much of the growth lies in new platforms. These platforms include the multitude of smartphones, such as iPhones and BlackBerrys, as well as netbooks and tablets, such as iPads. The major implications of new platforms mean consumers can access popular websites such as Facebook, Mashable, Twitter, and Foursquare.

Mobile and Smartphone Technology

More than 25 percent of the world's population—and and 60 percent of Canada's population owns a mobile phone.[46] It is no surprise then that the mobile platform is such an effective marketing tool—especially when targeting a younger audience. Smartphones up the

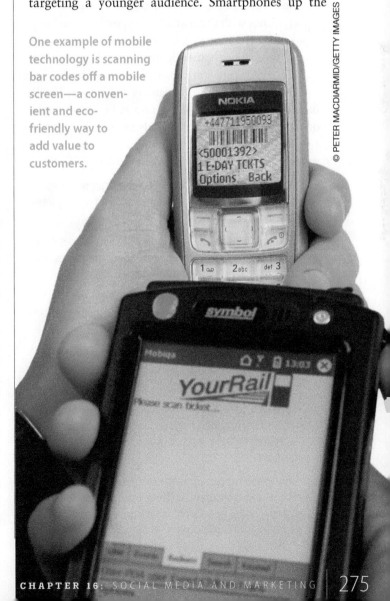

One example of mobile technology is scanning bar codes off a mobile screen—a convenient and eco-friendly way to add value to customers.

ante by allowing individuals to do nearly everything they can do with a computer—from anywhere. With a smartphone in hand, reading a blog, writing an email, scheduling a meeting, posting to Facebook, playing a multiplayer game, watching a video, taking a picture, using GPS, and surfing the Internet might all occur during one ten-minute car ride. Smartphone technology, often considered the crowning achievement in digital convergence and social media integration, has opened the door to modern mobile advertising as a viable marketing strategy.

The Interactive Advertising Bureau of Canada reported that mobile advertising revenue in 2009 reached $31.9 million, a 169 percent increase over 2008.[47] The recent popularity of mobile marketing can be traced to several factors. First, an effort to standardize mobile platforms has resulted in a low barrier to entry. Second, because mobile platforms cater to younger audiences, there are more consumers than ever acclimating to once-worrisome privacy and pricing policies. Third, because most consumers carry their smartphones with them at all times, mobile marketing is uniquely effective at garnering consumer attention in real time. Fourth, mobile marketing is measurable: Metrics and usage statistics make it an effective tool for gaining insight into consumer behaviour. Finally, mobile marketing's response rate is higher than that of traditional media types, such as print and broadcast advertisement. The following are some common mobile marketing tools include:

- *SMS (short message service):* 160-character text messages sent to and from cellphones. SMS is typically integrated with other tools.

- *MMS (multimedia messaging service):* Similar to SMS but allows the attachment of images, videos, ringtones, and other multimedia to text messages.

- *Mobile websites (MOBI and WAP websites):* websites designed specifically for viewing and navigation on mobile devices.

- *Mobile ads:* Visual advertisements integrated into text messages, applications, and mobile websites. Mobile ads are often sold on a cost-per-click basis.

- *Bluetooth marketing:* A signal is sent to Bluetooth-enabled devices, which allows marketers to send targeted messages to users based on their geographic locations.

- *Smartphone apps:* Software designed specifically for mobile and tablet devices. These apps include software to turn phones into scanners for various types of bar codes—including QR codes (as discussed in Chapter 17).

Rémy Martin, maker of high-end champagne cognac, used SMS, email, and website promotions to advertise VIP events held concurrently in six cities. To ensure younger generations' interest in the events, Rémy Martin also developed a WAP website called Rémy's Chill Zone, where, after opting in, users could gain additional information and engage with the brand on a deeper level. As a result, all six events sold out, and Rémy Martin began dialogues with younger customers who had never before experienced its product. As this example illustrates, mobile marketing is a great way to engage Generations X and Y.[48]

Applications and Widgets

Given the widespread adoption of Apple's iPhone, RIM's BlackBerry line, Android-based phones, and other smartphones, it's no surprise that millions of applications have been developed for the mobile market. Dozens of new and unique apps that harness mobile technology are added to mobile marketplaces every day. While many apps perform platform-specific tasks, others convert existing content into a mobile-ready format. Whether offering new or existing content, when an app is well branded and integrated into a company's overall marketing strategy, it can create buzz and generate customer engagement.

Volkswagen Group of America introduced the 2010 GTI sedan in an app called VW Real Racing GTI, which the GTI marketers promoted through Facebook, Twitter, YouTube, and other traditional channels. VW Real Racing GTI is a racing game that allows players to enjoy competitive racing on their mobile devices. VW Real Racing GTI connected with players—it is one of the most talked about apps from the Apple store, with nearly five million downloads.[49] While some marketers focus their apps on connectivity, Benjamin Moore Paint chose to focus on utility as an effective selling point, when it developed Colour Capture, an app that allows iPhone users to match colours in photos to shades in the Benjamin Moore colour collection. Users can also save their favourite colours and chip names for future use.[50]

Web widgets, also known as gadgets and badges, are software applications that run entirely within existing online platforms. Essentially, a Web widget allows a developer to embed a simple application such as a weather forecast, horoscope, or stock market ticker into a website, even if the developer did not write (or does not understand) the application's source code. From a marketing perspective, widgets allow customers to display company information (such as

HUMANITARIAN TEXTING

In January 2010, a **7.0 earthquake** struck Port-au-Prince, Haiti, and the surrounding areas. By the time the dust settled, 230,000 people had died and 1.9 million more had been left homeless. Among the organizations that pledged aid, the Canadian Red Cross's **text message-based donation campaign** proved to be the true breakthrough story of this crisis. By simply texting "HAITI" to 90999, individuals could make a $10 donation to the Canadian Red Cross that was charged to the donor's monthly mobile phone bill. More than $500,000 was raised in Canada through text messaging alone in the early days following the earthquake.

Several factors contributed to making the campaign successful. The long-term news coverage of the disaster, combined with the ease of texting a donation, gave many people a way to support relief efforts quickly and helped to ensure the success of the campaign. The innovative use of texting led the Red Cross to consider other uses. As part of its relief efforts, the Red Cross began texting earthquake survivors to inform them of a vaccination campaign in Port-au-Prince, sites where safe water was available, and other preventative health information. Texting allowed information to be quickly communicated to those in need.[52] The major disaster inspired long-term news coverage, and the ease of texting a donation gave many people a way to help after being exposed to the tragedy. A televised public service announcement by First Lady Michelle Obama prompted a significant spike in donations, as did an NFL play-off game segment during which commentators discussed the Red Cross campaign.[53]

SOURCES: Michael Bush, "Red Cross Delivers Real Mobile Results for a Real Emergency," *Advertising Age*, February 22, 2010, http://adage.com/digitalalist10/article?article_id=142204; and Nicole Wallace and Ian Wilhelm, "Charities Text Messaging Success Shakes Up the Fundraising World," *Chronicle of Philanthropy*, February 11, 2010, 7.

After the massive flooding in Pakistan displaced more than 14 million people, the Disasters Emergency Committee set up a texting donation service similar to that used in Haiti. It is promoted here by the boxer Amir Khan.

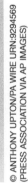

---

current promotions, coupons, or news) on their own websites. Widgets are often cheaper than apps to develop, can extend an organization's reach beyond existing platforms, will broaden the listening system, and can make an organization easier to find.[51]

Allowing customers to promote up-to-date marketing material on their own blogs and websites is very appealing, but before investing in a marketing-oriented widget, marketers should consider the following questions:

▶▶ Does my organization regularly publish compelling content, such as news, daily specials, or coupons, on its website or blog?

▶▶ Does my content engage individuals or appeal to their needs as customers?

▶▶ Is my content likely to inspire conversations with the company or with other customers? Will customers want to share my content with others?

If you can answer yes to these questions, a widget may be an effective tool for your organization.

The Changing World of Social Media

As you read through the chapter, some of the trends that are noted may already seem ancient to you. The rate of change in social media is astounding—usage statistics change daily for Facebook and Twitter. Some new developments that are in the rumour mill as we write this may have exploded in popularity; others may have fizzled out without even appearing on your radar. In Exhibit 16.3, we've listed some of the items that seem to be on the brink of exploding on to the social media scene. Take a moment to fill in the current state of each. Have you heard of it? Has it come and gone? Maybe it is still rumoured, or maybe it has petered out. This exercise highlights not only the speed with which social media changes but also the importance of keeping tabs on rumours. Doing so may result in a competitive advantage by being able to understand and invest in the next big social media site.

EXHIBIT 16.3
Social Media Trends

Site	Change	Where is it now?
Facebook	Threaded commenting, up/down voting comments.	
Twitter	Promoted tweets.	
Facebook/Bing	Linked searching in Bing. Search results include similar items liked by Facebook friends, and people searches pull information from your profile to find the correct person.	
Facebook Places/ Foursquare	Facebook Places is just introduced; Foursquare is gaining popularity away from major cities.	
Apple's Ping social music service	Released with iTunes 10, Ping allows users to like music, follow music stars and friends, post songs and albums, and find users with similar music tastes.	

© Cengage Learning 2011

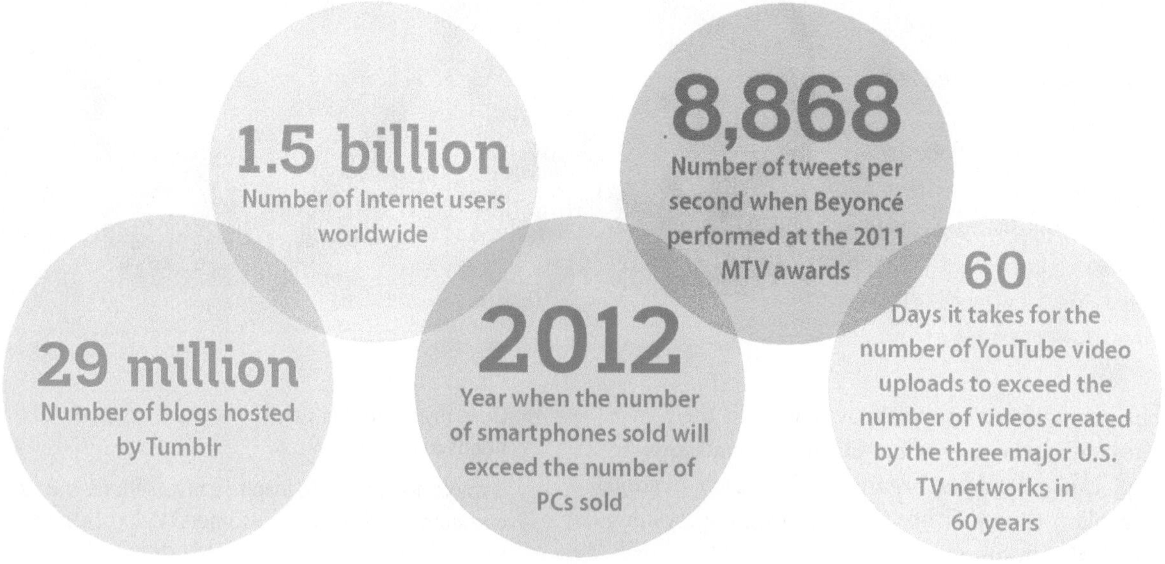

1.5 billion
Number of Internet users worldwide

8,868
Number of tweets per second when Beyoncé performed at the 2011 MTV awards

29 million
Number of blogs hosted by Tumblr

2012
Year when the number of smartphones sold will exceed the number of PCs sold

60
Days it takes for the number of YouTube video uploads to exceed the number of videos created by the three major U.S. TV networks in 60 years

LEARNING YOUR WAY

We know that no two students are alike. **MKTG** was developed to help you learn **marketing** in a way that works for you.

Not only is the format fresh and contemporary, it's also concise and focused. And **MKTG** is loaded with a variety of supplements, like chapter review cards, printable flashcards, and more!

At **www.icanmktg2.com**, you will find **interactive flashcards, crossword puzzles, quizzes, glossary of terms** and **more** to test your knowledge of key concepts. It includes plenty of resources to help you study, no matter what learning style you like best!

"I enjoy the cards in the back of the book and the fact that it partners with the website."

—Cassandra Jewell, Sir Sandford Fleming College

Visit **www.icanmktg2.com** to find the resources you need today!

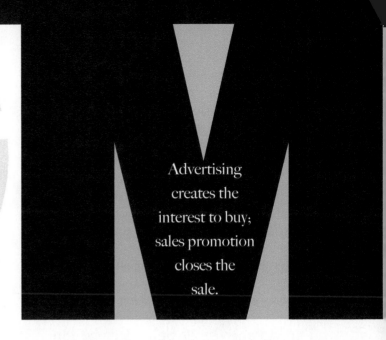

Advertising creates the interest to buy; sales promotion closes the sale.

LO 1 Sales Promotion

In addition to using advertising, public relations, direct marketing, and personal selling, marketing managers can use sales promotion to increase the effectiveness of their promotional efforts. *Sales promotion* refers to the marketing communication activities, other than advertising, personal selling, direct-response communication and public relations, in which a short-term incentive motivates consumers or members of the distribution channel to purchase a good or service immediately, either by lowering the price or by adding value.

Advertising offers the consumer a reason to buy; sales promotion offers an incentive to buy. Sales promotion is usually cheaper than advertising and easier to measure. A major national TV advertising campaign often costs more than $5 million to create, produce, and place. In contrast, sales promotional campaigns using the Internet or direct-marketing methods can cost significantly less. It is also very difficult to determine how many people buy a product or service as a result of radio or TV ads. By using sales promotion, marketers know the precise number of coupons redeemed, the number of clicks through to a website, or the number of contest entries.

Sales promotion is usually targeted toward either of two distinctly different markets. **Consumer sales promotion** is targeted to the ultimate consumer market. **Trade sales promotion** is directed to members of the marketing channel, such as

consumer sales promotion sales promotion activities targeting the ultimate consumer

trade sales promotion sales promotion activities targeting a marketing channel member, such as a wholesaler or retailer

What do you think?

Group coupon sites are just a passing fad.

| 1 | 2 | 3 | 4 | 5 | 6 | 7 |

STRONGLY DISAGREE   STRONGLY AGREE

© ISTOCKPHOTO.COM/TERRY J. ALCORN

wholesalers and retailers. Sales promotion expenditures have been steadily increasing over the last several years as a result of increased competition, the ever-expanding array of available media choices, consumers and retailers demanding more deals from manufacturers, and the continued reliance on accountable and measurable marketing strategies. In addition, those product and service marketers that have traditionally ignored sales promotion activities have discovered the marketing power of sales promotion. In fact, annual expenditures on promotion marketing in North America are now estimated to be more than $400 billion.

The Objectives of Sales Promotion

Sales promotion usually has more effect on behaviour than on attitudes. Immediate purchase is the goal of sales promotion, regardless of the form it takes. The objectives of a promotion depend on the general behaviour of target consumers (see Exhibit 17.1). For example, marketers who are targeting loyal users of their product need to reinforce existing behaviour or increase product usage. An effective tool for strengthening brand loyalty is the *frequent buyer program* that rewards consumers for repeat purchases. Other types of promotions are more effective with customers prone to brand switching or with those who are loyal to a competitor's product. A cents-off coupon, free sample, or eye-catching display in a store will often entice shoppers to try a different brand.

Once marketers understand the dynamics occurring within their product category and have determined the particular consumers and consumer behaviours they want to influence, they can then select the appropriate promotional tools to achieve these goals.

LO 2 Tools for Consumer Sales Promotion

Marketing managers must decide which consumer sales promotion devices to use in a specific campaign. The methods chosen must suit the objectives to ensure success of the overall promotion plan. The popular tools for consumer sales promotion discussed below have also been easily transferred to online versions to entice Internet users to visit sites, purchase products, or use services on the Web.

Coupons and Rebates

A **coupon** is a certificate that entitles consumers to an immediate price reduction when they buy the product. Coupons are a particularly good way to encourage product trial and repurchase. They are also likely to increase the amount of a product bought.

More than 325 billion coupons are distributed in the United States each year, about 100 times the number sent out in Canada. Coupons save Canadians about $120 million each year.[1] The increased online activity of Canadians coupled with the increasing availability of coupons online is expected to result in more coupon use by Canadians. Intense competition in the consumer packaged-goods category and the annual introduction of more than 1,200 new products have contributed to this trend. Using your smartphone at the counter to display an online coupon is so much easier than clipping a coupon, storing it where it can easily be found, and retrieving it for use once in the store.[2] Though coupons are often criticized for reaching consumers who have no interest in the product or for encouraging repeat purchase by regular users, recent studies indicate that coupons promote new-product use and are likely to stimulate purchases.

Freestanding inserts (FSI), the promotional coupon inserts found in newspapers, have been the traditional way of circulating printed coupons. But the volume of FSI coupons distributed is declining. To overcome the diminishing redemption rates, marketers are using new couponing strategies. Shortening the time during which coupons can be redeemed creates a greater sense of urgency to redeem the coupon. A key strategy is the distribution of coupons online, in

EXHIBIT 17.1
Types of Consumers and Sales Promotion Goals

Type of Buyer	Desired Results	Sales Promotion Examples
Loyal customers People who buy a particular brand most of the time or all of the time	Reinforce behaviour, increase consumption, change purchase timing	• Loyalty marketing programs, such as frequent buyer cards or frequent shopper clubs • Bonus packs that give loyal consumers an incentive to stock up or offer premiums in return for proof of purchase
Competitor's customers People who buy a competitor's product most of the time or all of the time	Break loyalty, persuade to switch to another brand	• Sampling to introduce another brand's superior qualities compared with competing brands • Sweepstakes, contests, or premiums that create interest in the product
Brand switchers People who buy a variety of products in the category	Persuade to buy one brand more often	• Any promotion that lowers the price of the product, such as coupons, price-off packages, and bonus packs • Trade deals that help make the product more readily available than competing products
Price buyers People who consistently buy the least expensive brand	Appeal with low prices or supply added value that makes price less important	• Coupons, price-off packages, refunds, or trade deals that reduce the price of the brand to match or undercut the price of the brand that would have otherwise been purchased

SOURCE: From *Sales Promotion Essentials*, 2nd edition., by Don E. Schulz, William A. Robinson, and Lisa A. Petrison. © 1998 NTC Publishing Group. Reprinted by permission of The McGraw-Hill Companies Inc.

particular through mobile phones. A survey by Instore Marketing Institute of U.S. consumers found that 34 percent of respondents were interested in receiving coupons via their mobile phones.[3]

In-store coupons are still popular because they are more likely to influence customers' buying decisions. Instant coupons on product packages and electronic coupons issued at the counter now achieve much higher redemption rates because consumers are making more in-store purchase decisions.

As mentioned earlier, as consumers embrace technology in every aspect of their life, Internet and online coupons will continue to grow in influence. Technology plays an increasingly significant role in the shopping process. Consumers view online flyers, visit Facebook to learn from friends about new products, and visit the websites of their favourite brands and retailers. In-store shoppers are comfortable using digital technologies that save them time

and add value. They have smartphones that can read quick response (QR) codes on product packages and shelf ads. These black barcodes arranged in a square pattern provide product information and can link consumers to product websites, where they can download coupons to their phones to use at the checkout.[4]

A new phenomenon in couponing is online group couponing. In April 2011, Toronto alone was estimated to have more than 35 online group couponing sites. Consumers participating in an online group couponing site, such as Groupon, WagJag, or a newcomer to Canada, Smart Betty, have a limited time to capitalize on the deal, which is effective only if a minimum number of people sign on for it. Social media sites such as Facebook are used to distribute information on the deal, and consumers who relay information about the deal are paid cash or given credits for their pushing efforts, which can create a coupon-buying frenzy. The key to the long-term success of the

COURTESY OF PROCTER & GAMBLE

online coupon sites will be how marketers use the information they capture and store in their database to deliver other marketing programs.

Rebates are cash refunds given for the purchase of a product during a specific period. They are similar to coupons in that they offer the purchaser a price reduction; however, because the purchaser must usually mail in a rebate form and some proof of purchase, the reward is not immediate. Manufacturers prefer rebates for several reasons. Rebates allow manufacturers to offer price cuts to consumers directly. Manufacturers have more control over rebate promotions because they can be rolled out and shut off quickly. Further, because buyers must fill out forms with their names, addresses, and other data, manufacturers use rebate programs to build customer databases. Perhaps the best reason of all to offer rebates is that although rebates are particularly good at enticing a purchase, most consumers never bother to redeem them. It is estimated that only half of consumers eligible for rebates collect them.[5]

Premiums

A **premium** is an extra item offered to the consumer, usually in exchange for some proof that the promoted product has been purchased. Premiums reinforce the consumer's purchase decision, increase consumption, and persuade non-users to switch brands. Premiums that are developed as collectibles can encourage brand loyalty. The best example of the use of premiums is McDonald's Happy Meal, which rewards children with a small toy.

Premiums can also include more product for the regular price, such as two-for-the-price-of-one bonus packs or packages that include more of the product. Kellogg's, for instance, added two more pastries to its Pop Tarts without increasing the price in an effort to

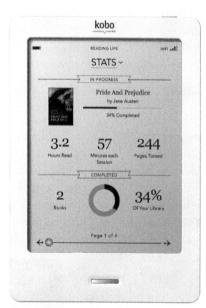

Kobo offered 100 free pre-loaded e-books so consumers could read from their Kobos right out of the box. The 100 e-books were all-time classics so there was a book for everyone.

boost market share lost to private-label brands and new competitors. The promotion was so successful the company decided to keep the additional product in its regular packaging. Another possibility is to attach a premium to the product's package.

Loyalty Marketing Programs

Loyalty marketing programs, or **frequent buyer programs**, reward loyal consumers for making multiple purchases. Loyalty marketing programs are designed to build long-term, mutually beneficial relationships between a company and its key customers. Eighty-six percent of Canadians participate in at least one loyalty program. The average Canadian household is active in more than nine programs. Consumers who belong to a loyalty program are 70 percent more likely to recommend the goods or services of loyalty program's provider to friends and family.[6] Loyalty marketing, which was popularized by the airline industry through its frequent flyer programs, enables companies to strategically invest sales promotion dollars in activities designed to capture greater profits from customers already loyal to the product or company. The oldest loyalty program in Canada is Canadian Tire money, and Canada's largest loyalty program is Air Miles.

Studies show consumer loyalty is on the decline. Only 12 to 15 percent of customers are loyal to a single retailer, according to the Center for Retail Management at Northwestern University. However up to 70 percent of company sales can be generated from that small group of loyal customers.[7] Research from Forrester shows that 54 percent of primary grocery shoppers belong to two or more supermarket loyalty programs. Although their multiple memberships speak to the popularity of loyalty cards, it also shows that customers are pledging their so-called loyalty to more than one store: 15 percent of primary grocery shoppers are cardholders in at least three programs.[8]

Through loyalty programs, shoppers receive discounts, alerts on new products, and other types of enticing offers. In exchange, retailers are able to build

In January 2006, Kraft Hockeyville was launched, providing communities across Canada with a unique opportunity to host a National Hockey League (NHL) pre-season game in their local arena by nominating their community as being Kraft Hockeyville, the place where hockey lives in Canada. The 2011 winner was Conception Bay South, Newfoundland and Labrador.

customer databases that help them better understand customer preferences. One of the most successful Canadian loyalty programs is the Shoppers Drug Mart Optimum Program. Shoppers Drug Mart listened to consumers who said they wanted a simple program with easily redeemable points that saved them money on everyday purchases. Shoppers Drug Mart in turn learns a great deal about its customers' shopping preferences and behaviours, which can be a valuable source of data for new product development, product line expansion, and promotions.

Cobranded credit cards are an increasingly popular loyalty marketing tool. In a recent year, almost one billion direct-marketing appeals for a cobranded credit card were sent to potential customers. Royal Bank, Scotiabank, Canadian Tire, Costco, Holt Renfrew, and Aeroplan are only a few of the companies sponsoring cobranded Visa, MasterCard, or American Express cards. Companies are increasingly using the Internet to build customer loyalty through email and blogs. More than 80 percent of supermarket chains are using email to register customers for their loyalty programs and to entice them with coupons, flyers, and promotional campaigns.[9]

The QR code on a product is ideal for retailers because it increases consumer engagement, thereby likely to also increase sales. It is also a good point-of-purchase product advertising tool because, like a silent salesperson, it provides consumers with all the information they need to make a purchase decision.

Contests and Sweepstakes

Contests and sweepstakes are generally designed to create interest in a good or service and, thereby, to encourage brand switching. *Contests* are promotions in which participants use some skill or ability to compete for prizes. A consumer contest usually requires entrants to submit a proof of purchase and answer questions, complete sentences, or write a paragraph about the product. Winning a *sweepstakes*, on the other hand, depends on chance, and participation is free. Sweepstakes usually draw about 10 times more entries than contests do. Online contests and sweepstakes are increasingly popular because of consumers' increased use of the Internet and the ease with which they can participate.

While contests and sweepstakes may draw considerable interest and publicity, they are generally not effective tools for generating long-term sales. To increase their effectiveness, sales promotion managers must make certain the award will appeal to the target market. Offering several smaller prizes to many winners instead of one huge prize to just one person often will increase the effectiveness of the promotion, but there's no denying the attractiveness of a jackpot-type prize. Tim Hortons' classic RRRoll Up the Rim to Win is an example of a sweepstakes that combines both large and small prizes to ensure many winners.

Sampling

Sampling allows the customer to try a product or service for free. Sampling can increase retail sales by as much as 40 percent, so it's no surprise that sampling has increased more than 20 percent annually in recent years.[10]

Samples can be directly mailed to the customer, delivered door-to-door, packaged with another product, or demonstrated or distributed at a retail store or service outlet. Sampling at special events is a popular, effective, and high-profile distribution method that permits marketers to piggyback onto fun-based consumer activities—including sporting events, college fests, fairs and festivals, beach events, and chili cook-offs.

Distributing samples to specific types of locations, such as health clubs, churches, or doctors' offices, is

> **sampling** a promotional program that allows the consumer the opportunity to try a product or service for free

one of the most efficient methods of sampling. What better way to get consumers to try a product than to offer a sample exactly when it is needed most? Frequent visitors to a health club are likely good prospects for a health-food product or vitamin supplement. At the end of an exercise class, health club instructors hand out not only these products but also body wash, deodorant, and face cloths to sweating participants.

Point-of-Purchase Promotion

Point-of-purchase (P-O-P) promotion includes any promotional display set up at the retailer's location to build traffic, advertise the product, or induce impulse buying. Point-of-purchase promotions include *shelf talkers* (signs attached to store shelves), shelf extenders (attachments that extend shelves so products stand out), ads on grocery carts and bags, end-of-aisle and floor-stand displays, television monitors at supermarket checkout counters, in-store audio messages, and audiovisual displays. One big advantage of P-O-P promotion is that it offers manufacturers a captive audience in retail stores. Another advantage is that between 70 and 80 percent of all retail purchase decisions are made in-store, so P-O-P promotions can be very effective, increasing sales by as much as 65 percent. Strategies to increase sales include adding header or riser cards, changing messages on base or case wraps, adding inflatable or digital displays, and using signs that advertise the brand's sports, movie, or charity tie-in.[11] The use of digital technology in store is being increasingly accepted by consumers as long as it continues to add value. Metro, the grocery retailer, recently installed digital display kiosks in select stores in Ontario. The kiosk has an LCD screen that loops 30-second videos of a meal being prepared. Consumers can use the touch screen display to search for a recipe amongst the 3,000 preloaded recipes by a number of search criterion. Brands can also advertise on the screens.[12]

Online Sales Promotion

Online sales promotions have expanded dramatically in recent years. Marketers are now spending billions of dollars annually on such promotions because they have

Trade shows and conventions are an increasingly important part of sales promotion; they are an effective way to introduce new products to the marketplace.

ALAN MARSH/FIRST LIGHT

COURTESY OF PEPSICO FOODS CANADA

proved to be effective and cost-efficient, generating response rates three to five times higher than those of their off-line counterparts. The most effective types of online sales promotions are free merchandise, sweepstakes, free shipping with purchases, and coupons.

Because today's consumer is web-savvy and mobile-savvy, promotions need to incorporate an online component to engage them. A great example of this is the Doritos® Guru promotion. The target audience was teens, and Doritos® wanted a new way to engage them. The contest asked consumers to create an ad and name the new flavour that Doritos® was distributing in a plain white bag. Consumer awareness of the contest was generated both through social media and conventional advertising methods. All messages drove the consumer to the contest website to learn more about the program and how to enter.

LO3 Tools for Trade Sales Promotion

Whereas consumer promotions *pull* a product through the channel by creating demand, trade promotions *push* a product through the distribution channel (see Chapter 12). When selling to members of the distribution channel, manufacturers use many of the same sales promotion tools used in consumer promotions—such as sales contests, premiums, and point-of-purchase displays. Several tools, however, are unique to manufacturers and intermediaries.

▸▸ *Trade allowances:* A **trade allowance** is a price reduction offered by manufacturers to intermediaries such as wholesalers and retailers. The price reduction or rebate is given in exchange for a specific activity, such as allocating space for a new product or buying a product during a promotional period. For example, a local Future Shop outlet could receive a special discount for running its own promotion on Sony surround sound systems.

▸▸ *Push money:* Intermediaries receive **push money** as a bonus for pushing the manufacturer's brand through the distribution channel. Often the push money is directed toward a retailer's salespeople. LinoColor, the leading high-end scanner company, produces a Picture Perfect Rewards catalogue filled with merchandise retailers can purchase with points accrued for every LinoColor scanner they sell.

▸▸ *Training:* Sometimes a manufacturer will train an intermediary's personnel if the product is rather complex—as frequently occurs in the computer and telecommunications industries. For example, representatives of a TV manufacturer such as Toshiba may train salespeople how to demonstrate to consumers the new features of the latest TV models.

▸▸ *Free merchandise:* Often a manufacturer offers retailers free merchandise in lieu of quantity discounts. Occasionally, free merchandise is used as payment for trade allowances normally provided through other sales promotions. Instead of giving a retailer a price reduction for buying a certain quantity of merchandise, the manufacturer may throw in extra merchandise for free (that is, at a cost that would equal the price reduction).

▸▸ *Store demonstrations:* Manufacturers can also arrange with retailers to perform an in-store demonstration. Food manufacturers often send representatives to grocery stores and supermarkets to let customers sample a product while shopping.

▸▸ *Business meetings, conventions, and trade shows:* Trade association meetings, conferences, and conventions are an important aspect of sales promotion and a growing, multibillion-dollar market. At these shows, manufacturers, distributors, and other vendors can display their goods and describe their services to customers and potential customers. Trade shows have been uniquely effective in introducing new products; they can establish products in the marketplace more quickly than advertising, direct marketing, or sales calls. Companies participate in trade shows to attract and identify new prospects, serve current customers, introduce new products, increase corporate image, test the market response to new products, enhance corporate morale, and gather competitive product information.

trade allowance a price reduction offered by manufacturers to intermediaries, such as wholesalers and retailers

push money money offered to channel intermediaries to encourage them to push products—that is, to encourage other members of the channel to sell the products

Trade promotions are popular among manufacturers for many reasons. Trade sales promotion tools help manufacturers gain new distributors for their products, obtain wholesaler and retailer support for consumer sales promotions, build or reduce dealer inventories, and improve trade relations. Car manufacturers annually sponsor dozens of auto shows for consumers. The shows attract millions of consumers, providing dealers with both increased store traffic and good leads.

LO4 Personal Selling

As mentioned in Chapter 14, *personal selling* is direct communication between a sales representative and one or more prospective buyers in an attempt to influence each other in a purchase situation. In a sense, all businesspeople are salespeople. An individual may become a plant manager, a chemist, an engineer, or a member of any profession and yet still have to sell. During a job search, applicants must sell themselves to prospective employers in an interview.

Personal selling offers several advantages over other forms of promotion. Personal selling may also work better than other forms of promotion given certain customer and product characteristics. Generally speaking, personal selling becomes more important as the number of potential customers decreases, as the complexity of the product increases, and as the value of the product grows (see Exhibit 17.2). For highly complex goods, such as business jets or private communication systems, a salesperson is needed to determine the prospective customer's needs, explain the product's basic advantages, propose the exact features

▸▸ Personal selling provides a detailed explanation or demonstration of the product. This capability is especially needed for goods and services that are complex or new.

▸▸ The sales message can be varied according to the motivations and interests of each prospective customer. Moreover, when the prospect has questions or raises objections, the salesperson is there to provide explanations. In contrast, advertising and sales promotion can only respond to the objections the copywriter thinks are important to customers.

▸▸ Personal selling can be directed only to qualified prospects. Other forms of promotion include some unavoidable waste because many people in the audience are not prospective customers.

▸▸ Personal selling costs can be controlled by adjusting the size of the sales force (and resulting expenses) in one-person increments. On the other hand, advertising and sales promotion must often be purchased in fairly large amounts.

▸▸ Perhaps the most important advantage is that personal selling is considerably more effective than other forms of promotion in obtaining a sale and gaining a satisfied customer.

and accessories that will meet the client's needs, and establish a support plan for installation and/or use.

LO5 Relationship Selling

Until recently, marketing theory and practice concerning personal selling focused almost entirely on a planned presentation to prospective customers for the sole purpose of making the sale. Marketers were most concerned with making a one-time sale and then moving on to the next prospect. Traditional personal selling methods attempted to persuade the buyer to accept a point of view or to convince the buyer to take some action. Frequently, the objectives of the salesperson were at the expense of the buyer, creating a win–lose outcome. Although this type of sales approach has not disappeared entirely, it is used less frequently by professional salespeople.

relationship selling (consultative selling) a multistage sales process that involves building, maintaining, and enhancing interactions with customers for the purpose of developing long-term satisfaction through mutually beneficial partnerships

EXHIBIT 17.2

Comparison of Personal Selling and Advertising/Sales Promotion

Personal selling is more important when...	Advertising and sales promotion are more important when...
The product has a high value.	The product has a low value.
It is a custom-made product.	It is a standardized product.
There are few customers.	There are many customers.
The product is technically complex.	The product is easy to understand.
Customers are concentrated.	Customers are geographically dispersed.
Examples: insurance policies, custom windows, airplane engines	**Examples:** soap, magazine subscriptions, cotton T-shirts

In contrast, modern views of personal selling emphasize the relationship that develops between a salesperson and a buyer. **Relationship selling**, or **consultative selling**, is a multistage sales process that involves building, maintaining, and enhancing interactions with customers for the purpose of developing long-term satisfaction through mutually beneficial partnerships. It typically emphasizes personalization and empathy as key ingredients when identifying prospects and developing them as long-term, satisfied customers. With relationship selling, the objective is to build long-term branded relationships with consumers and buyers. Thus, the focus is on building mutual trust between the buyer and seller through the delivery of anticipated, long-term, value-added benefits to the buyer.

Relationship or consultative salespeople, therefore, need to become consultants, partners, and problem solvers for their customers. They strive to build long-term relationships with key accounts by developing trust over time. The emphasis shifts from a one-time sale to a long-term relationship in which the salesperson works with the customer to develop solutions for enhancing the customer's bottom line. Research has shown that positive customer–salesperson relationships contribute to trust, increased customer loyalty, and the intent to continue the relationship with the salesperson.[13] Thus, relationship selling promotes a win–win situation for both buyer and seller. The immediacy of communication provided by email and mobile messaging allows the relationship between buyer and seller to develop more quickly and strengthen sooner.

The end result of relationship selling tends to be loyal customers who purchase from the company time after time. A relationship-selling strategy focused on retaining customers costs a company less than constantly prospecting and selling to new customers.

Relationship selling is more typical with selling situations for installation goods, such as heavy machinery or computer systems, and services, such as airlines and insurance, than for consumer goods. Exhibit 17.3 lists the key differences between traditional personal selling and relationship or consultative selling. These differences will become more apparent as we explore the personal selling process later in the chapter.

EXHIBIT 17.3

Key Differences between Traditional Selling and Relationship Selling

Traditional Personal Selling	Relationship or Consultative Selling
Sell products (goods and services)	Sell advice, assistance, and counsel
Focus on closing sales	Focus on improving the customer's bottom line
Limited sales planning	Consider sales planning as top priority
Spend most contact time telling customers about product	Spend most contact time attempting to build a problem-solving environment with the customer
Conduct product-specific needs assessment	Conduct discovery in the full scope of the customer's operations
Lone wolf approach to the account	Team approach to the account
Proposals and presentations are based on pricing and product features	Proposals and presentations are based on profit impact and strategic benefits to the customer
Sales follow-up is short term, focused on product delivery	Sales follow-up is long term, focused on long-term relationship enhancement

SOURCE: Robert M. Peterson, Patrick L. Schul, and George H. Lucas, Jr., "Consultative Selling: Walking the Walk in the New Selling Environment," National Conference on Sales Management, *Proceedings*, 140–41, March 1996.

LO 6 Steps in the Selling Process

Completing a sale actually requires several steps. The **sales process**, or **sales cycle**, is simply the set of steps a salesperson goes through to sell a particular product or service. The sales process or cycle can be unique for each product or service, depending on the features of the product or service, the characteristics of customer segments, and the internal processes in place within the firm, such as how leads are gathered.

Some sales take only a few minutes, but others may take much longer to complete. Sales of technical products such as a Boeing or Airbus airplane and customized goods and services typically take many months, perhaps even years, to complete. On the other end of the spectrum, sales of less technical products such as stationery are generally more routine and may take only a few days. Whether a salesperson spends a few minutes or a few years on a sale, seven basic steps comprise the personal selling process:

1. Generating leads
2. Qualifying leads
3. Approaching the customer and probing needs
4. Developing and proposing solutions
5. Handling objections
6. Closing the sale
7. Following up

Like other forms of promotion, these steps of selling follow the AIDA concept discussed in Chapter 14. Once a salesperson has located a prospect with the authority to buy, he or she tries to get the prospect's

sales process (sales cycle) the set of steps a salesperson goes through to sell a particular product or service

© ISTOCKPHOTO.COM/RYAN BALDERAS

IT COSTS BUSINESSES SIX TIMES MORE TO **GAIN A NEW CUSTOMER** THAN TO RETAIN A CURRENT ONE.

lead generation (prospecting) identification of those firms and people most likely to buy the seller's offerings

referral a recommendation to a salesperson from a customer or business associate

networking the use of friends, business contacts, coworkers, acquaintances, and fellow members in professional and civic organizations to identify potential clients

cold calling a form of lead generation in which the salesperson approaches potential buyers without any prior knowledge of the prospects' needs or financial status

attention. The salesperson can generate interest through an effective sales proposal and presentation that have been developed after a thorough needs assessment. After developing the customer's initial desire (preferably during the presentation of the sales proposal), the salesperson closes by trying to get an agreement to buy. Follow-up after the sale, the final step in the selling process, not only lowers cognitive dissonance (refer to Chapter 5) but also may open up opportunities to discuss future sales. Effective follow-up can also lead to repeat business in which the process may start all over again at the needs assessment step.

Traditional selling and relationship selling follow the same basic steps. They differ in the relative importance placed on key steps in the process. Traditional selling efforts are transaction oriented, focusing on generating as many leads as possible, making as many presentations as possible, and closing as many sales as possible. Minimal effort is placed on asking questions to identify customer needs and wants or matching these needs and wants to the benefits of the product or service. In contrast, the salesperson practising relationship selling emphasizes an upfront investment in the time and effort needed to uncover each customer's specific needs and wants and meet them with the product or service offering. By doing the homework upfront, the salesperson creates the conditions necessary for a relatively straightforward close. Let's look at each step of the selling process individually.

Step 1: Generating Leads

Initial groundwork must precede communication between the potential buyer and the salesperson. **Lead generation**, or **prospecting**, is the identification of those firms and people most likely to buy the seller's offerings. These firms or people become sales leads or prospects.

Sales leads can be obtained in several different ways, most notably through websites, advertising, trade shows and conventions, and direct-mail telemarketing and Web-based telemarketing. Favourable publicity also helps to create leads. Company records of past client purchases are another excellent source of leads.

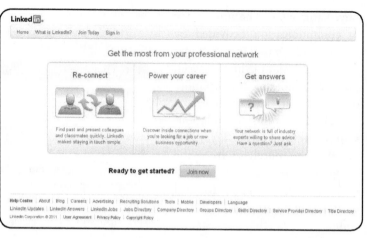

Another way to gather a lead is through a **referral**—a recommendation from a customer or business associate. The advantages of referrals over other forms of prospecting include highly qualified leads, higher closing rates, larger initial transactions, and shorter sales cycles. Referrals typically are as much as 10 times more productive in generating sales than are cold calls. Unfortunately, although most clients are willing to give referrals, many salespeople do not ask for them. Effective sales training can help to overcome this reluctance to ask for referrals.

Networking is using friends, business contacts, coworkers, acquaintances, and fellow members in professional and civic organizations to identify potential clients. Indeed, some national networking clubs have been started for the sole purpose of generating leads and providing valuable business advice. Increasingly, sales professionals are also using online networking sites such as LinkedIn to connect with targeted leads and clients around the world, 24 hours a day. LinkedIn is a business social networking site with more than 80 million registered users. LinkedIn allows its members to exchange knowledge, ideas, and opportunities in an online forum, 24 hours a day, 7 days a week.

Before the advent of more sophisticated methods of lead generation, such as direct mail and websites, most prospecting was done through **cold calling**—a form of lead generation in which the salesperson approaches potential buyers without any prior knowledge of the prospects' needs or financial status. Although this method is still used, many sales managers have realized the inefficiencies of having their top salespeople use their valuable selling time searching for the proverbial needle in a haystack. Passing the job of cold calling to a lower-cost employee, typically an internal sales support person, allows salespeople to spend their time more effectively by using their relationship-building skills on already identified prospects.

Step 2: Qualifying Leads

When a prospect shows interest in learning more about a product, the salesperson has the opportunity to follow up, or qualify, the lead.

Lead qualification involves determining whether the prospect has three factors:

1. *A recognized need:* The most basic criterion for determining whether someone is a prospect for a product is a need that is not being satisfied. The salesperson should first consider prospects who are aware of a need but should not discount prospects who have not yet recognized that they have a need. With a little more information about the product, such prospects may decide they do have a need for it. Preliminary interviews and questioning can often provide the salesperson with enough information to determine whether a need exists.

2. *Buying power:* Buying power involves both the authority to make the purchase decision and access to funds to pay for it. To avoid wasting time and money, the salesperson needs to identify the purchasing authority and the ability to pay before making a presentation. Organizational charts and information about a firm's credit standing can provide valuable clues.

3. *Receptivity and accessibility:* The prospect must be willing to see the salesperson and must be accessible to the salesperson. Some prospects simply refuse to see salespeople. Others, because of their stature in their organization, will see only a salesperson or sales manager with similar stature.

Personal visits to unqualified prospects wastes valuable salesperson time and company resources. Often the task of lead qualification is handled by a telemarketing group or a sales support person who *prequalifies* the lead for the salesperson. Prequalification systems relieve sales representatives from the time-consuming task of following up on leads to determine need, buying power, and receptivity. Prequalification systems may even set up initial appointments for the prospect and the salesperson to meet. The result is more time for the sales force to spend in front of interested customers who will answer the salesperson's questions, value their time, and be realistic about money and when they are prepared to buy. To assist in the task of qualifying leads, software is increasingly being used.

Companies are increasingly using their websites to qualify leads. When qualifying leads online, companies want visitors to register, indicate the products and services they are interested in, and provide information on their time frame and resources. Leads from the Internet can then be prioritized (those indicating a short time frame, for instance, are given a higher priority) and then transferred to salespeople. Enticing visitors to register also enables companies to customize their future electronic interactions.

Step 3: Approaching the Customer and Probing Needs

Before approaching the customer, the salesperson should learn as much as possible about the prospect's organization and its buyers. This process, called the **preapproach**, describes the research the salesperson must do before contacting a prospect. This research may include consulting standard reference sources, such as *The Financial Post Survey of Industrials, The Blue Book of Canadian Business, Scott's Directories*; visiting websites such as www.cbr.ca, or www.fpinfomart.ca; or contacting acquaintances or others who may have information about the prospect. Another preapproach task is to determine whether the actual approach should be a personal visit, a phone call, an email, or some other form of communication. During the sales approach, the salesperson

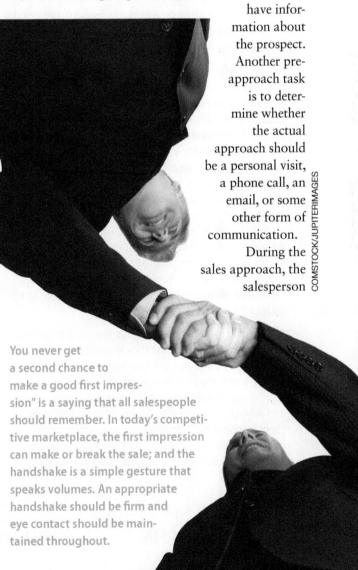

You never get a second chance to make a good first impression" is a saying that all salespeople should remember. In today's competitive marketplace, the first impression can make or break the sale; and the handshake is a simple gesture that speaks volumes. An appropriate handshake should be firm and eye contact should be maintained throughout.

COMSTOCK/JUPITERIMAGES

needs assessment
a determination of the customer's specific needs and wants and the range of options the customer has for satisfying them

either talks to the prospect or secures an appointment for a future time to probe the prospect further as to his or her needs. Relationship-selling theorists suggest that salespeople should begin developing mutual trust with their prospect during the approach. Salespeople must sell themselves before they can sell the product. Small talk that projects sincerity and some suggestion of friendship is encouraged to build rapport with the prospect, but remarks that could be construed as insincere should be avoided.

The salesperson's ultimate goal during the approach is to conduct a **needs assessment**, a determination of the customer's specific needs and wants and the range of options the customer has for satisfying them. In other words, the salesperson needs to find out as much as possible about the prospect's situation. The salesperson should determine how to maximize the fit between what the firm can offer and what the prospective customer wants. As part of the needs assessment, the consultative salesperson must know everything there is to know about the following:

▶▶ *The product or service:* Product knowledge is the cornerstone for conducting a successful needs analysis. The consultative salesperson must be an expert on his or her product or service, including technical specifications, the product's features and benefits, pricing and billing procedures, warranty and service support, performance comparisons with the competition, other customers' experiences with the product, and current advertising and promotional campaign messages. For example, a salesperson who is attempting to sell a computer network system to a doctor's office should be very knowledgeable about the various computers available for the doctor to purchase to install as part of the network, the capabilities of the computers, technical specifications, installation time, postpurchase service, and other related issues.

▶▶ *Customers and their needs:* The salesperson should know more about customers than they know about themselves. That's the secret to relationship and consultative selling, where the salesperson acts not only as a supplier of products and services but also as a trusted consultant and adviser. The professional salesperson brings each client business-building ideas and solutions to problems. For example, a computer system salesperson who asks the right questions should be able to identify areas where the doctor is being unproductive or where mistakes are being made due to the lack of computerization of the office or lack of staff training. The computer salesperson can act as a consultant, advising how the doctor's office can save money and time and be more efficient and effective with patients.

▶▶ *The competition:* The salesperson must know as much about the competitor's company and products as he or she knows about his or her own company. *Competitive intelligence* includes many factors: who the competitors are and what is known about them, how their products and services compare, advantages and disadvantages, and strengths and weaknesses.

▶▶ *The industry:* Knowing the industry involves active research on the part of the salesperson, which means attending industry and trade association meetings, reading articles published in industry and trade journals, keeping current with legislation and regulation that affect the industry, awareness of product alternatives and innovations from domestic and foreign competition, and having a feel for economic and financial conditions that may affect the industry. It is also important to be aware of economic downturns because businesses may be looking for less expensive financing options.

Creating a *customer profile* during the approach helps salespeople optimize their time and resources. This profile is then used to help develop an intelligent analysis of the prospect's needs in preparation for the next step, developing and proposing solutions. Customer profile information is typically stored and manipulated using sales force automation software packages designed for use on laptop computers. This software provides sales reps with a computerized and efficient method of collecting customer information for use during the entire sales process. Further, customer and sales data stored in a computer database can be easily shared among sales team members. The information can also be appended with industry statistics, sales or meeting notes, billing data, and other information that may be pertinent to the prospect or the prospect's company. The more salespeople know about their prospects, the better they can meet their needs.

Salespeople should wrap up their sales approach and need-probing mission by summarizing the prospect's need, problem, and interest. The salesperson should also get a commitment from the customer regarding some kind of action, whether it's reading

"THE **MORE** SALESPEOPLE KNOW ABOUT THEIR **PROSPECTS,** THE **BETTER** THEY CAN MEET THEIR NEEDS."

promotional material or agreeing to a demonstration. This commitment helps to further qualify the prospect and justifies additional time invested by the salesperson. The salesperson should reiterate the action he or she promises to take, such as sending information or calling back to provide answers to questions. At the conclusion of the sales approach, the salesperson should set the date and time of the next call and draft an agenda for the next call in terms of what the salesperson hopes to accomplish, such as providing a demonstration or presenting a solution.

Step 4: Developing and Proposing Solutions

Once the salesperson has gathered the appropriate information about the client's needs and wants, the next step is to determine whether his or her company's products or services match the needs of the prospective customer. The salesperson then develops a solution, or possibly several solutions, in which the salesperson's product or service solves the client's problems or meets a specific need.

These solutions are typically presented to the client in the form of a sales proposal presented at a sales presentation. A **sales proposal** is a written document or professional presentation that outlines how the company's product or service will meet or exceed the client's needs. The **sales presentation** is the formal meeting in which the salesperson presents the sales proposal to a prospective buyer. The presentation should be explicitly tied to the prospect's expressed needs. Further, the prospect should be involved in the presentation by being encouraged to participate in demonstrations or by exposure to computer exercises, slides, video or audio, flipcharts, photographs, and the like. Technology has become an important part of presenting solutions for many salespeople.

Because the salesperson often has only one opportunity to present solutions, the quality of both the sales proposal and presentation can make or break the sale. Salespeople must be able to present the proposal and handle any customer objections confidently and professionally. To deliver a powerful presentation, salespeople must be well prepared, use direct eye contact, ask open-ended questions, be poised, use hand gestures and voice inflection, focus on the customer's needs, incorporate visual elements that impart valuable information, know how to operate the audiovisual or computer equipment being used for the presentation, and ensure the equipment works.[14]

Nothing dies faster than a boring presentation. Often customers are more likely to remember how salespeople presented themselves than what they said.

Step 5: Handling Objections

Rarely does a prospect say "I'll buy it" right after a presentation. Instead, the prospect often raises objections or asks questions about the proposal and the product. The potential buyer may engage in a negotiation-type dialogue by insisting that the price is too high or that the good or service will not satisfy the present need.

One of the first lessons that every salesperson learns is that objections to the product should not be taken personally as confrontations or insults. A good salesperson considers objections a legitimate part of the purchase decision. To handle objections effectively, the salesperson should anticipate specific objections such as concerns about price, fully investigate the objection with the customer, be aware of what the competition is offering, and, above all, stay calm.

This highly sensitive situation requires skill because the salesperson must handle the objection without appearing argumentative. The best method for handling the objection is to probe for the exact nature of the obstacle and then use dialogue to jointly work toward a mutually satisfying solution.

sales proposal a formal written document or professional presentation that outlines how the salesperson's product or service will meet or exceed the prospect's needs

sales presentation a formal meeting in which the salesperson presents a sales proposal to a prospective buyer

PHOTODISC/GETTY IMAGES

If the salesperson is not confident in handling objections during the presentation, it is best to be honest, acknowledge the objection, and communicate to the buyer that he or she will get back to the customer with a possible solution.

Step 6: Closing the Sale

At the end of the presentation, the salesperson should ask the customer how he or she would like to proceed. If the customer exhibits signs of being ready to purchase, and all questions have been answered and objections have been met, then the salesperson can try to close the sale. Customers often give signals during or after the presentation that they are ready to buy or are not interested. Examples include facial expressions, gestures, and questions asked. The salesperson should look for these signals and respond appropriately.

Closing requires courage and skill. A salesperson should keep an open mind when asking for the sale and be prepared for either a yes or a no. The typical salesperson makes several hundred sales calls a year, many of which are repeat calls to the same client in an attempt to make a sale. Building a good relationship with the customer is very important. Often, if the salesperson has developed a strong relationship with the customer, only minimal efforts are needed to close a sale.

Negotiation often plays a key role in the closing of the sale. **Negotiation** is the process during which both the salesperson and the prospect offer special concessions in an attempt to arrive at a sales agreement. For example, the salesperson may offer a price cut, free installation, or a trial order. Effective negotiators, however, avoid using price as a negotiation tool. Because companies spend millions on advertising and product development to create value, when salespeople give in to price negotiations too quickly, they decrease the value of the product. Instead, effective salespeople should emphasize value to the customer, rendering price a nonissue. Salespeople should also be prepared to ask for trade-offs and should try to avoid giving unilateral concessions. Moreover, if the customer asks for a 5 percent discount, the salesperson should ask for something in return, such as higher volume or more flexibility in delivery schedules.

More and more Canadian companies are expanding their marketing and selling efforts into global markets. Salespeople selling in foreign markets should tailor their presentation and closing styles to each market. Different personalities and skills will be successful in some countries and absolute failures in others. For instance, if a salesperson is an excellent closer and always focuses on the next sale, doing business in Latin America might be difficult because Latin Americans typically want to take a long time building a personal relationship with their suppliers.

Step 7: Following Up

Salespeople's responsibilities do not end with making the sales and placing the orders. One of the most important aspects of their jobs is **follow-up**—the final step in the selling process, in which they must ensure that delivery schedules are met, that the goods or services perform as promised, and that the buyers' employees are properly trained to use the products.

In the traditional sales approach, follow-up with the customer is generally limited to successful product delivery and performance. A basic goal of relationship selling is to motivate customers to come back, again and again, by developing and nurturing long-term relationships. Exhibit 17.4 depicts the time requirements involved in the sales process and the relationship of high and low time expenditures in traditional and relationship selling approaches.

Most businesses depend on repeat sales, and repeat sales depend on thorough and continued follow-up by the salesperson. When customers feel abandoned, cognitive dissonance arises, and repeat sales decline.

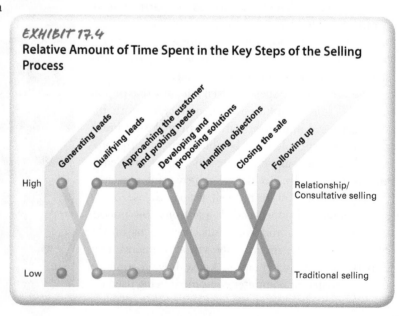

EXHIBIT 17.4
Relative Amount of Time Spent in the Key Steps of the Selling Process

Today, this issue is more pertinent than ever because customers are far less loyal to brands and vendors. Buyers are more inclined to look for the best deal, especially in the case of poor after-the-sale follow-up. Automated email follow-up marketing—a combination of sales automation and Internet technology—is enhancing customer satisfaction and generating more business for some marketers. After the initial contact with a prospect, a software program automatically sends a series of personalized emails over a period of time.

The Impact of Technology on Personal Selling

Will the increasingly sophisticated technology now available at marketers' fingertips eliminate the need for salespeople? Experts agree that a relationship between the salesperson and customer will always be necessary. Technology, however, can certainly help to improve that relationship. Cellphones, laptops, pagers, email, and electronic organizers allow salespeople to be more accessible to both clients and the company. Moreover, the Internet provides salespeople with vast resources of information on clients, competitors, and the industry. All of these new technologies, if used properly, can improve the effectiveness and efficiency of the salesperson.

E-business, or buying, selling, marketing, collaborating with partners, and servicing customers electronically using the Internet, has had a significant impact on personal selling. Virtually all large companies and most medium and small companies are involved in e-commerce and consider it to be necessary to compete in today's marketplace. For customers, the Web has become a powerful tool, providing accurate and up-to-date information on products, pricing, and order status. The Internet also cost-effectively processes orders and services requests. Although on the surface the Internet might look like a threat to the job security of salespeople, the Web actually releases sales reps from tedious administrative tasks, such as shipping catalogues, placing routine orders, or tracking orders. The result is more time to focus on the needs of their clients.

70%
Percentage of retail purchase decisions made in-store

999,368
Votes declaring Conception Bay South, Newfoundland and Labrador, the most passionate hockey town in Kraft's Hockeyville 2011 contest

Percentage of Canadians who would increase their coupon use in a slow economy
70%

1958
Year Canadian Tire introduced Canadian Tire money

7
Steps in the selling process

40
Number of Toyota RAVs Tim Hortons gave away during the 2010 RRRoll Up the-Rim to Win contest

Trying to set the right price is one of the most stressful and pressure-filled tasks of the marketing manager.

AFTER YOU FINISH THIS CHAPTER, GO TO WWW.ICANMKTG2.COM FOR STUDY TOOLS.

LO 1 The Importance of Price

Price means one thing to the consumer and something else to the seller. To the consumer, price is the cost of something. To the seller, price is revenue, the primary source of profits. In the broadest sense, price allocates resources in a free-market economy. Marketing managers are frequently challenged by the task of price setting.

price that which is given up in an exchange to acquire a good or service

What Is Price?

Price is that which is given up in an exchange to acquire a good or service. Price is typically the money exchanged for the good or service. Price may also include the time lost while waiting to acquire the good or service. For those who lose their jobs and must rely on charity, price might also include their lost dignity.

Consumers are interested in obtaining a reasonable price, which refers to the perceived reasonable value at the time of the transaction. The price paid is based on the satisfaction consumers *expect* to receive from a product and not necessarily the satisfaction they *actually* receive. Price can relate to anything with perceived

What do you think?

Buying an expensive brand of clothing makes me feel sophisticated.

| 1 | 2 | 3 | 4 | 5 | 6 | 7 |

STRONGLY DISAGREE   STRONGLY AGREE

© ISTOCKPHOTO.COM/KTSIMAGE

value, not just money. When goods and services are exchanged, the trade is called *barter*.

The Importance of Price to Marketing Managers

Prices are the key to revenues, which in turn are the key to profits for an organization. **Revenue** is the price charged to customers multiplied by the number of units sold. Revenue is what pays for every activity of the company: production, finance, sales, distribution, and so on. What's left over (if anything) is **profit**. Managers usually strive to charge a price that will earn a fair profit.

$$\text{Revenue} = \frac{\text{Price}}{\text{Unit}} \times \text{Units}$$

$$\text{Profit} = \text{Revenue} - \text{Expenses}$$

To earn a profit, managers must choose a price that is not too high or too low, a price that equals the perceived value to target consumers. If, in consumers' minds, a price is set too high, the perceived value will be less than the cost, and sale opportunities will be lost. Conversely, if a price is too low, the consumer may perceive it as a great value, but the firm loses revenue it could have earned.

Trying to set the right price is one of the most stressful and pressure-filled tasks of the marketing manager, as attested to by the following trends in the consumer market:

▸▸ Confronting a flood of new products, potential buyers carefully evaluate the price of each one against the value of existing products.

▸▸ The increased availability of bargain-priced private and generic brands has put downward pressure on overall prices.

▸▸ Many firms are trying to maintain or regain their market share by cutting prices.

▸▸ The Internet has made comparison shopping easier.

In the business market, buyers are also becoming more price sensitive and better informed. Computerized information systems enable organizational buyers to compare price and performance with great ease and accuracy. Improved communication and the increased use of direct marketing and computer-aided selling have also opened up many markets to new competitors. Finally, competition in general is increasing, so some installations, accessories, and component parts are being marketed as indistinguishable commodities.

LO 2 Pricing Objectives

To survive in today's highly competitive marketplace, companies need pricing objectives that are SMART (specific, measurable, attainable, relevant, and time-related). Realistic pricing goals then require periodic monitoring to determine the effectiveness of the company's strategy. For convenience, pricing objectives can be divided into three categories: profit oriented, sales oriented, and status quo.

Profit-Oriented Pricing Objectives

Profit-oriented objectives include profit maximization, satisfactory profits, and target return on investment.

Profit Maximization *Profit maximization* means setting prices so that total revenue is as large as possible relative to total costs. Profit maximization does not always signify unreasonably high prices, however. Both price and profits depend on the type of competitive environment a firm faces, such as whether it is in a monopoly position (i.e., the firm is the only seller) or in a much more competitive situation. Also, remember that a firm cannot charge a price higher than the product's perceived value. Many firms do not have the accounting data they need to maximize their profits.

Sometimes managers say that their company is trying to maximize profits; in other words, the company is trying to make as much money as possible. Although this goal may sound impressive to shareholders, it is not good enough for planning.

When attempting to maximize profits, managers can try to expand revenue by increasing customer satisfaction, or they can attempt to reduce costs by operating more efficiently. A third possibility is to attempt to do both. Recent research has shown that striving to enhance customer satisfaction leads to greater profitability (and customer satisfaction) than following a cost-reduction strategy or attempting to do both.[1] In other words, companies should consider allocating more resources to customer service initiatives, loyalty programs, and customer relationship management programs and allocating fewer resources to programs that are designed to improve efficiency and reduce costs. Both types of programs, of course, are critical to the success of the firm.

Satisfactory Profits Satisfactory profits are a reasonable level of profits. Rather than maximizing profits, many organizations strive for profits that are satisfactory to the shareholders and management—in other words, a level of profits consistent with the level of risk an organization faces. In a risky industry, a satisfactory profit may be 35 percent. In a low-risk industry, it might be 7 percent.

Target Return on Investment The most common profit objective is a target **return on investment (ROI)**, sometimes called the firm's return on total assets. ROI measures management's overall effectiveness in generating profits with the company's assets that have come from its investors. The higher the firm's ROI, the better off the firm is. Many companies use a target ROI as their main pricing goal. In summary, ROI is a percentage that puts a firm's profits into perspective by showing profits relative to investment.

Return on investment is calculated as follows:

$$\text{Return on investment (ROI)} = \frac{\text{Net profits (before taxes)}}{\text{Investment (owners' equity)}}$$

Assume that in 2011, Interior Tile Company, a small business in Alberta, had assets of $4.5 million, net profits of $550,000, and a target ROI of 10 percent. The following was the actual ROI:

$$\text{ROI} = \frac{\$550,000}{\$4,500,000}$$

$$= 12.2 \text{ percent}$$

As you can see, the ROI for Interior Tile Company exceeded its target, which indicates that the company prospered in 2011.

Comparing the 12.2 percent ROI with the industry average (11.2 percent) provides a more meaningful picture, however. Any ROI needs to be evaluated in terms of the competitive environment, risks in the industry, and economic conditions. Generally speaking, firms seek ROIs in the 10 to 30 percent range. In some industries, such as the grocery industry, however, a return of less than 5 percent is common and acceptable.

A company with a target ROI can predetermine its desired level of profitability. The

marketing manager can use the standard, such as 10 percent ROI, to determine whether a particular price and marketing mix are feasible. In addition, however, the manager must weigh the risk of a given strategy even if the return is in the acceptable range.

Sales-Oriented Pricing Objectives

Sales-oriented pricing objectives are based on either market share or dollar or unit sales.

Market Share **Market share** is a company's product sales as a percentage of total sales for that industry. Sales can be reported in dollars or in units of product. Knowing whether market share is expressed in revenue or units is important because the results may differ. Consider four companies competing in an industry with 2,000 total unit sales and total industry revenue of $4 million (see Exhibit 18.1). Company A has the largest unit market share at 50 percent, but it has only 25 percent of the revenue market share. In contrast, company D has only a 15 percent unit share but the largest revenue share: 30 percent. Usually, market share is expressed in terms of revenue and not units.

Many companies believe that maintaining or increasing market share is an indicator of the effectiveness of their marketing mix. Larger market shares have indeed often meant higher

return on investment (ROI)
ROI = Net Profits (before taxes) divided by the Investment (Owners' Equity)

market share a company's product sales as a percentage of total sales for that industry

EXHIBIT 18.1
Two Ways to Measure Market Share (Units and Revenue)

Company	Units Sold	Unit Price	Total Revenue	Unit Market Share	Revenue Market Share
A	1,000	$1,000	$1,000,000	50%	25%
B	200	4,000	800,000	10%	20%
C	500	2,000	1,000,000	25%	25%
D	300	4,000	1,200,000	15%	30%
Total	2,000		$4,000,000		

PROFITS DON'T AUTOMATICALLY FOLLOW FROM A LARGE MARKET SHARE.

Research organizations, such as Nielsen and Information Resources, Inc., provide excellent market share reports for many different industries. These reports enable companies to track their performance in various product categories over time.

Sales Maximization Rather than strive for market share, companies sometimes try to maximize sales. A firm with the objective of maximizing sales will ignore profits, competition, and the marketing environment as long as sales are rising.

If a company is strapped for funds or faces an uncertain future, it may try to generate a maximum amount of cash in the short run. Management's task when using this objective is to calculate which price–quantity relationship generates the greatest cash revenue. Sales maximization can also be effectively used on a temporary basis to sell off excess inventory.

Maximization of cash should never be a long-run objective because cash maximization may mean little or no profitability.

Status Quo Pricing Objectives

Status quo pricing seeks to maintain existing prices or to meet the competition's prices. This third category of pricing objectives has the major advantage of requiring little planning. It is essentially a passive policy.

Often, firms competing in an industry with an established price leader simply meet the competition's prices. These industries typically have fewer price wars than those with direct price competition. In other cases, managers regularly shop competitors' stores to ensure that their prices are comparable.

LO3 The Demand Determinant of Price

After marketing managers establish pricing goals, they must set specific prices to reach those goals. The price they set for each product depends mostly on two factors: the demand for the good or service and the cost to the seller for that good or service. When pricing

---

status quo pricing
a pricing objective that maintains existing prices or meets the competition's prices

profits, thanks to greater economies of scale, market power, and the ability to recruit and compensate top-quality management. Conventional wisdom also says that market share and return on investment are strongly related. For the most part they are; however, many companies with low market share survive and even prosper. To succeed with a low market share, companies need to compete in industries with slow growth and few product changes. Ferrari, the Italian sports car manufacturer, is one example of such a company. Otherwise, companies must vie in an industry that makes frequently purchased items, such as consumer convenience goods.

The conventional wisdom regarding market share and profitability isn't always reliable, however. Because of extreme competition in some industries, many market share leaders either do not reach their target ROI or actually lose money. Procter & Gamble switched from market share to ROI objectives after realizing that profits don't automatically follow as a result of a large market share. Still, for some companies, the struggle for market share can be all-consuming.

For decades, coffee and tea manufacturers have been locked in a struggle to dominate the hot beverage market. Numerous promotions, product extensions, and modifications have been tried in efforts to persuade drinkers to switch brands (or stay with their current brand). From 2000 to 2005, this industry lost some large manufacturers and grew by only 1.9 percent. But, niche manufacturers, such as Starbucks and some 40-plus small manufacturers, have had some success against the previous dominant companies in the industry, such as Folgers, Kraft Maxwell House, and others.

goals are mainly sales oriented, demand considerations usually dominate. Other factors, such as distribution and promotion strategies, perceived quality, demands of large customers, the Internet, and stage of the product life cycle, can also influence price.

The Nature of Demand

Demand is the quantity of a product that will be sold in the market at various prices for a specified period. The quantity of a product that people will buy depends on its price. The higher the price, the fewer goods or services consumers will demand. Conversely, the lower the price, the more goods or services they will demand.

This trend is illustrated in the following graph of the demand per week for gourmet cookies at a local retailer at various prices. This graph is called a *demand curve* (see Exhibit 18.2(a)). The vertical axis of the graph shows different prices of gourmet cookies, measured in dollars per package. The horizontal axis measures the quantity of gourmet cookies that will be demanded per week at each price. For example, at a price of $2.50, 50 packages will be sold per week; at $1, consumers will demand 120 packages—as the *demand schedule* shows (see Exhibit 18.2(b)).

Notice how the demand curve slopes downward and to the right, which indicates that more gourmet cookies are demanded as the price is lowered. In other words, if cookie manufacturers put a greater quantity on the market, then their hope of selling all of it will be realized only by selling it at a lower price.

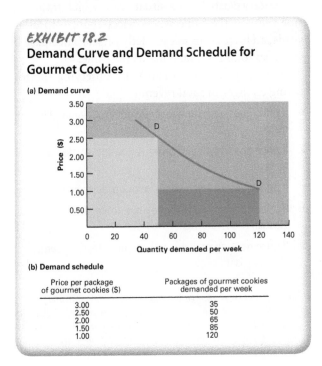

EXHIBIT 18.2
Demand Curve and Demand Schedule for Gourmet Cookies

(a) Demand curve

(b) Demand schedule

Price per package of gourmet cookies ($)	Packages of gourmet cookies demanded per week
3.00	35
2.50	50
2.00	65
1.50	85
1.00	120

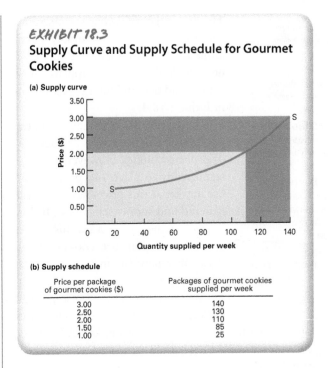

EXHIBIT 18.3
Supply Curve and Supply Schedule for Gourmet Cookies

(a) Supply curve

(b) Supply schedule

Price per package of gourmet cookies ($)	Packages of gourmet cookies supplied per week
3.00	140
2.50	130
2.00	110
1.50	85
1.00	25

One reason why more cookies are sold at lower prices than at higher prices is that lower prices attract new buyers. Also, with each reduction in price, the existing customers may buy extra.

Supply is the quantity of a product that will be offered to the market by a supplier or suppliers at various prices for a specified period. The graph (a) in Exhibit 18.3 above illustrates the resulting *supply curve* for gourmet cookies. Unlike the falling demand curve, the supply curve for gourmet cookies slopes upward and to the right. At higher prices, gourmet cookie manufacturers will obtain more resources (flour, eggs, chocolate) and produce more gourmet cookies. If the price consumers are willing to pay for gourmet cookies increases, producers can afford to buy more ingredients.

Output tends to increase at higher prices because manufacturers can sell more cookies and earn greater profits. The *supply schedule* (see Exhibit 18.3(b) above) shows that at $2 per package, suppliers are willing to place 110 packages of gourmet cookies on the market, but will offer 140 packages at a price of $3.

How Demand and Supply Establish Prices At this point, let's combine the concepts of demand and supply to see how competitive market prices are determined. So far, the premise is that if the price is *x*, then consumers will purchase *y* amount of gourmet cookies.

demand the quantity of a product that will be sold in the market at various prices for a specified period

supply the quantity of a product that will be offered to the market by a supplier at various prices for a specified period

price equilibrium
the price at which demand and supply are equal

elasticity of demand consumers' responsiveness or sensitivity to changes in price

elastic demand a situation in which consumer demand is sensitive to changes in price

inelastic demand a situation in which an increase or a decrease in price will not significantly affect demand for the product

unitary elasticity a situation in which total revenue remains the same when prices change

The demand curve cannot predict consumption, nor can the supply curve alone forecast production. Instead, we need to look at what happens when supply and demand interact, as shown in Exhibit 18.4.

At a price of $3 per package, the public would demand only 35 packages of gourmet cookies. However, suppliers stand ready to place 140 packages on the market at this price (data from the demand and supply schedules). If they do, they would create a surplus of 105 packages of gourmet cookies. How does a merchant eliminate a surplus? It lowers the price.

At a price of $1 per package, 120 packages would be demanded, but only 25 would be placed on the market. A shortage of 95 units would be created. If a product is in short supply and consumers want it, how do they entice the dealer to part with one unit? They offer more money—that is, they pay a higher price.

Now let's examine a price of $1.50 per package. At this price, 85 packages are demanded and 85 are supplied. When demand and supply are equal, a state called **price equilibrium** is achieved. A temporary price below the price equilibrium—say, $1—results in a shortage because at that price the demand for gourmet cookies is greater than the available supply. Shortages put upward pressure on price. As long as demand and supply remain the same, however, any temporary price increases or decreases tend to return to equilibrium. At equilibrium, prices have no inclination to rise or fall.

Prices may fluctuate during a trial-and-error period as the market for a good or service moves toward equilibrium. Sooner or later, however, demand and supply will settle into proper balance.

Elasticity of Demand

To appreciate demand analysis requires an understanding of the concept of elasticity. **Elasticity of demand** refers to consumers' responsiveness or sensitivity to changes in price. **Elastic demand** is a situation in which consumer demand is sensitive to changes in price. In other words, it occurs when consumers buy more or less of a product when the price changes. Conversely, **inelastic demand** is a situation in which an increase or a decrease in price will not significantly affect demand for the product.

Elasticity over the range of a demand curve can be measured by using this formula*:

$$\text{Elasticity } (E) = \frac{\text{Percentage change in quantity demanded of good A}}{\text{Percentage change in price of good A}}$$

If E is greater than 1, demand is elastic.
If E is less than 1, demand is inelastic.
If E is equal to 1, demand is unitary.

Unitary elasticity is a situation in which total revenue remains the same when prices change. In other words, an increase in sales exactly offsets a decrease in prices, so total revenue remains the same.

Elasticity can be measured by observing the following changes in total revenue:

▶▶ If price goes down and revenue goes up, demand is elastic.

▶▶ If price goes down and revenue goes down, demand is inelastic.

▶▶ If price goes up and revenue goes up, demand is inelastic.

▶▶ If price goes up and revenue goes down, demand is elastic.

▶▶ If price goes up or down and revenue stays the same, elasticity is unitary.

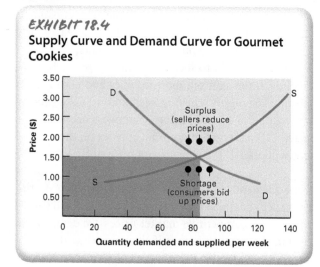

EXHIBIT 18.4
Supply Curve and Demand Curve for Gourmet Cookies

© ISTOCKPHOTO.COM/SERGEY KASHKIN

_____

* Since percentages change depending on which starting point is used, the midpoint method is commonly used rather than the traditional method shown below. The midpoint method takes the average of the two values for both quantity and price. See the calculation on page 303.

Elastic Demand The example of Sony digital cameras in Exhibit 18.5 shows a very elastic demand curve. When the price is dropped from $300 to $200, sales increase from 18,000 units to 59,000 units. Total revenue increases by $6.4 million (from $5.4 million to $11.8 million). An increase in total revenue when price falls indicates that demand is elastic.

Using this information, let's measure Sony's elasticity of demand when the price drops from $300 to $200 by applying the formula presented earlier:

$$E = \frac{\text{Change in quantity/(Sum of quantities/2)}}{\text{Change in price/(Sum of prices/2)}}$$

$$E = \frac{(59{,}000 - 18{,}000)/[(59{,}000 + 18{,}000)/2]}{(\$300 - \$200)/[(\$300 + \$200)/2]}$$

$$E = \frac{41{,}000/38{,}500}{\$100/\$250}$$

$$E = \frac{1.065}{0.4}$$

$$E = 2.66$$

Because E is greater than 1, demand is elastic

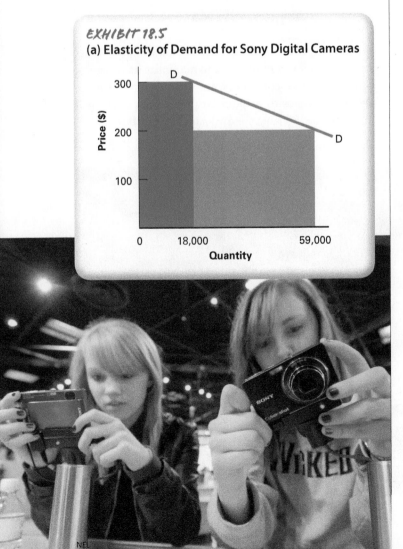

EXHIBIT 18.5
(a) Elasticity of Demand for Sony Digital Cameras

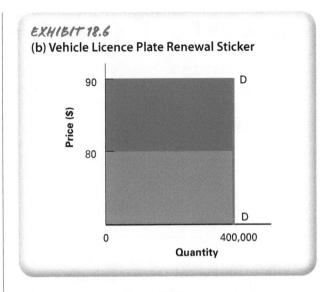

EXHIBIT 18.6
(b) Vehicle Licence Plate Renewal Sticker

Inelastic Demand When price and total revenue fall, demand is inelastic. When demand is inelastic, sellers can raise prices and increase their total revenue. Items that are relatively inexpensive but convenient tend to have inelastic demand. For example, vehicle licence plate renewal stickers have a completely inelastic demand curve (see Exhibit 18.6 above). If Ontario dropped its fee from $90 to $80, it would not cause people to buy more stickers. Demand is completely inelastic for stickers, which are required by law.

Factors That Affect Elasticity Several factors affect elasticity of demand, including the following:

▸▸ *Availability of substitutes:* When many substitute products are available, the consumer can easily switch from one product to another, making demand elastic. The same is true in reverse: a person will pay a higher price for a product that has no acceptable substitute. For example, the 20011 Mercedes-Benz SLS AMG, which has few substitutes, is priced at $200,000+.

▸▸ *Price relative to purchasing power:* If a price is so low that it comprises an inconsequential part of an individual's budget, demand will be inelastic. For example, Tim Hortons coffee, which is inexpensively priced, has inelastic demand.

▸▸ *Product durability:* Consumers often have the option of repairing durable products rather than replacing them, thus prolonging a product's useful life. In other words, people are sensitive to the price increase, and demand is elastic. Repairing a good pair of dress shoes instead of buying a new pair of shoes represents an elastic demand.

▸▸ *A product's other uses:* The greater the number of different uses for a product, the more elastic demand tends to be. If a product has only one use, as may be true of a new medicine, the quantity purchased probably will

eLASTICITY IN ACTION

In a recent summer, fans balked at the high prices for concerts. Promoters lost money, and some shows, including Lilith Fair, which featured such top female artists as Chantal Krevazuk, Indigo Girls, and Tegan and Sara were cancelled. This situation is price elasticity in action. By contrast, demand for some tickets was highly inelastic. Justin Bieber is still selling out concerts with tickets priced at up to $845.[2]

yield management systems (YMS) a technique for adjusting prices that uses complex mathematical software to profitably fill unused capacity by discounting early purchases, limiting early sales at these discounted prices, and overbooking capacity

not vary as price varies. A person will consume only the prescribed quantity, regardless of price. On the other hand, a product such as steel has many possible applications. As its price falls, steel becomes more economically feasible in a wider variety of applications, thereby making demand relatively elastic.

▶▶ *Rate of inflation:* Recent research has found that when a country's inflation rate (the rate at which the price level is rising) is high, demand becomes more elastic. In other words, rising price levels make consumers more price sensitive. During inflationary periods, consumers base their timing (when to buy) and quantity decisions on price promotions. This consumer behaviour suggests that a brand gains additional sales or market share as a result of either the product having been effectively promoted

or the marketing manager having kept the brand's price increases low, relative to the inflation rate.[3]

LO 4 The Power of Yield Management Systems

When competitive pressures are high, a company must know when it can raise prices to maximize its revenues. More and more companies are turning to yield management systems to help adjust prices. First developed in the airline industry, **yield management systems (YMS)** use complex mathematical software to profitably fill

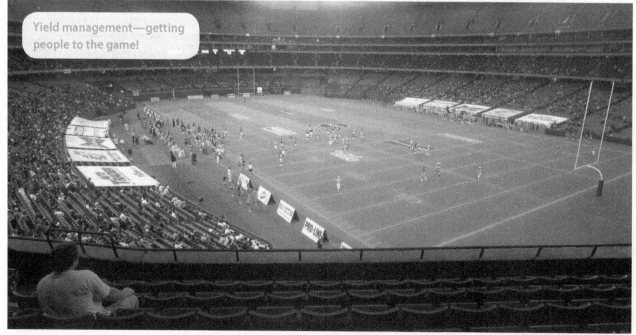

Yield management—getting people to the game!

unused capacity. The software employs techniques such as discounting early purchases, limiting early sales at these discounted prices, and overbooking capacity. YMS now are appearing in other services as well.[4]

Yield management systems are spreading beyond service industries as their popularity increases. The lessons of airlines and hotels aren't entirely applicable to other industries; however, because plane seats and hotel beds are perishable, if they go empty, the revenue opportunity is lost forever. So it makes sense to slash prices to move toward capacity if it's possible to do so without reducing the prices that other customers pay. Cars and steel aren't so perishable, but the capacity to make them is. An underused factory is a lost revenue opportunity. It makes sense to cut prices to use up capacity if it's possible to do so while getting other customers to pay full price.

Allstate uses a type of yield management system to determine insurance rates for drivers. In the past, customers for car insurance were divided into three categories. Now Allstate has more than 1,500 price levels. Agents used to simply refer to a manual to give customers a price; now they consult software that uses complex algorithms to analyze 16 credit report variables, such as late payments and card balances, and data such as claims history for specific car models. Safe drivers are rewarded, saving up to 20 percent over the old system, and high-risk drivers are penalized, paying up to 20 percent more. The system has worked so well that Allstate now applies it to other lines, such as homeowners' insurance.[5]

LO 5 The Cost Determinant of Price

Sometimes companies minimize or ignore the importance of demand and decide to price their products largely or solely on the basis of costs. Prices determined strictly on the basis of costs may be too high for the target market, thereby reducing or eliminating sales. On the other hand, cost-based prices may be too low, causing the firm to earn a lower return than it should. Nevertheless, costs should generally be part of any price determination, if only for determining a **floor price**, the price below which a good or service must not be priced in the long run. In other words, the floor price is the lowest price to which a company will allow a price to drop.

The idea of cost may seem simple, but it is actually a multifaceted concept, especially for producers of goods and services. A **variable cost** is a cost that varies with changes in the level of output, such as the cost of materials. Another variable cost is shrinkage cost, which results from theft and damage and may vary depending on such factors as location and the level of security. In contrast, a **fixed cost** does not change as output is increased or decreased. Examples include rent and executives' salaries.

To compare the cost of production to the selling price of a product, it is helpful to calculate costs per unit, or average costs. **Average variable cost (AVC)** equals total variable costs divided by quantity of output. **Average total cost (ATC)** equals total costs divided by output. As the graph in Exhibit 18.7(a) shows, AVC and ATC are basically U-shaped curves. In contrast, average fixed cost (AFC) declines continually as output increases because total fixed costs are constant.

Marginal cost (MC) is the change in total costs associated with a one-unit change in output. Exhibit 18.7(b) shows that when output rises from seven to eight units, the change in total cost increases from $640 to $750; therefore, the marginal cost is $110.

All the curves illustrated in Exhibit 18.7(a) have definite relationships:

▸▸ AVC plus AFC equals ATC.

▸▸ MC falls for a while and then turns upward, in this case after the fourth unit. At that point, diminishing returns set in, meaning that less output is produced for every additional dollar spent on variable input.

▸▸ MC intersects both AVC and ATC at their lowest possible points.

▸▸ When MC is less than AVC or ATC, the incremental cost will continue to pull the averages down. Conversely, when MC is greater than AVC or ATC, it pulls the averages up, and ATC and AVC begin to rise.

▸▸ The minimum point on the ATC curve is the least cost point for a fixed-capacity firm, although it is not necessarily the most profitable point.

Costs can be used to set prices in a variety of ways. Markup pricing is relatively simple. Profit maximization pricing and break-even pricing make use of the more complicated concepts of cost.

> **floor price** the lowest price to which a company will allow its price to drop
>
> **variable cost** a cost that varies with changes in the level of output
>
> **fixed cost** a cost that does not change as output is increased or decreased
>
> **average variable cost (AVC)** total variable costs divided by quantity of output
>
> **average total cost (ATC)** total costs divided by quantity of output
>
> **marginal cost (MC)** the change in total costs associated with a one-unit change in output

EXHIBIT 18.7

Hypothetical Set of Cost Curves and a Cost Schedule

(a) Cost Curves

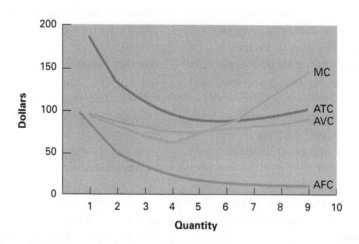

(b) Cost Schedule

	Total-Cost Data, per Week			Average-Cost Data, per Week			
(1) **Total Product (Q)**	**(2)** **Total Fixed Cost (TFC)**	**(3)** **Total Variable Cost (TVC)**	**(4)** **Total Cost (TC)**	**(5)** **Average Fixed Cost (AFC)**	**(6)** **Average Variable Cost (AVC)**	**(7)** **Average Total Cost (ATC)**	**(8)** **Marginal Cost (MC)**
			$TC = TFC + TVC$	$AFC = \dfrac{TFC}{Q}$	$AVC = \dfrac{TVC}{Q}$	$ATC = \dfrac{TC}{Q}$	$MC = \dfrac{\text{change in TC}}{\text{change Q}}$
0	$100	$ 0	$ 100	—	—	—	—
1	100	90	190	$100.00	$90.00	$190.00	$ 90
2	100	170	270	50.00	85.00	135.00	80
3	100	240	340	33.33	80.00	113.33	70
4	100	300	400	25.00	75.00	100.00	60
5	100	370	470	20.00	74.00	94.00	70
6	100	450	550	16.67	75.00	91.67	80
7	100	540	640	14.29	77.14	91.43	90
8	100	650	750	12.50	81.25	93.75	110
9	100	780	880	11.11	86.67	97.78	130
10	100	930	1,030	10.00	93.00	103.00	150

markup pricing the cost of buying the product from the producer plus amounts for profit and for expenses not otherwise accounted for; can be expressed as markup (cost) or markup (selling)

Markup Pricing

Markup pricing, the most popular method used by wholesalers and retailers to establish a selling price, does not directly analyze the costs of production. Instead, **markup pricing** represents the cost of buying the product from the producer, plus amounts for profit and for expenses not otherwise accounted for. The total determines the selling price.

When determining the markup price, the retailer adds a certain percentage to the cost of the merchandise received to arrive at the retail price. An item that costs the retailer $1.80 and is sold for $2.20 carries a markup of 40 cents, which is a markup of 22 percent of the cost ($0.40 ÷ $1.80). Recall from Chapter 13 that the difference between the retailer's cost and the selling price (in this example, 40 cents) is the gross margin. The following shows the calculation for determining the markup as a percentage of the cost.

$$\text{Markup (cost)} = \frac{\$\text{ Markup} \times 100\%}{\$\text{ Cost}}$$

$$= \frac{\$0.40 \times 100\%}{\$1.80}$$

$$= 22\%$$

Often in retailing, merchants tend to discuss markup (selling) in terms of its percentage of the retail price—in this example, the markup is 18 percent of the selling price ($0.40 ÷ $2.20).

$$\text{Markup (selling)} = \frac{\$\text{ Markup} \times 100\%}{\$\text{ Retail selling price}}$$

$$= \frac{\$0.40 \times 100\%}{\$2.20}$$

$$= 18\%$$

The reason that retailers and others speak of markups on selling price is that many important calculations in financial reports, such as gross sales and revenues, are sales figures, not cost figures. When retailers know the return they want on products (either as a fixed amount or as a percentage), they can use the following formula to calculate the final retail price:

$$\text{Retail price} = \frac{\text{Cost}}{1 - \text{Desired return on sales}}$$

$$= \frac{\$1.80}{1 - 0.18}$$

$$= \$2.20$$

If the retailer wants a 30 percent return, then:

$$\text{Retail price} = \frac{\$1.80}{1 - 0.30}$$

$$= \$2.57$$

To effectively use a markup that is based on cost or selling price, the marketing manager must calculate an adequate gross margin—the amount added to cost to determine price. The margin must ultimately provide adequate funds to cover selling expenses and profit. Once an appropriate margin has been determined, the markup technique has the major advantage of being easy to employ.

Markups are often based on experience. For example, many small retailers mark up merchandise 100 percent over cost. (In other words, they double the cost.) This tactic is called **keystoning**. Some other factors that influence markups are the merchandise's appeal to customers, past response to the markup (an implicit demand consideration), the item's promotional value, the seasonality of the goods, their fashion appeal, the product's traditional selling price, and competition. Most retailers avoid any set markup because of such considerations as promotional value and seasonality.

Price × 2 = Keystoning

Profit-Maximization Pricing

Producers tend to use more complicated methods of setting prices than distributors use. One method is **profit maximization**, which occurs when marginal revenue equals marginal cost. You learned earlier that marginal cost is the change in total costs associated with a one-unit change in output. Similarly, **marginal revenue (MR)** is the extra revenue associated with selling an extra unit of output. As long as the revenue of the last unit produced and sold is greater than the cost of the last unit produced and sold, the firm should continue manufacturing and selling the product. Exhibits 18.8(a), (b), and (c) show the revenues and costs for Lakeside Apple Growers (a hypothetical firm). Using the cost data from Exhibit 18.8(c), you will note that the difference between marginal revenue and marginal cost (i.e., MR−MC) is still slightly positive ($0.08/kg) at 45,000 kg but moves to a negative value (i.e., −$0.10/kg) by 50,000 kg. Thus, the profit-maximizing quantity (MR=MC) occurs at slightly more than 45,000 kg.

Because it will be difficult to determine the exact number of units between 45,000 and 50,000 kg where this balance occurs, it is helpful to do a more detailed analysis using smaller differences in production, say to the nearest 100 kg. However, because the price received may also vary depending on the quantity sold, determining the exact number of units can become a difficult exercise. Thus, it is best to refine the number of units as closely as possible, then produce until the profits are no longer increasing. Economists suggest producing up to the point where MR equals MC. If marginal revenue is just one penny greater than marginal costs, it will still increase total profits. In reality, determining the exact point at which MR equals MC can be a very difficult and time-consuming task.

Suppose, for example, that Lakeside Apple Growers, has fixed costs of $12,000 and its variable costs of labour and materials range from $0.45 to $0.28 for each unit produced (i.e., production efficiencies

keystoning the practice of marking up prices by 100 percent, or doubling the cost

profit maximization a method of setting prices so that marginal revenue equals marginal cost

marginal revenue (MR) the extra revenue associated with selling an extra unit of output, or the change in total revenue as a result of a one-unit change in output

EXHIBIT 18.8

Lakeside Apple Growers: Pricing, Demand, and Cost Factors for Apples

(a) Pricing, Demand, and Cost Factors

Demand (in kg)	Price/kg	Revenues	Variable Costs/kg	Profit Margin/Unit	Total Variable Cost	Fixed Costs	Total Costs	Profits
70,000	$0.50	$35,000	$0.28	$0.22	$19,600	$12,000	$31,600	$3,400
65,000	$0.55	$35,750	$0.30	$0.25	$19,500	$12,000	$31,500	$4,250
60,000	$0.60	$36,000	$0.32	$0.28	$19,200	$12,000	$31,200	$4,800
55,000	$0.65	$35,750	$0.34	$0.31	$18,700	$12,000	$30,700	$5,050
50,000	$0.70	$35,000	$0.35	$0.35	$17,500	$12,000	$29,500	$5,500
45,000	**$0.75**	**$33,750**	**$0.35**	**$0.40**	**$15,750**	**$12,000**	**$27,750**	**$6,000**
40,000	$0.80	$32,000	$0.36	$0.44	$14,400	$12,000	$26,400	$5,600
35,000	$0.85	$29,750	$0.36	$0.49	$12,600	$12,000	$24,600	$5,150
30,000	$0.90	$27,000	$0.39	$0.51	$11,700	$12,000	$23,700	$3,300
25,000	$0.95	$23,750	$0.42	$0.53	$10,500	$12,000	$22,500	$1,250
20,000	$1.00	$20,000	$0.44	$0.56	$8,800	$12,000	$20,800	−$800
15,000	$1.05	$15,750	$0.45	$0.60	$6,750	$12,000	$18,750	−$3,000

(b) Pricing, Demand, and Cost Factors

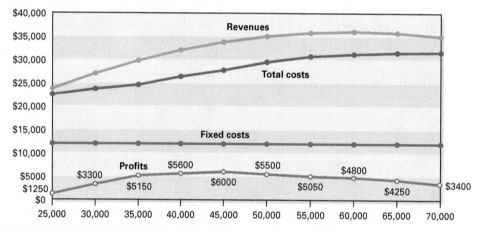

(c) Marginal Revenue and Marginal Cost

Demand (in kg)	Marginal Revenue	Marginal Cost	Marginal Revenue − Marginal Cost
70,000	−$0.15	$0.02	−$0.17
65,000	−$0.05	$0.06	−$0.11
60,000	$0.05	$0.10	−$0.05
55,000	$0.15	$0.24	−$0.09
50,000	$0.25	$0.35	−$0.10
45,000	**$0.35**	**$0.27**	**$0.08**
40,000	$0.45	$0.36	$0.09
35,000	$0.55	$0.18	$0.37
30,000	$0.65	$0.24	$0.41
25,000	$0.75	$0.34	$0.41
20,000	$0.85	$0.41	$0.44
15,000	$1.05	$1.25	−$0.20

reduce costs). Assume that the company can sell up to 70,000 kg of its product, but an increased supply also means lower prices (thus, a short supply would have a higher price of $1.05 per kg, but higher supply volumes could see the prices drop to $0.50 per kg). As Exhibits 18.8(a) and 18.8(b) illustrate, Lakeside Apple Growers profit maximization of $6,000 would occur if it sold 45,000 kg of apples. Thus, if the company took any greater volume to market, it would make less profit; or, if it could not produce this amount in the year (e.g., because of bad growing conditions), the company would also experience less profit.

Break-Even Pricing

Now let's take a closer look at the relationship between sales and cost. **Break-even analysis** determines the required sales volume to be reached before the company breaks even (its total costs equal total revenue) and no profits are earned. The typical break-even model assumes that at a set price, the total costs will comprise a given fixed cost and a constant average variable cost.

$$\text{BE (volume)} = \$12,000/(\$0.80 - \$0.36)/\text{kg}$$
$$= 27,273 \text{ kg}$$

$$\text{BE (dollars)} = \text{BE (kg)} \times \text{price/kg}$$
$$= 27,273 \text{ kg} \times \$0.80/\text{kg}$$
$$= \$21,818$$

As Exhibit 18.9(a) indicates, suppose that Lakeside Apple Growers' total variable costs increase by $0.36 every time one kilogram of apples is produced, and total fixed costs remain constant at $12,000 regardless of the level of output. Therefore, for 27,273 kg of output, Lakeside Apple Growers has $12,000 in fixed costs and $9,818.28 in total variable costs (27,273 kg × $0.36), or $21,818.28 in total costs. Revenue is also $21,818.40 (27,273 units, after rounding to the next kilogram × $0.80), yielding a net profit of essentially zero dollars ($0.12) at the break-even point of 27,273 kg units (notice that break-even units will need to be rounded up to the next whole unit measured for production for the firm to be above the break-even point.) The formula for calculating break-even quantities is simple:

$$\text{Break-even (quantity)} = \frac{\text{Total fixed costs}}{\text{Price} - \text{Variable costs}}$$
$$\left(\text{or } \frac{\text{Total fixed costs}}{\text{Fixed-cost contribution}} \right)$$

(Fixed-cost contribution = Price minus the average variable cost)

$$\text{BE (volume)} = \$12,000/ (\$0.80 - \$0.36)/\text{kg}$$
$$= 27,273 \text{ kg}$$

break-even analysis a method of determining what sales volume must be reached before total revenue equals total costs

EXHIBIT 18.9

(a) Lakeside Apple Growers: Break-Even Analysis for Apples

Break-even = Fixed costs/(Price − Variable costs)

Demand (in kg)	Price/kg	Revenues	Fixed Costs	Variable Costs/kg	Total Variable Costs	Total Costs	Profit	
15,000	$ 0.80	$12,000.00	$12,000.00	$0.36	$5,400.00	$17,400.00	−$5,400.00	
20,000	$ 0.80	$16,000.00	$12,000.00	$0.36	$7,200.00	$19,200.00	−$3,200.00	
25,000	$ 0.80	$20,000.00	$12,000.00	$0.36	$9,000.00	$21,000.00	−$1,000.00	
27,273	**$ 0.80**	**$21,818.40**	**$12,000.00**	**$0.36**	**$9,818.28**	**$21,818.28**	**$0.12**	**BE Point**
30,000	$ 0.80	$24,000.00	$12,000.00	$0.36	$10,800.00	$22,800.00	$1,200.00	
35,000	$ 0.80	$28,000.00	$12,000.00	$0.36	$12,600.00	$24,600.00	$3,400.00	
40,000	$ 0.80	$32,000.00	$12,000.00	$0.36	$14,400.00	$26,400.00	$5,600.00	
45,000	$ 0.80	$36,000.00	$12,000.00	$0.36	$16,200.00	$28,200.00	$7,800.00	
50,000	$ 0.80	$40,000.00	$12,000.00	$0.36	$18,000.00	$30,000.00	$10,000.00	
55,000	$ 0.80	$44,000.00	$12,000.00	$0.36	$19,800.00	$31,800.00	$12,200.00	
60,000	$ 0.80	$48,000.00	$12,000.00	$0.36	$21,600.00	$33,600.00	$14,400.00	
65,000	$ 0.80	$52,000.00	$12,000.00	$0.36	$23,400.00	$35,400.00	$16,600.00	
70,000	$ 0.80	$56,000.00	$12,000.00	$0.36	$25,200.00	$37,200.00	$18,800.00	

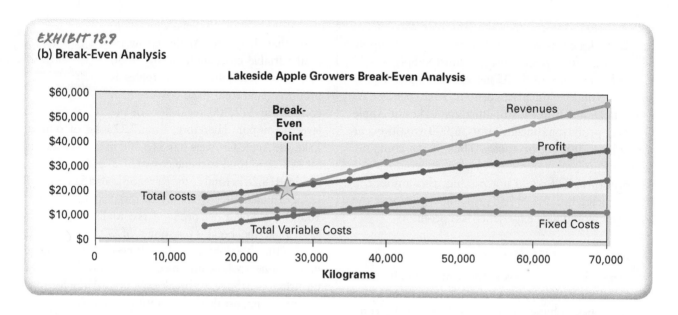

EXHIBIT 18.9
(b) Break-Even Analysis

Lakeside Apple Growers Break-Even Analysis

Revenues

Break-Even Point

Profit

Total costs

Fixed Costs

Total Variable Costs

Kilograms

Once the firm gets past the break-even point in dollars, the gap between total revenue and total costs widens because both functions are assumed to be linear.

BE (dollars) = BE (volume) × price/kg
= 27,273 kg × $0.80/kg
= $21,818

It can be seen in Exhibit 18.9(b) that profits grow from the break-even point in dollars as unit sales increase. Therefore, for Lakeside Apple Growers, the break-even quantity is 27,273 kg of apples, and profits will grow as it sells more beyond that break-even volume. Thus, the advantage of break-even analysis is that it provides a quick estimate of how much the firm must sell to break even and how much profit can be earned if a higher sales volume is obtained. If a firm is operating close to the break-even point, it may want to see what can be done to reduce costs or increase an extra unit of output. As long as the revenue of the last unit produced and sold is greater than the cost of the last unit produced and sold, the firm should continue manufacturing and selling the product.

However, break-even analysis is not without several important limitations. In a simple break-even analysis, it is not necessary to compute marginal costs and marginal revenues because price and average cost per unit are assumed to be constant. But as we noted earlier, supply can affect the price buyers are willing to pay and the business may be able to achieve efficiencies at different levels of production (see Exhibit 18.8). Also, because accounting data for marginal cost and revenue are frequently unavailable, it is convenient not to have to depend on that information. Moreover,

sometimes it is difficult to know whether a cost is fixed or variable. If labour wins a tough guaranteed-employment contract, are the resulting expenses a fixed cost? Changes in fixed costs will affect the break-even point. More important than cost determination is the fact that simple break-even analysis ignores demand. How does Lakeside Apple Growers know it can sell 25,000 kilograms at $0.80? Could it sell the same 25,000 units at $1 or even $1.20? Obviously, this information would profoundly affect the firm's pricing decisions.

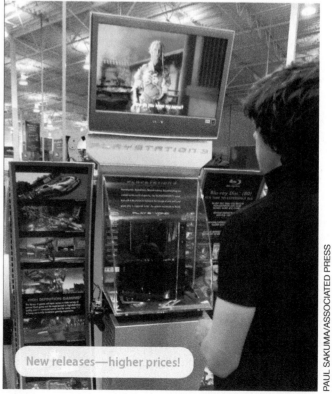

New releases—higher prices!

LO 6 Other Determinants of Price

Other factors besides demand and costs can influence price. For example, prices can be affected by the stages in the product life cycle, the competition, the product distribution strategy, the Internet and extranets, the promotion strategy, customer demands, and the perceived quality.

Stages in the Product Life Cycle

As a product moves through its life cycle (see Chapter 10), the demand for the product and the competitive conditions tend to change:

▶▶ *Introductory stage:* Management usually sets prices high during the introductory stage of a product. One reason is that the company hopes to recover its development costs quickly. In addition, demand originates in the core of the market (the customers whose needs ideally match the product's attributes) and thus is relatively inelastic. On the other hand, if the target market is highly price sensitive, management often finds it better to price the product at or below the market level.

▶▶ *Growth stage:* As the product enters the growth stage, prices generally begin to stabilize for several reasons. First, competitors have entered the market, increasing the available supply. Second, the product has begun to appeal to a broader market, often lower-income groups. Finally, economies of scale are lowering costs, and the savings can be passed on to the consumer in the form of lower prices.

▶▶ *Maturity stage:* Maturity usually brings further price decreases as competition increases and inefficient, high-cost firms are eliminated. Distribution channels become a significant cost factor, however, because of the need to offer wide product lines for highly segmented markets, extensive service requirements, and the sheer number of dealers necessary to absorb high-volume production. The manufacturers that remain in the market toward the end of the maturity stage typically offer similar prices. At this stage, price increases are usually cost initiated, not demand initiated. Nor do price reductions in the late phase of maturity stimulate much demand. Because demand is limited and producers have similar cost structures, the remaining competitors will probably match price reductions.

▶▶ *Decline stage:* The final stage of the life cycle may see further price decreases as the few remaining competitors try to salvage the last vestiges of demand. When only one firm is left in the market, prices begin to stabilize. In fact, prices may eventually rise dramatically if the product survives and moves into the specialty goods category, as have horse-drawn carriages and vinyl records.

The Competition

Competition varies during the product life cycle, of course, and so at times it may strongly affect pricing decisions. Although a firm may not have any competition at first, the high prices it charges may eventually induce another firm to enter the market.

Intense competition can sometimes lead to price wars. One company recently took action to avoid a calamitous price war by outsmarting its competition. A company (call it Acme) heard that its competitor was trying to steal some business by offering a low price to one of its best customers. Instead of immediately cutting prices, Acme reps visited three of its competitor's best clients and said they figured the client was paying X, the same price that the competitor had quoted to Acme's own customer. Within days, the competitor had retracted its low-price offer to Acme's client. Presumably, the competitor had received calls from three angry clients asking for the same special deal.

Distribution Strategy

An effective distribution network can often overcome other minor flaws in the marketing mix.[6] For example, although consumers may perceive a price as being slightly higher than normal, they may buy the product anyway if it is being sold at a convenient retail outlet.

Adequate distribution for a new product can often be attained by offering a larger-than-usual profit margin to distributors. A variation on this strategy is to give dealers a large trade allowance to help offset the costs of promotion and further stimulate demand at the retail level.

Manufacturers have gradually been losing control within the distribution channel to wholesalers and retailers, which often adopt pricing strategies that serve their own purposes. For instance, some distributors

BREAK-EVEN: THE "HOT SPOT" FOR BUSINESS.

are **selling against the brand**: they place well-known brands on the shelves at high prices while offering other brands—typically, their private-label brands, such as Life brand—at lower prices. Of course, sales of the higher-priced brands decline.

Wholesalers and retailers may also go outside traditional distribution channels to buy grey-market goods. As explained previously, distributors obtain the goods through unauthorized channels for less than they would normally pay, so they can sell the goods either with a bigger-than-normal markup or at a reduced price. Imports seem to be particularly susceptible to grey marketing. Although consumers may pay less for grey-market goods, they often find that the manufacturer won't honour the warranty.

Manufacturers can regain some control over price by using an exclusive distribution system, by franchising, or by avoiding doing business with price-cutting discounters. Manufacturers can also package merchandise with the **manufacturer's suggested retail price (MSRP)** marked on it or place goods on consignment. The best way for manufacturers to control prices, however, is to develop brand loyalty in consumers by delivering quality and value.

The Impact of the Internet and Extranets

The Internet, **extranets** (private electronic networks, such as corporate networks), and wireless setups are linking people, machines, and companies around the globe—and connecting sellers and buyers as never before. This link is enabling buyers to quickly and easily compare products and prices, which puts them in a better bargaining position. At the same time, the technology allows sellers to collect detailed data about customers' buying habits, preferences, and even spending limits so that sellers can tailor their products and prices.

Using Shopping Bots A shopping bot is a program that searches the Web for the best price for a particular item that a consumer wishes to purchase. *Bot* is short for *robot*. Shopping bots theoretically give pricing power to the consumer. The more information that the shopper has, the more efficient his or her purchase decision will be.

Shopping bots can be divided into two general types. The first is the broad-based type that searches a wide range of product categories such as mySimon.com, dealtime.com, bizmate.com, pricegrabber.com, and PriceSCAN.com. These sites operate by using a Yellow Pages type of model, listing every retailer they can find. The second is the niche-oriented type that searches for only one type of product such as computer equipment (CNET.com), books (Bookfinder.com), or CDs (CDPriceCompare.com).

Most shopping bots give preferential listings to those e-retailers that pay for the privilege. These so-called merchant partners receive about 60 percent of the click-throughs.[7] Typically, the bot lists its merchant partners first, not the retailer offering the lowest price.

Internet Auctions The Internet auction business is huge. Among the most popular consumer auction sites are the following:

▸▸ **www.auctions.amazon.com:** Links to Sotheby's for qualified sellers of high-end items.

▸▸ **www.ebay.ca:** The most popular auction site.

▸▸ **www.auctions.yahoo.com:** Free listings and numerous selling categories including international auctions.

Even though consumers are spending billions on Internet auctions, business-to-business auctions are likely to be the dominant form in the future. Recently, Whirlpool began holding online auctions. Participants bid on the price of the items that they would supply to Whirlpool, but with a twist: they had to include the date when Whirlpool would have to pay for the items. The company wanted to see which suppliers would offer the longest grace period before requiring payment. Five auctions held over five months helped Whirlpool uncover savings of close to $2 million and more than doubled the grace period.

Whirlpool's success is a sign that the business-to-business auction world is shifting from haggling over prices to niggling over parameters of the deal. Warranties, delivery dates, transportation methods, customer support, financing options, and quality have all become bargaining chips.

Promotion Strategy

Price is often used as a promotional tool to increase consumer interest. The weekly flyers sent out by grocery stores, for instance, advertise many products with special low prices.

Pricing can also be a tool for trade promotions. For example, Levi's Dockers (casual men's pants) are very popular. Sensing an opportunity, rival pants-maker Bugle Boy began offering similar pants at cheaper wholesale prices, which gave retailers a bigger gross margin than they were receiving through Dockers. Levi Strauss had to either lower its prices or risk its $400 million annual Dockers sales. Although Levi Strauss intended its cheapest Dockers to retail for $35, it started selling Dockers to retailers for $18 a pair. Retailers could then advertise Dockers at a very attractive retail price of $25.

Demands of Large Customers

Manufacturers find that their large customers such as department stores often make specific pricing demands that the suppliers must agree to. Department stores are making greater-than-ever demands on their suppliers to cover the heavy discounts and mark-downs on their own selling floors. They want suppliers to guarantee their stores' profit margins, and they insist on cash rebates should the guarantee not be met. They are also exacting fines for violations of ticketing, packing, and shipping rules. Cumulatively, the demands are nearly wiping out profits for all but the very biggest suppliers, according to fashion designers and garment makers.

With annual sales of $419 billion, Wal-Mart is the world's largest company, but it is also the largest customer of brands by Disney, Procter & Gamble, Kraft, Gillette, Campbell's soup, and most of North America's other leading branded manufacturers. Wal-Mart expects suppliers to offer their best price, period. There is no negotiation or ability to raise prices later. When suppliers have raised their prices, Wal-Mart has been known to remit payment that is based on the previous, lower prices.[8]

The Relationship of Price to Quality

When a purchase decision involves great uncertainty, consumers tend to rely on a high price as a predictor of good quality.[9] Reliance on price as an indicator of quality seems to occur for all products, but it reveals itself more strongly for some items than for others. Among the products that benefit from this phenomenon are coffee, Aspirin, salt, floor wax, shampoo, clothing, furniture, whisky, and many services. In the absence of other information, people typically assume that prices are higher because the products contain better materials, because they are made more carefully, or, in the case of professional services, because the provider has more expertise.

Research has found that products that are perceived to be of high quality tend to benefit more from price promotions than products perceived to be of lower quality.[10] However, when perceived high- and lower-quality products are offered in settings where consumers have difficulty making comparisons, then price promotions have an equal effect on sales. Comparisons are more difficult in end-of-aisle

COOL PRICE

Big White Ski Resort near

Kelowna, B.C., uses several different pricing strategies to attract different types of skiers and snowboarders to fill the resort. For example, on Fridays, night skiing and snowboarding costs just $5; in the spring, kids ski for free with their family; and a season's ski pass is discounted when purchased before the end of September. The previous season's rental equipment is sold off at $75 for a kid's package and $95 for a teenager's package; and both come with a free lift ticket and lesson and 50 percent off the purchase of year-end rental equipment.

PREMIUM DENIM?

In 2005, North Americans spent over **$13 billion on denim.** Of that, $650 million was for premium denim, defined as products priced at $75 or higher. Designer jeans that once commanded prices of $350 to $1,000 may be into the maturity phase. Designers such as Diesel, Christian Audigier, and others have been affected not only by the recession period of 2009 and onward but also by increased competition and the increasing costs of materials. The result has been prices dropping below the $300 mark.

STOCKBYTE/JUPITERIMAGES

---

prestige pricing
charging a high price to help promote a high-quality image

displays, feature advertising, and the like.

Knowledgeable merchants take these consumer attitudes into account when devising their pricing strategies. **Prestige pricing** is charging a high price to help promote a high-quality image. A successful prestige pricing strategy requires a retail price that is reasonably consistent with consumers' expectations. No one goes shopping at a Nike store and expects to pay $9.95 for a pair of running shoes. In fact, at such a low price, demand would fall drastically.

Some of the latest research on price–quality relationships has focused on consumer durable goods.

The researchers first conducted a study to ascertain the dimensions of quality, which were found to be the following: (1) ease of use; (2) versatility (the ability of a product to perform more functions, or be more flexible); (3) durability; (4) serviceability (ease of obtaining quality repairs); (5) performance; and (6) prestige. The researchers found that when consumers focused on prestige and/or durability to assess quality, price was a strong indicator of perceived overall quality. Price was less important as an indicator of quality if the consumer was focusing on one of the other four dimensions of quality.[11]

"CONSUMERS TEND TO RELY ON A **HIGH PRICE** AS A PREDICTOR OF **GOOD QUALITY**."

Satisfactory profit in low-risk industry
7%

Wal-Mart's 2011 sales total
$419 billion

When demand is elastic
$E>1$

$845
Price for a ticket to see Justin Bieber in Montreal

$430
Price for a ticket to see Lady Gaga in Montreal

1,500
Pricing levels in Allstate's yield management system (YMS)

$178
Lowest price point for True Religion jeans

71% The percentage of students who go online to study for a class.

LOG IN!

MKTG was designed for students just like you—busy people who want choices, flexibility, and multiple learning options.

MKTG delivers concise, electronic resources such as flashcards, interactive quizzes, crossword puzzles and more!

At **www.icanmktg2.com**, you'll find electronic resources such as **printable interactive flashcards, download-able study aids, games, quizzes,** and **videos** to test your knowledge of key concepts. These resources will help supplement your understanding of core **marketing** concepts in a format that fits your busy lifestyle.

"I really like how you use students' opinions on how to study and made a website that encompasses everything we find useful. Seeing this website makes me excited to study!"

—Abby Boston, Fanshawe College

Visit **www.icanmktg2.com** to find the resources you need today!

CHAPTER **19** **Setting the Right Price**

SALE $3.⁹⁹

Learning Outcomes

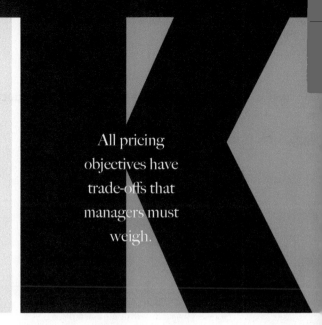

All pricing objectives have trade-offs that managers must weigh.

LO1 How to Set a Price on a Product

Setting the right price on a product is a four-step process (see Exhibit 19.1):

1. Establish pricing goals.
2. Estimate demand, costs, and profits.
3. Choose a price strategy to help determine a base price.
4. Fine-tune the base price by using pricing tactics.

Establish Pricing Goals

The first step in setting the right price is to establish pricing goals. Recall from Chapter 18 that pricing goals fall into three categories: profit oriented, sales oriented, and status quo. These goals are derived from the firm's overall objectives. A good understanding of the marketplace and of the consumer can sometimes tell a manager very quickly whether a goal is realistic.

All pricing goals have trade-offs that managers must weigh. A profit maximization goal may require a bigger initial investment than the firm can commit or wants to commit. A sales-oriented goal, such as reaching the desired market share, often means sacrificing short-term profit because without careful management, long-term

What do you think?

All pricing objectives have trade-offs that managers must weigh.

1	2	3	4	5	6	7
STRONGLY DISAGREE					STRONGLY AGREE	

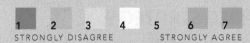

Find out what others think at the CourseMate for MKTG. Log in at NelsonBrain.com.

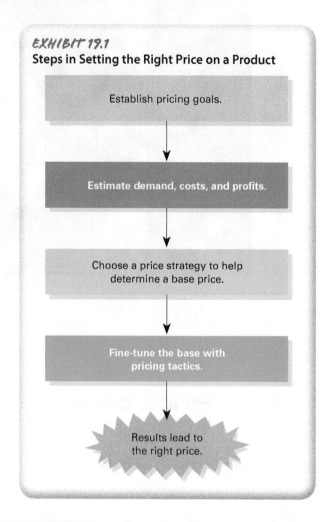

EXHIBIT 19.1
Steps in Setting the Right Price on a Product

Establish pricing goals.

↓

Estimate demand, costs, and profits.

↓

Choose a price strategy to help determine a base price.

↓

Fine-tune the base with pricing tactics.

↓

Results lead to the right price.

EXHIBIT 19.2
Product-Cycle Pricing Strategies

Competitive Environment	Introduction	Growth	Maturity	Decline
High	Penetration	Penetration	Status Quo (lead down)	
Medium	Status Quo	Status Quo (lead down)	Status Quo (maintain)	
Low	Skimming	Skimming	Skimming	Status Quo (maintain)

at a variety of prices. Next, they should determine the corresponding costs for each price. They are then ready to estimate how much profit, if any, and how much market share can be earned at each possible price. Managers can study the options in light of revenues, costs, and profits. In turn, this information can help determine which price can best meet the firm's pricing goals. (See Exhibits 19.1 and 19.2.)

Choose a Price Strategy

The basic, long-term pricing framework for a good or service should be a logical extension of the pricing goals. The marketing manager's chosen **price strategy** defines the initial price and the intended direction for price movements over the product life cycle. (See Exhibit 19.2 above.)

The price strategy sets a competitive price in a specific market segment that is based on a well-defined positioning strategy. Changing a price level from premium to super premium may require a change in the product itself, the target customers served, the promotional strategy, or the distribution channels.

A company's freedom in pricing a new product and devising a price strategy depends on the market conditions and the other elements of the marketing mix. If a firm launches a new item resembling several others already on the market, its pricing freedom will

price strategy a basic, long-term pricing framework that establishes the initial price for a product and the intended direction for price movements over the product life cycle

profit goals may not be met. Although meeting the competition is the easiest pricing goal to implement, it can also be short-sighted and costly.

In all situations, when managers set about establishing pricing goals, they must consider the product's demand, costs, profits, etc., as it progresses through its life cycle. This process usually means trade-offs occur in terms of meeting the target customer's needs, being competitive, having considerations for changing economic conditions, and meeting the company's overall objectives.

Estimate Demand, Costs, and Profits

Chapter 18 explained that total revenue is a function of price and quantity demanded and that quantity demanded depends on elasticity. After establishing pricing goals, managers should estimate total revenue

AS LONG AS DEMAND IS GREATER THAN SUPPLY, **SKIMMING** IS AN **ATTAINABLE STRATEGY.**

Often, companies will abandon a price skimming strategy over time, but at Chanel, that is not the case. Managers destroy unsold inventory as a way to maintain higher prices and avoid any suggestion of putting product on the market at a discount.

AP PHOTO/KOJI SASAHARA

be restricted. To succeed, the company will probably need to charge a price close to the average market price. In contrast, a firm that introduces a totally new product with no close substitutes will have considerable pricing freedom.

A recent study found that only approximately 8 percent of the companies surveyed conducted serious pricing research to support the development of an effective pricing strategy. In fact, 88 percent of companies surveyed did little or no serious pricing research. McKinsey & Company's Pricing Benchmark Survey estimated that only about 15 percent of companies do serious pricing research.[1]

Strategic pricing decisions tend to be made without an understanding of the likely response from either buyers or the competition. Managers often make tactical pricing decisions without reviewing how they may fit into the firm's overall pricing or marketing strategy. Many companies make pricing decisions and changes without an existing process for managing the pricing activity. As a result, many of them do not have a serious pricing strategy and do not conduct pricing research to develop their strategy.[2]

On the other hand, those companies that conduct both research and serious planning for creating a pricing strategy are endeavouring to understand the environment

HANDOUT/MCT/NEWSCOM

in which their product has entered or is currently in. These companies first consider their current product positioning (see Chapter 7), the product's demand and costs, the company long-term goals, and the product life-cycle stage, and then select from three basic approaches: price skimming, penetration pricing, and status quo pricing.

price skimming a high introductory price, often coupled with heavy promotion

Price Skimming Price skimming is sometimes called a *market-plus approach to pricing* because it denotes a high price relative to the prices of competing products. The term **price skimming**, referring to a high introductory price, often coupled with heavy promotion, is derived from the phrase "skimming the cream off the top." Companies often use this strategy for new products when

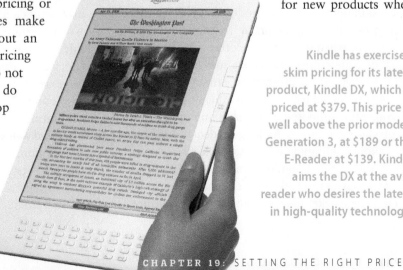

Kindle has exercised skim pricing for its latest product, Kindle DX, which is priced at $379. This price is well above the prior model, Generation 3, at $189 or the E-Reader at $139. Kindle aims the DX at the avid reader who desires the latest in high-quality technology.

DOLLAR STORES ARE PROFITABLE

Great Canadian Dollar Store

started in B.C. in 1993 and, by 2011, had grown to more than 100 locations across Canada. Locating small stores with low-cost everyday items in downtown neighbourhoods where shoppers live meets many customers' needs.

penetration pricing a relatively low price for a product initially as a way to reach the mass market

the product is perceived by the target market as having unique advantages. Often, companies will use skimming and then lower prices over time, known as *sliding down the demand curve*. Hardcover-book publishers, such as HarperCollins, lower the price when the books are re-released in paperback. Other manufacturers maintain skimming prices throughout a product's life cycle. A manager of the factory that produces Chanel purses (retailing for over $2,000 each) told one of the authors that it takes back and destroys unsold inventory rather than selling it at a discount.

Price skimming works best when the market is willing to buy the product even though it carries an above-average price. Firms can also effectively use price skimming when a product is well protected legally, when it represents a technological breakthrough, or when it has in some other way blocked the entry of competitors. Managers may follow a skimming strategy when production cannot be expanded rapidly because of technological difficulties, shortages, or constraints imposed by the skill and time required to produce a product. As long as demand is greater than supply, skimming is an attainable strategy.

A successful skimming strategy enables management to recover its product development costs quickly. Even if the market perceives an introductory price as

being too high, managers can lower the price. Firms often feel it is better to test the market at a high price and then lower the price if sales are too slow. Successful skimming strategies are not limited to products. Well-known athletes, lawyers, and hairstylists are experts at price skimming. Naturally, a skimming strategy will encourage competitors to enter the market.

Penetration Pricing Penetration pricing is at the opposite end of the spectrum from skimming. **Penetration pricing** means charging a relatively low price for a product initially as a way to reach the mass market. The low price is designed to capture a large share of a substantial market, resulting in lower production costs. If a marketing manager has decided that the firm's pricing object is to obtain a large market share, then penetration pricing is a logical choice.

Penetration pricing does mean lower profit per unit. Therefore, to reach the break-even point, the company requires a higher volume of sales than needed under a skimming policy. The recovery of product development costs may be slow. As you might expect, penetration pricing tends to discourage competition.

A penetration strategy tends to be effective in a price-sensitive market. Price should decline more rapidly when demand is elastic because the market can be expanded in response to a lower price. Also, price sensitivity and greater competitive pressure should lead either to a stable low price or to a lower initial price and then a later, relatively slow decline in the price.

Although Wal-Mart is typically associated with penetration pricing, other chains have also done an excellent job of following this strategy. Dollar stores, those bare-bones, strip-mall chains that sell staples at cut-rate prices, are now the fastest-growing retailers in North America. Dollar chains can locate their small stores right in downtown neighbourhoods, where their shoppers live. Parking is usually a snap, and shoppers can be in and out in less time than it takes to hike across a jumbo Wal-Mart parking lot.[3]

If a firm has a low fixed-cost structure, and each sale provides a large contribution to those fixed costs, penetration pricing can boost sales and provide large increases in profits—but only if the market size grows or if competitors choose not to respond. Low prices can attract additional buyers to the market. The increased sales can justify production expansion or the adoption of new technologies, both of which can reduce costs. And, if firms have excess capacity, even low-priced business can provide incremental dollars toward fixed costs.

Penetration pricing can also be effective if an experience curve will cause costs per unit to drop significantly. The experience curve proposes that per-unit costs will decrease as a firm's production experience increases. Manufacturers that fail to take advantage of these effects will find themselves at a competitive cost disadvantage relative to others that are further along the curve.

The big advantage of penetration pricing is that it typically discourages or blocks competition from entering a market. The disadvantage is that penetration means gearing up for mass production to sell a large volume at a low price. If the volume fails to materialize, the company will face huge losses from having built or converted a factory to produce the failed product.

Penetration pricing can also prove disastrous for a prestige brand that adopts the strategy in an effort to gain market share and fails. When Omega—once a more prestigious brand than Rolex—was trying to improve the market share of its watches, it adopted a penetration pricing strategy that destroyed the watch's brand image by flooding the market with lower-priced products. Omega never gained sufficient share on its lower-priced and lower-image competitors to justify destroying its brand image and high-priced position with upscale buyers.

Status Quo Pricing The third basic price strategy a firm may choose is status quo pricing, also called *meeting the competition or going-rate pricing* (see also Chapter 18). It means charging a price identical to or very close to the competition's price.

Although status quo pricing has the advantage of simplicity, its disadvantage is that the strategy may ignore demand or cost, or both. If the firm is comparatively small, however, meeting the competition may be the safest route to long-term survival.

LO 2 The Legality and Ethics of Price Strategy

As we mentioned in Chapter 2, some pricing decisions are subject to government regulation. Companies and marketers need to be aware of the laws within the Competition Act before establishing any strategy. The Act covers legal and ethical issues relating to deceptive pricing, price fixing, predatory pricing, resale price maintenance, and price discrimination. Both alleged and proven unethical pricing practices can have serious consequences for both the companies and the marketing managers involved.

Deceptive Pricing

Deceptive pricing refers to promoting a price or price saving that is not actually available. It occurs when the seller leads the purchaser to believe that he or she can or is receiving the good or service at the promoted or reduced price. Sellers who use deceptive pricing typically promote a low price on a product for which they have very little stock, or no stock at all, with the intent of selling the customer another, higher-priced product as a substitute. This tactic is called a *bait and switch*. To avoid the perception of using this tactic, marketers must ensure that they have adequate stock on hand or that they clearly indicate the limited quantities available at the reduced price; and if the stock quickly sells out, they should offer rain checks.

A second form of deceptive pricing occurs when a seller promotes a discount from a regular price that, in fact, has not been the regular price for a significant period of time. For example, in a recent case, the Forzani Group (operators of Sport Chek and Sport Mart) was fined $1.7 million for misleading the public by advertising reductions from prices that had not been in place for a significant period of time but had been inflated shortly before the sale.[4]

Other deceptive pricing practices include selling a product at a price above the advertised price (a civil court issue) and double ticketing, in which a product is sold for more than the lowest of two or more prices tagged on it (a criminal offence). Any company and its employees need to ensure that such deceptive pricing practices are not happening in their retail operations.

Price Fixing

Price fixing occurs when two or more companies conspire to set the prices for their products or services.

> **deceptive pricing** promoting a price or price saving that is not actually available
>
> **price fixing** an agreement between two or more firms on the price they will charge for a product

ARCH WHITE/GETSTOCK.COM

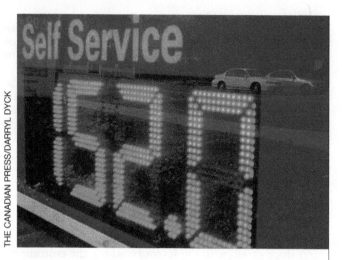
THE CANADIAN PRESS/DARRYL DYCK

predatory pricing
the practice of charging a very low price for a product with the intent of driving competitors out of business or out of a market

resale price maintenance
attempts by a producer to control a store's retail price for the product

It can be done by establishing a floor, or lowest price, in a bidding situation or by simply setting the market price that the consumer will pay. Proving an allegation of price fixing is often a very difficult and lengthy process. In one recent case on November 3, 2010, Panasonic Corporation pleaded guilty and was fined $1.5 million for charges under s. 45 of the *Competition Act* relating to the price fixing of hermetic refrigeration compressors sold in Canada. In a second case (the Quebec gasoline cartel case), 10 people and 11 companies were found guilty of conspiring to fix the gasoline prices paid by customers at the pump.[5] (A one-cent increase in gas prices over one year would have cost consumers an estimated $2 million.) The companies and some individuals in this case faced fines; other consequences of the charges could include lost consumer confidence, lost jobs, jail sentences, and potential loss of franchise rights.

Predatory Pricing

Although a normal business strategy might be to set prices low for the purpose of taking business away from the competition and gaining market, such action must be done within reason. **Predatory pricing** occurs when a company sets its prices very low with the intention of driving its competition out of either the market or the business. To do this, the company lowers its price below its average variable cost for an extended period of time—more time than is typical of any short-term loss leader that might be used to attract business or move excess inventory. Once the very low price has eliminated the competitor who cannot afford to operate at that price, the company will raise it prices. Predatory pricing situations are difficult to prove as evidence must show a wilful intent to destroy the competition. However, a charge of predatory pricing can still be damaging to the reputation of the accused company, as in WestJet's and Hawkair's 2003 allegations against Air Canada for its price reductions on specific routes[6] or the 2010 case in which the Supreme Court of British Columbia struck out Novus Entertainment's claims against Shaw Cablesystems regarding the abuse of dominance provisions of the Competition Act.[7]

Resale Price Maintenance

Producers usually take the time to research where they wish their products to be positioned in terms of price and quality, and in relation to their competitors, so that they achieve their desired profit goals. They cannot, however, dictate the retailer's selling price or determine a floor price. They may give their channel members a manufacturer's suggested retail price (MSRP) and even indicate the MSRP by way of a label on the product, but they cannot discriminate against any retailers that do not follow their recommendations. In Canada, **resale price maintenance**, producers' attempts to control the price of their products in retail stores, is illegal. However, companies operating both in Canada and in the United States will find that resale price maintenance is legal south of the border, and, thus, such firms may need two separate pricing policies.

Price Discrimination

Price discrimination is the practice of charging different prices to different buyers for goods of like grade and quality within relatively the same time period for the purpose of substantially reducing the competition. This type of price discrimination does not apply to services, end-users, or consumers; thus, movie theatres and dry cleaners, for example, can charge different prices for students and seniors or charge different prices on various days of the week.

Producers can legally offer promotional (push) incentives to channel members, but they must do so on a proportional basis; that is, sale prices and any

FINE-TUNING TECHNIQUES ARE **SHORT-RUN** APPROACHES THAT DO NOT CHANGE THE **GENERAL PRICE** LEVEL.

savings can be in relation to and proportional to transactional or logistical costs. Sellers may also lower their prices to buyers in their efforts to meet competitive challenges. Note that the Competition Act also makes it illegal for buyers to use their influence of purchasing power to force discriminator prices or services.

Six elements are necessary for a practice of price discrimination to occur:

1. Two or three instances of discrimination must have occurred over time.

2. The sales in question must have occurred within a relatively short period of time.

3. The products sold must be commodities or tangible goods.

4. The seller must charge different prices to two or more buyers for the same product.

5. The products sold must be of the same quality and grade.

6. The buyers of the good must be competitors.

LO 3 Tactics for Fine-Tuning the Base Price

After managers understand both the legal and the marketing consequences of price strategies, they should set a **base price**, the general price level at which the company expects to sell the good or service. The general price level is correlated with the pricing policy: a pricing level above the market price is price skimming, at the market price is status quo pricing, and below the market price is penetration pricing. The final step, then, is to fine-tune the base price.

Fine-tuning techniques are short-run approaches that do not change the general price level. They do, however, result in changes within a general price level.

These pricing tactics allow the firm to adjust for competition in certain markets, meet ever-changing government regulations, take advantage of unique demand situations, and meet promotional and positioning goals. Fine-tuning pricing tactics include various sorts of discounts, geographic pricing, and other pricing tactics.

Discounts, Allowances, Rebates, and Value-Based Pricing

A base price can be lowered through the use of discounts and the related tactics of allowances, rebates, low or zero percent financing, and value-based pricing. Managers use the various forms of discounts to encourage customers to do what they would not ordinarily do, such as paying cash rather than using credit, taking delivery out of season, or performing certain functions within a distribution channel.[8] The following are of the most common tactics:

▸▸ *Quantity discounts:* When buyers are charged a lower unit price when buying either in multiple units or more than a specified dollar amount, they are receiving a **quantity discount**. A **cumulative quantity discount** is a deduction from list price that applies to the buyer's total purchases made during a specific period; it is intended to encourage customer loyalty. In contrast, a **noncumulative quantity discount** is a deduction from list price that applies to a single order rather than to the total volume of orders placed during a certain period. It is intended to encourage orders in large quantities.

▸▸ *Cash discounts:* A **cash discount** is a price reduction offered to a consumer, an industrial user, or a marketing

base price the general price level at which the company expects to sell the good or service

quantity discount a unit price reduction offered to buyers buying either in multiple units or more than a specified dollar amount

cumulative quantity discount a deduction from list price that applies to the buyer's total purchases made during a specific period

noncumulative quantity discount a deduction from list price that applies to a single order rather than to the total volume of orders placed during a certain period

cash discount a price reduction offered to a consumer, an industrial user, or a marketing intermediary in return for prompt payment of a bill

JUSTIN SULLIVAN/GETTY IMAGES

intermediary in return for prompt payment of a bill (for example, 2/10, net 30). Prompt payment saves the seller carrying charges and billing expenses and allows the seller to avoid bad debt.

▸▸ *Functional discounts:* When distribution channel intermediaries, such as wholesalers or retailers, perform a service or function for the manufacturer (for example, setting up retail displays or extending credit), they must be compensated. This compensation, typically a percentage discount from the base price, is called a **functional discount** (or **trade discount**). Functional discounts vary greatly from channel to channel, depending on the tasks performed by the intermediary.

▸▸ *Seasonal discounts:* A **seasonal discount** is a price reduction for buying merchandise out of season (for example, buying new ski equipment in March and accepting delivery in July). It shifts the storage function to the purchaser. Seasonal discounts also enable manufacturers to maintain a steady production schedule year-round.

▸▸ *Promotional allowances:* A **promotional allowance** (also known as a **trade allowance**) is a payment to a dealer for promoting the manufacturer's products. It is both a pricing tool and a promotional device. As a pricing tool, a promotional allowance is like a functional discount. If, for example, a retailer runs an ad for a manufacturer's product, the manufacturer may offer a promotional allowance by paying half the cost.

▸▸ *Rebates:* A **rebate** is a cash refund given for the purchase of a product during a specific period. The advantage of a rebate over a simple price reduction for stimulating demand is that a rebate is a temporary inducement that can be withdrawn without altering the basic price structure (for example, Apple rebates on computers and printers). A manufacturer that uses a simple price reduction for a short time may meet resistance when trying to restore the price to its original, higher level.

▸▸ *Zero percent financing:* During the first six or seven years of the 2000s, new-car sales receded. To get people back into automobile showrooms, manufacturers offered zero percent financing, which enabled purchasers to pay for new cars by borrowing money at no interest charge. The tactic created a huge increase in sales but not without cost to the manufacturers. A five-year, interest-free car loan represented a cost of more than $3,000 on a typical vehicle sold during the zero percent promotion. But, because the recession of 2008–10 greatly affected auto sales, many automobile companies in 2011 were still using this financing option to entice buyers.

Value-Based Pricing **Value-based pricing**, also called *value pricing*, is a pricing strategy that has grown out of the quality movement. Instead of determining prices on the basis of costs or competitors' prices, value-based pricing starts with the customer, considers the competition, and then determines the appropriate price. The basic assumption is that the firm is customer driven, seeking to understand the attributes customers want in the goods and services they buy and the value of that bundle of attributes to customers. Because very few firms operate in a pure monopoly, however, a marketer using value-based pricing must also determine the value of competitive offerings to customers. Customers determine the value of a product (not just its price) relative to the value of alternatives. In value-based pricing, therefore, the price of the product is set at a level that seems to the customer to be a good price compared with the prices of other options.

Because of Wal-Mart's strong market entry into groceries, rival supermarkets are adopting value-based pricing as a defensive move. Shoppers in competitive markets are seeing prices fall as Wal-Mart pushes rivals to match its value prices. Numerous regional grocery chains have switched to value pricing. In the past, they offered weekly specials to attract shoppers and then made up the lost profit by keeping nonsale prices substantially higher. Now, Costco and Wal-Mart have conditioned consumers to expect inexpensive goods every day.[9]

Pricing Products Too Low Sometimes managers price their products too low, thereby reducing company profits.[10] Pricing too low seems to happen for two reasons. First, managers attempt to buy market share through aggressive pricing. Usually, however, these price cuts are quickly met by competitors. Thus, any gain in market share is short-lived, and overall industry profits end up falling. Second, managers have a natural tendency to want to make decisions that can be justified objectively.

The problem is that companies often lack hard data on the complex determinants of profitability, such as the relationship between price changes and sales volumes, the link between demand levels and costs, and the likely responses of competitors to price changes. In contrast, companies usually have rich, unambiguous information on costs, sales, market share, and competitors' prices. As a result, managers tend to make pricing decisions that are based on current costs, projected short-term share gains, or current competitor prices rather than on long-term profitability.

The problem of underpricing can be solved by linking information about price, cost, and demand within the same decision support system. The demand data can be developed via marketing research, which will enable managers to get the hard data they need to calculate the effects of pricing decisions on profitability.

Geographic Pricing

Because many sellers ship their wares to a nation-wide or even a worldwide market, the cost of freight can greatly affect the total cost of a product. Sellers may use several different geographic pricing tactics to moderate the impact of freight costs on distant customers. The following methods of geographic pricing are the most common:

▸▸ *FOB origin pricing:* **FOB origin pricing,** also called *FOB factory* or *FOB shipping point,* is a price tactic that requires the buyer to absorb the freight costs from the shipping point ("free on board"). The farther buyers are from sellers, the more they pay, because transportation costs generally increase with the distance merchandise is shipped.

▸▸ *Uniform delivered pricing:* If the marketing manager wants total costs, including freight, to be equal for all purchasers of identical products, the firm will adopt uniform delivered pricing, or postage stamp pricing. With **uniform delivered pricing**, the seller pays the actual freight charges and bills every purchaser an identical, flat freight charge.

▸▸ *Zone pricing:* A marketing manager who wants to equalize total costs among buyers within large geographic areas—but not necessarily all of the seller's market area—may modify the base price with a zone-pricing tactic. **Zone pricing** is a modification of uniform delivered pricing. Rather than using a uniform freight rate for its total market, the firm divides it into segments or zones and charges a flat freight rate to all customers in a given zone. Honda, for example, has standardized freight charges on its vehicles, which are based on costs from the point of origin to a specific region.

▸▸ *Freight absorption pricing:* In **freight absorption pricing**, the seller pays all or part of the actual freight charges and does not pass them on to the buyer. The manager may use this tactic in intensely competitive areas or as a way to break into new market areas.

▸▸ *Basing-point pricing:* With **basing-point pricing**, the seller designates a location as a basing point and charges all buyers the freight cost from that point, regardless of the city from which the goods are shipped. Thanks to several adverse court rulings, basing-point pricing has waned in popularity. Freight fees charged when none were actually incurred, called phantom freight, have been declared illegal.

Other Pricing Tactics

Unlike geographic pricing, other pricing tactics are unique and defy neat categorization. Managers use these tactics for various reasons—for example, to stimulate demand for specific products, to increase store patronage, and to offer a wider variety of merchandise at a specific price point. Other pricing tactics include a single-price tactic, flexible pricing, professional services pricing, price lining, leader pricing, bait pricing, odd–even pricing, price bundling, and two-part pricing.

Zone Pricing
shipped to Kelowna: $10
shipped to Toronto: $20

Single-Price Tactic A merchant using a **single-price tactic** offers all goods and services at the same price (or perhaps two or three prices). Netflix is an example of a single-price tactic where for $7.99 per month, members can watch unlimited movies and TV episodes on their TVs and computers. Dollar stores are another example of retailers using the single-price tactic.

Single-price selling removes price comparisons from the buyer's decision-making process. The retailer enjoys the benefits of

> **FOB origin pricing** the buyer absorbs the freight costs from the shipping point ("free on board")

> **uniform delivered pricing** the seller pays the actual freight charges and bills every purchaser an identical, flat freight charge

> **zone pricing** a modification of uniform delivered pricing that divides the total market into segments or zones and charges a flat freight rate to all customers in a given zone

> **freight absorption pricing** the seller pays all or part of the actual freight charges and does not pass them on to the buyer

> **basing-point pricing** charging freight from a given (basing) point, regardless of the city from which the goods are shipped

> **single-price tactic** offering all goods and services at the same price (or perhaps two or three prices)

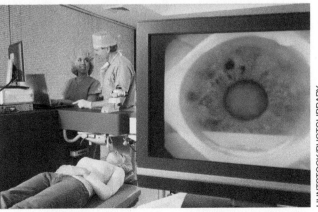

KHZ/SHUTTERSTOCK.COM

HUNTSTOCK/PHOTOLIBRARY

flexible pricing (variable pricing) different customers pay different prices for essentially the same merchandise bought in equal quantities

price lining offering a product line with several items at specific price points

leader pricing (loss-leader pricing) a product is sold near or even below cost in the hope that shoppers will buy other items once they are in the store

a simplified pricing system and minimal clerical errors. However, continually rising costs are a headache for retailers following this strategy. In times of inflation, they must frequently raise the selling price.

Flexible Pricing Flexible **pricing** (or **variable pricing**) means that different customers pay different prices for essentially the same merchandise bought in equal quantities. This tactic is often found in the sale of shopping goods, specialty merchandise, and most industrial goods except supply items. Car dealers and many appliance retailers commonly follow the practice. It allows the seller to adjust for competition by meeting another seller's price. Thus, a marketing manager with a status quo pricing objective might readily adopt the tactic. Flexible pricing also enables the seller to close a sale with price-conscious consumers.

The obvious disadvantages of flexible pricing are the lack of consistent profit margins, the potential ill will of high-paying purchasers, the tendency for salespeople to automatically lower the price to make a sale, and the possibility of a price war among sellers.

RESULTS OR A REBATE?

A simple philosophy is behind the promotions work that Rethink Communications of Vancouver, British Columbia, does for its clients: "If you don't get results, we shouldn't get our full fee."[11] Each year, the company and each client agree to a set of goals, both measurable and subjective, and Rethink sets aside up to 5 percent of the client's total fee—the rebate. Once a client receives its sales results for the year, it measures the effectiveness of Rethink's promotional work against the original objectives. On the basis of Rethink's score, the client pays Rethink some, or none, of the withheld rebate.

Professional Services Pricing Professional services pricing is used by people with lengthy experience, training, and often certification by a licensing board—for example, lawyers, physicians, and family counsellors. Professionals sometimes charge customers at an hourly rate, but sometimes fees are based on the solution of a problem or performance of an act (such as an eye examination) rather than on the actual time involved.

Those who use professional pricing have an ethical responsibility not to overcharge a customer. Because demand is sometimes highly inelastic, there may be a temptation to charge what the market will bear.[12]

Price Lining When a seller establishes a series of prices for a type of merchandise, it creates a price line. **Price lining** is the practice of offering a product line with several items at specific price points. The Limited may offer women's dresses at $40, $70, and $100, with no merchandise marked at prices between those figures. Instead of a normal demand curve running from $40 to $100, The Limited has three demand points (prices). Theoretically, the curve exists only because people would buy goods at the in-between prices if it were possible to do so.

Price lining reduces confusion for both the salesperson and the consumer. The buyer may be offered a wider variety of merchandise at each established price. Price lines may also enable a seller to reach several market segments. For buyers, the question of price may be quite simple: all they have to do is find a suitable product at the predetermined price. Moreover, price lining is a valuable tactic for the marketing manager because the firm may be able to carry a smaller total inventory than it could without price lines. The results may include fewer markdowns, simplified purchasing, and lower inventory-carrying charges.

Price lines also present drawbacks, especially if costs are continually rising. Sellers can offset rising costs in three ways. First, they can begin stocking lower-quality merchandise at each price point. Second, sellers can change the prices, although frequent price line changes may confuse buyers. Third, sellers can accept lower profit margins and hold quality and prices constant. This third alternative has short-run benefits, but its long-run handicaps may drive sellers out of business.

Leader Pricing Leader pricing (or **loss-leader pricing**) is selling a product near or even below cost in the hope that shoppers will buy other items once they are in the store. This type of pricing appears weekly in the newspaper advertising of supermarkets. Leader pricing is normally used on well-known items that consumers can easily recognize as bargains. The goal is not necessarily to sell large quantities of leader items, but to try to appeal to customers who might shop elsewhere.[13]

Leader pricing is not limited to products. Health and fitness clubs often offer a one-month free trial as a loss leader.

Bait Pricing In contrast to leader pricing, which is a genuine attempt to give the consumer a reduced price, bait pricing is deceptive. **Bait pricing** is a price tactic that tries to get the consumer into a store through false or misleading price advertising and then uses high-pressure selling to persuade the consumer to buy more expensive merchandise. You may have seen this ad or a similar one:

REPOSSESSED … Singer slant-needle sewing machine … take over 8 payments of $5.10 per month … ABC Sewing Centre.

This is bait. When a customer goes in to see the machine, a salesperson says that it has just been sold or else shows the prospective buyer a piece of junk. Then the salesperson says, "But I've got a really good deal on this fine new model." This is the switch that may cause a susceptible consumer to walk out with a $400 machine. The Competition Bureau considers bait pricing a deceptive act and has banned its use, but sometimes enforcement is lax.

Odd–Even Pricing Odd–even pricing (or psychological pricing) means pricing at odd-numbered prices to connote a bargain and pricing at even-numbered prices to imply quality. For years, many retailers have priced their products in odd numbers—for example, $99.95—to make consumers feel they are paying a lower price for the product. Even-numbered pricing is sometimes used to denote quality. The demand curve for such items would also be sawtoothed, except that the outside edges would represent even-numbered prices and, therefore, elastic demand.

Price Bundling Price bundling is marketing two or more products in a single package for a special price. For example, Microsoft offers suites of software that bundle spreadsheets, word processing, graphics, electronic mail, Internet access, and groupware for networks of microcomputers. Price bundling can stimulate demand for the bundled items if the target market perceives the price as a good value.

Hotels and airlines sell a perishable commodity (hotel rooms and airline seats) with relatively constant fixed costs. Bundling can be an important income stream for these businesses because the variable cost tends to be low—for instance, the cost of cleaning a hotel room. Therefore, most of the revenue can help cover fixed costs and generate profits.

Bundling has also been used in the telecommunications industry. Companies offer local service, long-distance service, DSL Internet service, wireless, and even cable TV in various menus of bundling. Telecom companies use bundling as a way to protect their market share and fight off competition by locking customers into a group of services. For consumers, comparison shopping may be difficult since they may not be able to determine how much they are really paying for each component of the bundle. A related price tactic is **unbundling**, or reducing the bundle of services that comes with the basic product. To help hold the line on costs, some stores require customers to pay for gift wrapping.

Clearly, price bundling can influence consumers' purchase behaviour. But what about the decision to consume a particular bundled product or service? Some of the latest research has focused on how people consume certain bundled products or services. According to this research, the key to consumption behaviour is how closely consumers can link the costs and benefits of the exchange.[14] In complex transactions, such as a holiday package, it may be unclear which costs are paying for which benefits. In such cases, consumers tend to mentally downplay their upfront costs for the bundled product, so they may be more likely to forgo a benefit that's part of the bundle, such as a free dinner.

Similarly, when people buy season's tickets to a concert series, sporting event, or other activity, the sunk costs (price of the bundle)

bait pricing a price tactic that tries to get consumers into a store through false or misleading price advertising and then uses high-pressure selling to persuade consumers to buy more expensive merchandise

odd–even pricing (psychological pricing) odd-numbered prices connote bargains and even-numbered prices imply quality

price bundling marketing two or more products in a single package for a special price

unbundling reducing the bundle of services that comes with the basic product

MIKE KEMP/RUBBERBALL PRODUCTIONS/GETTY IMAGES

two-part pricing
charging two separate amounts to consume a single good or service

consumer penalty
an extra fee paid by the consumer for violating the terms of the purchase agreement

and the pending benefit (going to see the events) become decoupled. The result is a reduced likelihood of consumption of all the events over time.

Theatregoers who purchase tickets to a single play are almost certain to use those tickets. This behaviour is consistent with the idea that in a one-to-one transaction (i.e., one payment, one benefit), the costs and benefits of that transaction are tightly coupled, resulting in strong sunk cost pressure to consume the pending benefit.

A theatre manager might expect a no-show rate of 20 percent when the percentage of season's ticket holders is high, but a no-show rate of only 5 percent when the percentage of season's ticket holders is low. When a theatre has a high number of season's ticket holders, a manager can oversell performances and maximize the revenue for the theatre.

The physical format of the transaction also figures in. A ski lift pass in the form of a booklet of tickets strengthens the cost–benefit link for consumers, whereas a single pass for multiple ski lifts weakens that link.

Although the price bundling of services can result in a lower rate of total consumption of that service, the same is not necessarily true for products. Consider the purchase of an expensive bottle of wine. When the wine is purchased as a single unit, its cost and eventual benefit are tightly coupled. As a result, the cost of the wine will be significant, and a person will likely reserve that wine for a special occasion. When the wine is purchased as part of a bundle (e.g., as part of a case of wine), however, the cost and benefit of that individual bottle of wine will likely become decoupled, reducing the impact of the cost on eventual consumption. Thus, in contrast to the price bundling of services, the price bundling of physical goods could lead to an increase in product consumption.

Two-Part Pricing **Two-part pricing** means charging two separate amounts to consume a single good or service. Health and fitness clubs charge a membership fee and then a flat fee each time a person uses certain equipment or facilities.

Consumers sometimes prefer two-part pricing because they are uncertain about the number and the types of activities they might use, such as at an amusement park. Also, the people who use a service most often pay a higher total price. Two-part pricing can increase a seller's revenue by attracting consumers who would not pay a high fee even for unlimited use.

Consumer Penalties

More and more businesses are adopting **consumer penalties**—extra fees paid by consumers for violating the terms of a purchase agreement. Businesses impose consumer penalties for two reasons: they will allegedly (1) suffer an irrevocable revenue loss and/or (2)

WICKED DEAL

Researchers found that theatregoers who purchased tickets to four plays were only 84 percent likely to use their first-play tickets and only 78 percent likely to use any given ticket across the four plays.[15]

If one of the plays in the bundle is Wicked, however, that might change things. Although the production eventually grossed $1.3 million a week in New York and broke box office records in Toronto, Wicked was not an instant success. Despite the show's initially low consumer awareness, producer Marc Platt was convinced that if he could just get people in the door, they would find the performance completely captivating. So he cut ticket prices by 30 percent and watched as patrons began to make repeat ticket purchases during intermission.

© KATHY WILLENS/ASSOCIATED PRESS

incur significant additional transaction costs should customers be unable or unwilling to complete their purchase obligations. Consumer penalties are commonly imposed when not showing up for reserved hotel accommodation and when failing to keep a doctor's or dentist's appointment. For the company, these customer payments are part of doing business in a highly competitive marketplace. With profit margins in many companies increasingly coming under pressure, organizations are looking to stem losses resulting from customers not meeting their obligations. However, the perceived unfairness of a penalty may affect some consumers' willingness to patronize a business in the future.

LO 4 Product Line Pricing

Product line pricing is setting prices for an entire line of products. Compared with setting the right price on a single product, product line pricing encompasses broader concerns. In product line pricing, the marketing manager tries to achieve maximum profits or other goals for the entire line rather than for a single component of the line.

Relationships among Products

The manager must first determine the type of relationship that exists among the various products in the line:

▸▸ If items are *complementary*, an increase in the sale of one good causes an increase in demand for the complementary product, and vice versa. For example, the sale of ski poles depends on the demand for skis, making these two items complementary.

▸▸ Two products in a line can also be *substitutes* for each other. If buyers buy one item in the line, they are less likely to buy a second item in the line. For example, a consumer who buys a cup of coffee is unlikely to also buy a cup of tea.

▸▸ A *neutral* relationship can also exist between two products. In other words, demand for one of the products is unrelated to demand for the other. For example, the demand for a textbook is unrelated to the demand for a pizza.

Joint Costs

Joint costs are costs that are shared in the manufacturing and marketing of several products in a product line. These costs pose a unique problem in product pricing. For example, the production of compact discs that combine photos and music.

Any assignment of joint costs is necessarily subjective because costs are actually shared. Suppose a company produces two products, X and Y, in a common production process, with joint costs allocated on a weight basis. Product X weighs 1,000 kilograms, and product Y weighs 500 kilograms. Thus, costs are allocated on the basis of $2 for X for every $1 for Y. Gross margins (sales less the cost of goods sold) might then be as follows:

	Product X	Product Y	Total
Sales	$20,000	$6,000	$26,000
Less: cost of goods sold	15,000	7,500	22,500
Gross margin	$ 5,000	($1,500)	$ 3,500

This statement reveals a loss of $1,500 on product Y. However, the firm must realize that overall it earned a $3,500 profit on the two items in the line. Also, weight may not be the appropriate way to allocate the joint costs. Instead, the firm might use other bases, including market value or quantity sold.

LO 5 Pricing during Difficult Economic Times

Pricing is always an important aspect of marketing, but it is especially crucial in times of inflation and recession. The firm that does not adjust to economic trends may lose ground that it can never make up.

Inflation

When the economy is characterized by high inflation, special pricing tactics are often necessary. They can be subdivided into cost-oriented and demand-oriented tactics.

Cost-Oriented Tactics One popular cost-oriented tactic is *culling products with a low profit margin* from the product line. However, this tactic may backfire for three reasons:

▸▸ A high volume of sales on an item with a low profit margin may still make the item highly profitable.

▸▸ Eliminating a product from a product line may reduce economies of scale, thereby lowering the margins on other items.

▶▶ Eliminating the product may affect the price-quality image of the entire line.

Another popular cost-oriented tactic is **delayed-quotation pricing,** which is used for industrial installations and many accessory items. Price is not set on the product until the item is either finished or delivered. Long production lead times force many firms to adopt this policy during periods of inflation. Builders of nuclear power plants, ships, airports, and office towers sometimes use delayed-quotation tactics.

Escalator pricing is similar to delayed-quotation pricing in that the final selling price reflects cost increases incurred between the time an order is placed and the time delivery is made. An escalator clause allows for price increases (usually across the board) that are based on the cost-of-living index or some other formula. As with any price increase, management's ability to implement such a policy is based on inelastic demand for the product. Often it is used only with new customers or for extremely complex products that take a long time to produce. Another tactic growing in popularity is to hold prices constant but add new fees. The rising price of fuel has forced many companies to cover their costs by adding or increasing a fuel surcharge. Canada Post's surcharge rose four times between March and August of 2008, moving from 7.75 percent to 12.25 percent in that six-month period.[16] In 2011, the surcharge is again expected to rise to 12.5 percent as fuel prices again started to increase.[17]

Any cost-oriented pricing policy that tries to maintain a fixed gross margin under all conditions can lead to a vicious circle. For example, a price increase will result in decreased demand, which in turn will increase production costs (because of lost economies of scale). Increased production costs then require a further

EA GAMES SCRIPPS HOWARD PHOTO SERVICE/NEWSCOM

Electronic Arts (EA) Canada, the developer and publisher of video games, faces demand for revision to its products not only from its consumers, avid gamers who want reality in the latest cars, but also because of changes in technology in the products by different companies, such as Nintendo and Sony. Some EA products can have as many as three revisions per year.

price increase, leading to further diminished demand, and so on.

Demand-Oriented Tactics Demand-oriented pricing tactics use price to reflect changing patterns of demand caused by inflation or high interest rates. Cost changes are considered, of course, but mostly in the context of how increased prices will affect demand.

Price shading is the use of discounts by salespeople to increase demand for one or more products in a line. Often, shading becomes habitual and is done routinely without much forethought.

To make the demand for a good or service more inelastic and to create buyer dependency, a company can use several strategies:

▶▶ *Cultivate selected demand:* Marketing managers can target prosperous customers who will pay extra for convenience or service. In cultivating close relationships with affluent organizational customers, marketing managers should avoid putting themselves at the mercy of a dominant firm. They can more easily raise prices when an account is readily replaceable. Finally, in companies where engineers exert more influence than purchasing departments, performance is favoured over price. Often a preferred vendor's pricing range expands if other suppliers prove technically unsatisfactory.

▶▶ *Create unique offerings:* Marketing managers should study buyers' needs. If the seller can design distinctive goods or services uniquely fitting buyers' activities, equipment, and procedures, a mutually beneficial relationship will evolve. By satisfying targeted buyers in a superior way, marketing managers can make them dependent on the brand. Companies such as Microsoft and Sony, makers of the Xbox and PlayStation game consoles, have gaming software such as Need for Speed designed specifically for their systems by companies such as EA Canada in Burnaby, British Columbia. This system-specific software encourages gamers to be more loyal to their hardware.

▶▶ *Change the package design:* Another way companies pass on higher costs is to shrink product sizes but keep prices

CHRIS SHACKLEFORD/SHUTTERSTOCK.COM

the same, for example, by putting fewer sheets on a roll of paper towels.

▶▶ *Heighten buyer dependence:* Owens Corning supplies an integrated insulation service that includes commercial and scientific training for distributors and seminars for end-users. This practice freezes out competition and supports higher prices.

Recession

A recession is a period of reduced economic activity. Reduced demand for goods and services, accompanied by higher rates of unemployment, is a common trait of a recession. Yet astute marketers can often find opportunity during recessions. A recession is an excellent time to build market share because competitors are struggling to make ends meet.

Two effective pricing tactics to hold or build market share during a recession are value-based pricing and bundling. *Value-based pricing*, discussed earlier in the chapter, stresses to customers that they are getting a good value for their money. *Bundling* or *unbundling* can also stimulate demand during a recession. If features are added to a bundle, consumers may perceive the offering as having greater value. Conversely, companies can unbundle offerings and lower base prices to stimulate demand.

Recessions are a good time for marketing managers to study the demand for individual items in a product line and the revenue they produce. Pruning unprofitable items can save resources that can be better used elsewhere.

Prices often fall during a recession as competitors try desperately to maintain demand for their wares. Even if demand remains constant, falling prices mean lower profits or no profits. Falling prices, therefore, are a natural incentive to lower costs. During the past recession, companies implemented new technology to improve efficiency and then slashed payrolls. They also discovered that suppliers were an excellent source of cost savings; the cost of purchased materials accounts for slightly more than half of most North American manufacturers' expenses. Specific strategies that companies use with suppliers include the following:

▶▶ *Renegotiating contracts:* Sending suppliers letters demanding price cuts of 5 percent or more; putting out for rebid the contracts of those that refuse to cut costs.

▶▶ *Offering help:* Dispatching teams of experts to suppliers' plants to help reorganize and suggest other productivity-boosting changes; working with suppliers to make parts simpler and cheaper to produce.

▶▶ *Keeping the pressure on:* To make sure that improvements continue, setting annual, across-the-board cost reduction targets, often of 5 percent or more per year.

▶▶ *Paring down suppliers:* To improve economies of scale, slashing the overall number of suppliers, sometimes by up to 80 percent, and boosting purchases from those suppliers that remain.

Tough tactics like these help keep companies afloat during economic downturns.

8%
Percentage of companies that do serious pricing research

2009
Latest year for revisions to Competitions Act of 1986

4
Steps to setting the right price

5%
Percentage of performance-based price rebate offered by Rethink

$2.7 million in fines and 44 months in jail for four individuals
The penalty imposed for the price fixing of gasoline

30,000
Number of items generally carried by supermarkets

CHAPTER **20** **Developing a Global Vision**

Over the past two decades, world trade has climbed from $200 billion a year to over $7 trillion.

LO 1 Rewards of Global Marketing

AFTER YOU FINISH THIS CHAPTER, GO TO WWW. ICANMKTG2.COM FOR STUDY TOOLS.

Today, global revolutions are under way in many areas of our lives: management, politics, communications, and technology. The word *global* has assumed a new meaning, referring to a boundless mobility and competition in social, business, and intellectual arenas. **Global marketing**—marketing that targets markets throughout the world—has become an imperative for business.

Canadian managers must develop a **global vision** not only to recognize and react to international marketing opportunities but also to remain competitive at home. Often a Canadian firm's toughest domestic competition comes from foreign companies. Moreover, a global vision enables a manager to understand that customer and distribution networks operate worldwide, blurring geographic and political barriers and making them increasingly irrelevant to business decisions. In summary, having a global vision means recognizing and reacting to international marketing opportunities, using effective global marketing strategies, and being aware of threats from foreign competitors in all markets.

Over the past two decades, world trade has climbed from $200 billion a year to over $7 trillion. Countries and companies that were never considered major

global marketing
marketing that targets markets throughout the world

global vision
recognizing and reacting to international marketing opportunities, using effective global marketing strategies, and being aware of threats from foreign competitors in all markets

What do you think?

What a business decides to do overseas doesn't affect me.

1 2 3 4 5 6 7
STRONGLY DISAGREE   STRONGLY AGREE

© WORLDFOTO/ALAMY

Find out what others think at the CourseMate for MKTG. Log in at NelsonBrain.com.

players in global marketing are now influential, and some of them show great skill. As a result, today's marketers face many challenges to their customary practices. Product development costs are rising, the life of products is getting shorter, and new technology is spreading around the world faster than ever. But, instead of fearing change, marketing winners relish its unrelenting pace.

Adopting a global vision can be very lucrative for a company. Gillette, for example, generates about two-thirds of its annual revenue from international divisions, and PepsiCo (the owner of Frito-Lay) brings in more than $3.25 billion annually from its overseas snack business. Another company with a global vision is Pillsbury, whose iconic Pillsbury Doughboy sells a product in India that the company had just about abandoned in North America: flour. To reach Indian housewives, the Doughboy speaks six regional languages and has adopted Indian customs, such as bowing in the traditional Indian greeting.

Global marketing is not, however, a one-way street, whereby only Canadian companies sell their wares and services throughout the world. Foreign competition in the domestic market, once relatively rare, is now found in almost every industry. In fact, in many industries, Canadian businesses have lost significant market share to imported products. In electronics, cameras, automobiles, fine china, tractors, leather goods, and a host of other consumer and industrial products, Canadian companies have struggled at home to maintain their market shares against foreign competitors.

Importance of Global Marketing to Canada

Canada's reliance on international commerce will increase as global markets become easier for Canadian firms to access. Globalization also means that foreign firms will find Canada an appealing market for their products and services. This trend toward increased globalization is a result of the world becoming smaller through advances in technology and telecommunications, improved and less costly transportation, and a

reduction in trade barriers. Canada's future growth will largely depend on our ability to effectively compete in the global marketplace.

As of 2009, exports and imports accounted for 45 percent of our gross domestic product (GDP). Our largest trading partner, by far, is the United States, which is the destination for 75 percent of our exports and the source of 55 percent of our imports.[1] Clearly, the United States is important to our economy and prosperity. However, our overreliance on the United States has led to encouragement, from all levels of government, for firms of all sizes to seek out new opportunities in almost every region of the world. These efforts are beginning to bear fruit as Asian economies are increasing their share of trade with Canadian businesses.

Most small- and medium-sized firms are essentially nonparticipants in global trade and marketing.

CANADA'S TOP 10 EXPORT MARKETS

Country	Export Value (in billions of dollars)
United States	269.8
United Kingdom	12.1
China	11.2
Japan	8.3
Mexico	4.8
Germany	3.7
South Korea	3.5
Netherlands	2.8
France	2.7
India	2.1

SOURCE: Canada's top ten trading partners 2009: http://www.international.gc.ca/economist-economiste/performance/state-point/state_2010_point/2010_5.aspx?lang=eng, accessed January 31, 2011.

EXPORTS AND IMPORTS ACCOUNT FOR **45 PERCENT** OF CANADA'S GROSS DOMESTIC PRODUCT.

In the past, only the very large multinational companies have seriously attempted to compete worldwide; however, this trend is beginning to change.

The Fear of Trade and Globalization The protests during meetings of the World Trade Organization, the World Bank, and the International Monetary Fund (these three organizations are discussed later in the chapter) show that many people fear world trade and globalization. Protesters' main arguments include the following:

▸ Millions of North Americans have lost jobs due to an increase in imports, production being shifted abroad, or the outsourcing of jobs to other countries. Most displaced workers find new jobs—but often for less pay.

▸ Millions of others fear losing their jobs, especially at those companies operating under competitive pressure.

▸ Employers often threaten to outsource jobs if workers do not accept pay cuts.

▸ Service and white-collar jobs are increasingly vulnerable to operations moving offshore.

Benefits of Globalization According to traditional economic theory, globalization relies on competition to drive down prices and increase product and service quality. Businesses go to the countries that operate most efficiently and/or those that have the technology to produce what is needed. Many companies for which the bulk of the work is labour intensive, requiring few skills, move their factories to countries where work can be done more efficiently because of an abundance of less educated workers. In return, these countries buy more higher-valued goods made by skilled workers in developed countries.

Thus, globalization expands economic freedom, spurs competition, and raises the productivity and living standards of people in countries that open themselves to the global marketplace. For less developed countries, globalization also offers access to foreign capital, global export markets, and advanced technology while breaking the monopoly of inefficient and protected domestic producers. Faster growth, in turn, reduces poverty, encourages democratization, and promotes higher labour and environmental standards. Although government officials may face more difficult choices as a result of globalization, their citizens enjoy greater individual freedom. In this sense, globalization acts as a check on governmental power by making it more difficult for governments to abuse the freedom and property of their citizens.

LO 2 Multinational Firms

Many large Canadian companies are global marketers, and many have been very successful. A company that is heavily engaged in international trade, beyond exporting and importing, is called a multinational corporation. **Multinational corporations** move resources, goods, services, and skills across national boundaries without regard to the country in which the headquarters is located.

Multinationals often develop their global business in stages. In the first stage, companies operate in one country and sell into others. Second-stage multinationals set up foreign subsidiaries to handle sales in one country. In the third stage, they operate an entire line of business in another country. The fourth stage has evolved primarily due to the Internet and involves mostly high-tech companies. For these firms, the executive suite is virtual. Their top executives and core corporate functions may be located in different countries, wherever the firms can gain a competitive edge through the availability of talent or capital, low costs, or proximity to their most important customers. A multinational company may have several worldwide headquarters, depending on the locations of certain markets or technologies.

A good example of a fourth-stage company is Trend Micro, an Internet antivirus software company.[2] The main virus response centre is in the Philippines, where 250 ever-vigilant engineers work evening and midnight shifts as needed. Six other labs are scattered from Munich to Tokyo. Trend Micro's financial headquarters is in Tokyo, where it went public; product development is in Ph.D.-rich Taiwan; and most of its sales are in Silicon Valley—inside the giant American market. When companies fragment this way, they are no longer limited to the strengths, or hobbled by the weaknesses, of their native lands. Such fourth-stage multinationals are being created around the world.

The role of multinational corporations in developing nations is a subject of controversy. Multinationals' ability to tap financial, physical, and human resources from all over the world and combine them economically and profitably can be of benefit to any country. They also often possess and can transfer the most up-to-date technology. Critics, however, claim that often the wrong kind of technology is transferred to developing

multinational corporation a company that is heavily engaged in international trade, beyond exporting and importing

CANADA'S TOP 10 CORPORATIONS BY REVENUE, 2010

Company	Revenue (in billions of dollars)
Manulife Financial	40.11
Royal Bank of Canada	38.14
Power Corp. of Canada	33.21
Power Financial	32.76
George Weston	31.88
Loblaw Companies	30.74
Great-West Life Co.	30.52
Sun Life Financial	27.89
Suncor Energy	27.54
Toronto-Dominion Bank	25.42

SOURCE: "Rankings of Canada's Top 1000 Public Companies by Profit," *The Globe and Mail*, June 19, 2010, http://www.theglobeandmail.com/report-on-business/rob-magazine/top-1000/rankings-of-canadas-top-1000-public-companies-by-profit/article1608779/, accessed January 31, 2011.

THE CANADIAN PRESS/MARIO BEAUREGARD

---

capital intensive
using more capital than labour in the production process

global marketing standardization
production of uniform products that can be sold the same way all over the world

nations. Usually, it is **capital intensive** (requiring a greater expenditure for equipment than for labour) and thus does not substantially increase employment. A *modern sector* then emerges in the nation, employing a small proportion of the labour force at relatively high productivity and income levels and with increasingly capital-intensive technologies. In addition, multinationals sometimes support reactionary and oppressive regimes if doing so is in their best interests. Other critics say that the firms take more wealth out of developing nations than they bring in, thus widening the gap between rich and poor nations.

Global Marketing Standardization

Traditionally, marketing-oriented multinational corporations have used a strategy of providing different product features, packaging, advertising, and so on, in each country where they operate. McDonald's global success is—believe it or not—based on variation rather than standardization. McDonald's changes its salad dressings and provides self-serve espresso for French tastes, bulgogi burgers in South Korea, falafel burgers in Egypt, beer in Germany, and sake in Japan.

In contrast to the idea of tailoring marketing mixes to meet the needs and wants of consumers in different countries, **global marketing standardization** involves producing uniform products that can be sold in the same way all over the world. Communication and technology have made the world smaller so that almost all consumers everywhere want all the things they have heard about, seen, or experienced. Global marketing standardization presumes that the markets throughout the world are becoming more alike, so, by practising uniform production, companies should be able to lower production and marketing costs and increase profits.

Today, many multinational companies use a combination of global marketing standardization and variation. Procter & Gamble calls its new philosophy *global planning*. The idea is to determine which product modifications are necessary from country to country while trying to minimize those modifications. P&G has at least four products that are marketed similarly in most parts of the world: Camay soap, Crest toothpaste, Head & Shoulders shampoo, and Pampers diapers. However, the smell of Camay, the flavour of Crest, the formula of Head & Shoulders, and the advertising for all three vary from country to country.

> "A MULTINATIONAL COMPANY MAY HAVE SEVERAL **WORLDWIDE HEADQUARTERS,** DEPENDING ON THE LOCATIONS OF CERTAIN MARKETS AND TECHNOLOGIES."

LO3 External Environment Facing Global Marketers

A global marketer or a firm considering global marketing must consider the external environment. Many of the same environmental factors that operate in the domestic market also exist internationally. These factors include culture, economic and technological development, political structure and actions, demographic makeup, and natural resources.

Culture

Central to any society is the common set of values shared by its citizens that determines what is socially acceptable. Culture underlies the family, the educational system, religion, and the social class system. The network of social organizations generates overlapping roles and status positions. These values and roles have a tremendous effect on people's preferences and thus on marketers' options. Language is another important aspect of culture. Marketers must take care in translating product names, slogans, instructions, and promotional messages so as not to convey the wrong meaning.

Each country has its own customs and traditions that determine business practices and influence negotiations with foreign customers.

The literal translation of Coca-Cola in Chinese characters is "bite the wax tadpole."

In many countries, personal relationships are more important than financial considerations. Negotiations in Japan often include long evenings of dining, drinking, and entertaining; and only after a close personal relationship has been formed do business negotiations begin.

Making successful sales presentations abroad requires a thorough understanding of the country's culture. The English, for example, want plenty of documentation for product claims and are less likely to simply accept the word of the sales representative. Compared with managers in other countries, managers in Scandinavian and Dutch companies are more likely to approach business transactions as Canadian managers do.

Economic and Technological Development

A second major factor in the external environment facing the global marketer is the level of economic development in the countries where it operates. In general, complex and sophisticated industries are found in developed countries, and more basic industries are found in less developed nations. Average family incomes are higher in the more developed countries compared with in the less developed markets. Larger incomes mean greater purchasing power and demand, not only for consumer goods and services but also for the machinery and workers required to produce consumer goods.

The combined gross national income (GNI) of the 234 nations for which data are available is approximately $74.54 trillion. Divide that up among the world's 6.7 billion inhabitants, and you get approximately $11,125 for every man, woman, and child on Earth.[3]

In low-income countries where the annual GNI per capita is $745 or less, the average life expectancy is only 58.9 years, compared with 81 years in Canada. Eighty out of every 1,000 newborns die in low-income countries each year, versus only five in Canada. Just

SALES SUCCESS **ABROAD** REQUIRES A **THOROUGH UNDERSTANDING** OF THE COUNTRY'S **CULTURE.**

WHO ARE THE RICHEST CITIZENS ON THE PLANET? RESIDENTS OF LUXEMBOURG, WITH PER CAPITA GNI OF $81,800.

© ISTOCKPHOTO/DHARUMA

59.8 percent of children are immunized against measles in those nations, compared with 94 percent of children in Canada. But just because a country has a low GNI per capita doesn't mean that everyone is poor. In fact, some of these countries have large and growing pockets of wealth.

Political Structure and Actions

Political structure is a third important variable facing global marketers. Government policies run the gamut from no private ownership and minimal individual freedom to little central government and maximum personal freedom. As rights of private property increase, government-owned industries and centralized planning tend to decrease. But rarely will a political environment be at one extreme or the other. More often, countries combine multiple elements into a unique political and economic identity. India, for instance, is a republic whose political ideology includes elements of socialism, monopoly capitalism, and competitive capitalism.

A recent World Bank study found that government regulations can have varying effects on different economic sectors depending on the country's larger political orientation. Regulations can also be effective to varying degrees within a country, depending on the presence of special-interest groups. The conventional wisdom has been that countries with

Mercosur the largest Latin American trade agreement, which includes Argentina, Bolivia, Brazil, Chile, Colombia, Ecuador, Paraguay, Peru, and Uruguay

Uruguay Round an agreement created by the World Trade Organization to dramatically lower trade barriers worldwide

the least regulations tend to be most efficient; however, this argument has been increasingly questioned by the rapid rise of centrally planned economies, such as China.

Legal Considerations Closely related to and often intertwined with the political environment are legal considerations. Many of the following legal structures are designed to either encourage or limit trade:

- ▸▸ *Tariff:* a tax levied on the goods entering a country.
- ▸▸ *Quota:* a limit on the amount of a specific product that can enter a country. Companies request quotas as a means of protection from foreign competition.
- ▸▸ *Boycott:* the exclusion of all products from certain countries or companies. Governments use boycotts to exclude products from countries with which they have a political dispute.
- ▸▸ *Exchange control:* a law compelling a company earning foreign exchange from its exports to sell it to a control agency, usually a central bank. A company wishing to buy goods abroad must first obtain foreign currency exchange from the control agency. For instance, Avon Products drastically cut back new production lines and products in the Philippines because exchange controls prevented the company from converting pesos to dollars to ship back to the home office. The pesos had to be used in the Philippines.
- ▸▸ *Market grouping (also known as a common trade alliance):* occurs when several countries agree to work together to form a common trade area that enhances trade opportunities.
- ▸▸ *Trade agreement:* an agreement to stimulate international trade. Not all government efforts are meant to stifle imports or investment by foreign corporations. The Uruguay Round of trade negotiations is an example of an effort to encourage trade. The largest Latin American trade agreement is **Mercosur**, which includes Argentina, Bolivia, Brazil, Chile, Colombia, Ecuador, Paraguay, Peru, and Uruguay. The elimination of most tariffs among the trading partners has resulted in trade revenues of over $16 billion annually. The economic boom created by Mercosur will undoubtedly cause other nations to seek trade agreements on their own or to enter Mercosur.

Uruguay Round and Doha Round The **Uruguay Round** is an agreement that has dramatically lowered trade barriers worldwide. Adopted in 1994, the agreement has been signed by 148 nations. It is the most ambitious global trade agreement ever negotiated. The agreement has reduced tariffs by one-third worldwide—a move that is expected to raise global income by $235 billion annually. Perhaps most notable is the recognition of new global realities. For the first time, an agreement covers services, intellectual property rights, and trade-related investment measures such as exchange controls.

The Uruguay Round made several major changes to world trading practices:

▸▸ *Entertainment, pharmaceuticals, integrated circuits, and software:* The rules protect patents, copyrights, and trademarks for 20 years. Computer programs receive 50 years' protection and semiconductor chips receive 10 years' protection. But many developing nations were given a decade to phase in patent protection for drugs.

▸▸ *Financial, legal, and accounting services:* Services came under international trading rules for the first time, creating a vast opportunity for these competitive Canadian industries. Now it is easier for managers and key personnel to be admitted to a country. Licensing standards for professionals, such as doctors, cannot discriminate against foreign applicants. That is, foreign applicants cannot be held to higher standards than domestic practitioners.

▸▸ *Agriculture:* Europe is gradually reducing farm subsidies, opening new opportunities for such Canadian farm exports as wheat and corn. Japan and Korea are beginning to import rice.

▸▸ *Textiles and apparel:* Strict quotas limiting imports from developing countries are being phased out, causing further job losses in the Canadian clothing trade. But retailers and consumers are the big winners, because past quotas have added $15 billion a year to clothing prices.

▸▸ *A new trade organization:* The **World Trade Organization (WTO)** replaced the old **General Agreement on Tariffs and Trade (GATT)**, which was created in 1948. The old GATT contained extensive loopholes that enabled countries to avoid the trade-barrier reduction agreements—a situation similar to obeying the law only if you want to! Today, all WTO members must fully comply with all agreements under the Uruguay Round. The WTO also has an effective dispute settlement procedure with strict time limits to resolve disputes.

The latest round of WTO trade talks began in Doha, Qatar, in 2001. For the most part, the periodic meetings of WTO members under the Doha Round have been very contentious. Typically, the discussions find developing countries on one side of the argument and the rich developed countries on the other. This round has not progressed very far.

The trend toward globalization has resulted in the creation of additional agreements and organizations: the North American Free Trade Agreement, the Central America Free Trade Agreement, the European Union, the World Bank, the International Monetary Fund, and the G20, a group of the largest and fastest growing top 20 economies of the world.

North American Free Trade Agreement At the time it was instituted, the **North American Free Trade Agreement (NAFTA)** created the world's largest free trade zone. The agreement includes Canada, the United States, and Mexico, with a combined population of 360 million and a combined economy of $6 trillion. Canada, the largest U.S. trading partner, entered a free trade agreement with the United States in 1988, so the main impact of NAFTA was to open the Mexican market to Canadian and U.S. companies. When the treaty went into effect, it removed a web of Mexican licensing requirements, quotas, and tariffs that limited transactions in Canadian and U.S. goods and services.

The real question is whether NAFTA can continue to deliver rising prosperity in all three countries. Canada has certainly benefited from cheaper imports and more investment opportunities abroad. U.S. trade with both Canada and Mexico exceeds $1.5 billion a day.[4] Although Mexico has thrived under NAFTA, its advantage as a low-cost producer is being lost to countries such as India and China. American and Canadian businesses complain that Mexico has a dysfunctional judicial system, unreliable power supplies, poor roads, high corporate tax rates, and unfriendly labour relations. These complaints have given companies pause when considering investing in Mexico. Mexico still has a lot to offer, but it must improve its infrastructure.

Canada and Free Trade Agreements Apart from a free trade agreement with the United States and Mexico (NAFTA), Canada is continuously improving its mutually beneficial trade relations with other countries. Canada has signed free trade agreements (FTAs) with Panama, Jordan, Colombia, Peru, Costa Rica, Chile, Israel, and the European Free Trade Association. Canada is in negotiations with several other countries regarding FTAs, including India, Turkey, Ukraine, Korean Singapore, and Dominican Republic. Canada is also negotiating with other countries to enhance its current FTAs and to join other pre-existing FTA blocs, such as the Andean Community Countries Free Trade

World Trade Organization (WTO) a trade organization that replaced the old General Agreement on Tariffs and Trade (GATT)

General Agreement on Tariffs and Trade (GATT) a trade agreement that contained loopholes that enabled countries to avoid trade-barrier reduction agreements

North American Free Trade Agreement (NAFTA) an agreement between Canada, the United States, and Mexico that created the world's largest free trade zone

Agreement, the Caribbean Community Free Trade Agreement, and the Free Trade Area of the Americas.[5]

Canada's Top 10 Import Markets, 2009

Country	Import Value (in billions of dollars)
United States	186.8
China	39.7
Mexico	16.5
Japan	15.2
Germany	10.7
United Kingdom	9.4
South Korea	5.9
France	5.6
Italy	4.4
Algeria	3.8

SOURCE: Foreign Affairs and International Trade Canada, "Canada's State of Trade: Trade and Investment Update 2010," http://www.international.gc.ca/economist-economiste/performance/state-point/state_2010_point/2010_5.aspx?lang=eng, accessed January 31, 2011.

European Union One of the world's most important free trade zones is the **European Union**, which now encompasses most of Europe. In 2004, the European Union (EU) expanded from 15 members (Austria, Belgium, Denmark, Finland, France, Germany, Greece, Ireland, Italy, Luxembourg, the Netherlands, Portugal, Spain, Sweden, and the United Kingdom) to 25 members with a combined population of 450 million. The new members were Cyprus, the Czech Republic, Estonia, Hungary, Latvia, Lithuania, Malta, Poland, Slovakia, and Slovenia. These entrants differ in several ways from the older members. Eight of the new members are former Soviet satellites and remain saddled with inefficient government offices, state-controlled enterprises, and large, protected farm sectors. Most economists predict that it will take 50 years or longer before productivity and living standards in these entrants catch up to those in Western Europe. In 2007, Bulgaria and Romania also joined the EU, bringing the member total to 27.

The primary goal of the EU is to create a unified European market. Other goals include instituting a common foreign policy, security policy, and defence policy and a European citizenship, whereby any EU citizen can live, work, vote, and run for office anywhere in the member countries. The EU is creating standardized trade rules and coordinated health and safety standards. Duties, customs procedures, and taxes have been standardized. The standardized rules have helped to create an estimated 2.5 million jobs since 1993.

Nevertheless, many regulations still are not standardized. Since 1997, Kellogg's has faced obstacle after obstacle as it tries to persuade regulators in different EU countries to allow it to put the same vitamins in all of its Corn Flakes. Denmark doesn't want any vitamins added, fearing that cereal eaters who already take multivitamins might exceed their recommended daily doses, which some experts say can damage internal organs. Dutch officials don't believe that either vitamin D or folic acid is beneficial, so they don't want them added. Finland likes vitamin D more than other countries; it helps Finns make up for sun deprivation.[6] With more than 15 different languages and individual national customs, Europe will always be far more diverse than North America, and product differences will continue.

An entirely different type of problem facing global marketers is the possibility of a protectionist movement by the EU against outsiders. In addition, the EU is a very tough antitrust enforcer. In 2005, the European offices of Intel were raided by EU antitrust officials looking for evidence of monopoly power abuse. Advanced Micro Devices (AMD) claimed that Intel had achieved its 90 percent share of the global market through threats and kickbacks.[7]

The World Bank and International Monetary Fund Two international financial organizations are instrumental in fostering global trade. The **World Bank**, an international bank, offers low-interest loans to developing nations. Originally, the purpose of the loans was to help these nations build infrastructure such as roads, power plants, schools, drainage projects, and hospitals. Now the World Bank offers loans to help developing nations relieve their debt burdens. To receive the loans, countries must pledge to lower trade barriers and aid private enterprise. In addition to making loans, the World Bank is a major source of advice and information for developing nations.

The **International Monetary Fund (IMF)** was founded in 1945, one year after the creation of the World Bank, to promote trade through financial cooperation and eliminate trade barriers in the process. The

European Union a free trade zone encompassing 27 European countries

World Bank an international bank that offers low-interest loans, advice, and information to developing nations

International Monetary Fund (IMF) an international organization that acts as a lender of last resort, providing loans to troubled nations, and also works to promote trade through financial cooperation

© JOANNA WNUK/ SHUTTERSTOCK

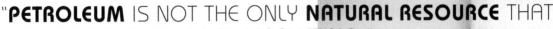

"PETROLEUM IS NOT THE ONLY NATURAL RESOURCE THAT AFFECTS INTERNATIONAL MARKETING."

IMF makes short-term loans to member nations that are unable to meet their budgetary expenses. It operates as a lender of last resort for troubled nations. In exchange for these emergency loans, IMF lenders frequently extract significant commitments from the borrowing nations to address the problems that led to the crises. These steps may include curtailing imports or even devaluing the currency.

Demographic Makeup

The three most densely populated nations in the world are China, India, and Indonesia. For marketers, though, that fact alone is not particularly useful; they also need to know whether the population is mostly urban or rural. Countries with a higher population living in urban settings represent more attractive markets. Just as important as population is personal income within a country.

Another key demographic consideration is age. A wide age gap separates the older populations of the industrialized countries from the vast working-age populations of developing countries. This gap has enormous implications for economies, businesses, and the competitiveness of individual countries. While Europe and Japan struggle with pension schemes and the rising cost of health care, China, Brazil, and Mexico reap the fruits of a demographic dividend: falling labour costs, a healthier and more educated population, and the entry of millions of women into the workforce. The demographic dividend is a gift of falling birthrates, which causes a temporary bulge in the number of working-age people.

Natural Resources

A final factor in the external environment that has become more evident in the past decade is the shortage of natural resources. Petroleum resources have created huge amounts of wealth for oil-producing countries such as Norway, Saudi Arabia, and the United Arab Emirates, where both consumer and industrial markets have blossomed. On the flip side, industrial countries such as Japan, the United States, Canada, and much of Western Europe experienced an enormous transfer of wealth to the petroleum-rich nations.

Petroleum is not the only natural resource that affects international marketing. Warm climate and

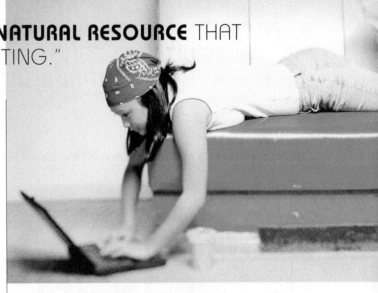

lack of water mean that many of Africa's countries will remain importers of foodstuffs. Vast differences in natural resources create international dependencies, huge shifts of wealth, inflation and recession, export opportunities for countries with abundant resources, and even a stimulus for military intervention.

PHOTODISC/GETTY IMAGES

LO 4 Global Marketing by the Individual Firm

A company should consider entering the global marketplace only after its management has a solid grasp of the global environment.

Companies decide to *go global* for a number of reasons. Perhaps the most important reason is to earn additional profits. Managers may feel that international sales will result in higher profit margins or more added-on profits. A second stimulus is that a firm may have a unique product or technological advantage not available to other international competitors. Such advantages should result in major business successes abroad. In other situations, management may have exclusive market information regarding foreign customers, marketplaces, or market situations not known to others. Although exclusivity can provide an initial motivation for international marketing, managers can expect that competitors will catch up with the firm's temporary information advantage. Finally, saturated domestic markets, excess capacity, and potential for economies of scale can also be motivators to go global. Economies of scale mean that average per-unit production costs fall as output is increased.

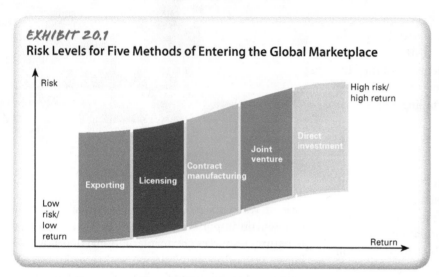

EXHIBIT 20.1
Risk Levels for Five Methods of Entering the Global Marketplace

export, which is usually treated as a domestic customer by the domestic manufacturer. The buyer for export assumes all risks and sells internationally for its own account. The domestic firm is involved only to the extent that its products are bought in foreign markets.

A second type of intermediary is the **export broker**, who plays the traditional broker's role by bringing buyer and seller together. The manufacturer still retains title and assumes all the risks. Export brokers operate primarily in agricultural products and raw materials.

Export agents, a third type of intermediary, are foreign sales agent–distributors who live in the foreign country and perform the same functions as domestic manufacturers' agents, helping with international financing, shipping, and so on. Export Development Canada provides help for Canadian firms seeking agents or distributors in almost every country. A second category of agents resides in the manufacturer's country but represents foreign buyers. This type of agent acts as a hired purchasing agent for foreign customers operating in the exporter's home market.

Many firms form multinational partnerships—called strategic alliances—to assist them in penetrating global markets; strategic alliances were examined in Chapter 6. Five other methods of entering the global marketplace are, in order of risk, exporting, licensing and franchising, contract manufacturing, the joint venture, and direct investment (see Exhibit 20.1 above).

Exporting

When a company decides to enter the global market, exporting is usually the least complicated and least risky method of entry. **Exporting** is selling domestically produced products to buyers in another country. A company can sell directly to foreign importers or buyers. Exporting is not limited to huge corporations. Smaller Canadian companies have found many export market opportunities for their products and services. The United States is the world's largest exporter.

Instead of selling directly to foreign buyers, a company may decide to sell to intermediaries located in its domestic market. The most common intermediary is the export merchant, also known as a **buyer for**

Licensing and Franchising

Another effective way for a firm to move into the global arena with relatively little risk is to sell a licence to manufacture its product to someone in a foreign country. **Licensing** is the legal process whereby a licensor allows another firm to use its manufacturing process, trademarks, patents, trade secrets, or other proprietary knowledge. The licensee, in turn, pays the licensor a royalty or fee agreed on by both parties. Because licensing has many advantages, U.S. companies have eagerly embraced the concept. The trend is not limited to big corporations; numerous smaller firms have seized lucrative opportunities by signing licensing agreements with businesses in developing countries.[8]

A licensor must ensure it can exercise sufficient control over the licensee's activities to ensure proper quality, pricing, distribution, and so on. Licensing

---

exporting selling domestically produced products to buyers in another country

buyer for export an intermediary in the global market that assumes all ownership risks and sells globally for its own account

export broker an intermediary who plays the traditional broker's role by bringing buyer and seller together

export agent an intermediary who acts like a manufacturer's agent for the exporter. The export agent lives in the foreign market

licensing the legal process whereby a licensor agrees to let another firm use its manufacturing process, trademarks, patents, trade secrets, or other proprietary knowledge may also create a new competitor in the long run, if the licensee decides to void the licence agreement. International law is often ineffective in stopping such actions. Two common ways of maintaining effective control over licensees are shipping one or more critical components from Canada or registering patents and trademarks locally to the Canadian firm, not to the licensee. Garment companies maintain control by delivering only so many labels per day; they also supply their own fabric, collect the scraps, and complete accurate unit counts.

Franchising is a form of licensing that has grown rapidly in recent years. Over half of all international franchises are for fast-food restaurants and business services.

Contract Manufacturing

Firms that do not want to become involved in either licensing or global marketing may choose to engage in **contract manufacturing**, which is private-label manufacturing by a foreign company. The foreign company produces a certain volume of products to specification, with the domestic firm's brand name on the goods. The domestic company usually handles the marketing. Thus, the domestic firm can broaden its global marketing base without investing in overseas plants and equipment. After establishing a solid base, the domestic firm may switch to a joint venture or direct investment. Marketers should exercise caution in selecting contract manufacturers abroad, however. Particularly in China, contract manufacturers have been making overruns and selling the excess production directly to either consumers or retailers.[9]

Joint Venture

Joint ventures are similar to licensing agreements. In an international **joint venture**, the domestic firm either buys part of a foreign company or joins with a foreign company to create a new entity. A joint venture is a quick and relatively inexpensive way to go global and to gain needed expertise.[10]

Joint ventures can be very risky. Many fail; others fall victim to a takeover, in which one partner buys out the other. Sometimes joint venture partners simply can't agree on management strategies and policies.

CANADA'S TOP 5 EXPORTS, 2009 ($ MILLIONS)

1.	Crude petroleum oils and oils obtained from bituminous minerals	42,700
2.	Motor vehicles for passenger transport (other than buses/public transport)	26,565
3.	Liquefied petroleum or hydrocarbon gases	18,214
4.	Oil (non-crude)	11,970
5.	Gas turbines	4,750

SOURCE: Foreign Affairs and International Trade Canada, "Canada's State of Trade: Trade and Investment Update 2010," http://www.international.gc.ca/economist-economiste/performance/state-point/state_2010_point/2010_5.aspx?lang=eng, accessed February 1, 2011. Reproduced with the permission of Her Majesty the Queen in Right of Canada, represented by the Minister of Foreign Affairs, 2011.

When a joint venture is successful, however, both parties gain valuable skills from the alliance.

Direct Investment

Active ownership of a foreign company or of overseas manufacturing or marketing facilities is **direct foreign investment**. Direct foreign investment by Canadian firms was approximately $523 billion in 2006. Direct investors have either a controlling interest or a large minority interest in the firm. Thus, they hold both the greatest potential reward and the greatest potential risk. Sometimes firms make direct investments because they can find no suitable local partners. Also, direct investments avoid the communication problems and conflicts of interest that can arise with joint ventures. Other firms simply don't want to share their technology, which they fear may be stolen or ultimately used against them by creating a new competitor.

A firm may make a direct foreign investment by acquiring an interest in an existing company or by building new facilities. It might do so because it has difficulty either transferring some resource to a foreign operation or sourcing that resource locally. One important resource is personnel, especially managers.

contract manufacturing private-label manufacturing by a foreign company

joint venture a domestic firm's purchase of part of a foreign company or a domestic firm joining with a foreign company to create a new entity

direct foreign investment active ownership of a foreign company or of overseas manufacturing or marketing facilities

YUM BRAND'S **KFC** FRIED-CHICKEN CHAIN HAS **3,700 FRANCHISES IN CHINA** AND OPENED THAT COUNTRY'S FIRST DRIVE-THROUGH IN 2002.

Honda Canada's Alliston, Ontario, plant opened in 1986, making it the first plant built in Canada by a Japanese car manufacturer. Alliston now has two more Honda plants supplying cars and engines for Japan, the United States, South America, and other countries.

If the local labour market is tight, the firm may buy an entire foreign firm and retain all its employees instead of paying higher salaries than competitors.

The United States is a popular place for direct investment by foreign companies. By 2007, the value of foreign-owned businesses in the United States was more than $500 billion.

LO 5 The Global Marketing Mix

To succeed, firms seeking to enter into foreign trade must adhere to the principles of the marketing mix. Information gathered on foreign markets through research is the basis for the four Ps of global marketing strategy: product, place (distribution), promotion, and price. Marketing managers who understand the advantages and disadvantages of different ways of entering the global market and the effect of the external environment on the firm's marketing mix have a better chance of reaching their goals.

The first step in creating a marketing mix is developing a thorough understanding of the global target market. Often this knowledge can be obtained through the same types of marketing research used in the domestic market (see Chapter 4). However, global marketing research is conducted in vastly different environments. Conducting a survey can be difficult in developing countries, where telephone ownership is growing but is not always common, and mail delivery is slow or sporadic. Drawing samples that are based on known population parameters is often difficult because of the lack of data. Moreover, the questions a marketer is able to ask may differ in other cultures. In some cultures, people tend to be more private than in Canada and will not respond to personal questions on surveys.

Product and Promotion

With the proper information, a good marketing mix can be developed. One important decision is whether to alter the product or the promotion for the global marketplace. Other options are to radically change the product or to adjust either the promotional message or the product to suit local conditions.

One Product, One Message The strategy of global marketing standardization, which was discussed earlier, means developing a single product for all markets and promoting it the same way throughout the world. Global media—especially satellite and cable TV networks such as CNN International, MTV Networks, and British Sky Broadcasting—make it possible to beam advertising to audiences unreachable a few years ago. Eighteen-year-olds in Paris often have more in common with 18-year-olds in Halifax than with their own parents. Almost all of MTV's advertisers run unified, English-language campaigns in the 28 nations the firm reaches. The audiences buy the same products, go to the same movies, listen to the same music, and sip the same colas. Global advertising merely works on that premise.

Unchanged products may fail simply because of cultural factors. Any type of war game tends to do very poorly in Germany, even though Germany is by far the world's biggest game-playing nation. A successful game in Germany has plenty of details and a thick rulebook. Despite cultural hurdles, numerous multinational firms are applying uniform branding on products around the world. Sometimes the desire for absolute standardization must also give way to practical considerations and local market dynamics. For example, because of the feminine connotations of the word *diet*, the European version of Diet Coke is known

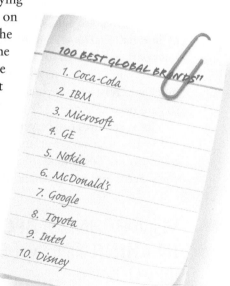

100 BEST GLOBAL BRANDS

1. Coca-Cola
2. IBM
3. Microsoft
4. GE
5. Nokia
6. McDonald's
7. Google
8. Toyota
9. Intel
10. Disney

as Coca-Cola Light. Sometimes, even if the brand name differs by market, managers can create a strong visual relationship by uniformly applying the brandmark and graphic elements on packaging.[12]

Product Invention In the context of global marketing, product invention can be taken to mean either creating a new product for a market or drastically changing an existing product. For example, to cater to the Japanese market, Nabisco had to remove the cream filling from its Oreo cookies because Japanese children thought the cookies were too sweet. Frito-Lay's most popular potato chip in Thailand is shrimp flavoured.

Consumers in different countries use products differently. For example, in many countries, clothing is worn much longer between washings than in Canada, so a more durable fabric must be produced and marketed. For the Peruvian market, Goodyear developed a tire that differs from its other tire lines; a higher percentage of natural rubber and better treads are needed to handle the tough Peruvian driving conditions.

Product Adaptation Another alternative for global marketers is to slightly alter a basic product to meet local conditions. In Britain, Starbucks' menu includes cheese and Marmite sandwiches. (Marmite is a black yeast spread that only the British seem able to stomach.) Its local product-development team has also come up with Strawberries and Cream Frappuccino, a cold beverage now available in Canadian stores. On the whole, though, British Starbucks are much like any Starbucks in North America.[13]

Sometimes marketers can simply change the package size. In India, Unilever sells single-use sachets of Sunsilk shampoo for 2 to 4 cents. Unilever's Rexona brand deodorant sticks sell for 16 cents and up. They are big hits in India, the Philippines, Bolivia, and Peru—where Unilever has grabbed 60 percent of the deodorant market.[14] On electronic products, power sources and voltage must be changed. It may be necessary, for example, to change the size and shape of the electrical plug.

Message Adaptation Another global marketing strategy is to maintain the same basic product but alter the promotional strategy. Bicycles are mainly pleasure vehicles in Canada. In many parts of the world,

however, they are a family's main mode of transportation. Thus, promotion in these countries should stress durability and efficiency. In contrast, Canadian advertising may emphasize escaping and having fun.

Kit Kat bars are a hit the world over, but Nestlé didn't have much luck selling them in Japan—until it redesigned its message for the teen market. In Japan, the product's name is pronounced *kitto katsu*, which roughly translates to "I hope you win." Fuelling a rumour that Kit Kats bring success at crucial school exams, Nestlé rolled out packages combining the candy with other good-luck charms. Now 90 percent of Japanese schoolkids say they've heard of Kit Kat bars, and Kit Kat sales have soared 28 percent.[15]

Some cultures view a product as having less value if it has to be advertised. In other nations, claims that seem commonplace by Canadian standards may be viewed negatively or even not allowed. Germany does not permit advertisers to state that their products are the best or better than those of competitors, a description commonly used in Canadian advertising. The hardsell tactics and sexual themes so common in Canadian advertising are taboo in many countries. Language barriers, translation problems, and cultural differences have generated numerous headaches for international marketing managers.

Place (Distribution)

Solving promotional and product problems does not guarantee global marketing success. The product still needs to be adequately distributed. Innovative distribution systems can create a competitive advantage for savvy companies. Planes taking tourists by day to Kenya's Nairobi Airport return to their European hubs by night crammed with an average 25 tonnes apiece of fresh beans, bok choy, okra, and other produce that was harvested and packaged just the day before.

In many developing nations, channels of distribution and the physical infrastructure are inadequate. Both inadequate and poorly maintained highways, distribution centres, and storage facilities mean that a significant portion of fruits and vegetables spoil while being transported from the farm to the market, resulting in higher costs and shortages. Therefore, the main modes of transport are truck and train. India's highway network stretches just 200,000 km. Many

ROSE ALCORN

Indian roads are simple, two-lane affairs, maintained badly, if at all. Shipping goods by rail costs twice as much as in developed countries and three times as much as in China.[16]

Pricing

Once marketing managers have determined a global product and promotion strategy, they can select the remainder of the marketing mix. Pricing presents some unique problems in the global sphere.[17] For example, exporters must not only cover their production costs but must also consider transportation costs, insurance, taxes, and tariffs. When deciding on a final price, marketers must also determine what customers are willing to spend on a particular product and ensure that their foreign buyers will pay the price. Because developing nations lack mass purchasing power, selling to them often poses special pricing problems. Sometimes a product can be simplified in order to lower the price. The firm must not assume that low-income countries are willing to accept lower quality, however. Although the nomads of the Sahara are very poor, they still buy expensive fabrics to make their clothing. Their survival in harsh conditions and extreme temperatures requires this expense. Additionally, certain expensive luxury items can be sold almost anywhere.

Exchange Rates

The exchange rate is the price of one country's currency in terms of another country's currency. If a country's currency *appreciates*, less of that country's currency is needed to buy another country's currency. If a country's currency *depreciates*, more of that currency will be needed to buy another country's currency.

Appreciation and depreciation affect the prices of a country's goods. If the Canadian dollar depreciates relative to the Japanese yen, Canadian residents will need to pay more dollars to buy Japanese goods. To illustrate, suppose the dollar price of a yen is $0.012 and that a Toyota is priced at 2 million yen. At this exchange rate, a Canadian resident pays $24,000 for a Toyota ($0.012 × 2 million yen = $24,000). If the dollar depreciates to $0.018 to one yen, however, the Canadian resident will have to pay $36,000 for the same Toyota.

As the dollar depreciates, the prices of Japanese goods rise for Canadian residents, so they buy fewer Japanese goods—thus, Canadian imports may decline. At the same time, as the dollar depreciates relative to the yen, the yen appreciates relative to the dollar. This means prices of Canadian goods fall for the Japanese, so they buy more Canadian goods—and Canadian exports rise.

Currency markets operate under a system of **floating exchange rates**. Prices of different currencies float up and down on the basis of the demand for and the supply of each currency. Global currency traders create the supply of and demand for a particular country's currency on the basis of that country's investment, trade potential, and economic strength.

Dumping Dumping is generally considered to be the sale of an exported product at a price lower than that charged for the same or a like product in the home market of the exporter. This practice is regarded as a form of price discrimination that can potentially harm the importing nation's competing industries. Dumping may occur as a result of exporter business strategies that include (1) trying to increase an overseas market share, (2) temporarily distributing products in overseas markets to offset slack demand in the home market, (3) lowering unit costs by exploiting large-scale production, and (4) attempting to maintain stable prices during periods of exchange rate fluctuations.

Historically, the dumping of goods has presented serious problems in international trade. As a result, dumping has led to significant disagreements among countries and diverse views about its harmfulness. Some trade economists view dumping as harmful only when it involves the use of predatory practices that intentionally try to eliminate competition and gain monopoly power in a market. They believe that predatory dumping rarely occurs and that antidumping rules are a protectionist tool whose cost to consumers and import-using industries exceeds the benefits to the industries receiving protection.

Countertrade Global trade does not always involve cash. Countertrade is a fast-growing way to conduct global business. In **countertrade**, all or part of the payment for goods or services is in the form of other goods or services. Countertrade is thus a form of barter (swapping goods for goods), an age-old

PHOTODISC/GETTY IMAGES

COUNTERTRADE IS A FORM OF **BARTER.**

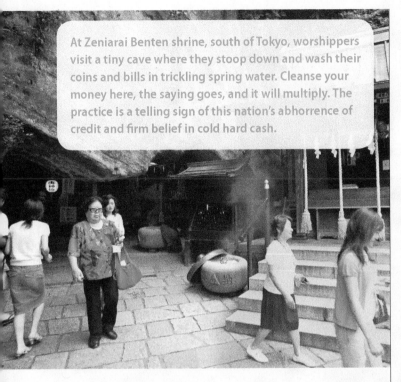

At Zeniarai Benten shrine, south of Tokyo, worshippers visit a tiny cave where they stoop down and wash their coins and bills in trickling spring water. Cleanse your money here, the saying goes, and it will multiply. The practice is a telling sign of this nation's abhorrence of credit and firm belief in cold hard cash.

© SHIZUO KAMBAYASHI/ ASSOCIATED PRESS

practice whose origins have been traced back to cave dwellers. The U.S. Department of Commerce says that roughly 30 percent of all global trade is countertrade.

One common type of countertrade is straight barter. For example, the Malaysian government recently bought 20 diesel-powered locomotives and paid for them with palm oil. Another form of countertrade is the compensation agreement. Typically, a company provides technology and equipment for a plant in a developing nation and agrees to take full or partial payment in goods produced by that plant. For example, General Tire Company supplied equipment and know-how for a Romanian truck tire plant. In turn, General Tire sold the tires it received from the plant in the United States under the Victoria brand name. Both parties benefit even though neither party uses cash.

LO 6   The Impact of the Internet

Opening an e-commerce site on the Internet immediately puts a company in the international marketplace. Sophisticated language translation software can make any site accessible to people around the world. Global shippers such as UPS, FedEx, and DHL help solve international e-commerce distribution complexities. Currency conversion software allows companies to post prices in Canadian dollars, then ask their customers what currency they wish to use for payment. But despite many advancements, the promises of borderless commerce and the global Internet economy are still being restrained by the old rules, regulations, and habits. For example, Canadians spend an average of $6,500 per year by credit card, whereas Japanese spend less than $2,000. Many Japanese don't even have a credit card, making it difficult to conduct regular business over the Internet.

Percentage of Canadian GDP generated from global trade
45%

$6,500
Average Canadian's annual credit card expenditure

$1 billion
Daily trade between the United States and Canada

2002
Year first drive-through restaurant opened in China

71% The percentage of students who go online to study for a class.

© Anderson Ross/Getty Images

GET ONLINE

The easy-to-navigate website for **MKTG** offers guidance on key topics in **marketing** in a variety of engaging formats. You have the opportunity to refine and check your understanding via interactive quizzes and flashcards. Videos and audio summaries provide inspiration for your own further exploration. And, in order to make **MKTG** an even better learning tool, we invite you to speak up about your experience with **MKTG** by completing a survey form and sending us your comments.

Get online and discover the following resources:
- Printable PowerPoint Slides
- Flashcards
- Interactive Quizzing
- Crossword Puzzles
- Audio Summaries

"I think this book is awesome for students of all ages. It is a much simpler way to study."

—Yasmine Al-Hashimi, Fanshawe College

Glossary

accessory equipment Goods such as portable tools and office equipment that are less expensive and shorter-lived than major equipment. 96

adopter A consumer who was happy enough with his or her trial experience with a product to use it again. 163

advergaming Placing advertising messages in Web-based or video games to advertise or promote a product, service, organization, or issue. 253

advertising Impersonal, one-way mass communication about a product or organization that is paid for by a marketer. 226

advertising appeal A reason for a person to buy a product. 246

advertising campaign A series of related advertisements focusing on a common theme, slogan, and set of advertising appeals. 246

advertising objective A specific communication task that a campaign should accomplish for a specified target audience during a specified period. 246

advertising response function A phenomenon in which spending for advertising and sales promotion increases sales or market share up to a certain level but then produces diminishing returns. 244

advocacy advertising A form of advertising in which an organization expresses its views on a particular issue or cause. 245

AIDA concept A model that outlines the process for achieving promotional goals in terms of stages of consumer involvement with the message; the acronym stands for *attention, interest, desire,* and *action.* 235

applied research An attempt to develop new improved products. 24

aspirational reference groups Groups that an individual would like to join. 78

assurance The knowledge and courtesy of employees and their ability to convey trust. 173

atmosphere The overall impression conveyed by a store's physical layout, décor, and surroundings. 220

attitude A learned tendency to respond consistently toward a given object. 87

audience selectivity The ability of an advertising medium to reach a precisely defined market. 254

automatic vending The use of machines to offer goods for sale. 212

average total cost (ATC) Total costs divided by quantity of output. 305

average variable cost (AVC) Total variable costs divided by quantity of output. 305

baby boomers People born between 1947 and 1965. 19

bait pricing A price tactic that tries to get consumers into a store through false or misleading price advertising and then uses high-pressure selling to persuade consumers to buy more expensive merchandise. 327

base price The general price level at which the company expects to sell the good or service. 323

basic research Pure research that aims to confirm an existing theory or to learn more about a concept or phenomenon. 24

basing-point pricing Charging freight from a given (basing) point, regardless of the city from which the goods are shipped. 325

BehaviorScan A scanner-based research program that tracks the purchases of 3,000 households through store scanners in each research market. 64

belief An organized pattern of knowledge that an individual holds as true about his or her world. 87

benefit segmentation The process of grouping customers into market segments according to the benefits they seek from the product. 114

blog A publicly accessible Web page that functions as an interactive journal, whereby readers can post comments on the author's entries. 253

brainstorming The process of getting a group to think of unlimited ways to vary a product or solve a problem. 159

brand A name, term, symbol, design, or combination thereof that identifies a seller's products and differentiates them from competitors' products. 146

brand equity The value of company and brand names. 146

brand loyalty A consistent preference for one brand over all others. 146

brand mark The elements of a brand that cannot be spoken. 146

brand name That part of a brand that can be spoken, including letters, words, and numbers. 146

break-even analysis A method of determining what sales volume must be reached before total revenue equals total costs. 308

business analysis The second stage of the screening process, where preliminary figures for demand, cost, sales, and profitability are calculated. 159

business marketing The marketing of goods and services to individuals and organizations for purposes other than personal consumption. 91

business product (industrial product) A product used to manufacture other goods or services, to facilitate an organization's operations, or to resell to other customers. 142

business services Expense items that do not become part of a final product. 97

business-to-business electronic commerce The use of the Internet to facilitate the exchange of goods, services, and information between organizations. 101

business-to-business online exchange An electronic trading floor that provides companies with integrated links to their customers and suppliers. 93

buyer A department head who selects the merchandise for his or her department and may also be responsible for promotion and for personnel. 208

buying centre All those people in an organization who become involved in the purchase decision. 98

buyer for export An intermediary in the global market that assumes all ownership risks and sells globally for its own account. 342

campaign management Developing product or service offerings customized for the appropriate customer segment and then pricing and communicating these offerings for the purpose of enhancing customer relationships. 135

cannibalization Situation that occurs when sales of a new product cut into sales of a firm's existing products. 118

capital intensive Using more capital than labour in the production process. 336

cash cow In the portfolio matrix, a business unit that usually generates more cash than it needs to maintain its market share. 40

cash discount A price reduction offered to a consumer, an industrial user, or a marketing intermediary in return for prompt payment of a bill. 323

category killers Specialty discount stores that heavily dominate their narrow merchandise segment. 210

cause-related marketing A type of sponsorship involving the association of a for-profit company with a nonprofit organization; through the sponsorship the company's product or service is promoted, and money is raised for the nonprofit. 259

central-location telephone (CLT) facility A specially designed phone room used to conduct telephone interviewing. 53

chain stores Stores owned and operated as a group by a single organization. 206

channel A medium of communication—such as a voice, radio, or newspaper—used for transmitting a message. 231

channel conflict A clash of goals and methods among distribution channel members. 195

channel control A situation in which when one marketing channel member intentionally affects another member's behaviour. 194

channel leader (channel captain) A member of a marketing channel who exercises authority and power over the activities of other channel members. 194

channel members All parties in the marketing channel that negotiate with one another, buy and sell products, and facilitate the change of ownership between buyer and seller in the course of moving the product from the manufacturer into the hands of the final consumer. 186

channel partnering (channel cooperation) The joint effort of all channel members to create a supply chain that serves customers and creates a competitive advantage. 196

channel power A marketing channel member's capacity to control or influence the behaviour of other channel members. 194

closed-ended question An interview question that asks the respondent to make a selection from a limited list of responses. 54

cobranding Placing two or more brand names on a product or its package. 148

code of ethics A guideline to help marketing managers and other employees make better decisions. 30

cognitive dissonance Inner tension that a consumer experiences after recognizing an inconsistency between behaviour and values or opinions. 71

cold calling A form of lead generation in which the salesperson approaches potential buyers without any prior knowledge of the prospects' needs or financial status. 290

commercialization The decision to market a product. 162

communication The process by which we exchange or share meanings through a common set of symbols. 229

comparative advertising A form of advertising that compares two or more competing brands on one or more specific attributes. 245

Competition Bureau The federal department charged with administering most marketplace laws. 24

competitive advantage The set of unique features of a company and its products that are perceived by the target market as significant and superior to the competition. 37, 226

competitive advertising A form of advertising designed to influence demand for a specific brand. 245

competitive intelligence (CI) An intelligence system that helps managers assess their competition and vendors in order to become more efficient and effective competitors. 65

compiled list A customer list that was developed by gathering names and addresses gleaned from telephone directories and membership rosters, sometimes enhanced with information from public records, such as census data, auto registrations, birth announcements, business start-ups, or bankruptcies. 131

component lifestyles Choosing goods and services that meet one's diverse needs and interests rather than conforming to a single, traditional lifestyle. 16

component parts Either finished items ready for assembly or products that need very little processing before becoming part of some other product. 97

computer-assisted personal interviewing The interviewer reads the questions from a computer screen and enters the respondent's data directly into the computer. 53

computer-assisted self-interviewing The respondent reads questions off a computer screen and directly keys his or her answers into a computer or other electronic recording device. 53

concentrated targeting strategy Strategy used to select one segment a market for targeting marketing efforts. 117

concept test Evaluation of a new-product idea, usually before any prototype has been created. 159

consumer behaviour How consumers make purchase decisions and how they use and dispose of purchased goods or services; also includes the factors that influence purchase decisions and product use. 67

consumer decision-making process A five-step process used by consumers when buying goods or services. 68

consumer penalty An extra fee paid by the consumer for violating the terms of the purchase agreement. 328

consumer product A product bought to satisfy an individual's personal wants. 142

consumer sales promotion Sales promotion activities targeting the ultimate consumer. 281

continuous media schedule A media scheduling strategy in which advertising is run steadily throughout the advertising period; used for products in the latter stages of the product life cycle. 255

contract manufacturing Private-label manufacturing by a foreign company. 343

control Provides the mechanisms both for evaluating marketing results in light of the plan's objectives and for correcting actions that do not help the organization reach those objectives within budget guidelines. 44

convenience product A relatively inexpensive item that merits little shopping effort. 142

convenience sample A form of nonprobability sample using respondents who are convenient, or readily accessible, to the researcher—for example, employees, friends, or relatives. 57

convenience store A miniature supermarket, carrying only a limited line of high-turnover convenience goods. 210

cooperative advertising An arrangement in which the manufacturer and the retailer split the costs of advertising the manufacturer's brand. 250

core service The most basic benefit the consumer is buying. 175

corporate blogs Blogs that are sponsored by a company or one of its brands and maintained by one or more of the company's employees. 260

corporate social responsibility A business's concern for society's welfare. 27

cost competitive advantage Being the low-cost competitor in an industry while maintaining satisfactory profit margins. 37

cost per contact The cost of reaching one member of the target market. 254

countertrade A form of trade in which all or part of the payment for goods or services is in the form of other goods or services. 346

coupon A certificate that entitles consumers to an immediate price reduction when they buy the product. 282

coverage ensuring product availability in every outlet where potential customers might want to buy it. 193

credence quality A characteristic that consumers may have difficulty assessing even after purchase because they do not have the necessary knowledge or experience. 172

crisis management A coordinated effort to handle all the effects of either unfavourable publicity or an unexpected unfavourable event. 260

cross-tabulation A method of analyzing data that shows the analyst the responses to one question in relation to the responses to one or more other questions. 58

crowdsourcing Channelling the power of online crowds to gather feedback on marketing programs for almost immediate improvements and changes; using consumers to develop and market product. 233

culture The set of values, norms, attitudes, and other meaningful symbols that shape human behaviour and the artifacts, or products, of that behaviour as they are transmitted from one generation to the next. 74

cumulative quantity discount A deduction from list price that applies to the buyer's total purchases made during a specific period. 323

customer-centric A philosophy under which the company customizes its product and service offering based on data generated through interactions between the customer and the company. 127

customer relationship management (CRM) A company-wide business strategy designed to optimize profitability, revenue, and customer satisfaction by focusing on highly defined and precise customer groups. 125

customer satisfaction Customers' evaluation of a good or service in terms of whether it has met their needs and expectations. 8

customer value The relationship between benefits and the sacrifice necessary to obtain those benefits. 7

dashboard Display of computer-generated visual output easily accessed by employees for the purpose of maximizing customer relationship marketing interactions. 48

database A collection of data, especially one that can be accessed and manipulated by computer software. 131

database marketing The creation of a large computerized file of customers' and potential customers' profiles and purchase patterns. 48

data mining An analytical process that compiles actionable data on the purchase habits of a firm's current and potential customers. 127

data warehouse A central repository of data from various functional areas of the organization that are stored and inventoried on a centralized computer system so that the information can be shared across all functional departments of the business. 131

deceptive pricing Promoting a price or price saving that is not actually available. 321

decision support system (DSS) An interactive, flexible computerized information system that enables managers to obtain and manipulate information as they are making decisions. 47

decline stage A long-run drop in sales. 167

decoding Interpretation of the language and symbols sent by the source through a channel. 231

delayed-quotation pricing Pricing that is not set until the item is either finished or delivered; used for industrial installations and many accessory items. 330

demand The quantity of a product that will be sold in the market at various prices for a specified period. 301

demographic segmentation Segmenting markets by age, gender, income, ethnic background, and family life cycle. 109

demography The study of people's vital statistics, such as their age, race and ethnicity, and location. 17

department store A store housing several departments under one roof. 208

derived demand The demand for business products. 92

destination stores Stores that consumers purposely plan to visit. 219

development The stage in the product development process in which a prototype is developed and a marketing strategy is outlined. 159

diffusion The process by which the adoption of an innovation spreads. 163

direct channel A distribution channel in which producers sell directly to consumers. 189

direct foreign investment Active ownership of a foreign company or of overseas manufacturing or marketing facilities. 343

direct mail A printed form of direct-response communication that is delivered directly to consumers' homes. 257

direct marketing (direct-response marketing) Techniques used to get consumers to make a purchase from their home, office, or another nonretail setting. 213

direct-response broadcast Advertising that uses television or radio and includes a direct call to action asking the consumer to respond immediately. 256

direct-response communication Communication of a message directly from a marketing company and directly to an intended individual target audience. 228

direct-response print Advertising in a print medium that includes a direct call to action. 257

direct-response television (DRTV) Advertising that appears on television and encourages viewers to respond immediately. 256

direct retailing The selling of products by representatives who work door-to-door, office-to-office, or at home parties. 212

discount store A retailer that competes on the basis of low prices, high turnover, and high volume. 210

discrepancy of assortment The lack of all the items a customer needs to receive full satisfaction from a product or products. 186

discrepancy of quantity The difference between the amount of product produced and the amount an end-user wants to buy. 186

disintermediation The elimination of intermediaries such as wholesalers or distributers from a marketing channel. 103

distribution resource planning (DRP) An inventory control system that manages the replenishment of goods from the manufacturer to the final consumer. 199

diversification A strategy of increasing sales by introducing new products into new markets. 42

dog In the portfolio matrix, a business unit that has low growth potential and a small market share. 41

Do Not Call List (DNCL) A free service whereby Canadians register their telephone number to reduce or eliminate phone calls from telemarketers. 257

drugstore A retail store that stocks pharmacy-related products and services as its main draw. 209

dual distribution (multiple distribution) The use of two or more channels to distribute the same product to target markets. 190

dumping The sale of an exported product at a price lower than that charged for the same or a like product in the home market of the exporter. 346

earned media A public relations term connoting free media such as mainstream media coverage. 267

80/20 principle A principle holding that 20 percent of all customers generate 80 percent of the demand value. 114

elastic demand A situation in which consumer demand is sensitive to changes in price. 302

elasticity of demand Consumers' responsiveness or sensitivity to changes in price. 302

electronic data interchange (EDI) Information technology that replaces the paper documents that usually accompany business transactions, such as purchase orders and invoices, with electronic transmission of the needed information to reduce inventory levels, improve cash flow, streamline operations, and increase the speed and accuracy of information transmission. 198

electronic distribution A distribution technique that includes any kind of product or service that can be distributed electronically, whether over traditional forms such as fibre-optic cable or through satellite transmission of electronic signals. 202

empathy Caring, individualized attention to customers. 173

empowerment Delegation of authority to solve customers' problems quickly—usually by the first person who learns of the customer's problem. 9, 128

encoding The conversion of a sender's ideas and thoughts into a message, usually in the form of words or signs. 230

environmental management When a company implements strategies that attempt to shape the external environment within which it operates. 16

environmental scanning Collection and interpretation of information about forces, events, and relationships in the external environment that may affect the future of the organization or the implementation of the marketing plan. 37

escalator pricing Pricing that reflects cost increases incurred between the time the order is placed and the time delivery is made. 330

ethics The moral principles or values that generally govern the conduct of an individual or a group. 28

ethnographic research The study of human behaviour in its natural context; involves observation of behaviour and physical setting. 55

European Union A free trade zone encompassing 27 European countries. 340

evaluation Gauging the extent to which the marketing objectives have been achieved during the specified time period. 44

evoked set (consideration set) A group of the most preferred alternatives resulting from an information search, which a buyer can further evaluate to make a final choice. 70

exchange People giving up one thing to receive another thing they would rather have. 4

exclusive distribution A form of distribution that involves only one or a few dealers within a given area. 194

executive interview A type of survey that involves interviewing business people at their offices concerning industrial products or services. 53

experience curves Curves that show costs declining at a predictable rate as experience with a product increases. 38

experience quality A characteristic that can be assessed only after use. 172

experiment A method a researcher uses to gather primary data to determine cause and effect. 56

export agent An intermediary who acts like a manufacturer's agent for the exporter. The export agent lives in the foreign market. 342

export broker An intermediary who plays the traditional broker's role by bringing buyer and seller together. 342

exporting Selling domestically produced products to buyers in another country. 342

express warranty A written guarantee. 153

extensive decision making The most complex type of consumer decision making, used when considering the purchase of an unfamiliar, expensive product or an infrequently purchased item; requires the use of several criteria for evaluating options and much time for seeking information. 72

external information search The process of seeking information in the outside environment. 69

extranet A private electronic network that links a company with its suppliers and customers. 312

factory outlet An off-price retailer that is owned and operated by a manufacturer. 211

family brand Marketing several different products under the same brand name. 148

family life cycle (FLC) A series of stages determined by a combination of age, marital status, and the presence or absence of children. 113

feedback The receiver's response to a message. 231

field service firm A firm that specializes in interviewing respondents on a subcontracted basis. 57

fixed cost A cost that does not change as output is increased or decreased. 305

flexible pricing (variable pricing) Different customers pay different prices for essentially the same merchandise bought in equal quantities. 326

flighted media schedule A media scheduling strategy in which ads are run heavily every other month or every two weeks, to achieve a greater impact with an increased frequency and reach at those times. 255

floating exchange rates Prices of different currencies move up and down based on the demand for and the supply of each currency. 346

floor price The lowest price to which a company will allow its price to drop. 305

FOB origin pricing The buyer absorbs the freight costs from the shipping point ("free on board"). 325

focus group Seven to ten people who participate in group discussion led by a moderator. 54

follow-up The final step of the selling process, in which the salesperson ensures that delivery schedules are met, that the goods or services perform as promised, and that the buyers' employees are properly trained to use the products. 294

four Ps Product, place, promotion, and price, which together make up the marketing mix. 43

frame error A sample drawn from a population differs from the target population. 57

franchise The right to operate a business or to sell a product. 206

franchisee An individual or business that is granted the right to sell a franchisor's product. 215

franchiser The originator of a trade name, product, methods of operation, and so on that grants operating rights to another party to sell its product. 215

freight absorption pricing The seller pays all or part of the actual freight charges and does not pass them on to the buyer. 325

frequency The number of times an individual is exposed to a given message during a specific period. 254

frequent buyer program A loyalty program in which loyal consumers are rewarded for making multiple purchases of a particular good or service. 284

full-line discount stores A retailer that offers consumers very limited service and carries a broad assortment of well-known, nationally branded "hard goods." 210

functional discount (trade discount) A discount to wholesalers and retailers for performing channel functions. 324

gap model A model identifying five gaps that can cause problems in service delivery and influence customer evaluations of service quality. 173

General Agreement on Tariffs and Trade (GATT) A trade agreement that contained loopholes that enabled countries to avoid trade-barrier reduction agreements. 339

Generation X People born between 1966 and 1978. 19

Generation Y People born between 1979 and 1994. 18

generic product A no-frills, no-brand-name, low-cost product that is simply identified by its product category. 147

generic product name A term that identifies a product by class or type and cannot be trademarked. 150

geodemographic segmentation Segmenting potential customers into neighbourhood lifestyle categories. 113

geographic segmentation Segmenting markets by region of a country or the world, market size, market density, or climate. 109

global brand A brand where at least 20 percent of the product is sold outside its home country or region. 146

global marketing Marketing that targets markets throughout the world. 333

global marketing standardization Production of uniform products that can be sold the same way all over the world. 336

global vision Recognizing and reacting to international marketing opportunities, using effective global marketing strategies, and being aware of threats from foreign competitors in all markets. 333

green marketing The development and marketing of products designed to minimize negative effects on the physical environment. 28

gross margin The amount of money the retailer makes as a percentage of sales after the cost of goods sold is subtracted. 207

growth stage The second stage of the product life cycle when sales typically grow at an increasing rate, many competitors enter the market, large companies may start acquiring small pioneering firms, and profits are healthy. 166

heterogeneity The variability of the inputs and outputs of services, which causes services to tend to be less standardized and uniform than goods. 173

horizontal conflict A channel conflict that occurs among channel members on the same level. 195

ideal self-image The way an individual would like to be. 83

implementation The process that turns a marketing plan into action assignments and ensures that these assignments are executed in a way that accomplishes the plan's objectives. 44

implied warranty An unwritten guarantee that the good or service is fit for the purpose for which it was sold. 153

independent retailers Retailers owned by a single person or partnership and not operated as part of a larger retail institution. 206

individual branding Using different brand names for different products. 148

inelastic demand A situation in which an increase or a decrease in price will not significantly affect demand for the product. 302

inflation A measure of the decrease in the value of money, expressed as the percentage reduction value since the previous year. 23

infomercial A 30-minute or longer advertisement that looks more like a TV talk show than a sales pitch. 251

informational labelling Package labelling designed to help consumers make proper product selections and to lower their cognitive dissonance after the purchase. 152

InfoScan A scanner-based sales-tracking service for the consumer packaged goods industry. 64

innovation A product perceived as new by a potential adopter. 163

inseparability The inability of the production and consumption of a service to be separated; consumers must be present during the production. 172

institutional advertising A form of advertising designed to enhance a company's image rather than promote a particular product. 244

intangibility The inability of services to be touched, seen, tasted, heard, or felt in the same manner that goods can be sensed. 172

integrated marketing communications (IMC) The careful coordination of all promotional messages for a product or a service to assure the consistency of messages at every contact point where a company meets the consumer. 240

intensive distribution A form of distribution aimed at having a product available in every outlet where target customers might want to buy it. 193

interaction The point at which a customer and a company representative exchange information and develop learning relationships. 128

internal information search The process of recalling information stored in one's memory. 69

internal marketing Treating employees as customers and developing systems and benefits that satisfy their needs. 180

International Monetary Fund (IMF) An international organization that acts as a lender of last resort, providing loans to troubled nations, and also works to promote trade through financial cooperation. 340

interpersonal communication Direct, fact-to-face communication between two or more people. 230

introductory stage The full-scale launch of a new product into the marketplace. 166

inventory control system A method of developing and maintaining an adequate assortment of materials or products to meet a manufacturer's or a customer's demand. 199

involvement The amount of time and effort a buyer invests in the search, evaluation, and decision processes of consumer behaviour. 72

joint costs Costs that are shared in the manufacturing and marketing of several products in a product line. 329

joint demand The demand for two or more items used together in a final product. 92

joint venture A domestic firm's purchase of part of a foreign company or a domestic firm joining with a foreign company to create a new entity. 343

just-in-time production (JIT) A process that redefines and simplifies manufacturing by reducing inventory levels and delivering raw materials just when they are needed on the production line. 198

keiretsu A network of interlocking corporate affiliates. 104

keystoning The practice of marking up prices by 100 percent, or doubling the cost. 307

knowledge management The process by which learned information from customers is centralized and shared for the purpose of enhancing the relationship between customers and the organization. 128

leader pricing (loss-leader pricing) A product is sold near or even below cost in the hope that shoppers will buy other items once they are in the store. 326

lead generation (prospecting) Identification of those firms and people most likely to buy the seller's offerings. 290

lead qualification Determination of a sales prospect's (1) recognized need, (2) buying power, and (3) receptivity and accessibility. 291

learning A process that creates changes in behaviour, immediate or expected, through experience and practice; in a CRM environment, the informal process of collecting customer data through customer comments and feedback on product or service performance. 86; 128

licensing The legal process whereby a licensor agrees to let another firm use its manufacturing process, trademarks, patents, trade secrets, or other proprietary knowledge. 342

lifestyle A mode of living as identified by a person's activities, interests, and opinions. 83

lifetime value (LTV) analysis A data manipulation technique that projects the future value of the customer over a period of years using the assumption that marketing to repeat customers is more profitable than marketing to first-time buyers. 134

limited decision making The type of decision making that requires a moderate amount of time for gathering information and deliberating about an unfamiliar brand in a familiar product category. 72

location-based social networking sites Websites that combine the fun of social networking with the utility of location-based GPS technology. 274

logistics The process of strategically managing the efficient flow and storage of raw materials, in-process inventory, and finished goods from point of origin to point of consumption. 196

logistics information system The link that connects all of the logistics functions of the supply chain. 196

loyalty marketing program A promotional program designed to build long-term, mutually beneficial relationships between a company and its key customers. 284

major equipment (installations) Such capital goods as large or expensive machines, mainframe computers, blast furnaces, generators, airplanes, and buildings. 96

mall intercept interview Interviewing people in the common areas of shopping malls. 52

management decision problem A broad-based problem that uses marketing research in order for managers to take proper actions. 49

manufacturer's brand The brand name of a manufacturer. 147

manufacturers' suggested retail price (MSRP) the price recommended by the Manufacturer to aid controlling price competition and unit sales and, thereby ensure fair margins. 312

marginal cost (MC) The change in total costs associated with a one-unit change in output. 305

marginal revenue (MR) The extra revenue associated with selling an extra unit of output, or the change in total revenue as a result of a one-unit change in output. 307

market People or organizations with needs or wants and the ability and willingness to buy. 107

market development A marketing strategy that involves attracting new customers to existing products. 41

marketing The activity, set of institutions, and processes for creating, communicating, delivering, and exchanging offerings that have value for customers, clients, partners, and society at large. 3

marketing audit A thorough, systematic, periodic evaluation of the objectives, strategies, structure, and performance of the marketing organization. 45

marketing channel (channel of distribution) A set of interdependent organizations that ease the transfer of ownership as products move from producer to business user or consumer. 185

marketing concept The idea that the social and economic justification for an organization's existence is the satisfaction of customers' wants and needs while meeting organizational objectives. 5

marketing-controlled information source A product information source that originates with marketers promoting the product. 69

marketing information Everyday information about developments in the marketing environment that managers use to prepare and adjust marketing plans. 47

marketing mix A unique blend of product, place, promotion, and pricing strategies designed to produce mutually satisfying exchanges with a target market. 43

marketing myopia Defining a business in terms of goods and services rather than in terms of the benefits that customers seek. 35

marketing objective A statement of what is to be accomplished through marketing activities. 36

marketing plan A written document that acts as a guidebook of marketing activities for the marketing manager. 34

marketing planning Designing activities relating to marketing objectives and the changing marketing environment. 34

marketing research The process of planning, collecting, and analyzing data relevant to a marketing decision. 48

marketing research aggregator A company that acquires, catalogues, reformats, segments, and resells reports already published by marketing research firms. 50

marketing research issue A statement that defines the focus for the information that is to be collected to aid any marketing decision making. 49

marketing research objective The specific information needed to solve a marketing research issue. 49

marketing strategy The activities of selecting and describing one or more target markets and developing and maintaining a marketing mix that will produce mutually satisfying exchanges with target markets. 42

market opportunity analysis (MOA) The description and estimation of the size and sales potential of market segments that are of interest to the firm and the assessment of key competitors in these market segments. 42

market orientation A philosophy that involves obtaining information about customers, competitors, and markets; examining the information from a total business perspective; determining how to deliver superior customer value; and implementing actions to provide value to customer. 6

market penetration A marketing strategy that tries to increase market share among existing customers. 41

market segment A subgroup of people or organizations sharing one or more characteristics that cause them to have similar product needs. 107

market segmentation The process of dividing a market into meaningful, relatively similar, and identifiable segments or groups. 108

market share A company's product sales as a percentage of total sales for that industry. 299

markup pricing The cost of buying the product from the producer plus amounts for profit and for expenses not otherwise accounted for; can be expressed as markup (cost) or markup (selling). 306

Maslow's hierarchy of needs A method of classifying human needs and motivations into five categories in ascending order of importance: physiological, safety, social, esteem, and self-actualization. 86

mass communication The communication of a concept or message to large audiences. 230

mass customization (build-to-order) A production method whereby products are not made until an order is placed by the customer; products are made according to customer specifications. 197

mass merchandising A retailing strategy using moderate to low prices on large quantities of merchandise and lower levels of service to stimulate high turnover of products. 210

materials-handling system A method of moving inventory into, within, and out of the warehouse. 200

materials requirement planning (MRP) (materials management) An inventory control system that manages the replenishment of raw materials, supplies, and components from the supplier to the manufacturer. 199

maturity stage A period during which sales increase at a decreasing rate. 167

measurement error An error that occurs when the information desired by the researcher differs from the information provided by the measurement process. 57

media mix The combination of media to be used for a promotional campaign. 254

media planning The series of decisions advertisers make regarding the selection and use of media, allowing the marketer to optimally and cost-effectively communicate the message to the target audience. 249

media schedule Designation of the media, the specific publications or programs, and the insertion dates of advertising. 255

media sharing sites Websites that allow users to upload and distribute multimedia content, such as videos and photos. 273

medium The channel used to convey a message to a target market. 249

Mercosur The largest Latin American trade agreement, which includes Argentina, Bolivia, Brazil, Chile, Colombia, Ecuador, Paraguay, Peru, and Uruguay. 338

microblogs Blogs with strict limits on the length of posts. 271

mission statement A statement of the firm's business based on a careful analysis of benefits sought by present and potential customers and an analysis of existing and anticipated environmental conditions. 35

modified rebuy A situation where the purchaser wants some change in the original good or service. 100

morals The rules people develop as a result of cultural values and norms. 28

motive A driving force that causes a person to take action to satisfy specific needs. 86

multiculturalism When all major ethnic groups in an area—such as a city, county, or census tract—are roughly equally represented. 20

multinational corporation A company that is heavily engaged in international trade, beyond exporting and importing. 335

multiplier effect (accelerator principle) Phenomenon in which a small increase or decrease in consumer demand can produce a much larger change in demand for the facilities and equipment needed to make the consumer product. 92

multisegment targeting strategy Strategy that chooses two or more well-defined market segments and develops a distinct marketing mix for each. 118

mystery shoppers Researchers posing as customers who gather observational data about a store. 55

need recognition Result of an imbalance between actual and desired states. 68

needs assessment A determination of the customer's specific needs and wants and the range of options the customer has for satisfying them. 292

negotiation The process during which both the salesperson and the prospect offer special concessions in an attempt to arrive at a sales agreement. 294

networking The use of friends, business contacts, coworkers, acquaintances, and fellow members in professional and civic organizations to identify potential clients. 290

new buy A situation requiring the purchase of a product for the first time. 100

new product A product new to the world, new to the market, new to the producer, new to the seller, or new to some combination of these. 155

new-product strategy A plan that links the new-product development process with the objectives of the marketing department, the business unit, and the corporation. 157

niche One segment of a market. 117

niche competitive advantage The advantage achieved when a firm seeks to target and effectively serve a single segment of the market. 39

noise Anything that interferes with, distorts, or slows down the transmission of information. 231

nonaspirational reference groups (dissociative groups) Groups that influence our behaviour because we try to maintain distance from them. 79

noncorporate blogs Independent blogs that are not associated with the marketing efforts of any particular company or brand. 260

noncumulative quantity discount A deduction from list price that applies to a single order rather than to the total volume of orders placed during a certain period. 323

nonmarketing-controlled information source A product information source not associated with advertising or promotion. 69

nonprobability sample Any sample in which little or no attempt is made to have a representative cross-section of the population. 57

nonprofit organization An organization that exists to achieve some goal other than the usual business goals of profit, market share, or return on investment. 180

nonprofit organization marketing The effort by nonprofit organizations to bring about mutually satisfying exchanges with target markets. 180

nonstore retailing Shopping without visiting a store. 212

norms The values and attitudes deemed acceptable by a group. 78

North American Free Trade Agreement (NAFTA) An agreement between Canada, the United States, and Mexico that created the world's largest free trade zone. 339

North American Industry Classification System (NAICS) An industry classification system developed by the United States, Canada, and Mexico to classify North American business establishments by their main production processes. 101

observation research A research method that relies on four types of observation: people watching people, people watching an activity, machines watching people, and machines watching an activity. 55

odd–even pricing (psychological pricing) Odd-numbered prices to connote bargains and even-numbered prices to imply quality. 327

off-price retailer A retailer that sells at prices 25 percent or more below traditional department store prices because it pays cash for its stock and usually doesn't ask for return privileges. 211

one-to-one marketing An individualized marketing method that utilizes customer information to build long-term, personalized, and profitable relationships with each customer. 118

online marketing Two-way communication of a message delivered through the Internet to the consumer. 229

online retailing A type of shopping available to consumers who have personal computers and access to the Internet. 214

open-ended question An interview question that encourages an answer phrased in the respondent's own words. 54

opinion leader An individual who influences the opinions of others. 79

optimizers Business customers who consider numerous suppliers, both familiar and unfamiliar, solicit bids, and study all proposals carefully before selecting one. 116

order processing system A system whereby orders are entered into the supply chain and filled. 198

original equipment manufacturers (OEMs) Individuals and organizations that buy business goods and incorporate them into the products that they produce for eventual sale to other producers or to consumers. 94

outsourcing (contract logistics) A manufacturer's or supplier's use of an independent third party to manage an entire function of the logistics system, such as transportation, warehousing, or order processing. 201

owned media Online content that an organization creates and controls. 267

paid media Content paid for by a company to be placed online. 267

penetration pricing A relatively low price for a product initially as a way to reach the mass market. 320

perception The process by which people select, organize, and interpret stimuli into a meaningful and coherent picture. 84

perceptual mapping A means of displaying or graphing, in two or more dimensions, the location of products, brands, or groups of products in customers' minds. 120

perishability The inability of services to be stored, warehoused, or inventoried. 173

personality A way of organizing and grouping the consistency of an individual's reactions to situations. 83

personal selling A purchase situation involving a personal paid-for communication between two people in an attempt to influence each other. 228

persuasive labelling Package labelling that focuses on a promotional theme or logo, and consumer information is secondary. 151

pioneering advertising A form of advertising designed to stimulate primary demand for a new product or product category. 245

planned obsolescence The practice of modifying products so those that have already been sold become obsolete before they actually need replacement. 145

planning The process of anticipating future events and determining strategies to achieve organizational objectives in the future. 34

point-of-purchase display (P-O-P) A promotional display set up at the retailer's location to build traffic, advertise the product, or induce impulse buying. 286

point-of-sale interactions Communications between customers and organizations that occur at the point of sale, usually in a store. 129

portfolio matrix A tool for allocating resources among products or strategic business units on the basis of relative market share and market growth rate. 40

position The place a product, brand, or group of products occupies in consumers' minds relative to competing offerings. 120

positioning A process that influences potential customers' overall perception of a brand, product line, or organization in general. 119

preapproach A process that describes the research a salesperson must do before contacting a prospect. 291

predatory pricing The practice of charging a very low price for a product with the intent of driving competitors out of business or out of a market. 322

predictive modelling A data manipulation technique in which marketers try to determine, based on some past set of occurrences, the odds that some other occurrence, such as an inquiry or purchase, will take place in the future. 134

premium An extra item offered to the consumer, usually in exchange for some proof of purchase of the promoted product. 284

prestige pricing Charging a high price to help promote a high-quality image. 314

price That which given up in an exchange to acquire good or service. 297

price bundling Marketing two or more products in a single package for a special price. 327

price equilibrium The price at which demand and supply are equal. 302

price fixing An agreement between two or more firms on the price they will charge for a product. 321

price lining Offering a product line with several items at specific price points. 326

price shading The use of discounts by salespeople to increase demand for one or more products in a line. 330

price skimming A high introductory price, often coupled with heavy promotion. 319

price strategy A basic, long-term pricing framework that establishes the initial price for a product and the intended direction for price movements over the product life cycle. 318

primary data Information that is collected for the first time and is used for solving the particular problem under investigation. 51

primary membership groups groups with which individuals interact regularly in an informal, face-to-face manner. 78

private brand A brand name owned by a wholesaler or a retailer. 147

probability sample A sample in which every element in the population has a known statistical likelihood of being selected. 56

problem child (question mark) In the portfolio matrix, a business unit that shows rapid growth but poor profit margins. 40

processed materials Products used directly in manufacturing other product. 97

product Everything, both favourable and unfavourable, received in an exchange. 141

product advertising A form of advertising that promotes the benefits of a specific good or service. 245

product category All brands that satisfy a particular type of need. 165

product development A marketing strategy that involved the creation of new products for current customers; the process of converting applications for new technologies into marketable products. 41; 158

product differentiation A positioning strategy that some firms use to distinguish their products from those of competitors. 120

production orientation A philosophy that focuses on the internal capabilities of the firm rather than on the desires and needs of the marketplace. 4

product item A specific version of a product that can be designated as a distinct offering among an organization's products. 143

product life cycle (PLC) A concept that traces the stages of a product's acceptance, from its introduction (birth) to its decline (death). 165

product line A group of closely related product items. 143

product line depth The number of product items in a product line. 143

product line extension Adding additional products to an existing product line to compete more broadly in the industry. 145

product line pricing Setting prices for an entire line of products. 329

product mix All products that an organization sells. 143

product mix width The number of product lines an organization offers. 143

product modification Changing one or more of a product's characteristics. 144

product offering The mix of products offered to the consumer by the retailer; also called the product assortment or merchandise mix. 217

product placement A public relations strategy that involves getting a product, service, or company name to appear in a movie, television show, radio program, magazine, newspaper, video game, video or audio clip, book, or commercial for another product; on the Internet; or at special events. 258

product/service differentiation competitive advantage The provision of a unique benefit that is valuable to buyers beyond simply offering a low price. 39

profit Revenue minus expenses. 298

profit maximization A method of setting prices so that marginal revenue equals marginal cost. 307

promotion Communication by marketers that informs, persuades, and reminds potential buyers of a product for the purpose of influencing an opinion or eliciting a response. 225

promotional allowance (trade allowance) A payment to a dealer for promoting the manufacturer's products. 324

promotional mix The combination of promotional tools—including advertising, public relations, sales promotion, personal selling, direct-response communication, and online marketing—used to reach the target market and fulfill the organization's overall goals. 226

promotional strategy A plan for the optimal use of the elements of promotion: advertising, direct marketing, public relations, personal selling, sales promotion, and online marketing. 225

psychographic segmentation Market segmentation on the basis of personality, motives, lifestyles, and geodemographics categories. 113

psychological influences Tools that consumers use to recognize, gather, analyze, and self-organize to aid in decision making. 84

publicity Public information about a company, product, service, or issue appearing in the mass media as a news item. 227

public relations The marketing function that evaluates public attitudes, identifies areas within the organization the public may be interested in, and executes a program of action to earn public understanding and acceptance. 227

public service advertisement (PSA) An announcement that promotes a program of a nonprofit organization or of a federal, provincial or territorial, or local government. 182

pull strategy A marketing strategy that stimulates consumer demand to obtain product distribution. 239

pulsing media schedule A media scheduling strategy that uses continuous scheduling throughout the year coupled with a flighted schedule during the best sales periods. 256

purchasing power A comparison of income versus the relative cost of a set standard of goods and services in different geographic areas. 22

push money Money offered to channel intermediaries to encourage them to push products—that is, to encourage other members of the channel to sell the products. 287

push strategy A marketing strategy that uses aggressive personal selling and trade advertising to convince a wholesaler or a retailer to carry and sell particular merchandise. 239

pyramid of corporate social responsibility A model that suggests corporate social responsibility is composed of economic, legal, ethical, and philanthropic responsibilities and that the firm's economic performance supports the entire structure. 27

quantity discount A unit price reduction offered to buyers buying either in multiple units or more than a specified dollar amount. 323

random error The selected sample is an imperfect representation of the overall population. 57

random sample A sample arranged in such a way that every element of the population has an equal chance of being selected as part of the sample. 57

raw materials Unprocessed extractive or agricultural products, such as mineral ore, lumber, wheat, corn, fruits, vegetables, and fish. 96

reach The number of target consumers exposed to a commercial at least once during a specific period, usually four weeks. 254

real self-image The way an individual actually perceives himself or herself. 83

rebate A cash refund given for the purchase of a product during a specific period. 284, 324

receiver The person who decodes a message. 231

recency-frequency-monetary (RFM) analysis The analysis of customer activity as to recency, frequency, and monetary value. 133

recession A period of economic activity characterized by negative growth, which reduces demand for goods and services. 23

reciprocity A practice where business purchasers choose to buy from their own customers. 94

recruited Internet sample Pre-recruited respondents must qualify to participate and then e-mailed a questionnaire or directed to a secure website. 61

reference group A group in society that influences an individual's purchasing behaviour. 78

referral A recommendation to a salesperson from a customer or business associate. 290

relationship commitment A firm's belief that an ongoing relationship with another firm is so important that the relationship warrants maximum efforts at maintaining it indefinitely. 104

relationship marketing A strategy that focuses on keeping and improving relationships with current customers. 8

relationship selling (consultative selling) A multistage sales process that involves building, maintaining, and enhancing interactions with customers for the purpose of developing long-term satisfaction through mutually beneficial partnerships. 288

reliability The ability to perform a service dependably, accurately, and consistently. 173

repositioning Changing consumers' perceptions of a brand in relation to competing brands. 121

resale price maintenance Attempts by a producer to control a store's retail price for the product. 322

research design Specifies which research questions must be answered, how and when the data will be gathered, and how the data will be analyzed. 51

response list A customer list that includes the names and addresses of individuals who have responded to an offer of some kind, such as by mail, telephone, direct-response television, product rebates, contests or sweepstakes, or billing inserts. 131

responsiveness The ability to provide prompt service. 173

retailer A channel intermediary that sells mainly to consumers. 188

retailing All the activities directly related to the sale of goods and services to the ultimate consumer for personal, nonbusiness use. 205

retailing mix A combination of the six Ps— product, place, promotion, price, presentation, and personnel—to sell goods and services to the ultimate consumer. 217

return on investment (ROI) ROI = Net Profits (before taxes) divided by Investment (Owner's Equity). 299

revenue The price charged to customers multiplied by the number of units sold. 298

review sites Websites that allow consumers to post, read, rate, and comment on opinions regarding all kinds of products and services. 274

routine response behaviour The type of decision making exhibited by consumers buying frequently purchased, low-cost goods and services; requires little search and decision time. 72

sales orientation The idea that people will buy more goods and services if aggressive sales techniques are used and that high sales result in high profits. 5

sales presentation A formal meeting in which the salesperson presents a sales proposal to a prospective buyer. 293

sales process (sales cycle) The set of steps a salesperson goes through to sell a particular product or service. 289

sales promotion Marketing activities—other than personal selling, advertising, and public relations—that stimulate consumer buying and dealer effectiveness. 228

sales proposal A formal written document or professional presentation that outlines how the salesperson's product or service will meet or exceed the prospect's needs. 293

sample A subset from a larger population. 56

sampling A promotional program that allows the consumer the opportunity to try a product or service for free. 285

sampling error A sample that does not represent the target population. 57

satisficers business customers who place their order with the first familiar supplier to satisfy their Product and delivery requirements. 116

scaled-response question A closed-ended question designed to measure the intensity of a respondent's answer. 54

scanner-based research A system for gathering information from a single group of respondents by continuously monitoring the advertising, promotion, and pricing they are exposed to and the products they buy. 63

scrambled merchandising The tendency to offer a wide variety of nontraditional goods and services under one roof. 209

screened Internet sample An Internet sample with quotas that are based on desired sample characteristics. 60

screening The first filter in the product development process, which eliminates ideas that are inconsistent with the organization's new-product strategy or are obviously inappropriate for some other reason. 159

search quality A characteristic that can be easily assessed before purchase. 172

seasonal discount A price reduction for buying merchandise out of season. 324

seasonal media schedule A media scheduling strategy that runs advertising only during times of the year when the product is most likely to be used. 256

secondary data Data previously collected for any purpose other than the one at hand. 49

secondary membership groups groups with which individuals interact less consistently and more formally than with primary membership groups. 78

segmentation bases (variables) Characteristics of individuals, groups, or organizations. 109

selective distortion A process whereby consumers change or distort information that conflicts with their feelings or beliefs. 84

selective distribution A form of distribution achieved by screening dealers to eliminate all but a few in any single area. 194

selective exposure The process whereby a consumer decides which stimuli to notice and which to ignore. 84

selective retention A process whereby consumers remember only information that supports their personal beliefs. 84

self-concept How consumers perceive themselves in terms of attitudes, perceptions, beliefs, and self-evaluations. 83

self-regulation Programs voluntarily adopted by business groups to regulate the activities of their members. 26

selling against the brand Stocking well-known branded items at high prices in order to sell store brands at discounted prices. 312

sender The originator of the message in the communication process. 230

service The result of applying human or mechanical efforts to people or objects. 171

service mark A trademark for a service. 149

shopping product A product that requires comparison shopping because it is usually more expensive than a convenience product and is found in fewer stores. 142

simulated (laboratory) market testing The presentation of advertising and other promotion materials for several products, including a test product, to members of the product's target market. 162

simultaneous product development A team-oriented approach to new-product development. 160

single-price tactic Offering all goods and services at the same price (or perhaps two or three prices). 325

social class A group of people who are considered nearly equal in status or community esteem, who regularly socialize among themselves both formally and informally, and who share behavioural norms. 77

social commerce A subset of e-commerce that involves the interaction and user contribution aspects of social online media to assist online buying and selling of products and services. 265

socialization process The passing down of cultural values and norms to children. 81

social media Any tool or service that uses the Internet to facilitate conversations. 263

social networking sites (social media sites) Websites where users create and share information about themselves, brands, and other mutual interests; websites that allow individuals to connect—or network—with friends, peers, and business associates. 233; 272

social news sites Websites that allow users to decide which content is promoted on a given website by voting that content up or down. 273

societal marketing orientation The idea that an organization exists not only to satisfy customers' wants and needs and to meet organizational objectives but also to preserve or enhance individuals' and society's long-term best interests. 6

sociometric leader A low-profile, well-respected collaborative professional who is socially and professionally well connected. 79

spatial discrepancy The difference between the location of a producer and the location of widely scattered markets where the product is desired. 187

specialty discount store A retail store that offers a nearly complete selection of single-line merchandise and uses self-service, discount prices, high volume, and high turnover. 210

specialty product A particular item that consumers search extensively for and are very reluctant to accept substitutes for. 142

specialty store A retail store specializing in a given type of merchandise. 209

sponsorship A public relations strategy in which a company spends money to support an issue, cause, or event that is consistent with corporate objectives, such as improving brand awareness or enhancing corporate image. 259

status quo pricing A pricing objective that maintains existing prices or meets the competition's prices. 300

stickiness A measure of a website's effectiveness; calculated by multiplying the frequency of visits by both the duration of the visits and the number of pages viewed during each visit (site reach). 102

star In the portfolio matrix, a business unit that is a fast-growing market leader. 40

stimulus Any unit of input affecting one or more of the five senses: sight, smell, taste, touch, hearing. 68

straight rebuy A situation in which the purchaser reorders the same goods or services without looking for new information or new suppliers. 100

strategic alliance (strategic partnership) A cooperative agreement between business firms. 103

strategic business unit (SBU) A subgroup of a single business or a collection of related businesses within the larger organization. 36

strategic channel alliance A cooperative agreement between business firms to use one of the manufacturer's already established distribution channels. 191

strategic planning The managerial process of creating and maintaining a fit between the organization's objectives and resources and evolving market opportunities. 33

subculture A homogeneous group of people who share elements of the overall culture and also have their own unique cultural elements. 76

supercentre A retail store that combines groceries and general merchandise goods with a wide range of services. 210

supermarket A large, departmentalized, self-service retailer that specializes in food and some nonfood items. 209

supplementary services A group of services that support or enhance the core service. 175

supplies Consumable items that do not become part of the final product. 97

supply The quantity of a product that will be offered to the market by a supplier at various prices for a specified period. 301

supply chain The connected chain of all of the business entities, both internal and external to the company, that perform or support the marketing channel functions. 186

supply chain management A management system that coordinates and integrates all of the activities performed by supply chain members into a seamless process, from the source to the point of consumption, resulting in enhanced customer and economic value. 191

supply chain team An entire group of individuals who orchestrate the movement of goods, services, and information from the source to the consumer. 196

survey research The most popular technique for gathering primary data, in which a researcher interacts with people to obtain facts, opinions, and attitudes. 52

sustainability The idea that socially responsible companies will outperform their peers by focusing on the world's social problems and viewing them as opportunities to build profits and help the world at the same time. 27

sustainable competitive advantage an advantage that cannot be copied by the competition. 39

SWOT analysis Identifying internal strengths (S) and weaknesses (W) and also examining external opportunities (O) and threats (T). 37

tangibles The physical evidence of a service, including the physical facilities, tools, and equipment used to provide the service. 173

target market A defined group most likely to buy a firm's product; a group of people or organizations for which an organization designs, implements, and maintains a marketing mix intended to meet the needs of that group, resulting in mutually satisfying exchanges. 15; 116

teamwork Collaborative efforts of people to accomplish common objectives. 10

telemarketing The use of the telephone to sell directly to consumers; the use of telecommunications to sell a product or service; involves both outbound calls and inbound calls. 213; 257

temporal discrepancy A situation in which a product is produced but a customer at that time is not ready to buy it. 187

test marketing The limited introduction of a product and a marketing program to determine the reactions of potential customers in a market situation. 161

touch points All possible areas of a business where customers have contact with that business. 129

trade allowance A price reduction offered by manufacturers to intermediaries, such as wholesalers and retailers. 287

trademark The exclusive right to use a brand or part of a brand. 149

trade sales promotion Sales promotion activities targeting a marketing channel member, such as a wholesaler or retailer. 281

trust The condition that exists when one party has confidence in an exchange partner's reliability and integrity. 104

two-part pricing Charging two separate amounts to consume a single good or service. 328

unbundling Reducing the bundle of services that comes with the basic product. 327

undifferentiated targeting strategy Marketing approach that views the market as one big market with no individual segments and thus uses a single marketing mix. 117

uniform delivered pricing The seller pays the actual freight charges and bills every purchaser an identical, flat freight charge. 325

unique selling proposition Desirable, exclusive, and believable advertising appeal selected as the theme for a campaign. 247

unitary elasticity A situation in which total revenue remains the same when prices change. 302

universal product codes (UPCs) A series of thick and thin vertical lines (bar codes), readable by computerized optical scanners that match the codes to brand names, package sizes, and prices. 152

universe The population from which a sample will be drawn. 56

unrestricted Internet sample A survey in which anyone with a computer and Internet access can fill out the questionnaire. 60

unsought product A product unknown to the potential buyer or a known product that the buyer does not actively seek. 143

Uruguay Round An agreement created by the World Trade Organization to dramatically lower trade barriers worldwide. 338

usage-rate segmentation Dividing a market by the amount of product bought or consumed. 114

value The enduring beliefs shared by a society that a specific mode of conduct is personally or socially preferable to another mode of conduct. 75

value-based pricing Setting the price at a level that seems to the customer to be a good price compared with the prices of other options. 324

variable cost A cost that varies with changes in the level of output. 305

vertical conflict A channel conflict that occurs between different levels in a marketing channel, most typically between the manufacturer and wholesaler or between the manufacturer and retailer. 195

want A particular product or service that the customer believes could satisfy an unfulfilled need. 68

warehouse membership clubs Limited-service merchant wholesalers that sell a limited selection of brand-name appliances, household items, and groceries on a cash-and-carry basis to members, small businesses, and groups. 211

warranty A confirmation of the quality or performance of a good or service. 153

World Bank An international bank that offers low-interest loans, advice, and information to developing nations. 340

World Trade Organization (WTO) A trade organization that replaced the old General Agreement on Tariffs and Trade (GATT). 339

yield management systems (YMS) A technique for adjusting prices that uses complex mathematical software to profitably fill unused capacity by discounting early purchases, limiting early sales at these discounted prices, and overbooking capacity. 304

zone pricing a modification of uniform delivered pricing that divides the total market into segments or zones and charges a flat freight rate to all customers in a given zone. 325

Endnotes

1

1. Anique Gonzalez, "Peter F. Drucker: Business Sage," http://www.marketingcrossing.com/article/220112/Peter-F-Drucker-Business-Sage/, accessed August 22, 2011.

2. American Marketing Association, "AMA Definition of Marketing," http://www.marketing-power.com/Community/ARC/Pages/Additional/Definition/default.aspx, accessed June 28, 2010.

3. Gonzalez, "Peter F. Drucker: Business Sage."

4. lululemon athletica, "Create Your Ideal Life with Vision and Goals," http://www.lululemon.com/education/goalsetting, accessed August 22, 2011.

5. Philip Kotler, *Marketing Management*, 11th ed. (Upper Saddle River, NJ: Prentice-Hall, 2003), 12.

6. Zipcar, "Mission," www.zipcar.com, accessed September 26, 2010.

7. Kristin Laird, "Hitting the Mark," *Marketing Magazine*, April 30, 2010, http://www.marketingmag.ca/news/marketer-news/hitting-the-mark-2471, accessed July 25, 2011.

8. Ann Harrington, "America's Most Admired Companies," *Fortune*, March 8, 2004, 100.

9. Associated Press, "Research In Motion Releasing PlayBook Tablet to Rival Apple's iPad," September 28, 2010, http://www.marketingmag.ca/news/media-news/research-in-motion-releasing-playbook-tablet-to-rival-apples-ipad-5155, accessed September 26, 2010.

10. Interbrand, "Best Global Brands 2010: Brand Leaders Conversations," http://www.interbrand.com/en/best-global-brands/Best-Global-Brands-2010/Disney-Matthew-Ryan.aspx, accessed September 21, 2010.

11. Valerie A. Zeithaml, Mary Jo Bitner, and Dwayne D. Gremler, *Services Marketing*, 4th ed. (New York: McGraw-Hill Irwin, 2006), 110.

12. "Building Business around Customers: Know Thy Customer," *BusinessWeek*, September 12, 2005, 8.

13. Vadim Kotelnikov, "Customer Retention—Driving Profits through Giving Customers Lots of Reasons," http://www.1000ventures.com/business_guide/crosscuttings/customer_retention.html, accessed September 26, 2010.

14. Richard Branson, "Opinion: Weak Links in the Chain of Good Service," *Canadian Business*, April 8, 2011, http://www.canadianbusiness.com/article/11378--opinion-weak-links-in-the-chain-of-good-service, accessed July 25, 2011.

15. Ibid.

16. Zeithaml, Bitner, and Gremler, *Services Marketing*.

17. Interbrand, "Best Global Brands 2010: Brand Leaders Conversations."

18. CNW Group Ltd., "J.D. Power and Associates Reports Customer Satisfaction with Retail Banks in Canada Increases as Industry Strengthens Following Global Financial Crisis," news release, July 22, 2010, http://www.newswire.ca/en/releases/archive/July2010/22/c6012.html, accessed September 19, 2010.

19. TD Canada Trust, "TD's Guiding Principles," www.td.com/guidingprinciples.jsp, accessed September 19, 2010.

20. CNW Group Ltd., "J.D. Power and Associates Reports Customer Satisfaction with Retail Banks in Canada."

21. Polaroid, "Polaroid Unveils New Product Line-up at CES," January 6, 2010, http://www.polaroid.com/en/news/2010/1/7/polaroid-unveils-new-product-line-ces, accessed August 24, 2011.

22. Jordan Adler, "Nissan Site Lets Consumers Learn about Juke," *Marketing*, June 25, 2010, http://www.marketingmag.ca/news/marketer-news/nissan-site-lets-consumers-learn-about-juke-3446, accessed August 25, 2011.

2

1. The Vanier Institute of the Family, "Definition of Family," https://www.vifamily.ca/node/2, accessed July 25, 2011.

2. The Vanier Institute of the Family, "Thinking about Families: An Interview with Katherine Scott, Director of Programs, Vanier Institute of the Family," Transition Magazine, winter 2010, 5–7.

3. Ibid.

4. Ibid.

5. Karen Mazurkewich, "Tweens & Technology," *National Post*, August 10, 2010, www.mhoneill.com/106B/articles/tween%20power.pdf, accessed August 29, 2011.

6. Sharon Lem, "TDSB Says No to Expanding Video Advertising in Schools," *Toronto Sun*, March 9, 2011, http://www.torontosun.com/news/torontoandgta/2011/03/09/17558486.html, accessed August 29, 2011.

7. "Despite Economic Upheaval Generation Y Is Still Feeling Green: RSA," Newswire, October 28, 2010, http://www.newswire.ca/en/releases/archive/October2010/28/c6663.html, accessed August 29, 2011.

8. Kate Engineer, "Generation Y is the New Face of Luxury," *Marketing*, September 29, 2010, http://bibmanagement.com/generation-y-is-the-new-face-of-luxury/, accessed August 29, 2011.

9. Karen Akers, "Generation Y: Marketing to the Young and the Restless," *Successful Promotions*, January/February 2005, 33–38.

10. "The Gen X Budget," *American Demographics*, July/August 2002, S5.

11. Dick Chay, "New Segments of Boomers Reveal New Marketing Implications," *Marketing News*, March 15, 2005, 24.

12. Louise Lee, "Love Those Boomer," *Business Week*, October 24, 2005, 94–101.

13. Brian Steinberg, "Neilsen Makes the Case for Targeting Boomers," *Marketing Magazine*, July 19, 2010, http://www.marketingmag.ca/news/marketer-news/nielsen-makes-the-case-for-targeting-boomers-3984, accessed August 20, 2010.

14. Statistics Canada, "Census metropolitan area (CMA) and census agglomeration (CA)," http://www12.statcan.ca/english/census06/reference/dictionary/geo009.cfm, accessed September 2008.

15. Martin Turcotte and Mireille Vézina, "Migration from Central and Surrounding Municipalities in Toronto, Montréal and Vancouver," Canadian Social Trends, Statistics Canada catalogue no. 11-008-X, June 8, 2010, http://www.statcan.gc.ca/pub/11-008-x/2010002/article/11159-eng.pdf, accessed September 20, 2010.

16. Statistics Canada, "2006 Census: Immigration, Citizenship, Language, Mobility and Migration," *The Daily*, December 4, 2007, http://www.statcan.gc.ca/daily-quotidien/071204/dq071204a-eng.htm, accessed September 20, 2010

17. Statistics Canada, "Population Projections of Visible Minority Groups, Canada, Provinces, and Regions," Catalogue no 91-541-XIE.

18. Ibid.

19. City of Toronto, "Diversity," http://www.toronto.ca/quality_of_life/diversity.htm.

20. Duane Stanford, "Coke's World Cup Song Is a Marketing Winner," *Bloomberg News*, July 15, 2010, http://www.businessweek.com/magazine/content/10_30/b4188024314746.htm, accessed September 4, 2010.

21. Statistics Canada, "Visible Minority Population by Age," http://www.statscan.ca, accessed September 20, 2010.

22. "Making Multicultural Work," *Marketing*, Cultural Diversity in Canada Supplement, May 2005, 5; "The Web Goes Multicultural," *Advertising Age*, November 29, 1999, 51, 54.

23. Statistics Canada, "Median Total Income, by Family Type, by Province and Territory," http://www40.statcan.ca/l01/cst01/famil108a-eng.htm, accessed August 28, 2011.

24. Ibid.

25. Human Resources and Skills Development, "Special Reports—What Difference Does Education Make to Financial Security," http://www4.hrsdc.gc.ca/.3ndic.1t.4r@-eng.jsp?iid=54, accessed August 28, 2011.

26. Marc Gunther, "The Green Machine," *Fortune*, August 7, 2006, 42–57.

27. Julian Beltrame, "Canada's Recession Wasn't That Bad After All: Statistics Canada," Canadian Press, April 15, 2010, http://www.fftimes.com/node/232752, accessed August 29, 2011.

28. Ipsos Reid, Deloitte, Tourism Industry Association of Canada, *"Navigate: New Directions in Tourism, Hospitality and Leisure*, winter 2010, 4–11.

29. See Competition Bureau website, http://www.competitionbureau.gc.ca

30. Jonathon Pauls, "ASC Exaggerates the Truth," *Strategy Magazine*, February 2011, 19–26.

31. Jonathan Paul, "No-so-secret Origins: Lay's and Starbucks," *Strategy Magazine*, February 1, 2011, http://www.strategyonline.ca/articles/magazine/20110201/upfrontlays.html, accessed August 28, 2011.

32. Marc Gunther, "Will Social Responsibility Harm Business?" *Wall Street Journal*, May 18, 2005, A2.

33. This section is adapted from Archie B. Carroll, "The Pyramid of Corporate Social Responsibility: Toward the Moral Management of Organizational Stakeholders," *Business Horizons*, July/August 1991, 39–48. See also Kirk Davidson, "Marketers Must Accept Greater Responsibilities," *Marketing News*, February 2, 1998, 6.

34. "Globally, Companies are Giving Back" *HR Magazine*, June 1, 2007, 30.

35. S. C. Johnson, "Our Greenlist Process," http://www.scjohnson.com/en/commitment/focus-on/greener-products/greenlist.aspx, accessed August 28, 2011.

36. Mountain Equipment Co-op, "Ethical Sourcing," http://www.mec.ca/Main/content_text.jsp?FOLDER%3C%3Efolder_id=1408474396038947, accessed August 28, 2011.

37. Based on Edward Stevens, *Business Ethics* (New York: Paulist Press, 1979). Used with permission of Paulist Press.

38. Anusorn Singhapakdi, Skott Vitell, and Kenneth Kraft, "Moral Intensity and Ethical Decision Making of Marketing Professionals," *Journal of Business Research*, March 1996, 245–255; Ishmael Akaah and Edward Riordan, "Judgments of Marketing Professionals about Ethical Issues in Marketing Research: A Replication and Extension," *Journal of Marketing Research*, February 1989, 112–120.

3

1. http://www.bcg.com; http://www.wikipedia.org.

2. Kathryn Kranhold, "The Immelt Era, Five Years Old, Transforms GE," *Wall Street Journal*, September 11, 2006, B1.

3. Ray A. Smith, "Buying a Suit That's Not Hot," *Wall Street Journal Online*," July 7, 2005.

4. Geoff Keighly, "The Phantasmagoria Factory," *Business 2.0*, January/February 2004, 103; Christopher J. Chipello, "Cirque du Soleil Seeks Partnerships to Create Entertainment Centers," *WSJ.com*, July 18, 2001; Steve Friess, "Cirque Dreams Big," *Newsweek*, July 14, 2003, 42; "Bravo Announces Programming Alliance with Cirque du Soleil; Original Series, Specials, and Documentaries to Air on Bravo, 'The Official U.S. Network of Cirque du Soleil,'" *Business Wire*, June 19, 2000; "Inhibitions Take the Night Off for International Gala Premiere of ZUMANITY; Another Side of Cirque du Soleil™ at New York–New York Hotel and Casino," *PR Newswire*, September 21, 2003; Laura Del Rosso, "'O' Dazzles with Air, Underwater Acrobatics," *Travel Weekly*, August 5, 2002; Gigi Berardi, "Circus + Dance = Cirque du Soleil," *Dance Magazine*, September 2002.

5. Sharon Edelson, "Cirque du Soleil Builds Brand beyond the Ring," *WWD.com*, February 9, 2006.

6. Verne G. Kopytoff, "H.P. Profit Up 5%, but PC Sales Are Declining," *New York Times*, May 18, 2011, http://www.nytimes.com/2011/05/18/technology/18hewlett.html.accessed June 20, 2011.

4

1. Ann Breese and Donald Bruzzone, "A Definite Impact," *Quirk's Marketing Research Review*, April 2004, 22–31.

2. Kettle Valley Research, "City of Kelowna: 2006 Citizen Survey Detailed Report," http://www.city.kelowna.bc.ca/CityPage/Docs/PDFs/Communications/2006%20Citizen%20Survey%20Report.pdf, 1–2, accessed July 2008.

3. Alison Stein Wellner, "Watch Me Now," *American Demographics*, October 2002, S1–S8.

4. "How Cool Is That?" *Smart Money*, June 2005, 13.

5. Statistics Canada, *Internet Use Survey 2010*, May 25, 2011.

6. Karl Feld, "Do You Know Where Your Data Came From?" *Quirk's Marketing Research Review*, November 2007, 24–31.

7. For information on building a panel, see Brian Wansink and Seymour Sudman, "Building a Successful Convenience Panel," *Marketing Research*, Fall 2002, 23–27.

8. Conversation with Jerry Thomas, *CEO Decision Analyst*, September 20, 2005. This firm has one of the largest Internet panels in the world.

9. Pallavi Gogoi, "Smells Like Teen Marketing; 3iYing Teams Up with Design-Conscious Teen Girls in a Radical Approach to Pushing Everything from Tampons to Cell Phones," *Business Week Online*, November 11, 2005.

10. This information on blogging comes from "Intelliseek to Provide AOL with Daily Blog Trend Analysis," *PR Newswire*, October 17, 2005, http://www.intelliseek.com; Justin Martin, "BLOGGING FOR DOLLARS: How Would You Like to Survey 20 Million Consumers in Two Minutes?" *Fortune*, December 12, 2005, 178; "Intelliseek's Enhanced BlogPulse Offers Data-Rich Blog Profiles," *PR Newswire*, July 21, 2005.

11. Carl McDaniel and Roger Gates, *Marketing Research*, 6th ed. (Mason, OH: Thomson South-Western, 2005).

12. Normandy Madden, "Leo Burnett Behind New System to Blunt Counterfeiting in China," *AdvertisingAge*, January 31, 2011.

13. Stephanie Hughes and Fred Beasley, "An Examination of the Existence and Usage of Competitive Intelligence in Professional Sports," *Journal of Competitive Intelligence and Management*, 2007, 108.

5

1. "What's Hot in the Living Spaces of Young Adults?" *American Demographics*, September 2003, 14.

2. Ronald Alsop, "The Best Corporate Reputations in America: Johnson & Johnson (Think Babies!) Turns Up Tops," *Wall Street Journal*, September 23, 1999, B1. See also Alsop, "Survey Rates Companies' Reputations, and Many Are Found Wanting," *Wall Street Journal*, February 7, 2001, B1.

3. Princeton Research Survey Associates, "Consumer Behavior, Experiences and Attitudes: A Comparison by Age Groups," *AARP*, March 1999.

4. Amy Goldwasser, "What Is the Good Life? An A–Z Guide to Living Large," *Inc.*, October 2003, 71.

5. http://www.mystictan.com, accessed February 2006.

6. Stephanie Thompson, "Marketers Embrace Latest Health Claims," *Advertising Age*, February 28, 2000, 20–22. See also John Urquhart, "A Health Food Hits Big Time," *Wall Street Journal*, August 3, 1999, B1, B4.

7. Cathleen Egan, "Kellogg, General Mills Battle over Bars," *Wall Street Journal*, March 26, 2001, B10.

8. "LeBron James Hits $90M Jackpot," *CBS News*, February 11, 2009.

9. John Gaffney, "The Kids Are Doing It. Should You? *Business 2.0*, November 2001, 141

10. "The Buzz Starts Here: Finding the First Mouth for Word-of-Mouth Marketing," *Knowledge@Wharton*, March 4, 2009.

11. Rachel Dodes, "Bloggers Get Under the Tent," *Wall Street Journal*, September 12, 2006, B1, B2.

12. Matthew Klein, "He Shops, She Shops," *American Demographics*, March 1998, 34–35.

13. "Nintendo's Women Gamers Could Transform Market," *Times Online*, October 10, 2007.

14. Khanh T. L. Tran, "Women Assert Computer Games Aren't Male Preserve," *Wall Street Journal*, February 26, 2001, B1. See also Meeyoung Song, "Credit-Card Companies Cater to Korean Women," *Wall Street Journal*, June 6, 2001, B4.

15. Jack Neff, "Time to Rethink Your Message: Now the Cart Belongs to Daddy," *Advertising Age*, January 17, 2011, 1.

16. Linda Crane, "YouthPulseSM 2010," *Trends & Tudes*, November 2010.

17. Nora J. Rifon and Molly Catherine Ziske, "Using Weight Loss Products: The Roles of Involvement, Self-Efficacy and Body Image," in *1995 AMA Educators' Proceedings*, ed. Barbara B. Stern and George M. Zinkhan (Chicago: American Marketing Association, 1995), 90–98.

18. Lisa Vickery, Kelly Greene, Shelly Branch, and Emily Nelson, "Marketers Tweak Strategies as Age Groups Realign," *Wall Street Journal*, May 15, 2001, B1.

19. Sarah Hall, "What Color Is Your Cart?" *Self*, September 1999, 150, http://www.godiva.com, accessed January 2006.

20. "BMW Subliminal Ad Burns Logo onto Your Eyelids. Effectiveness in Influencing Customers Has Not Been Determined as of Yet," video, David Kiley (HYPERLINK "/bloggers/david-kiley/rss.xml" RSS feed) on Dec 17th 2010 at 4:55PM, accessed August 28, 2011.

21. Joshua Rosenbaum, "Guitar Maker Looks for a New Key," *Wall Street Journal*, February 11, 1998, B1, B5.

22. Elizabeth J. Wilson, "Using the Dollarmetric Scale to Establish the Just Meaningful Difference in Price," in *1987 AMA Educators' Proceedings*, ed. Susan Douglas et al. (Chicago: American Marketing Association, 1987), 107.

23. Sunil Gupta and Lee G. Cooper, "The Discounting of Discounts and Promotion Thresholds," *Journal of Consumer Research*, December 1992, 401–411.

24. Mark Stiving and Russell S. Winer, "An Empirical Analysis of Price Endings with Scanner Data," *Journal of Consumer Research*, June 1997, 57–67. See also Robert M. Schindler and Patrick N. Kirby, "Patterns of Rightmost Digits Used in Advertised Price: Implications for Nine-Ending

Effects," *Journal of Consumer Research*, September 1997, 192–201.

6

1. Michael D. Hutt and Thomas W. Speh, *Business Marketing Management* (Cincinnati: South-Western, 2004), 4.
2. Statistics Canada, Public Sector Statistics, http://cansim2.statcan.ca, accessed September 2008.
3. Inc. Staff, "How to Sell to Northrup Grumman," *Inc.*, April 5, 2010, www.inc.com/magazine/20100401/how-to-sell-to-northrop-grumman,html; Inc. Staff, "How to Sell to Dell," *Inc.*, April 5, 2010, www.inc.com/magazine/20100401/how-to-sell-to-coca-cola.html.
4. *Marketing News*, July 15, 2005, 29.
5. http://www.clickz.com/stats/sectors/b2b/article/php, online.
6. NetGenesis, E-Metrics: Business Metrics for the New Economy, http://www.netgenesis.com/downloads/Papers.cfm.
7. Wikipedia, the Free Encyclopedia, July 26, 2005; Janet Adamy, "Retail Exchanges Plan Merger to Vie With Wal-Mart," *Wall Street Journal*, April 26, 2005, B7.
8. "B2B Ain't What It Used to Be," *eMarketer*, June 24, 2005, online.
9. James Bandler, "As Kodak Eyes Digital Future, A Big Partner Starts to Fade," *Wall Street Journal*, January 23, 2004, online; "Walgreens switching back to Kodak Digital Photo Kiosks, August 30, 2005, online at http://www.gokis.net/self-service/archives/001108.html.
10. Andy Pasztor, Jonathan Karp, and J. Lynn Lunsford, "Boeing, Lockheed Agree to Form Rocket Joint Venture, Ending Feud," *Wall Street Journal*, May 3, 2005, A3.
11. Robert M. Morgan and Shelby D. Hunt, "The Commitment-Trust Theory of Relationship Marketing," *Journal of Marketing*, 58: 4, 1994, 23.
12. Ibid.
13. Leila Abboud, "How Eli Lilly's Monster Deal Faced Extinction—but Survived," *Wall Street Journal*, April 27, 2005, online.

7

1. Michelle Halpern, "Cute but Scary," *Marketing Magazine*, August 9, 2004.
2. "Marketing to Online Teens," *eMarketer*, May 11, 2004.
3. "Canadian Teenagers Are Leading the Online Revolution? Maybe Not..." http://www.ipsos-na.com/news-polls/pressrelease.aspx?id=3829, *Ipsos.com*, accessed February 6, 2011.
4. Aimee Deeken, "Teenage Tasteland," *Spring Magazine*, March 1, 2004, 22–24.
5. Ibid.
6. From Charles W. Lamb Jr., Joseph F. Hair Jr., Carl McDaniel, A.J. Faria and William J. Wellington, *Marketing*, 4th Canadian edition (Toronto: Nelson Education Ltd., 2009), p. 169.
7. Michelle Halpern, "A&W Brings Back Another Blast from Its Past," *Marketing Magazine*, June 18, 2004.
8. Halpern, "Cute, but Scary."
9. Newsline, "Dentures Get Sexed Up," *Marketing Magazine*, September 9, 2002, 16.
10. Khanh T. L. Tran, "Women Assert Computer

Games Aren't Male Preserve," *Wall Street Journal*, February 26, 2001, B1, B8.
11. "Holiday Proposal Dos and Don'ts," http://weddings.weddingchannel.com/wedding-planning-ideas/proposals-engagement-advice/articles/holiday-proposal-dos-and-donts.aspx, accessed August 2, 2011.
12. Lisa Vickery, Kelly Greene, Shelly Branch, and Emily Nelson, "Marketers Tweak Strategies as Age Groups Realign," *Wall Street Journal*, May 15, 2001, B1.
13. Statistics Canada, "Average Income after Tax by Economic Family Types," http://www40.statcan.ca/l01/cst01/famil21a-eng.htm, accessed February 6, 2011.
14. Loretta Lam, "Music to Ethnic Ears," *Marketing Magazine*, May 19, 2003, 10–11.
15. Deborah L. Vence, "You Talkin to Me?," *Marketing News*, March 1, 2004, 1, 9–11.
16. Juan Garcia and Roberto Gerdes, "To Win Latino Market, Know Pitfalls, Learn Rewards," *Marketing News*, March 1, 2004, 14, 19.
17. Statistics Canada, "Couple Families by Presence of Children Aged 24 and under in Private Households, 2006 Counts, for Canada, Provinces and Territories—20% Sample Data." http://www12.statcan.ca/census-recensement/2006/dp-pd/hlt/97-553/pages/page.cfm?Lang=E&Geo=PR&Code=01&Table=1&Data=Count&Age=2&StartRec=1&Sort=2&Display=Page
18. Statistics Canada, "Census Families, Number and Average Size," http://www40.statcan.ca/l01/cst01/famil40-eng.htm
19. From Charles W. Lamb Jr., Joseph F. Hair Jr., Carl McDaniel, A.J. Faria and William J. Wellington, *Marketing*, Fourth Canadian Edition (Toronto: Nelson Education Ltd., 2009), 169–170.
20. Carolyn Poirot, "If It Fuels Good, Eat It," *Fort Worth Star-Telegram*, August 11, 2003, E1.
21. Joanna Pachner, "Faster Hotter Sooner," *Financial Post*, *National Post*, March 6, 2007.
22. Eve Lazarus, "Fat Chances," *Marketing Magazine*, April 3, 2006.
23. Lior Arussy, "Be a Bag," *Customer Relationship Management*, March 2005, 24.
24. Danny Kucharsky, "Mega Bloks Target Kids at Retail," *Marketing Magazine*, November 12, 2001, 4.
25. Popbytes, "Rihanna Tops the Charts with Milk—Video!," http://allwomenstalk.com/rihanna-tops-the-charts-with-milk-video/, accessed September 1, 2011.
26. Vijay Mahajan and Yoram Wind, "Get Emotional Product Positioning," *Marketing Management*, May/June 2002, 36–41.
27. "Cottonelle Turns into Cashmere in New Campaign," *Marketing Daily*, June 15, 2005.

8

1. Joseph Hair, Robert Bush, and David Ortinau, *Marketing Research: Within a Changing Information Environment*, 3d ed. (Burr Ridge, IL: McGraw-Hill/Irwin, 2006), 114.
2. http://www.ondemand5.com.
3. Jeff Sweat, "Keep 'Em Happy," *Internet Week.com*, January 28, 2002.
4. http://www.playstation.ca/; SAP Customer Success Story, "Playstation.com Chooses mySAP CRM," http://h71028.www7.hp.com/enterprise/downloads/playstation.pdf, accessed August 3, 2011.

5. Student Price Card, "About the Card," http://www.spccard.ca/about.aspx, accessed August 31, 2011.
6. British Columbia Automobile Association (BCAA), "When a Company Believes in Doing the Right Thing It Shows," http://www.bcaa.com/wps/portal/BCAA/careers?rdePathInfo=xchg/bcaa-com/hs.xsl/360.htm, accessed August 31, 2011.
7. http://www.playstation.ca/; SAP Customer Success Story, "Playstation.com Chooses mySAP CRM."
8. *Random House Webster's Dictionary*.
9. Evan Shuman, "Wal-Mart Plans for Its 4PB Data Warehouse," Ziff Davis, August 3, 2007, online at http://www.eweek.com/c/a/Data-Storage/WalMart-Plans-for-Its-4PB-Data-Warehouse/.
10. "The Key to Effective CRM: Building an Interactive Dialog," http://www.marketing3.nl, presentation in Utrecht, the Netherlands, December 4, 2003; http://www.theknot.com; "The Knot Ties in Consumers with Personalization," *Consumer-Centric Benchmarks for 2001 & Beyond*, http://www.risnews.com; Jack Schofield, "Casino Rewards Total Loyalty," http://technology.guardian.co.uk/online/story/0,3605,1122850,00.html, accessed April 2006; Christina Binkley, "Lucky Numbers: A Casino Chain Finds a Lucrative Niche—The Small Spenders," *Wall Street Journal*, May 4, 2000, A1, A10; "Personal Touch for VIPs: Client-Tracking System Helps Harrah's Tailor Sales Efforts for Frequent Visitors," *Information Week*, November 4, 2003.
11. B. Weitz, S. Castleberry, and J. Tanner, *Selling* (Burr Ridge, IL: McGraw-Hill/Irwin, 2004), 184–185.
12. Jaimie Seaton, "Stave Solves the Relationship Puzzle," *1to1 Magazine*, August 4, 2003, http://www.1to1.com.
13. Lesley Young, "When Three Heads are Better than One," *Marketing Magazine*, December 8, 2003.
14. Karen Schwartz, "Kraft Data Mining Transforms Marketing and Margins," *Consumer Goods Magazine*, September 2000, http://www.consumergoods.com.
15. Insights taken from a conversation with Campion CEO Brock Elliot, June 13, 2008.
16. Kit Davis, "Track Star, RFID Is Racing to Market," *Consumer Goods Magazine*, June 2003, http://www.consumergoods.com.

9

1. Todd Wasserman, "P&G Tries to Absorb More Low-End Sales," *BrandWeek*, September 26, 2005, 4.
2. Todd Wasserman, "P&G Seeks Right Ingredient to Wash Out Laundry Woes," *BrandWeek*, August 8, 2005, 5.
3. Kenneth Hein, "Parade of Drinks May Clog Channel," *BrandWeek*, February 7, 2005, 4.
4. Janet Adamy, "Heinz Sets Overhaul Plans in Motion," *Wall Street Journal*, September 20, 2005, A4.
5. "Nielsen: Store Brand Consumers Evolving in Canada," http://www.pgstorebrands.com/top-story-nielsen__store_brand_consumers_evolving_in_canada-709.html, accessed February 9, 2011.
6. William Bulkeley, "Got a Better Letter Opener? Staples Solicits Inventive Ideas from the Public for Products It Can Brand, Sell, Exclusively," *Wall Street Journal*, July 13, 2006, B1.

7. "Private Label Widely Seen as 'Good Alternative' to Other Brands, According to A.C. Neilson Global Survey," http://biz.yahoo.com, August 14, 2005.

8. Gina Chon, "Henry Ford's Model A Would Be at Home in the Car-Name Game," *Wall Street Journal*, April 12, 2006, B1.

9. Deborah L. Vence, "Product Enhancement," *Marketing News*, May 1, 2005, 19.

10. Ibid.

11. Erin White, "Burberry Wants the Knockoffs to Knock It Off," *Fort Worth Star Telegram*, May 28, 2003, 6F.

12. Deborah Ball, "The Perils of Packaging: Nestlé Aims for Easier Openings," *Wall Street Journal*, November 17, 2005, B1.

10

1. Patricia Sellers, "P&G: Teaching an Old Dog New Tricks," *Fortune*, May 31, 2004, 168–178.

2. "A Creative Corporation Toolbox," *Business Week*, August 2005, online.

3. Bruce Nussbaum, "Get Creative," *Business Week*, August 1, 2005, 64.

4. Renee Hopkins Callahan, Gwen Ishmael, and Leyla Namiranian, "The Case for In-the-Box Innovation," *Innovation Brochure* (Arlington, TX: Decision Analyst, 2005).

5. Matthew Boyle, "Reinventing Your Company," *Fortune*, September 6, 2004, 226.

6. "Changing the World," *Entrepreneur*, October 2003, 30.

7. Sellers, "P&G: Teaching an Old Dog New Tricks," 168.

8. David Welch, "The Second Coming of Cadillac," *Business Week*, November 24, 2003, 79–80.

9. Jeremy Cato, "Mercedes-Benz Takes Crown from BMW," *Globe and Mail*, January 11, 2011, http://www.theglobeandmail.com/globe-drive/new-cars/auto-news/mercedes-benz-takes-crown-from-bmw/article1876179/, accessed February 10, 2011.

10. Callahan et al., "The Case for In-the-Box Innovation."

11. Chris Penttila, "Keeping It Fresh," *Entrepreneur*, April 2005, 88.

12. Gary Fraser and Bryan Mattimor, "Slow Down, Speed Up New Product Growth," *Brandweek*, January 10, 2005, 18.

13. Bridget Finn, "Mining Blogs for Marketing Insight," *Business 2.0*, September 2005, 35.

14. Sellers, "P&G: Teaching an Old Dog New Tricks," 174.

15. David Kirkpatrick, "Innovation Do's and Don't's," *Fortune*, September 6, 2004, 240.

16. Sellers, "P&G: Teaching an Old Dog New Tricks," 174.

17. Pentilla, "Keeping It Fresh."

18. "2009 Global R&D Funding Forecast Update," http://www.rdmag.com/Featured-Articles/2009/06/2009-Global-R-D-Funding-Forecast-Update/, accessed February 10, 2011.

19. John Battelle, "The CTO in a GTO," *Business 2.0*, July 2004, 91.

20. Sarah Ellison and Charles Forelle, "Gillette's Smooth Bet: Men Will Pay More for Five-Blade Razor," *Wall Street Journal*, September 15, 2005, B1, B5.

21. Paul Lukas, "How Many Blades Is Enough," *Fortune*, October 31, 2005, 40.

22. Pete Engardio, "Scouring the Planet for Brainiacs," *Business Week*, October 11, 2004, 106.

23. Ibid.

24. Robert D. Hof, "The Power of Us," *Business Week*, June 20, 2005, 78–80.

25. Ibid., 77.

26. John Gaffney, "How Do You Feel about a $44 Tooth-Bleaching Kit," *Business 2.0*, October 2001, 125–127.

27. Ibid.

28. Sellers, "P&G: Teaching an Old Dog New Tricks," 168.

29. Kevin J. Clancy and Peter C. Krieg, "Product Life Cycle: A Dangerous Idea," *Brandweek*, March 1, 2004, 26.

30. "When Will It Fly," *The Economist*, August 9, 2003, 332.

31. James Bandler, "Ending Era, Kodak Will Stop Selling Most Film Cameras," *Wall Street Journal*, January 14, 2004, B1.

32. James Daly, "Restart, Redo, Recharge," *Business 2.0*, May 1, 2001, 11.

11

1. Statistics Canada, "Employment by Industry and Sex," http://www40.statcan.gc.ca/l01/cst01/labor10a-eng.htm, accessed on April 13, 2011.

2. The Canadian Services Coalition and The Canadian Chamber of Commerce, *Canadian Services Sector: A New Success Story*, June 2006, http://www.canadianservicescoalition.com/CanadianServicesSectorANewSuccessStory.pdf, accessed April 18, 2011.

3. Charles Riley, "IKEA Workers Get Wheels (Assembly Required)," http://money.cnn.com/2010/12/10/news/companies/ikea_bike_gift/index.htm, accessed April 19, 2011.

4. Valerie A. Zeithaml, Mary Jo Bitner, and Dwayne Gremler, *Services Marketing* (New York: McGraw-Hill, 2006).

5. Ibid.

6. Much of the material in this section is based on Christopher H. Lovelock and Jochen Wirtz, *Services Marketing*, 5th ed. (Upper Saddle River, NJ: Prentice Hall, 2004).

7. Lululemon Athletica, "Career Opportunities: Lululemon Possibilities," http://www.lululemon.com/about/careers, accessed April 19, 2011.

8. Hamilton Health Sciences, "Changes at Hamilton Health Sciences Enhance Care, Improve System Sustainability," press release, April 4, 2011, http://www.mcmasterchildrenshospital.ca/workfiles/PR/ABC%20-%20April%204,%20 2011%20News%20Release%20and%20 Backgrounder.doc, accessed April 19, 2011.

9. Lovelock and Wirtz, *Services Marketing*.

10. Ibid.

11. Much of the material in this section is based on Leonard L. Berry and A. Parasuraman, *Marketing Services*, (New York: Free Press, 1991), 132–150.

12. Richard Yerema and Kristina Leung, "Employer Review: TD Bank Financial Group," *Mediacorp Canada Inc.*, http://www.eluta.ca/top-employer-td-bank, accessed March 3, 2011.

13. Foreign Affairs and International Trade Canada, "Canada's State of Trade: Trade and Investment Update, 2011," http://www.inter-national.gc.ca/economist-economiste/perfor-mance/state-point/state_2011_point/2011_2.aspx?lang=eng&view=d, accessed August 28, 2011.

14. Imagine Canada, "Charities & Nonprofit Organizations," http://www.imaginecanada.ca/node/32, accessed April 19, 2010.

15. Ibid.

12

1. Nicole Harris, "'Private Exchanges' May Allow B-to-B Commerce to Thrive After All," *Wall Street Journal*, March 16, 2001, B1; Michael Totty, "The Next Phase," *Wall Street Journal*, May 21, 2001, R8.

2. "Pepsi, Starbucks Teaming Up," *Supermarket News*, October 31, 1994, 31; *Starbucks Annual Report, 2006*.

3. Jonathan Welsh, "Auto Makers Now 'Slam' Cars Right in the Factory," *Wall Street Journal*, October, 30, 2001, B1.

4. Owen Keates, "Flow Control," *Management*, March 2001, 28.

5. http://www.toyotaforklift.com; http://www.toyotaforklift.com/about_us/company_profile/toyo-taphilosophy.aspx; Elena Eptako Murphy, "Buying on Price Alone Can Lead to High Operating Costs," Purchasing.com, September 4, 2003.

6. Leigh Muzslay, "Shoes That Morph from Sneakers to Skates Are Flying Out of Stores," *Wall Street Journal*, July 26, 2001, B1; http://www.heelys.com, January 2006.

7. "Apple Stores in China Outsell Fifth Avenue as Nation Outgrows Gray Market," *Bloomberg News*, January 26, 2011.

8. J. Bandler, "Losing Focus: As Kodak Eyes Digital Future, a Big Partner Starts to Fade," *Wall Street Journal*, January 23, 2004, A1.

9. http://www.dell.com; Stacy Perman, "Automate or Die," *Business 2.0 Online*, July 2003.

10. Julie Schlosser, "Just Do It," *Fortune*, December 13, 2004, http://www.fortune.com.

11. Carlita Vitzthum, "Just-in-Time Fashion," *Wall Street Journal*, May 18, 2001, B1; Julie Creswell, "Confessions of a Fashion Victim," *Fortune*, December 10, 2001, 48; http://www.zara.com, February 2006.

12. Bill Canis, "The Motor Vehicle Supply Chain: Effects of the Japanese Earthquake and Tsunami," *Congressional Research Service*, May 23, 2011.

13. http://www.amazon.com, February 2006.

14. "Item-Level RFID Takes a Step Forward," http://www.newsfactor.com/news, January 2006; "Walgreen to Use Tagged Displays," http://www.rfidjournal.com, and http://www.ncr.com, February 2006.

15. "Leveraged Procurement," http://www.outsourcing-supply-chain-management.com/lever-aged.html, http://www.sysco.ca.

16. Mei Fong, "Ikea Hits Home in China," *Wall Street Journal*, March 3, 2006, B1.

17. Toby Herscovitch, "Wide Range: Cutting the Cost of Crossing Borders," *ExportWise*, Winter 2006, 8–9.

18. Kevin Hogan, "Borderline Savings," *Business 2.0*, May 17, 2001, 34.

13

1. Paul M. Jacobson, "The Structure of Retail in Canada," Retail 2004, Industry Canada, http://www.strategis.ic.gc.ca.

2. Statistics Canada, "Annual Retail Trade 2005," *The Daily*, March 27, 2007, http://www.statscan.ca; Statistics Canada, "Canadian Economic Accounts," *The Daily*, March 2, 2007, http://www.statscan.ca; Statistics Canada, "Retail Trade," February 2011, http://www.statscan.ca.

3. Walmart, "About Us," http://walmartstores.com/aboutus/, accessed August 29, 2011; "Walmart Canada to Take Over Target's 39 Zellers Locations," Canadian Press, June 27,

2011; www.canadian grocer.com, accessed August 29, 2011.

4. http://www.restaurant.org/trendmapper/, February 2006.

5. Canadian Restaurant and Foodservices Association, "Survey Shows B.C. Restaurants Hit Hard By HST," press release, August 3, 2010, http://www.crfa.ca/aboutcrfa/newsroom/2010/survey_shows_bc_restaurants_hit_hard_by_hst.asp, accessed September 1, 2011.

6. Statistics Canada, "Retail Non Store Industries—Vending," March 2011, http://www40.statcan.ca/l01/cst01/trad40a-eng.htm, accessed August 30, 2011.

7. Avon Products Inc., http://www.meetmark.com/PRSuite/home/home.jsp, accessed August 30, 2011.

8. Statistics Canada, "Retail Non Store Industries—Electronic & Mail Order, March 2011. www40.statcan.ca/l01/cst01/trad40a-eng.htm, accessed August 30, 2011.

9. Dell Web site, http://www.dell.com/us/en/gen/corporate, February 2006.

10. Statistics Canada, "E-Commerce: Shopping on the Internet 2005," *The Daily*, November 1, 2006.

11. McDonald's Corporation, Inside the U.S. Franchising Fact Sheet, http://www.mcdonalds/corp/franchise/faqs.html, January 2006.

12. http://www.bluefly.com.

13. http://www.thebestofchicago.com; http://www.Fridgedoor.com.

14. Viswanath Venkatesh, V. Ramesh, and Anne P. Massey, "m-Commerce: Breaking through the Adoption Barriers," *Research at Smith*, Fall 2003, 4:1; http://www.bearingpoint.com; http://www.bearingpoint.com/solutions/wireless_internet_solutions/mcommerce.html; "The Swipe and Sip Soda: Pepsi Taste-Tests New Wireless Credit Card System for Vending Machines," *m-pulse: A Cooltown Magazine*, November 23, 2003; http://www.cooltown.hp.com.

15. http://www.usatech.com

14

1. General Motors, "2011 Chevrolet Cruze Overview," http://www.gm.ca/gm/english/vehicles/chevrolet/cruze/overview?adv=98824&k_clickid=782f8889-a223-b848-0b2d-0000336d4683, accessed January 9, 2011.

2. Kellogg Company, "Health and Nutrition," http://www2.kelloggs.ca/General.aspx?ID=1657, accessed October 31, 2010; Kellogg Company, "Kellogg Company Joins National Initiative to Help Reduce Obesity," www.kelloggcompany.com/company.aspx?id=3008, accessed October 31, 2010.

3. Emily Wexler, "McDonald's Plans to Win," *Strategy*, September 2009, http://strategyonline.ca/2009/09/01/bizmcdonalds-20090901/, accessed August 10, 2011.

4. Ipsos Reid, "Canada's Love Affair with Online Social Networking Continues" July 14, 2011, http://www.ipsos-na.com/news-polls/pressrelease.aspx?id=5286, accessed September 29, 2011.

5. Kristin Laird, "Salty Tears Spilled Over New Knorr's Sidekicks," http://www.marketingmag.ca/creative/salty-tears-spilled-over-new-knorrs-sidekicks-10512, accessed May 12, 2010.

6. BMO Financial Group, "BMO Report: Majority of Canadian Businesses Using Social Media 'Digg' It," news release, September 27, 2010, http://www2.bmo.com/news/

article_pf/0,1085,contentCode-10418_divId-4_langId-1_navCode-112,00.html, accessed May 12, 2010.

7. Ibid.

8. Matt Rocheleau, "Senior Citizens Carve Their Own Niche with Laptops and Facebook," *Christian Science Monitor*, July 24, 2010, http://www.csmonitor.com/Innovation/Tech/2010/0724/Senior-citizens-carve-their-own-niche-with-laptops-and-Facebook, accessed May 15, 2010.

9. Michael Dewing, Social Media: 2. Who Uses Them? Publication No. 2010-05E, Social Affairs Division, Parliamentary Information and Research Service, Library of Parliament, http://www2.parl.gc.ca/Content/LOP/ResearchPublications/2010-05-e.htm, accessed May 12, 2010.

10. Gap Inc., "Gap Listens to Customers and Will Keep Classic Blue Box Logo," press release, October 11, 2010, http://www.gapinc.com/content/gapinc/html/media/pressrelease/2010/med_pr_GapLogoStatement10112010.html, accessed December 13, 2010.

11. The AIDA concept is based on the classic research of E. K. Strong, Jr., as theorized in *The Psychology of Selling and Advertising* (New York: McGraw-Hill, 1925) and "Theories of Selling," Journal of Applied Psychology, 9 (1925): 75–86.

12. Peter Svenson, "Apple Casts a Hefty Shadow over Top Electronics Show," *The Hamilton Spectator*, January 4, 2011, p. A9.

13. Thomas E. Barry and Daniel J. Howard, "A Review and Critique of the Hierarchy of Effects in Advertising," *International Journal of Advertising*, 9 (1990): 121–135.

14. Chris Powell, "GM Back Cruze with Major Media Investment," *Marketing*, October 29, 2010, http://www.marketingmag.ca/news/marketer-news/gm-canada-backs-cruze-with-major-media-investment-5690, accessed October 31, 2010.

15

1. Television Bureau of Canada, "Canadian Net Advertising Revenue by Medium, 200–2009," http://www.tvb.ca/pages/nav2_htm, accessed September 1, 2010.

2. CTV News, "Tories Blasted over $130 M Advertising Budget," September 21, 2010; http://www.ctv.ca/CTVNews/Canada/20100921/government-advertising-100921/, accessed September 21, 2010.

3. Michael R. Solomon, *Consumer Behavior*, 6th ed. (Upper Saddle River, NJ: Prentice Hall, 2004), 275.

4. Tom Duncan, *Integrated Marketing Communications* (Burr Ridge, IL: McGraw-Hill, 2002), 257.

5. Laura Q. Hughes and Wendy Davis, "Revival of the Fittest," *Advertising Age*, March 12, 2001, 18–19; http://www.hersheys.com/chocolateworld/, accessed January 2006.

6. Geoffrey Fowler, "For P&G in China, It's Wash, Rinse, Don't Repeat," *Wall Street Journal*, June 9, 2006, A11.

7. Radio Marketing Bureau, "Why Radio?" http://www.rmb.ca/why_radio.aspx?id=8208, accessed August 28, 2011.

8. Chris Isidore, "GM on a Roll: 1st Super Bowl Ads in Three Years," *CNN Money*, January 11, 2011; http://money.cnn.com/2011/01/11/news/companies/gm_super_bowl_ad/index.htm?section=money_news_companies, accessed January 15, 2011.

9. Doritos, "Crash the Super Bowl Contest," http://www.crashthesuperbowl.com/#/contest-inf, accessed January 15, 2011.

10. Brian Steinberg and Ethan Smith, "Rocking Madison Ave.: Advertisers Are Hunting for Fresh Pop Hits That Haven't Been Heard in Commercials Before," *Wall Street Journal*, June 9, 2006, A11.

11. Katie Bailey, "PVR Users Still Watch Ads: TVB," *Media in Canada*, August 12, 2010; http://www.mediaincanada.com/articles/mic/20100812/tvb_pvr.html, accessed January 12, 2011.

12. Canadian Media Directors' Council, *Media Digest* 09/10, 71.

13. eMarketer, January 29, 2007, http://www.eMarketer.com.

14. Canadian Media Directors' Council, *Media Digest* 09/10, 71.

15. Christopher Lawton, "Videogame Ads Attempt Next Level," *Wall Street Journal*, July 25, 2005, B6; "Video Game Advertising Gets a Boost," *USA Today*, December 16, 2004, B1; Derek Sooman, "World's First Video Game Advertising Network," October 20, 2004, http://www.techspot.com; http://www.massiveincorporated.com, accessed January 2006.

16. eMarketer Digital Intelligence, "Canadian Mobile Subscriptions to Climb 20% by 2014," http://www.emarketer.tv/Article.aspx?R=1007747, accessed [January 15, 2011.

17. "Telemarketer Faces Record Fine for Violating Do Not Call List," The *Globe and Mail*, December 10, 2010, http://www.theglobeandmail.com/news/national/telemarketer-faces-record-fine-for-violating-do-not-call-list/article1842450/, accessed January 19, 2011.

18. Craig MacBride, "Warner Has A-maze-ing Plans for Inception Launch," Media in Canada, December 6, 2010; http://www.mediaincanada.com/articles/mic/20101206/inception.html, accessed January 15, 2011.

19. http://www.hbc.com/hbc/hbc_csr_eng/comm_principal1.html; "Consumer Behavior Study Confirms Cause-Related Marketing Can Exponentially Increase Sales," http://www.ca.finance.yahoo.com, accessed October 2008, based on Sarah Kerkian's "Past, Present, Future: The 25th Anniversary of Cause Branding."

20. http://www.playstation.com, accessed January 2006.

21. "Embattled BP Chief: I Want My Life Back," Times Online, May 31, 2010, http://business.timesonline.co.uk/tol/business/industry_sectors/natural_resources/article7141137.ece, accessed August 11, 2011.

16

1. Brian Solis, *Engage: The Complete Guide for Brands and Businesses to Build, Cultivate and Measure Success in the New Web* (Hoboken, NJ: John Wiley & Sons, 2010), 37.

2. "Social Media for Non Profits," *Primalmedia*, February 18, 2009, www.primalmedia.com/blog/social-media-non-profits.

3. David Scholz and Laurie Smith, "Social Media Reality Check, 2011 Research Findings," http://www.legermarketing.com/documents/SPCLM/11681ENG.pdf, accessed September 1, 2011.

4. "Bieber's Baby Most Viewed Video at YouTube," March 28, 2011, http://www.physorg.com/news/2011-03-bieber-baby-viewed-video-youtube.html, accessed August 31, 2011.

5. Salma Jafri, "Lady Gaga's Social Media Success and Strategy," Suite101.com, June 5, 2010, http://marketingpr.suite101.com/article.cfm/lady-gagas-social-media-success-and-strategy; Dorothy Pomerantz, "Lady Gaga Leads List of Celeb 100 Newcomers," *Forbes*, June 28, 2010, www.forbes.com/2010/06/22/lady-gaga-kristin-stewart-business-entertainment-celeb-100-10-newcomers.html.

6. Andrew Hampp, "Gaga, Oooh La La: Why the Lady Is the Ultimate Social Climber," *Advertising Age*, February 22, 2010, http://adage.com/digitalalist10/article?article_id=142210.

7. Scholz and Smith, "Social Media Reality Check."

8. Solis, *Engage*.

9. "The World Was A-Twitter," August 31, 2011, http://www.thespec.com/print/article/586844, accessed August 31, 2011.

10. Solis, *Engage*.

11. Scholz and Smith, "Social Media Reality Check."

12. "The 2010 Canada Digital Year in Review," comScore, Inc., http://www.comscore.com/Press_Events/Presentations_Whitepapers/2011/2010_Canada_Digital_Year_in_Review, accessed August 31, 2011.

13. *Media Digest* 10/11, (Toronto: Canadian Media Directors' Council), 2010, p. 60.

14. Shane Snow, "iPad by the Numbers," *Mashable*, July 2010, http://mashable.com/2010/06/07/ipad-infographic-2.

15. Paul Marsden, "Simple Definition of Social Commerce," *Social Commerce Today*, June 2010, http://socialcommercetoday.com/social-commerce-definition-word-cloud-definitive-definition-list.

16. "The 2010 Canada Digital Year in Review."

17. Shar VanBoskirk, "U.S. Interactive Marketing Forecast 2009 to 2014," *Forrester Research*, July 6, 2009, www.forrester.com/rb/Research/us_interactive_marketing_forecast,_2009_to_2014/q/id/47730/t/2.

18. "2010 Canadian Online Advertising Revenue Grows to $2.23 Billion, Surpassing Daily Newspapers," http://www.iabcanada.com/blog/2010-internet-revenue-survey, accessed September 1, 2011.

19. *Marketing News Staff*, "Digital Dozen: Step Up to The Bar," *Marketing News*, March 15, 2010, www.marketingpower.com/ResourceLibrary/Publications/MarketingNews/2010/3_15_10/Digital Dozen.pdf.

20. Ibid.

21. Jeff Howe, *Crowdsourcing: Why the Power of the Crowd Is Driving the Future of Business* (New York, NY: Three Rivers Press, 2009), 32.

22. Amy-Mae Elliott, "Power to the People: 3 Tasty Crowdsourcing Case Studies," http://mashable.com/2011/02/20/crowdsourcing-case-studies/, accessed September 1, 2011.

23. Sean Corcoran, "Defining Earned, Owned and Paid Media," Forrester Blogs, December 16, 2009, http://blogs.forrester.com/interactive_marketing/2009/12/defining-earned-owned-and-paid-media.html; Brian Solis, "Why Brands Are Becoming Media," *Mashable*, February 11, 2010.

24. Ibid.

25. Jonathon Hensley, "How to Build Trust Online," *Marketing News*, March 15, 2010.

26. Jim Sterne, *Social Media Metrics* (Hoboken, NJ: John Wiley & Sons, 2010).

27. Erik Bratt, "Social Media ROI Success Stories," *MarketingProfs*, 2009, www.

marketingprofs.com/store/product/27/social-media-roi-success-stories.

28. Scholz and Smith, "Social Media Reality Check."

29. David Berkowitz, "100 Ways to Measure Social Media," *Inside the Marketers Studio*, November 17, 2009, www.marketersstudio.com/2009/11/100-ways-to-measure-social-media-.html.

30. Charlene Li and Josh Bernoff, *"Groundswell": Winning in a World Transformed by Social Technologies*, (Boston, MA: Harvard Business Press, 2009).

31. *North American Technographics Interactive Marketing Online Survey*, Forrester Research, June 2009, www.forrester.com/ER/Research/Survey/Excerpt/1,10198,726,00.html.

32. Juan Carlos Perez, "Forrester Notes Social Media Contributor Slowdown," *Computerworld*, September 28, 2010, www.computerworld.com/s/article/9188538/Forrester_notes_social_media_contributor_slowdown.

33. Dan Zarella, *The Social Media Marketing Book* (Beijing, China: O'Reilly, 2010).

34. Marcus Hondro, "Twits: Justin Bieber Hits 12 Million Twitter Followers," August 20, 2011, http://www.suite101.com/news/twits-justin-bieber-hits-12-million-twitter-followers-a385277, accessed September 6, 2011.

35. Dan Kislenko, "And Cupcakes for All," *Hamilton Spectator*, May 19, 2011, http://www.thespec.com/living/food/article/533995--and-cupcakes-for-all, accessed September 1, 2011.

36. Marketing Profs, "Adobe Systems," *Facebook Success Stories*, 2009, www.marketingprofs.com/store/product/35/facebook-success-stories.

37. Marketing Profs, *LinkedIn Success Stories*, 2009, www.marketingprofs.com/store/product/37/linkedin-success-stories.

38. Ramya Raghavan, "Using Video to Connect with Your Donors and Prospects," International Fundraising eConference, May 12–14, 2009.

39. BMO Financial Group, "Podcasts, Business Coach," http://www.bmo.com/podcast/en/?businessCoach, accessed August 31, 2011.

40. Zarella, *The Social Media Marketing Book*.

41. Solis, *Engage*, 54.

42. Solis, *Engage*, 97.

43. Zarella, *The Social Media Marketing Book*.

44. Solis, *Engage*, 51.

45. "Social Gaming Integral to Social Networking," *Marketing Profs*, February 19, 2010, www.marketingprofs.com/charts/2010/3425/social-gaming-integral-to-social-networking.

46. The Economist, "Three Is the Magic Number," http://www.economist.com/blogs/newsbook/2011/02/canadas_mobile_phone_market, accessed September 1, 2011.

47. IAB Canada, "Canadian Mobile Advertising Revenue for 2009 Grows to $31.9 Million, 169% over 2008 Totals," http://www.iabcanada.com/blog/canadian-mobile-advertising-revenue-for-2009-grows-to-31-9-million-169-over-2008-totals, accessed September 5, 2011.

48. Marketing Profs, *Mobile Marketing Success Stories*, 2009, www.marketingprofs.com/store/product/36/mobile-marketing-success-stories.

49. "Real Racing GTI," Volkswagen, www.vw.com/realracinggti/en/us (accessed October 14, 2010).

50. *Marketing News* Staff, "Digital Dozen: Benjamin Moore Paints App Success," *Marketing News*, March 15, 2010, www.marketingpower.com/ResourceLibrary/Publications/MarketingNews/2010/3_15_10/Digital Dozen.pdf.

51. Beth Kanter, "Screencast: Using Widgets to Build Community on Blogs Featured on NTEN Blog,"

Beth's Blog, March 20, 2007, http://beth.typepad.com/beths_blog/2007/03/screncast_using.html.

52. Canadian Red Cross, "Stories from the Field, Messages of Health and Hope," May 3, 2010, http://www.redcross.ca/haiti2010/hope/sms.asp, accessed September 1, 2011.

53. Michael Bush, "Red Cross Delivers Real Mobile Results for a Real Emergency" *Advertising Age*, February 22, 2010, http://adage.com/digitalalist10/article?article_id=142204; Nicole Wallace and Ian Wilhelm, "Charities Text Messaging Success Shakes Up the Fundraising World," *Chronicle of Philanthropy*, February 11, 2010, 7.

17

1. Siri Agrell, "The Return of the Coupon," The *Globe and Mail*, August 26, 2008.

2. Trendwatching.com, "11 Crucial Consumer Trends for 2011," http://trendwatching.com/trends/11trends2011/#pricing, accessed January 16, 2011.

3. "Untapped Potential for Mobile Loyalty Programs, *eMarketer*, January 4, 2011, www.emarketer.com/Articles/Print.aspx?1008147, accessed January 19, 2011.

4. "Marketing to Shoppers at Every Touch Point," *eMarketer*, January 13, 2011, http://www.emarketer.com/Articles/Print.aspx?1008171, accessed January 19, 2011.

5. Bruce Mohl, "Retailers Simplify the Rebate Process," *Boston Globe*, November 7, 2004.

6. Chris Atchison, "What Small Business Can Learn from Shoppers' Optimum Program," The *Globe and Mail*, October 10, 2010, http://m.theglobeandmail.com/report-on-business/your-business/grow/customer-experience/what-small-businesses-can-learn-from-shoppers-optimum-program/article1750498/comments/?service=mobile, accessed January 16, 2011.

7. "Loyalty Programs," *CRMTrends*, http://www.crmtrends.com/loyalty.html, accessed January 19, 2011.

8. Matthew Haeberle, "Loyalty Is Dead: Great Experiences, Not Price, Will Create Loyal Customers," *Chain Store Age*, January 2004, 17.

9. "Grocers' Use of E-Mail Growing," *Promo P&I*, August 2005, http://www.promomagazine.com, accessed January 2006.

10. Lafayette Jones, "Ethnic Product Sampling: The Hidden Opportunity," *Retail Merchandiser*, August 2001, 45; Tim Parry, "Sampling—Teaching Tools," *PROMO Magazine*, http://www.promomagazine.com, accessed January 2006.

11. "Point-of-Purchase: $17 Billion," *PROMO Magazine*, October 29, 2001, 3; "In Praise of Promotion," *PROMO Xtra*, http://promomagazine.com, accessed January 2006.

12. Melita Kuburas, "Metro's Recipe TV Hits the Sweet Spot," *Strategy Online*, June 1, 2010; http://www.strategyonline.ca/articles/magazine/20100601/upfrontmetro.html, accessed January 16, 2011.

13. Michael Beverland, "Contextual Influences and the Adoption and Practice of Relationship Selling in a Business-to-Business Setting: An Exploratory Study," *Journal of Personal Selling & Sales Management*, Summer 2001, 207.

14. http://www.presentations.com.

18

1. Roland Rust, Christine Moorman, and Peter R. Dickson, "Getting Return on Quality: Revenue

Expansion, Cost Reduction, or Both?" *Journal of Marketing*, October 2002, 7–24.

2. http://www.ticketsinventory.com/concert/justin-bieber-tickets/1716707.php, accessed September 1, 2011

3. Tammo H. A. Bijmolt, Harald J. van Heerde, and Rik G. M. Pieters, "New Empirical Generalizations on the Determinants of Price Elasticity," *Journal of Marketing Research*, May 2005, 141–156; Christian Homburg, Wayne Hoyer, and Nicole Koschate, "Customers' Reactions to Price Increases: Do Customer Satisfaction and Perceived Motive Fairness Matter?" *Journal of the Academy of Marketing Science*, Winter 2005, 36–49; and Gadi Fibich, Arieh Gavious, and Oded Lowengart, "The Dynamics of Price Elasticity of Demand in the Presence of Reference Price Effects," *Journal of the Academy of Marketing Science*, Winter 2005, 66–78.

4. "The Price Is Really Right," *Business Week*, March 31, 2003, 62–66.

5. "Telling the Risky from the Reliable," *Business Week*, August 1, 2005, 57–58.

6. See Joseph Cannon and Christian Homburg, "Buyer-Supplier Relationships and Customer Firm Costs," *Journal of Marketing*, January 2001, 29–43.

7. Ashutosh Dixit, Karin Braunsberger, George Zinhan, and Yue Pan, "Information Technology-Enhanced Pricing Strategies: Managerial and Public Policy Implications," *Journal of Business Research*, September 2005, 1169–1177.

8. "One Nation under Wal-Mart," *Fortune*, March 3, 2003, 65–78.

9. R. Chandrashekaran, "The Implications of Individual Differences in Reference to Price Utilization for Designing Effective Price Communications," *Journal of Business Research*, August 2001, 85–92.

10. Katherine Lemon and Stephen Nowlis, "Developing Synergies between Promotions and Brands in Different Price-Quality Tiers," *Journal of Marketing Research*, May 2002, 171–185. See also Valerie Taylor and William Bearden, "The Effects of Price on Brand Extension Evaluations: The Moderating Role of Extension Similarity," *Journal of the Academy of Marketing Science*, Spring 2002, 131–140; and Raj Sethuraman and V. Srinivasan, "The Asymmetric Share Effect: An Empirical Generalization on Cross-Price Effects," *Journal of Marketing Research*, August 2002, 379–386.

11. Merrie Brucks, Valarie Zeithaml, and Gillian Naylor, "Price and Brand Name as Indictors of Quality Dimensions for Consumer Durables," *Journal of the Academy of Marketing Science*, Summer 2000, 359–374; Wilfred Amaldoss and Sanjay Jain, "Pricing of Conspicuous Goods: A Competitive Analysis of Social Effects," *Journal of Marketing Research*, February 2005, 30–42.

19

1. Kent Monroe and Jennifer Cox, "Pricing Practices That Endanger Profits," *Marketing Management*, September/October 2001, 42–46.

2. Thomas T. Nagle and George Cressman, "Don't Just Set Prices, Manage Them," *Marketing Management*, November/December 2002, 29–33; Jay Klompmaker, William H. Rogers and Anthony Nygren, "Value, Not Volume," *Marketing Management*, June 2003, 45–48; and Alison Wellner, "Boost Your Bottom Line by Taking the Guesswork Out of Pricing," *Inc.*, June 2005, 72–82.

3. "Out-Discounting the Discounter," *Business Week*, May 10, 2004, 78–79; an interesting article on shoppers who use penetration pricing to their advantage is: Edward J. Fox and Stephen J. Hoch, "Cherry-Picking," *Journal of Marketing*, January 2005, 46–62.

4. Patrick Brethour and Janet McFarland, "Forzani Agrees to Pay Record Fine," The *Globe and Mail*, July 7, 2004, B1, B22.

5. Canadian Press, "Gas Stations Busted for Price Fixing in Quebec," *Kelowna Daily Courier*, June 13, 2008, A1, A5; "Quebec Gas Companies Charged with Price Fixing," June 12, 2008, http://www.ctv.ca, accessed September 2008.

6. Nicolas Van Praet, "Profitable WestJet Accuses Air Canada of Using Court-Protection to Reduce Air Fares Below Cost," *CanWest News*, October 20, 2003, 1; "Small B.C. Airline Accuses Insolvent Air Canada of Predatory Pricing," *Canadian Press News Wire*, April 16, 2003.

7. Phillip Dampier, "BC Supreme Court Tosses Out Novus Entertainment's Lawsuit against Shaw Cable," *Stop the Cap!*, August 18, 2010, http://stopthecap.com/2010/08/18/bc-supreme-court-tosses-out-novus-entertainments-lawsuit-against-shaw-cable/, accessed September 1, 2011.

8. Bruce Alford and Abhijit Biswas, "The Effects of Discount Level, Price Consciousness, and Sale Proneness on Consumers' Price Perception and Behavioral Intention," *Journal of Business Research*, September 2002, 775–783. See also V. Kumar, Vibhas Madan, and Srini Srinivasan, "Price Discounts or Coupon Promotions: Does It Matter?" *Journal of Business Research*, September 2004, 933–941.

9. "Price War in Aisle 3," *Wall Street Journal*, May 27, 2003, B1, B16. See also: Kathleen Seiders and Glenn Voss, "From Price to Purchase," *Marketing Management*, December 2004, 38–43; "Grocery Stores Cut Out the Weekly Specials," *Wall Street Journal*, July 20, 2005, D1, D3; and Gerald E. Smith and Thomas Nagle, "A Question of Value," *Marketing Management*, July/August 2005, 39–44.

10. Joel Urbany, "Are Your Prices Too Low?" *Harvard Business Review*, October 2001, 26–27.

11. http://www.rethink.ca.

12. To learn more about pricing fairness, see Lan Xia, Kent Monroe, and Jennifer Cox, "The Price Is Unfair! A Conceptual Framework of Price Fairness Perceptions," *Journal of Marketing*, October 2004, 1–15.

13. David Bell, Ganesh Iyer, and V. Padmanabhar, "Price Competition under Stockpiling and Flexible Consumption," *Journal of Marketing Research*, August 2002, 292–303.

14. Dilip Soman and John Gourville, "Transaction Decoupling: The Effects of Price Bundling on the Decision to Consume," MSI Report No. 98–131, 2002; Stefan Stremersch and Gerard J. Tellis, "Strategic Bundling of Products and Prices: A New Synthesis for Marketing," *Journal of Marketing*, January 2002, 55–71; and "Forget Prices and Get People to Use the Stuff," *Wall Street Journal*, June 3, 2004, A2.

15. Dilip Soman and John Gourville, "Transaction Decoupling: How Price Bundling Affects the Decision to Consume," *Journal of Marketing Research*, February 2001, 30–44.

16. Canada Post surcharge rates found at http://www.canadapost.ca/business/corporate/about/announcements/fuel_surcharge/default-e.asp, accessed September 2008.

17. Canada Post, "Fuel Surcharge," http://www.canadapost.ca/cpo/mc/aboutus/news/fuel/default.jsf, accessed August 30, 2011.

20

1. Foreign Affairs and International Trade Canada, "Canada's State of Trade: Trade and Investment Update 2010," http://www.international.gc.ca/economist-economiste/performance/state-point/state_2010_point/2010_5.aspx?lang=eng, accessed January 31, 2011.

2. "Borders Are So 20th Century," *Business Week*, September 22, 2003, 68.

3. Central Intelligence Agency, "The World Fact Book," https://www.cia.gov/library/publications/the-world-factbook/geos/xx.html, accessed August 30, 2011.

4. Office of the United States Trade Representative, "North American Free Trade Agreement (NAFTA)," http://www.ustr.gov/trade-agreements/free-trade-agreements/north-american-free-trade-agreement-nafta, accessed August 30, 2011.

5. Foreign Affairs and International Trade Canada, "Negotiations and Agreements," http://www.international.gc.ca/trade-agreements-accords-commerciaux/agr-acc/index.aspx, accessed February 1, 2011.

6. Justin Lahart, "Corn Flakes Clash Shows the Glitches in European Union," *Wall Street Journal*, November 1, 2005, A1, A9.

7. "Intel Raided in EU Antitrust Investigation," The *Globe and Mail*, July 13, 2005, B8.

8. Justin Lahart, "For Small Businesses, Big World Beckons," *Wall Street Journal*, January 26, 2001, http://online.wsj.com/article/SB10001424052748703951704576092010276714424.html?KEYWORDS=licensing+global+market, accessed February 1, 2011.

9. "A Sneaker Maker Says China Partner Became Its Rival," *Wall Street Journal*, December 14, 2002, A1, A8.

10. Zeynep Emden, Attila Yaprak, and S. Tamer Causugil, "Learning From Experience in International Alliances: Antecedents and Firm Performance Implications," *Journal of Business Research*, July 2005, 883–901; Jane Lu and Louis Hébert, "Equity Control and the Survival of International Joint Ventures: A Contingency Approach," *Journal of Business Research*, June 2005, 736–745.

11. "100 Best Global Brands," *Business Week*, September 29, 2009, 50.

12. "Capturing a Piece of the Global Market," *Brand Week*, June 20, 2005, 20.

13. "Lattes Lure Brits to Coffee," *Wall Street Journal*, October 20, 2005, B1, B6.

14. "Small Is Profitable," *Business Week*, August 26, 2002, 112–114.

15. "If Only 'Krispy Kreme' Meant Makes You Smarter," *Business 2.0*, August 2005, 108.

16. "India's Bumpy Ride," *Fortune*, October 31, 2005, 149–153.

17. Matthew Myers, "Implications of Pricing Strategy—Venture Strategy Experience: An Application Using Optimal Models in an International Context," *Journal of Business Research*, June 2004, 591–600.

Index

customer satisfaction customers' evaluation of a good or service in terms of whether it has met their needs and expectations

customer value the relationship between benefits and the sacrifice necessary to obtain those benefits

empowerment delegation of authority to solve customers' problems quickly—usually by the first person that the customer notifies regarding a problem

exchange people giving up one thing to receive another thing they would rather have

marketing the activity, set of institutions, and processes for creating, communicating, delivering, and exchanging offerings that have value for customers, clients, partners, and society at large

marketing concept the idea that the social and economic justification for an organization's existence is the satisfaction of customers' wants and needs while meeting organizational objectives

market orientation a philosophy that involves obtaining information about customers, competitors, and markets; examining the information from a total business perspective; determining how to deliver superior customer value; and implementing actions to provide value to customers

production orientation a philosophy that focuses on the internal capabilities of the firm rather than on the desires and needs of the marketplace

relationship marketing a strategy that focuses on keeping and improving relationships with current customers

sales orientation the idea that people will buy more goods and services if aggressive sales techniques are used and that high sales result in high profits

societal marketing orientation the idea that an organization exists not only to satisfy customers' wants and needs and to meet organizational objectives but also to preserve or enhance individuals' and society's long-term best interests

teamwork collaborative efforts of people to accomplish common objectives

LO 1 Define the term *marketing*. Marketing is the activity, set of institutions, and processes for creating, communicating, delivering, and exchanging offerings that have value for customers, clients, partners, and society at large.

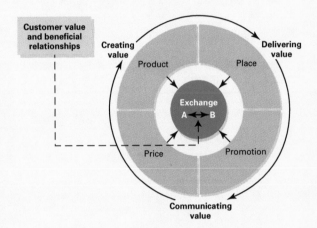

LO 2 Describe four marketing management philosophies. The role of marketing and the character of marketing activities within an organization are strongly influenced by the organization's philosophy and orientation. A production-oriented organization focuses on the internal capabilities of the firm rather than on the desires and needs of the marketplace. A sales orientation is based on the beliefs that people will buy more products if aggressive sales techniques are used and that high sales volumes produce high profits. A market-oriented organization focuses on satisfying customer wants and needs while meeting organizational objectives. A societal marketing orientation goes beyond a market orientation to include the preservation or enhancement of individuals' and society's long-term best interests.

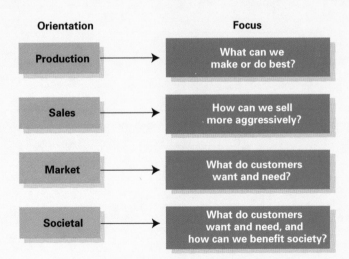

LO 3 Understand the differences between sales and market orientations. First, sales-oriented firms focus on perfecting sales techniques; market-oriented firms focus on customers' needs and preferences. Second, sales-oriented companies consider themselves to be deliverers of goods and services, whereas market-oriented companies view themselves as satisfiers of customers. Third, sales-oriented firms direct their products to everyone; market-oriented firms aim at specific segments of the population. Fourth, although the primary goal of both types of firms is profit, sales-oriented businesses pursue maximum sales

volume through aggressive selling, whereas market-oriented businesses pursue customer satisfaction through coordinated activities.

	What is the organization's focus?	What business are you in?	To whom is the product directed?	What is your primary goal?	How do you seek to achieve your goal?
Sales Orientation	Inward, on the organization's needs	Selling goods and services	Everybody	Profit through maximum sales volume	Primarily through intensive sales activities
Market Orientation	Outward, on the wants and preferences of customers	Satisfying customer wants and needs and delivering superior value	Specific groups of people	Profit through customer satisfaction	Through coordinated marketing and interfunctional activities

LO 4

Describe several reasons for studying marketing. First, marketing affects the allocation of goods and services that influence a nation's economy and standard of living. Second, an understanding of marketing is crucial to understanding most businesses. Third, career opportunities in marketing are diverse, profitable, and expected to increase significantly during the coming decade. Fourth, understanding marketing makes consumers more informed.

Marketing affects you every day!

applied research an attempt to develop new improved products

baby boomers people born between 1947 and 1965

basic research pure research that aims to confirm an existing theory or to learn more about a concept or phenomenon

code of ethics a guideline to help marketing managers and other employees make better decisions

Competition Bureau the federal department charged with administering most marketplace laws

component lifestyles choosing goods and services that meet one's diverse needs and interests rather than conforming to a single, traditional lifestyle

corporate social responsibility a business's concern for society's welfare

demography the study of people's vital statistics, such as their age, race and ethnicity, and location

environmental management when a company implements strategies that attempt to shape the external environment within which it operates

ethics the moral principles or values that generally govern the conduct of an individual or a group

Generation X people born between 1966 and 1978

Generation Y people born between 1979 and 1994

green marketing the development and marketing of products designed to minimize negative effects on the physical environment

inflation a measure of the decrease in the value of money, expressed as the percentage reduction value since the previous year

morals the rules people develop as a result of cultural values and norms

multiculturalism when all major ethnic groups in an area—such as a city, county, or census tract—are roughly equally represented

purchasing power a comparison of income versus the relative cost of a set standard of goods and services in different geographic areas

pyramid of corporate social responsibility a model that suggests corporate social responsibility is composed of economic, legal, ethical, and philanthropic responsibilities and that the firm's economic performance supports the entire structure

recession a period of economic activity characterized by negative growth, which reduces demand for goods and services

self-regulation programs voluntarily adopted by business groups to regulate the activities of their members

LO 1 Discuss the external environment of marketing, and explain how it affects a firm.

The external marketing environment consists of social, demographic, economic, technological, political and legal, and competitive variables. Marketers generally cannot control the elements of the external environment. Instead, they must understand how the external environment is changing and the impact of that change on the target market. Marketing managers can then create a marketing mix to effectively meet the needs of target customers.

LO 2 Describe the social factors that affect marketing.

Within the external environment, social factors are perhaps the most difficult for marketers to anticipate. Several major social trends are currently shaping marketing strategies. First, people of all ages have a broader range of interests, defying traditional consumer profiles. Second, changing gender roles are bringing more women into the workforce and increasing the number of men who shop. Third, having a greater number of dual-career families creates demand for time-saving goods and services.

LO 3 Explain the importance to marketing managers of current demographic trends.

Age	Gen Y	Gen X	Baby Boom	Seniors
	1979–1994	1966–1978	1947–1965	Before 1946
	6.4 million	70 million	9.0 million	6.0 million

Today, several basic demographic patterns are influencing marketing mixes. Because the Canadian population is growing at a slower rate, marketers can no longer rely on profits from generally expanding markets. Marketers are also faced with increasingly experienced consumers among the younger generations, such as tweens and Gen-Yers. And because the population is also growing older, marketers are offering more products that appeal to middle-aged and elderly consumers.

LO 4 Explain the importance to marketing managers of multiculturalism and growing ethnic markets.

Multiculturalism occurs when all major ethnic groups in an area are roughly equally

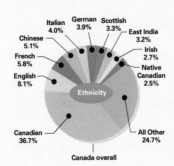

Italian 4.0%
German 3.9%
Scottish 3.3%
East India 3.2%
Chinese 5.1%
Irish 2.7%
French 5.8%
Native Canadian 2.5%
English 8.1%
Ethnicity
Canadian 36.7%
All Other 24.7%

Canada overall

SOURCE: Based on reported ethnic origin of households. Statistics Canada, *Population by Selected Ethnic Origins*, July 2, 2007.

Visible Minority Population in Selected Major Canadian Cities

	2001	2006	2017
Vancouver	36.9%	42.2%	51.0%
Toronto	36.8	41.9	50.5
Calgary	17.5	19.5	23.6
Ottawa	17.0	20.8	27.4
Edmonton	14.6	15.3	17.5
Montreal	13.6	15.4	19.4
Windsor	12.9	15.8	21.4
Winnipeg	12.5	13.3	15.7
Kitchener	10.7	12.0	15.1
Hamilton	9.8	11.1	14.5

SOURCE: Adapted from the Statistics Canada publication "Population Projections of Visible Minority Groups, Canada, Provinces and Regions," 2001 to 2017, Catalogue 91-541, released March 22, 2005, URL: http://www.statcan.ca/english/freepub/91-541-XIE/91-541-XIE2005001.pdf.

sustainability the idea that socially responsible companies will outperform their peers by focusing on the world's social problems and viewing them as opportunities to build profits and help the world at the same time

target market a defined group most likely to buy a firm's product

represented. Growing multiculturalism makes the marketer's task more challenging. Many companies are now creating departments and product lines to effectively target multicultural market segments. Companies have quickly found that ethnic markets are not homogeneous.

LO 5 Identify consumer and marketer reactions to the state of the economy.

In recent years, many households have gone into debt as the rise in consumer spending has outpaced the

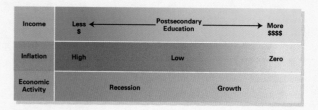

	Less $		Postsecondary Education		More $$$$
Income					
Inflation	High		Low		Zero
Economic Activity		Recession		Growth	

growth in income. At the same time, the financial power of women has increased, and they are making the purchasing decisions for many products in traditionally male-dominated areas. During a time of inflation, marketers generally attempt to maintain level pricing to avoid losing customer brand loyalty. During times of recession, many marketers maintain or reduce prices to counter the effects of decreased demand; they also concentrate on increasing production efficiency and improving customer service.

LO 6 Identify the impact of technology on a firm.
Monitoring new technology is essential to keeping up with competitors in today's marketing environment. Canada excels in basic research and, in recent years, has dramatically improved its track record in applied research. Innovation is increasingly becoming a global process. Without innovation, Canadian companies can't compete in global markets.

LO 7 Discuss the political and legal environment of marketing.
All marketing activities are subject to provincial and federal laws and the rulings of regulatory agencies. Marketers are responsible for remaining aware of and abiding by such regulations. Many laws, including privacy laws, have been passed to protect the consumer.

LO 8 Explain the basics of foreign and domestic competition.
The competitive environment encompasses the number of competitors a firm must face, the relative size of the competitors, and the degree of interdependence within the industry. Declining population growth, rising costs, and shortages of resources have heightened domestic competition.

LO 9 Discuss corporate social responsibility.
Responsibility in business refers to a firm's concern for the way its decisions affect society. Social responsibility has four components: economic, legal, ethical, and philanthropic. These components are intertwined, yet the most fundamental responsibility is earning a profit. If a firm does not earn a profit, the other three responsibilities are moot. Most business people believe they should do more than pursue profits. Although a company must consider its economic needs first, it must also operate within the law, do what is ethical and fair, and be a good corporate citizen. The concept of sustainability is that socially responsible companies will outperform their peers by focusing on the world's social problems and viewing them as an opportunity to earn profits and help the world at the same time.

Philanthropic responsibilities
Be a good corporate citizen.
Contribute resources to the community; improve the quality of life.

Ethical responsibilities
Be ethical.
Do what is right, just, and fair. Avoid harm.

Legal responsibilities
Obey the law.
Law is society's codification of right and wrong. Play by the rules of the game.

Economic responsibilities
Be profitable.
Profit is the foundation on which all other responsibilities rest.

LO 10 Describe the role of ethics and ethical decisions in business.
Business ethics may be viewed as a subset of the values of society as a whole. The ethical conduct of business people is shaped by societal elements, including family, education, religion, and social movements. As members of society, business people are morally obligated to consider the ethical implications of their decisions.

Ethical decision making is approached in three basic ways. The first approach examines the consequences of decisions. The second approach relies on rules and laws to guide decision making. The third approach is based on a theory of moral development that places individuals or groups in one of three developmental stages: preconventional morality, conventional morality, or postconventional morality.

Many companies develop a code of ethics to help their employees make ethical decisions. A code of ethics can help employees identify acceptable business practices, be an effective internal control on behaviour, help employees avoid confusion when determining whether decisions are ethical, and facilitate discussion about what is right and wrong.

4 Decision Support Systems and Market Research

BehaviorScan a scanner-based research program that tracks the purchases of 3,000 households through store scanners in each research market

central-location telephone (CLT) facility a specially designed phone room used to conduct telephone interviewing

closed-ended question an interview question that asks the respondent to make a selection from a limited list of responses

competitive intelligence (CI) an intelligence system that helps managers assess their competition and vendors in order to become more efficient and effective competitors

computer-assisted personal interviewing the interviewer reads the questions from a computer screen and enters the respondent's data directly into the computer

computer-assisted self-interviewing the respondent reads questions off a computer screen and directly keys his or her answers into a computer or other electronic recording device

convenience sample a form of nonprobability sample using respondents who are convenient, or readily accessible, to the researcher—for example, employees, friends, or relatives

cross-tabulation a method of analyzing data that shows the analyst the responses to one question in relation to the responses to one or more other questions

dashboard display of computer-generated visual output easily accessed by employees for the purpose of maximizing customer relationship marketing interactions

database marketing the creation of a large computerized file of customers' and potential customers' profiles and purchase patterns

decision support system (DSS) an interactive, flexible computerized information system that enables managers to obtain and manipulate information as they are making decisions

ethnographic research the study of human behaviour in its natural context; involves observation of behaviour and physical setting

executive interview a type of survey that involves interviewing business people at their offices concerning industrial products or services

experiment a method a researcher uses to gather primary data to determine cause and effect

field service firm a firm that specializes in interviewing respondents on a subcontracted basis.

focus group seven to ten people who participate in group discussion led by a moderator

LO 1
Explain the concept and purpose of a marketing decision support system. A decision support system (DSS) makes data instantly available without outside assistance to marketing managers. This allows even novice computer users to manipulate data in a variety of ways and to answer "what if" questions that can aid their marketing decision making. Four characteristics that make good DSSs especially useful to marketing managers are: interactivity, flexibility, discovery orientation, and accessibility.

LO 2
Define marketing research and explain its importance to marketing decision making. Marketing research is a process of collecting and analyzing data for the purpose of solving specific marketing problems. Marketers use marketing research to explore the profitability of marketing strategies. They can examine why particular strategies failed and analyze characteristics of specific market segments. Managers can use research findings to help keep their current customers. Moreover, marketing research allows management to behave proactively, rather than reactively, by identifying newly emerging patterns in society and the economy.

Why marketing research?
- ☑ Improve quality of decision making
- ☑ Trace problems
- ☑ Focus on keeping existing customers
- ☑ Understand changes in marketplace

LO 3
Describe the steps involved in conducting a marketing research project. The marketing research process involves several basic steps. First, the researcher and the decision maker must agree on a research issue and on the set of research objectives. The researcher then creates an overall research design to specify how primary data will be gathered and analyzed.

Before collecting data, the researcher decides whether the group to be interviewed will be a probability or nonprobability sample. Field service firms are often hired to carry out data collection. Once data have been collected, the researcher analyzes them using statistical analysis. The researcher then prepares and presents oral and written reports, including conclusions and recommendations, to management. As a final step, the researcher determines whether the recommendations were implemented and what could have been done to make the project more successful.

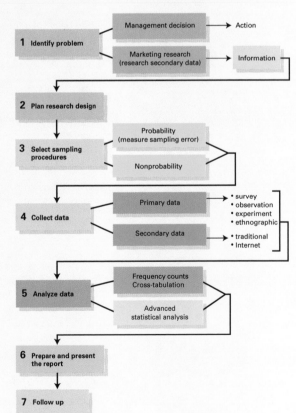

frame error a sample drawn from a population differs from the target population.

InfoScan a scanner-based sales-tracking service for the consumer packaged goods industry

mall intercept interview interviewing people in the common areas of shopping malls

management decision problem a broad-based problem that uses marketing research in order for managers to take proper actions

marketing information everyday information about developments in the marketing environment that managers use to prepare and adjust marketing plans

marketing research the process of planning, collecting, and analyzing data relevant to a marketing decision

marketing research aggregator a company that acquires, catalogues, reformats, segments, and resells reports already published by marketing research firms

marketing research issue a statement that defines the focus for the information that is to be collected to aid any marketing decision making

marketing research objective the specific information needed to solve a marketing research issue

measurement error an error that occurs when the information desired by the researcher differs from the information provided by the measurement process

mystery shoppers researchers posing as customers who gather observational data about a store

nonprobability sample any sample in which little or no attempt is made to have a representative cross-section of the population

observation research a research method that relies on four types of observation: people watching people, people watching an activity, machines watching people, and machines watching an activity

open-ended question an interview question that encourages an answer phrased in the respondent's own words

primary data information that is collected for the first time and is used for solving the particular problem under investigation

probability sample a sample in which every element in the population has a known statistical likelihood of being selected

random error the selected sample is an imperfect representation of the overall population

random sample a sample arranged in such a way that every element of the population has an equal chance of being selected as part of the sample

recruited Internet sample pre-recruited respondents must qualify to participate and then e-mailed a questionnaire or directed to a secure website

research design specifies which research questions must be answered, how and when the data will be gathered, and how the data will be analyzed

sample a subset from a larger population

LO 4
Discuss the profound impact of the Internet on marketing research. The Internet has vastly simplified the secondary data search process, placing more sources of information in front of researchers than ever before. Internet survey research is surging in popularity. Internet surveys can be created rapidly and reported in real time. They are also relatively inexpensive and can easily be personalized. Often researchers can use the Internet to contact respondents who are difficult to reach by other means. The Internet can also be used to conduct focus groups, to distribute research proposals and reports, and to facilitate collaboration between the client and the research supplier. Clients can access real-time data and analyze the information as the collection process continues.

LO 5
Discuss the growing importance of scanner-based research. A scanner-based research system enables marketers to monitor a market panel's exposure and reaction to such variables as advertising, coupons, store displays, packaging, and price. By analyzing these variables in relation to the panel's subsequent buying behaviour, marketers gain useful insight into sales and marketing strategies.

BehaviorScan
Panel information from specific groups of people, enables researchers to manipulate variables and see real results

InfoScan
Aggregate consumer information on all bar-coded products

LO 6
Explain when marketing research should be conducted. Acquiring marketing information can require a great deal of time and expense. As such, the willingness to acquire additional decision-making information depends on managers' perceptions of its quality, price, and timing. Research, therefore, should be undertaken only when the expected value of the information is greater than the cost of obtaining it.

When Should Research be Conducted
☐ Information is needed for a Decision
☐ Benefits > Costs
☐ Time is available

LO 7
Explain the concept of competitive intelligence. Competitive intelligence (CI) helps managers assess their competition and their vendors in order to become more efficient and effective competitors. Intelligence is analyzed information; it becomes decision-making intelligence when it has implications for the organization.

By helping managers assess their competition and vendors, CI leads to fewer surprises. CI is part of a sound marketing strategy; it helps companies respond to competitive threats and helps reduce unnecessary costs.

sampling error a sample does not represent the target population

scaled-response question a closed-ended question designed to measure the intensity of a respondent's answer

scanner-based research a system for gathering information from a single group of respondents by continuously monitoring the advertising, promotion, and pricing they are exposed to and the products they buy

screened Internet sample an Internet sample with quotas that are based on desired sample characteristics

secondary data data previously collected for any purpose other than the one at hand

survey research the most popular technique for gathering primary data, in which a researcher interacts with people to obtain facts, opinions, and attitudes

universe the population from which a sample will be drawn

unrestricted Internet sample a survey in which anyone with a computer and Internet access can fill out the questionnaire

aspirational reference groups groups that an individual would like to join

attitude a learned tendency to respond consistently toward a given object

belief an organized pattern of knowledge that an individual holds as true about his or her world

cognitive dissonance inner tension that a consumer experiences after recognizing an inconsistency between behaviour and values or opinions

consumer behaviour how consumers make purchase decisions and how they use and dispose of purchased goods or services; also includes the factors that influence purchase decisions and product use

consumer decision-making process a five-step process used by consumers when buying goods or services

culture the set of values, norms, attitudes, and other meaningful symbols that shape human behaviour and the artifacts, or products, of that behaviour as they are transmitted from one generation to the next

evoked set (consideration set) a group of the most preferred alternatives resulting from an information search, which a buyer can further evaluate to make a final choice

extensive decision making the most complex type of consumer decision making, used when considering the purchase of an unfamiliar, expensive product or an infrequently purchased item; requires the use of several criteria for evaluating options and much time for seeking information

external information search the process of seeking information in the outside environment

ideal self-image the way an individual would like to be

internal information search the process of recalling information stored in one's memory

involvement the amount of time and effort a buyer invests in the search, evaluation, and decision processes of consumer behaviour

learning a process that creates changes in behaviour, immediate or expected, through experience and practice

lifestyle a mode of living as identified by a person's activities, interests, and opinions

limited decision making the type of decision making that requires a moderate amount of time for gathering information and deliberating about an unfamiliar brand in a familiar product category

Maslow's hierarchy of needs a method of classifying human needs and motivations into five categories in ascending order of importance: physiological, safety, social, esteem, and self-actualization

marketing-controlled information source a product information source that originates with marketers promoting the product

motive a driving force that causes a person to take action to satisfy specific needs

LO 1 Explain why marketing managers should understand consumer behaviour.
Consumer behaviour describes how consumers make purchase decisions and how they use and dispose of the products they buy. An understanding of consumer behaviour reduces marketing managers' uncertainty when they are defining a target market and designing a marketing mix.

LO 2 Analyze the components of the consumer decision-making process.
The consumer decision-making process begins with need recognition, when stimuli trigger awareness of an unfulfilled want. If additional information is required to make a purchase decision, the consumer may engage in an internal or external information search. The consumer then evaluates the additional information and establishes purchase guidelines. Finally, a purchase decision is made.

Consumer postpurchase evaluation is influenced by prepurchase expectations, the prepurchase information search, and the consumer's general level of self-confidence. Cognitive dissonance is the inner tension that a consumer experiences after recognizing a purchased product's disadvantages. When a purchase creates cognitive dissonance, consumers tend to react by seeking positive reinforcement for the purchase decision, avoiding negative information about the purchase decision, or revoking the purchase decision by returning the product.

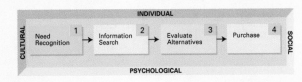

LO 3 Identify the types of consumer buying decisions and discuss the significance of consumer involvement.
Consumer decision making falls into three broad categories. First, consumers exhibit routine response behaviour for frequently purchased, low-cost items that require very little decision effort; routine response behaviour is typically characterized by brand loyalty. Second, consumers engage in limited decision making for occasional purchases or for unfamiliar brands in familiar product categories. Third, consumers practise extensive decision making when making unfamiliar, expensive, or infrequent purchases. High-involvement decisions usually include an extensive information search and a thorough evaluation of alternatives. In contrast, low-involvement decisions are characterized by brand loyalty and a lack of personal identification with the product. The main factors affecting the level of consumer involvement are previous experience, interest, perceived risk of negative consequences (financial, social, and psychological), situation, and social visibility.

LO 4 Identify and understand the cultural factors that affect consumer buying decisions.
Cultural influences on consumer buying decisions include culture and values, subculture, and social class. Culture is the essential character of a society that distinguishes it from other cultural groups. The underlying elements of every culture are the values, language, myths, customs, rituals, laws, and the artifacts, or products, transmitted from one generation to the next. The

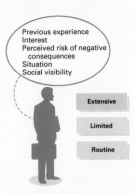

need recognition result of an imbalance between actual and desired states

nonaspirational reference groups (dissociative groups) groups that influence our behaviour because we try to maintain distance from them

nonmarketing-controlled information source a product information source not associated with advertising or promotion.

norms the values and attitudes deemed acceptable by a group

opinion leader an individual who influences the opinions of others

perception the process by which people select, organize, and interpret stimuli into a meaningful and coherent picture

personality a way of organizing and grouping the consistency of an individual's reactions to situations

primary membership groups groups with which individuals interact regularly in an informal, face-to-face manner

psychological influences tools that consumers use to recognize, gather, analyze, and self-organize to aid in decision making

real self-image the way an individual actually perceives himself or herself

reference group a group in society that influences an individual's purchasing behaviour

routine response behaviour the type of decision making exhibited by consumers buying frequently purchased, low-cost goods and services; requires little search and decision time

secondary membership groups groups with which individuals interact less consistently and more formally than with primary membership groups

selective distortion a process whereby consumers change or distort information that conflicts with their feelings or beliefs

selective exposure the process whereby a consumer decides which stimuli to notice and which to ignore

selective retention a process whereby consumers remember only information that supports their personal beliefs

self-concept how consumers perceive themselves in terms of attitudes, perceptions, beliefs, and self-evaluations

social class a group of people who are considered nearly equal in status or community esteem, who regularly socialize among themselves both formally and informally, and who share behavioural norms

socialization process the passing down of cultural values and norms to children

sociometric leader a low-profile, well-respected collaborative professional who is socially and professionally well connected

stimulus any unit of input affecting one or more of the five senses: sight, smell, taste, touch, hearing

subculture a homogeneous group of people who share elements of the overall culture and also have their own unique cultural elements

value the enduring belief shared by a society that a specific mode of conduct is personally or socially preferable to another mode of conduct

want a particular product or service that the customer believes could satisfy an unfulfilled need

most defining element of a culture is its values—the enduring beliefs shared by a society that a specific mode of conduct is personally or socially preferable to another mode of conduct. A culture can be divided into subcultures on the basis of demographic characteristics, geographic regions, national and ethnic background, political beliefs, and religious beliefs. Subcultures share elements of the overall culture as well as cultural elements unique to their own group. A social class is a group of people who are considered nearly equal in status or community esteem, who regularly socialize among themselves both formally and informally, and who share behavioural norms.

LO 5 Identify and understand the social factors that affect consumer buying decisions.

Social factors include such external influences as reference groups, opinion leaders, and family. Consumers seek out others' opinions for guidance on new products or services and products with image-related attributes or because attribute information is lacking or uninformative. Consumers may use products or brands to identify with or become a member of a reference group. Opinion leaders are members of reference groups who influence others' purchase decisions. Family members also influence purchase decisions; children tend to shop in similar patterns as their parents.

Reference Groups	Direct		Indirect	
	Primary	Secondary	Aspirational	Nonaspirational

Opinion Leaders	People you know	Celebrities

Family	Socialization Process		
	Initiators	Decision Makers	Consumers
	Influencers		Purchasers

LO 6 Identify and understand the individual factors that affect consumer buying decisions.
Individual factors that affect consumer buying decisions include gender; age and family life-cycle stage; and personality, self-concept, and lifestyle. Beyond obvious physiological differences, men and women differ in their social and economic roles, which affects their consumer buying decisions. How old a consumer is generally indicates what products he or she may be interested in purchasing. Marketers often define their target markets in terms of consumers' life-cycle stage, following changes in consumers' attitudes and behavioural tendencies as they mature. Finally, certain products and brands reflect consumers' personality, self-concept, and lifestyle.

LO 7 Identify and understand the psychological factors that affect consumer buying decisions.
Psychological factors include perception, motivation, learning, values, beliefs, and attitudes. These factors allow consumers to interact with the world around them, recognize their feelings, gather and analyze information, formulate thoughts and opinions, and take action. Perception allows consumers to recognize their consumption problems. Motivation is what drives consumers to take action to satisfy specific consumption needs. Almost all consumer behaviour results from learning, which is the process that creates changes in behaviour through experience. Consumers with similar beliefs and attitudes tend to react alike to marketing-related inducements.

Perception	Selective Exposure	
	Selective Retention	Selective Distortion

Motivation	Needs				
	Physiological	Safety	Social	Esteem	Self-Actualization

Learning	Stimulus Generalization	Stimulus Discrimination

Beliefs & Attitudes	Changing Beliefs about Attributes	Changing Importance of Beliefs	Adding New Beliefs

6 | Business Marketing

accessory equipment goods such as portable tools and office equipment that are less expensive and shorter-lived than major equipment

business marketing the marketing of goods and services to individuals and organizations for purposes other than personal consumption

business services expense items that do not become part of a final product

business-to-business electronic commerce the use of the Internet to facilitate the exchange of goods, services, and information between organizations

business-to-business online exchange an electronic trading floor that provides companies with integrated links to their customers and suppliers

buying centre all those people in an organization who become involved in the purchase decision

component parts either finished items ready for assembly or products that need very little processing before becoming part of some other product

derived demand the demand for business products

disintermediation the elimination of intermediaries such as wholesalers or distributers from a marketing channel

joint demand the demand for two or more items used together in a final product

keiretsu a network of interlocking corporate affiliates

major equipment (installations) such capital goods as large or expensive machines, mainframe computers, blast furnaces, generators, airplanes, and buildings

modified rebuy a situation where the purchaser wants some change in the original good or service

multiplier effect (accelerator principle phenomenon in which a small increase or decrease in consumer demand can produce a much larger change in demand for the facilities and equipment needed to make the consumer product

new buy a situation requiring the purchase of a product for the first time

North American Industry Classification System (NAICS) an industry classification system developed by the United States, Canada, and Mexico to classify North American business establishments by their main production processes

original equipment manufacturers (OEMs) individuals and organizations that buy business goods and incorporate them into the products that they produce for eventual sale to other producers or to consumers

processed materials products used directly in manufacturing other product

LO 1 Describe business marketing. Business marketing provides goods and services that are bought for use in business rather than for personal consumption. Intended use, not physical characteristics, distinguishes a business product from a consumer product.

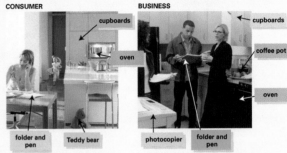

REGINE MAHAUX/ PHOTOGRAPHER'S CHOICE/ GETTY IMAGES

RYAN MCVAY/PHOTODISC/ JUPITER IMAGES

LO 2 Explain the major differences between business and consumer markets. In business markets, demand is derived, price-inelastic, joint, and fluctuating. Purchase volume is much larger than in consumer markets, customers are fewer in number and more geographically concentrated, and distribution channels are more direct. Buying is approached more formally using professional purchasing agents, more people are involved in the buying process, negotiation is more complex, and reciprocity and leasing are more common. And, finally, selling strategy in business markets normally focuses on personal contact rather than on advertising.

Characteristic	Business Market	Consumer Market
Demand	Organizational	Individual
Purchase volume	Larger	Smaller
Number of customers	Fewer	Many
Location of buyers	Geographically concentrated	Dispersed
Distribution structure	More direct	More indirect
Nature of buying	More professional	More personal
Nature of buying influence	Multiple	Single
Type of negotiations	More complex	Simpler
Use of reciprocity	Yes	No
Use of leasing	Greater	Lesser
Primary promotional method	Personal selling	Advertising

LO 3 Identify the four major categories of business market customers. Producer markets consist of for-profit organizations and individuals that buy products to use in producing other products, as components of other products, or in facilitating business operations. Reseller markets consist of wholesalers and retailers that buy finished products to resell for profit. Government markets include federal, provincial, and city governments that buy goods and services to support their own operations and serve the needs of citizens. Institutional markets consist of very diverse nonbusiness institutions whose main goals do not include profit.

raw materials unprocessed extractive or agricultural products, such as mineral ore, lumber, wheat, corn, fruits, vegetables, and fish

reciprocity a practice where business purchasers choose to buy from their own customers

relationship commitment a firm's belief that an ongoing relationship with another firm is so important that the relationship warrants maximum efforts at maintaining it indefinitely

stickiness a measure of a website's effectiveness; calculated by multiplying the frequency of visits by both the duration of the visits and the number of pages viewed during each visit (site reach)

straight rebuy a situation in which the purchaser reorders the same goods or services without looking for new information or new suppliers

strategic alliance (strategic partnership) a cooperative agreement between business firms

supplies consumable items that do not become part of the final product

trust the condition that exists when one party has confidence in an exchange partner's reliability and integrity

LO 4 **Describe the seven types of business goods and services.** Major equipment includes capital goods, such as heavy machinery. Accessory equipment is typically less expensive and shorter-lived than major equipment. Raw materials are extractive or agricultural products that have not been processed. Component parts are finished or near-finished items to be used as parts of other products. Processed materials are used to manufacture other products. Supplies are consumable and not used as part of a final product. Business services are intangible products that many companies use in their operations.

LO 5 **Discuss the unique aspects of business buying behaviour.** Business buying behaviour is distinguished by five fundamental characteristics. First, buying is normally undertaken by a buying centre consisting of many people who range widely in authority level. Second, business buyers typically evaluate alternative products and suppliers on the basis of their quality, service, and price—in that order. Third, business buying falls into three general categories: new buys, modified rebuys, and straight rebuys. Fourth, the ethics of business buyers and sellers are often scrutinized. Fifth, customer service before, during, and after the sale plays a big role in business purchase decisions.

LO 6 **Explain the North American Industry Classification System.** The NAICS provides a way to identify, analyze, segment, and target business and government markets. Organizations can be identified and compared by using the NAICS numeric code, which indicates the business sector, subsector, industry group, industry, and country industry. NAICS is a valuable tool for analyzing, segmenting, and targeting business markets.

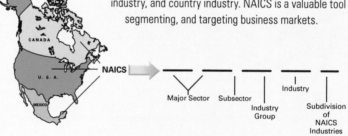

LO 7 **Describe the role of the Internet in business marketing.** The rapid expansion and adoption of the Internet have made business markets more competitive than ever before. The number of business buyers and sellers using the Internet is rapidly increasing. Firms are seeking new and better ways to expand markets and sources of supply, increase sales and decrease costs, and better serve customers. As a result of the Internet, every business in the world is potentially a local competitor.

LO 8 **Discuss the role of relationship marketing and strategic alliances in business marketing.** Relationship marketing entails seeking and establishing long-term alliances or partnerships with customers. A strategic alliance is a cooperative agreement between business firms. Firms form alliances to leverage what they do well by partnering with others that have complementary skills.

benefit segmentation the process of grouping customers into market segments according to the benefits they seek from the product

cannibalization situation that occurs when sales of a new product cut into sales of a firm's existing products

concentrated targeting strategy strategy used to select one segment a market for targeting marketing efforts

demographic segmentation segmenting markets by age, gender, income, ethnic background, and family life cycle

80/20 principle a principle holding that 20 percent of all customers generate 80 percent of the demand

family life cycle (FLC) a series of stages determined by a combination of age, marital status, and the presence or absence of children

geodemographic segmentation segmenting potential customers into neighbourhood lifestyle categories

geographic segmentation segmenting markets by region of a country or the world, market size, market density, or climate

market people or organizations with needs or wants and the ability and willingness to buy

market segment a subgroup of people or organizations sharing one or more characteristics that cause them to have similar product needs

market segmentation the process of dividing a market into meaningful, relatively similar, and identifiable segments or groups

multisegment targeting strategy strategy that chooses two or more well-defined market segments and develops a distinct marketing mix for each

niche one segment of a market

one-to-one marketing an individualized marketing method that utilizes customer information to build long-term, personalized, and profitable relationships with each customer

optimizers business customers who consider numerous suppliers, both familiar and unfamiliar, solicit bids, and study all proposals carefully before selecting one

perceptual mapping a means of displaying or graphing, in two or more dimensions, the location of products, brands, or groups of products in customers' minds

position the place a product, brand, or group of products occupies in consumers' minds relative to competing offerings

positioning a process that influences potential customers' overall perception of a brand, product line, or organization in general

product differentiation a positioning strategy that some firms use to distinguish their products from those of competitors

LO 1 **Describe the characteristics of markets and market segments.** A market is composed of individuals or organizations that have both the ability and willingness to make purchases to fulfill their needs or wants. A market segment is a group of individuals or organizations with similar product needs as a result of one or more common characteristics.

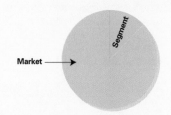

LO 2 **Explain the importance of market segmentation.** Before the 1960s, few businesses targeted specific market segments. Today, segmentation is a crucial marketing strategy for nearly all successful organizations. Market segmentation enables marketers to tailor marketing mixes to meet the needs of particular population segments. Segmentation helps marketers identify consumer needs and preferences, areas of declining demand, and new marketing opportunities.

LO 3 **Discuss criteria for successful market segmentation.** Successful market segmentation depends on four basic criteria: (1) a market segment must be substantial and have enough potential customers to be viable; (2) a market segment must be identifiable and measurable; (3) members of a market segment must be accessible to marketing efforts; and (4) a market segment must respond to particular marketing efforts in a way that distinguishes it from other segments.

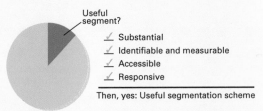

Useful segment?
- ☑ Substantial
- ☑ Identifiable and measurable
- ☑ Accessible
- ☑ Responsive

Then, yes: Useful segmentation scheme

LO 4 **Describe the bases commonly used to segment consumer markets.** Five bases are commonly used for segmenting consumer markets. Geographic segmentation is based on region, size, density, and climate characteristics. Demographic segmentation is based on age, gender, income level, ethnicity, and family life-cycle characteristics. Psychographic segmentation includes personality, motives, and lifestyle characteristics. Benefits sought is a type of segmentation that identifies customers according to the benefits they seek in a product. Finally, usage segmentation divides a market by the amount of product purchased or consumed.

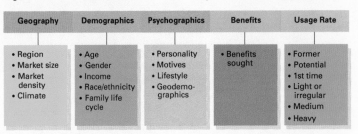

Geography	Demographics	Psychographics	Benefits	Usage Rate
• Region • Market size • Market density • Climate	• Age • Gender • Income • Race/ethnicity • Family life cycle	• Personality • Motives • Lifestyle • Geodemographics	• Benefits sought	• Former • Potential • 1st time • Light or irregular • Medium • Heavy

LO 5 **Describe the bases for segmenting business markets.** Business markets can be segmented on two general bases. First, businesses segment markets on the basis of company characteristics, such as customers' geographic location, type of company, company size, and product use. Second, companies may segment customers on the basis of the buying processes those customers use.

psychographic segmentation market segmentation on the basis of personality, motives, lifestyles, and geodemographics categories

repositioning changing consumers' perceptions of a brand in relation to competing brands

satisficers business customers who place their order with the first familiar supplier to satisfy their product and delivery requirements

segmentation bases (variables) characteristics of individuals, groups, or organizations

target market a group of people or organizations for which an organization designs, implements, and maintains a marketing mix intended to meet the needs of that group, resulting in mutually satisfying exchanges

undifferentiated targeting strategy marketing approach that views the market as one big market with no individual segments and thus uses a single marketing mix

usage-rate segmentation dividing a market by the amount of product bought or consumed

LO 6 **List the steps involved in segmenting markets.** Six steps are involved when segmenting markets: (1) selecting a market or product category for study; (2) choosing a basis or bases for segmenting the market; (3) selecting segmentation descriptors; (4) profiling and evaluating segments; (5) selecting target markets; and (6) designing, implementing, and maintaining appropriate marketing mixes.

| **1** Select a market or product category for study. | **2** Choose a basis or bases for segmenting the market. | **3** Select segmentation descriptors. | **4** Profile and analyze segments. | **5** Select target markets. | **6** Design, implement, and maintain appropriate marketing mixes. |

Note that steps 5 and 6 are actually marketing activities that follow market segmentation (steps 1 through 4).

LO 7 **Discuss alternative strategies for selecting target markets.** Marketers select target markets using three different strategies: undifferentiated targeting, concentrated targeting, and multisegment targeting. An undifferentiated targeting strategy assumes that all members of a market have similar needs that can be met by using a single marketing mix. A concentrated targeting strategy focuses all marketing efforts on a single market segment. Multisegment targeting is a strategy that uses two or more marketing mixes to target two or more market segments.

LO 8 **Explain one-to-one marketing.** One-to-one marketing is an individualized marketing method that utilizes customer information to build long-term, personalized, and profitable relationships with each customer. Successful one-to-one marketing comes from understanding customers and collaborating with them, rather than using them as targets for generic messages. Database technology makes it possible for companies to interact with customers on a personal, one-to-one basis.

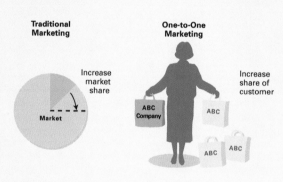

LO 9 **Explain how and why firms implement positioning strategies and how product differentiation plays a role.** Positioning is used to influence consumer perceptions of a particular brand, product line, or organization in relation to competitors. The term position refers to the place that the offering occupies in consumers' minds. To establish a unique position, many firms use product differentiation, emphasizing the real or perceived differences between competing offerings. Products may be differentiated on the basis of attribute, price and quality, use or application, product user, product class, or competitor.

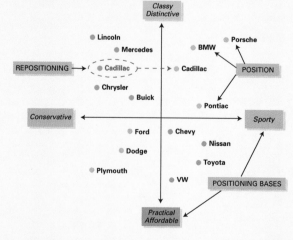

Each car occupies a position in consumers' minds.
Cars can be positioned according to attribute (sporty, conservative, etc.), to price/quality (affordable, classy, etc.), or other bases.
With edgier ads, Cadillac has repositioned itself as a car for younger drivers.

8 Customer Relationship Management (CRM)

campaign management developing product or service offerings customized for the appropriate customer segment and then pricing and communicating these offerings for the purpose of enhancing customer relationships

compiled list a customer list that was developed by gathering names and addresses gleaned from telephone directories and membership rosters, sometimes enhanced with information from public records, such as census data, auto registrations, birth announcements, business start-ups, or bankruptcies

customer-centric a philosophy under which the company customizes its product and service offering based on data generated through interactions between the customer and the company

customer relationship management (CRM) a company-wide business strategy designed to optimize profitability, revenue, and customer satisfaction by focusing on highly defined and precise customer groups

database a collection of data, especially one that can be accessed and manipulated by computer software

data mining an analytical process that compiles actionable data on the purchase habits of a firm's current and potential customers.

data warehouse a central repository of data from various functional areas of the organization that are stored and inventoried on a centralized computer system so that the information can be shared across all functional departments of the business

empowerment delegation of authority to solve customers' problems quickly—usually by the first person who learns of the customer's problem

interaction the point at which a customer and a company representative exchange information and develop learning relationships

knowledge management the process by which learned information from customers is centralized and shared for the purpose of enhancing the relationship between customers and the organization

learning in a CRM environment, the informal process of collecting customer data through customer comments and feedback on product or service performance

lifetime value (LTV) analysis a data manipulation technique that projects the future value of the customer over a period of years using the assumption that marketing to repeat customers is more profitable than marketing to first-time buyers

point-of-sale interactions communications between customers and organizations that occur at the point of sale, usually in a store

LO 1 Define customer relationship management.
Customer relationship management (CRM) is a company-wide business strategy designed to optimize profitability, revenue, and customer satisfaction by focusing on highly defined and precise customer groups. This strategy is accomplished by organizing the company around customer segments, encouraging and tracking customer interaction with the company, fostering customer-satisfying behaviours, and linking all processes of a company from its customers through its suppliers.

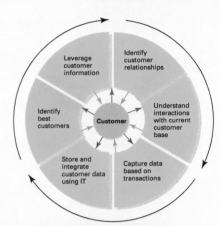

LO 2 Explain how to identify customer relationships with the organization.
Companies that implement a CRM system adhere to a customer-centric focus or model. A customer-centric company focuses on learning the factors that build long-lasting relationships with valuable customers and then builds its system to satisfy and retain those customers. Building relationships through CRM is a strategic process that focuses on learning, managing customer knowledge, and empowerment.

LO 3 Understand interactions with the current customer base.
The interaction between the customer and the organization is considered to be the foundation on which a CRM system is built. Only through effective interactions can organizations learn about the expectations of their customers, generate and manage knowledge about customers, negotiate mutually satisfying commitments, and build long-term relationships. Effective management of customer interactions recognizes that customers provide information to organizations across a wide variety of touch points. Consumer-centric organizations are implementing new and unique approaches for establishing interactions specifically for this purpose. They include Web-based interactions, point-of-sale interactions, and transaction-based interactions.

LO 4 Outline the process of capturing customer data.
Vast amounts of information can be obtained from the interactions between the organization and its customers. In a CRM system, the issue is not how much data can be obtained, but rather what type of data should be acquired and how those data can be used effectively for relationship enhancement. The channel, transaction,

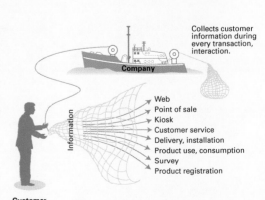

Collects customer information during every transaction, interaction.

- Web
- Point of sale
- Kiosk
- Customer service
- Delivery, installation
- Product use, consumption
- Survey
- Product registration

predictive modelling a data manipulation technique in which marketers try to determine, based on some past set of occurrences, the odds that some other occurrence, such as an inquiry or purchase, will take place in the future

recency-frequency-monetary (RFM) analysis the analysis of customer activity as to recency, frequency, and monetary value

response list a customer list that includes the names and addresses of individuals who have responded to an offer of some kind, such as by mail, telephone, direct-response television, product rebates, contests or sweepstakes, or billing inserts

touch points all possible areas of a business where customers have contact with that business

and product or service consumed constitute the touch points between a customer and the organization. These touch points represent possible areas within a business where customer interactions can take place and, hence, the opportunity for acquiring data from the customer.

LO 5 Describe the use of technology to store and integrate customer data.

Customer data gathering is complicated because information needed by one unit of the organization (e.g., sales and marketing) is often generated by another area of the business or even a third-party supplier (e.g., an independent marketing research firm). Because of the lack of standard structure and interface, organizations rely on technology to capture, store, and integrate strategically important customer information. The process of centralizing data in a CRM system is referred to as data warehousing. A data warehouse is a central repository of customer information collected by an organization.

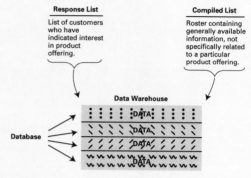

LO 6 Describe how to identify the best customers.

Customer relationship management, as a process strategy, attempts to manage the interactions between a company and its customers. To be successful, organizations must identify customers who yield high profitability or high potential profitability. To accomplish this task, significant amounts of information must be gathered from customers, stored and integrated in the data warehouse, and then analyzed for commonalities that can produce segments that are highly similar, yet different from other customer segments. A useful approach to identifying the best customers is recency-frequency-monetary (RFM) analysis. Data mining uses RFM, predictive modelling, and other approaches to identify significant relationships among several customer dimensions within vast data warehouses. These significant relationships enable marketers to better define the most profitable customers and prospects.

LO 7 Explain the process of leveraging customer information throughout the organization.

One of the benefits of a CRM system is the capacity to share information throughout the organization. This sharing of information allows an organization to interact with all functional areas to develop programs targeted to its customers in a process commonly referred to as campaign management. Campaign management involves developing customized product/service offerings for the appropriate customer segment and pricing and communicating these offerings for the purpose of enhancing customer relationships. When a company employee has access to customer information by using a dash board (which shows the most important information on one screen), the employee can instantly view a customer's profile and use this information to improve communications with the customer.

Marketing Information

CRM Database

Applications

✓ Campaign management

✓ Retaining loyal customers

✓ Cross-selling other products and services

✓ Designing targeted marketing communications

✓ Reinforcing customer purchase decisions

✓ Inducing product trial by new customers

✓ Increasing effectiveness of distribution channel marketing

✓ Improving customer service

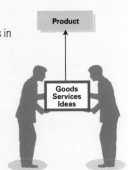

brand a name, term, symbol, design, or combination thereof that identifies a seller's products and differentiates them from competitors' products

brand equity the value of company and brand names

brand loyalty a consistent preference for one brand over all others

brand mark the elements of a brand that cannot be spoken

brand name that part of a brand that can be spoken, including letters, words, and numbers

business product (industrial product) a product used to manufacture other goods or services, to facilitate an organization's operations, or to resell to other customers

cobranding placing two or more brand names on a product or its package

consumer product a product bought to satisfy an individual's personal wants

convenience product a relatively inexpensive item that merits little shopping effort

express warranty a written guarantee

family brand marketing several different products under the same brand name

generic product a no-frills, no-brand-name, low-cost product that is simply identified by its product category

generic product name a term that identifies a product by class or type and cannot be trademarked

global brand a brand where at least 20 percent of the product is sold outside its home country or region

implied warranty an unwritten guarantee that the good or service is fit for the purpose for which it was sold

individual branding using different brand names for different products

informational labelling package labelling designed to help consumers make proper product selections and to lower their cognitive dissonance after the purchase

manufacturer's brand the brand name of a manufacturer

persuasive labelling package labelling that focuses on a promotional theme or logo, and consumer information is secondary

planned obsolescence the practice of modifying products so those that have already been sold become obsolete before they actually need replacement

private brand a brand name owned by a wholesaler or a retailer

product everything, both favourable and unfavourable, received in an exchange

LO 1 Define the term product. A product is anything, desired or not, that a person or organization receives in an exchange. The basic goal of purchasing decisions is to receive the tangible and intangible benefits associated with a product. Tangible aspects include packaging, style, colour, size, and features. Intangible qualities include service, the retailer's image, the manufacturer's reputation, and the social status associated with a product. An organization's product offering is the crucial element in any marketing mix.

LO 2 Classify consumer products. Consumer products are classified into four categories: convenience products, shopping products, specialty products, and unsought products. Convenience products are relatively inexpensive and require limited shopping effort. Shopping products are of two types: homogeneous and heterogeneous. Because of the similarity of homogeneous products, they are differentiated mainly by price and features. In contrast, heterogeneous products appeal to consumers because of their distinct characteristics. Specialty products possess unique benefits that are highly desirable to certain customers. Finally, unsought products are either new products or products that require aggressive selling because they are generally avoided or overlooked by consumers.

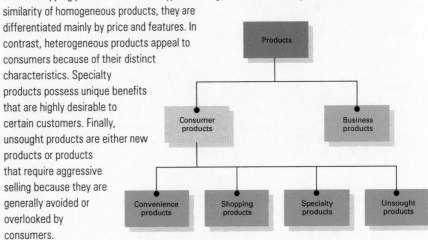

LO 3 Define the terms product item, product line, and product mix. A product item is a specific version of a product that can be designated as a distinct offering among an organization's products. A product line is a group of closely related products offered by an organization. An organization's product mix includes all the products it sells. Product mix width refers to the number of product lines an organization offers. Product line depth is the number of product items in a product line. Firms modify existing products by changing their quality, functional characteristics, or style. Product line extension occurs when a firm adds new products to existing product lines.

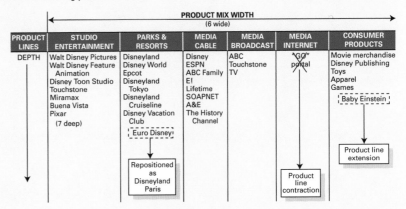

NEL

product item a specific version of a product that can be designated as a distinct offering among an organization's products

product line a group of closely related product items

product line depth the number of product items in a product line

product line extension adding additional products to an existing product line to compete more broadly in the industry

product mix all products that an organization sells

product mix width the number of product lines an organization offers

product modification changing one or more of a product's characteristics

service mark a trademark for a service

shopping product a product that requires comparison shopping because it is usually more expensive than a convenience product and is found in fewer stores

specialty product a particular item that consumers search extensively for and are very reluctant to accept substitutes for

trademark the exclusive right to use a brand or part of a brand

universal product codes (UPCs) a series of thick and thin vertical lines (bar codes), readable by computerized optical scanners that match the codes to brand names, package sizes, and prices

unsought product a product unknown to the potential buyer or a known product that the buyer does not actively seek

warranty a confirmation of the quality or performance of a good or service

LO 4 **Describe marketing uses of branding.** A brand is a name, term, or symbol that identifies and differentiates a firm's products. Established brands encourage customer loyalty and help new products succeed. Branding strategies require decisions about individual, family, manufacturers', and private brands.

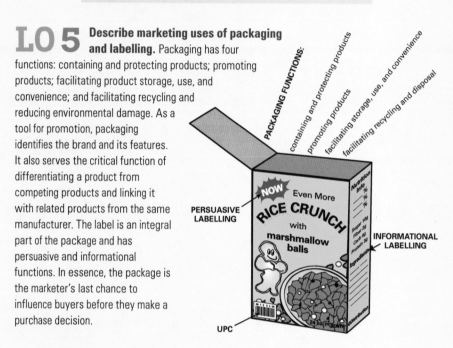

LO 5 **Describe marketing uses of packaging and labelling.** Packaging has four functions: containing and protecting products; promoting products; facilitating product storage, use, and convenience; and facilitating recycling and reducing environmental damage. As a tool for promotion, packaging identifies the brand and its features. It also serves the critical function of differentiating a product from competing products and linking it with related products from the same manufacturer. The label is an integral part of the package and has persuasive and informational functions. In essence, the package is the marketer's last chance to influence buyers before they make a purchase decision.

LO 6 **Discuss global issues in branding and packaging.** In addition to brand piracy, international marketers must address a variety of concerns regarding branding and packaging, including choosing a brand-name policy, translating labels and meeting host-country labelling requirements, making packages aesthetically compatible with host-country cultures, and offering the sizes of packages preferred in host countries.

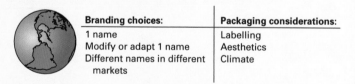

Branding choices:	Packaging considerations:
1 name	Labelling
Modify or adapt 1 name	Aesthetics
Different names in different markets	Climate

LO 7 **Describe how and why product warranties are important marketing tools.** Product warranties are important tools because they offer consumers protection and help them gauge product quality.

Express warranty = written guarantee
Implied warranty = unwritten guarantee

Developing and Managing Products

adopter a consumer who was happy enough with his or her trial experience with a product to use it again

brainstorming the process of getting a group to think of unlimited ways to vary a product or solve a problem

business analysis the second stage of the screening process, where preliminary figures for demand, cost, sales, and profitability are calculated

commercialization the decision to market a product

concept test evaluation of a new-product idea, usually before any prototype has been created

decline stage a long-run drop in sales

development the stage in the product development process in which a prototype is developed and a marketing strategy is outlined

diffusion the process by which the adoption of an innovation spreads

growth stage the second stage of the product life cycle when sales typically grow at an increasing rate, many competitors enter the market, large companies may start acquiring small pioneering firms, and profits are healthy

innovation a product perceived as new by a potential adopter

introductory stage the full-scale launch of a new product into the marketplace

maturity stage a period during which sales increase at a decreasing rate

new product a product new to the world, new to the market, new to the producer, new to the seller, or new to some combination of these

new-product strategy a plan that links the new-product development process with the objectives of the marketing department, the business unit, and the corporation

product category all brands that satisfy a particular type of need

product development a marketing strategy that involves the creation of marketable new products; the process of converting applications for new technologies into marketable products

product life cycle (PLC) a concept that traces the stages of a product's acceptance, from its introduction (birth) to its decline (death)

screening the first filter in the product development process, which eliminates ideas that are inconsistent with the organization's new-product strategy or are obviously inappropriate for some other reason

LO 1

Explain the importance of developing new products and describe the six categories of new products. New products are important to sustain growth and profits and to replace obsolete items. New products can be classified as new-to-the-world products (discontinuous innovations), new product lines, additions to existing product lines, improvements or revisions of existing products, repositioned products, or lower-priced products. To sustain or increase profits, a firm must innovate.

New products power long-term value
- New-to-the-world
- New product lines
- Additions to existing product lines
- Improvements to existing products
- Repositioned products
- Lower-priced products

Company

Long-term value

LO 2

Explain the steps in the new-product development process. First, a firm forms a new-product strategy by outlining the characteristics and roles of future products. Then new-product ideas are generated by customers, employees, distributors, competitors, vendors, and internal R&D personnel. Once a product idea has survived initial screening by an appointed screening group, it undergoes business analysis to determine its potential profitability. If a product concept seems viable, it progresses into the development phase, in which the technical and economic feasibility of the manufacturing process is evaluated. The development phase also includes laboratory and use testing of a product for performance and safety. Following initial testing and refinement, most products are introduced in a test market to evaluate consumer response and marketing strategies. Finally, test market successes are propelled into full commercialization. The commercialization process involves starting up production, building inventories, shipping to distributors, training a sales force, announcing the product to the trade, and advertising to consumers.

Number of new product ideas / Time

- Idea generation
- Idea screening
- Business analysis
- Development
- Test marketing
- Commercialization

LO 3

Discuss global issues in new-product development. A marketer with global vision seeks to develop products that can easily be adapted to suit local needs. The goal is not simply to develop a standard product that can be sold worldwide. Smart global marketers also look for good product ideas worldwide.

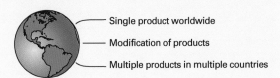

- Single product worldwide
- Modification of products
- Multiple products in multiple countries

LO 4

Explain the diffusion process through which new products are adopted. The diffusion process is the spread of a new product from its producer to ultimate adopters. Adopters in the diffusion process belong to five categories: innovators, early adopters, the early majority, the late majority, and laggards. Product characteristics that affect the rate of adoption include product complexity, compatibility with existing social values, relative

simulated (laboratory) market testing the presentation of advertising and other promotion materials for several products, including a test product, to members of the product's target market

simultaneous product development a team-oriented approach to new-product development

test marketing the limited introduction of a product and a marketing program to determine the reactions of potential customers in a market situation

advantage over existing substitutes, visibility, and "trialability." The diffusion process is facilitated by word-of-mouth communication and communication from marketers to consumers.

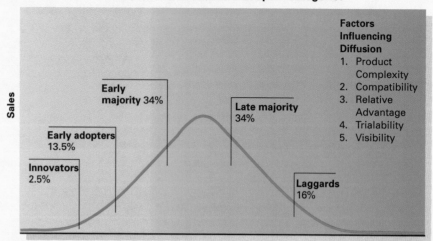

Diffusion of Innovations—Adopter Categories

Factors Influencing Diffusion
1. Product Complexity
2. Compatibility
3. Relative Advantage
4. Trialability
5. Visibility

LO 5 **Explain the concept of product life cycles.** All brands and product categories undergo a life cycle with four stages: introduction, growth, maturity, and decline. The rate at which products move through these stages varies dramatically. Marketing managers use the product life cycle concept as an analytical tool to forecast a product's future and devise effective marketing strategies.

	Product Life Cycle Stage			
Marketing Mix Strategy	**Introductory**	**Growth**	**Maturity**	**Decline**
Product Strategy	Limited number of models; frequent product modifications	Expanded number of models; frequent product modifications	Large number of models	Elimination of unprofitable models and brands
Distribution Strategy	Distribution usually limited, depending on product; intensive efforts and high margins often needed to attract wholesalers and retailers	Expanded number of dealers; intensive efforts to establish long-term relationships with wholesalers and retailers	Extensive number of dealers; margins declining; intensive efforts to retain distributors and shelf space	Unprofitable outlets phased out
Promotion Strategy	Develop product awareness; stimulate primary demand; use intensive personal selling to distributors; use sampling and couponing for consumers	Stimulate selective demand; advertise brand aggressively	Stimulate selective demand; advertise brand aggressively; promote heavily to retain dealers and customers	Phase out all promotion
Pricing Strategy	Prices are usually high to recover development costs (see Chapter 18)	Prices begin to fall toward end of growth stage as result of competitive pressure	Prices continue to fall	Prices stabilize at relatively low level; small price rises are possible if competition is negligible

Time

Sales

assurance the knowledge and courtesy of employees and their ability to convey trust

core service the most basic benefit the consumer is buying

credence quality a characteristic that consumers may have difficulty assessing even after purchase because they do not have the necessary knowledge or experience

empathy caring, individualized attention to customers

experience quality a characteristic that can be assessed only after use

gap model a model identifying five gaps that can cause problems in service delivery and influence customer evaluations of service quality

heterogeneity the variability of the inputs and outputs of services, which causes services to tend to be less standardized and uniform than goods

inseparability the inability of the production and consumption of a service to be separated; consumers must be present during the production

intangibility the inability of services to be touched, seen, tasted, heard, or felt in the same manner that goods can be sensed

internal marketing treating employees as customers and developing systems and benefits that satisfy their needs

nonprofit organization an organization that exists to achieve some goal other than the usual business goals of profit, market share, or return on investment

nonprofit organization marketing the effort by nonprofit organizations to bring about mutually satisfying exchanges with target markets

perishability the inability of services to be stored, warehoused, or inventoried

public service advertisement (PSA) an announcement that promotes a program of a nonprofit organization or of a federal, provincial or territorial, or local government

reliability the ability to perform a service dependably, accurately, and consistently

LO 1 Discuss the importance of services to the economy.
The service sector plays a crucial role in the Canadian economy, employing more than 78 percent of the workforce and accounting for a similar percentage of the gross domestic product.

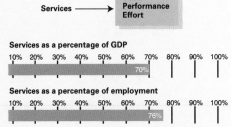

Services ⟶ Deed Performance Effort

Services as a percentage of GDP
10% 20% 30% 40% 50% 60% 70% 80% 90% 100%
70%

Services as a percentage of employment
10% 20% 30% 40% 50% 60% 70% 80% 90% 100%
76%

LO 2 Discuss the differences between services and goods.
Services are distinguished by four characteristics. Services are intangible performances because they lack clearly identifiable physical characteristics, making it difficult for marketers to communicate their specific benefits to potential customers. The production and consumption of services occur simultaneously. Services are heterogeneous because their quality depends on such elements as the service provider, individual consumer, location, and so on. Finally, services are perishable in the sense that they cannot be stored or saved. As a result, synchronizing supply with demand is particularly challenging in the service industry.

Intangible

Inseparable

Heterogeneous

Perishable

LO 3 Describe the components of service quality and the gap model of service quality.
Service quality has five components: reliability (ability to perform the service dependably, accurately, and consistently), responsiveness (providing prompt service), assurance (knowledge and courtesy of employees and their ability to convey trust), empathy (caring, individualized attention), and tangibles (physical evidence of the service).

SERVICE
Reliability Responsiveness Assurance Empathy Tangibles

The gap model identifies five key discrepancies that can influence customer evaluations of service quality. When the gaps are large, service quality is low. As the gaps shrink, service quality improves. Gap 1, the Knowledge Gap, is found between customers' expectations and management's perceptions of those expectations. Gap 2, the Standard Gap, is found between management's perception of what the customer wants and specifications for service quality. Gap 3, the Delivery Gap, is found between service quality specifications and delivery of the service. Gap 4, the Communications Gap, is found between service delivery and what the company promises to the customer through external communication. Gap 5, the Perception Gap, is found between customers' service expectations and their perceptions of service performance.

LO 4 Develop marketing mixes for services using the 8 Ps of services marketing.

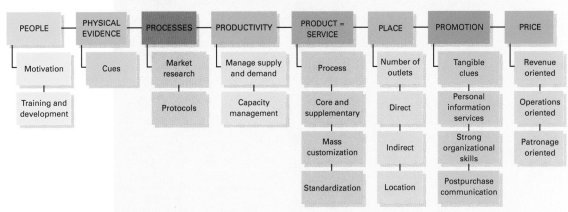

PEOPLE	PHYSICAL EVIDENCE	PROCESSES	PRODUCTIVITY	PRODUCT = SERVICE	PLACE	PROMOTION	PRICE
Motivation	Cues	Market research	Manage supply and demand	Process	Number of outlets	Tangible clues	Revenue oriented
Training and development		Protocols	Capacity management	Core and supplementary	Direct	Personal information services	Operations oriented
				Mass customization	Indirect	Strong organizational skills	Patronage oriented
				Standardization	Location	Postpurchase communication	

LO 5 Discuss relationship marketing in services.

Relationship marketing in services involves attracting, developing, and retaining customer relationships. Relationship marketing has three levels: level 1 focuses on pricing incentives; level 2 uses pricing incentives and social bonds with customers; and level 3 uses pricing, social bonds, and structural bonds to build long-term relationships.

3 Creating value-added services not available elsewhere — STRUCTURAL SOCIAL FINANCIAL

2 Designs services to meet customer needs — SOCIAL FINANCIAL

1 Pricing incentives — FINANCIAL

LO 6 Explain internal marketing in services.

Internal marketing means treating employees as customers and developing systems and benefits that satisfy their needs. Employees who like their jobs and are happy with the firm they work for are more likely to deliver good service.

Management   Employees   Customers

Good service flows from management to customers through employees.

LO 7 Discuss global issues in services marketing.

To be successful globally, service firms must adjust their marketing mix for the environment of each target country.

LO 8 Describe nonprofit organization marketing.

Nonprofit organizations pursue goals other than profit, market share, and return on investment. Nonprofit organization marketing facilitates mutually satisfying exchanges between nonprofit organizations and their target markets. Several unique characteristics distinguish nonbusiness marketing strategy, including a concern with services and social behaviours rather than manufactured goods and profit; a difficult, undifferentiated, and in some ways marginal target market; a complex product that may have only indirect benefits and may elicit very low involvement; distribution that may or may not require special facilities depending on the service provided; a relative lack of resources for promotion; and prices only indirectly related to the exchange between the producer and the consumer of services.

Nonprofit Organization Marketing

PRODUCT
- Benefit complexity
- Benefit strength
- Involvement

PLACE
- Special facilities

TARGET
- Apathetic or strongly opposed
- Undifferentiated segmentation
- Complementary positioning

PROMOTION
- Professional volunteers
- Sales
- Public service advertising

PRICE
- Nonfinancial
- Indirect payment
- Separation between payers and users
- Below-cost pricing

channel conflict a clash of goals and methods among distribution channel members

channel control a situation in which when one marketing channel member intentionally affects another member's behaviour

channel leader (channel captain) a member of a marketing channel who exercises authority and power over the activities of other channel members

channel members all parties in the marketing channel that negotiate with one another, buy and sell products, and facilitate the change of ownership between buyer and seller in the course of moving the product from the manufacturer into the hands of the final consumer

channel partnering (channel cooperation) the joint effort of all channel members to create a supply chain that serves customers and creates a competitive advantage

channel power a marketing channel member's capacity to control or influence the behaviour of other channel members

coverage ensuring product availability in every outlet where potential customers might want to buy it

direct channel a distribution channel in which producers sell directly to consumers

discrepancy of assortment the lack of all the items a customer needs to receive full satisfaction from a product or products

discrepancy of quantity the difference between the amount of product produced and the amount an end user wants to buy

distribution resource planning (DRP) an inventory control system that manages the replenishment of goods from the manufacturer to the final consumer

dual distribution (multiple distribution) the use of two or more channels to distribute the same product to target markets

electronic data interchange (EDI) information technology that replaces the paper documents that usually accompany business transactions, such as purchase orders and invoices, with electronic transmission of the needed information to reduce inventory levels, improve cash flow, streamline operations, and increase the speed and accuracy of information transmission

electronic distribution a distribution technique that includes any kind of product or service that can be distributed electronically, whether over traditional forms such as fibre-optic cable or through satellite transmission of electronic signals

exclusive distribution a form of distribution that involves only one or a few dealers within a given area

horizontal conflict a channel conflict that occurs among channel members on the same level

intensive distribution a form of distribution aimed at having a product available in every outlet where target customers might want to buy it

inventory control system a method of developing and maintaining an adequate

LO 1 Explain what a marketing channel is and why intermediaries are needed.
A marketing channel is a business structure of interdependent organizations that reach from the point of product origin to the consumer with the purpose of physically moving products to their final consumption destination, representing place or distribution in the marketing mix and encompassing the processes involved in getting the right product to the right place at the right time. Members of a marketing channel create a continuous and seamless supply chain that performs or supports the marketing channel functions. Channel members provide economies to the distribution process in the form of specialization and division of labour; overcoming discrepancies in quantity, assortment, time, and space; and providing contact efficiency.

LO 2 Define the types of channel intermediaries and describe their functions and activities.
The most prominent difference separating intermediaries is whether they take title to the product. Retailers and merchant wholesalers take title, but agents and brokers do not. Retailers are firms that sell mainly to consumers. Merchant wholesalers are those organizations that facilitate the movement of products and services from the manufacturer to producers, resellers, governments, institutions, and retailers. Agents and brokers facilitate the exchange of ownership between sellers and buyers. Channel intermediaries perform three basic types of functions. Transactional functions include contacting and promoting, negotiating, and risk taking. Logistical functions performed by channel members include physical distribution, storing, and sorting functions. Finally, channel members may perform facilitating functions, such as researching and financing.

LO 3 Describe the channel structures for consumer and business products and discuss alternative channel arrangements.
Marketing channels for consumer and business products vary in degree of complexity.

LO 4 Define supply chain management and discuss its benefits.
Supply chain management coordinates and integrates all of the activities performed by supply chain members into a seamless process from the source to the point of consumption. The responsibilities of a supply chain manager include developing channel design strategies, managing the relationships of supply chain members, sourcing and procurement of raw materials, scheduling production, processing orders, managing inventory and storing product, and selecting transportation modes. The supply chain manager is also responsible for managing customer service and the information that flows through the supply chain. The benefits of supply chain management include reduced costs in inventory management, transportation, warehousing, and packaging; improved service through such techniques as time-based and make-to-order deliveries; and enhanced revenues, which result from such supply chain–related achievements as higher product availability and more customized products.

LO 5 Discuss the issues that influence channel strategy.
When determining marketing channel strategy, the supply chain manager must first decide on the market, product, and producer factors, which will influence the choice of channel. In making these decisions and to ensure success, the manager must consider the 3C distribution objectives of coverage, cost, and control. These objectives will enable the manager to select the appropriate level of distribution intensity. Intensive distribution is distribution aimed at maximum market coverage. Selective distribution is achieved by screening dealers to eliminate all but a few in any single area. The most restrictive form of market coverage is exclusive distribution, which involves only one or a few dealers within a given area.

assortment of materials or products to meet a manufacturer's or a customer's demand

just-in-time production (JIT) a process that redefines and simplifies manufacturing by reducing inventory levels and delivering raw materials just when they are needed on the production line

logistics the process of strategically managing the efficient flow and storage of raw materials, in-process inventory, and finished goods from point of origin to point of consumption

logistics information system the link that connects all of the logistics functions of the supply chain

marketing channel (channel of distribution) a set of interdependent organizations that ease the transfer of ownership as products move from producer to business user or consumer

mass customization (build-to-order) a production method whereby products are not made until an order is placed by the customer; products are made according to customer specifications

materials-handling system a method of moving inventory into, within, and out of the warehouse

materials requirement planning (MRP) (materials management) an inventory control system that manages the replenishment of raw materials, supplies, and components from the supplier to the manufacturer

order processing system a system whereby orders are entered into the supply chain and filled

outsourcing (contract logistics) a manufacturer's or supplier's use of an independent third party to manage an entire function of the logistics system, such as transportation, warehousing, or order processing

retailer a channel intermediary that sells mainly to end-using consumers

selective distribution a form of distribution achieved by screening dealers to eliminate all but a few in any single area

spatial discrepancy the difference between the location of a producer and the location of widely scattered markets where the product is desired

strategic channel alliance a cooperative agreement between business firms to use one of the manufacturer's already established distribution channels

supply chain the connected chain of all of the business entities, both internal and external to the company, that perform or support the logistics function

supply chain management a management system that coordinates and integrates all of the activities performed by supply chain members into a seamless process, from the source to the point of consumption, resulting in enhanced customer and economic value

supply chain team an entire group of individuals who orchestrate the movement of goods, services, and information from the source to the consumer

temporal discrepancy a situation in which a product is produced but a customer at that time is not ready to buy it

vertical conflict a channel conflict that occurs between different levels in a marketing channel, most typically between the manufacturer and wholesaler or between the manufacturer and retailer

LO 6

Explain channel leadership, conflict, and partnering. Power, control, leadership, conflict, and partnering are the main social dimensions of marketing channel relationships. Channel power refers to the capacity of one channel member to control or influence other channel members. Channel control occurs when one channel member intentionally affects another member's behaviour. Channel leadership is the exercise of authority and power. Channel conflict occurs when a clash of goals and methods occurs among the members of a distribution channel. Channel conflict can be either horizontal, such as between channel members at the same level, or vertical, such as between channel members at different levels of the channel. Channel partnering is the joint effort of all channel members to create a supply chain that serves customers and creates a competitive advantage. Collaborating channel partners meet the needs of consumers more effectively by ensuring that the right products reach shelves at the right time and at a lower cost, boosting sales and profits.

LO 7

Describe the logistical components of the supply chain. The logistics supply chain consists of several interrelated and integrated logistical components: (1) sourcing and procurement of raw materials and supplies, (2) production scheduling, (3) order processing, (4) inventory control, (5) warehousing and materials handling, and (6) transportation. Integrating and linking all of the logistics functions of the supply chain is the logistics information system. Information technology connects the various components and partners of the supply chain into an integrated whole. The supply chain team, in concert with the logistics information system, orchestrates the movement of goods, services, and information from the source to the consumer. Supply chain teams typically cut across organizational boundaries, embracing all parties who participate in moving product to market. Procurement deals with the purchase of raw materials, supplies, and components according to production scheduling. Order processing monitors the flow of goods and information (order entry and order handling). Inventory control systems regulate when and how much to buy (order timing and order quantity). Warehousing provides storage of goods until needed by the customer while the materials-handling system moves inventory into, within, and out of the warehouse. Finally, the major modes of transportation include railroads, motor carriers, pipelines, waterways, and airways.

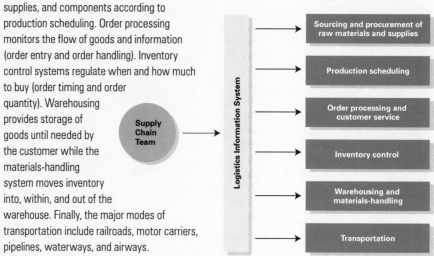

LO 8

Discuss new technology and emerging trends in supply chain management. Several emerging trends are changing the job of today's supply chain manager. Technology and automation are bringing up-to-date distribution information to the decision maker's desk. Technology is also linking suppliers, buyers, and carriers for joint decision making, and it has created a new electronic distribution channel. Many companies are saving money and time by outsourcing to third-party carriers to handle some or all aspects of the distribution process.

LO 9

Discuss channels and distribution decisions in global markets. Global marketing channels are becoming more important to Canadian companies seeking growth abroad. Manufacturers that introduce products in foreign countries must consider these issues. Global distribution expertise is also emerging as an important skill for supply chain managers as many countries are removing trade barriers.

- Distribute directly or through foreign partners
- Different channel structures than in domestic markets
- Illegitimate "grey" marketing channels
- Legal and infrastructure differences

atmosphere the overall impression conveyed by a store's physical layout, décor, and surroundings

automatic vending the use of machines to offer goods for sale

buyer a department head who selects the merchandise for his or her department and may also be responsible for promotion and for personnel

category killers specialty discount stores that heavily dominate their narrow merchandise segment

chain stores stores owned and operated as a group by a single organization.

convenience store a miniature supermarket, carrying only a limited line of high-turnover convenience goods

department store a store housing several departments under one roof

destination stores stores that consumers purposely plan to visit

direct marketing (direct-response marketing) techniques used to get consumers to make a purchase from their home, office, or another nonretail setting

direct retailing the selling of products by representatives who work door-to-door, office-to-office, or at home parties

discount store a retailer that competes on the basis of low prices, high turnover, and high volume

drugstore a retail store that stocks pharmacy-related products and services as its main draw

factory outlet an off-price retailer that is owned and operated by a manufacturer

franchise the right to operate a business or to sell a product

franchisee an individual or business that is granted the right to sell a franchisor's product

franchiser the originator of a trade name, product, methods of operation, and so on that grants operating rights to another party to sell its product

full-line discount stores a retailer that offers consumers very limited service and carries a broad assortment of well-known, nationally branded "hard goods"

gross margin the amount of money the retailer makes as a percentage of sales after the cost of goods sold is subtracted

independent retailers retailers owned by a single person or partnership and not operated as part of a larger retail institution

mass merchandising a retailing strategy using moderate to low prices on large quantities of merchandise and lower levels of service to stimulate high turnover of products

nonstore retailing shopping without visiting a store

LO 1 Discuss the importance of retailing in the Canadian economy.
Retailing plays a vital role in the Canadian economy for two main reasons. First, retail businesses contribute to our high standard of living by providing a vast number and diversity of goods and services. Second, retailing employs a large portion of the Canadian working population.

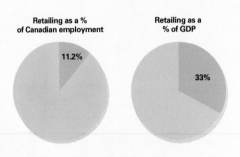

LO 2 Explain the dimensions by which retailers can be classified.
Many different kinds of retailers exist. A retail establishment can be classified according to its ownership, level of service, product assortment, and price. On the basis of ownership, retailers can be broadly differentiated as independent retailers, chain stores, or franchise outlets. The level of service retailers provide can be classified along a continuum of high to low. Retailers also classify themselves by the breadth and depth of their product assortments; some retailers have concentrated product assortments, whereas others have extensive product assortments. Last, general price levels also classify a store, from discounters offering low prices to exclusive specialty stores where high prices are the norm. Retailers use the three variables of level of service, product assortment, and price to position themselves in the marketplace.

- Ownership
- Level of service
- Product assortment
- Price

LO 3 Describe the major types of retail operations.
The major types of retail stores are department stores, specialty retailers, supermarkets, drugstores, convenience stores, discount stores, and restaurants. Department stores carry a wide assortment of shopping and specialty goods, are organized into relatively independent departments, and offset higher prices by emphasizing customer service and décor. Specialty retailers typically carry a narrower but deeper assortment of merchandise, emphasizing distinctive products and a high level of customer service. Supermarkets are large self-service retailers that offer a wide variety of food products and some nonfood items. Drugstores are retail formats that sell mostly prescription and over-the-counter medications, health and beauty aids, cosmetics, and specialty items. Convenience stores carry a limited line of high-turnover convenience goods. Discount stores offer low-priced general merchandise and consist of four types: full-line discounters, specialty discount retailers, warehouse clubs, and off-price retailers.

Finally, restaurants straddle the line between the retailing and services industries; although restaurants sell a product, food and drink, to final consumers, they can also be considered service marketers because they provide consumers with the service of preparing food and providing table service.

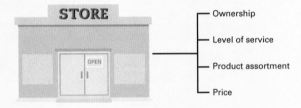

Scrambled merchandising

off-price retailer a retailer that sells at prices 25 percent or more below traditional department store prices because it pays cash for its stock and usually doesn't ask for return privileges

online retailing a type of shopping available to consumers who have personal computers and access to the Internet

product offering the mix of products offered to the consumer by the retailer; also called the product assortment or merchandise mix

retailing all the activities directly related to the sale of goods and services to the ultimate consumer for personal, nonbusiness use

retailing mix a combination of the six Ps— product, place, promotion, price, presentation, and personnel—to sell goods and services to the ultimate consumer

scrambled merchandising the tendency to offer a wide variety of nontraditional goods and services under one roof

specialty discount store a retail store that offers a nearly complete selection of single-line merchandise and uses self-service, discount prices, high volume, and high turnover

specialty store a retail store specializing in a given type of merchandise

supercentre a retail store that combines groceries and general merchandise goods with a wide range of services

supermarket a large, departmentalized, self-service retailer that specializes in food and some nonfood items

telemarketing the use of the telephone to sell directly to consumers

warehouse membership clubs limited-service merchant wholesalers that sell a limited selection of brand-name appliances, household items, and groceries on a cash-and-carry basis to members, small businesses, and groups

LO 4 **Discuss nonstore retailing techniques.** Nonstore retailing, which is shopping outside a store setting, has three major categories. Automatic vending uses machines to offer products for sale. In direct retailing, the sales transaction occurs in a home setting, typically through door-to-door sales or party plan selling. Direct marketing refers to the techniques used to get consumers to buy from their homes or place of business. Those techniques include direct mail, catalogues and mail order, telemarketing, and electronic retailing, such as home shopping channels and online retailing using the Internet.

LO 5 **Define franchising and describe its two basic forms.** Franchising is a continuing relationship in which a franchiser grants to a franchisee the business rights to operate or to sell a product. Modern franchising takes two basic forms. In product and trade name franchising, a dealer agrees to buy or sell certain products or product lines from a particular manufacturer or wholesaler. Business format franchising is an ongoing business relationship in which a franchisee uses a franchiser's name, format, or method of business in return for several types of fees.

LO 6 **List the major tasks involved in developing a retail marketing strategy.** Retail management begins with defining the target market, typically on the basis of demographic, geographic, or psychographic characteristics. After determining the target market, retail managers must develop the six variables of the retailing mix: product, promotion, place, price, presentation, and personnel.

LO 7 **Describe new developments in retailing.** Two major trends are evident in retailing today. First, adding interactivity to the retail environment is one of the most popular strategies in retailing in recent years. Both small retailers and national chains are using interactivity to involve customers and set themselves apart from the competition. Second, m-commerce (mobile e-commerce) is gaining in popularity. M-commerce enables consumers to purchase goods and services using wireless mobile devices, such as smartphones, pagers, personal digital assistants (PDAs), and handheld computers.

Nonstore Retailing

Vending

Direct retailing

Direct marketing — direct mail, catalogues, telemarketing

Electronic retailing — online, shop at home

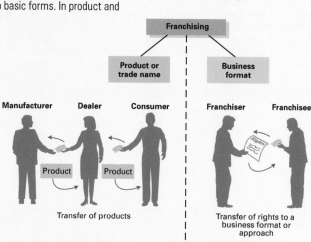

Franchising

Product or trade name

Business format

Manufacturer — Dealer — Consumer

Product — Product

Transfer of products

Franchiser — Franchisee

Transfer of rights to a business format or approach

PRODUCT Width and depth of product assortment
PLACE Location and hours
PROMOTION Advertising, publicity, public relations
PRICE
PRESENTATION Layout and atmosphere
PERSONNEL Customer service and personal selling
TARGET

Interactivity gets consumers involved in retail experience.

M-commerce is purchasing goods through mobile devices.

advertising impersonal, one-way mass communication about a product or organization that is paid for by a marketer

AIDA concept a model that outlines the process for achieving promotional goals in terms of stages of consumer involvement with the message; the acronym stands for *attention, interest, desire,* and *action*

channel a medium of communication—such as a voice, radio, or newspaper—used for transmitting a message

communication the process by which we exchange or share meanings through a common set of symbols

competitive advantage the set of unique features of a company and its products that are perceived by the target market as significant and superior to the competition

crowdsourcing channelling the power of online crowds to gather feedback on marketing programs for almost immediate improvements and changes

decoding interpretation of the language and symbols sent by the source through a channel

direct-response communication communication of a message directly from a marketing company and directly to an intended individual target audience

encoding the conversion of a sender's ideas and thoughts into a message, usually in the form of words or signs

feedback the receiver's response to a message

integrated marketing communications (IMC) the careful coordination of all promotional messages for a product or a service to assure the consistency of messages at every contact point where a company meets the consumer

interpersonal communication direct, fact-to-face communication between two or more people

mass communication the communication of a concept or message to large audiences

noise anything that interferes with, distorts, or slows down the transmission of information

online marketing two-way communication of a message delivered through the Internet to the consumer

personal selling a purchase situation involving a personal paid-for communication between two people in an attempt to influence each other

promotion communication by marketers that informs, persuades, and reminds potential buyers of a product for the purpose of influencing an opinion or eliciting a response

LO 1 Discuss the role of promotion in the marketing mix.
Promotion is communication by marketers that informs, persuades, and reminds potential buyers of a product for the purpose of influencing an opinion or eliciting a response. Promotional strategy is the plan for using the elements of promotion—advertising, direct-response communication, public relations, sales promotion, personal selling, and online marketing—to meet the firm's overall objectives and marketing goals. Using these objectives, marketers combine the elements of the promotional strategy to form a coordinated promotion plan. The promotion plan then becomes an integral part of the total marketing strategy for reaching the target market, in addition to product, distribution, and price.

Promotional Strategy

Promotional mix
Advertising
Direct-Response
Communication
Public Relations
Sales Promotion
Personal Selling
Online Marketing

Competitive advantage

Marketer

Consumer

LO 2 Discuss the elements of the promotional mix.
The elements of the promotional mix include advertising, public relations, sales promotion, personal selling, direct-response communication, and online marketing. Advertising is a form of impersonal, one-way mass communication paid for by the source. Public relations is the function of promotion concerned with a firm's public image. Firms can't buy good publicity, but they can take steps to create a positive company image. Sales promotion is typically used to back up other components of the promotional mix by stimulating immediate demand. Personal selling typically involves direct communication, in person or by telephone; the seller tries to initiate a purchase by informing and persuading one or more potential buyers. Direct-response communication is designed to generate profitable business results through targeted communications to a specific audience. Direct-response communication uses a combination of relevant messaging and offers that can be tracked, measured, analyzed, stored, and leveraged to drive future marketing initiatives. Online marketing is communication delivered through the Internet.

LO 3 Describe the communication process.
The communication process has several steps. When an individual or organization has a message to convey to a target audience, it encodes that message using language and symbols familiar to the intended receiver and sends the message through a channel of communication. Noise in the transmission channel distorts the source's intended message. Reception occurs if the message falls within the receiver's frame of reference. The receiver decodes the message and usually provides feedback to the source. Normally, feedback is direct for interpersonal communication and indirect for mass communication.

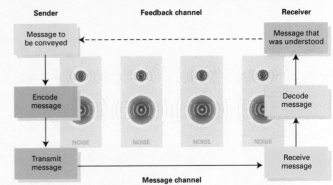

Sender	Feedback channel	Receiver
Message to be conveyed	← - - - - - - - - -	Message that was understood
Encode message		Decode message
	NOISE NOISE NOISE NOISE	
Transmit message	→	Receive message
	Message channel	

LO 4 Outline the goals and tasks of promotion.
The fundamental goals of promotion are to induce, modify, or reinforce behaviour by informing, persuading, and reminding. Informative promotion explains a good's or service's purpose and benefits. Promotion that informs the consumer is typically used to increase demand for a general product

promotional mix the combination of promotional tools—including advertising, public relations, sales promotion, personal selling, direct-response communication, and online marketing—used to reach the target market and fulfill the organization's overall goals

promotional strategy a plan for the optimal use of the elements of promotion: advertising, direct marketing, public relations, personal selling, sales promotion, and online marketing

publicity public information about a company, product, service, or issue appearing in the mass media as a news item

public relations the marketing function that evaluates public attitudes, identifies areas within the organization the public may be interested in, and executes a program of action to earn public understanding and acceptance

pull strategy a marketing strategy that stimulates consumer demand to obtain product distribution

push strategy a marketing strategy that uses aggressive personal selling and trade advertising to convince a wholesaler or a retailer to carry and sell particular merchandise

receiver the person who decodes a message

sales promotion marketing activities—other than personal selling, advertising, and public relations—that stimulate consumer buying and dealer effectiveness

sender the originator of the message in the communication process

social networking sites (social media sites) websites where users create and share information about themselves, brands, and other mutual interests

category or to introduce a new good or service. Persuasive promotion is designed to stimulate a purchase or an action. Promotion that persuades the consumer to buy is essential during the growth stage of the product life cycle, when competition becomes fierce. Reminder promotion is used to keep the product and brand name in the public's mind. Promotions that remind are generally used during the maturity stage of the product life cycle.

LO 5 Discuss the AIDA concept and its relationship to the promotional mix.
The AIDA model outlines the four basic stages in the purchase decision-making process, which are initiated and propelled by promotional activities: (1) attention, (2) interest, (3) desire, and (4) action. The components of the promotional mix have varying levels of influence at each stage of the AIDA model. Advertising is a good tool for increasing awareness and knowledge of a good or service. Sales promotion is effective when consumers are at the purchase stage of the decision-

	Attention	Interest	Desire	Action
Advertising	✓+	✓+	✓	✓−
Direct-Response Communication	✓+	✓	✓	✓+
Public Relations	✓+	✓+	✓+	✓−
Sales Promotion	✓	✓	✓+	✓
Personal Selling	✓	✓+	✓+	✓+
Online Marketing	✓+	✓+		✓−

making process. Personal selling is most effective in developing customer interest and desire.

LO 6 Examine the factors that affect the promotional mix.
Promotion managers consider many factors when creating promotional mixes. These factors include the nature of the product, product life-cycle stage, target market characteristics, the type of buying decision involved, availability of funds, and feasibility of push or pull strategies. Because most business products tend to be custom-tailored to the buyer's exact specifications, the marketing manager may choose a promotional mix that relies more heavily on personal selling. On the other hand, consumer products are generally mass-produced and lend themselves more to mass promotional efforts, such as advertising and sales promotion. As products move through different stages of the product life cycle, marketers will choose to use different promotional elements. For example, advertising is emphasized more in the introductory stage of the product life cycle than in the decline stage. Characteristics of the target market, such as geographic location of potential buyers and brand loyalty, influence the promotional mix as does whether the buying decision is complex or routine. The amount of funds a firm has to allocate to promotion may also help determine the promotional mix. Small firms with limited funds may rely more heavily on public relations, whereas larger firms may be able to afford broadcast or print advertising. Last, if a firm uses a push strategy to promote the product or service, the marketing manager may choose to use aggressive advertising and personal selling to wholesalers and retailers. If a pull strategy is chosen, then the manager often relies on aggressive mass promotion, such as advertising and sales promotion, to stimulate consumer demand.

LO 7 Discuss the concept of integrated marketing communications.
Integrated marketing communications is the careful coordination of all promotional messages for a product or service to ensure the consistency of messages at every contact point where a company meets the consumer—advertising, sales promotion, personal selling, public relations, as well as direct marketing, packaging, and other forms of communication. Marketing managers carefully coordinate all promotional activities to ensure that consumers see and hear one message. Integrated marketing communications has received more attention in recent years due to the proliferation of media choices, the fragmentation of mass markets into more segmented niches, and the decrease in advertising spending in favour of promotional techniques that generate an immediate sales response.

advergaming placing advertising messages in Web-based or video games to advertise or promote a product, service, organization, or issue

advertising appeal a reason for a person to buy a product

advertising campaign a series of related advertisements focusing on a common theme, slogan, and set of advertising appeals

advertising objective a specific communication task that a campaign should accomplish for a specified target audience during a specified period

advertising response function a phenomenon in which spending for advertising and sales promotion increases sales or market share up to a certain level but then produces diminishing returns

advocacy advertising a form of advertising in which an organization expresses its views on a particular issue or cause

audience selectivity the ability of an advertising medium to reach a precisely defined market

blog a publicly accessible Web page that functions as an interactive journal, whereby readers can post comments on the author's entries

cause-related marketing a type of sponsorship involving the association of a for-profit company with a nonprofit organization; through the sponsorship the company's product or service is promoted, and money is raised for the nonprofit

comparative advertising a form of advertising that compares two or more competing brands on one or more specific attributes

competitive advertising a form of advertising designed to influence demand for a specific brand

continuous media schedule a media scheduling strategy in which advertising is run steadily throughout the advertising period; used for products in the latter stages of the product life cycle

cooperative advertising an arrangement in which the manufacturer and the retailer split the costs of advertising the manufacturer's brand

corporate blogs blogs that are sponsored by a company or one of its brands and maintained by one or more of the company's employees

cost per contact the cost of reaching one member of the target market

crisis management a coordinated effort to handle all the effects of either unfavourable publicity or an unexpected unfavourable event

direct mail a printed form of direct-response communication that is delivered directly to consumers' homes

direct-response broadcast advertising that uses television or radio and includes a direct call to action asking the consumer to respond immediately

LO 1 **Discuss the effects of advertising on market share and consumers.** Advertising helps marketers increase or maintain brand awareness and, subsequently, market share. Typically, more is spent to advertise new brands that have a small market share than to advertise older brands. Brands with a large market share use advertising mainly to maintain their share of the market. Advertising affects consumers' daily lives and their purchases. Although advertising can seldom change strongly held consumer attitudes and values, it may transform a consumer's negative attitude toward a product into a positive one. Additionally, when consumers are highly loyal to a brand, they may buy more of that brand when advertising is increased. Last, advertising can also change the importance of a brand's attributes to consumers. By emphasizing different brand attributes, advertisers can change their appeal in response to consumers' changing needs or try to achieve an advantage over competing brands.

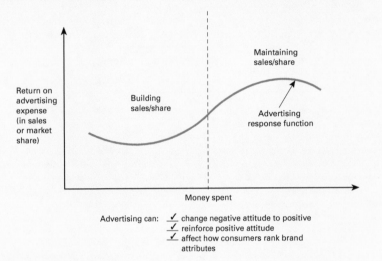

Advertising can: ✓ change negative attitude to positive
✓ reinforce positive attitude
✓ affect how consumers rank brand attributes

LO 2 **Identify the major types of advertising.** Advertising is any form of nonpersonal, paid communication in which the sponsor or company is identified. The two major types of advertising are institutional advertising and product advertising. Institutional advertising is not product oriented; rather, its purpose is to foster a positive company image among the general public, investment community, customers, and employees. Product advertising is designed mainly to promote goods and services, and it is classified into three main categories: pioneering, competitive, and comparative. A product's place in the product life cycle is a major determinant of the type of advertising used to promote it.

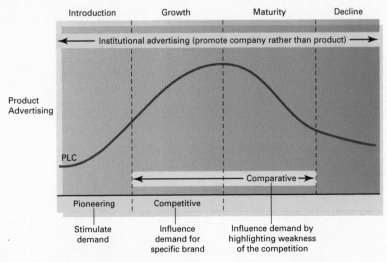

direct-response print advertising in a print medium that includes a direct call to action

direct-response television (DRTV) advertising that appears on television and encourages viewers to respond immediately

Do Not Call List (DNCL) a free service whereby Canadians register their telephone number to reduce or eliminate phone calls from telemarketers

flighted media schedule a media scheduling strategy in which ads are run heavily every other month or every two weeks, to achieve a greater impact with an increased frequency and reach at those times

frequency the number of times an individual is exposed to a given message during a specific period

infomercial a 30-minute or longer advertisement that looks more like a TV talk show than a sales pitch

institutional advertising a form of advertising designed to enhance a company's image rather than promote a particular product

media mix the combination of media to be used for a promotional campaign

media planning the series of decisions advertisers make regarding the selection and use of media, allowing the marketer to optimally and cost-effectively communicate the message to the target audience

media schedule designation of the media, the specific publications or programs, and the insertion dates of advertising

medium the channel used to convey a message to a target market

noncorporate blogs independent blogs that are not associated with the marketing efforts of any particular company or brand

pioneering advertising a form of advertising designed to stimulate primary demand for a new product or product category

product advertising a form of advertising that promotes the benefits of a specific good or service

product placement a public relations strategy that involves getting a product, service, or company name to appear in a movie, television show, radio program, magazine, newspaper, video game, video or audio clip, book, or commercial for another product; on the Internet; or at special events

pulsing media schedule a media scheduling strategy that uses continuous scheduling throughout the year coupled with a flighted schedule during the best sales periods

reach the number of target consumers exposed to a commercial at least once during a specific period, usually four weeks

seasonal media schedule a media scheduling strategy that runs advertising only during times of the year when the product is most likely to be used

sponsorship a public relations strategy in which a company spends money to support an issue, cause, or event that is consistent with corporate objectives, such as improving brand awareness or enhancing corporate image

telemarketing the use of telecommunications to sell a product or service; involves both outbound calls and inbound calls

unique selling proposition a desirable, exclusive, and believable advertising appeal selected as the theme for a campaign

LO 3 **Discuss the creative decisions in developing an advertising campaign.** Before any creative work can begin on an advertising campaign, marketers need to determine the goals or objectives the advertising should achieve. The objectives of a specific advertising campaign often depend on the overall corporate objectives and the product being advertised. Once objectives are defined, creative work can begin on the advertising campaign. Creative decisions include identifying the product's benefits, developing possible advertising appeals, evaluating and selecting the advertising appeals, executing the advertising message, and evaluating the effectiveness of the campaign.

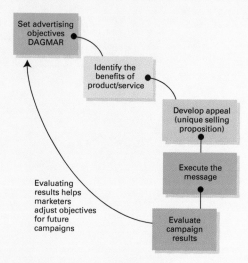

Set advertising objectives DAGMAR → Identify the benefits of product/service → Develop appeal (unique selling proposition) → Execute the message → Evaluate campaign results

Evaluating results helps marketers adjust objectives for future campaigns

LO 4 **Describe media evaluation and selection techniques.** Media evaluation and selection comprise a crucial step in the advertising campaign process. Major types of advertising media include newspapers, magazines, radio, television, outdoor advertising such as billboards and bus panels, and the Internet. Promotion managers choose the advertising campaign's media mix on the basis of the following variables: cost per contact, reach, frequency, characteristics of the target audience, flexibility of the medium, noise level, and the lifespan of the medium. After choosing the media mix, a media schedule designates when the advertisement will appear and the specific vehicles it will appear in.

Media Choices

Type: Newspaper, Magazine, Radio, Television, Outdoor, Internet, Alternative

Considerations:	
Mix	(How much of each?)
Cost per contact	(How much per person?)
Reach	(How many people?)
Frequency	(How often?)
Audience selectivity	(How targeted is audience?)

flexibility
noise
life span
fragmentation

LO 5 **Discuss the role of direct-response communication in the promotional mix.** Direct-response communication is often referred to as direct marketing. It involves the development of relevant messages and offers that can be tracked, measured, analyzed, stored, and leveraged. Popular direct-marketing tools include direct-response broadcast, direct-response print, telemarketing, and direct mail. Direct-response communication is designed to generate an immediate response from the consumer through the inclusion of a key element—the offer.

LO 6 **Discuss the role of public relations in the promotional mix.** Public relations is a vital part of a firm's promotional mix. A company fosters good publicity to enhance its image and promote its products. Popular public relations tools include new-product publicity, product placement, consumer education, event sponsorship, issue sponsorship, and websites. An equally important aspect of public relations is managing unfavourable publicity in a way that is least damaging to a firm's image.

Public Relations versus **Publicity**

Originates with the company | May or may not originate with the company

• new-product publicity
• product placement
• consumer education
• sponsorship
• websites

Major Public Relations TOOLS

Unfounded publicity | Crisis management

– respond quickly
– respond truthfully
– have a communication plan in place

earned media a public relations term connoting free media such as mainstream media coverage

location-based social networking sites websites that combine the fun of social networking with the utility of location-based GPS technology

media sharing sites websites that allow users to upload and distribute multimedia content, such as videos and photos

microblogs blogs with strict limits on the length of posts

owned media online content that an organization creates and controls

paid media content paid for by a company to be placed online

review sites websites that allow consumers to post, read, rate, and comment on opinions regarding all kinds of products and services

social commerce a subset of e-commerce that involves the interaction and user contribution aspects of social online media to assist online buying and selling of products and services

social media any tool or service that uses the Internet to facilitate conversations

social networking sites websites that allow individuals to connect—or network—with friends, peers, and business associates

social news sites websites that allow users to decide which content is promoted on a given website by voting that content up or down

LO 1 Describe social media, how it is used, and its relation to integrated marketing communications.
Social media, commonly thought of as digital technology, is a way for marketers to communicate one-on-one with consumers and measure the effects of those interactions. Social media includes social networks, microblogs, and media sharing sites, all of which are used by the majority of adults. Smartphones and tablet computers have given consumers greater freedom to access social media on the go, which has increased the usage of social media sites. Many advertising budgets are allotting more money to online marketing, including social media, mobile marketing, and search marketing.

Categories of Media Types

Owned Media	Earned Media	Paid Media
Blogs	Word of mouth	Newspapers
Websites	Online buzz	Television
Facebook Pages	Viral videos	Radio
	Retweets	Magazines
	Comments on blogs	Out of home
	Publicity	Direct mail
		Display
		Paid search
		Other direct online advertising

LO 2 Explain how to create a social media campaign.
A social media campaign should take advantage of the three media categories: *owned media, earned media,* and *paid media.* To use these types of media in a social media campaign, first implement an effective listening system. Marketers can interact with negative feedback, make changes, and effectively manage their online presence. Paying attention to the ways that competing brands attract and engage with their customers can be particularly enlightening for both small businesses and global brands. Second, develop a list of objectives that reflects how social media dynamically communicates with customers and builds relationships.

Social Media Objectives

listen and learn

build relationships and awareness

promote products and services

manage reputation

improve customer service

LO 3 Evaluate the various methods of measurement for social media.
Hundreds of metrics have been developed to measure social media's value, but these metrics are meaningless unless they are tied to key performance indicators. The three areas of media measurement are social media measurement (track return on investment of each social media tool), public relations (PR) measurement (calculate the impact of social media on press coverage and other elements of PR), and social media monitoring (customer service improvement, brand management, and prospecting).

LO 4 Explain consumer behaviour on social media.
To effectively leverage social media, marketers must understand who uses social media and how they use it. If a brand's target market does not use social media, a social media campaign might not be useful. There are six categories of social media users: creators, critics, collectors, joiners, spectators, and inactives. A new category is emerging called "conversationalists," who post status updates on social networking sites or microblogs.

LO 5 **Describe the social media tools in a marketer's toolbox and how they are useful.** A marketer has many tools to implement a social media campaign. However, new tools emerge daily, so these resources will change rapidly. Some of the strongest social media platforms are blogs, microblogs, social networks, media creation and sharing sites, social news sites, location-based social networking sites, and virtual worlds and online gaming. Blogs allows marketers to create content in the form of posts, which ideally build trust and a sense of authenticity in customers. Microblogs, such as Twitter, allow brands to follow, retweet, respond to potential customers' tweets, and tweet content that inspires customers to engage the brand, laying a foundation for meaningful two-way conversation. Social networks allow marketers to increase awareness, target audiences, promote products, forge relationships, attract event participants, perform research, and generate new business. Media sharing sites give brands an interactive channel to disseminate content. Social news sites are useful to marketers to promote campaigns, create conversations, and build website traffic. Location-based social networking sites can forge lasting relationships and loyalty in customers. Review sites allow marketers to respond to customer reviews and comments about their brand. Virtual worlds are fertile ground for branded content, and online gaming allows marketers to integrate their message onto a game platform.

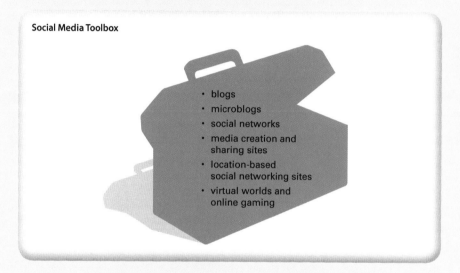

Social Media Toolbox

- blogs
- microblogs
- social networks
- media creation and sharing sites
- location-based social networking sites
- virtual worlds and online gaming

LO 6 **Describe the impact of mobile technology on social media.** There are five reasons for the popularity of mobile marketing: (1) standardized mobile platforms, (2) fewer consumer concerns regarding privacy and pricing policies, (3) real-time advertising, (4) mobile marketing is measurable, and (5) a higher response rate compared with traditional advertising. Because of the rapid growth of smartphones, well-branded, integrated apps allow marketers to create buzz and generate customer engagement. Widgets allow customers to post a company's information to its site, are less expensive than apps, and broaden that company's exposure.

cold calling a form of lead generation in which the salesperson approaches potential buyers without any prior knowledge of the prospects' needs or financial status

consumer sales promotion sales promotion activities targeting the ultimate consumer

coupon a certificate that entitles consumers to an immediate price reduction when they buy the product

follow-up the final step of the selling process, in which the salesperson ensures that delivery schedules are met, that the goods or services perform as promised, and that the buyers' employees are properly trained to use the products

frequent buyer program a loyalty program in which loyal consumers are rewarded for making multiple purchases of a particular good or service

lead generation (prospecting) identification of those firms and people most likely to buy the seller's offerings

lead qualification determination of a sales prospect's (1) recognized need, (2) buying power, and (3) receptivity and accessibility

loyalty marketing program a promotional program designed to build long-term, mutually beneficial relationships between a company and its key customers

needs assessment a determination of the customer's specific needs and wants and the range of options the customer has for satisfying them

negotiation the process during which both the salesperson and the prospect offer special concessions in an attempt to arrive at a sales agreement

networking the use of friends, business contacts, coworkers, acquaintances, and fellow members in professional and civic organizations to identify potential clients

point-of-purchase display (P-O-P) a promotional display set up at the retailer's location to build traffic, advertise the product, or induce impulse buying

preapproach a process that describes the research a salesperson must do before contacting a prospect

premium an extra item offered to the consumer, usually in exchange for some proof of purchase of the promoted product

push money money offered to channel intermediaries to encourage them to push products—that is, to encourage other members of the channel to sell the products

rebate a cash refund given for the purchase of a product during a specific period

referral a recommendation to a salesperson from a customer or business associate

LO 1 Define and state the objectives of sales

promotion. Sales promotion consists of those marketing communication activities, other than advertising, personal selling, and public relations, in which a short-term incentive motivates consumers or members of the distribution channel to purchase a good or service immediately, either by lowering the price or by adding value. The main objectives of sales promotion are to increase trial purchases, consumer inventories, and repeat purchases. Sales promotion is also used to encourage brand switching and to build brand loyalty. Sales promotion supports advertising activities.

LO 2 Discuss the most common forms of consumer sales promotion.

Consumer forms of sales promotion include coupons and rebates, premiums, loyalty marketing programs, contests and sweepstakes, sampling, and point-of-purchase displays. Coupons are certificates entitling consumers to an immediate price reduction when they purchase a product or service. Coupons are a particularly good way to encourage product trial and brand switching. Similar to coupons, rebates provide purchasers with a price reduction, although it is not immediate. To receive a rebate, consumers generally must mail in a rebate form with a proof of purchase. Premiums offer an extra item or incentive to the consumer for buying a product or service. Premiums reinforce the consumer's purchase decision, increase consumption, and persuade nonusers to switch brands. Rewarding loyal customers is the basis of loyalty marketing programs. Loyalty programs are extremely effective at building long-term, mutually beneficial relationships between a company and its key customers. Contests and sweepstakes are generally designed to create interest, often to encourage brand switching. Because consumers perceive risk in trying new products, sampling is an effective method for gaining new customers. Finally, point-of-purchase displays set up at the retailer's location build traffic, advertise the product, and induce impulse buying.

CONSUMER SALES PROMOTION

Coupons and rebates

Premiums

Loyalty marketing program

Contests and sweepstakes

Sampling

P-O-P

Online

LO 3 **List the most common forms of trade sales promotion.** Manufacturers use many of the same sales promotion tools used in consumer promotions, such as sales contests, premiums, and point-of-purchase displays. In addition, manufacturers and channel intermediaries use several unique promotional strategies: trade allowances, push money, training programs, free merchandise, store demonstrations, and meetings, conventions, and trade shows.

Trade Sales Promotion Tools

LO 4 **Describe personal selling.** Personal selling is direct communication between a sales representative and one or more prospective buyers in an attempt to influence each other in a purchase situation. Broadly speaking, all business people use personal selling to promote themselves and their ideas. Personal selling offers several advantages over other forms of promotion. Personal selling allows salespeople to thoroughly explain and demonstrate a product. Salespeople have the flexibility to tailor a sales proposal to the needs and preferences of individual customers. Personal selling can be more efficient than other forms of promotion because salespeople target qualified prospects and avoid wasting efforts on unlikely buyers. Personal selling affords greater managerial control over promotion costs. Finally, personal selling is the most effective method of closing a sale and producing satisfied customers.

Personal Selling Advantages

- ✓ Detailed explanation or demonstration
- ✓ Variable sales message
- ✓ Directed at qualified prospects
- ✓ Controllable adjustable selling costs
- ✓ Effective at obtaining sale and gaining customer satisfaction

LO 5 **Discuss the key differences between relationship selling and traditional selling.** Relationship selling is the practice of building, maintaining, and enhancing interactions with customers for the purpose of developing long-term satisfaction through mutually beneficial partnerships. Traditional selling, on the other hand, is transaction focused. That is, the salesperson is most concerned with making one-time sales and moving on to the next prospect. In contrast, salespeople who practise relationship selling typically spend more time understanding a prospect's needs and developing solutions to meet those needs.

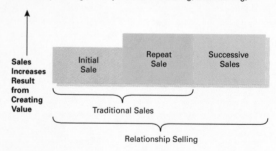

Sales Increases Result from Creating Value

Initial Sale | Repeat Sale | Successive Sales

Traditional Sales

Relationship Selling

LO 6 **List the steps in the selling process.** The selling process is composed of seven basic steps: (1) generating leads, (2) qualifying leads, (3) approaching the customer and probing needs, (4) developing and proposing solutions, (5) handling objections, (6) closing the sale, and (7) following up.

Closing the sale
Handling objections
Developing and proposing solutions
Approaching customer
Qualifying leads
Generating leads
Follow Up
A Continuing Process

average total cost (ATC) total costs divided by quantity of output

average variable cost (AVC) total variable costs divided by quantity of output

break-even analysis a method of determining what sales volume must be reached before total revenue equals total costs

demand the quantity of a product that will be sold in the market at various prices for a specified period

elastic demand a situation in which consumer demand is sensitive to changes in price

elasticity of demand consumers' responsiveness or sensitivity to changes in price

extranet a private electronic network that links a company with its suppliers and customers

fixed cost a cost that does not change as output is increased or decreased

floor price the lowest price to which a company will allow its price to drop

inelastic demand a situation in which an increase or a decrease in price will not significantly affect demand for the product

keystoning the practice of marking up prices by 100 percent, or doubling the cost

manufacturers' suggested retail price (MSRP) the price recommended by the manufacturer to aid controlling price competition and unit sales and, thereby ensure fair margins

marginal cost (MC) the change in total costs associated with a one-unit change in output

marginal revenue (MR) the extra revenue associated with selling an extra unit of output, or the change in total revenue as a result of a one-unit change in output

market share a company's product sales as a percentage of total sales for that industry

markup pricing the cost of buying the product from the producer plus amounts for profit and for expenses not otherwise accounted for; can be expressed as markup (cost) or markup (selling)

prestige pricing charging a high price to help promote a high-quality image

price that which given up in an exchange to acquire good or service

price equilibrium the price at which demand and supply are equal

profit revenue minus expenses

profit maximization a method of setting prices so that marginal revenue equals marginal cost

return on investment (ROI) ROI = Net Profits (before taxes) divided by Investment (Owners' Equity)

LO 1 Discuss the importance of pricing decisions to the economy and to the individual firm.
Pricing plays an integral role in the economy by allocating goods and services among consumers, governments, and businesses. Pricing is essential in business because it creates revenue, which is the basis of all business activity. In setting prices, marketing managers strive to find a level high enough to produce a satisfactory profit.

> Price × Sales unit = Revenue
> Revenue − Costs = Profit
> Profit drives growth, salary increases, and corporate investment

LO 2 List and explain a variety of pricing objectives.
Establishing realistic and measurable pricing objectives is a critical part of any firm's marketing strategy. Pricing objectives are commonly classified into three categories: profit oriented, sales oriented, and status quo. Profit-oriented pricing is based on profit maximization, a satisfactory level of profit, or a target return on investment. The goal of profit maximization is to generate as much revenue as possible in relation to cost. Often, a more practical approach than profit maximization is setting prices to produce profits that will satisfy management and stockholders. The most common profit-oriented strategy is pricing for a specific return on investment relative to a firm's assets. The second type of pricing objective is sales oriented, and it focuses on either maintaining a percentage share of the market or maximizing dollar or unit sales. The third type of pricing objective aims to maintain the status quo by matching competitors' prices.

LO 3 Explain the role of demand in price determination.
Demand is a key determinant of price. When establishing prices, a firm must first determine demand for its product. A typical demand schedule shows an inverse relationship between quantity demanded and price: When price is lowered, sales increase; and when price is increased, the quantity demanded falls. For prestige products, however, a direct relationship may exist between demand and price: the quantity demanded will increase as price increases.

Marketing managers must also consider demand elasticity when setting prices. Elasticity of demand is the degree to which the quantity demanded fluctuates with changes in price. If consumers are sensitive to changes in price, demand is elastic; if they are insensitive to price changes, demand is inelastic. Thus, an increase in price will result in lower sales for an elastic product and little or no loss in sales for an inelastic product.

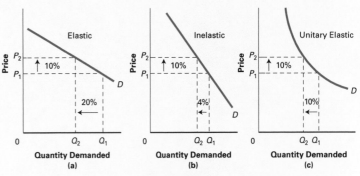

What affects elasticity?
- Availability of substitutes
- Price relative to purchasing power
- Product durability
- Product's other uses
- Inflation rate

LO 4 Understand the concept of yield management systems.

Yield management systems use complex mathematical software to profitably fill unused capacity. The software uses techniques such as discounting early purchases, limiting early sales at these discounted prices, and overbooking capacity. These systems are used in service and retail businesses and are substantially raising revenues.

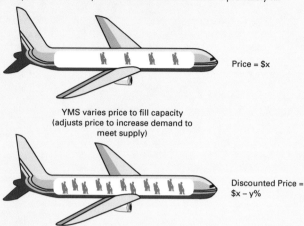

Price = $x

YMS varies price to fill capacity (adjusts price to increase demand to meet supply)

Discounted Price = $x – y%

LO 5 Describe cost-oriented pricing strategies.

The other major determinant of price is cost. Marketers use several cost-oriented pricing strategies. To cover their own expenses and obtain a profit, wholesalers and retailers commonly use markup pricing: tacking an extra amount onto the manufacturer's original price. Another pricing technique is to maximize profits by setting price where marginal revenue equals marginal cost. Still another pricing strategy determines how much a firm must sell to break even and uses this amount as a reference point for adjusting price.

Markup: Cost + x% = Price
Profit Maximization: Price set at point where MR = MC

MC

$

MR

Quantity

Break-Even: Price set at point where total cost = total revenue

Total revenue

$ BE   Total costs

Quantity

LO 6 Demonstrate how price can be affected by the product life cycle, competition, distribution and promotion strategies, customer demands, the Internet and extranets, and perceptions of quality.

The price of a product normally changes as it moves through the life cycle and as demand for the product and competitive conditions change. Management often sets a high price at the introductory stage, and the high price tends to attract competition. The competition usually drives prices down because individual competitors lower prices to gain market share.

Adequate distribution for a new product can sometimes be obtained by offering a larger-than-usual profit margin to wholesalers and retailers. The Internet enables consumers to compare products and prices quickly and efficiently. Price is also used as a promotional tool to attract customers. Special low prices often attract new customers and entice existing customers to buy more. Large buyers can extract price concessions from vendors. Such demands can squeeze the profit margins of suppliers.

Perceptions of quality can also influence pricing strategies. A firm trying to project a prestigious image often charges a premium price for a product. Consumers tend to equate high prices with high quality.

Price/quality relationship
– Uncertain consumers tend to rely on price to indicate quality ("You get what you pay for.")

PLC
Introduction
Growth
Maturity
Decline

Competition
– Other firms enter market
– Price wars

Demands of large customers
– Large customers pressure suppliers for price reductions and guaranteed margins

Price

– Convenience
– Selling against the brand
– Exclusive distribution

Distribution

Promotion strategy
Price used as a promotional tool

– Consumers use shopping bots to hunt for bargains
– Increased competition
– Internet auctions

Internet and extranets

bait pricing a price tactic that tries to get consumers into a store through false or misleading price advertising and then uses high-pressure selling to persuade consumers to buy more expensive merchandise

base price the general price level at which the company expects to sell the good or service

basing-point pricing charging freight from a given (basing) point, regardless of the city from which the goods are shipped

cash discount a price reduction offered to a consumer, an industrial user, or a marketing intermediary in return for prompt payment of a bill

consumer penalty an extra fee paid by the consumer for violating the terms of the purchase agreement

cumulative quantity discount a deduction from list price that applies to the buyer's total purchases made during a specific period

deceptive pricing promoting a price or price saving that is not actually available

delayed-quotation pricing pricing that is not set until the item is either finished or delivered; used for industrial installations and many accessory items

escalator pricing pricing that reflects cost increases incurred between the time the order is placed and the time delivery is made

flexible pricing (variable pricing) different customers pay different prices for essentially the same merchandise bought in equal quantities

FOB origin pricing the buyer absorbs the freight costs from the shipping point ("free on board")

freight absorption pricing the seller pays all or part of the actual freight charges and does not pass them on to the buyer

functional discount (trade discount) a discount to wholesalers and retailers for performing channel functions

joint costs costs that are shared in the manufacturing and marketing of several products in a product line

leader pricing (loss-leader pricing) a product is sold near or even below cost in the hope that shoppers will buy other items once they are in the store

noncumulative quantity discount a deduction from list price that applies to a single order rather than to the total volume of orders placed during a certain period

odd–even pricing (psychological pricing) odd-numbered prices to connote bargains and even-numbered prices to imply quality

penetration pricing a relatively low price for a product initially as a way to reach the mass market

LO 1 **Describe the procedure for setting the right price.** The process of setting the right price on a product involves four major steps: (1) establishing pricing goals; (2) estimating demand, costs, and profits; (3) choosing a price policy to help determine a base price; and (4) fine-tuning the base price with pricing tactics. A price strategy establishes a long-term pricing framework for a good or service. The three main types of price policies are price skimming, penetration pricing, and status quo pricing. A price-skimming policy charges a high introductory price, often followed by a gradual reduction. Penetration pricing offers a low introductory price to capture a large market share and attain economies of scale. Finally, status quo pricing strives to match competitors' price.

LO 2 **Identify the legal and ethical constraints on pricing decisions.** Government regulation helps monitor four major areas of pricing: unfair trade practices, price fixing, predatory pricing, and price discrimination. Some provinces have enacted unfair trade practice regulations that protect small businesses from large firms that operate efficiently on extremely thin profit margins; the acts prohibit charging below-cost prices. The federal government's Competition Act prohibits both price fixing, which is an agreement between two or more firms on a particular price, and predatory pricing, in which a firm undercuts its competitors with extremely low prices to drive them out of business, and makes it illegal for firms to discriminate between two or more buyers in terms of price.

LO 3 **Explain how discounts, geographic pricing, and other pricing tactics can be used to fine-tune the base price.** Several techniques enable marketing managers to adjust prices within a general range in response to changes in competition, government regulation, consumer demand, and promotional and positioning goals. Techniques for fine-tuning price are: discounts, allowances, rebates, value-based pricing, geographic pricing, and a variety of other specific pricing tactics such as single pricing, flexible pricing, professional services pricing, etc.

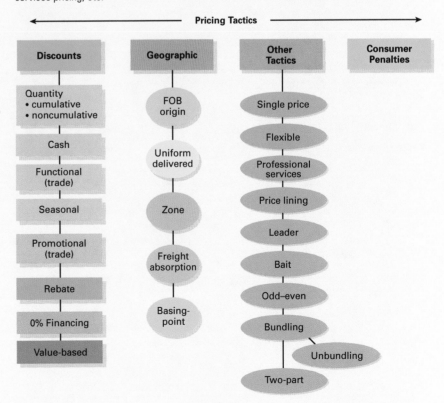

Pricing Tactics

Discounts
- Quantity
  - cumulative
  - noncumulative
- Cash
- Functional (trade)
- Seasonal
- Promotional (trade)
- Rebate
- 0% Financing
- Value-based

Geographic
- FOB origin
- Uniform delivered
- Zone
- Freight absorption
- Basing-point

Other Tactics
- Single price
- Flexible
- Professional services
- Price lining
- Leader
- Bait
- Odd–even
- Bundling
- Unbundling
- Two-part

Consumer Penalties

predatory pricing the practice of charging a very low price for a product with the intent of driving competitors out of business or out of a market

price bundling marketing two or more products in a single package for a special price

price fixing an agreement between two or more firms on the price they will charge for a product

price lining offering a product line with several items at specific price points

price shading the use of discounts by salespeople to increase demand for one or more products in a line

price skimming a high introductory price, often coupled with heavy promotion

price strategy a basic, long-term pricing framework that establishes the initial price for a product and the intended direction for price movements over the product life cycle

product line pricing setting prices for an entire line of products

promotional allowance (trade allowance) a payment to a dealer for promoting the manufacturer's products

quantity discount a unit price reduction offered to buyers buying either in multiple units or more than a specified dollar amount

rebate a cash refund given for the purchase of a product during a specific period

resale price maintenance attempts by a producer to control a store's retail price for the product

seasonal discount a price reduction for buying merchandise out of season

single-price tactic offering all goods and services at the same price (or perhaps two or three prices)

two-part pricing charging two separate amounts to consume a single good or service

unbundling reducing the bundle of services that comes with the basic product

uniform delivered pricing the seller pays the actual freight charges and bills every purchaser an identical, flat freight charge

value-based pricing setting the price at a level that seems to the customer to be a good price compared with the prices of other options

zone pricing a modification of uniform delivered pricing that divides the total market into segments or zones and charges a flat freight rate to all customers in a given zone

The first type of tactic gives lower prices to those that pay promptly, order a large quantity, or perform some function for the manufacturer. Value-based pricing starts with the customer, considers the competition and costs, and then determines a price. Additional tactics in this category include seasonal discounts, promotion allowances, and rebates (cash refunds).

Geographic pricing tactics—such as FOB origin pricing, uniform delivered pricing, zone pricing, freight absorption pricing, and basing-point pricing—are ways of moderating the impact of shipping costs on distant customers.

A variety of other pricing tactics stimulate demand for certain products, increase store patronage, and offer more merchandise at specific prices.

More and more customers are paying price penalties, which are extra fees for violating the terms of a purchase contract. The perceived fairness or unfairness of a penalty may affect some consumers' willingness to patronize a business in the future.

LO 4
Discuss product line pricing. Product line pricing maximizes profits for an entire product line. When setting product line prices, marketing managers determine which type of relationship exists among the products in the line: complementary, substitute, or neutral. Managers also consider joint (shared) costs among products in the same line.

LO 5
Describe the role of pricing during periods of inflation and recession. Marketing managers employ cost-oriented and demand-oriented tactics during periods of economic inflation. Cost-oriented tactics include dropping products with a low profit margin, using delayed-quotation pricing and escalator pricing, and adding fees. Demand-oriented pricing methods include price shading and increasing demand through cultivating selected customers, creating unique offerings, changing the package size, and heightening buyer dependence.

To stimulate demand during a recession, marketers use value-based pricing, bundling, and unbundling. Recessions are also a good time to prune unprofitable items from product lines. Managers strive to cut costs during recessions in order to maintain profits as revenues decline. Implementing new technology, cutting payrolls, and pressuring suppliers for reduced prices are common techniques used to cut costs. Companies also create new value-added products.

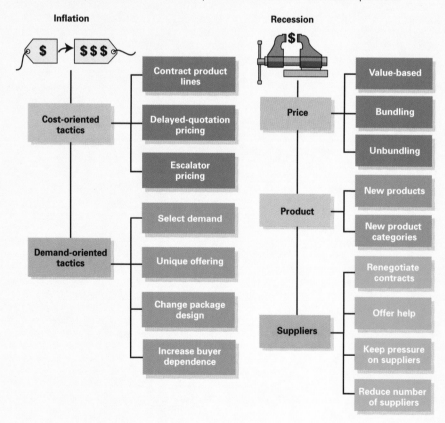

buyer for export an intermediary in the global market that assumes all ownership risks and sells globally for its own account

capital intensive using more capital than labour in the production process

contract manufacturing private-label manufacturing by a foreign company

countertrade a form of trade in which all or part of the payment for goods or services is in the form of other goods or services

direct foreign investment active ownership of a foreign company or of overseas manufacturing or marketing facilities

dumping the sale of an exported product at a price lower than that charged for the same or a like product in the home market of the exporter

European Union a free trade zone encompassing 27 European countries

export agent an intermediary who acts like a manufacturer's agent for the exporter. The export agent lives in the foreign market.

export broker an intermediary who plays the traditional broker's role by bringing buyer and seller together

exporting selling domestically produced products to buyers in another country

floating exchange rates prices of different currencies move up and down based on the demand for and the supply of each currency

General Agreement on Tariffs and Trade (GATT) a trade agreement that contained loopholes that enabled countries to avoid trade-barrier reduction agreements

global marketing marketing that targets markets throughout the world

global marketing standardization production of uniform products that can be sold the same way all over the world

global vision recognizing and reacting to international marketing opportunities, using effective global marketing strategies, and being aware of threats from foreign competitors in all markets

International Monetary Fund (IMF) an international organization that acts as a lender of last resort, providing loans to troubled nations, and also works to promote trade through financial cooperation

joint venture a domestic firm's purchase of part of a foreign company or a domestic firm joining with a foreign company to create a new entity

licensing the legal process whereby a licensor agrees to let another firm use its manufacturing process, trademarks, patents, trade secrets, or other proprietary knowledge

Mercosur the largest Latin American trade agreement, which includes Argentina, Bolivia, Brazil, Chile, Colombia, Ecuador, Paraguay, Peru, and Uruguay

LO 1
Discuss the importance of global marketing. Business people who adopt a global vision are better able to identify global marketing opportunities, understand the nature of global networks, create effective global marketing strategies, and compete against foreign competition in domestic markets.

LO 2
Discuss the impact of multinational firms on the world economy. Multinational corporations are international traders that regularly operate across national borders. Because of their vast size and financial, technological, and material resources, multinational corporations have a great influence on the world economy. They have the ability to overcome trade problems, save on labour costs, and tap new technology.

LO 3
Describe the external environment facing global marketers. Global marketers face the same environmental factors as they do domestically: cultural, economic and technological development, political structure and actions, demography, and natural resources. Cultural considerations include societal values, attitudes and beliefs, language, and customary business practices. A country's economic and technological status depends on its stage of industrial development, which, in turn, affects average family incomes. The political structure is shaped by political ideology and such policies as tariffs, quotas, boycotts, exchange controls, trade agreements, and market groupings. Demographic variables include the size of a population and its age and geographic distribution.

multinational corporation a company that is heavily engaged in international trade, beyond exporting and importing

North American Free Trade Agreement (NAFTA) an agreement between Canada, the United States, and Mexico that created the world's largest free trade zone

Uruguay Round an agreement created by the World Trade Organization to dramatically lower trade barriers worldwide

World Bank an international bank that offers low-interest loans, advice, and information to developing nations

World Trade Organization (WTO) a trade organization that replaced the old General Agreement on Tariffs and Trade (GATT)

LO 4 **Identify the various ways of entering the global marketplace.** Firms use the following strategies to enter global markets, in descending order of risk and profit: direct investment, joint venture, contract manufacturing, licensing and franchising, and exporting.

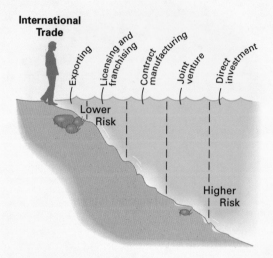

LO 5 **List the basic elements involved in developing a global marketing mix.** A firm's major consideration is how much it will adjust the four Ps—product, promotion, place (distribution), and price—within each country. One strategy is to use one product and one promotion message worldwide. A second strategy is to create new products for global markets. A third strategy is to keep the product basically the same but alter the promotional message. A fourth strategy is to slightly alter the product to meet local conditions.

Global Marketing Mix		
Product + Promotion	**Place (Distribution)**	**Price**
One Product, One Message	Channel Choice	Dumping
Product Invention	Channel Structure	Countertrade
Product Adaption	Country Infrastructure	Exchange Rates
Message Adaption		Purchasing Power

LO 6 **Discover how the Internet is affecting global marketing.** Simply opening a website can open the door to international sales. International carriers, such as UPS, can help solve logistics problems. Language translation software can help an e-commerce business become multilingual. Yet cultural differences and old-line rules, regulations, and taxes hinder rapid development of e-commerce in many countries.